CARING FOR VETERANS AND THEIR FAMILIES

A GUIDE FOR NURSES AND HEALTHCARE PROFESSIONALS

RITA F. D'AOUST
PHD, ANP-BC, CNE, FAANP, FNAP, FAAN
ASSOCIATE DEAN FOR TEACHING AND LEARNING
ASSOCIATE PROFESSOR
JOINT APPOINTMENT, SCHOOL OF MEDICINE
JOHNS HOPKINS UNIVERSITY SCHOOL OF NURSING
BALTIMORE, MARYLAND

ALICIA GILL ROSSITER
DNP, APRN, FNP, PPCNP-BC, FAANP, FAAN
LIEUTENANT COLONEL (RETIRED)
UNITED STATES AIR FORCE RESERVE NURSE CORPS
CHIEF OFFICER OF MILITARY AND VETERAN AFFAIRS
UNIVERSITY OF SOUTH FLORIDA
COLLEGE OF NURSING
TAMPA, FLORIDA

JONES & BARTLETT
LEARNING

World Headquarters
Jones & Bartlett Learning
25 Mall Road
Burlington, MA 01803
978-443-5000
info@jblearning.com
www.jblearning.com

Jones & Bartlett Learning books and products are available through most bookstores and online booksellers. To contact Jones & Bartlett Learning directly, call 800-832-0034, fax 978-443-8000, or visit our website, www.jblearning.com.

Substantial discounts on bulk quantities of Jones & Bartlett Learning publications are available to corporations, professional associations, and other qualified organizations. For details and specific discount information, contact the special sales department at Jones & Bartlett Learning via the above contact information or send an email to specialsales@jblearning.com.

Production Credits
VP, Product Management: Marisa Urbano
VP, Product Operations: Christine Emerton
Director, Product Management: Matt Kane
Product Manager: Tina Chen
Content Strategist: Christina Freitas
Project Manager: Kristen Rogers
Senior Project Specialist: Alex Schab
Digital Project Specialist: Rachel DiMaggio
Senior Marketing Manager: Lindsay White
Product Fulfillment Manager: Wendy Kilborn
Composition: S4Carlisle Publishing Services
Project Management: S4Carlisle Publishing Services
Cover Design: Scott Moden
Text Design: Scott Moden
Senior Media Development Editor: Troy Liston
Rights & Permissions Manager: John Rusk
Rights Specialist: Maria Leon Maimone
Cover Image (Title Page, Part Opener, Chapter Opener):
© Steve Cukrov/Shutterstock
Printing and Binding: LSC Communications

Library of Congress Cataloging-in-Publication Data
Names: D'Aoust, Rita F., editor. | Rossiter, Alicia Gill, editor.
Title: Caring for veterans and their families : a guide for healthcare professionals / edited by Rita F. D'Aoust, Alicia Gill Rossiter.
Description: First edition. | Burlington, MA : Jones & Bartlett Learning, [2023] | Includes bibliographical references and index.
Identifiers: LCCN 2021027542 | ISBN 9781284171341 (paperback)
Subjects: MESH: Veterans Health Services | Military Family | Veterans--psychology | Military Nursing | United States
Classification: LCC UB369 | NLM WA 360 | DDC 362.1086/97--dc23
LC record available at https://lccn.loc.gov/2021027542

6048

Printed in the United States of America
25 24 23 22 21 10 9 8 7 6 5 4 3 2 1

Dedication and Preface

Rita F. D'Aoust, PhD, ANP-BC, CNE, FAANP, FNAP, FAAN

This book began as a labor of love for every veteran and family who has served and every healthcare provider who has cared for a veteran or family member. To my fellow healthcare professionals: to whom much is given, much is expected. As such, we carry a great responsibility to honor those who have put themselves in harms' way by providing the best care and services. I thank my patients who have given me this honor. This book provides context, best evidence, evaluation and management strategies, and resources to care for veterans and their families.

Military service offers opportunity and is based on servant leaders where true leaders serve and true servants lead. We owe a debt to care and advocate for those who have served in harm's way. I acknowledge and thank the service members and veterans who have served and their families. My service is as a military and family member, as well as healthcare provider. Every veteran deserves recognition and I wish to personally acknowledge a few. I thank my co-editor for her service and ongoing commitment to veteran issues. Ten years ago, we embarked on a journey to develop a course on military and veteran health care, followed by a veteran to nursing program, and many consultations and publications to extend this work.

I owe a debt to my immigrant grandfather, Antonio Ferrari, who joined the U.S. Army and served during World War I to obtain U.S. citizenship. I am reminded of my Uncle Bob's sacrifices over two decades of active service and how we would send care packages while he served overseas. I am indebted to my dear friend, Margaret Briody, who served in the U.S. Army Reserve Nurse Corps and still laugh about her annual ritual of "making weight."

To my treasured mentor and friend, Jeanne, who taught me the meaning of sacrifice when she lost her son, a true servant leader. While all gave some, some gave all. Captain William "Bill" Grace served as a C-5 Aircraft Commander and died in a training accident on December 2, 1996. Capt. Grace took his responsibilities seriously and himself lightly and gave the ultimate sacrifice to our country. Never forget his name, legacy, and sacrifice.

I am humbled by my son-in-law Matthew Butlin's ingrained sense of leadership and concern for those under his care, first as a naval aviator and officer and now as a spouse and dad. I am impressed with my daughter Maria's passion and commitment as she tirelessly advocates and represents veterans and their families' rights, services, and policies. I wish to acknowledge my daughters Diana and Laura, who quietly serve by providing dental and pediatric care for veterans and their families.

Most of all, I am in awe of my husband Ray's sense of duty when he responded to a call to serve in Vietnam upon college graduation. His modesty and pride as a veteran amaze me. I pray that no veteran is ever treated with hostility or apathy for their service as were Vietnam veterans. His service medals are no longer hidden in a storage box, but it took a while. I thank him for his unwavering love and support, even as he would (im)patiently ask "How's that book coming along?" And yes, Ray, we will always check for the family sponsored bricks at the hometown Veterans of Foreign War Memorial.

Alicia Gill Rossiter, DNP, APRN, FNP, PPCNP-BC, FAANP, FAAN, Lieutenant Colonel (Retired), U.S. Army Nurse Corps/U.S.A.F. Reserve Nurse Corps

While the greatest honor of my life has been serving my country, my greatest privilege has been serving with, caring for, and educating those who have served in harm's way. For those who serve, we live by the creed to "leave no man or woman behind." As I was preparing my first presentation of many on educating nurses to care for veterans, I remember opening an email with a link to an article in the *Journal of the American Medical Association* entitled "The Unasked Question." After reading the article I realized that while we may have left no man or woman behind on the battlefield, we have left many behind on the homefront, especially in regard to transitioning our service members from the military and back into the civilian sector.

Like the author Dr. Jeffrey Brown, I too realized that never had any provider ever asked about my military service nor had it ever occurred to me to let them know that I had served. Had anyone asked, what would I have told them and how could sharing that information impact my physical and psychological health? Asking one simple question—Have you ever served?—is critically important because no one who serves leaves the military unchanged. It was in that moment that the trajectory of my career changed, and the foundation of this book was laid. This book is the culmination of a decade of work with my co-editor—I can think of no one I would have wanted to work on this project with than her. My inspirations are the friends that I served with and the veterans I have cared for. There is no greater bond than serving: we leave no comrade behind whether it be on the battlefield or at home where the battle is often relived.

I come from a multigenerational military family: my grandfather, Private James W. Bostick (U.S. Army Infantry and Purple Heart recipient) and my great-aunt, Captain Julia R. Maloney (U.S. Army Nurse Corps) served in World War II; my dad and my uncles, John Kevin Gill (Master Chief Petty Officer, U.S. Coast Guard) and John McKeever (Lieutenant Colonel, U.S. Army) in/during Vietnam, I served in Operation Desert Shield/Desert Storm, and most recently, my brother Hank Gill (Specialist, United States Army) in Operation Iraqi Freedom/Operation Enduring Freedom. We have served in every branch, including the Army, Navy, Air Force, Marines, and Coast Guard. To each of them I thank I them for their selfless service and sacrifice, and for imparting those values on the lives of those they served with and those they touched, including me.

I dedicate this book to those who have served, are currently serving, and will serve, and to the families who support them on the homefront, because when one serves, all serve. Nowhere is this more evident than within my own family. My service is a direct result of my dad's—Captain Henry A. Gill, Jr. (U.S. Marines and U.S. Navy)—example. I am forever grateful to him for his wisdom and for instilling in me these core values—integrity, loyalty, leadership, duty, honor, country. To my mom, Peggy, who watched her father, aunt, husband, and two children leave for war, you are braver than you know. To my brothers, Hank and Jay, the two "military brats'" I had the joy of growing up with, life as a military-connected child was never dull. And finally, to my husband, Tommy, and my three daughters, Kylee, Molly, and Hayley, thank you for allowing me to serve, and thank you for your love and support. I firmly believe that being a military family member is the hardest job out there. I love you all to the moon and back.

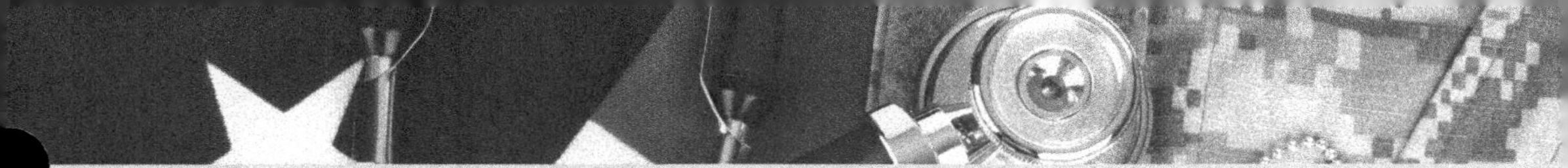

Brief Contents

Foreword	**xix**
About the Authors	**xxi**
Acknowledgments	**xxiv**
Contributors	**xxv**
Introduction	**xxix**

PART I **Introduction to Military and Veteran Health** **1**

CHAPTER 1 **Military Culture** 3

CHAPTER 2 **Military Healthcare System** 19

CHAPTER 3 **Active Duty, Reserve, National Guard: Are There Differences?** 31

CHAPTER 4 **History of Women Who Have Served and Their Service Connected Health Risks** 45

CHAPTER 5 **Caring for Female Veterans** 65

CHAPTER 6 **Transition from Military to Civilian Life: Considerations for Providers** 93

CHAPTER 7 **Veterans Health Administration** 105

CHAPTER 8 **Service-Associated Conditions and Veterans Health Administration Eligibility** ... 121

CHAPTER 9 **The Use of Service, Emotional Support, and Companion Animals as a Complementary Health Approach for Military Veterans: Information for Healthcare Providers** 139

PART II Physical Wounds of War 153

CHAPTER 10 **Polytrauma Care Across the Continuum** 155

CHAPTER 11 **Military Occupational Exposures** 187

CHAPTER 12 **Caring for Veterans with TBI in the Private Sector** 203

CHAPTER 13 **Military Caregivers of Veterans and Service Members with Traumatic Brain Injury** 219

CHAPTER 14 **Pain and Pain Management in the Veteran** 235

CHAPTER 15 **Identifying the Unique Needs of Veterans That Influence End-of-Life Care** 251

PART III Psychological Wounds of War 265

CHAPTER 16 **PTSD in Military Veterans: What Civilian Providers Should Know** 267

CHAPTER 17 **Suicide Risk Evaluation and Management Among Veterans Receiving Community-Based Care** 295

CHAPTER 18 **Caring for Veterans with Substance Use Disorders (SUD)** 319

CHAPTER 19 **Treating Victims of Military Sexual Trauma** 335

CHAPTER 20 **Assessing and Addressing Health Care for Veterans Experiencing Homelessness** 351

CHAPTER 21 **Identifying Soul Injury: A Self-Awareness Inventory** 375

CHAPTER 22 **Moral Stress and Injury in the Military and Veterans** 387

PART IV The Military Family **401**

CHAPTER 23 **Impact of Parental Military Service on Military-Connected Children** 403

CHAPTER 24 **Military Spouses** 421

CHAPTER 25 **Second Service: Military and Veteran Caregivers Among Us** 433

CHAPTER 26 **Supporting the Sidelines: Encounters with Stress and Loss Related to Military Service** 443

PART V Preparing Professionals to Care for Service Members, Veterans, and Their Families **455**

CHAPTER 27 **To Know Them Is to Care for Them Better: Educating Healthcare Providers on Caring for Veterans** 457

CHAPTER 28 **It Starts with One Question—Have You Ever Served?** 471

Index **477**

Contents

Foreword xix

About the Authors xxi

Acknowledgments xxiv

Contributors xxv

Introduction xxix

PART I Introduction to Military and Veteran Health **1**

CHAPTER 1 Military Culture **3**

Introduction 3
Military Language 3
Military Ethos and Mindset 4
Branches of Service 6
- Reserves and National Guard 6
- Special Operations Command 7

Military Rank 8
Jobs in the Military 8
- Joining the Military 9

Female Veterans and Military Service 10
Sexual Orientation, Gender Identity, and the Military 10
Era of Service 11
Military Families 12
The Military Healthcare System 13
- The Veterans Health Administration (VHA) 14
- Medications 15
- Nonprescription Substances 15

Conclusion 16
References 16

CHAPTER 2 Military Healthcare System **19**

The Military Healthcare System (MHS) 19
Battlefield Medicine and Transition of Care for Wounded Warriors 19
The Role of the Military Healthcare System in OCONUS and CONUS as well as during Peacetime and War 20
- Role 1 – 4 20
- Examine the Role of the Medical Home within the MHS 21

Mission of the MHS and Mission Readiness 23
- Healthcare Missions between the Services 24

Scope and Allocations of Care 24
Access to Care for Military Members and Families: Private Sector Partnerships and Department of Veteran Affairs (VA) Partnerships 25
Tricare Insurance 26
Education and Training Requirements of the MHS Team 26
Patient Satisfaction and Loyalty in the MHS 26
Conclusion 28
References 28
Useful Websites 29

CHAPTER 3 Active Duty, Reserve, National Guard: Are There Differences? 31

Introduction 31
Who Are the Reserve Components? 32
Entitlements 35
Related Health Benefits 36
The Deployment Cycle 36
Impact of 9/11 on the Reserve Components 41
Conclusion 43
References 44

CHAPTER 4 History of Women Who Have Served and Their Service Connected Health Risks 45

Data and Subject Issues 45
Historical Review of Women in the Military 46
Civil War (1861–1865) 47
Spanish-American War (1898–1902) 47
World War I (1917–1918) 48
World War II (1941–1945) 48
1950–1961 49
Vietnam War (1964–1973) 49
Total Force Concept 50
Reserves/National Guard Personnel 50
Gulf War I (1991) 51
Iraq and Afghanistan Wars (2001–2014+) 51
OIF/OEF/OND Military Women *51*
OIF/OEF/OND Women Veterans *52*
First, Identification 53
Military Children Identification 53
Does "Healthy Solider Effect" Still Apply? 53
Possible Deployment Consequences 54
Behavioral Health Issues Leading to Physical Complications 54
Depression *54*
Posttraumatic Stress Disorder *56*
Military Sexual Trauma (MST) *57*
Suicide Thoughts and Behavior (STB) *58*
Urological Deployment Hazards 58
Urinary Tract Infections and Acute Dysuria 59
Overactive Bladder 59
Pelvic Organ Prolapse (POP) 59
Bladder Pain Syndrome (BPS) 60
Trauma Outcomes and Urogenital Health (TOUGH) Project 60
Interventions 60
Therapeutic Relationships 60
Healthcare System 60
Clinical Care Environment 61
References 61

CHAPTER 5 Caring for Female Veterans 65

Changing Profile of the U.S. Military 66
Rethinking Veterans: Who Is the Woman Veteran? 67
Understanding the Culture of the Department of Veteran Affairs 68
Institutional Barriers Faced by Female Veterans 69
Healthcare Issues for Women Who Served in Major Conflicts 70
Integrative Health Care: Treating the Whole Person 71
Caring for the Physical Health of Female Veterans 72
Well-Woman Exam 73
Physical Exam 73
Caring for the Emotional and Mental Health of Female Veterans: A Biopsychosocial-Spiritual Perspective 79
The Biological Domain: Past 81
The Biological Domain: Present 82
The Psychological Domain: Past 83
The Psychological Domain: Present 84
The Social Domain 84
The Spiritual Domain 84

Emerging Issues for Female Veterans . . . 84
Military Sexual Trauma . . . 85
Homelessness Among Female Veterans . . . 86
Intimate Partner Violence (IPV) and Domestic Violence . . . 87
Summary . . . 88
References . . . 89

CHAPTER 6 Transition from Military to Civilian Life: Considerations for Providers . . . 93

Individual Considerations . . . 94
Demographics . . . 94
Psychological Factors . . . 95
Information/Skills . . . 95
Purpose/Meaning . . . 96
Belonging . . . 96
Interpersonal Considerations . . . 97
Community/Society/System Issues . . . 98
Health Care Related . . . 98
Logistics of Transition . . . 99
Relationship with the Veterans Administration . . . 100
Resilience and Growth . . . 101
Conclusion . . . 102
References . . . 102

CHAPTER 7 Veterans Health Administration . . . 105

"For Those Who Have Borne the Battle" . . . 106
Eligibility for VA Healthcare Services and Programs . . . 107
U.S. Department of Veterans Affairs . . . 107
Mission of the VA Healthcare System . . . 109
Eligibility and Enrollment for Care . . . 109
VA Healthcare System . . . 109
Caring for Veterans in the 21st Century . . . 112
Afghanistan: Operation Enduring Freedom (OEF) and Iraq: Operation Iraqi Freedom (OIF) . . . 114
A Way Forward . . . 115
Phoenix . . . 116
The Way Forward . . . 117
References . . . 118

CHAPTER 8 Service-Associated Conditions and Veterans Health Administration Eligibility . . . 121

Veterans . . . 122
Veteran Benefits . . . 123
Active Service . . . 123
Length of Service . . . 124
Military Discharge . . . 124
DD Form 214 (Certificate of Release or Discharge from Active Service) . . . 124
The Character of Discharge and Associated Veteran Benefits . . . 124
Honorable Discharge . . . 126
General Discharge . . . 126
A Discharge Under Other Than Honorable Conditions (OTH) . . . 126
Bad Conduct Discharge (BCD) . . . *126*
Dishonorable Discharge (DD) . . . 127
Bad Paper . . . 127
Taking Care of the Veteran Community . . . 127
Eligibility for Care . . . 127
Enrollment Priority Groups . . . 128
(US Department of Veteran Affairs, 2017) . . . 128
Priority Group 1 . . . *128*
Priority Group 2 . . . *128*
Priority Group 3 . . . *128*
Priority Group 4 . . . *128*
Priority Group 5 . . . *128*
Priority Group 6 . . . *129*
Priority Group 7 . . . *129*
Priority Group 8 . . . *129*
Veteran Benefits vs. Entitlements . . . 129
The VHA Claims and Appeals . . . 130
Claims . . . *130*
Appeal Options for Disability Claims . . . *131*

Service-Connected Disability 132
Disability Rating and Priority Systems of Care 132
VA Criteria for Disability-Priority Treatment Groups. 133
Other Than Honorable Discharges 133
Barriers to Benefitted Entitlements 134
Resources 135
Military Sexual Trauma 135
References 137

CHAPTER 9 The Use of Service, Emotional Support, and Companion Animals as a Complementary Health Approach for Military Veterans: Information for Healthcare Providers 139

Introduction 139
Benefits of the Human-Animal Bond 140
Service Animals: Beyond the Task . . . 141
Service Animal Case Study 141
Emotional Support Animals: Salve for Hidden Wounds 144
Emotional Support Animals Case Study 144
Companion Animals: Comforting Comrades 145
Companion Animal Case Study 145
Animal Welfare. 147
Acknowledgments 150
References 150

PART II Physical Wounds of War 153

CHAPTER 10 Polytrauma Care Across the Continuum 155

Introduction 155
Polytrauma Care Across the Continuum 155
Training. 156
Trauma Combat Casualty Care Course 156
Clinical Practice Guidelines 156
Comprehensive Medical Readiness Program 156
Civilian Sector Training Opportunities. . . . 157
Planning and Response. 157
Polytrauma 157
Types of Injuries 158
Blasts 158
Penetration Injuries 159
Soft Tissue Injury and Internal Trauma 159
Orthopedic Trauma and Amputation 160
Burns 160
Spinal Cord Injuries 161
Clinical Treatment Considerations 161
Risks to Service Members. 162
Environmental Exposure Risks 162
Infection Risks and Considerations. 162
Emergency Response 163
Triage 163
Damage Control Resuscitation 163
Pain Management 164
Introduction to Patient Movement . . . 164
Intra-Theater and Inter-Theater Patient Movement 165
Intra-Theater Patient Movement 166
MEDEVAC 166
Intra-Theater Aeromedical Evacuation. 168
Inter-Theater Patient Movement 168
Aeromedical Evacuation. 168
Patient Movement Regulation Center 168
En Route Patient Staging System 169
Aeromedical Evacuation Crew 169
Critical Care Air Transport Teams 169
Physiological Stressors of Flight 169
Patient Movement Summary. 173
Hospital Care 173
Rehabilitation. 173
Admission 174
Discharge 176

Considerations for War-Injured Service Members . . . 176
Healthcare Costs . . . 176
Multimorbidity . . . 177
Technological Advancements . . . 179
Support System Considerations . . . 180
Individual . . . *180*
Family Members and Caregivers . . . *180*
Resources . . . 181
For Healthcare Providers . . . 181
For the Veteran or Service Member . . . 182
For the Caregiver and Family Members . . . 183
Summary . . . 183
References . . . 184

CHAPTER 11 Military Occupational Exposures . . . 187

Toxic Exposures During Military Deployments . . . 187
Agent Orange and Herbicidal Exposure . . . 188
Gulf War Illness . . . 189
Depleted Uranium . . . 190
Burn Pits . . . 191
Toxic Exposures in the United States . . . 191
Military-Specific Occupational Exposures . . . 192
Eyes . . . 192
Military Background . . . *192*
Military Ocular Health and Injury Prevention Programs . . . *193*
Veteran Ocular Health Assessment . . . *193*
Ears . . . 194
Military Background . . . *194*
Military Hearing Conservation Programs . . . *194*
Veteran Auditory Health Assessment . . . *195*
Pulmonary . . . 195
Military Background . . . *195*
Veteran Pulmonary Health Assessment . . . *196*
Musculoskeletal . . . 197
Military Background . . . *197*
Veteran Musculoskeletal Health Assessment . . . *198*
Neurological . . . 198
Military Background . . . *198*
Veteran Neurological Health Assessment . . . 199
Conclusion . . . 200
References . . . 200

CHAPTER 12 Caring for Veterans with TBI in the Private Sector . . . 203

Introduction . . . 203
TBI Reintegration: The Military/Civilian Divide . . . 203
Definition of Community Reintegration . . . 204
TBI Definition and Severity Levels . . . 204
Mild TBI . . . 205
Symptoms . . . *205*
Moderate and Severe TBI . . . 206
TBI Screening . . . 206
Environments of Care . . . 206
Polytrauma System of Care . . . 207
Blast Injuries . . . 207
TBI as a Chronic Condition . . . 209
Common Post-Concussion Symptoms . . . 209
Sleep disorders . . . *209*
Cognitive symptoms . . . *209*
Visual symptoms . . . *210*
Chronic pain . . . *210*
Behavioral/Mental health diagnoses . . . *210*
Polytrauma clinical triad . . . *210*
Treatment Considerations and Resources . . . 210
Conclusion . . . 212
Training and Resources for Private Sector Providers . . . 212
Mission Act Resources . . . 212
Resources for the Military Family/Caregiver . . . 213
References . . . 213

CHAPTER 13 Military Caregivers of Veterans and Service Members with Traumatic Brain Injury....219

Incidence of TBI 219
Impact of TBI on Caregivers 220
Unique Characteristics of Military Caregivers of Individuals with TBI 221
Increased Medical Complexity 221
Family Strain and Deployment-Related Changes 221
Navigation of Complex Healthcare Systems 222
How Military Caregiver Outcomes Differ from Civilian Caregivers 222
Financial 222
Mental Health 223
HRQoL 223
Sleep 224
Clinical Recommendations 224
Assistance with Managing Cognitive and Emotional Difficulties for the SMV 225
Assistance with Self-Management of Emotions and Stress 225
Assistance with Obtaining Needed Services and with Everyday Needs 226
Summary and Conclusion 227
References 227

CHAPTER 14 Pain and Pain Management in the Veteran.... 235

Introduction 235
Definitions of Pain 236
Pain Descriptors and Pain Physiology 236
Acute Pain 236
Chronic Pain 237
Cancer Pain 237
Acute or Chronic Pain 238
Veterans and Pain 238
Management of Pain in the Veterans Health Administration (VHA) 239
Pharmacological Pain Management 240
Interventions for the Management of Pain in Veterans 244
Integrative Medicine and Complementary Therapies for Chronic Pain Management 244
Chronic Pain and Its Impact on Veterans and Their Families 246
Abuse Disorders Related to Chronic Pain 246
Summary 247
References 247

CHAPTER 15 Identifying the Unique Needs of Veterans That Influence End-of-Life Care....251

Stoicism: A Help and a Hindrance 251
Healthcare Practice Tips for Stoic Veterans 252
PTSD At-Risk Environments: Dangerous Duty Military Assignments 252
Healthcare Practice Tips for Veterans with PTSD 252
Guilt and Shame: Emotions That Might Surface as Veterans Prepare to "Meet Their Maker" 254
Guilt, Shame, and Soul Injury Practice Considerations 255
"Thank You" Is Not Enough: Helping Veterans UNBURDEN 256
Case Example: Exert Care That "Image" Does Not Inadvertently Silence the Untold Story *256*
Specialized Consideration: Vietnam Veterans 257
Case Example: "Welcoming Home" Vietnam Veterans 258
Often Forgotten: Women Veterans 259

Resources and Support for Veteran Healthcare Providers 259
A Final Word to a Dying Veteran from a Hospice Nurse 262
References 262

PART III Psychological Wounds of War 265

CHAPTER 16 PTSD in Military Veterans: What Civilian Providers Should Know. 267

What Is Post-Traumatic Stress Disorder? 268
Criterion A: Traumatic Experience 269
Criterion B: Intrusive Symptoms. 269
Criterion C: Avoidance and Numbing 270
Criterion D: Negative Cognitive and Mood Symptoms. 270
Criterion E: Marked alterations in arousal and reactivity 271
Military Sexual Trauma 271
Moral Injury 272
What Is Unique About PTSD in Veterans 273
Training and Culture. 273
Conditions of Deployments 273
Military Occupational Specialty 273
Frequency of Deployment and Dwell Time 273
Traumatic Brain Injury 274
Polytrauma 274
Risk and Protective Factors for Developing PTSD 275
Screening for PTSD 275
Behaviors Encountered in a Clinical Setting 277
Autonomic Reactivity 277
Inattention and Distraction. 277
Skills for inattention/distraction 278
Irritability and Anger 278
De-escalation Techniques 278
Suicidal Thoughts. 279
Treatment for PTSD 279
Evidence-Based Psychotherapies. 281
Emerging and Adjunctive Therapies 282
Family Considerations. 283
Helping Veterans Seek Assistance 287
Supporting Family Members. 288
Managing and Helping Children. 288
Resources for Family Members of Veterans 288
References 289

CHAPTER 17 Suicide Risk Evaluation and Management Among Veterans Receiving Community-Based Care 295

Suicide Risk Identification, Evaluation, Stratification, and Management 296
Suicide Risk Screening 297
Evaluation of Suicide Risk. 299
Demographic Characteristics 299
History of SDV Thoughts and Behaviors 299
Psychiatric Conditions and Symptoms. . . . 300
Physical Health Conditions. 300
Biopsychosocial Stressors 301
Deployment and Combat-Related Experiences 301
Access to Lethal Means. 301
Warning Signs 302
Protective Factors 302
Risk Stratification 303
Suicide Risk Management. 303
Non-pharmacologic Treatments 306
Safety Planning Interventions. 306
Cognitive Behavioral Therapy for Suicide Prevention (CBT-SP) 307
Problem-Solving Therapy. 307
Pharmacologic Treatments 308
Treatment Options for Suicidal Behavior in Individuals with Specific Psychiatric Conditions 308
Post-Acute Care 308

Technology-Based Modalities 309
Means Safety Counseling 309
Challenges in Veteran Suicide Prevention 310
Conclusion 312
References 313

CHAPTER 18 Caring for Veterans with Substance Use Disorders (SUD) 319

Substance Use Disorders (SUD) 319
Prevalence and Risk Factors 319
Drinking Behaviors 321
Early Intervention 322
Screening 322
Brief Intervention *322*
Signs and Symptoms of Withdrawal and Delirium Tremens 324
Withdrawal Interventions and Safety 324
Family Involvement 325
Trauma and Substance Abuse 325
Suicide 326
Conclusion 332
References 332

CHAPTER 19 Treating Victims of Military Sexual Trauma 335

Why Prepare for MST Patients? 335
Defining MST and Sexual Assault and Sexual Harassment 336
Traumatic Effects of SA 336
Comorbidities 337
Barriers to Reporting SA 337
MST Victims Are Reluctant Patients 338
How to Prepare for Sexual Assault Patients 338
First, Be Aware 338
Second, Prepare *339*
Third, Act *339*
Diagnosing MST 339
Treating MST 340
Follow-up and Referrals 341
Importance of Documentation 341
Know the Law, Follow the Law 341
References 342
Appendix A: Differences between Military and Civilian Sexual Assault Definitions, Laws, and Guidelines 345
Appendix B: Post-Assault Clinical Flow Sheet 347
Appendix C: MST Resources for Civilian Providers 350

CHAPTER 20 Assessing and Addressing Health Care for Veterans Experiencing Homelessness 351

Introduction 351
Risk Factors Leading to Veteran Homelessness 354
Psychosocial Risks 354
Post-Traumatic Stress Disorder *354*
Substance Use Disorders *354*
Incarceration 355
Transition to Civilian Life 356
Federal Policies to Reduce Veteran Homelessness 357
Veterans Administration 358
Other-Than-Honorable Discharge *358*
The Decision-Making Process Used by Homeless Veterans in Accessing Health Care 359
Symbolic Interactionism 359
Homeless Vietnam Veteran (HVV) Healthcare Utilization Theory 360
Healthcare Needs 360
Psychiatric Needs 362
Post-Traumatic Stress Disorder *362*
Combat and Operational Stress Reaction *362*
Suicide Ideation and Suicide Attempt *363*
Military Sexual Trauma 364
Transgender Veterans 365
Street Medicine/Health Care 365
COVID-19 Employment and Housing Efforts 366

Housing 368
Community First! Village 369
Harbor Care, Nashua, NH 369
Bud Clark Commons with Home Forward and Health Share of Oregon. . . 371
Swords to Plowshares 371
Swords to Plowshares 372
Summary 372
References 373

CHAPTER 21 Identifying Soul Injury: A Self-Awareness Inventory 375

Wounds of Suffering: PTSD, Moral Injury, Soul Injury 376
Soul Injury: An Overview 379
Soul Injury Self-Awareness Inventory (SISAI) 380
Using the Tool to Facilitate Meaningful Conversations 381
Validation of the Soul Injury Self-Awareness Inventory 383
Responding to Soul Injury 384
Self-Help Tools 385
Summary 386
References 386

CHAPTER 22 Moral Stress and Injury in the Military and Veterans 387

Introduction 387
Moral Injury 387
Moral Injury in Military Healthcare Providers 389
Differences Between Moral Injury and PTSD 392
Highlighting the Research Gap: Female Veterans and Families 394
Legal Issues 394
Treatment for Moral Injury 395
Moral Resilience 396
Screening 396
Screening Tools 396
Strategy 397
Treatment Strategies 397
Conclusion 398
References 398

PART IV **The Military Family 401**

CHAPTER 23 Impact of Parental Military Service on Military-Connected Children 403

Crunching Numbers 404
Pros and Cons of Military Life 404
Academics 405
Relocations 405
Social Issues 405
Family Dynamics 405
Benefits 406
Gold Star and Blue Star Families 406
Services for Military Children 406
Family Care Plans 407
The Impact of Military Service on Children 407
Physical and Psychological Risk Factors 407
Infants (Newborn–12 Months) 408
Toddlers and Preschoolers (Ages 1 Year–5 Years) 408
School Age Children (Ages 6 Years–12 Years) 409
Adolescents (Ages 13 Years–18 Years) . . . 409
The Deployment Cycle 409
Pre-deployment 410
Deployment 410
Reunification 410
Risks to Children 411

The Exceptional Family Member Program 411
Education and the Military Child 413
Factors Affecting Resilience 413
I Serve 2 414
Resources for Caring for Military-Connected Children 414
References 415
Appendix: I Serve 2 418

CHAPTER 24 Military Spouses. . . . 421

Introduction 421
The Importance of the Military Spouses—Looking at the "So What" 421
Historical Perspective 422
Contemporary Spouse 422
National Guard and Reserve 422
Demographics 423
Education 423
Occupations/Employment 424
Programs to Promote Military Spousal Education and Employment 426
Health and Well-Being 426
Impact of Military Life Cycle 426
Deployment Cycle 427
Availability of Resources 428
Specific Population Considerations 428
Caregivers 429
Male Spouses 429
Gold Star Spouses 429
Summary 430
References 430

CHAPTER 25 Second Service: Military and Veteran Caregivers Among Us 433

Who Are Military and Veteran Caregivers 433
Characteristics of Military and Veteran Caregivers 434
Needs of Military and Veteran Caregivers 435
Implications of Caregiving 435
Case Scenarios 435
Case Scenario 1 435
Case Scenario 2 436
Case Scenario 3 436
Case Scenario 4 436
Case Scenario 5 436
Caregivers Assisting Veterans with Polytrauma 437
Health and Well-being Based on a Psychosocial Construct 438
Current Initiatives and Programs 439
Caregiver Experience Journey Map 439
Health Assessment for Loved Ones 439
Conclusion 441
References 442

CHAPTER 26 Supporting the Sidelines: Encounters with Stress and Loss Related to Military Service 443

Encounters with Stress: Stressors for Military Members and Families 443
Military Impact on Coping Strategies 445
Opportunities to Assess Health Needs 447
Resources 447
Encounters with Loss: Bereavement and Grief 448
Unique Aspects of Bereavement for Military Families 450
Assessing for Further Mental Health Needs 450
Supports for Grieving 451
References 452

PART V **Preparing Professionals to Care for Service Members, Veterans, and Their Families 455**

CHAPTER 27 To Know Them Is to Care for Them Better: Educating Healthcare Providers on Caring for Veterans 457

Introduction to the Program 458
Student Learning Activities 458
Clinical Experiences 459
Program Field Experiences......... 460
Available Resources............... 461
Volunteer Opportunities 462
Finding Veteran Opportunities 462
Additional Veteran Educational Resources 462
Lessons Learned 463
Transitioning from Combat to Classroom.................. 465
References 467
Appendix: Culture Practicum Skills Assessment 468
Final Reflective Writing 469
Expected Learning Outcome........ 469
Reflective Writing Questions........ 469
Commonly Asked Questions Regarding the Reflective Writing... 469
To whom am I writing?............. 469
Do I need to use APA format?......... 470
What length should my paper be? 470
Reflective Writing Grading Rubric ... 470

CHAPTER 28 It Starts with One Question—Have You Ever Served?..........................471

Have You Ever Served? Initiative..... 472
The Unasked Question No More..... 475
References 476

Index 477

Foreword

Advancing Private Sector Health Care for Military Veterans

My Perspective

I am honored to offer perspective on why this book is value-added for the healthcare industry. During my 22 years as a public servant/federal employee with a 14 year tenure as a national level executive for the Department of Veterans Affairs (VA) https://www.va.gov/health-care/, it became clear to me that my prior private sector experience was significantly devoid of understanding the unique aspects of caring for military veterans. I am grateful to have served in various nursing leadership VA roles. I hold the Department of Veterans Affairs–Veterans Health Administration in high regard for providing specialized care based upon dedicated research and education for veterans' health care. I understand that many veterans receive care in the private sector outside the VA. Early in my career, in my private sector roles, I never gave a thought to the fact that I had provided direct care to veterans and nursing leadership to those who care for veterans. It is indisputable that I could have served veterans better if I had been exposed to the relevant aspects of their military experiences and the influence of veteran-specific healthcare conditions. Additionally, I am saddened to think of the missed opportunities to learn about the power of inspirational veteran stories . . . if I had only known to ask and listen.

Why the Book Is Value-Added

This first of its kind book provides a comprehensive view of what is so very important to providing health care to our nation's heroes in all settings of the private sector. Approximately 60% of America's veterans receive all of their health care in the private sector.

The Department of Veterans Affairs is authorized by Congress to provide health care to veterans who meet specific enrollment criteria. Approximately nine million veterans are enrolled for VA healthcare benefits. National statistics indicate that there are approximately 20.4 million U.S. military veterans (2016). The Veterans Health Administration is America's largest integrated healthcare system, providing care at 1,255 healthcare facilities, including 170 medical centers and 1,074 outpatient sites of care of varying complexity (VHA outpatient clinics). Many veterans who are enrolled in VA care also received care from private sector providers.

The book provides private sector healthcare clinicians with guidance on how to address culturally competent care for veterans and their family members. The book is a primer on military cultural competence, defines who a veteran is, and provides insight into the various branches of the military and how that impacts the veteran. It discusses the role of the military and veteran healthcare systems. The book provides insight and guidance on key topics focused on understanding healthcare needs of military veterans and their families. Finally, it provides education, research, and clinical guidance for addressing the unique physical and psychosocial healthcare needs of military veterans and their family members.

About Editors/Authors

Dr. Alicia Rossiter and Dr. Rita D'Aoust are recognized clinicians, academicians, authors, speakers, and researchers. They are professionals who are clearly committed to advancing the science and practice of nursing as evidenced by their extensive publications and community based contributions. Much of their work has focused on health care for military veterans and their families. Their expertise puts them on solid ground for editing invited manuscripts for this book in addition to their authoring several chapters.

Drs. Rossiter and D'Aoust sought chapter authors who have substantive experience as active duty clinicians, veterans, civilians, providers, VA clinicians, and family members. The in-depth expertise of these authors underscores the validity of guidance provided in this book as being clearly reliable. The invited authors demonstrate commitment to presenting instructive advice for interdisciplinary teams of clinicians.

Dr. Alicia Rossiter is an associate professor at the University of South Florida College of Nursing Tampa, Florida. She is a fellow in the American Academy of Nurse Practitioners and the American Academy of Nursing. I became familiar with Dr. Alicia Rossiter's work when introduced to her by a mutual colleague, William (Bill) Bester. At the time when I met Alicia, Bill and I were senior advisors for the Jonas Center for Nursing and Veteran Healthcare (https://www.thejonascenter.com/). Previously, Bill and I had worked closely together as Federal Nursing Service Chiefs; I was the Chief Nursing Officer-Department of Veterans Affairs (2000–2014) and Bill was the Chief Nursing Officer of the United States Army Nurse Corps. Alicia was an active Jonas Scholar during our tenure as Senior Advisors for the Jonas Center. Dr. Rossiter became Vice Chair, Board Member for the Jonas Scholar Alumni Advisory Council.

Dr. Rita D'Aoust is an associate professor and associate dean at The Johns Hopkins School of Nursing. Her work at Hopkins focuses on mentoring doctoral students with interests in veteran care through their DNP scholarly projects. In her mentor role, Dr. D'Aoust facilitates congressional policy trips with the House Committee on Veterans Affairs, Health Subcommittee. Prior to her work at Hopkins, she served in the roles of associate dean and associate professor at the University of South Florida where she created a veteran health care course and the veteran to BS in nursing program. She served as a co-director for the Veterans Administration Nursing Academy Program for USF and James A. Haley VA. She has conducted veteran healthcare research. She is a Fellow in the American Academy of Nurse Practitioners, the National Academies of Practice, and the American Academy of Nursing. I salute Dr. D'Aoust's son-in-law who served as a naval aviator for 10 years, husband who is a Vietnam veteran with a service connected disability, and her husband's father and uncles who also served our country.

Cathy Rick

Catherine (Cathy) Rick, RN, NEA-BC, FAAN
Healthcare Consultant – CJR Consulting
Former Chief Nursing Officer-Department of Veterans Affairs Headquarters (2000–2014)
Editor and Author: *Realizing the Future of Nursing: VA Nurses Tell Their Stories* (2015)

End Note

I am grateful to Drs. Rossiter and D'Aoust for taking on the challenge of highlighting the special healthcare needs of military veterans and their families. Our nation's heroes are deserving of the recognition and understanding of the impact that their service has had on their health and well-being. Referencing the collection of informative guidance provided in this book will improve private sector health care for those who were willing to secure our nation's safety and freedom.

About the Authors

Dr. Rita F. D'Aoust is an associate professor and associate dean for teaching and learning at the Johns Hopkins University School of Nursing and holds a joint appointment in the School of Medicine, Department of General Internal Medicine.

Dr. D'Aoust earned her bachelor of science and master of science degrees and two post-master's certificate in acute care nurse practitioner and adult nurse practitioner from the University of Rochester School of Nursing. She earned her PhD from the University of Rochester Warner Graduate School of Education and Human Development. She completed a mini-fellowship in geriatrics at the David Geffen School of Medicine, University of California, Los Angeles. She is a board-certified adult nurse practitioner and serves medically underserved communities and is a certified nurse educator.

Dr. D'Aoust has served from the sidelines as a spouse and family member for military and veteran service and as a nurse practitioner caring for veterans in community settings. She has made significant contributions to educate nurses caring for veterans. She served as the co-director for the Veterans Affairs Nursing Academy (VANA) and subsequent Veterans Affairs Nursing Academic Partnerships (VANAP) at the James A. Haley Veterans Hospital and University of South Florida. With federal funding, she served as the primary investigator and led the development, implementation, and evaluation of the Veteran to Bachelor of Science Program at the University of South Florida. She developed an innovative approach to eliminate barriers and provide recognition of prior learning by developing an approach to award upper-division academic credit for nursing courses through an evaluation of American Council of Education (ACE) transcripts for military medics and corpsmen and recognizing prior coursework regardless of completion date. She led the development of an online course, Introduction to Military and Veteran Healthcare. She has served as a Jonas Scholar mentor for doctoral students at Johns Hopkins School of Nursing and the University of South Florida.

Her research contributions to the impact of military service on veteran health include the use of a novel therapy, Accelerated Resolution Therapy (ART) to treat post-traumatic stress disorder in homeless veterans, PTSD secondary to military sexual trauma, and the incidence of fibromyalgia symptomology in community-dwelling women veterans. Dr. D'Aoust has mentored numerous doctoral students on policy issues for veterans, nurse practitioner roles in veteran care, and quality improvement initiatives in VA settings.

Dr. D'Aoust is an expert in interprofessional education, community service, and providing access to care for vulnerable populations. Dr. D'Aoust has long made her mark where the business of education and health care intersect. She has led advances in curriculum and classroom technology that match an understanding of ways to construct learning with the philosophy of education and a mastery of financial issues in higher education. At the Johns Hopkins School of Nursing, she continues to lead the development and implementation of innovative teaching and learning strategies. Dr. D'Aoust is a nationally recognized leader in education program development, evaluation, and administration. She brings multiple PI grant expertise, especially in the areas of program evaluation and academic-service collaborations, quality improvement initiatives in acute care and community settings, and integrating geriatrics in primary care. At Johns Hopkins School of Nursing, she led the development and transition for an online program for Doctors of Nursing Practice Advanced Practice (nurse practitioners, clinical nurse specialists). She led the development of an advanced diagnostic and clinical procedures courses for nurse practitioners. Currently, she leads the development and testing of a nurse practitioner clinical competency development and assessment. Dr. D'Aoust also brings an understanding of the nursing workforce and recruitment from underserved populations. Additional research and scholarship contributions include the impact of chronic stress on sleep and depression for caregivers of persons with dementia and left ventricular assist devices. She is an active member of a nursing workforce study team that examines the impact of nurse practitioner full practice authority on changes to health access, NP income, and practice characteristics.

She was inducted as a fellow in the American Association of Nurse Practitioners in 2011, National Academies of Practice in 2012, and in the American Academy of Nursing in 2017.

Dr. Alicia Gill Rossiter is an associate professor and the chief officer of Military and Veteran Affairs at the University of South Florida College of Nursing. Prior to transitioning into her current role, she served as the director of the Veteran to Bachelor of Science in Nursing (VBSN) program. The VBSN program is a program for military medics and corpsmen that builds upon their military healthcare education, training, and experience, and provides a more efficient pathway and education ladder from veteran, to student, to baccalaureate-prepared nursing professional. She graduated with her bachelor of science in nursing from the University of Alabama and her master of science and doctor of nursing practice from the University of South Florida. She is a board-certified pediatric nurse practitioner.

Dr. Rossiter served in the U.S. Army Nurse Corps on active duty for four years, which included two deployments: a humanitarian mission to Honduras, Central America and a combat deployment to Saudi Arabia during Operation Desert Shield/Desert Storm. She branch-transferred into the U.S. Air Force Reserve Nurse Corps in 1995 and served as an Individual Mobilization Augmentee until she retired in June 2015. In her last assignment, she served as adjunct faculty at the Daniel K. Inouye Graduate School of Nursing at the University of the Health Sciences in Bethesda, Maryland, the nation's only federal/military health science university.

Her military experience has the been the impetus behind her research and scholarly work, which includes women veterans and military sexual trauma, the effects of parental military service on military-connected children, and transitioning needs of medics and corpsmen into the professional role of nursing. She was instrumental in the development of a first-of-its-kind College of Nursing online "Introduction to Military and Veteran Health" course. Dr. Rossiter completed her doctor of nursing practice in May 2015. Her groundbreaking work with Accelerated Resolution Therapy for Military Sexual Trauma related post-traumatic stress disorder (PTSD) led to integration of this innovative, highly effective treatment into Department of Defense PTSD treatment protocols and inclusion as trauma-based therapy for PTSD in the Substance Abuse and Mental Health Services Administration (SAMHSA) National Registry of Evidence Based Programs and Practices.

During her doctoral program at USF, she was selected as a Bob Woodruff Jonas Veteran

Healthcare Scholar and an American Academy of Nursing Jonas Policy Scholar with the Military and Veteran Health Expert Panel. She was inducted as a fellow in the American Association of Nurse Practitioners in 2014 and in the American Academy of Nursing in 2018 where she currently serves as the chair for the Military/Veteran Health Expert Panel.

Acknowledgments

The editors gratefully acknowledge the exceptional contributions of our expert authors who have contributed to this book. Many of the authors have served in uniform, caring for our service members and their families both on the battlefield and in military treatment facilities around the world. Other authors have cared for veterans and their families either within the Veteran Healthcare Administration or within community settings, where those who serve are hidden and their military connection may not be known. Many authors have also worked to advance policy and education to improve health service access and outcomes for our veterans. We thank you for sharing your knowledge and expertise with the readers. We owe a debt of gratitude to those who serve, both during their service and once they leave service.

We also thank Jones & Bartlett Learning for their support and patience in the development of our book, *Caring for Veterans and Their Families: A Guide for Nurses and Healthcare Providers*. A special shout-out to Christina Freitas, Tina Chen, Maria Leon Maimone, Roxanne Klaas, and Bharathi Sanjeev—thank you for helping to put our passion on paper.

**The views expressed in this book are those of the contributors and do not reflect the official policy or position of the Departments of the Army, Navy, Air Force, or Space Force; Department of Defense; Department of Homeland Security; Veteran Health Administration; U.S. government; or the authors' respective institutions.

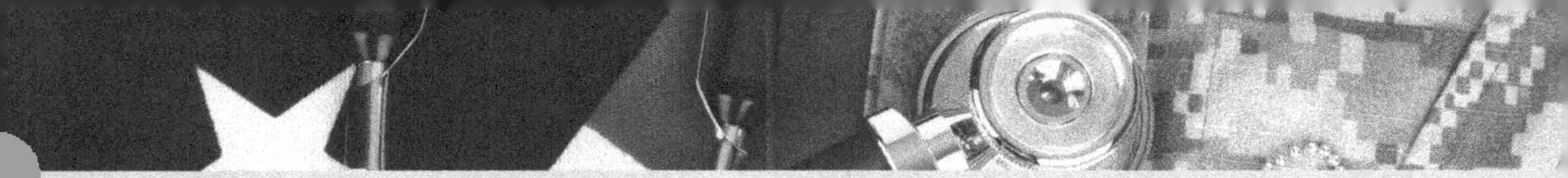

Contributors

Myrna L. Armstrong, EdD, RN, ANEF, FAAN
Texas Tech University Health Sciences Center
School of Nursing
Lubbock, Texas

Kent D. Blad, DNP, FNP-BC, ACNP-BC, FCCM, FAANP
Brigham Young University
College of Nursing
Provo, Utah

James Blankenship, MSN, CFNP
Loudon Free Clinic
Leesburg, Virginia

Allison E. Boyrer, MS, MA, BSN, RN
Department of Veterans Affairs
Rocky Mountain Regional Medical Center
Denver, Colorado

Connie J. Braybrook, DNP, MSN, PMHNP-BC
United States Navy
Nurse Corps
Key West, Florida

Lisa A. Brenner, PhD, ABPP
University of Colorado, Anschutz Medical Campus
School of Medicine/Departments of PM&R, Psychiatry, and Neurology
Rocky Mountain Regional VA
Rocky Mountain Mental Illness Research, Education, and Clinical Center
Aurora, Colorado

Tanya S. Capper, Major, MSN Ed, RN, CMSRN, CPN
United States Air Force
Nurse Corps
Panama City, Florida

Noelle E. Carlozzi, PhD
University of Michigan
Department of Physical Medicine & Rehabilitation
Ann Arbor, Michigan

Alison M. Cogan, PhD, OTR/L
VA Greater Los Angeles Healthcare System
Center for the Study of Healthcare Innovation, Implementation, and Policy
Los Angeles, California

Ronald D. Cole, DNP-c, MPH, BSN, RN, PHNA-BC
Public Health Command-Pacific
Director Human Health Services
Tripler, Hawaii

Patricia L. Conard, PhD, RN
University of Arkansas, Fort Smith
School of Nursing
Fort Smith, Arkansas

LuAnn J. Conforti-Brown, MSW, PhD
University of South Florida
School of Social Work
Tampa, Florida

Rita F. D'Aoust, PhD, ANP-BC, CNE, FAANP, FNAP, FAAN
Johns Hopkins University
School of Nursing
Baltimore, Maryland

Peter J. Delany, PhD, LCSW-C, RADM (Retired), United States Public Health Service
Catholic University of America
National Catholic School of Social Service
Washington, District of Columbia

Roxana E. Delgado, PhD, MS
University of Texas Health San Antonio
Department of Medicine, General and Hospital Medicine Division
San Antonio, Texas

Christina (Tina) Dillahunt-Aspillaga, PhD, CRC, CVE, ICVE, CLCP, CBIST, FACRM
University of South Florida
College of Behavioral and Community Sciences
Tampa, Florida

Tracy Dustin, MSN-Ed, CNE
Salt Lake City Department of Veteran's Affairs Medical Center
Salt Lake City, Utah

Tina M. Fanello, LCSW
University of Colorado
Anschutz Medical Campus–Marcus Institute for Brain Health
Aurora, Colorado

Stephanie Felder, PhD, LCSW, LCSS-A
Catholic University of America
National Catholic School of Social Service
Washington, District of Columbia

Jeanne T. Grace, RN, PhD
University of Rochester
School of Nursing
Rochester, New York

Deborah L. Grassman, MSN, APRN
Opus Peace
St. Petersburg, Florida

Catherine J. Hernandez, DNP, APRN, CPNP-PC
Springhill, Florida

Renee Semonin Holleran, FNP-B, RN-BC, PhD, FAEN
George E. Wahlen Veterans Health Administration
APRN Anesthesia Chronic Pain
Salt Lake City, Utah

Heather L. Johnson, DNP, FNP-BC, FAANP, Lt Col, USAF (Retired)
The Uniformed Services University of the Health Sciences Daniel K. Inouye Graduate School of Nursing
Walter Reed National Military Medical Center Cabrera Family Health Center
Bethesda, Maryland

Catharine Johnston-Brooks, PhD, ABPP-CN
Marcus Institute for Brain Health
University of Colorado School of Medicine
Aurora, Colorado

Abi Katz, DO, MS, HMDC
Amedisys, Inc.
Baton Rouge, LA
Boonshoft School of Medicine, Wright State University
Dayton, Ohio

Katherine G. Kemp, BSc
Veterans Services
National Hospice & Palliative Care Organization
Alexandria, Virginia

Deborah J. Kenny, PhD, RN, FAAN
University of Colorado, Colorado Springs
Johnson Beth-El College of Nursing and Health Sciences
Colorado Springs, Colorado

Adam R. Kinney, PhD, OTR/L
University of Colorado Anschutz School of Medicine
Department of Physical Medicine and Rehabilitation
Department of Veterans Affairs
Rocky Mountain MIRECC for Suicide Prevention
Aurora, Colorado

Jennifer A. Korkosz, DNP, WHNP-BC, APRN
University of Delaware
VA Medical Center
Women's Health Clinic
Wilmington, Delaware

Cheryl A. Krause-Parello, PhD, RN, FAAN
Florida Atlantic University
Christine E. Lynn College of Nursing
Boca Raton, Florida

Susan K. Lee, PhD, RN, CNE, CPXP, FAAN
The University of Texas
MD Anderson Cancer Center Healthcare Disparities, Diversity, and Advocacy Program
School of Health Professions
Houston, Texas

Wendy J. Lee, DNP, FNP-BC, FAANP
University of Texas Health San Antonio
School of Nursing
San Antonio, Texas

Paul C. Lewis, PhD, FNP-BC, Colonel (Retired), U.S. Army Nurse Corps
University of Cincinnati
College of Nursing
Cincinnati, OH

Catherine G. Ling, PhD FNP-BC CNE FAANP FAAN
Johns Hopkins University
School of Nursing
Baltimore, Maryland

Christi D. Luby, PhD, MPH, MCHES®, CFE
Hedgesville, West Virginia

Konstance C. Mackie, DNP, APRN, CPNP-PC, LCDR, USN
Naval Medical Center Camp Lejeune
Pediatrics
Camp Lejeune, North Carolina

Charles R. McMichael, Major, MSHS, RN, CEN
U.S. Air Force
Nurse Corps
San Antonio, Texas

Emma I. Meyer, RN, BSN
Bondurant, Iowa

S. Juliana Moreno
Florida Atlantic University
Christine E. Lynn College of Nursing
Boca Raton, Florida

Dianne Morrison-Beedy, PhD, RN, FNAP, FAANP, FAAN
The Ohio State University
College of Nursing
Columbus, Ohio

Morgan E. Nance, MA
University of Colorado, Anschutz Medical Campus
School of Medicine/Department of PM&R
Rocky Mountain Regional VA
Rocky Mountain Mental Illness Research, Education, and Clinical Center
Aurora, Colorado

Kimberly S. Peacock, EdD
University of Texas Health San Antonio
Department of Medicine
San Antonio, Texas

Richard M. Prior, DNP, FNP-BC, FAANP, Colonel (Retired), U.S. Army Nurse Corps
University of Cincinnati
College of Nursing
Cincinnati, Ohio

Mary Jo Pugh, PhD, RN
University of Utah
VA Salt Lake City
Department of Medicine and IDEAS Center
Salt Lake City, Utah

Catherine (Cathy) J. Rick, RN, NEA-BC, FAAN
Healthcare Consultant, CJR Consulting
Surprise, Arizona
Former Chief Nursing Officer-Headquarters, Department of Veterans Affairs (2000–2014) Washington, District of Columbia

Alicia Gill Rossiter, DNP, APRN, FNP, PPCNP-BC, FAANP, FAAN, Lieutenant Colonel (Retired), United States Army Nurse Corps, United States Air Force Reserve Nurse Corps
University of South Florida
College of Nursing
Tampa, Florida

Angelle M. Sander, PhD
Baylor College of Medicine
H. Ben Taub Department of Physical Medicine and Rehabilitation
TIRR Memorial Hermann
Brain Injury Research Center
Houston, Texas

Joel D. Scholten, MD
Department of Veterans Affairs
Veterans Health Administration
Physical Medicine & Rehabilitation (12RPS6)
Washington, District of Columbia

Jami L. Skarda Craft, MS, CCC-SLP
Traumatic Brain Injury Intrepid Spirit Center
Madigan Army Medical Center
Tacoma, Washington

Linda Spoonster Schwartz, RN, MSN, DrPH. FAAN, Colonel USAF Retired
Yale University
School of Nursing
New Haven, Connecticut

Lillian F. Stevens, PhD
Formerly with Hunter Holmes McGuire Veterans Affairs Medical Center
Mental Health Service
Richmond, Virgina

Ali R. Tayyeb, PhD, RN, NPD-BC, PHN
California State University, Los Angeles
Patricia A. Chin School of Nursing
Los Angeles, California

Judith Vanderryn, PhD
Denver, Colorado

William Washington, MD, MPH, FACPM
U.S. Army
Medical Corps
Preventive Medicine Consultant and Public Health Emergency Officer
Regional Health Command-Europe

Pamela Willson, PhD, APRN, FNP-BC, CNE, NE-BC, FAANP
Texas State University
Office of Distance and Extended Learning
San Marcos, Texas

Margaret Chamberlain Wilmoth, PhD, MSS, RN, FAAN, Major General, U.S. Army (Retired)
University of North Carolina
School of Nursing
Chapel Hill, North Carolina

Josephine F. Wilson, DDS, PhD
Wright State University
Boonshoft School of Medicine, Department of Population & Public Health Sciences
Dayton, Ohio

Spencer R. Young, BA
University of Colorado, Anschutz Medical Campus
School of Medicine/Department of PM&R
Rocky Mountain Regional VA
Rocky Mountain Mental Illness Research, Education, and Clinical Center
Aurora, Colorado

Jessica L. Zumba, MSN, RN
University of Colorado College of Nursing
Aurora, Colorado

Introduction

Preparing Healthcare Providers to Care for Veterans and Their Families: Moving from "Do No Harm" to "Do Great Good"

Dianne Morrison-Beedy, Alicia Gill Rossiter, and Rita F. D'Aoust

This introduction, and our experience with veteran and military health competencies, began in a similar way as the parable of the blind men and the elephant. Like many people who do not have experience with veteran and military health "elephants," the provider's and caregiver's experience of health for both active duty and those who have served is shaped largely by the small piece, experience, or history that they directly touch, which may be very limited or nonexistent. Yet that small "touch of the elephant" shapes how one interacts with, and cares for, veteran clients and their families. Each blind man (or provider) believes that they understand (from their limited touchpoint) what "an elephant" is like, and thus providers often bring a narrow or constrained understanding of the complex factors and needs impacting veteran health and well-being. Our quest for building educational competencies for providers was fueled by the need to move beyond the limited subjective experiences that may exist for one provider that may ignore other's limited, subjective experiences (which may be equally true), to provide a more inclusive approach needed for relevant, tailored care for our veterans. This introduction hopes to move us forward in our actions, beyond a "do no harm" approach for addressing the unique needs of veterans, to building capacity in educational programs to provide gold-standard, up-to-date care, and services to them. Given the number of veterans in the United States and their varied deployment, combat, employment, and service experiences, these competencies will address significant challenges in the healthcare sector.

Accounting for active duty, reservists and the National Guard, over 2.6 million Americans have served in the military since 9/11 (National Center for Veterans Analysis and Statistics, 2016). In fact, over one in ten citizens over the age of 18 years are classified as veterans in the United States (Newport, 2012). This demographic patient segment represents not only the entire Veterans Healthcare System (VA) but, given that the majority of veterans receive their healthcare in the civilian sector (Moss, Moore, & Selleck, 2015), they represent a significant section of healthcare consumers across the United States. The VHA serves approximately nine million veterans enrolled in the VA healthcare system (United States Department of Veterans Affairs, 2021). Approximately 12 million veterans receive care in the civilian sector. These veterans either: (a) do not have a service-connected disability, (b) do not qualify for VHA, or (c) have not been appropriately screened, referred and subsequently determined to have a service-connected disability. To receive VHA care as a covered benefit, the patient must: (1) meet veteran eligibility service, (2) have proof of a service-connected disability, and (3) receive a determination of disability.

Historically, military and veteran health care has been siloed, either in the Defense Healthcare System for active duty service members and their families, or the VA Healthcare System for veterans with service-connected health issues. The emphasis for preparing healthcare providers has traditionally been focused on those who provide care in these two agencies and not necessarily civilian providers in the community who may have limited or sporadic engagement with the military and/or veteran community. The longevity of the wars in Iraq and Afghanistan, coupled with the shift in appropriations to the DHS and the passing of the Choice Act of 2014 and the MISSION Act of 2018, has led to an increasing number of service members, veterans, and their families receiving care in the civilian sector. These providers in the civilian sector may be unaware of their client's connection to the military and may lack the knowledge and expertise to provide culturally competent care to military-connected patients.

The Joining Forces Initiative launched by First Lady Michelle Obama and Dr. Jill Biden in 2011 was a nationwide call to action for the health, education, and employment sectors of communities across the country that was aimed at rallying support and awareness of the service, sacrifice, and unique education, health, and employment needs of service members, veterans, and their families. A key component to this initiative was educating the civilian community regarding the strengths and needs of those who serve in harm's way and the families that support them on the home front. One of the key pillars of the Joining Forces' initiative was ensuring that the unique healthcare needs of service members, veterans, and their families were met. This included not only identifying and providing care for service members and veterans who have experienced the visible and invisible wounds of war, but also occupational health issues and exposures associated with military service either as a service member, spouse, or military-connected child (Joining Forces, 2011).

At the invitation of First Lady Obama and Dr. Biden, college of nursing deans from around the country were invited to pledge that nurses join forces with the White House to improve health outcomes of service members, veterans, and their family members. This could be accomplished, in part, by including veteran health competencies in nursing education and expanding opportunities for research and training focused on veteran's health. This event led to an outpouring of support from the nursing community; more than 500 nursing schools and 160 nursing organizations pledged their support for the initiative. The American Association of Colleges of Nursing created a veteran toolkit for nurse educators, the National League of Nursing developed veteran-specific simulation experiences for educating students, the American Academy of Nursing launched their "Have You Ever Served?" Campaign, and the American Association of Nurse Practitioners had their first call for abstracts focused solely on providing culturally competent care to veterans in clinical practice. As co-authors, we helped initiate a first-ever international conference on these issues in nursing academia (Morrison-Beedy, Passmore, & D'Aoust, 2015; Visovsky & Morrison-Beedy, 2016). From there, other health professions and health agencies joined forces, leading to collaborations with the civilian health sector, the Department of Defense, the VHA, and veteran's service organizations in the community (Saver, 2012).

Given these large population sub-sets, and resulting variation in possible care settings, a broad array of personnel were identified who can be responsible for the care of veteran clients. There is an ever-growing awareness of the correlation between military service and unique physical and psychological health comorbidities (Fredricks & Nakazawa, 2015). Yet there is still a dearth of knowledge and expertise across the healthcare provider and caregiver sectors when it comes to recognizing service-related impact on health and well-being and necessary knowledge and skills needed to address a veteran's distinctive health experience (Fredricks & Nakazawa, 2015). Veteran health competencies are essential to all providers regardless of settings. There is often an assumption that military experience, even within the military health arena, or experience as a health professional in the VHA/VA, constitutes "veteran health competency." This assumption has led to care that is less than holistic, tailored, and evidence-based; thus the need for competency-based education.

Early in this book, Chapters 1 to 9 focus largely on providing our readers an understanding of the military system, culture, and branches of service. We present the unique challenges faced by female veterans and those experienced by military members as they leave active duty. Considerable detail is provided there on the VA healthcare system and other support services. Recent initiatives such as the "Have you ever served?," "I Serve 2," the VA Military Health History Pocket Card for Health Professions Trainees & Clinicians, and "IDing Veterans" provides users of this book pragmatic approaches to garnering needed information to address the needs of those who have served and their family members.

This information and background "sets the stage" as we move into a more focused lens on the physical and psychological "wounds of war." Whether these wounds are superficial or deep, what is clear is that these impacts can affect both the active duty or reserve/National Guard, the individual, or their loved ones. In the chapters that follow, we provide detailed background information as well as strategies and resources directly related to the physical or psychological concern. Topical areas range from those physical wounds resulting from direct trauma or environmental exposures across the life spectrum as well as impact on caregivers. The varied and complex psychological impacts affecting those who have served time in the military are detailed and the needs and challenges faced by their family members are thoughtfully described in that section. The diversity of providers and caregivers delivering care for our veterans is quite broad. These personnel can be: (a) hired as employee provider or contracted providers for the VHA or a VA facility, (b) civilian sector personnel practicing across very different non-VA/VHA settings and agencies for veterans without an identified service-associated disability, or (c) civilian providers practicing through the MISSION Act of 2018.

The MISSION Act is fundamentally transforming VA health care by giving veterans greater access to health care in VA facilities and the community. More than 5,000 veterans per week are using new Urgent Care benefits through the 6,400 local urgent care providers that have partnered with VA. The urgent care network covers 90% of all veterans (United States Department of Veterans Affairs, 2021). The Veteran Population Model 2018 indicates that there are 19.5 million veterans in the United States, with approximately 50% of veterans having served in the Gulf War Era (National Center for Veterans Analysis and Statistics, 2020). As required by the VA Mission Act of 2018, the VA implemented the Veterans Community Care Program (VCCP). Under the Mission Act, the VCCP is a permanent program that has consolidated or replaced VAs' previous community care program and established designated access standards and contracts with third-party administrators to build networks of community providers to increase access for veteran care. The VCCP allows VA various options to purchase community care in the civilian section, including through regional contracts called Community Care Networks (CCN), and set direct agreements with community providers for care not included in those contracts, known as Veterans Care Agreements. Additionally, the VA uses contract providers to supplement in-house compensation and pension (C&P) exam program. These examinations are critical for determination of service-associated disability compensation. The VA is moving to outsource all C&P exams to improve timely decisions as well as reduce the backlog of C&P exams that has increased by 200,000 (Shane, 2020).

Improvements in the scheduling process for VCCP remains a challenge. The lack of a comprehensive policy, an electronic provider-profile management system, decision support tools, and referral manager may limit the VA's ability to reduce veterans' wait time for care (United States Government Accountability Office, 2020). Yet despite these limitations, the number of veterans cared for in the civilian sector through VCCP increased 77% from 2014 through 2019.

With the numerous and complex challenges facing veterans and family members, there exists a need for moving beyond the overarching structural organization of concepts identified as unique to this population, to an approach that provides the structure and process for performance and assessment. When developing educational or training programs for caring for this special population, much discussion has taken place within educational and healthcare organizations across disciplines about the need for a consistent set of knowledge and skills, "a core set of competencies." These "competencies" are not just a "to do checklist of skills" (although these may be included as part of the competency); they are instead an integration of knowledge, skills, and affective qualities that are needed to competently meet the needs of the service member, caregiver, or family member, that can be observed and measured (Giddens, 2020). Competencies required by those who care for or attend the veteran population continue to be developed, tailored, and refined. In 2015, Moss and colleagues identified 10 core competency areas. These areas include military and veteran culture, understanding the VA healthcare system, polytrauma, substance use, exposure to environmental hazards, military sexual trauma (MST), traumatic brain injury (TBI), post-traumatic stress disorder (PTSD), suicide, and homelessness (Moss et al., 2015).

In 2007, the Veterans Affairs (VA) Health Care System partnered with selected top schools of nursing with the goal of increasing compassionate, tailored nursing care for the nation's veterans. This mutually beneficial enterprise helped provide both faculty and staff development addressing veteran-specific needs as well as increasing the graduation numbers of highly educated nurses who had received VA setting training that facilitated recruitment into career paths in the VA system (Bowman et al., 2011). This VA Nursing Academy (VANA), which subsequently evolved into the VA Nursing Academic Partnerships (VANAP), initiated a set of competencies for nurses focused primarily on clients in the VA health system. These competencies encompassed the knowledge, skills, and attitudes that should serve as a base for caring for veterans with specific health conditions. These issues, although not exclusive to military service, were often identified more commonly in this population. These included military culture, post-traumatic stress disorder (PTSD), environmental/chemical exposures, substance use disorders (SUD), military sexual trauma (MST), traumatic brain injury (TBI), suicide, end of life, homelessness, amputation/assistive devices, and VA healthcare administration. Similarly, Vest and colleagues (2018, 2019) and Fredericks (2015) identified physician knowledge, comfort, and educational needs required for effective VHA consultation and referral much in line with those competency areas identified. Adding to these recommendations, the Substance Abuse and Mental Health Services Administration (SAMHSA) advocated for proficiencies specific to mental health and, and they described it, "[military] cultural competency" (2020).

Building upon these competencies, Rossiter, Morrison-Beedy, Capper, and D'Aoust

(2018) extended this understanding by developing educational curricular modules that could be provided in online format, as an elective, or integrated within current curriculum. Originally targeted to baccalaureate nursing students, the goal of developing these modules was to establish a baseline of understanding in all nursing students to be able to identify and address the unique needs of veterans whether inside a VA or other outside non-military health settings. These modules were later expanded to increase their utility across disciplines and levels of care providers or attendees.

In the development of these competencies we noted that, for the veteran client, the mental and physical health impact of military service is not always evident at the time of separation. For example, service members understand that exposure to certain dangerous conditions and hazards are a part of their military service. They understand that they may serve overseas or in areas that could pose a significant risk to their health and well-being. However, few men and women serving in the military expect exposure to hazards at the military base on which they work and call home even if only temporary. Exposure to drinking water contaminated with perfluoroalkyl and polyfluoroalkyl substances (PFAS) is now a problem for many veterans and service members. PFAS has been used in firefighting foam on military bases. PFAS has contaminated military base groundwater as well as the surrounding communities. Thus, thousands of military personnel may have been exposed to PFAS-contaminated water. PFAS can be a factor in several developing health conditions such as hepatic injury, fertility, changes in child and fetal development, immune system dysfunction, increased risk of thyroid disease, and asthma. While the science improves that supports the link between exposure and certain conditions, providers in the civilian and VHA sector need to know about service-connected environmental exposure and impact on service member health over time. Importantly, knowing how to screen and test, even when testing may not be currently covered by the VA is important (United States Department of Veterans Affairs, 2020; United States Environmental Protection Agency, 2021).

Moving beyond the ten topical areas identified by Moss et al. (2015), these competencies contained targeted objectives and content addressing knowledge, attitudes, and skills for each competency area. Importantly, we developed an approach that is inclusive of all health professionals who care for veterans, whether in the civilian sector or VHA setting. Building upon our previous work (Morrison-Beedy et al., 2015; Morrison-Beedy, 2016; Rossiter et al., 2018), we have expanded these general groupings to include, and differentiate, those laddered competencies needed by entry or staff level professionals and those needed by health providers (e.g., MD, PA, NP, ClinPsych, LCSW). Furthermore, we provide a framework that includes conditions, screening, and resources.

Understanding that the attitude component of these competencies serves as the overarching approach, we provide this holistic approach to working with veterans, military members, and their families. Whether providers are addressing educational, knowledge-based needs, or clinical skills components when caring for veterans, a needed base of understanding and sensitivity serves as the starting point for all encounters with the veteran or his/her family members. Certainly, authenticity in approach and seeking to understand, from the lens of a veteran, their experience is first and foremost. Providing care in a supportive and non-judgmental manner helps lay the foundation for a positive, ongoing relationship between client and provider. Imbedded within this empathetic and honest approach is the ability to express appreciation for a veteran's service. Honoring both the complex personal and organizational sacrifice that exists within the military experience for both the veteran and their family members is essential. Coupled within these experiences are a complexity of responses from those impacted by service. These can range from stoicism, to quiet or unacknowledged suffering, to reflective understanding of a job well done. Certainly, the old adage holds true for those providers addressing uncertain, complex, and discomforting situations for the first time—"get comfortable being uncomfortable"—but with each encounter your skills and emotional reactions to these difficult conversations will improve.

This book addresses the latest iterations of these competencies and each chapter provides in detail content-intensive background information as well as strategies specific to screening and care provision as well as targeted resources for the reader. In an international conference focused on veterans and military health issues, "Joining Forces to Restore Lives," Brigadier General Kevin Beaton spoke about his and many others' involvement in across the globe and directed this moving comment to all attendees regarding the world's veterans: "We must help them find the path forward." Certainly, this book represents the commitment of so many across diverse backgrounds, disciplines, and experiences to communicate, share, and band together to ensure our military and veterans find a path forward (Morrison-Beedy, 2016). In this effort, all contributors and readers are also a "band of brothers (and sisters)." Our commitment is to truly "do great good" for all who have served.

References

Bowman, C. C., Johnson, L., Cox, M., Rick, C., Dougherty, M., Alt-White, A. C., . . . Dobalian, A. (2011). The department of veterans affairs nursing academy (VANA): Forging strategic alliances with schools of nursing to address nursing's workforce needs. *Nursing Outlook, 59*(6), 299-307.

Fredricks, T. R., & Nakazawa, M. (2015). Perceptions of physicians in civilian medical practice on veterans' issues related to health care. *The Journal of the American Osteopathic Association, 115*(6), 360-368.

Giddens, J. (2020). Demystifying concept-based and competency-based approaches. *Journal of Nursing Education, 59*(3), 123-124.

Joining Forces. (2011). About joining forces. Retrieved from https://obamawhitehouse.archives.gov/joiningforces/about

Morrison-Beedy, D. (2016). Finding a path forward: A focus on military and veterans health. *Nursing Outlook, 64*(5), 403-405.

Morrison-Beedy, D., Passmore, D., & D'Aoust, R. (2015). Military and veteran's health integration across missions: How a college of nursing "joined forces." *Nursing Outlook, 63*(4), 512-520.

Moss, J. A., Moore, R. L., & Selleck, C. S. (2015). Veteran competencies for undergraduate nursing education. *Advances in Nursing Science, 38*(4), 306-316.

National Center for Veterans Analysis and Statistics. (2016). Profile of post-9/11 veterans: 2014. Retrieved from https://www.va.gov/vetdata/docs/specialreports/post_911_veterans_profile_2014.pdf

National Center for Veterans Analysis and Statistics. (2020). Veteran population projection model 2018. Retrieved from https://www.va.gov/vetdata/docs/Demographics/New_Vetpop_Model/Vetpop_Infographic2020.pdf

Newport, F. (2012). In US, 24% of men, 2% of women are veterans. Retrieved from http://www.gallup.com/poll/158729/men-women-veterans.aspx.

Rossiter, A. G., Morrison-Beedy, D., Capper, T., & D'Aoust, R. F. (2018). Meeting the needs of the 21st century veteran: Development of an evidence-based online veteran healthcare course. *Journal of Professional Nursing: Official Journal of the American Association of Colleges of Nursing, 34*(4), 280-283.

Saver, C. (2012). Nurse leaders, dr. jill biden, and first lady michelle obama join forces to announce new initiative to help veterans and their families. *American Nurse*, Retrieved from https://www.myamericannurse.com/nurse-leaders-dr-jill-biden-and-first-lady-michelle-obama-join-forces-to-announce-new-initiative-to-help-veterans-and-their-families/

Shane, L. (2020). VA moving ahead with plans to outsource all compensation and pension exams. Retrieved from https://www.militarytimes.com/news/pentagon-congress/2020/11/16/va-moving-ahead-with-plans-to-outsource-all-compensation-and-pension-exams/

Substance Abuse and Mental Health Services Administration. (2020). Cultural competency for serving the military and veterans. Retrieved from https://www.samhsa.gov/section-223/cultural-competency/military-veterans

United States Department of Veterans Affairs. (2020). Public health military exposures, PFAS. Retrieved from https://www.publichealth.va.gov/exposures/pfas.asp

United States Department of Veterans Affairs. (2021). About Veterans health administration. Retrieved from https://www.va.gov/health/aboutvha.asp#:~:text=The%20Veterans%20Health%20Administration%20(VHA,Veterans%20enrolled%20in%20the%20VA

United States Environmental Protection Agency. (2021). Per- and polyfluoroalkyl substances (PFAS). Retrieved from https://www.epa.gov/pfas

United States Government Accountability Office. (2020). *Veterans community care program: Improvements need to help ensure timely access to care.* Retrieved from https://www.gao.gov/products/GAO-20-643

Vest, B. M., Kulak, J. A., & Homish, G. G. (2019). Caring for veterans in US civilian primary care: Qualitative interviews with primary care providers. *Family Practice, 36*(3), 343-350.

Vest, B. M., Kulak, J., Hall, V. M., & Homish, G. G. (2018). Addressing patients' veteran status: Primary care providers' knowledge, comfort, and educational needs. *Family Medicine, 50*(6), 455.

Visovsky, C., & Morrison-Beedy, D. (2016). A template for building global partnerships: The joining forces conference goes across the atlantic from the US to the UK. *Nurse Education Today, 47*, 99-100.

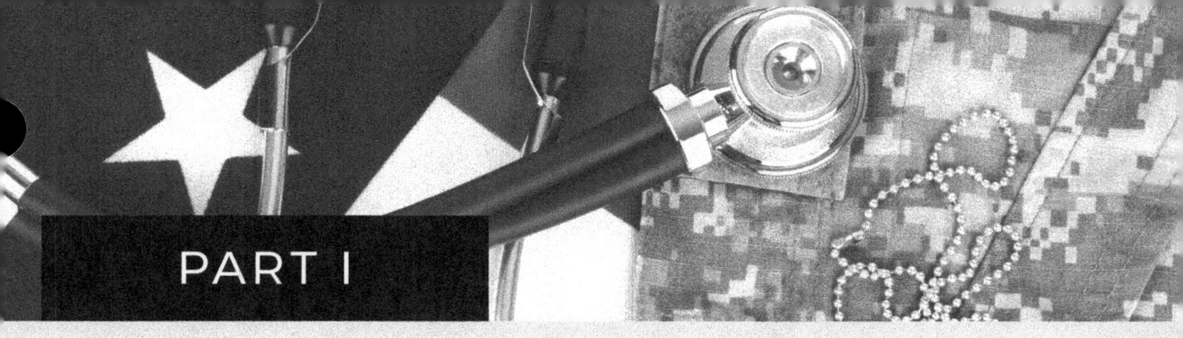

PART I

Introduction to Military and Veteran Health

CHAPTER 1 Military Culture 3

CHAPTER 2 Military Healthcare System 19

CHAPTER 3 Active Duty, Reserve, National Guard: Are There Differences? 31

CHAPTER 4 History of Women Who Have Served and Their Service Connected Health Risks. 45

CHAPTER 5 Caring for Female Veterans 65

CHAPTER 6 Transition from Military to Civilian Life: Considerations for Providers. 93

CHAPTER 7 Veterans Health Administration. 105

CHAPTER 8 Service-Associated Conditions and Veterans Health Administration Eligibility 121

CHAPTER 9 The Use of Service, Emotional Support, and Companion Animals as a Complementary Health Approach for Military Veterans: Information for Healthcare Providers 139

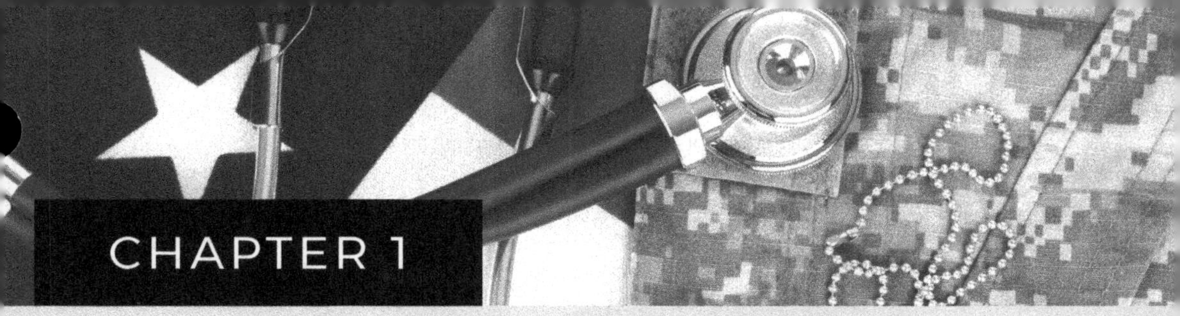

CHAPTER 1

Military Culture

Tina M. Fanello, Jami Skarda Craft, and Catharine H. Johnston-Brooks

The views expressed in this chapter are those of the authors and do not reflect the official policy of the Department of the Army, Department of Defense, or the U.S. government.

Introduction

The intent of this chapter is to offer civilian healthcare providers a better understanding of the perspective veterans may bring to their healthcare encounters in civilian life. Exhibiting knowledge and cultural competency by acknowledging and incorporating awareness of military culture can lead to improved patient satisfaction and enhanced health outcomes (Alizadeh & Chavan, 2016; Meyer et al., 2016). The military has a shared set of behaviors, beliefs, and values that impact how one thinks, communicates, interacts, and views one's role in life and in health care. What is unique about culture in the context of the military is the mindset shift from self-reliance to one of an interdependence, with the collective mission to protect our country by rising above any one individual's needs. Many aspects of military culture contribute to and reinforce this group mindset, including training, uniforms, use of rank, and use of language. Recognizing the presence of subcultures within branches, ranks, and job categories is important to understand the larger culture of the military. The impact of expectations and values within these subcultures further influences veterans' views and experiences within healthcare settings.

Trust is essential to the process of creating an effective working relationship between patients and providers. Having a basic knowledge of military structure and demographics can serve as a foundation on which to build trust so that even without personal service in the military, civilian providers can effectively address the many complex physical and psychological healthcare needs of this population.

Military Language

Familiarizing oneself with the language of military culture includes understanding key terms and jargon, and recognizing the style of direct, concise, and honest communication commonly demonstrated within the military community. This familiarity will significantly enhance the development of a relationship between the civilian provider and the patient.

There are many commonplace terms unique to the military, with numerous acronyms, abbreviations, and military concepts. Although civilian providers may not use this language, understanding key terms can be helpful to comprehend what a veteran is explaining and can support development of a therapeutic relationship. Terms or jargon can vary from one branch to another. For example, a service member (SM, actively serving in the military) is referred to differently across branches of the military. An individual currently serving or having served in the Army should be referred to as a "soldier." In contrast, Air Force members are "airmen and airwomen"; individuals in the Navy are referred to as "sailors," while members of the Marine Corps are simply referred to as "Marines." These distinctions may seem minor, but they can represent one of the most important uses of language that demonstrate respect for the veteran's branch of the service and acknowledgment of an important component of military culture.

Communication in the military is often directive and concrete. The military commonly communicates by providing only the amount of information necessary for the situation, without extensive explanation or emotion. This style of communication can come across as rude or demanding to those not familiar with the culture, but it is the language style to which veterans are accustomed. When building rapport, the civilian provider should be aware of how the veteran communicates. Being direct and providing the "what, why, and when" of information can ensure that the communication exchange is positive and accurate.

Within the healthcare setting, numerous terms that provide information regarding injury or health history may sound unfamiliar to a civilian provider. Geographic locations and timelines of injury are often provided within a military health record. Terms often used when discussing where an injury occurred are CONUS (continental United States—lower 48), OCONUS (outside the continental United States), and "theater" or "theatre" (geographic area of war operations). The medical evacuation of wounded personnel from a battlefield following an injury or medical event is communicated with the acronym MEDEVAC. Timeline of injuries or time of service may be designated by acronyms such as GWOT (Global War on Terrorism), referring to the conflicts that began after September 11, 2001. The most recent wars in the Middle East, including OEF (Operation Enduring Freedom [the war in Afghanistan]), OIF (Operation Iraqi Freedom), and OND (Operation New Dawn), can be referred to collectively as GWOT. As of 2020, troops continue to be deployed to the Middle East and across the world.

Military Ethos and Mindset

All branches of the military subscribe to the same fundamental set of beliefs and attitudes represented by the Military/Warrior Ethos (U.S. Army, 2020a). Strategies used to shift these beliefs and attitudes individuality to the unified group mentality that is essential to the success of the military begin at basic training and are reinforced through every aspect of the lived military experience.

I will always place the mission first.
I will never accept defeat.
I will never quit.
I will never leave a fallen comrade.

The term *mindset* refers to a unifying aspect of military culture that is used as a foundational component to teach perseverance, responsibility, motivation, adaptation, and service above self. A U.S. Army Research Institute report describes one intervention on the first day of new soldier training: "Typically, the days are regimented, and most activities are designed to make all Trainees look and act alike. Their individual identities and personalities are temporarily removed in the attempt to produce the basic Soldier." The intent of this intervention is to "inculcate

Warrior Ethos into Soldiers and leaders" and is referred to as "Soldierization" (Riccio et al., 2004). These actions include shaving recruits' hair, issuing uniforms, and memorizing of the Warrior Ethos, which begins to strip away individualism and create a member of the Armed Forces.

Table 1-1 demonstrates six specific traits, along with consequential strengths and vulnerabilities, recognized by the Center for Deployment Psychology as reinforced by the Warrior Ethos: selflessness (others above self), loyalty (commitment to mission and protecting others), stoicism (toughness), moral code (what is right and wrong), social order (defending societal values), and excellence (being the best) (Uniformed Services University, 2018). For many SMs, these traits become a permanent part of their identity and, as such, may have a powerful influence on how they engage with healthcare services.

To briefly illustrate, these traits will be considered as they might apply to a veteran having served as a combat medic in the Army. Medic training is comprised of a 10-week basic course and a 16-week advanced training course. Although medics are considered nonlicensed medical personnel, they are frequently referred to by peers as "doc" and are individually responsible for approximately 40 troops (Cooper, 2013).

Medics are indispensable on the battlefield and known for their selfless courage as they must put other's lives before their own. Many combat medics have seen "the worst" on the battlefield; therefore, they may view their own needs as minute in comparison. When contemplating if they should get their own injuries evaluated, medics may be inclined to decide that others' care is more important and forgo their own medical needs. This pattern, the vulnerability or downside of selflessness, may continue even years after leaving the military.

The loyalty and commitment involved in saving a wounded comrade in combat is immense. For this reason, medics might be driven to dismiss their own injuries, or even hide them, so as not to "abandon" the team. This vulnerability of loyalty can lead to minimizing personal injuries or symptoms—an "others have it worse" attitude—or even the

Table 1-1 The Warrior Ethos

Strength	Trait	Vulnerability
Placing the welfare of others above one's own welfare	**Selflessness**	Not seeking help for health problems because personal health is not a priority
Commitment to accomplishing missions and protecting comrades in arms	**Loyalty**	Survivor guilt and complicated bereavement after losing friends
Toughness and ability to endure hardships without complaint	**Stoicism**	Not acknowledging significant symptoms and suffering after returning home
Following an internal moral compass to choose "right" over "wrong"	**Moral Code**	Feeling frustrated and betrayed when others fail to follow a moral code
Meaning and purpose when defending societal values	**Social Order**	Loss of meaning or betrayal when rejected by society
Becoming the best and most effective professional possible	**Excellence**	Feeling ashamed of (or not acknowledging) imperfections

rejection of care if they perceive that they could have done more to help someone on the battlefield. Similarly, a vulnerability of excellence may be demonstrated by a self-perception of failure that can lead to complex psychological trauma, moral injury, and maladaptive behavior such as substance abuse.

In this example of a combat medic, the persistence of selflessness, loyalty, and excellence are values that may supersede the inclination to ask for help. As a healthcare provider, recognizing and addressing these vulnerabilities, and inquiring about the veterans' experience, can help patients move beyond the barriers to asking for help by demonstrating insight and fostering rapport.

Branches of Service

The Armed Forces of the United States consists of four main branches within the Department of Defense: Army, Air Force, Navy, and Marine Corps (U.S. Department of Defense, 2020). Another branch, the U.S. Coast Guard, falls within the Department of Homeland Security and operates under the Department of the Navy during times of war. The newest branch, Space Force, established in December 2019, operates under the Department of the Air Force. The overall collective mission of the military is to protect the United States and its territories. Each branch has its own specific focus, including a unique set of values and expectations, within this collective mission. The four main branches of the military account for the vast majority of the military veteran population and will be the primary focus of this section.

The **U.S. Army** is the largest branch of the military and is most engaged in land-based warfare. The Army's stated mission is "to deploy, fight, and win our Nation's wars by providing ready, prompt, and sustained land dominance" (U.S. Army, 2011). Most of the training and combat missions take place on foot or using ground military vehicles. Army troops tend to have the longest deployments, with an average of 9.66 months per deployment compared to all active duty (AD) branches' average of 7.52 months (Institute of Medicine, 2013).

The **U.S. Air Force** serves as the aerial warfare branch and the mission is "to fly, fight and win in air, space and cyberspace" (Gettle, 2007). Air Force training and combat support take place primarily in the air. The Air Force, on average, has the shortest deployments with an average of 4.89 months (Institute of Medicine, 2013).

The **U.S. Navy's** mission is "to maintain, train and equip combat ready Naval forces capable of winning wars, deterring aggression and maintain freedom of the seas," essentially protecting the United States "on, under and over the water" (Naval Medical Research Center, 2020). Another vital responsibility is training chaplains and nonlicensed medical personnel called corpsmen, serving both the Navy and the Marine Corps.

The **U.S. Marine Corps** is a part of the Department of the Navy but is considered a separate branch of the military. The mission of the Marine Corps is "to win our Nation's battles swiftly and aggressively in times of crisis" on land, sea, and air (U.S. Marine Corps, 2020). Essentially, the Marine Corps is "first to fight," and trained to be the most aggressive fighters in any environment. Of all branches, Marines tend to have the strongest branch-specific pride and enthusiasm demonstrated by their recruiting slogan: "The Few. The Proud. The Marines" (Schogol, 2017).

Reserves and National Guard

The **reserve components** refer to two organizations within the U.S. military: the Reserves and the National Guard. Five branches of the military (Army, Navy, Air Force, Marine, Coast Guard) have reserve components, with the Army and Air Force having additional National Guard elements. Reserve and National

Guard components are generally required to serve one weekend a month and two weeks a year unless mobilized to full-time AD for a mission. Members of both reserve components are considered members of the military, but they are only considered full-time military personnel if they are activated to deploy. Most members of these reserve components work full- or part-time civilian jobs and can live anywhere they choose in the United States. Members of both reserve components may be eligible for veteran benefits if they meet certain criteria (U.S. Department of Veterans Affairs, 2012). For further reference, visit https://www.benefits.va.gov/guardreserve.

There are a few differences between the two reserve components. The **Reserves** are a federal reserve force that augments each of the active military components as personnel resource needs dictate. The **National Guard**, on the other hand, has both federal and state missions. Activated by state governors, the National Guard's primary mission is to support the United States in times of natural and human-made disasters. The National Guard can also be activated by the president for federal service to support in times of national emergency, national disasters, or war.

The U.S. military has heavily relied on reserve components in the wars in Iraq and Afghanistan. At its peak, in 2003, approximately 40% of the total U.S. military fighting forces were Reserve and National Guard components (Segal & Segal, 2005).

There are several disparities between Reserve and Guard members when compared to full-time AD SMs; one of the most salient is access to culturally responsive health care following a deployment. Members of the Reserve and Guard have 180 days following deployment to access health care from the Military Health System (MHS). However, members of reserve components commonly forgo access to military medicine after a deployment due to travel distance and the logistics that may delay returning to homes, families, and jobs. Instead, these SMs rely on civilian healthcare entities in their home communities. As civilian healthcare providers, understanding limitations to healthcare access for reserve components is a vital consideration when discussing military service and may further inform assessment and treatment.

Special Operations Command

The **U.S. Special Operations Command** (**USSOCOM** or **SOCOM**) is the command center for a group of elite members of the military that spans across the four main branches of the U.S. military. It includes AD, National Guard, and Reserves. These specially trained members are called Special Operations Forces (SOF). Special operations require unique modes of employment, tactical techniques, equipment, and training. These operations are often conducted in hostile or politically sensitive environments and involve high-risk training and missions (Feickert, 2020).

The most common and familiar SOF organizations include:

- Army: Delta Force, Green Berets, and the 75th Ranger Regiment
- Air Force: Special Tactics Airmen, Pararescue Jumpers (PJs) specializing in personnel recovery and Special Operations Aviators
- Marine Corp: Marine Corps Forces, Special Operations Command (MARSOC) Raiders
- Navy: Navy SEALs (Sea, Air, Land)

Many SOF members transition into high-security government jobs such as the Department of Intelligence or other private military security companies after leaving the military. Due to their unique training, members of this population are often held to higher standards of performance and may face negative implications when deciding to seek medical or psychological care during and following military service. Loyalty (commitment to mission) often results in a higher rate of deployments with less recovery time to address medical or psychological health concerns. This loyalty increases the long-term possibilities of untreated, often overlapping physical and psychological injuries. Excellence (being the best) is also a source of pride, and any perceived imperfections may be another prohibitive barrier to asking for help. An approach to building trust with this military subculture is that integrity, "straight shooting," and good judgment are essential. Civilian providers who are honest and display sound professional judgement, rather than merely asserting their competence, will be more likely to gain the trust of veterans with whom they work (Gayton & Kehoe, 2016).

Military Rank

Rank represents a position of authority and is a symbol of respect. Rank also determines pay grade, level of responsibility, housing, and social status. Rank establishes a clear chain of command by delegating a hierarchy of authority. Each SM has a specific individual to report to in the chain of command as established by rank. All military branches follow the same general command structure with two types of rank: enlisted and officer. Circumventing the chain of command can result in disciplinary action. Pay grades are designated salary levels, and these range from 1 to 10.

Enlisted E-1 up to E-4 are personnel usually within the first few years of their military career. **Enlisted Noncommissioned Officers (NCOs) E-5 up to E-9** are promoted through the enlisted ranks. They have advanced training in their military occupational specialty and provide direct supervision and leadership of other enlisted members of the military. **Commissioned Officers O-1 up to O-10** plan and direct personnel operations and materials management. Officers are required to have a four-year college degree. **Warrant Officers WO-1 up to CWO-5** fall between the ranks of enlisted personnel and commissioned officers, selected for technical skills and expertise in their field. For more information on rank within each branch, a rank structure chart can be very helpful (e.g., www.defense.gov/Resources/Insignia/). Members of the military are expected to utilize rank, but it is not appropriate for civilians to do so.

At any level, the responsibility of leadership brings an inherent attitude toward physical and mental health care. Traits of loyalty (accomplishing missions and protecting others) and excellence (being the best) are reinforced as an SM rises through the ranks. In addition, higher rank is associated with increased reluctance to seek health care due to stoicism (toughness) and the wish not to be perceived as weak. This shift in attitude may be attributed to a sense of accountability, responsibility, or a perception of dedication to the larger mission. Healthcare providers should be cognizant that higher rank may result in an initial guardedness until trust is established.

Jobs in the Military

Jobs in the military are assigned a combination of letters and/or numbers, referred to in the Army and Marine Corps as a Military Occupation Specialty (MOS), in the Air Force as Air Force specialty code (AFSC), and in the Navy as Navy enlisted classification (NEC). There are more than 800 job categories in the military; some examples include infantry, intelligence, military police, logistics, engineer, communications, medic, transportation, and aviation. All applicants take an Armed Forces Vocational Aptitude Battery (ASVAB) to determine for which branch and job they are best suited in the military. Once applicants have received their score on the ASVAB, other factors such as qualifications, security clearance, and physical requirements are considered. It is important for civilian providers to understand that all SMs from all job categories are eligible for combat deployment and may experience combat exposure.

Within the larger construct of military culture, some job categories instill unique skillsets and values that shape attitudes about accessing health care. Given the high-risk nature of job categories such as SOF and explosive ordnance disposal (EOD), SMs may habitually focus on the here and now, while ignoring the implications of their job on long-term physical and psychological health. In addition, personnel in high-risk job categories tend to have a strong appetite for adrenalin-inducing activities, causing further wear and tear on a body already affected by years of harsh, high-stress circumstances. Veterans in these job categories may have experienced repeated blast exposures (even hundreds depending on the length of their military career), leaving them at high risk for traumatic brain injury, hearing loss, and headaches, as well as psychological impacts or personality changes. Acknowledging this mindset is critical to recognizing military attitudes toward personal health, moving past the toughness and sometimes dismissive attitude about health care that may have become part of the veteran's identity.

There are several helpful websites that detail various types of military jobs (e.g., www.todaysmilitary.com/careers-benefits/explore-careers).

Joining the Military

Fewer than one-half of 1% of the U.S. population currently serves as AD military personnel. Joining the U.S. military requires an individual to be a U.S. citizen or lawful permanent resident between the ages of 17 and 39 (age limit varies by branch), to be in good physical and psychological health, and to hold at least a high school diploma or GED (USA.gov, 2020). Individuals join the military from a variety of ethnic, social, geographic, and cultural backgrounds, and therefore the factors that influence a decision to serve in the Armed Forces are unique to each person. A 2018 RAND study found that the top three reasons recruits chose to join the military are (1) travel and adventure, (2) benefits such as health care and education, and (3) a response to a call to serve. Other reasons include perception of honor, job training, and pay (Helmus et al., 2018).

AD demographics paint a picture of a predominantly young population, with 71% of enlisted SMs age 30 or younger (the Marine Corps has the largest percentage of enlisted members age 30 or younger, at 86.4%). In addition, 69% of all AD SMs identify as White with the second largest population being Black (17.1%). Of all AD SMs, 16.5% identify as women, increasing from 14.7% in 2000, and the percentage is expected to continue to rise (Department of Defense, 2018). The six states providing the highest number of recruits are California, Texas, Florida, Georgia, North Carolina, and New York (Department of Defense, 2018).

The 2018 U.S. Census Bureau reports that approximately 18.2 million people, or 7% of the adult population, are veterans of the U.S. Armed Forces (Vespa, 2020). The overall number of veterans is predicted to steadily decline over the next 30 years to 13.6 million due to increasing mortality rates of World War II, Korean conflict, and Vietnam era veterans. Census data reveal that the median age of all living veterans is 65. The median age of post-9/11 veterans is 37, while Vietnam era (the largest living cohort, at 6.4 million) and World War II veterans have median ages of 71 and 93, respectively (Vespa, 2020).

States with the highest number of veterans are California (1.47 million), Texas (1.4 million), and Florida (1.4 million), while the state with the highest percentage of veterans is Alaska, at 10.7%. Post-9/11 veterans, on average, have a 43% chance of having a service-connected disability compared to Gulf War (27%) and Vietnam era veterans (16%).

Reasons for this increase are complex and include improved lifesaving measures in the battlefield (fewer people died on the battlefield in recent wars) and improved recognition by the Veterans Affairs (VA) of service-related disabilities (Vespa, 2020).

Female Veterans and Military Service

Women have proudly served their country throughout the history of the United States, but the extent of their involvement and recognition of their contributions have changed dramatically over time. Prior to being formally recognized as part of the U.S. Armed Forces with the Army Nurse Corps in 1901, women served during the American Revolution and Civil War disguised as male soldiers (U.S. Army, 2020b). Since the early 1900s, women served primarily as nurses, but have slowly integrated into other roles such as flying aircraft, gathering intelligence, and engaging in communications operations with minimal recognition for their contributions. The wars in Iraq and Afghanistan have significantly changed the roles of women in the military. For example, women have been involved in combat with limited acknowledgment for many years. In 2015, the Pentagon lifted a ban on women serving in combat arms units, allowing women to apply for any job available to men, provided that they meet the same physical requirements (U.S. Army, 2020b).

Women currently make up approximately 9% (1.7 million) of the veteran population. By 2040 that number is projected to rise to 17% (Vespa, 2020). Although the proportion of female SMs and veterans is growing, they are still significantly outnumbered by their male counterparts. Given these numbers and the history of women's service, there are aspects of a woman's military experience that continue to be unique and challenging, such as ill-fitting gear, navigating family life, and unique healthcare challenges.

Sadly, one of the most significant health issues facing female veterans is military sexual trauma (MST), a term used to describe sexual assault or harassment that takes place during military service. While men also report MST, women report it in much higher numbers. One in 4 women and 1 in 100 men screened at the VA reported MST (Wilson, 2018). Frequently, MST is not disclosed until leaving the military because despite a strict no-tolerance policy, many victims fear retaliation from the perpetrator or believe that nothing will be done about the incident even if it is reported. This lack of disclosure is particularly true when the perpetrator is someone in the individual's chain of command upon whom the individual must rely for safety and well-being (Andresen et al., 2019). Screening for MST is a crucial healthcare consideration for these veterans, as it is strongly associated with mental health conditions including posttraumatic stress disorder (PTSD), dissociative disorders, eating disorders, and personality disorders. In addition, veterans with MST are at a higher risk for suicide and intentional self-harm, as compared to their peers without MST. This further reinforces the need for heightened awareness of, and screening for, suicide risk in the female veteran population (Kimerling et al., 2007).

Sexual Orientation, Gender Identity, and the Military

The formal targeting of homosexuality in the military began in 1942 when psychological examinations were used to screen homosexuals out of military service, including males demonstrating "feminine-like behaviors" (Rubin et al., 2012). In 1981, the military outlawed any form of homosexuality and discharged any individual, regardless of gender, suspected of homosexual activity. With the evolution of social attitudes, the familiar policy of "Don't Ask, Don't Tell, Don't Pursue" (DADT) was signed into law in 1993, prohibiting the military from screening for homosexual behaviors. Once in the service, SMs could not be asked about sexual orientation. This policy also meant that individuals were forced to conceal their sexual orientation; choosing to reveal it put them at risk for being dishonorably discharged and potentially losing their military career and all military benefits. As social attitudes continued to change, a repeal of DADT went into effect in 2011. As of 2020, gay, lesbian, and bisexual individuals openly serve in the military without any lawful repercussions of disclosure (Rubin et al., 2012).

Obtaining sexual identity and orientation history is best practice for any healthcare assessment, including that involving veterans. It is important not to assume that, because a veteran is married or has been married to someone of the opposite gender in the past, the individual has not also had same-sex partners. Gay and lesbian veterans may have married someone of the opposite sex as an avenue of safety during times when their personal safety or career may have been jeopardized as a result of being suspected of being gay.

In 2016, the Pentagon announced a new policy to allow transgender individuals to serve in the military, and for those who were already serving, to do so openly. In 2018, the policy was reversed and as of 2020, individuals who identify as transgender are banned from serving in the U.S. military (Council on Foreign Relations, 2020). During this short period of time, both the MHS and the VA offered some medical and psychological gender transitioning services, only to be revoked in 2018 when the policy was reversed (Human Rights Campaign, 2020).

Relevant to healthcare assessment and treatment of this population in the civilian healthcare sector, understanding that gender identity and sexual orientation may often be hidden while serving in the military is important. Individuals may only feel safe to disclose this information upon leaving the military. For many lesbian-gay-bisexual-transgender (LGBT) patients, discrimination in health care is associated with negative perceptions of health care (Ruben et al., 2019). This situation further reinforces the importance of creating a trusting and a safe relationship to truly help these individuals with what are often complex medical and psychological health needs.

Era of Service

Healthcare providers should also be mindful about the era in which an individual served. Societal attitudes about the era of service, and a veteran's experience with that era of service, may elicit different attitudes about sharing service-related mental or physical health concerns. For example, many Vietnam veterans returned home to widespread antiwar protests while often enduring physical conditions from environmental exposure to Agent Orange and psychological burdens from atrocities they experienced during deployment (Llorente & Ritchie, 2020). Shame and guilt related to the political and social climate of the Vietnam War may have left some veterans guarded about even disclosing their service during this time.

Not all veterans have been provided the same access to healthcare services, especially related to psychological health. It was not until the Vietnam era that mental health challenges such as PTSD were truly acknowledged and treated by the healthcare community. Over time, more physical, cognitive, and psychological healthcare resources have become available to treat these "invisible war wounds," but the stigma of asking for help persists (Sharp et al., 2015).

Unique health concerns of the Vietnam era veterans are exposure to Agent Orange, along with the high prevalence of hepatitis C, PTSD, and homelessness. Those exposed to herbicides such as Agent Orange between the years 1962 and 1975 in Vietnam, as well as other locations (e.g., Korea and Thailand), may be at higher risk for certain medical conditions including AL amyloidosis, ischemic heart disease, noninsulin-dependent diabetes mellitus, Parkinson disease, peripheral neuropathy, skin conditions, and various types of cancers (Board on Population Health and Public Health Practice Health and Medicine Division & Committee to Review the Health Effects in Vietnam Veterans of Exposure to Herbicides, 2018). These conditions may be eligible for care and compensation through the VA (U.S. Department of Veteran Affairs, 2020a).

Often referred to as "signature wounds" of the wars in Iraq and Afghanistan, traumatic brain injury (TBI) and PTSD, both addressed elsewhere, are essential to consider, especially in GWOT veterans. However, there are other important physical and psychological health considerations of this era. The impact of multiple blast exposures impacts the brain and other systems of the body, often resulting in sleep disorders, hearing loss, chronic pain, and gastrointestinal issues (Przekwas et al., 2019). The psychological implications of war and the stress of multiple deployments, with inadequate access to acute treatment, may result in not only PTSD but also anxiety disorders, depression, and other stress-related conditions (Macgregor et al., 2014). In addition, exposure to burn pits (incinerated waste including chemicals, weapons and ammunition, plastics, medical waste, rubber, and human waste) is common in Iraq and Afghanistan veterans and can potentially result in respiratory diseases and other health risks (Sotolongo et al., 2020). These considerations help explain why veterans from this era are at such high risk for polysubstance abuse, depression, anxiety, and other stress-related conditions.

Many of the wounds of service and war are shared by veterans despite their era of service. Although risks may be greater during time of war, injuries and psychological trauma can occur outside wartime. Military training is dangerous, and many injuries and deaths occur every year due to vehicle accidents, accidental gunshot wounds, large weapon system accidents, or psychological trauma from losing a comrade due to an accident or suicide. Using an open-ended question such as "What was your experience with serving during that time?" saves providers from trying to guess what might be relevant and allows patients to share what is most important to them.

Military Families

Military life comes with its own set of rules, traditions, and restrictions that must be observed and followed by all members of the SM's family. Family plays a central role within military culture and is often involved in support of readiness, meaning that if an SM's family needs are not met, the entire mission can be impacted. This concept is another example of the military cultural value of placing the collective group over individual needs. It may mean family members delay or limit recommended health care due to a move, deployment of a family member, or general demands of military life.

There are many unpredictable variables that limit opportunities and create stress for families. Fears of death or injury are obviously stressful situations during training and deployment, but also of concern to the overall health of a family unit is the isolation of a single parent who must manage a household and children for long periods of time. Depending on the branch of service, job training, missions, and deployments can vary in length from a few weeks to many months. At the height of the GWOT, for example, some combat deployments lasted 15 to 18 months. Not only is the time an SM is away from the family stressful due to worry, single parenting, and missing loved ones, but also significant is the time following the return home when family members must adjust to different parenting styles, schedules, shifts in roles, and expectations. If an SM is returning home from a difficult combat deployment there may be psychological or physical injuries to contend with as well. Children may not understand why their parent is acting differently, and spouses may be dealing with changes in the marital dynamic. Research has indicated that children of deployed military members are apt to abuse substances and have higher rates of externalizing behaviors (e.g., physical fights, carrying weapons). There is also evidence of higher rates of suicidal ideation in children with a deployed parent as compared to civilian children (Williamson et al., 2018).

Adjustment and change can be particularly challenging if the child of a military family has special needs. This added burden can impact psychological and social development. Military families are seven times more likely to relocate than civilians, and with each move come new schools, new friends and neighbors, and different housing conditions. Adult children of military members report that geographic mobility is the single most stressful aspect of growing up in the military (Ender, 2000). For spouses, meaningful career paths can be difficult without an established support system or adequate child care in new locations. Of female military spouses, 90% report being underemployed with respect to their education and experience, and tend to make 38% less income than their civilian counterparts (Community Salute, 2017).

There are a few considerations to keep in mind when working with veterans and their families with respect to the caregiver role and the diversity of support systems. A spouse, adult child, or extended family member may take on a caregiver role if the veteran is struggling with issues such as memory loss, physical injuries, or psychological difficulties as a result of military service. The VA provides compensation for eligible veterans requiring a caregiver due to their service-connected disabilities (see, for example, https://www.va.gov/family-member-benefits/comprehensive-assistance-for-family-caregivers/). SMs and their families may have diverse support systems beyond their immediate family unit. Often parents or in-laws, as well as friends, neighbors, and extended family members, may be involved as primary supports.

In summary, it is important to recognize that military families are a relevant component of military culture. Many of the cultural components that are life principles for veterans, such as group mindset and Warrior Ethos traits including loyalty and social order, also extend to military families and have similar implications.

The Military Healthcare System

"The Military Health System (MHS) is the global health system for the Department of Defense (DoD) with a principal mission of readiness: maintaining a medically ready fighting force, and a ready medical system that is prepared to respond to the full spectrum of military operations" (Department of Defense, 2020). The MHS delivers care to AD SMs and their families in more than 50 military hospitals and 600 clinics worldwide, and is supported by private sector providers on a referral basis under Tricare coverage (Department of Defense, 2020).

The civilian healthcare system is very different from the military healthcare system. In civilian health care, patients are required to articulate their own health needs, navigate insurance benefits, find providers, and make their own appointments, often requiring self-advocacy and persistence. Military healthcare culture, much like military culture as a whole, is directed by others. Service members are often told where to go and what to do to address their health needs, in order to meet the principal mission of readiness. An annual medical assessment called the Periodic Health Assessment (PHA) is required and used to evaluate medical readiness (Military Health System, 2020). Veterans may be required to have certain conditions evaluated and cleared in order to do their job, such as a pilot requiring medical clearance following a concussion or an SM being required by the commander to seek psychological services for symptoms of PTSD that are impacting the ability to perform acceptably.

Civilian health care requires a certain amount of self-advocacy that may be unfamiliar to veterans. Therefore, it may be advantageous for the provider to be direct and specific by giving concrete and clear recommendations for medications and follow-up care. Providing written recommendations or speaking to a family member may also be helpful.

The Veterans Health Administration (VHA)

The VA provides a comprehensive system of benefits to assist with the transition back to civilian life, one of which is health care provided under the VHA. Some of the more popular VA benefits include assistance with education, home loans, and life insurance. The structure of the VHA, commonly referred to as "the VA," is comprised of approximately 170 large VA medical centers located in major cities across the United States that offer traditional hospital-based services and some specialty care. In addition, the VHA offers medical and/or mental health services at approximately 1,400 outpatient sites:

- Community-Based Outpatient Clinics (CBOC) provide veterans with common outpatient services such as primary care and mental health services.
- Community Living Centers are skilled nursing facilities for veterans with stable chronic conditions who need rehabilitation or require hospice care.
- Vet Centers offer free readjustment counseling to all combat veterans (U.S. Department of Veteran Affairs, 2020b).

With some exceptions, anyone having served 24 months of AD with an honorable discharge is eligible for VA healthcare benefits. Since there are exceptions to the minimum duty requirements, the VA encourages all veterans to apply to determine enrollment eligibility. Any veteran can apply for healthcare benefits at a local VA facility. To find the closest VA facility, visit www.va.gov/find-locations/.

Veterans can receive care for medical and psychological conditions at no cost if these conditions have been determined to be "service connected." Service-connected conditions are any medical or psychological health diagnoses that had their onset during time of service. Veterans may also receive care at the VA for nonservice-connected conditions with low-cost copayments based on a financial assessment by the VA. After a medical or psychological condition is determined to be service-connected, the VA has a complex evaluation system to determine "service-connected disability ratings" determining both monetary compensation and access to other VA resources. A lack of a service-connected disability for a specific condition does not necessarily mean that the injury did not occur. For example, an SM may have sustained an injury during time in service but because the VA evaluation did not find the condition disabling enough to warrant compensation, or the event was not documented properly while the individual was in AD, a disability rating may not be assigned.

Like many large government organizations, the VA system can be challenging to navigate, and this process leaves some veterans feeling dismissed. Although most individuals have positive experiences at the VA (Veterans of Foreign Wars, 2019), others may not, and this perception may be precisely the reason care is sought from a civilian provider. It can be easy to get drawn into a veteran's negative past experiences with VA healthcare providers, and it can be disruptive to a veteran's sense of safety and stability when specific providers or past care are openly criticized. The best approach is to employ empathy and listen carefully to what specific concerns exist about previous care, as these may be the areas needing extra attention and consideration. The act of truly listening without judgment assists with the crucial task of building trust.

Medications

The many medical and psychological problems experienced by veterans imply that medications are often prescribed and being taken. An accurate history of medication use is therefore pivotal in the care of these patients. There are two significant healthcare culture considerations when discussing medication history with the veteran population: multiple prescribers and medication adherence.

Referred to as "dual healthcare system use," some veterans have multiple avenues to healthcare resources, depending on their benefits, including the VA, the MHS, civilian health care, and private pay health care. As a result, veterans may have multiple prescribers. They may possibly have two different primary care providers, one at the VA and another in the community under Medicare or private insurance. That same patient may have a psychiatrist, psychiatric nurse practitioner, or other specialty care providers such as a cardiologist or neurologist at the VA, in the community, or both. Outside clinics such as hormone replacement centers or substance treatment programs may also prescribe certain medications. Data reported by the VA in 2018 reported one in five VA enrollees are "dual" users of healthcare systems. Unless disclosed by the patient, there is no formal way to track where patients receive all their medications. Nevertheless, providers should ask veterans if they are receiving medication from more than one prescriber to avoid problems such as high-risk adverse drug interactions and the perpetuation of addiction or overuse.

Medication adherence is another crucial cultural consideration in the veteran population. Some veterans self-discontinue medications, often psychotropic drugs, because they think the medication is not working, they feel they should be able to manage their mood without medication, or they have undesirable side effects (Fortney et al., 2011). It is important for civilian providers to investigate a veteran's attitudes and beliefs about taking medications before prescribing.

Supporting veterans in properly adhering to medication use is another example of the importance of developing trust to foster honesty about their experiences with medications. One specific example might be a veteran experiencing erectile dysfunction as a side effect of a psychotropic medication. Being direct and creating safety by displaying openness to discuss problems further may help build trust and allow the patient to be more informed and communicative about personal concerns. In summary, the following considerations are important when taking a medication history from veterans:

- Ask if more than one source is prescribing medication, including medical, mental health, and other outside settings such as hormone therapy clinics.
- List all prescribed medications and the reasons for taking them (remember that some drugs are used off-label).
- Ask if patients are taking the medications as prescribed. It is not uncommon for some patients to take their daily medications "as needed" rather than as prescribed.
- Inquire about any adverse experiences from medications in the past (not just allergies). Individuals may have had multiple trials of psychotropic or headache medications—two of the more common medication categories—while they were in the military or at the VA, and it is meaningful to understand why these medications did not work or produced an adverse response.

Nonprescription Substances

Asking about nonprescription substances such as alcohol and marijuana, both of which are frequently used to manage symptoms such as sleep disturbance, anxiety, and pain, is also important. In addition to alcohol and marijuana, some veterans resort to other unconventional substances to manage their symptoms such as hallucinogenic mushrooms (psilocybin), peyote, and ayahuasca. These plant medicines are not legal for use in the United States, apart from some religious exemptions. However, veterans may participate in retreats to the Amazon of South America or other regions such as Costa Rica where some individuals report experiencing profound psychological transformations as highlighted in the 2018 documentary *From Shock to Awe* (Cote, 2018).

A recent comprehensive review of psychedelic drugs such as MDMA, ketamine, classic psychedelics (psilocybin, LSD, dimethyltryptamine), and cannabinoids concluded that all of these drugs have some therapeutic potential (Krediet et al., 2020). Although much is unknown about the risks, it is important to be cautious about displaying judgment when discussing use of these substances with veteran patients. Veterans have likely encountered judgment in other healthcare settings, which may leave them guarded about fully disclosing important health information. Acknowledging that many veterans are feeling desperate to get relief from their symptoms and exhibiting curiosity about their use of these substances is the path to help build trust in this realm.

Conclusion

The aim of this chapter has been to provide an understanding of components of military culture as a way of better understanding perspectives some veterans bring to their civilian healthcare encounters. Specific aspects of military culture such as training, rank, and language that are used to cultivate and maintain the culture of a unified mindset have been highlighted. Traits representing both strengths and vulnerabilities were identified in the Military/Warrior Ethos and used as a framework to explore attitudes and beliefs that may impact how some veterans view health care. In addition, recognizing subcultures within the larger construct of the military such as branch, rank, and job categories was emphasized as offering additional insight into veterans' beliefs about their health. Finally, possessing a basic knowledge about the demographics of veteran populations, and the complex structure of the military, can serve as an important avenue to the building of trust.

Establishing trust is at the heart of the message in this chapter. Knowing if an individual served and in what capacity is the first step. The foundation for building trust truly begins by assessing what is most meaningful, and this process can naturally start with a question such as "What was your experience with serving in the military and do you have any health concerns related to your service?" Applying basic knowledge and understanding of military culture as an avenue to successfully creating a positive therapeutic alliance will provide a road map forward to address some of the most relevant and critical health concerns of veterans.

References

Alizadeh, S., & Chavan, M. (2016). Cultural competence dimensions and outcomes: A systematic review of the literature. *Health & Social Care in the Community, 24*(6), e117–e130. doi:10.1111/hsc.12293

Andresen, F. J., Monteith, L. L., Kugler, J., Cruz, R. A., & Blais, R. K. (2019). Institutional betrayal following military sexual trauma is associated with more severe depression and specific posttraumatic stress disorder symptom clusters. *Journal of Clinical Psychology, 75*(7), 1305–1319. doi:10.1002/jclp.22773

Board on Population Health and Public Health Practice Health and Medicine Division, & Committee to Review the Health Effects in Vietnam Veterans of Exposure to Herbicides. (2018). *Veterans and Agent Orange: Update 11 (2018)*. National Academies Press.

Community Salute. (2017). *Supporting veterans and military families: Understanding the community*. https://www.imls.gov/sites/default/files/publications/documents/supporting-veterans-and-military-families-understanding.pdf

Cooper, C. E. (Producer). (2013). Combat medics are always in the fight. https://www.army.mil/article/98620/combat_medics_are_always_in_the_fight#:~:text=The%20combat%20medic%20was%20established,responsible%20for%20about%2040%20troops

Cote, L. (Writer). (2018). *From shock to awe* [Film]. In K. Kraus (Maxi Cohen). U.S.A.

Council on Foreign Relations. (2020). Demographics of the U.S. military. https://www.cfr.org/backgrounder/demographics-us-military

Department of Defense. (2018). *Profile of the military community*. https://download.militaryonesource.mil/12038/MOS/Reports/2018-demographics-report.pdf

Department of Defense. (2020). *Fact sheet: Overview of the Department of Defense's Military Health System*. https://archive.defense.gov/home/features/2014/0614_healthreview/docs/Fact_Sheet_Overview.PDF

Ender, M. (2000). Beyond adolescence: The experiences of adult children of military parents. In J. Martin, L. Rosen, and L. Sparacino (Eds.), *The military family: A practice guide for human service providers* (pp. 241–255). Praeger Publishers.

Feickert, A. (2020). *U.S. special operations forces (SOF): Background and issues for Congress*. https://fas.org/sgp/crs/natsec/RS21048.pdf

Fortney, J. C., Pyne, J. M., Edlund, M. J., Stecker, T., Mittal, D., Robinson, D. E., & Henderson, K. L. (2011). Reasons for antidepressant nonadherence among veterans treated in primary care clinics. *Journal of Clinical Psychiatry, 72*(6), 827–834. doi:10.4088/JCP.09m05528blu

Gayton, S. D., & Kehoe, E. J. (2016). The character strengths of special forces personnel: Insights for civilian health care practitioners. *Military Medicine, 181*(9), 996–1001. doi:10.7205/milmed-d-15-00440

Gettle, M. (2007). *Air Force fosters a "warrior ethos" in all airmen*. https://www.af.mil/News/Article-Display/Article/127527/air-force-fosters-warrior-ethos-in-all-airmen/#:~:text=The%20warrior%20ethos%20is%20also,aging%20aircraft%20and%20space%20inventories

Helmus, T. C., Zimmerman, S. R., Posard, M. N., Wheeler, J. L., Ogletree, C., Stroud, Q., & Harrell, M. C. (2018). *Life as a private: A study of the motivations and experiences of junior enlisted personnel in the U.S. Army*. RAND Corporation.

Human Rights Campaign. (2020). *Transgender military service*. https://www.hrc.org/resources/transgender-military-service

Institute of Medicine. (2013). *Returning home from Iraq and Afghanistan: Assessment of readjustment needs of veterans, service members, and their families*. National Academies Press.

Kimerling, R., Gima, K., Smith, M. W., Street, A., & Frayne, S. (2007). The Veterans Health Administration and military sexual trauma. *American Journal of Public Health, 97*(12), 2160–2166. doi:10.2105/ajph.2006.092999

Krediet, E., Bostoen, T., Breeksema, J., Van Schagen, A., Passie, T., & Vermetten, E. (2020). Reviewing the potential of psychedelics for the treatment of PTSD. *International Journal of Neuropsychopharmacology, 23*(6), 385–400. doi:10.1093/ijnp/pyaa018

Llorente, M., & Ritchie, E. C. (2020). Moral injury in Vietnam veterans: What community providers need to know. *American Journal of Geriatric Psychiatry, 28*(4), S5–S6. doi:10.1016/j.jagp.2020.01.019

Macgregor, A. J., Heltemes, K. J., Clouser, M. C., Han, P. P., & Galarneau, M. R. (2014). Dwell time and psychological screening outcomes among military service members with multiple combat deployments. *Military Medicine, 179*(4), 381–387. doi:10.7205/milmed-d-13-00314

Meyer, E. G., Writer, B. W., & Brim, W. (2016). The importance of military cultural competence. *Current Psychiatry Reports, 18*(3). doi:10.1007/s11920-016-0662-9

Military Health System. (2020). Periodic health assessment. https://archive.defense.gov/home/features/2014/0614_healthreview/

Naval Medical Research Center. (2020). The Navy ethos. https://www.med.navy.mil/sites/nmrc/pages/navy_ethos.htm

Przekwas, A., Garimella, H. T., Tan, X. G., Chen, Z. J., Miao, Y., Harrand, V., Kraft, R. H., & Gupta, R. K. (2019). Biomechanics of blast TBI with time-resolved consecutive primary, secondary, and tertiary loads. *Military Medicine, 184*(1), S195–S205. doi:10.1093/milmed/usy344

Riccio, G., Sullivan, R., Klein, G., Salter, M., & Kinnison, H. (2004). Warrior ethos: Analysis of the concept and initial development of applications. The Wexford Group International.

Ruben, M. A., Livingston, N. A., Berke, D. S., Matza, A. R., & Shipherd, J. C. (2019). Lesbian, gay, bisexual, and transgender veterans' experiences of discrimination in health care and their relation to health outcomes: A pilot study examining the moderating role of provider communication. *Health Equity, 3*(1), 480–488. doi:10.1089/heq.2019.0069

Rubin, A., Weiss, E., & Coll, J. (2012). *Handbook of military social work*. John Wiley & Sons.

Schogol, J. (2017). *Marines are once again "the few, the proud."* https://www.marinecorpstimes.com/news/your

-marine-corps/2017/03/30/marines-are-once-again-the-few-the-proud/

Segal, D. R., & Segal, M. W. (2005). *U.S. military's reliance on the reserves*. https://www.prb.org/usmilitarysrelianceonthereserves/

Sharp, M. L., Fear, N. T., Rona, R. J., Wessely, S., Greenberg, N., Jones, N., & Goodwin, L. (2015). Stigma as a barrier to seeking health care among military personnel with mental health problems. *Epidemiologic Reviews, 37*(1), 144–162. doi:10.1093/epirev/mxu012

Sotolongo, A., Falvo, M., Santos, S., Johnson, I., Arjomandi, M., Hines, S., Krefft, S., & Osterholzer, J. (2020). Military burn pits. *American Journal of Respiratory and Critical Care Medicine, 201*(7), P13–P14. doi:10.1164/rccm.2017P13

Uniformed Services University. (2018). Military culture: Core competencies for healthcare professionals. https://deploymentpsych.org/military-culture-course-modules

U.S. Army. (2011). *Our mission*. https://www.army.mil/about/

U.S. Army. (2020a). *Warrior ethos: US Army values*. https://www.army.mil/values/warrior.html

U.S. Army. (2020b). *Women in the Army*. https://www.army.mil/women/history/

U.S. Department of Defense. (2020). *Our forces*. https://www.defense.gov/Our-Story/Our-Forces/

U.S. Department of Veterans Affairs. (2012). Summary of VA benefits for National Guard and Reserve members and veterans. In *VA PAM 27-12-5*. Veterans Benefits Administration.

U.S. Department of Veteran Affairs. (2020a). *Agent Orange exposure and VA disability compensation*. https://www.va.gov/disability/eligibility/hazardous-materials-exposure/agent-orange/

U.S. Department of Veteran Affairs. (2020b). Office of Rural Health. https://www.ruralhealth.va.gov/aboutus/structure.asp

U.S. Marine Corps. (2020). *Our mission*. U.S. Naval Academy. https://www.usna.edu/MarineCorps/index.php

USA.gov. (2020). Join the military. https://www.usa.gov/join-military

Vespa, J. E. (2020). *Those who served: America's veteran's from World War II to the war on terror*. https://www.census.gov/content/dam/Census/library/publications/2020/demo/acs-43.pdf

Veterans of Foreign Wars. (2019). *Our care: A report evaluating veterans health care*. https://www.va.gov/opa/pressrel/pressrelease.cfm?id=5328

Williamson, V., Stevelink, S. A. M., Da Silva, E., & Fear, N. T. (2018). A systematic review of wellbeing in children: A comparison of military and civilian families. *Child and Adolescent Psychiatry and Mental Health, 12*(1). doi:10.1186/s13034-018-0252-1

Wilson, L. C. (2018). The prevalence of military sexual trauma: A meta-analysis. *Trauma, Violence, & Abuse, 19*(5), 584–597. doi:10.1177/1524838016683459

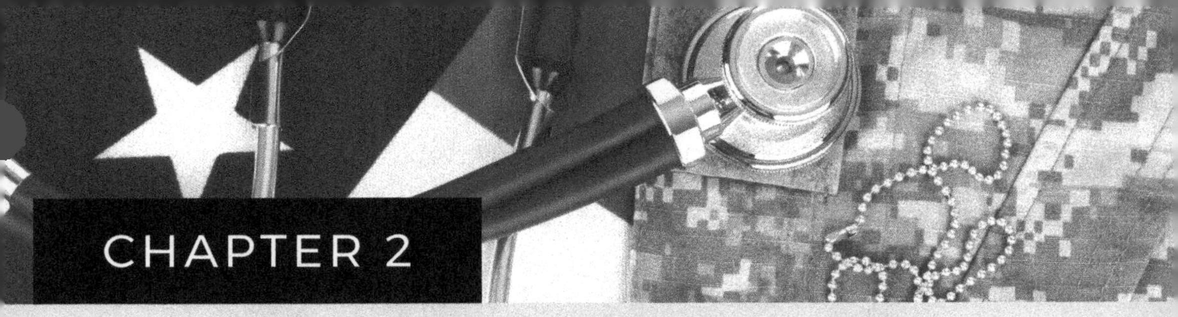

CHAPTER 2

Military Healthcare System

Ron Cole and William Washington

The Military Healthcare System (MHS)

The Defense Health Agency (DHA) provides an integrated healthcare delivery system of medical treatment facilities (MTF), including hospitals, medical centers, and clinics, all with a particular emphasis on population health and medical readiness. The overreaching mission of the DHA is to provide necessary medical support to military operations, service members, and their families. In 2017 Congress directed the Department of Defense (DoD) to consolidate all DoD military treatment facilities of the Army, Navy (including the Marine Corps), and Air Force under the DHA. Each branch of service has the responsibility of managing medical operations for their respective soldiers, airmen, sailors, and marines (Adirim, 2019) (**Figure 2-1**).

Battlefield Medicine and Transition of Care for Wounded Warriors

Healthcare delivery in the battlefield setting sets the DHA mission apart from that of the civilian healthcare system in significant ways. During wartime, the military has the responsibility to develop, communicate, and operationalize strategies to deliver needed health care in very austere and unpredictable circumstances on the battlefield, while still caring for those back home. The cost of not meeting the demand of this mission is directly measured in decreased operational mission readiness, insufficient care to dependents, and (most significantly) loss of our valuable assets—or service members (SMs). The military has executed this mission with exceptional success for many years. In fact, many lifesaving

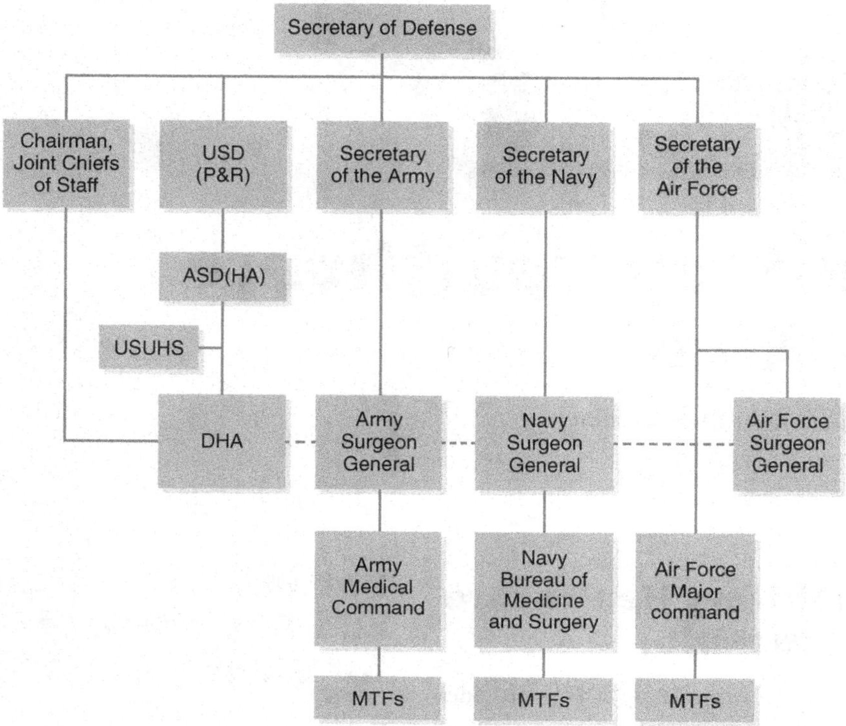

Figure 2-1 Integrated healthcare delivery system.

Modified from Department of Defense. (2014). Overview of the Department of Defense's military health system. https://archive.defense.gov/home/features/2014/0614_healthreview/docs/Fact_Sheet_Overview.PDF

antibiotics, surgical procedures, and general medical practices can be linked directly to battlefield medicine (Cubano, 2018). The mission is not only to deliver health care in these unique situations, but also to do so while maintaining a standard of care that is commensurate with non-battlefield settings. This feat requires extensive training and preparation of the military medical personnel on the front lines of the healthcare delivery system.

Another critical component of battlefield medicine is patient transport and transfer. The DHA coordinates military and logistical assets to facilitate the seamless transfer of sick and injured SMs from the battle zone to the appropriate level of care facility. While it may seem simplistic, this often requires procurement of a complex combination of point-of-injury ground assets, medical air evacuation support, unique naval capabilities, and military fires to protect medical personnel and transportation assets during execution of the movement. These unique challenges represent just a fraction of the no-fail mission sets taken on by the military medical delivery network.

The Role of the Military Healthcare System in OCONUS and CONUS as well as during Peacetime and War

Role 1 – 4

Field Manual (FM) 4–02 (2013) lays out the roles or echelons of care for active beneficiaries, which spans from the unit level to general hospitals. Level I is unit level care (e.g., buddy aid, combat stress support, and evacuations support), level II is care provided by medical battalions or medical companies (e.g., level I care with the addition of surgical, dental, and radiological support), level III care is conducted in the MTF (Evacuation Hospitals or Combat Support Hospitals) (e.g., conduct surgery, recover for return to duty, stabilize for evacuation), and level IV care is conduct in Field or General Hospitals away from the combat zone (e.g., rehabilitation, orthopedics, OB/GYN, dental, and optometry).

The DHA must tailor healthcare delivery to many different locations, operational missions, and patient populations. During wartime, this mission spans from the front lines of the battle to the long-term rehabilitation complex, and every step in between. The configuration of MTFs along the continuum of care must encompass a wide range of capabilities, and the DHA must ensure provider competency in all required specialties. There is a large network of educational and training organizations within the DHA that play an invaluable role in this regard. Considering that the United States has existed in a steady state of wartime operations for decades, the DHA has become extremely resourceful and resilient at operationalizing the delivery of its healthcare products.

Moreover, recent years have seen an escalation of tensions at the demilitarized zone between North and South Korea where many SMs and their families live and work. SMs stationed in Japan also are in danger of the increasing ability of North Korea to strike Japan with deadly force. In addition to traditional military treats, infectious diseases have threatened the readiness of our troops and the well-being of their families worldwide. Depending on where SMs work, imminent threat of war, vectorborne illness, pandemic infectious disease, water/food security, among other issues must be mitigated to ensure operational readiness.

Military public health personnel work tirelessly to provide sound and effective preventive medical plans to minimize the impact of infectious disease and trauma, manage behavioral health treats, and overcome other risks to SMs and their families. Prevention protocols are also specific to location of military operations, population, and other factors. Preventive measures are arguably the efforts across the force healthcare delivery network that pay the highest dividends and have the longest history in the U.S. military, which dates to World War 1 (Fox et al., 2010).

Examine the Role of the Medical Home within the MHS

The patient-centered medical home (PCMH) concept was introduced in the United States in 1967 to combat rising medical costs, optimize resources, and address increased demand for care, poor health outcomes, and unacceptable patient satisfaction. A council of leading medical professional agencies endorsed the PCMH model in 2002, with a focus on seven core principles to be implemented within the primary care setting (**Table 2-1**) (Marshall et al., 2011).

Within the MHS, the PCMH is physically located within military treatment facilities and provides high-quality care to SMs and their families. The PCMH minimizes disruption of care and decreases the time active duty (AD) civilians, SMs, retirees, and their beneficiaries are out of the workplace for medical appointments. PCMHs offer a patient empowerment model, which actively involves patients in their own care and places them at the center of the care plan where they are encouraged to have an active role. The PCMH model focuses on the patients' health goals in locations where they work, play, and live. Medical homes offer primary care and other ancillary services such as laboratory, pharmacy, and radiology services. The PCMH model can provide

Table 2-1 Patient-Centered Medical Home (PCHM) Principles

Types of Care	Definition
Personal Physician	Each patient has an ongoing relationship with a personal physician trained to provide first contact, continuous, and comprehensive care.
Physician-Directed Medical Practice	The personal physician leads a team of individuals at the practice level who collectively take responsibility for the ongoing care of patients.
Whole-Person Orientation	The personal physician is responsible for providing all the patient's healthcare needs or taking responsibility for appropriately arranging care with other qualified professionals. This includes care for all stages of life: acute care, chronic care, preventive services, and end-of-life care.
Coordinated and/or Integrated Care	Care is coordinated and/or integrated across all elements of the complex healthcare system (e.g., subspecialty care, hospitals, home health agencies, nursing homes) and the patient's community (e.g., family, public and private community-based services). Care is facilitated by registries, information technology, health information exchange, and other means to ensure that patients get the indicated care in a culturally and linguistically appropriate manner when and where they need it.
Quality and Safety	Quality and safety are hallmarks of the medical home. Practices advocate for their patients to support the attainment of optimal, patient-centered outcomes that are defined by a care planning process driven by a compassionate, robust partnership between physicians, patients, and the patient's family. ■ Evidence-based medicine and clinical decision support tools guide decision making. ■ Physicians in the practice accept accountability for continuous quality improvement through voluntary engagement in performance measurement and improvement. ■ Patients actively participate in decision making, and feedback is sought to ensure patient expectations are being met. ■ Information technology is utilized appropriately to support optimal patient care, performance measurement, patient education, and enhanced communication. ■ Practices go through a voluntary recognition process by an appropriate nongovernmental entity to demonstrate that they have the capabilities to provide patient-centered services consistent with the medical home model. ■ Patients and families participate in quality improvement activities at the practice level.
Enhanced Access	Enhanced access to care is available through systems such as open scheduling, expanded hours, and new options for communication between patients, their personal physician, and practice staff.
Payment Reform	Payment appropriately recognizes the added value provided to patients who have a PCMH. The payment structure should: ■ Reflect the value of physician and nonphysician staff of patient-centered care management that falls outside of the face-to-face visit.

Types of Care	Definition
	■ Pay for services associated with coordination of care both within a given practice and between consultants, ancillary providers, and community resources. ■ Support adoption and use of health information technology for quality improvement. ■ Support provision of enhanced communication access such as secure email and telephone consultation. ■ Recognize the value of physician work associated with remote monitoring of clinical data using technology. ■ Allow for separate fee-for-service payments for face-to-face visits. Payments for care management services that fall outside of the face-to-face visit, as described earlier, should not result in a reduction in the payments for face-to-face visits. ■ Recognize case mix differences in the patient population being treated within the practice. ■ Allow physicians to share in savings from reduced hospitalizations associated with physician-guided care management in the office setting. ■ Allow for additional payments for achieving measurable and continuous quality improvements.

Table was created based on extracted definitions provided in the MHSPCMH guide (MHSPCMH, 2011).

shorter times away from military units, work, or home, and the centralized team structure improves readiness by decreasing emergency room (ER) visits (Marshall et al., 2011).

The military has three distinct populations that include SMs, retirees, and their family members. Caring for these unique populations must focus on the end-state of "readiness." Overall, the medical home in the MHS focuses on combat medical readiness for SMs, family readiness for the beneficiaries, and readiness for all retirees and AD civilians who support the warfighter. To ensure that all beneficiaries receive adequate care, the MHS deployed two platforms to enhance access to care. Soldier-centered medical homes (SCMHs) and family-centered medical homes (FCMHs) were operationalized to increase access to care and to leverage embedded medical assets. SCMHs are housed on the military installation near brigade level units where much of the SM population lives, while FCMHs are strategically placed in local communities to facilitate easy accessibility for beneficiaries. By creating these two new clinical platforms of integrated care for SMs and their families, the MHS effectively increased access to care, improved patient satisfaction and readiness, decreased cost, and improved the quality of care (Army Medicine, n.d.).

Mission of the MHS and Mission Readiness

The complex mission of the DHA includes ensuring the health and well-being of millions of AD and reserve SMs and their families. SMs must be trained, retrained, and ready to provide the highest level of medical care in support of operational missions across the globe.

Moreover, the United States has maintained a military presence in many countries with whom they have historically been at war. With SMs and their families living and working in countries and cities worldwide, military medical assets must also follow to ensure continuity of medical readiness. The DHA has intensely invested resources, and the DoD has heavily budgeted for seamless access to care of all SMs, no matter where they are asked to serve. Alongside access to care for SMs and their families, quality and safety are of great concern to the DHA. With large medical centers, community hospitals, and clinics spanning the globe, DHA MTF safety is consistently rated as comparable to that found in the civilian sector based on averages from nationally standardized surveys of employee perceptions and patient response rates (Secretary of Defense, 2019).

Healthcare Missions between the Services

For all branches of the military, the goal is to provide high-quality healthcare products to SMs. Due to the differences in missions, vehicle platforms, and several other key factors, there are significant differences in the way that healthcare delivery is managed across the DoD footprint. Navy, Air Force, and Army providers must have mission-specific training, which makes for some differences in patient management across the Armed Forces. In many cases, there is no single set of metrics that can be monitored to assess performance of healthcare delivery, quality, safety, access, and other parameters across the enterprise. Additionally, purchased care that occurs outside of the DHA network of MTFs carry their own set of metrics, medical records systems, and providers, which compound the problem of tracking and comparing healthcare delivery across the entire DoD footprint (Washington et al., 2018).

Scope and Allocations of Care

The MHS provides care for some 9.5 million beneficiaries: AD, retirees, their qualified family members, and survivors (Tricare, n.d.). The MHS provides the same preventive care and every type of medical/surgical service as healthcare systems in the private sector and is managed by Tricare, a state-of-the-art comprehensive military health maintenance organization (HMO). The level of access to care at military treatment facilities is based on the beneficiary category, of which there are two major groups:

1. AD, retired, and guard/reserve members
2. Dependents (spouses and children under age 23 who are registered in the medical record database)

A beneficiary's category determines the enrollment qualification and the subsequent coverage group. Tricare Prime, Tricare Prime Remote, Tricare Prime Overseas, Tricare Prime Remote Overseas, Tricare Select, Tricare Select Overseas, Tricare Young Adult, Tricare For Life, Tricare Reserve Select, Tricare Retired Reserves, and U.S. Family Health Plan are the different programs being offered (Tricare, n.d.). While enrollment can seem overwhelming, Tricare services offer assistance for determining which option is best for each beneficiary.

AD and their families are top priority in the provider portfolio in military treatment facilities. This group is front-loaded for all medical and surgical appointments within available provider profiles. Many AD SMs and their families are enrolled in one of the Tricare Prime options, which have no associated co-pays or monthly costs. Generally, there are no out-of-pocket expenses, even if the beneficiary is seen in the private sector. Additionally, travel reimbursement for specialty care not provided within the local MTF is available to offset any costs the beneficiary may incur.

Retirees are prioritized second in military MTF. In most instances, retirees are in what is called space available (SPACE A) categories for appointments. This means that any empty appointments after the demand from the AD group has been satisfied can be scheduled for a retiree. Dependent children may be seen under certain circumstances depending on the

SM's marital status during the time of service. Unfortunately, Reservists and National Guard members cannot be serviced at the military MTF on a regular basis. This group is only entitled to medical care at the MTFs when they are on AD orders, in which case they are considered first priority just like other AD SMs and their families.

Access to Care for Military Members and Families: Private Sector Partnerships and Department of Veteran Affairs (VA) Partnerships

Not all installations have the same level of military treatment facility coverage. Depending on the size of the military community, location, and the missions, different levels of military emergency facilities, military medical centers, community hospitals, or clinics may vary. Beneficiaries will move from one state or country to another when changing duty stations, so their type of enrollment may change (e.g., a move from the United States to Germany requires an enrollment change from Tricare Prime to Tricare Prime Overseas). To facilitate continuity of care, military electronic health records (EHR) are uniform across all states and continents.

Special assignments such as training with industry partners, long-term health education and training, or recruitment are other times when the beneficiary's type of enrollment may change. If there is no nearby MTF, the plan will change from Tricare Prime to Tricare Prime Remote, or U.S. Family Health Plan, which gives coverage to contracted private sector providers at no cost, including medications. The Assistant Secretary of Defense (ASD) of Health Affairs oversees Tricare, but it is managed by the military and private sector partnerships. There are several types of private sector partnerships (**Table 2-2**) that require registration as a network or nonnetwork entity (Smith et al., 2017).

Military members with over 20 years of service, or those who have qualifying medical injuries, may leave AD and become a retiree. All others who separate are considered veterans. The VA healthcare system does not service AD SMs but is the primary source of access to health care for retirees. Since the VA does not see AD SMs, no record sharing routinely occurs between the two populations. For years, the MHS and VA have been working toward developing a method of record sharing

Table 2-2 Provider Types

Professional providers (other than applied behavior analysis [ABA]) include medical doctors and doctors of osteopathy (MDs/DOs), physician assistants (PAs), nurse practitioners (NPs), urgent care providers, psychiatrists, psychologists, masters-level mental health providers, and physical, speech, and occupational therapists (PTs, STs, OTs).	**ABA providers** include Tricare-authorized Board-Certified Behavior Analysts® (BCBAs), BCBA doctorals (BCBA-Ds), licensed behavior analysts (LBAs), or other qualified Tricare-authorized independent providers with a scope of practice for independent practice of ABA.
Facilities and ancillary type providers include hospitals, ambulatory surgical centers, hospices, skilled nursing facilities, psychiatric facilities, home health agencies, and durable medical equipment and medical supply companies.	To enroll: www.tricare.mil

TRICARE. (n.d.). *Become a Tricare provider*. https://www.tricare-west.com/content/hnfs/home/tw/prov/become-a-provider.html

between VA healthcare facilities and MTFs. The Virtual Lifetime Electronic Record (VLER) Health Initiative and eHealth Exchange (a network of exchange partners who securely share clinical information across the United States) are data management platforms that allow participating medical organizations to share medical records. Several VA facilities in the United States are leveraging the VLER and are sharing military EHRs between the military MTF, VA, and participating civilian healthcare partners to provide continuity of care and reduce errors and redundancies (Tricare, n.d.).

Tricare Insurance

The DHA delivers health care to millions of SMs and their dependents. To accomplish this, the system relies on both MTFs and purchased care, which is used when MTFs are over capacity. The purchased care option employs assets from civilian network hospitals to augment the reach and capacity of DHA assets. The military healthcare delivery network is managed through Tricare, which handles over 9.5 million beneficiaries (Tricare, n.d.). Also, compared to civilian healthcare delivery systems, the DHA generally covers a younger, healthier, and more compliant patient population. The systems, too, within the DHA tend to be more integrated and easier to access for SMs and their families (Army Medicine, n.d.).

Education and Training Requirements of the MHS Team

To augment healthcare delivery, the ASD of Health Affairs places a high value on medical education and training of healthcare providers through several outlets across the country. The Uniformed Services University of the Health Sciences (USUHS) is, perhaps, the flagship of the medical education efforts across the DHA, but there are many other medical military training programs throughout the country as well. Additionally, the DHA has prominent research and development operations that are active in production of vaccines, medications, and other healthcare knowledge products, materials, and services.

The USUHS trains a significant number of healthcare professionals annually, but to meet the demand of the DHA, private civilian training programs are employed as well. Physicians, nurses, behavioral health providers, and many other medical professionals are routinely recruited from the private sector to become medical officers in the DoD. Several incentive programs are available to civilian-trained healthcare professionals through the DHA that function to expand the capabilities and proficiency of the DHA provider force. Additionally, programs to certify providers, nurses, veterinarians, medics, and other healthcare professionals are provided across the force to ensure that providers remain up to date with new medical developments and are consistently provided DHA beneficiaries with cutting-edge medical care (Army Medicine, n.d.).

Patient Satisfaction and Loyalty in the MHS

Healthcare outcomes are the measure for quality of all healthcare systems, and the MHS system is no exception. The personal expectation in contrast to the experience is what will determine the quality of care that the MHS is delivering. Research on the MHS discovers that many military beneficiaries were less than pleased with the care received and suggested improvement to decrease the gap between beneficiaries' expectations and their experience (Jennings & Loan, 1999; Jennings et al., 2005). As the DoD evaluates medical systems for the military, the National Defense Authorization Act (NDAA, 1992) mandated the establishment of an annual survey program that is benchmarked against healthcare norms.

MHS healthcare scientists gather data to analyze beneficiary satisfaction and to support strategic marketing and planning. Data scientists also work to increase access to and quality of care, and to maintain a proactive posture for responding to changing needs of the DoD. The needed information is extracted from a series of surveys, including the Health Care Survey of DoD Beneficiaries (HCSDB), Tricare Inpatient Satisfaction Survey (TRISS), and Joint Outpatient Experience Survey (JOES). HCSDB is conducted annually for system improvement and assesses how efficiently the system administers benefits to Tricare members. The TRISS and JOES are based on individual encounters both inpatient and outpatient, respectively. Every visit with a provider within the MHS will trigger a survey depending on the type of encounter (Army Medicine, n.d.). The MHS generates annual reports to assess results of the surveys, and these reports are shared with senior leaders and NDAA. Reports can be obtained through the MHS Army Medicine website.

Figure 2-2 is a snapshot from the DHA survey evaluating satisfaction with care.

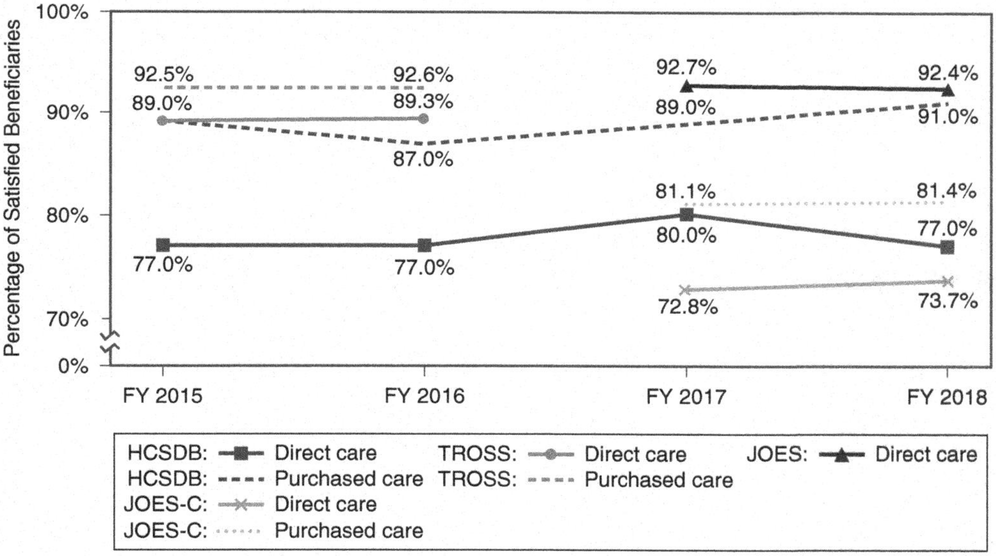

Notes:
- Results for each survey above are weighted to appropriately represent the composition of the MHS population.
- TROSS results for FY 2016 continue from October 2015 to May 2016 for direct care, and from October 2015 to April 2016 for purchased care.
- Results for HCSDB are for Prime enrollees only. "HCSDB Purchased Care" is defined as those who are assigned to an MCSC. "Satisfaction With Care is worded very similarly in each survey as the following statement: "Overall, I am satisfied with the health care I received on this visit" The five-point scale for this question ranges from "Strongly Disagree" to "Strongly Agree." The results provided above are for those beneficiaries who reported either "Somewhat Agree" or "Strongly Agree."
- Sites that migrated to MHS GENESIS were sampled in FY 2018 Q3 after migration, respective to the JOES and JOES-C surveys.
- For visual display, numbers in parentheses on the graph indicate the number of overlapping data points.

Figure 2-2 HCSDB, TRISS, JOES, and JOES-C ratings of satisfaction with care, FYs 2015–2018.
DHA/SP&FI (J-5)/Decision Support, HCSDB, TROSS, and JOES, compiled May 12, 2018.

Several recent studies regarding quality of and access to care for retirees and veterans reveal that many private sector providers lack the needed level of familiarity with the healthcare needs of military beneficiaries (Dyhouse, 2018). This disconnect provides barriers to care for many military families. The military has a specific culture, comradery, environment, and community that must be considered by civilian medical systems. Military beneficiaries can develop a sense of loss and undue stress if these variables are not considered (Daniels, 2017; Elnitsky & Kilmer, 2017). Providers within the MHS are colleagues, neighbors, brothers and sisters in arms with the people they serve. The convenience and a sense of familiarity with this system make it easy for the beneficiaries to remain loyal. Additionally, the MHS is staffed largely by veterans and AD professionals who have firsthand experience with the nuances of military life.

Conclusion

Every healthcare system is expected to provide the best care possible, and there are no exemptions for the MHS. We have reviewed the missions, operations, populations, and partnerships of this complex system. Hopefully, we have shed light on some to the unique situations associated with caring for our SMs who defend the United States and its allies. In addition to maintaining the highest standards, the MHS is responsible for the medical readiness of the fighting Armed Forces of our nation (Kellermann, 2017). For more information on the MHS, refer to the resource list at the end of this chapter.

References

Adirim, T. (2019). A military health system for the twenty-first century. *Health Affairs, 38*(8), 1268–1273.

Army Medicine. (n.d.). http://www.armymedicine.mil/

Cubano, M. A. (2018). *Emergency war surgery* (Rev. 5th ed.). Government Printing Office. https://medcoe.army.mil

Daniels, W. C. (2017). A phenomenological study of the process of transitioning out of the military and into civilian life from the acculturation perspective. Thesis paper. UNLV University Libraries.

Dyhouse, J. (2018). Most private doctors not prepared to treat veterans. *VFW Magazine, 105*(9), 10.

Elnitsky, C. A., & Kilmer, R. P. (2017). Facilitating reintegration for military service personnel, veterans, and their families: An introduction to the special issue. *American Journal of Orthopsychiatry, 87*(2), 109.

Field Manual (FM) 4–02. (2013). Army Health System (AHS). https://armypubs.army.mil/epubs/DR_pubs/DR_a/ARN31133-FM_4-02-000-WEB-1.pdf

Fox, M., Curriero, F., Kulbicki, K., Resnick, B., & Burke, T. (2010). Evaluating the community health legacy of WWI chemical weapons testing. *Journal of Community Health, 35*(1), 93–103.

Jennings, B. M., & Loan, L. A. (1999). Patient satisfaction and loyalty among military healthcare beneficiaries enrolled in a managed care program. *The Journal of Nursing Administration, 29*(11), 47–55. https://doi.org/10.1097/00005110-199911000-00011

Jennings, B. M., Loan, L. A., Heiner, S. L., Hemman, E. A., & Swanson, K. M. (2005). Soldiers' experiences with military health care. *Military Medicine, 170*(12), 999–1004.

Kellermann, A. (2017). Rethinking the United States' military health system. *Health Affairs Blog*. https://www.healthaffairs.org/do/10.1377/hblog20170427.059833/full/

Marshall, R. C., Doperak, M., Milner, M., Motsinger, C., Newton, T., Padden, M., Pastoor, S., Hughes, C. L., LeFurgy, J., & Mun, S. K. (2011). Patient-centered medical home: An emerging primary care model and the military health system. *Military Medicine, 176*(11), 1253–1259. https://doi.org/10.7205/milmed-d-11-00109

Military Health System Patient Centered Medical Home Guide (MHSPCMH). (2011). https://www.milsuite.mil/book/servlet/JiveServlet/previewBody/340421-102-1-577206/PCMH%20Guide.pdf

National Defense Authorization Act (NDAA). (1992). Public Law No. 102-484, §724, 106 Stat. 2315, 2440.

Secretary of Defense. (2019). Memorandum for secretaries of the military departments chairman of the joint chiefs of staff under secretary of defense for personnel and readiness chiefs of the military services (pp. 149–153). http://www.defense.gov

Smith, D. J., Bono, R. C., & Slinger, B. J. (2017). Transforming the military health system. *JAMA*, *318*(24), 2427–2428.

Tricare. (n.d.). http://www.armymedicine.mil/

Washington, W., Maby, J. I., Weber, N., Cowan, D. N., Kelly, A. L., Rushin, C. B., Feng, X., Jackson, R., Gary, J. K., & Murray, J. K. (2018, fourth quarter). Accession medical standards analysis & research activity. Annual report. AMSARA.

Useful Websites

1. Tricare: https://tricare.mil/
2. Defense Health Agency (DHA): https://www.health.mil/About-MHS/OASDHA/Defense-Health-Agency
3. Surgeon Generals—Army, Navy, Air Force
4. Military and Veteran Benefits: http://www.Military.com
5. Military Healthcare System Review http://archive.defense.gov/pubs/140930_MHS_Review_Final_Report_Main_Body.pdf
6. Uniformed Services University of the Health Sciences (USUHS): https://www.usuhs.edu/home
7. Health: https://health.mil/About-MHS
8. Army Medicine: https://armymedicine.health.mil/Patient-Centered-Medical-Home
9. Uniformed Service Academy of Family Physicians: http://www.usafp.org/Patient-Centered-Medical-Home-Page.html
10. Patient Centered Primary Care Collaborative: http://www.pcpcc.net/
11. American College of Physicians PCMH Resource Site: http://www.acponline.org/running_practice/pcmh/understanding/
12. NCQA Recognition Website: http://www.ncqa.org/tabid/631/default.aspx
13. American Academy of Pediatrics Center for Medical Home Implementation: http://www.medicalhomeinfo.org/how/care_delivery/pediatric_subspecialists.aspx
14. AHRQ PCMH Resource Center: http://www.pcmh.ahrq.gov/portal/server.pt/community/pcmh__home/1483
15. American College of Physicians PCMH Website: http://www.acponline.org/running_practice/pcmh/
16. American Academy of Family Physicians PCMH Checklist: http://www.usafp.org/PCMH-Files/AAFP-Files/PCMHChecklist.pdf
17. American Academy of Family Physicians: http://www.aafp.org/online/en/home/membership/initiatives/futurefamilymed.html
18. Patient-Centered Primary Care Collaborative: http://www.pcpcc.net3
19. American College of Physicians: http://www.acponline.org/running_practice/pcmh/demonstrations/jointprinc_05_17.pdf
20. Become a Tricare Provider: https://www.tricare-west.com/content/hnfs/home/tw/prov/become-a-provider.html
21. U.S. Department of Veterans Affairs: www.va.gov
22. Overview of the Department of Defense's Military Health System: https://archive.defense.gov/home/features/2014/0614_healthreview/docs/Fact_Sheet_Overview.PDF
23. Accessions Medical Standards Analysis and Research Activity: https://www.amsara.amedd.army.mil/AMSARAAR.aspx

CHAPTER 3

Active Duty, Reserve, National Guard: Are There Differences?

Peggy Wilmoth

Introduction

Yes, Virginia, there are differences! And while these differences may be nuanced and often confusing to many, it is often wiser to focus on the consistencies among them. The ties that bind are strong and indelible. The members of the Uniformed Services all volunteer to serve the country and take the same oath to protect and defend the Constitution. The bonds forged among them are stronger than those many civilians will ever experience.

It helps if one thinks of this like a funnel. The Uniformed Services is the overarching term given to the eight uniformed services. The term is codified in the U.S. Code Service 31 USCS § 3701 as those who serve the public through the federal government. The U.S. Code is the set of policies grounded in law that guide everything from the existence of a specific force to the authorities for calling them for duty (**Table 3-1**).

Five of those Uniformed Services fall under the guidance and direction of the Department of Defense and are collectively referred to as the Armed Forces since they are typically "armed" with weapons. The Armed Forces are comprised of the personnel of the Army, Navy, Air Force, and Marine Corps, and the nascent Space Force, governed by 10 U.S. Code. The Armed Forces are further divided into components: active component (AC) or active duty (AD) and the reserve components (RCs). The RCs are further divided into the Title 10 Reserve forces and those under Title 32, better known as the National Guard. A key grammatical point is, when referred to collectively, they are the RCs (plural); when discussing only one of them, such as the Army Reserve, it is singular component, or RC.

The AD force of the Armed Forces, regardless of service, serves 365 days per year. They are federal forces, meaning under control of the federal government and are governed by Title 10 U.S. Code (https://www.law.cornell.edu/uscode/text/10). While we typically think of these individuals as living on or near military posts and bases, many live in civilian communities all across the country and around the world. (The Army calls them "posts"; other

Table 3-1 Uniformed Services

The seven uniformed services are, in order of precedence by ceremonial formation and primary function:

Service	Primary Function	Agency
U.S. Army	Provides the ground forces	Department of Defense (DoD)
U.S. Marine Corps	Maintains amphibious and ground units for contingency and combat operations	Department of Defense
U.S. Navy	Force on, above, and below the surface of the water	Department of Defense
U.S. Air Force	Provides lethal air capability	Department of Defense
U.S. Coast Guard	Provides law and maritime safety enforcement, marine and environmental protection, and military naval support	Department of Homeland Security
U.S. Public Health Service Commissioned Corps	Mission is to deliver public health and disease prevention expertise at home and abroad as well as to disaster areas and areas affected by U.S. military operations	Department of Health and Human Services
National Oceanic and Atmospheric Administration Commissioned Corps	Offers expertise on anything from meteorology to geology to oceanography to DoD, National Aeronautics and Space Administration, Merchant Marines, others	National Oceanic and Atmospheric Administration
U.S. Space Corps	Equips space forces to protect U.S. and Allied interests	Department of Defense

services refer to them as "bases.") They may work as recruiters in your town or in a lab engaged in research in a foreign country, or as a liaison in an embassy. Those serving on AD regardless of service generally receive the same benefits: 30 days of vacation or "leave" per year, medical and dental coverage, access to a defined "blended" retirement system, educational benefits, housing or a housing allowance, long-term care/life insurance, and access to the commissary and base exchange system. Enlisted members are provided or "issued" their uniforms while officers must pay out of pocket for theirs. Members of the AD component and their families move on a fairly frequent basis from one duty station to another, and these moves are called permanent change of station (PCS) moves.

Who Are the Reserve Components?

The term RCs is another umbrella term that refers to the seven individual reserve components of the Armed Forces: the Army National Guard of the United States, the Army Reserve, the Navy Reserve, the Marine Corps Reserve, the Air National Guard of the United States, the Air Force Reserve, and the Coast Guard Reserve. These seven reserve components exist to "provide trained units and qualified persons available for active duty in the armed forces, in time of war or national emergency, and at such other times as the national security may require, to fill the needs of the armed forces whenever more units and persons are needed than are in the regular components" (10 U.S.C. §10102).

By law, the Title 10 elements of the reserve are entitled to 48 inactive duty for training (or drill) days per year and 14 days on AD for annual training (10 U.S.C. § 10147). Many do much more duty than that, and since 2001 the RC has moved from being a strategic force in the reserve to one that is operational and engaged in a more frequent manner in the current operations taking place around the world. There are multiple authorities that can bring members of the RC on to an AD status, and each of these has different rules regarding eligibility for benefits such as health care (**Table 3-2**).

The National Guard, comprised of both the Army and the Air Guard, is both a federal and state entity. The National Guard regulated by 32 U.S. Code (https://www.law.cornell.edu/uscode/text/32) is composed of 54 separate

Table 3-2 Reserve Access Authorities

Statute	Utilization Process	Intended Use	Requirements
Involuntary			
Section **12301(a)** of Reference (d) Full Mobilization	Congressional Declaration of War or National Emergency	Rapid expansion of military services to meet an external threat to national security	■ No personal limitation ■ Duration of war or national emergency plus 6 months ■ Applicable to all reservists (including inactive and retired)
Section **12302** of Reference (d) Partial Mobilization	Presidential Declaration of National Emergency	Manpower required to meet external threat to national security or domestic emergency	■ Maximum 1,000,000 Ready Reservists on active duty ■ Not more than 24 consecutive months
Section **12304** of Reference (d) Presidential Selected Reserve Call-Up	President determines reserve component (RC) augmentation is required other than during war or national emergency	Augment the active forces for any named operational mission, or to provide assistance for responding to an emergency involving the use or threatened use of a weapon of mass destruction, or a terrorist attack or threatened terrorist attack in the United States that could result in significant loss of life or property	■ Maximum 200,000 members of Selected Reserve/Individual Ready Reserve on active duty ■ May include up to 30,000 Individual Ready Reserve ■ Limited to 365 consecutive days active duty ■ Prohibited for support of federal government or a state during a domestic serious natural or manmade disaster, accident or catastrophe ■ Prohibited for use in repelling invasions suppressing insurrections, rebellions, domestic violence, unlawful combinations, or conspiracies, or executing U.S. laws

(continues)

Table 3-2 Reserve Access Authorities *(continued)*

Statute	Utilization Process	Intended Use	Requirements
Section **12304a** of Reference (d) Reserve Emergency Call-Up	Secretary of Defense authority in response to governor's request for federal assistance in accordance with Section 5121 *et seq*. of Title 42, U.S.C. (Reference *(aa)*); presidential determination of major disaster or emergency required	Manpower required for response to a major disaster or emergency in the United States and its territories	■ No personnel limitation ■ Limited to continuous period of not more than 120 days ■ Does not apply to National Guard or Coast Guard Reserve ■ Secretaries of the military departments may approve 12304a activations provided the orders are 30 days or less in duration
Section **12304b** of Reference (d) Reserve Preplanned Call-Up	Secretary of Military Department authority to order any unit of the Selected Reserve to active duty for preplanned and prebudgeted missions	Augment AC (Active Component) for any preplanned missions in support of CCMD (Combatant Command) requirements	■ Maximum 60,000 on active duty at any one time ■ Limited to 365 consecutive days ■ Manpower and costs are specifically included and identified in the submitted defense budget for anticipated demand ■ Budget information includes description of the mission and the anticipated length of time for involuntary order to active duty ■ Secretary invoking section 12304b of Reference (d) must submit to Congress a written report detailing circumstances of call-up
Section **12301(b)** of Reference (d) 15-Day Statue	Service Secretary authority to order to active duty without consent of persons affected	Annual training or operational mission	■ 15 days active duty once per year, governor's consent required for National Guard
Voluntary			
Section **12301(d)** of Reference (d)	An authority designated by a Service Secretary may order an RC member to active duty with consent of the member	Active duty in excess of annual training requirements. May be used for training special work, operational support, etc.	■ No set duration ■ Consent of the governor or other appropriate authority of the state concerned required for members of the National Guard

Department of Defense. (2017). *Instruction (NUMBER 1235)*. Author. https://www.esd.whs.mil/Portals/54/Documents/DD/issuances/dodi/123512p.pdf?ver=2019-02-26-152340-327

National Guard organizations: one for each state, and one for Puerto Rico, Guam, the U.S. Virgin Islands, and the District of Columbia. The organizations in all entities except the District of Columbia National Guard operate as state or territorial organizations under the control of the governor. The District of Columbia National Guard is under federal control since Washington, D.C., is not yet a state. Given this dual state and federal set of authorities, the National Guard can be called to action either by the governor on state duty or for federal duty through various federal mechanisms, all of which are outlined in the U.S. Code.

Entitlements

There is a vast array of entitlements or "pay and benefits" provided to those who volunteer to serve the country in uniform. Benefits are tiered with those on AD and their eligible dependents having full access, with those in the RCs having lesser access. Benefits generally fall into six broad categories: education, health care, morale, welfare and recreation, family programs, commissary and exchange, and miscellaneous others such as legal assistance, space available travel, life insurance, and a few others (Department of Defense, 2012)

The ability to obtain medical and dental care is one of the most sought after benefits, with the details of these benefits outlined in Chapter 55 of Title 10 in the U.S. Code. The health benefits for the Armed Forces are administered through the Military Health System (MHS), which had 9.4 million beneficiaries in 2018 (Mendez, 2018). The essential mission of the MHS is twofold: (1) ensure the health and wellness of military personnel so they can carry out their military missions and (2) be prepared to deliver health care during wartime. Traditionally, AD forces have had access to medical and dental care through the MHS with care delivered on military bases by healthcare providers who may be either in uniform on AD or civilian employees of the MHS. This access has been defined based on published regulatory priorities:

- Priority 1: AD service member
- Priority 2: AD family members enrolled in Tricare Prime
- Priority 3: Retirees, their family members, and survivors enrolled in Tricare Prime
- Priority 4: AD family members not enrolled in Tricare Prime and Tricare Reserve Select enrollees (U.S. Code)

The key to accessing benefits is to be deemed eligible and to have this eligibility documented in the Defense Enrollment Eligibility Reporting System (DEERS). This is similar to any employer certifying one's eligibility for benefits. DEERS is the gatekeeper for all health-related entitlements. In addition to the service member who is automatically eligible for care (called the sponsor), eligible family members, referred to as dependents, can also access care. Dependent is a term defined in 10 U.S.C. §1072 with eligible familial relationships clearly delineated, (e.g., spouses [including same-sex spouses], children, certain un-remarried former spouses, and dependent parents) (Mendez, 2018). Health care and dental care for the uniformed member is generally provided at no cost at an AD MTF. The AD member who is assigned to a duty station at a distance from an MTF will have access to care through the military's health insurance program, Tricare.

What is known as Tricare today actually began in 1956 with the passage of the Dependents Medical Care Act of 1956 (P.L. 84-569). This law provided a statutory basis for dependents of AD members, retirees, and dependents of retirees to seek care at MTFs. This law also gave DoD the authority to contract for a health insurance plan for coverage of civilian hospital services for AD dependents. This evolved, and in 1966 the Civilian Health and Medical Program of the Uniformed Services (CHAMPUS) was created. CHAMPUS was reformed into Tricare by Congress as a nationwide managed care program in 1994 through the DoD Appropriations Act for Fiscal year 1994 (Dolfini-Reed & Jebo, 2000). As with most health plans, they continue to evolve and change with the intended goal of cost savings while simultaneously improving health outcomes (Mendez, 2019b).

Today Tricare is a health insurance–like program that pays for care delivered by civilian providers, outside of an MTF. There are three primary benefit plans: a health maintenance organization option (Tricare Prime), a preferred provider option (Tricare Select), and a Medicare wraparound option (Tricare for Life) for Medicare-eligible retirees. Other Tricare plans include Tricare Young Adult, Tricare Reserve Select, and Tricare Retired Reserve. Also included in Tricare is a pharmacy program and optional dental or vision plans. Once again, DEERS eligibility is key with other factors such as sponsor's duty status and geographic location playing a role in the final determination of level of access. Reimbursement rates are modeled on Medicare for inpatient and outpatient as well as for other related services. The authority that guides reimbursement is 10 U.S.C. §1079(h) and (j), which require that payment levels for healthcare services provided under Tricare be aligned with Medicare's fee schedule as much as practical (Mendez, 2019).

What benefits does Tricare provide and for whom? It depends. Refer to **Table 3-3** for a quick oversight. For more detail, refer to the reports from the Congressional Research Service (CRS) noted in the Reference List.

Related Health Benefits

Tricare also has a pharmacy benefit that was created in 2000 (P.L. 106-65) that allows eligible beneficiaries three ways to utilize this benefit: via MTF pharmacies, Tricare retail pharmacies, and/or the Tricare Mail Order Program. Participation in this benefit does not cost any additional amount, but there are adjusted co-payment amounts. Beneficiaries can also take part in the Extended Care Health Option (ECHO) program for defined services. This program provides supplemental health care and nonmedical services and supplies for eligible beneficiaries. There are three categories of ECHO benefits: general services/supplies, home health care, and applied behavioral analysis for autism spectrum disorder. The one caveat to use of this benefit is that ECHO is used last, after accessing services through federal, state, and local services such as Medicaid's home and community-based services.

Reservists in reserve status are limited in the type of healthcare benefits they are eligible to receive (**Table 3-4**). Mobilization and subsequent deployment allow them to have access to the same medical benefits as AD personnel, and make their family members eligible for expanded benefits through Tricare. There are many nuances about access to benefits related to the authority used to place the reservist on AD that is not covered in this chapter.

The Deployment Cycle

The term *deployment cycle* can have multiple meanings, including referencing which phase of the cycle a unit is in and what types of activities are required to occur. It may also be used as a framework for understanding the stresses on both the SM and their family when called to go to war or serve in a contingency operation. When referencing the deployment cycle in relation to a unit's rotation, there are generally four phases: predeployment, deployment, postdeployment, and reintegration. Activities in the predeployment phase will include meeting the health and training requirements of the combatant command prior to moving into the designated theater of operations. The length of this period of time is generally longer for those in the RCs since they have to leave their civilian employment and report to their reserve unit prior to moving to an AD installation for

Table 3-3 Key Tricare Options

	Tricare Prime*#%	Tricare Select#	Tricare for Life	Tricare Reserve Select**
Type of Option	Managed health option similar to HMO*-style option	Self-managed, preferred-provider option	Wraparound benefit plan	Premium-based health plan; those on FEHBP** not eligible
Who Is Eligible	Required: Active duty living near MTF*** Some retirees if living within a designated PSA****	Available worldwide for those eligible	Retired enrollees in Medicare. Must pay for Medicare B premiums to retain this coverage	Those in SELRES#
Annual Enrollment Fee	Yes, for retirees	Yes and must enroll annually	No	Yes
Annual Deductible	No	Yes	Unknown	Unknown
Co-payments	Minimal	Variable co-pay amounts depending on in-network civilian provider versus out of network provider	No out-of-pocket expenses for services covered by both Medicare and Tricare for Life	

*Subsets of Tricare Prime include Tricare Prime Remote and Tricare Prime Overseas/Prime Remote Overseas
**Subset of Tricare Select for which members pay a monthly premium
#Tricare Young Adult: Unmarried dependent children who do not have private health insurance through an employer may remain in Tricare until age 26 under a parent's coverage via TYA Select or TYA Prime. Premiums are required for both.
%Offered only in Prime Service Area (PSA)
*HMO= Health Maintenance Organization
**FEHBP=Federal Employee Health Benefits Plan
***MTF= Military Treatment Facility
****PSA= Prime Service Area
#SELRES=Selected Reserve
Data from Military Times. (n.d.). *Tricare changes: What you need to know*. https://www.militarytimes.com/pay-benefits/2019/06/09/your-2019-guide-to-military-pay-and-benefits/#tricare

final preparation. This period of time may range from hours for some AD units up to 6 months for some reserve elements.

The deployment phase is the period of time that the unit is in the theater of operations engaging in its mission. Postdeployment begins as the unit returns home and completes physical exams, turns in equipment, and has briefings on various topics. For those in the RC, these briefings include their postdeployment benefits for which they and their immediate family are eligible. This should be a period of time for the SM to return to a more regular sleep cycle and to reflect on and make

Table 3-4 Benefits Reserve and Active Duty

Benefit	Description	Inactive Duty	Annual Training	AD/FTNGD ≤30 Days	AD/FTNGD ≥31 Days	Contingency Operation	Extended Active Duty
Medical and dental benefits: member	Comprehensive care for members on AD for >30 days	Not eligible	Not eligible	Not eligible	Yes	Yes	Yes
Medical and dental treatment: member	Treatment for injury, illness, or disease incurred or aggravated in line of duty for members on AD for ≤30 days or performing inactive duty	Yes	Yes	Yes	No	No	No
Medical care (delayed effective date AD order)	Medical and dental care for reserve component members and dependents up to 180 days before commencement of AD when the member is covered by an order to AD in support of a contingency operation	No	No	No	No	Yes	No

Transitional health care	Medical and dental care for 180 days following release from AD, or for 180 days following the diagnosis of the condition that was identified during the member's 180-day transition period (but only for the postrelease condition)	No	No	No	Yes, if: ■ involuntarily separated from AD ■ discharged because of sole survivorship ■ a member of the individual Ready Reserve and agrees to serve in the Selected Reserve	Yes, if period of AD is >30 days	Yes, if: ■ involuntarily separated ■ separated and agrees to serve in the Selected Reserve ■ discharged because of sole survivorship
Tricare Reserve Select (TRS)	Tricare for Selected Reserve members and their eligible dependents. Must not be eligible for, or enrolled in, the Federal Employees Health Benefits Program	Eligible	Eligible	Eligible	No (covered under comprehensive AD health care)	No (covered under comprehensive AD health care)	No
Tricare dental program: member	Premium-sharing, cost-sharing dental insurance program for reserve component members not on AD >30 days	Eligible	Eligible	Eligible	No (covered under comprehensive AD health care)	No (covered under comprehensive active duty health care)	No
Medical care: dependents	Tricare and space available care at a military treatment facility	No	No	No	Yes	Yes	Yes

(continues)

Table 3-4 Benefits Reserve and Active Duty *(continued)*

Benefit	Description	Inactive Duty	Annual Training	AD/FTNGD ≤30 Days	AD/FTNGD ≥31 Days	Contingency Operation	Extended Active Duty
Tricare Dental Program: dependents	Premium-sharing, cost-sharing dental insurance program for dependents of AD and RC members	Eligible					Eligible
Tricare for Retirees	Tricare plan options for retired members and their eligible dependents	Eligible, if receiving retired pay and <65 years of age					Eligible, if receiving retired pay and <65 years of age
Tricare Retired Reserve (TRR)	A premium-based health plan under Tricare for retired RC members under age 60 and their eligible dependents. Must not be eligible for, or enrolled in, the Federal Employees Health Benefits Program	Eligible	Eligible	Eligible	Eligible, but would have comprehensive health coverage while on AD and TRR would be suspended	Eligible, but would have comprehensive health coverage while on AD and TRR would be suspended	No
Tricare for Life	Tricare (as a second payer) for retirees who have both Medicare Parts A and B	Eligible, if enrolled in Medicare Parts A and B					Eligible, if enrolled in Medicare Parts A and B

Note: Current as of May 2012; AD: active duty, FTNGD: full-time National Guard duty.

meaning out of the deployment experiences. Unfortunately for too many, this is a compressed period of time, filled with briefings and appointments in order to shorten the phase and return to the family.

Finally, the reintegration phase differs in length depending on the type and length of deployment and the command policy. This can be a very stressful time for both the SM and the family. AD units may be given a period of block leave during which everyone is on vacation, spending time reacclimating to being at home. It includes a return to family and community life and a slow return to regular military duties. For Reservists, some of whom may not have any accumulated paid military leave, the demands of their civilian employer may cut this time short and they may be expected back on the job in a matter of days or weeks. There have been problems since 9/11 with Reservists returning home to find that their job had been eliminated due to restructuring, that they were passed over for a promotion, or finding that their fellow employees were upset about having to pick up their duties during the deployment. There are laws that help protect reservists, under the Uniformed Services Employment and Redeployment Rights Act (USERRA) (https://www.dol.gov/agencies/vets/programs/userra) for which all employers should be well versed if they have a Reservist in their organization.

The deployment cycle has also been used as a framework for research and around which Congress and the DoD has structured programmatic funding, health assessments, and entitlements. One example of programmatic support is the Yellow Ribbon Reintegration Program (YRRP) mandated by Congress that began in 2008 (P.L. 110-181) to support the RC (https://www.yellowribbon.mil). This program is run by the DoD but implemented by each respective RC to meet their unique service culture.

Mentioned previously are the Deployment Health Assessments that are completed during each of the deployment cycles (DoD, 2019). These are mandated physical and mental health screenings that are designed to document health-related fitness and well-being of the SM at each phase of the cycle and which are then used to help identify individuals for referral and treatment. The goal is to anticipate, recognize, monitor, evaluate, communicate, and mitigate health threats (DoD, 2019). These are generally focused on those who deploy outside of the United States for longer than 30 days. An overview can be found at https://www.pdhealth.mil/clinical-guidance/deployment-health-assessments.

Impact of 9/11 on the Reserve Components

The world changed a great deal on September 11, 2001, for millions of Americans, including for those who serve in one of the RCs. On that day the RCs went from being a strategic force to an operational one. Prior to 9/11 the RCs were viewed as a "force in waiting" for a major conflict that would rapidly expand the Armed Forces (Commission on the National Guard and Reserve, 2008). Reservists attended once-a-month drills and their annual training events but did not anticipate being called to AD unless there was a world war. On 9/11 the RCs became operational as they became integrated into the rest of the force and placed into the cycle of deployments, hence the terminology that has been embraced: The RC is an operational force. This was codified in DoD Directive 1200.17, dated October 29, 2008 (https://www.esd.whs.mil/Portals/54/Documents/DD/issuances/dodd/120017p.pdf).

The CRS reports that as of June 15, 2020, 1,007,061 members of the RCs have been both involuntarily and voluntarily called to duty since 9/11 (Kapp & Torreon, 2020). Some have been called to duty within the United States, to backfill AD forces who were sent overseas, to staff training and mobilization/demobilization sites or to more fully staff reserve units. Others have been deployed to Germany to work at logistic bases or at Landstuhl Regional Medical Center, while others have been deployed to the theater of operations.

The impact of becoming an operational force has led to many changes within the RCs, including frequency of deployments, changing the nature and frequency of what used to be weekend drills to battle assemblies, and upgrading annual training to focus more on both individual battle skills and units to practice their wartime mission. This has led to strain among civilian employers as well as increased pressure on the RC family.

The Employer Support for Guard and Reserve (ESGR) is a DoD program created in 1972 to promote cooperation and understanding between RC SMs and their civilian employers (https://www.esgr.mil). The volunteers who staff the state-level programs are frequently called upon to assist in resolving conflicts arising from an employee's military commitment. ESGR is able to mediate many conflicts and is an invaluable resource for the RC. This author has personally called upon ESGR to intervene when a former supervisor engaged in retribution about the demands of her RC commitment.

As discussed previously, there are several different types of authorities that can be used to mobilize and/or deploy an individual reservist. **Figure 3-1** shows the steps employed

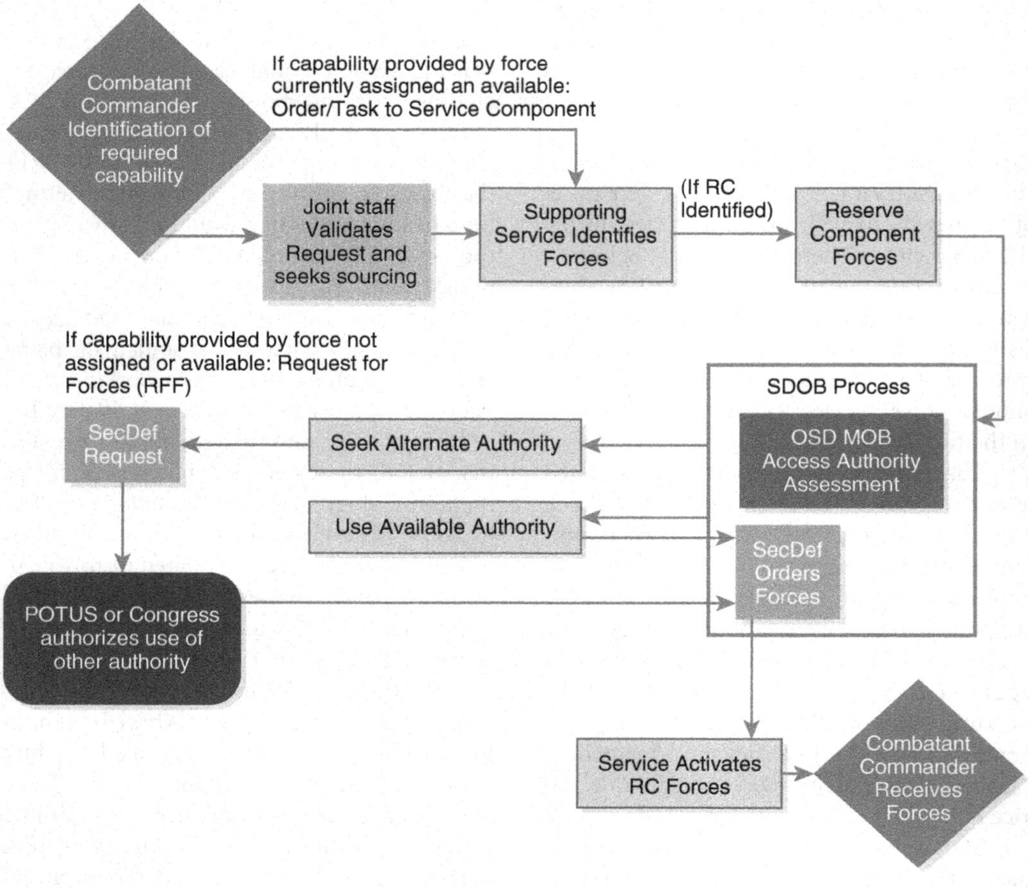

Figure 3-1 RC access flowchart.

to begin and complete this process. As complex as this process is, there is equal complexity regarding the types of benefits that the individual reservist and the family are able to access during a mobilization/deployment and in the immediate period postdeployment. First, it is important to note that all reservists must be mobilized or called to AD to assemble at their unit of record. Deployment refers to the actual movement of a unit to and from an operational area, and in jargon typically means moved to a location outside of the United State (Office of the Chairman, 2020).

The years since 9/11 have taken a toll on Reserve families as well as their employers. Resources for the family based on phase of the deployment cycle can be found at https://www.militaryonesource.mil/military-life-cycle/deployment. However, how much of a toll on RC families versus AC families is hard to determine since most of the information about RC families tends to be more anecdotal than data based. There simply has been little concentrated research focusing on how becoming an operational force has affected them. Much of the published research focuses solely on AD families or has a relatively small number of RC families as part of the sample. For example, the RAND Report on the Deployment Life Cycle (Meadows et al., 2016) included only 721 families of RC members out of 2,724 total families, which reflected 26% of the sample size. This underreporting of the experiences of RC-connected families is very troubling, especially when one considers that 50% of the entire Army is composed of the National Guard and Army Reserve.

Key findings from the RAND Deployment Life Cycle Study (2016) included service members reporting improved family environments during deployment while spouses reported no changes. Nor were there significant effects on persistent psychological or behavioral health outcomes for either spouse unless the SM experienced some trauma while deployed. Children and teens also coped well in general, although increases in emotional problems and depression were reported. The most turbulent time for the SM and family was upon redeployment and reintegrating into the family and more support for the family during this time was recommended (Meadows et al., 2016). This is especially important for those in the RCs.

There are periodic internal surveys done of RC spouses, with the one done in 2017 available publicly (OPA, 2017). This survey had an 18% response rate with about two-thirds reporting satisfaction with the "Reserve way of life" and reporting a comfortable family financial picture, which was consistent with prior surveys. Reports of somewhat increased stress experienced by the spouse at home and some increase in negative behaviors of children were reported but were consistent with previous reports when deployments were at a higher pace. The one issue of higher need reported was the need for child care, which is not subsidized for reservists who are mobilized and deployed unless they live near an AD installation that is able to accommodate them.

Conclusion

Developing an appreciation for and understanding of the culture of the Armed Forces will provide the civilian clinician with context as they care for a veteran or reservist. Clearly there are many nuances to military life and culture that cannot be captured in writing, but being willing to listen, trying to understand this unique culture in American life, and valuing the importance they place on patriotism and defense of the Constitution will go a long way to both appreciating their service and engaging in the differential diagnosis process.

References

Commission on the National Guard and Reserve (2008). *Commission on the National Guard and Reserves: Transforming the National Guard and Reserves into a 21st-century operational force*. Author.

Department of Defense. (2012). *Report of the eleventh quadrennial review of military compensation*. The Pentagon. https://militarypay.defense.gov/Portals/3/Documents/Reports/11th_QRMC_Main_Report_FINAL.pdf?ver=2016-11-06-160559-590

Department of Defense. (2019). *Deployment health*. DOD Instruction 6490.03. The Pentagon.

Dolfini-Reed, M. & Jebo, J. (2000). *The evolution of the military health care system: Changes in public law and DOD regulations*. Center for Naval Analyses.

Kapp, L. & Torreon, B. S. (2018). *Reserve component personnel issues: Questions and answers* (RL 30802, Version 7-5700). Congressional Research Service.

Kapp, L. & Torreon, B. S. (2020). *Reserve component personnel issues: Questions and answers* (RL 30802, Version 23, June 15, 2020). Congressional Research Service.

Meadows, S. O., Tanielian, T., & Karney, B. R. (Eds.). (2016). *The deployment life study: Longitudinal analysis of military families across the deployment cycle*. RAND.

Mendez, B. H. P. (December 20, 2018). *Military medical system: Frequently asked questions* (Summary R45399, version 4). Congressional Research Service.

Mendez, B. H. P (July 26,2019a). *Military health system reform*. In Focus 11273. Congressional Research Service. https://crsreports.congress.gov

Mendez, B. H. P. (December 18, 2019b). *Defense primer: Military health system*. In Focus: IF10530. Congressional Research Service.

Office of the Chairman of the Joint Chiefs of Staff. (2020). *DoD dictionary of military and associated terms*. The Joint Staff. https://www.jcs.mil/Portals/36/Documents/Doctrine/pubs/dictionary.pdf

Office of People Analytics. (2017). *2017 survey of reserve component spouses* (2017 RCSS). Department of Defense.

U.S. Code. (n.d.). *Title 10. Armed forces, subtitle. A. General military law, part II. Personnel, chapter 5*. 10 U.S. Code chapter 55–Medical and dental care. Government Printing Office.

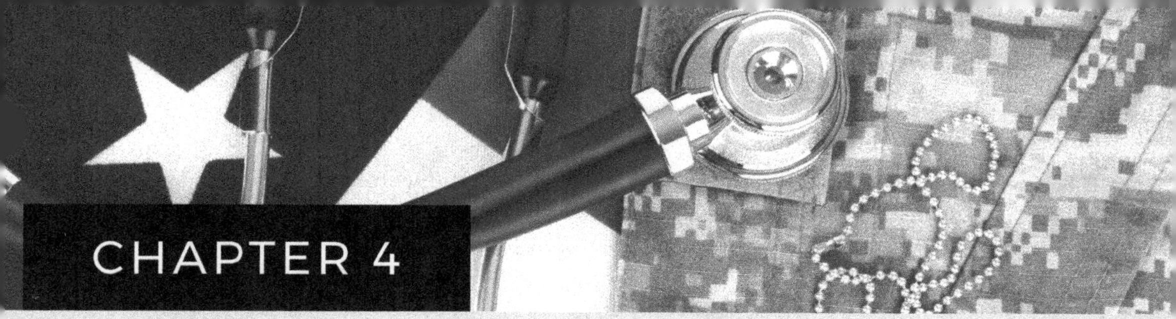

CHAPTER 4

History of Women Who Have Served and Their Service Connected Health Risks

Patricia L. Conard and Myrna L. Armstrong

This manuscript is dedicated to the over 250,000 women veterans who are serving (or have served) on deployed active duty for the Iraq and Afghanistan wars.

"It is hard to fail, but it is worse never to have tried to succeed . . . In this life, we get nothing save by effort."

—**Theodore Roosevelt** (Chicago, April 10, 1899)

This chapter explores the amazing previous journeys, and some of the present-day interactions, women have had with the U.S. military, regardless of the environment (regional, national, or international), the purpose (skirmishes or humanitarian efforts), or the occasion (war or peacetime). Besides the women's involvement in the early historical wars, some of their physical and behavioral health issues from each of the specific wars since 1965 are discussed. Their presence during the Vietnam War was capped by congressional mandates of less than 2%, but to date women military service members' (WMSM) presence is now stronger and more interactive than ever (Murphy & Hans, 2014; U.S. Department of Veteran Affairs, 2007). They should be proud, as women are almost 16% of the total fighting force of the military, and there are almost 2 million women veterans today (U.S. Department of Veteran Affairs, 2019b).

Data and Subject Issues

Nursing has a valuable central role to play in the fundamental delivery of gender-centered care with advocacy, assessment, intervention, and evaluation for the psychosocial and physical care needs of the WMSM, the women veterans (WV), and their family/loved ones. This premise is important as the WMSM presence, accomplishments, and health concerns are often still not well quantified. In addition, sometimes significant equality, safety, and collegiality issues remain, as they work alongside their military counterparts. In this chapter the holistic care concerns of those deployed WMSM and WV from the Iraq and Afghanistan wars are provided as an example of this premise.

Interestingly as this topic of military and veteran women is pursued, several issues should be noted. Data are only as good as the timely collection and dissemination of information. Most numbers of participation regarding women serving in and with the military, especially before approximately 1975, are listed as estimates partially due to poor/fair accounting and limited personnel management (U.S. Department of Veteran Affairs, 2007). To date it can still be noted that different literature sources provide different estimates of women military participation (Feller & Moore, 1996; Schwartz, 1987; U.S. Department of Veteran Affairs, 2007, 2019b). Sometimes the comprehensive data were totally lost to destructive fires, as in the Civil War and the Confederacy personnel and their injured (Schuette & Armstrong, 2019).

Almost all of the information about veterans comes from the Veterans Administration (VA). While WMSM had large numbers of participants, especially in World War II (1941–1945), it was another 40-plus years before Congress authorized and implemented healthcare services for them through the Veterans Health Administration (VHA) of the VA (Conard & Armstrong, 2018). Women in the military were not given veteran status until 1948. Even after that implementation, research about veterans was mainly conducted on the dominant population of men in the military for many years. To date, the VHA data still only reflect information gleaned from those that are registered, use the system, and/or receive benefits from the VA. Of the 19 million total U.S. veterans in 2019, approximately 45–55% use any part of the VA; thus there is an entire segment of over 9 million veterans that are not represented when the data about veterans are published (Atkins & Lipson, 2015; U.S. Department of Veteran Affairs, 2019b). The remainder, as well as some of those who use the VA, are obtaining their health care in the civilian sector. Women from the Iraq and Afghanistan wars are becoming the most rapidly increasing segment of the veteran population, thus both military and veteran gender-specific studies and/or research are finally being funded and conducted (Atkins & Lipson, 2015). In addition, even though the literature reports are titled close to the published year, conducting large datasets for research often takes a minimum 3–5 years of planning, approval, implementing, and analyzing, so when it is circulated it still only reflects the picture of events at the time of collection.

Historical Review of Women in the Military

The initial 125 years of service of women working in the military was mostly behind the scenes, often devalued and provided with limited recognition. Yet they continued to serve. Imagine the mantra "I served to care" the many wives, mothers, and daughters could have spoken who attended the wounded under dangerous conditions during the nation's early military conflicts and wars efforts (U.S. Department of Veteran Affairs, 2007). Historically, women often disguised themselves as males to carry out tasks as cooks, caregivers, and nurses during the early nation's wars. During the Revolutionary War (1775–1783), nurses received $2 monthly for their services plus one ration daily (Feller & Moore, 1996). After the war no one believed there was a continued need for permanent health personnel or a centralized Medical Department of the military, so everything was dissolved and not reestablished until after the War of 1812–1815, by Congress in 1818 (U.S. Department of Veteran Affairs, 2007).

Civil War (1861–1865)

At the start of the Civil War, medicine in the 1860s was described as "primitive and developing . . . without knowledge of the cause and effects of germs upon infections and diseases; medicine could offer little for cure" (Schuette & Armstrong, 2019, p. 2). Nurse Dorothea L. Dix was appointed in 1861 to explore, then implement, care for the mentally ill, which she did by establishing a short course in nursing and eventually training over 6,000 women to provide assistance (Feller & Moore, 1996). With the serious fighting beginning in the Civil War, many soldiers provided the day-to-day patient care responsibilities in open bay environments while over 400 nurses worked in hospitals far behind the combat fighting lines (U.S. Department of Veteran Affairs, 2007). Nurses were paid $12 per month along with a daily ration (Feller & Moore, 1996). In addition, Drummer Boys (9–14 years of age) were the extra help then; they became stretcher bearers, found straw to make the cots more comfortable, sharpen surgical instruments, and frequently helped the surgeons with sick calls and amputations (Schuette & Armstrong, 2019).

Dr. Mary Walker is often listed as the first (and only) woman to receive the Medal of Honor for her astounding work in the Civil War (Meyer, 2016). Although educated as a surgeon, she first worked as a nurse (unpaid) while for 3 years requesting continuously to perform her medical occupation in the Union Army; she even gave care to surrounding civilians. Finally, she became a contract surgeon and often volunteered to slip behind enemy lines to pass along important messages to the Union Army generals. Later, she was caught and imprisoned for 4 months, then eventually labeled as a possible spy. After the war she was awarded the Medal of Honor, then it was rescinded, and her name removed from the listing of honors because she was a noncombatant. She refused adamantly to surrender the Medal of Honor, although with her untimely death she never knew her name and Medal were reinstated in 1977 (Meyer, 2016). At the end of the Civil War, Congress established a permanent Army Medical Department so "military doctors would never again be part-time personnel anymore" and there would be established healthcare training programs for injured soldiers (Feller & Moore, 1996; Schuette & Armstrong, 2019, p. 2).

Spanish-American War (1898–1902)

During the Spanish-American War over 1,500 civilian nurses were appointed under contract for service in hostile territories with benefits of a monthly $30 salary and daily ration. This time nurses again demonstrated even more feminine boldness with their deliberate and effective healthcare and administrative responsibilities. Their pay was eventually increased to $40 monthly, and if they had international assignments their pay was increased to $50. Yet after the war ended, as with previous wars, they were again promptly dismissed (Feller & Moore, 1996). Finally, at the turn of the 20th century, their vision and collective effort began to gain momentum. Their outstanding actions produced incremental results, and their accomplishments paved the way soon thereafter for the formation of the Army (1901) and Navy (1908) Nurse Corps. Congressional stipulations in place created the first Army regular (full-time) nurses (N = >200), although they were appointed and not commissioned until 1947. If nurses were willing to serve in emergencies, they could become part of the first Reserve Corp (N = 37) but only if these nurses had prior active duty (AD) time (Feller & Moore, 1996). In 1909 the American Red Cross was founded by Jane Delano, a visionary nurse and active worker in the organization. She arranged to have nurses (N = 4,000) serving in disasters for this organization, where they could also become a supplemental cohort to fill Army Reserve nurse positions, if needed.

World War I (1917-1918)

During World War I over 12,000 women served as nurses (2,000 full time and 10,000 Reserve). Base pay was increased to $60 monthly (Feller & Moore, 1996). By 1918 nursing's numbers rose to over 21,000, and almost half of them had international assignments. Unfortunately, over 400 nurses were killed in the line of duty during this time. Women were now working in the Army, as well as the Navy, Marines, and Coast Guard (U.S. Department of Veteran Affairs, 2007). Shortly after their war efforts, the Army Reorganization Act of 1920 granted nurses officer status but limited their promotion ranks to Second Lieutenant through Major (only four positions compared to more than seven in the present-day rank system). Their pay was not equalized. By 1921, peacetime became apparent, so a large demobilization (dismissal) again occurred, although this time (1926) the World War I nurses were entitled to retirement benefits, based on their length of service (Feller & Moore, 1996). Another 23,000 women began to serve in administrative staff positions during World War I, often initially because of an acute manpower shortage, then later because they were quite efficient (U.S. Department of Veteran Affairs, 2007). After the war, many of these military clerical positions remained, similar to the significant impact of women working in the civilian sector.

World War II (1941-1945)

On Pearl Harbor Day (December 7, 1941), there were 7,000 full-time Army and 1,700 Navy nurses present in the military. Within 6 months after the Declaration of War there were more than 12,000 nurses mobilized, and by 1943 there were over 36,000 serving on AD. By Victory in Japan (V-J) Day in September 1945, the Army's topmost strength was over 57,000 nurses and the Navy had over 11,000 nurses (Feller & Moore, 1996; U.S. Department of Veteran Affairs, 2007). The Coast Guard also had large numbers of nurses involved in their military strength. With such a large wartime demand of nurses by this time, the United States was facing a critical shortage of the nation's registered nurses (RN). To remedy the situation Congress created the U.S. Cadet Nurse Corp, although rather than establish another new school of nursing they reinforced existing civilian schools of nursing in the nation (Feller & Moore, 1996). Federally funded, astoundingly "over 124,000 graduate nurses completed their programs from 1,125 of the nation's 1,300 schools of nursing" during that time; many of them were from hospital schools of nursing (Feller & Moore, 1996, p. 15).

Women support staff provided other valuable military employment with new positions, such as in intelligence, cryptography, postal service, pilots, and parachute rigging. Thus, in World War II, the brave service of more than 400,000 women, with their expanded roles and responsibilities conducted in global locations, seemed to become the pivotal event for women's future military occupations (U.S. Department of Veteran Affairs, 2007). Finally their contributions were recognized. Despite some congressional concerns, General Eisenhower, who was Army Chief of Staff at the time, became a strong advocate for legislation accepting, then propelling, women within the military. Although partial pay and rank level remained, what did become a highlight was the signing of the Servicemen's Readjustment Act, also known as the G.I. (Government Issue) Bill of Rights of 1944. This included educational benefits, low-interest home and business loans, employment assistance, and unemployment benefits for returning World War II veterans. Over 64,000 women (19.5%) attended college on these resources (U.S. Department of Veteran Affairs, 2007). Later, in 1948, President Truman's Armed Services Integration Act provided women permanent military status and entitled them with veteran designation and some benefits (U.S. Department of Veteran Affairs, 2007). It also ended racial segregation in the Armed Forces.

1950–1961

Over 1,500 nurses were involved in the Korean Conflict (1950–1953); later (1955), men who were RNs were equally acknowledged by the military and commissioned. Additionally in 1960, the prior AD service criteria was eliminated for nurses who wanted to serve in the Army Reserve program; civilian nurses could then obtain a Direct Commission into the Reserve program (Feller & Moore, 1996). In total, the number of military women during the Korean Conflict was almost 49,000, declining to about 35,000 by war's end in June 1955 (U.S. Department of Veteran Affairs, 2007). It is interesting to note the discrepancies of words here, as the so-called Korean Conflict (or skirmish or police action) finally was called a war in the 1990s by Congress (Wright, 2013). The use of consistent terminology is important as later it can make a difference regarding VA entitlement issues (Wright, 2013). With the ongoing political truce relationships with North Korea, some sources describe the resigning of the truce (and ending of the war) as 1953, while others maintain the termination date of 1955 (U.S. Department of Veteran Affairs, 2007; Wright, 2013).

Later, during the Cold War era, to increase military strength during international pressure from the Soviets, nursing skills, as part of over 20 Reserve Component (RC) units, were tested out in 1961 during their activation for the Berlin War crisis (Feller & Moore, 1996). Over 43,000 men and women service members (SMs) were sent to that area to patrol the divided Germany nation until the Berlin Wall was destroyed in 1989.

Vietnam War (1964–1973)

By 1962 the first cohort of nurses (10) were assigned to operationalize a hospital within the Republic of Vietnam, and by 1966 over 300 nurses from the three service branches (Army, Navy, Air Force) were stationed there. Overall, in the Vietnam War, there were almost 11,000 military women that volunteered to serve, and 80% were deployed as nurses (Schwarz, 1987). Their volunteerism was necessary as military draft regulations only applied for men. Another more than 250,000 women were in the military during the Vietnam War (U.S. Department of Veteran Affairs, 2007). Outstandingly, their laudable performance prompted equal military benefits, promotions, and retirement for women and men SMs in 1967, as well as a smoother transition for women to serve in the Army Reserve Corps, with the signing of Public Law 0-130 by President Johnson (Feller & Moore, 1996). During this time each of the service branches had a military woman that achieved the rank of General (one star) (U.S. Department of Veteran Affairs, 2007).

Although when compared to more recent wars, after their Vietnam service little became known about the physical health issues of these prior-era women veterans. Multiple reasons were present, including virtually no VA access for gender-specific care due to the lack of congressional funding, sparse data collection for epidemiological data about them, as well as limited public support and acknowledgment when they returned home (Kang et al., 2014). In addition, incomplete military rosters listing women Vietnam veterans' service activities protracted the ability to gather pertinent data about them. Slowly information has come forward, and currently these Vietnam era women veterans are entering an age range where medical needs are increasing. For many, there are apparent lingering health issues from the war (Kang et al., 2014). Although the women veterans were not officially involved in combat or application of herbicides, they still could have been exposed to combat and/or harmful environmental concerns (Kang et al., 2014). Many were exposed to Agent Orange or other herbicides. A range of birth defects were found to be linked to their Vietnam service such as spina bifida in their children (U.S. Department of Veterans Affairs, 2019a). Some have been exposed to infectious diseases, pesticides around the military installations, waste anesthetic gases, and ethylene oxide gas used in the sterilization of medical equipment (Bond, 2004).

Behavioral health issues were also present. Many of these military women included newly graduated nurses that were deployed to difficult working environments soon after entering the military, with limited healthcare experience and military service. The Vietnam War was the first focal discussion of a mental health issue that was later termed posttraumatic stress disorder (PTSD) (U.S. Department of Veteran Affairs, 2007). Many of these women veterans suffered significant rates of depression and PTSD after the war, partly because of the sexual harassment, trauma, and discrimination they encountered (Kang et al., 2014). They also reported poorer psychological and physical health, more readjustment problems following discharge, and a greater incidence of unemployment due to these behavioral health problems. Often it has taken a long time (for some >40 years) for the personal PTSD problems to be acknowledged (Kang et al., 2014).

Total Force Concept

In 1973, the change to an all-volunteer military system from the previous draft process produced a new total force concept, with more entry opportunities for women including admissions (1976) to the service academies (West Point, Annapolis, Colorado Springs) (U.S. Department of Veteran Affairs, 2007; 2019b). While military women in their occupational roles were performing at significant levels, it also became apparent that personnel demands for the total force volunteer concept could not be achieved with only men; women also had to step up and fill those needed military positions (U.S. Department of Veteran Affairs, 2007). At that time there were about 55,000 women in the AD military, making up about 2.5% of the total force (U.S. Department of Veteran Affairs, 2007). These admission opportunities included increasing the amount of additional occupations for all personnel, including nurses, in the service branches of the Army, Navy, Air Force, Marines, and Coast Guard. This also included more Reserve forces from all of the service branches, as well as the two types of National Guard (Army, Air Force) personnel. Thus, the WMSM mantra could now be modified to "I serve with honor," as well as serving with caring. After completing their basic military education, WMSM could individually progress through different advanced education, assignments, roles, experiences, equal accountability, and responsibilities before their discharge and acquisition of the veteran designation (U.S. Department of Veteran Affairs, 2018d). Similar to their military men counterparts, during their service intense, distinctive military values of loyalty, duty, respect, selfless service, honor, integrity, and personal courage became mandatory and were often imprinted for life (Street et al., 2009).

Reserves/National Guard Personnel

Reserves/National Guard personnel (aka RC) are part-time military personnel who ordinarily train approximately 39 days per year. They are granted veteran distinction if they have served at least 29 consecutive days of full-time AD in total during their time of service. What makes them distinctive is that almost all RC hold full- or part-time civilian employment while fulfilling those responsibilities effectively. If and when they are activated or mobilized for a mission serving their country, they are also expected to perform their military occupations with the same proficiency as their full-time military counterparts. This time of AD deployment and reintegration to nondeployment conditions can happen as often as necessary to serve their country. As an RC, they also can become a veteran, regardless of their service branch, as well as achieve retirement benefits. Thus, both the full- and part-time military SMs deserve timely, effective, safe, and equitable individual-centered care with "respect, nurture, and empowering appreciation for their service and sacrifice" (Tanielian et al., 2018). Women make up approximately 20% of the total RC, with more in the Reserves (18%) than the National Guard (10%) due to more assigned stand-by military healthcare providers (Department of Defense, 2019).

Gulf War I (1991)

During the short 42-day Gulf War I, an extraordinary amount of full- and part-time military SMs were deployed to protect the Persian Gulf region. In total over 700,000 military SMs were deployed, including at that time the highest amount of military women (over 7%) (U.S. Department of Veteran Affairs, 2007). Over 40,000 RC women were on AD for a vast array of roles and assignment expectations, often within combat zone environments (Pierce, 2005; U.S. Department of Veteran Affairs, 2019b). While these military women were still not able to officially serve in combat, they were in combat zones as they were "attached" to a combat unit, just not assigned. Preparation for deployment included multiple vaccines and prophylactic medication (Pierce, 2005). Military SMs often lived in crowded, unsanitary conditions and experienced exposure to harsh environmental conditions that included the weather, oil fires, fuels, and other chemicals (Pierce, 2005). Currently between 25% and 33% of those SMs deployed to the Persian Gulf region are still suffering from a medically unexplained illness, once called Gulf War syndrome and now termed chronic multisymptom illness by the VHA (U.S. Department of Veterans Affairs, 2018a). While some chronic conditions have a latency period of years or decades such as cancer and neurological diseases, it will be imperative to monitor the Gulf War I veterans' health (Coughlin, 2016).

Iraq and Afghanistan Wars (2001–2014+)

This post-9/11 group contains the largest share of veterans (7.1 million) from the Iraq and Afghanistan wars (Operation Iraqi Freedom [OIF], Operation Enduring Freedom [OEF], and Operation New Dawn [OND]) (Bialik, 2017; U.S. Department of Veterans Affairs, 2018e). By September 30, 2005, the number of women on AD nearly quadrupled to more than 202,000, making up nearly 14% of the U.S. total forces (U.S. Department of Veterans Affairs, 2007).

OIF/OEF/OND Military Women

Now, there has been even more of a military transformation with almost 700,000 women having served in the U.S. military in support of the Iraq and Afghanistan wars (U.S. Department of Veteran Affairs, 2019b). These post-9/11 deployed SMs are distinctive. OIF/OEF/OND included more AD women warriors in every service branch than in previous conflicts, whether from military bases (15.2%) or RC units (18.5%) (Braun et al., 2016; Institute of Medicine [IOM], 2013; U.S. Department of Defense, 2019). Their numbers have increased yearly (>15.1%) in contrast to the decreased amount of military men (84.5%) (U.S. Department of Defense, 2017). Demographically, these military women were younger than prior-era wars, had achieved higher educational levels, and were often divorced (20%) and/or a single parent, with increased diversity (Hispanics [7%] and Blacks [12%]). RC women were older and at the time of OIF/OEF/OND received "less overall military training and may have been less prepared to deal with family and civilian life separation . . . [later] they tended to have less access to and awareness of military resources that could provide assistance during the reintegration process" (Maung et al., 2017, p. 67).

Despite continued combat exclusion rules for WMSM, during their deployment many OIF/OEF/OND military women were still attached (not assigned) to greater than 95% of the military infantry, engineering, and artillery roles, tasked with one or more of the different (>250,000) positions

(Wilson & Nelson, 2012). While overall they had less actual combat, their duty assignments kept them in the battle zones, similar to their male counterparts, with no front lines to retreat and recoup. Snipers were camouflaged throughout the area, while improvised explosive devices and penetrating fragments were everywhere (Flynn & Hassan, 2010). Everyone was in constant danger, all the time. Their OIF/OEF/OND assignments were "as gunners, security, fuel truck drivers, radar operators, helicopter mechanics, and even counter-insurgency warfare," as well as logistic and health care; leadership responsibilities included increased command positions (Conard & Armstrong, 2018). As never before, this all-volunteer women force involved in OIF/OEF/OND wars experienced long and sustained combat, often resulting in multiple deployments, as their military counterparts (Tepe et al., 2016).

For protection in combat zones during the first 8 years of OIF/OEF/OND, these military women were often issued body armor designed for men (Naclerio et al., 2011; Spelman et al., 2012). Subsequently, the chest plates did not accommodate busts, were longer in length creating difficulty to adequately bend at the waist, were bulky enough to inhibit/decrease their marksman skills, often created "chafing, bruising, and abrasions," while increasing their musculoskeletal injuries (20%), as compared to military men (4%) (Jackson, 2018; Naclerio et al., 2011). Their associated danger and roles were evidenced by over 140 military women killed and almost 1,000 wounded in action while supporting OIF/OEF/OND (Street et al., 2009). Now, fortunately the protective vest has been totally redesigned (Jackson, 2018).

OIF/OEF/OND Women Veterans

Presently, there is an increased demand for women veterans' health care, and many of these women are in a quandary regarding their health care (Tanielian et al., 2018). While general VHA care for women veterans finally and slowly emerged in the late 1980s, today there are over 2 million women veterans, or 1 in 13 veterans (9%); by 2035 it will be 1 in 7 (15%) (U.S. Department of Veterans Affairs, 2018e). The further discussion in this chapter will examine post-9/11 era women veterans and their visible genitourinary (GU) difficulties, as well as extrapolate specific invisible behavioral health issues from the growing body of literature that could be part of their holistic health concerns. Information about this newest generation of women veterans and their unique military experiences can assist nurses in providing applicable integrated biopsychosocial care for them as their nontraditional combat circumstances may be otherwise hard to envision.

Currently OIF/OEF/OND women veterans represent the fastest growing segment of the VHA (36%), for some, or all, of their yearly and varying health services at one of the 170 VHA medical centers and/or 1,061 outpatient sites (U.S. Department of Veterans Affairs, 2018d). This VHA population of women veterans will increase 22% by 2021. Enrollment in the VHA is dependent on qualifying for a priority designation, so some may not be eligible for care due to economic, service, or discharge elements (Tanielian et al., 2018). Logistical and economic issues continue to be barriers for them, including long driving distances and time to seek care, as well as increased costs for caregiver duties, work responsibilities, transportation, and healthcare availability (Washington et al., 2013). Now, when compared to nonveteran women, these women veterans could be unemployed (4.1%), up to four times as likely to be homeless (18–29 years of age), and five to six times more likely to commit suicide (Gerber et al., 2014; Koblinsky et al., 2017; U.S. Department of Veterans Affairs, 2018d).

While they served in OIF/OEF/OND, over 95% of post-9/11 era women veterans were in their reproductive years, yet interestingly their current major VHA use for service-connected disabilities includes behavioral health, musculoskeletal/connective tissue issues, and migraine assistance, along with total hysterectomies (Braun et al., 2016; National Center for Veterans Analysis and Statistics, 2017). Further care for most of their postservice gynecological, genitourinary, and maternity care has been in community facilities, often due to the lack of VHA medical support and timelessness for these health needs (Conard & Armstrong, 2018). With new congressional action for collaborative private sector service to improve access, more OIF/OEF/OND women veterans will be taking advantage of the local contracted provider-purchased VHA care or already could be patients within community health facilities (Tanielian et al., 2018). Thus, addressing women veterans' needs will be an important part of the nurse's clinical practice (Tanielian et al., 2018).

First, Identification

Women veterans are often not questioned (Mohler & Sankey-Deemer, 2017), acknowledged, or sometimes respected for their service-related nontraditional military responsibilities as a so-called real soldier or real veteran (Conard & Armstrong, 2018; Street et al., 2009). Nurses can change that with clinicians routinely screening, asking the universal assessment question, "Have you served in the military?" before starting the health history. Rather than missing or misdiagnosing the genitourinary problem(s) and related holistic concerns, which may further decrease the women veterans' quality of life, asking the right questions can further assess their military background experiences, current service-connected clinical concerns, and relevant occupational or environmental exposures that could be interrelated (Conard et al., 2015; Conrad & Armstrong, 2018; Mohler & Sankey-Deemer, 2017; Rossiter et al., 2016). Currently 25–40% of veterans' disabilities are not often observed (Mohler & Sankey-Deemer, 2017). The valuable Military Health History Pocket Card for Clinicians (available at https://www.va.gov/oaa/pocketcard/overview.asp) also is helpful to further establish rapport and address women veterans' health concerns for possible timely access to the applicable medical resources (U.S. Department of Veterans Affairs, 2018b).

Military Children Identification

For those nurses that interact with families with children, many deployed SMs were parents (44%), so SM families could have been affected by their separation, combat injury, and death (Department of Defense, 2010). What is being noted now is that more than 2 million children of veterans could also have "collateral wounds of war" while trying to cope with a deployed household member (Rossiter et al., 2016, p. 485). As many as 0.5 million of these children have been examined for clinical depression (Rossiter et al., 2016). The initiative "I Serve 2" was designed to prompt healthcare providers to query military children with the expanding assessment question, "Do you have a parent who ever served in the military?" (Rossiter et al., 2016).

Does "Healthy Solider Effect" Still Apply?

Throughout their career the many demands of keeping fit and training required that OIF/OEF/OND military women remain in optimal health, especially when preparing and enduring deployment (Steele & Yoder, 2013). Many have experienced continual health coverage and key assessment/preventive screening. Based on that, one of the natural assumptions upon discharge becomes the "protective healthy solider effect" (Conard & Armstrong, 2018) that some believe is present with WMSM, especially when comparing their health to civilian counterparts. One recent report cites women veterans as being in very good or excellent health (56.4%), yet more likely to face behavioral health challenges and have more chronic diseases such as arthritis (16%), cancer (15%), cardiovascular (16%), chronic obstructive pulmonary disease (19%), and functional impairment (29%) in higher rates than their civilian counterparts (United Health Foundation, 2017).

To achieve this good health and physical conditioning, effective clinician review/support during deployment is also required. In one study, between 15% and 44% of OIF/OEF/OND military women felt they did not have adequate predeployment information or access to good care in their deployed settings (Wilson & Nelson, 2012). These combat zone situations for OIF/OEF/OND military women (69%) presented major genitourinary care barriers, including a lack of confidence when seeking medical assistance. Many of the medics/corps personnel were primarily trained in emergency medical treatment, resuscitation, and little/no gender-specific health issues (Wilson et al., 2017). In addition, WMSM experienced embarrassment and nonconfidentiality when seen by their coworkers or someone in their chain of command (Lowe & Ryan-Wenger, 2003; Naclerco et al., 2011; Wilson et al., 2017). Their access to care was also hampered by austere locations, transport availability, and laboratory capabilities (Trego et al., 2018). Instead, they often sought internet self-help sources, peer-to-peer guidance, or delayed seeking assistance; unfortunately, any or all of these could create worse symptomatology and eventually warrant specialist care (Wilson et al., 2017). Better point-of-care gender-specific healthcare algorithms have now been established for the medics/corps personnel (Office of the Assistant Secretary of Defense Health Affairs, 2015).

Possible Deployment Consequences

Military combat zone experiences change almost everyone (Flynn & Hassan, 2010). With OIF/OEF/OND military women serving in many similar roles and environments as their male counterparts, few return home unscathed. "Interestingly, some of the acquired survival skills used during OIF/OEF/OND (emotional control, focused aggression, and hyperawareness) [become] troublesome" when they are trying to adjust their value-laden, structured military life to the civilian world (Conard & Armstrong, 2018, p. 165). Physical and/or behavioral health factors could surface, whether their service-related urologic concerns occurred during their deployment or soon after. Outcomes could produce lifelong health challenges or could peak several decades after their military service.

If these GU reintegration issues have surfaced, there could be significantly increased rates of comorbid interrelationships adversely affecting both their physical urological problems and behavioral health concerns (Bradley et al., 2017; Tanielian et al., 2018). Nurses should be aware of the physical and behavioral health overlaps with the possibility of the OIF/OEF/OND women veterans underreporting them, thus producing obstacles for adequate assistance and treatment. It is always easier to present (and respond to) physical symptoms than behavioral health issues so frequent monitoring at each visit should be conducted to elicit any unreported military circumstances and/or symptomology (**Table 4-1**).

Behaviorally, any lowered social support, strain, and/or chronic anger experienced during deployment could produce a long, difficult journey and little/no family support with women veterans' civilian readjustment period (Hawkins & Crowe, 2018). Highlighting the clinical necessity of their current problems and planning for early intervention would help to anticipate some of their future holistic needs (IOM, 2013).

Behavioral Health Issues Leading to Physical Complications

Depression

Besides a deep, prolonged, and painful sadness, depression (14%) also includes diminished

Table 4-1 Various Assessment Instruments for Query of Women Veteran Health Concerns

Type	Items	Instrument Availability
Alcohol	3	Alcohol Use Disorders Identification Test (AUDIT; auditscreen.org/)
Depression/ Suicide	2 or 9	Asking questions about suicidal ideation, intent, plan, and attempts is not easy as about 3% entertain suicide thoughts with no certain way to predict who will go on to attempt suicide. Start out with the two-item survey (www.cqaimh.org/pdf/tool_phq2.pdf) and, if positive, continue on with the nine-item Patient Health Questionnaire (https://www.uspreventiveservicestaskforce.org/Home/GetFileByID/218)
IPV	5	Hurts-Insult-Threaten-Scream (HITS) Tool (www.getdomesticviolencehelp.com/hits-screening-tool.html)
Medical Issues	20	Assesses general mental and physical health (https://www.rand.org/health/surveys_tools/mos/12-item-short-form.html)
(Military Sexual Trauma) MST	2	(Veteran Health Administration) VHA version: When you were in the military, a. did you ever receive uninvited and unwanted sexual attention? b. did anyone ever use force or the threat of force to have sex with you against your will?
(Post Traumatic Stress Disorder) PTSD	17	PTSD Checklist—Civilian Version (https://www.ptsd.va.gov/professional/assessment/screens/civilian-ptsd-checklist.asp; five item)
Sleep	3	Sleep Difficulties Scale (contributes to dx of PTSD also) adapted from the Insomnia Severity Index (U.S. military): In past 4 weeks, have you experienced difficulties (a) falling asleep, (b) staying asleep, or (c) waking too early? (Steele & Fogarty, 2017)
(Traumatic Brain Injury) TBI	4	VHA TBI Screening ToolL (VATBITS)BITBIS) screen (http://militarymedicine.amsus.org/doi/xml/10.7205/MILMED-D-14-00255)
Urinary	7	Urogenital Distress Inventory used to assess urogenital symptoms frequency and bother, then three subscales for stress, irritative, and obstructive issues. Incontinence IIQ-7 assesses functional impact related to urinary symptoms. Both forms can be found at http://www.womenshealthapta.org/wp-content/uploads/2013/12/IIQ.pdf

Reproduced from Conard, P. L., & Armstrong, M. L. (2018). Nursing care of women veterans of the Iraq and Afghanistan wars. *Nursing for Women's Health, 22*(2), 158–173. https://doi.org/10.1016/j.nwh.2018.02.007

self-worth, frequently compounded with exhaustion, fatigue, and social isolation (Cohen et al., 2012; Koblinsky et al., 2017). Nightmares, insomnia, irritability, and sleep apnea are common (Spelman et al., 2012). Some women veterans perceive they were not a real participant, so they had "tried to work harder to prove themselves" during deployment (Street et al., 2009; Wilson et al., 2017). Other OIF/OEF/OND military women express a bothersome notion of "perceived burdensomeness, a belief their existence had a negative impact on others" (Blais et al., 2018, p. 55). Remarks could include "I should have done more," "I didn't pull my weight," "They were always watching me," and "I knew I couldn't make a mistake or ask a question" (Maung et al., 2017, p. 67). Financial stability could also be a significant predictor of depressive symptoms (Sairsingh et al., 2018). This behavioral avoidance/withdrawal can hinder women veterans from seeking out resources, and they may often turn to alcohol to deal with the stressors (Maung et al., 2017). Later, increased depression can turn into risks for osteoporosis, cardiovascular disease, metabolic syndrome, dementia, and mortality in postmenopausal women (Resnick et al., 2012). Depression has also been associated with poorer adherence to treatment prescribed for lipid reduction, hypertension, and smoking cessation, as well as poorer control of diabetes (Lutwak, 2013).

Posttraumatic Stress Disorder

The invisible behavioral wounds of PTSD are possible any time anyone faces fear, helplessness, or horror from a stressful situation (e.g., combat, disaster, rape, assault) (Allen et al., 2013; Rivera & Johnson, 2014). Proactively the military, with an increased medical awareness of this prevalent wartime behavioral health issue, as well as a 2-year individual case cost of almost $20,000, has conducted more timely diagnostic assessments before and during OIF/OEF/OND (Geiling et al., 2012; IOM, 2013). Before discharge and 90–180 days after deployment, again frequent PTSD evaluations were prevalent. Accompanying health education to the OIF/OEF/OND military women stressed that occurrences may persist more than a few months, or begin later, waning throughout one's life (IOM, 2013; U.S. Department of Veterans Affairs, 2017). Repetition of this type of education will be important.

The invisible cluster of reexperiencing, avoidance, emotional numbing, and hyperarousal symptoms are often accompanied with intense guilt, self-loathing, depression, traumatic brain injury (TBI), pain, and substance abuse use disorder (Murphy & Hans, 2014). Untreated, chronic PTSD affects almost every bodily system producing significant poorer health and functional problems such as violence aggression, intimate partner violence, digestive system disorders, and sexual dysfunction, all that can further compound an allostatic stress load, which is predictive of cardiac disease (Mohler & Sankey-Deemer, 2017; Resnick et al., 2012; Spelman et al., 2012). Changes in health behaviors such as smoking and decreased physical activity may lead to greater risk of heart disease from resulting PTSD (Lutwak, 2013). Chronic pain has been shown to increase and sustain PTSD, whereas PTSD is also known to retain chronic pain (IOM, 2013; Resnick et al., 2012). Estimated individual case costs for PTSD in 2035 could exceed $50,000, and without any treatment and health promotion programs this chronic situation could well tally over $1 million (Geiling et al., 2012). Studies are now examining several stress response neurohormones such as allopregnanolone (ALLO) and risk, recovery, and comorbidity effects with PTSD (Resnick et al., 2012). Additionally, higher than usual risk taking and perceived invincibility can be present with many veterans, including women veterans, especially with motor vehicles and increased vehicular accidents/fatalities (Cohen et al., 2012).

Gynecologically, several studies link PTSD with increased neurotransmitter and hormone levels to other health conditions such as abnormal pap smears, sexually transmitted infections, menstrual disorders, infertility polycystic ovarian syndrome, chronic pelvic pain, and pelvic inflammatory conditions (Cohen et al., 2012). OIF/OEF/OND women veterans are also concerned about behavioral health pharmacotherapy affecting sexual dysfunction and pregnancy (Blais et al., 2018).

The VHA reports women veterans have been the largest OIF/OEF/OND group coming forward to report PTSD. Other variables include the amount of support and individual help they obtained after the traumatic events. Yet, some suggest that when unisex screening tools are used within VHA evaluations that OIF/OEF/OND women veterans very quickly receive the primary diagnosis of depression (23%), compared with their male counterparts (17%) (Cohen et al., 2012; Sairsingh et al., 2018). Around 20% of OIF/OEF/OND women veterans have been given a PTSD diagnosis (U.S. Department of Veterans Affairs, 2017), and over 48,000 women veterans are receiving compensation for it. This accounts for roughly 12% of all women veterans with this service-connected disability (National Center for Veterans Analysis and Statistics, 2017). Additionally, many WMSM may have been exposed historically to premilitary sexual violence/abuse (39%), compared to men (13%), creating an accumulative or even greater susceptibility and impact to any type of trauma in the deployed setting (Braun et al., 2016; Flynn & Hassan, 2010; Street et al., 2009).

Military Sexual Trauma (MST)

Defined by the Department of Veterans Affairs, MST is a "sexual assault, or repeated, threatening sexual harassment experienced by the veteran during their military service." Others call it a "non-combat violent assault" and a "high betrayal trauma" (Allen et al., 2013; IOM, 2013, p 3). "Solitary duty, poor barracks security, and insufficient perimeter lighting," as well as an inherent male-dominated authoritative command control are some of the risks associated with combat environments (Naclerio et al., 2011; Street et al., 2009). These risks are listed as predisposing factors to MST for WMSM. While traumatic exposure is more common and frequent in men, MST in women veterans produces a higher risk/impact shock for them. Those affected often experience the "enemy within," frequently knowing their assailant(s), then still having to work and interact daily with them to accomplish mutual goals (Street et al., 2009), while feeling damaged (Naclerio et al., 2011). Upon contact, they experience a stronger and longer intensity to the traumatic event, especially if there was a lengthy exposure (IOM, 2013; Resnick et al., 2012). Many of these situations are still unreported (80–90%), especially when they are attempting to realign themselves to military values, compounding the shame, and/or they have perceptions of being a weak troop (Maung et al., 2017). Unfortunately, MST is not blind to gender with 1 in 4 women and 1 in 100 men veterans reporting the situation(s) (Naclerio et al., 2011; U.S. Department of Veteran Affairs, 2018c). While the numbers appear smaller in military men, with the greater percentage of men in the service, the proportional incidence is about the same.

Caring for veterans with MST is challenging. The VHA emphasizes in their literature a complete commitment to helping those with MST while they also describe MST as an "experience, not a diagnosis, or behavioral health condition" (U.S. Department of Veterans Affairs, 2018c). Unfortunately, those with MST are nine times more likely to develop PTSD (IOM, 2013; Koblinsky et al., 2017; Naclerio et al., 2011), in addition to experiencing shame, hopelessness, poor emotional functioning, and low social support. Many with MST suffer from comorbidities (Hickey et al., 2017), such as anxiety, depression, substance abuse, suicide attempts, sexual problems, weight or eating difficulties, diabetes, fatigue, and gastrointestinal issues (U.S. Department of Veteran Affairs, 2018c). A study by Cichowski et al. (2017) revealed a number of chronic pain conditions associated with MST such as irritable bowel syndrome, chronic pelvic pain, back pain, joint pain, fibromyalgia, and headaches. MST may also lead to cardiac health problems, which can be significant especially for WMSM and/or women veterans who are menopausal

(Lutwak, 2013). Obesity has also been associated with MST, which further burdens the risk for cardiac disease (Pandey et al., 2018). MST has become a costly combat remnant with the Department of Defense (DoD). Already in 2010, the DoD noted the spending of almost $100,000 for legal and attrition costs, while the VHA reported individual case costs of $11,000 (Geiling et al., 2012).

Suicide Thoughts and Behavior (STB)

One suicide is too many! As troublesome as suicides are for any veteran, the numbers continue to hover daily around 20, with at least 14 of them never seeking any care from the VHA (Kelly, 2017). OIF/OEF/OND women veterans are a part of this difficult picture (>20%), especially when they have a dyad or triad of increased pain, MST, PTSD, depression, impulsivity, sleep deprivation, substance abuse, unemployment, homelessness, and/or anger management issues (Conard et al., 2015). Civilian women make more suicide attempts, but OIF/OEF/OND women veterans with firearm knowledge, accessibility, and/or possession assist them to completion. Other higher risks include those who are married or living with a companion, between 35 and 50 years of age, reporting past attempts (6%), and current suicidal thoughts (Sairsingh et al., 2018). Significant low arousal and sexual satisfaction, often associated with sexual dysfunction, are also indicators of suicidal ideation (Blais et al., 2018). Lesbian, gay, bisexual, and transgender women veterans (>0.5 million) can also be affected with failed interpersonal stressors, experiencing chronic fear from discrimination, and/or hiding their sexual orientation (Koblinsky et al., 2017). Veteran screening for suicide should be conducted at each visit (see Table 4-1). Common assessment questions should include, "Have you thought about hurting yourself?" and, if positive, "Do you have a plan, and what is your plan?"

Urological Deployment Hazards

Geography, terrain, and infrastructure are just some of the usual deployment conditions affecting combat zone experiences (Lowe & Ryan-Wenger, 2003). OIF/OEF/OND circumstances generated distracting urologic gender-specific challenges (Trego et al., 2018) with extreme daily heat of >100°F and subfreezing temperatures at night (Spelman et al., 2012) in sandy and dirty environments. WMSM battle uniforms were worn almost continuously, made from tightly woven fabric that did not stimulate airflow (Lowe & Ryan-Wenger, 2003; Wilson & Nelson, 2012). Many times these WMSM lived in close quarters (tents, permanent structures, or ships) with their male counterparts. This often meant shared hygiene facilities, lack of privacy, and no/limited laundry (Steele & Yoder, 2013). Anatomic differences in female GU structures and undressing with >40 lbs of full battle gear (outerwear, chemical and armor protective gear, and weapons) made urination a miserable, daunting task in unsafe unsanitary austere conditions (Lowe & Ryan-Wenger, 2003; Spelman et al., 2012; Steele & Yoder, 2013). Bombs were even present by the side of the road.

These challenges led to decreased hydration to avoid urination, voluntarily holding urine for prolonged periods, wearing perineal pads, or using urination bottles/bags/cans, all potentiating urinary tract infections (UTIs) as well as vaginitis (Braun et al., 2016; Reed et al., 2018; Steele & Yoder, 2013; Street et al., 2009; Tepe et al., 2016; Trego et al., 2018). This also had military ramifications as it affected unit readiness when some WMSM were medically evacuated from their combat zone locations and did not return to their duty stations resulting in a need to obtain replacements (Wilson & Nelson, 2012). The result was close to three times the proportion of OIF/OEF/OND women evacuated for nonbattle

GU injuries and/or lost days of work than that of their male counterparts (Office of Assistant Secretary, 2015). Just for OIF, a GU diagnosis made up 16% of all diseases and nonbattle injuries (Wilson & Nelson, 2012). Later, the DoD reported more GU concerns for women (7%) than for men (1.5%). Since their reintegration, the VHA has reported over 56,000 OIF/OEF/OND women veteran visits for GU system problems (43%), as compared to their male counterparts (>125,000; 13.5%) (Murphy & Hans, 2014).

Urinary Tract Infections and Acute Dysuria

Within the civilian sector over 8 million community clinic visits (84%) and emergency department visits (21%) are due to UTIs made by U.S. women as well as 150 million cases globally. While several have reported that the most common GU disorder of OIF/OEF/OND women veterans was UTIs, epidemiology figures vary from 10–18.4% (Murphy & Hans, 2014; Steele & Yoder, 2013; Wilson & Nelson 2012). The cause was often due to an occurring uropathogenic agent colonization of ascending, hematogenous, or periurogenital spread. Infrequent urination then led to bladder distention, ischemia, and UTIs (Davis, 2005). Symptoms of dysuria reflected either urinary or vaginal difficulties or both, especially in hot or cold environments (Davis, 2005).

While prevention was key, often the UTI was left untreated. Now these women veterans are prone to serious risk of pyelonephritis, increased medical costs, lost employment time, and poor quality of life (Steele & Yoder, 2013). What is now known is that after the single UTI occurrence, 30–44% can have a recurrent UTI and the second one will be within 6 months; 50% will have a third occurrence often within 12 months (Brubaker et al., 2018). Recently the American Urogynecologic Society published a best-practice statement, "Recurrent Urinary Tract Infection in Adult Women" (Brubaker et al, 2018).

Overactive Bladder

Currently a significantly higher number of OIF/OEF/OND women veterans (>22%) have reported troublesome urinary urgency, frequency, and incontinence symptoms, when compared to the general women population of the same age (17%), and women under 45 years of age (5–10%) (Bradley et al., 2012, 2014). Besides negatively affecting their quality of life (Bradley et al., 2014), further research (Bradley et al., 2017) confirmed that these women veterans often present with related association of behavioral health conditions (anxiety, depression) and prior sexual assault. The multifaceted neuropharmacologic relationships of behavioral issues and bladder muscles suggest further complex alterations and "also explains the association between prior sexual assault and urinary symptoms" (Bradley et al., 2012, p. 502.e6). Of women veterans, 11% will develop new overactive bladder symptoms yearly and one-third will have resolution of these symptoms after 1 year (Bradley et al., 2014, 2017).

Pelvic Organ Prolapse (POP)

The usual risk factors of age, number of vaginal and multiple deliveries, high birthweight deliveries, chronic cough, and genetic susceptibility, along with the continual efforts for strenuous activity, could predispose the OIF/OEF/OND woman veteran to the muscular weakening of the pelvic floor muscles and connective tissue, producing POP. One observational study of 144 nulliparous women at a military academy with a mean age of 19.6 years noted that 50% had some loss of pelvic floor support (stages 1 and II) on exam; 19% reported incontinence upon running. These findings were similar to an Australian study with nonmilitary personnel (Larson & Yavorek, 2006).

Bladder Pain Syndrome (BPS)

In one study (Resnick et al., 2012), OIF/OEF/OND women veterans were found to have more than twice the occurrence of BPS than men. The pain accompanies the urinary bladder being filled, which greatly impacts such women's quality of life.

Trauma Outcomes and Urogenital Health (TOUGH) Project

One purpose for the TOUGH project was to establish baseline data for long-term effects of vulvovaginal and other GU injuries before future military women would be included in all combat-related positions (Reed et al., 2018). Currently sustained GU injury data in OIF/OEF/OND military women include explosions (8) and gunshots (1) from battle injuries, as well as nonbattle injuries from gunshots (2), falls (2), and other blunt injury accidents (7). Resultant damages included their kidneys (12), vulva (4), vagina (3), and bladder (1); regional injuries included colorectal issues (5) and lower extremity amputations (2) (Reed et al., 2018). Greater internal protection of the GU and reproductive tracts were the major reason the study authors believe WMSM's injuries were different than men (Reed et al., 2018).

Interventions

Acknowledging the concerns of GU issues and advocating for the women veterans' holistic care should be a priority as their health needs will require complex care coordination (Conard & Armstrong, 2018). Also, often the risk factors affect both the urologic and gynecologic systems such as vaginitis and UTIs (Lowe & Ryan-Wenger, 2003). Additionally, their response to trauma and injury provides further evidence that women often react differently than men during those situations (Conard & Armstrong, 2018; Rivera & Johnson, 2014). Active listening and understanding of their wartime experiences will be critical to initiate further compliance with their treatment process (Koblinsky et al., 2017). Three recommendations include enhancing an interdisciplinary coordinated, comprehensive, interventional approach.

Therapeutic Relationships

Just as family and friends may not understand, often OIF/OEF/OND woman veterans may doubt whether healthcare providers will also understand their military experiences and present situations, which can create an internal and personal barrier for treatment (Maung et al., 2017). Promoting an "empathic, and consistent care" relationship to engage them as full partners in the development of best urologic practice should be beneficial for their care (Koblinsky et al., 2017). Explore with them unmet needs. This will be crucial to whether OIF/OEF/OND women veterans will continue with both their urologic care and any behavioral health interaction as "one unpleasant visit could have long-standing negative impacts" (Koblinsky et al., 2017).

Healthcare System

Nurses are an important component to promote seamless continuity and clinical coordination, not only for the OIF/OEF/OND women veterans but for women veterans in general. The growing number of WMSM is unprecedented and is expected to increase (Rivera & Johnson, 2014), as well as the population of women veterans. The latter is due to "(a) of the increasing number and proportion of women entering (and leaving) the military, (b) a more favorable survival rate of women compared to men at any given age, and (c) the younger age distribution of WV compared to male veterans, which means relatively more women at younger ages, with lower mortality rates"

(U.S. Department of Veteran Affairs, 2007, p. 7). What will be important is to guide advocacy and healthcare policy to improve their quality of life, provide a holistic diagnosis, and facilitate an appropriate collaborative alliance approach (Tanielian et al., 2018). Frequent posted health education hotline messaging about all the behavioral health issues, and especially suicide, within the clinical practice treatment areas will be vital (Koblinsky et al., 2017) (**Box 4-1**). The veterans suicide hotline is 1-800-273-TALK (http://veterancrisisline.net/).

As best practice, nurses can remove the significant gaps for culturally competent high-quality care delivery with the creation of applicable interdisciplinary health teams composed of primary care, behavioral health, and social workers (Spelman et al., 2012). Frequent screening to accomplish applicable holistic care will be important (Conard et al., 2015; Conard & Armstrong, 2018).

Box 4-1 Example of Messaging for Collaborative Practice

She served, she deserves the best care anywhere.
Women's Health Services: www.womenshealth.va.gov
Women Veterans Call Center: 1-855-VA-WOMEN (1-855-829-6636)
Locate the nearest VA facility: www.va.gov/directory
Check VA eligibility: www.va.gov/healtheligibility
VA benefit information: www.vba.va.gov/VBA
VA homeless program: www.va.gov/homeless
Veteran Crisis Hotline: 1-800-273-8255, press 1
eBenefits: www.ebenefits.va.gov

Women's Health Services, Department of Veterans Affairs. (n.d.). *Women veterans*. https://www.minneapolis.va.gov/services/women/index.asp

Clinical Care Environment

Nurses should increase their ability to provide evidence-based "talk," not just about urologic concerns but, if necessary, the integrative approaches about depression, PTSD, MST, and safe sexual practices for women veterans. Taking the time to implement frequent screening tools, as well as frequent suicide monitoring, to facilitate any discussion of these issues will be important. In addition, build collaborative interprofessional team support for any VHA behavioral health treatment (Koblinsky et al., 2017). A reminder, OIF/OEF/OND women veterans will be very cautious about overuse of antidepressant medications and their side effects, especially since many are of child-bearing age (Koblinsky et al., 2017).

References

Allen, P., Armstrong, M., Conard, P., Saladiner, J., & Hamilton, M. (2013). Veteran's healthcare considerations for today's nursing curricula. *Journal of Nursing Education, 52*, 632–640.

Atkins, D., & Lipson, L. (2015). The role of research in a time of rapid change: Lessons from research on women veterans' health. *Medical Care, 53*(4, Suppl 1), S5–S7.

Bialik, K. (2021). *The changing face of America's veteran population*. http://www.PewResearch.org/fact-tank/2017/11/10/the-changing-face-of-America's-veteran-population https://www.pewresearch.org/fact-tank/2021/04/05/the-changing-face-of-americas-veteran-population/#:~:text=There%20are%20around%2019%20million,the%20total%20U.S.%20adult%20population.

Blais, R. K., Monteith, L. L., & Kugler, J. (2018). Sexual dysfunction is associated with suicidal ideation in female service members and veterans. *Journal of Affective Disorders, 226*, 52–57.

Bond, E. (2004). Women's physical and mental health sequella of wartime service. *Nursing Clinics of North America, 39*(1), 53–68.

Bradley, C., Nygaard, I., Mengeling, M., Torner, J., Hills, S. L., Johnson, S., & Sadler, A. (2014). Overactive bladder and mental health symptoms in recently deployed women veterans. *The Journal of Urology, 191*(5), 1327–1332.

Bradley, C., Nygaard, I., Mengeling, M., Torner, J., Stockdate, C. K., Booth, B. M., & Sadler, A. G. (2012). Urinary incontinence, depression and posttraumatic stress disorder in women veterans. *American Journal of Obstetrics & Gynecology, 206*, 502.e1–e6.

Bradley, C. S., Nygaard, I. E., Hillis, S. L., Torner, J. C., & Sadler, A. G. (2017). Longitudinal associations between mental health conditions and overactive bladder in women veterans. *American Journal of Obstetrics & Gynecology, 217*(10), 430.e1–430.e8.

Braun, L. A., Kennedy, H. P., Womack, J. A., & Wilson, C. (2016). Integrative literature review: U.S. military women's genitourinary and reproductive health. *Military Medicine, 181*(1), 35–49.

Brubaker, L., Carberry, C., Nardos, R., Carter-Brooks, C., & Lowder, J. L. (2018). American urogynecologic society best-practice statement: Recurrent urinary tract infection in adult women. *Female Pelvic Medicine & Reconstructive Surgery, 24*(5), 321–333.

Cichowski, S., Rogers, R., Clark, E., Murata, E., & Murata, A. (2017). Military sexual trauma in female veterans is associated with chronic pain. *Military Medicine, 182*, e1895–e1899.

Cohen, B. E., Maguen, S., Bertenthal, S. Y., Jacoby, V., & Seal, K. (2012). Reproductive and other health outcomes in Iraq and Afghanistan women veterans using VA health care: Association with mental health diagnoses. *Women's Health Issues*, 22, e461–e471.

Conard, P., Allen, P., & Armstrong, M. (2015). Preparing staff to care for veterans in a way they need and deserve. *The Journal of Continuing Education in Nursing, 46*(3), 109–118.

Conard, P., & Armstrong, M. L. (2018). Nursing care of women veterans of the Iraq and Afghanistan wars. *AHWONN, 22*(2), 158–173.

Coughlin, S. (2016). Letter to the editor: Need for studies of the health of Gulf War women veterans. *Military Medicine, 181*, 198.

Davis, G. D. (2005). Acute dysuria among female soldiers. *Military Medicine, 179*(9), 735–738.

Department of Defense. (2010). *The impacts of deployment of deployed members of the Armed Forces on their dependent children.* http://download.militaryonesource.mil/12038/MOS/Reports/Report_to_Congress_on_Impact_of_Deployment_on_Military_Children.pdf.

Dever, M. (2016). *Vietnam-era women veterans: The unknown trauma.* https://www.dav.org/learn-more/news/2016/vietnam-era-women-veterans-the-unknown-trauma/

Donnelly, K. T., Donnelly, J. P., Dunnam, M., Warner, G. C., Kittleson, C. J., Constance, J. E., . . . & Alt, M. (2011). Reliability, sensitivity, and specificity of the VA traumatic brain injury screening tool. *The Journal of head trauma rehabilitation, 26*(6), 439–453.

Feller, C. M., & Moore, C. J. (1996). *Highlights in the history of the Army Nurse Corps.* CMH Pub 85-1. U.S Army Center of Military History.

Flynn, M., & Hassan, A. (2010). Unique challenges of war in Iraq and Afghanistan. *Journal of Social Work, 48*(2), 169–173.Geiling, J., Rosen, J., & Edwards, R. (2012). Medical costs of war in 2035: Long-term care challenges for veterans of Iraq and Afghanistan. *Military Medicine, 177*, 1235–1244.

Gerber, M. D., Iverson, K. A., Dichter, M. E., Klap, R., & Latta, R. E. (2014). Women veterans and intimate partner violence: Current state of knowledge and future directions. *Journal of Women's Health, 23*(4), 302–309. doi:10:1089/jwh.2013/4513

Hawkins, B. L., & Crowe, B. M. (2018). Contextual facilitators and barriers of community reintegration among injured female military veterans: A qualitative study. *Archives of Physical Medicine and Rehabilitation, 99*(2S), S65–S71. doi:org/10.1016/j.apmr.2017.07.018

Hickey, T., Kirwin, P., Gardner, E., & Feinleib, J. (2017). Patient-centered perioperative care for a victim of military sexual trauma. *Military Medicine, 182*, e1807–e1811.

Institute of Medicine. (2013). *Returning home from Iraq and Afghanistan: Assessment of readjustment needs of veterans, service members, and their families.* National Academies Press.

Jackson, K. (2018). *House approves funding for women specific body armor.* http://connectingvets.com/articles/house-approves-funding-women-specific-body-armor

Kang, H., Cypel, Y., Kilbourne, A., Magruder, K., Serpi, T., Collins, J.,Frayne, S., Furey, J., Huang, G., Kimerling, R., Reinhard, M., Schumacher,K., & Spiro, A. (2014). HealthVIEWS: Mortality study of female US Vietnam era veterans, 1965-2010. *American Journal of Epidemiology, 179*(6), 721–730.

Kelly, L. (2017). Shulkin: VA will address high suicide rates in veteran population. *The Washington Times.* https//www.washingtontimes.com/news/2017/set/27/david-shulkin

Koblinsky, S. A., Schroeder, A. L., & Leigh, L. A (2017). "Give us respect, support and understanding": Women veterans of Iraq and Afghanistan recommend strategies for improving their mental health care. *Social Work in Mental Health, 15*(2), 121–142.

Larson, W. I., & Yavorek, T. A. (2006). Pelvic organ prolapse and urinary incontinence in nulliparous women at the United States Military Academy. *International Urogynecology, 17*(3), 208–210.

Lowe, N., & Ryan-Wenger, N. (2003). Military women's risk factors for and symptoms of genitourinary infections during deployment. *Military Medicine, 168*, 569–574.

Lutwak, N. (2013). Military sexual trauma increases risk of post-traumatic stress disorder and depression thereby amplifying the possibility of suicidal ideation and cardiovascular disease. *Military Medicine, 178*(4), 359–361.

Maguen, S., Lau, K. M., Madden, E., & Seal, K. (2012). Factors associated with completing comprehensive traumatic brain injury evaluation. *Military medicine, 177*(7), 797–803.

Maung, J., Milsson, J. E., Berkel, L. A., & Kelly, P. (2017). Women in the National Guard: Coping and barriers to care. *Journal of Counseling & Development, 95*, 67–75.

Meyer, C. E. (2016). Mary Edwards Walker: The only woman awarded the Medal of Honor. *Military Medicine, 181*(5), 502–503. doi:10.7205/MILMED-D-15-00573

Mohler, K. M., & Sankey-Deemer, C. (2017). Primary care providers and screening for military service and PTSD. *American Journal of Nursing, 117*(11), 22–29.

Murphy, F. M., & Hans, S. (2014). *Women veterans: The long journey home*. Disabled American Veterans (DAV). http://www.dav.org/women-veterans-study

Naclerio, A., Stola, J., Tregp, L., & Flaherty, E. (2011). *The concerns of women currently serving in the Afghanistan Theater of Operations*. Health Service Support Assessment Team, UC, Afghanistan. www.globalsecurity.org/military/library/report/2011/women-concerns-afghanistan.pdf; https://www.army.mil/e2/c/downloads/262501.pdf

National Center for Veterans Analysis & Statistics. (2017). *Women veterans: The past, present, and future of women veterans*. U.S. Department of Veterans Affairs.

Office of the Assistant Secretary of Defense Health Affairs. (2015). *Deployment health for women*. House Report 113-446 (p. 164). https://www.congress.gov/congressional-report/113th-congress/house-report/446/1

Pandey, N., Ashfaq, S., Dauterive, E., MacCarthy, A., & Copeland, L. (2018). Military sexual trauma and obesity among women veterans. *Journal of Women's Health, 27*(3), 305–310.

Pierce, P. (2005). Federal Nursing Service Award: Monitoring the health of Persian Gulf War veteran women. *Military Medicine, 170*, 349–354.

Reed, A. M., Janak, J. C., Orman, J. A., & Hudak, S. J. (2018). Genitourinary injuries among female U.S. service members during Operation Iraqi Freedom and Operation Enduring Freedom: Findings from the Trauma Outcomes and Urogenital Health (TOUGH) project. *Military Medicine, 183*(7/8), e304–e308.

Resnick, E. M., Mallampalli, M., & Carter, C. (2012). Current challenges in female veterans health. *Journal of Women's Health, 21*(9), 895–900.

Rivera, J., & Johnson, A. (2014). Female veterans of Operations Enduring Freedom: Status and future directions. *Military Medicine, 179*, 133–136.

Rossiter, A. G., Dumas, M. A., Wilmoth, M. C., & Patrician, P. A. (2016). "I serve 2": Meeting the needs of military children in civilian practice. *Nursing Outlook, 64*, 485–490.

Sairsingh, H., Solomon, P., Helstrom, A., & Treglia, D. (2018). Depression in female veterans returning from deployment: The role of social factors. *Military Medicine, 183*(3/4), e133–e139.

Schuette, W., & Armstrong, M. L. (2019). Civil War drummer boys: Musicians, messengers, and medical assistants. *Military Medicine, 184*(1/2), 1–4. doi:10.1093/milmed/usy258

Schwarz, L. (1987). Women and the Vietnam experience. *Image: Journal of Nursing Scholarship, 19*(4), 168–173.

Spelman, J. F., Hunt, S. C., Seal, K. H., & Burgo-Blac, A. L. (2012). Post deployment care for returning combat veterans. *Journal of General Internal Medicine, 27*(9), 1200–1209.

Stalsburg, B. (2010). *Military sexual trauma: The quick facts*. https://vawnet.org/sites/default/files/assets/files/2016-09/SWAN-MSTFactSheet.pdf

Steele, N. M., & Fogarty, G. J. (2017). Screening for anger and sleep difficulties. *Military medicine, 182*(3-4), e1628-e1633.

Steele, N., & Yoder, L. H. (2013). Military women's urinary patterns, practices and complications in deployment settings. *Urologic Nursing, 33*(2), 61–71, 78.

Street, A. E., Vogt, D., & Dutra, L. (2009). A new generation of women veterans: Stressors faced by women deployed to Iraq and Afghanistan. *Clinical Psychology Review, 29*, 685–694.

Tanielian, T., Farmer, C. M., Burns, R. M., Duffy, E. L., & Setodji, C. M. (2018). *Ready or not? Assessing the capacity of New York State health care providers to meet the needs of veterans*. Rand Health. http://www.rand.org

Tepe, V., Yarnell, A., Nindl, B. C., Van Arsdale, S., & Deuster, P. A. (2016). Women in combat: Summary of findings and a way ahead. *Military Medicine, 181*(1), 109–118.

Timeline: A history of women in the US military. https://taskandpurpose.com/timeline-history-women-us-military

Trego, L. L., Steele, N. M., & Jordan, P. (2018). Using the RE_AIM model of health promotion to implement a military women's health promotion program for austere settings. *Military Medicine, 183*(3/4), 538–546.

United Health Foundation. (2017). *America's Health Rankings® Health of Women Who Have Served* Report. https://www.americashealthrankings.org/

U.S. Department of Defense (2019) Fact Sheet: Women in Service Review (WISR). https://dod.defense.gov/Portals/1/Documents/pubs/Fact_Sheet_WISR_FINAL.pdf

U.S. Department of Veterans Affairs. (2007). *Women veterans: Past, present, and future*. https://www.va.gov/womenvet/docs/womenvet_history.pdf

U.S. Department of Veterans Affairs. (2017). *Traumatic stress in female veterans*. https://www.ptsd.va.gov/professional/treat/type/trauma_female_veterans.asp

U.S. Department of Veterans Affairs. (2018a). *Gulf War veterans medically unexplained illnesses*. https://www.publichealth.va.gov/exposures/gulfwar/medically-unexplained-illness.asp

U.S. Department of Veterans Affairs. (2018b). *Military health history pocket card for clinicians*. https://www.va.gov/oaa/pocketcard/overview.asp

U.S. Department of Veterans Affairs. (2018c). *Military sexual trauma*. https://www.ptsd.va.gov/public/types/violence/military-sexual-trauma-general.asp

U.S. Department of Veterans Affairs. (2018d). *VA benefits & health care utilization*. https://www.va.gov/vetdata/docs/pocketcards/fy2018q2.pdf

U.S. Department of Veterans Affairs. (2018e). *Veteran population projections: FY2010-FY2040*. https//www.va.gov/vetdata/docs/QuickFacts/Population_quickfacts.pdf

U.S. Department of Veterans Affairs. (2019a). *Birth defects of children of Vietnam and Korea veterans*. https://www.publichealth.va.gov/exposures/agentorange/birth-defects/index.asp

U.S. Department of Veterans Affairs. (2019b). *Women veterans health: Women veterans history month*. https://www.womenshealth.va.gov/WOMENSHEALTH/outreachmaterials/womenveteransmakehistory/campaigns_makehistory.asp

Washington, D., Bean-Mayberry, B., Hamilton, A., Cordasco, K., & Yano, E. (2013). Women veterans healthcare delivery preferences and use by military service era: Findings from the National Survey of Women Veterans. *Journal of General Internal Medicine, 28*(2), S571–S576.

Wilson, C., & Nelson, J. P. (2012). Exploring the patterns, practices, and experiences of military women who managed genitourinary symptoms in deployed settings. *JOGNN, 41*, 293–302.

Wilson, C., Corrigan, R., & Braun, L. (2017). Deployed women's illness behaviors while managing genitourinary symptoms: An exploratory theoretical synthesis of two qualitative studies. *Nursing Outlook, 65*, S17–S25.

Women's Memorial. (n.d.). *History highlights—including World War I, World War II, educational benefits*. https://www.womensmemorial.org/.

Wright, J. (2013). What we learned from the Korean War. *The Atlantic*. http://www.theatlantic.com/international/archive/2013/07/what-we-learned-from-the-Korean-War

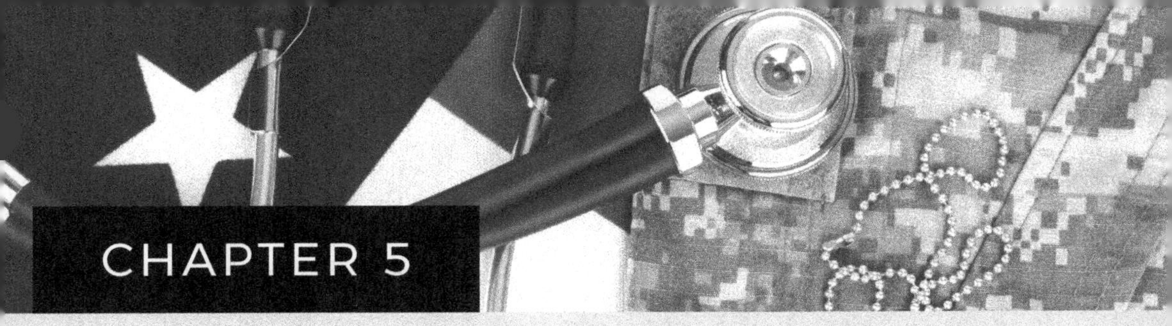

CHAPTER 5

Caring for Female Veterans

Stephanie Felder, James Blankenship, and Peter Delany

We, at VA, must be visionary and agile enough to anticipate and adjust not only to the coming increase in women Veterans but also to the accompanying complexity and longevity of treatment needs they will bring with them.

—**VA Secetary Eric Shinseki** (2009-2014)

Women veterans are the fastest growing population of veterans, and they present unique healthcare challenges. In 2019, there were approximately 2 million women veterans in the United States, and this number is expected to increase at an average rate of 18,000 women per year over the next 6 years (Department of Labor, 2019; National Center for Veterans Analysis and Statistics, 2017). To address the needs of all veterans and enhance the access to timely care, the U.S. Department of Veterans Affairs (VA) expanded service availability in 2018 when the MISSON Act was signed. The VA stated that "the MISSION Act gives Veterans greater access to health care in VA facilities and the community, expands benefits for caregivers, and improves VA's ability to recruit and retain the best medical providers" (Department of Veterans Affairs, 2020). The signing of this act, along with the VA's commitment to care, will undoubtedly lead to more veterans, including female veterans, seeking care in the community. This will provide opportunities for community practitioners to continue the quality care provided by the VA and meet the distinctive needs of female veterans.

This chapter will focus on providing health care for female veterans. Topics mentioned in earlier chapters, such as the history of women veterans and service-connected comorbidities, will be discussed in relation to their impact on care of the female veteran population. Additionally, the chapter includes information on screenings and how to conduct a physical and mental health assessment with the female veteran population. The chapter presents an integrative medicine approach to providing treatment to female veterans. The information is intended for medical and mental health professionals to assist them in caring for female veterans. The integrative approach focuses on the patient at the center of their treatment. It takes a holistic approach to care by addressing the physical, mental, emotional, environmental, social, and spiritual influences on a person's health. In addition, Appendix A provides a list of relevant referrals for serving female veterans. Other appendices are referred to in the chapter.

Changing Profile of the U.S. Military

The U.S. military has always been known as the model for race and gender relations. Regarding race, Executive Order 9981 signed by President S. Truman on July 26, 1948, established the President's Committee on Equality of Treatment and Opportunity with the sole purpose of integrating the military. This led the way for affirming the existence of women in the military concurrently with implementing desegregation practices in the workforce—both building a path to a unified force. The impact of Executive Order 9981 also led to a change in the veteran population profile. Since the Afghanistan and Iraq wars, the veteran population began to include more women and younger women with different healthcare needs than older women veterans. The number of female veterans has been rising for quite some time. From 2010–2021, the number of female veterans doubled from 160,000 to 310,000. Additionally, given the military's coordinated efforts to diversify the force, the number of minorities in the military also increased. It is not too surprising, therefore, that the military is experiencing a rise in minority female service members among the ranks. Currently, there are more minority female recruits entering the military than male enlisted. According to the VA, these trends are expected to continue to significantly increase. **Figures 5-1** and **5-2** display the VA's 30-year projections for the female veteran and minority veteran populations.

Given the continual increase of female and minority active duty (AD) service members, there is a growing need for culturally sensitive interventions for women in both AD and veteran care settings. Therefore, it is essential for civilian providers to understand this increase in female veterans and their characteristics.

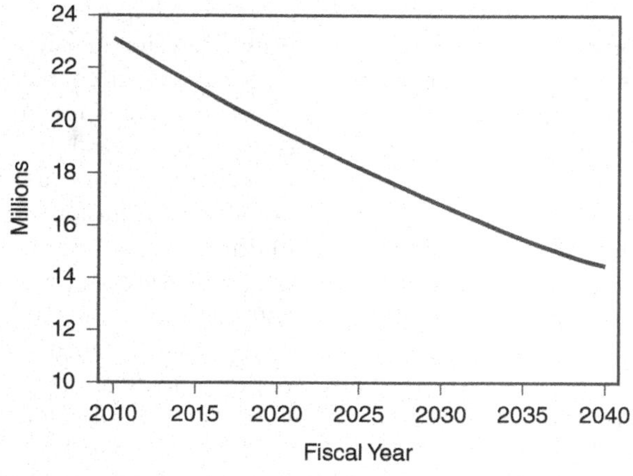

Figure 5-1 Projected female veteran population 2010–2040.

Office of the Actuary. (2011). *Quick facts [PowerPoint]*. Department of Veterans Affairs. https://www.va.gov/vetdata/docs/QuickFacts/population_quickfacts.pdf

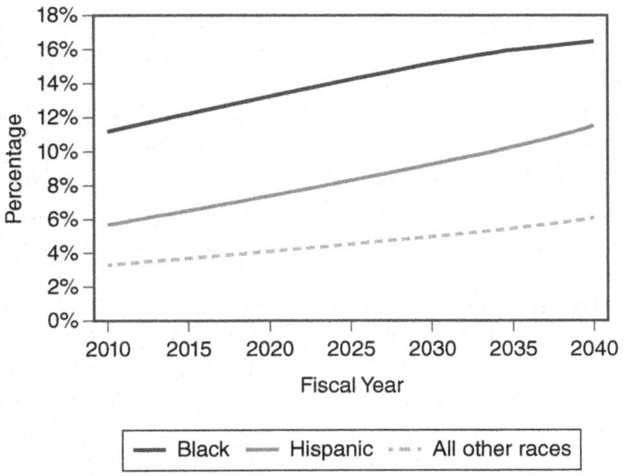

Figure 5-2 Projected percent of minority veteran population 2010–2040.

Office of the Actuary. (2011). *Quick facts [PowerPoint]*. Department of Veterans Affairs. https://www.va.gov/vetdata/docs/QuickFacts/population_quickfacts.pdf

Rethinking Veterans: Who Is the Woman Veteran?

She is returning from war or long deployments overseas.
She is bringing home the physical and emotional scars of combat.
She is a Veteran once she has been honorably discharged from the U.S Armed Forces.
She is also a Veteran if she has been deployed to a combat zone as a National Guard or Reservist.
She may be a Veteran while still actively serving in the Guard or Reserve.
(Women Veterans Health Care, 2012)

This quote captures the psychological and physiological impact of military service on female veterans and encompasses experiences that many may not associate with the term *female veteran*. It is important to recognize that the experience of each veteran is unique and should be acknowledged.

The following demographics, reported in the *Sourcebook: Women Veterans in the Veterans Health Administration, Volume 4* (Frayne, 2018) and prepared by the Women's Health Evaluation Initiative using the Veterans Health Administration (VHA) databases, cover data at 5-year intervals (FY00, FY05, FY10, and FY15):

- In FY15, approximately 43% of women veteran VHA patients were 18–44 years old, 46% were 45–64 years old, and 12% were 65+ years old. From FY00–FY15, the number of women in these age groups from youngest to oldest increased 2.3-fold, 4.3-fold, and 1.7-fold, respectively. The 55–64-year-old subgroup grew more than 7-fold over the 16-year period.
- Across this 16-year period, women were consistently younger on average than were men, although the age gap narrowed over time. By FY15, almost 90% of women were younger than 65 years old, whereas the majority of men were 65+ years old.
- The proportion of women veteran VHA patients belonging to a racial/ethnic

minority group increased from 30% in FY00 to 42% in FY15.

- Among veteran VHA patients under 65 years old, women were more heterogeneous than their male counterparts on race/ethnicity in every year examined, and this difference between women and men grew wider over time.
- The proportion of women veteran VHA patients with a service-connected disability rating increased from 48% in FY00 to 63% in FY15.
- A higher proportion of women than men had service-connected disability ratings in both FY00 and FY15 among 18–44-year-olds and 45–64-year-olds, but not among 65+ year-olds.
- Between FY00 and FY15, the number of women veteran VHA patients using mental health/substance use disorder (SUD) specialty care increased nearly 5-fold, reaching 176,526 women by FY15. During the same period, the number of men using mental health/SUD specialty care increased 2-fold.
- The proportion of women veteran VHA patients with any mental health/SUD encounters increased from 23% in FY00 to 40% in FY15.
- The number of female veteran women age 35 years or older with childbirth deliveries increased 16-fold from FY00 to FY15.

Understanding the Culture of the Department of Veteran Affairs

As a civilian healthcare provider, it is critical to understand the contextual underpinning of female veterans' access to health care. Since the VA healthcare structure was intended for male veterans, the VA has been challenged in meeting the unique needs of female veterans. The impact of receiving care in an institution that was not originally designed to meet their needs may carry over when female veterans seek care. Understanding the framework of their previous care will be helpful as providers navigate building an alliance with the patient and determining the best course for treatment.

Historically, the VA has been challenged in meeting the unique needs of female veterans (Hamilton et al., 2012; Perl, 2015; Tsai et al., 2012a). The VA system, as a whole, was designed to meet the needs of its primary users—males. Women in the military were not given veteran status until 1948, although they served in recognized AD roles since 1901 when Congress allowed the Army to create the nursing corps. As the role of women in the military evolved, an increasing number of female veterans required access to care, which resulted in the need for the VA to modify its ability to cater to this distinct group (Perl, 2015). In efforts to address the male-dominated culture and provide better health care to women in 1994, the VA formed the Center for Women Veterans when Congress signed Public Law 103-446. The center was to perform the following roles: coordinate and monitor gender-specific healthcare benefits, provide administrative services for female veterans, lead the cultural transformation of the VA both internally and externally (i.e., raise awareness of women veterans' service), and increase awareness of the responsibility of the VA to treat women veterans with respect and dignity.

The Center for Women Veterans (2019) indicated that "women are one of the fastest growing subgroup of Veterans and are signing up for VA healthcare and benefits at higher rates than ever before" (para. 1). The Center for Women Veterans has hosted numerous events and continues to advocate for the unique needs of women veterans. Given its reports it is clear that the male-dominated healthcare structure has impacted the care female veterans receive and, at the minimal, the perception of their care.

Institutional Barriers Faced by Female Veterans

Working with female veterans can be a complicated process that requires skill. Being able to pick up on subtle verbal and nonverbal cues is essential to providing effective care for this population. A social worker who worked with the Department of Veteran Affairs for years provided the context for how intricate this process can be. When asked for her perspective on the profile of the female veteran she stated:

> Female veterans are usually resilient, resourceful, and extremely intelligent. However, they are often dealing with PTSD, sexual trauma, suicidal ideations, and low self-esteem. When working with female veterans to address these issues, providers should remember to routinely conduct a brief mental health screening and remind them that it's okay to ask for and accept help when needed. Providers should empower female veterans by providing tools and suggestions on how to cope, as they prefer to be self-sufficient and are usually eager to learn about anything that is going to improve them or their situation. Providers should also be aware of possible people, places, sounds, smells, etc. that could serve as triggers to this population. Helping veterans identify their triggers is the key to enabling them to address them.

Although this social worker worked with female and male veterans for over 8 years, she was very clear on the level of assessment and understanding needed to work with female veterans. The information provided by this social worker is not surprising. Female veterans learned early in their careers that it is important to show strength and resilience in the face of adversity. Additionally, although women served in the U.S. military since the Revolutionary War and were recognized since 1948, medical services for women were not readily accessible until 1988 with the establishment of the Women Veterans Health Program. In the face of a growing concern, the Women Veterans Health Program was developed to address the increasing number of female veterans (at that time it was approximately 4.4%) and their unique needs (Department of Veteran Affairs, n.d.; Women Veterans Health Care, 2020). This lag in development of gender-specific services undoubtedly fostered a culture that ultimately led female veterans to be reluctant to seek care or even express the need for care. The stoic presentation, along with the lapse of care for female veterans, has led to a female veteran persona that can make caring for them multifaceted and complicated.

Further complicating the female veteran profile is the issue that, for a long time, female service members did not even know that they were qualified as veterans once they left the service. For instance, a female veteran interviewed for a study (Felder, 2019) on homelessness stated:

> But I got out in 1991, 1990 to '91, and it was before 2008 before I even knew that I could file for anything [she did not know she was deemed a veteran and could file as such]. Then when I filed, they denied me. Then 2009 I was going to give up. I said forget it. Then, you know, I got to have it and they denied me again. I filed again and they denied me. In 2010, they finally approved me, but gave me a zero percent compensation. Well, yeah, you have this condition but we're not paying you for it. Well, hell, what is it—what good do you think it is to tell me yeah and then not pay me for it? I want the money. So I got me a representative at the regional office and I appealed it, that decision, and they gave me 30 percent...

This quote provides one example of a female veteran who left the service in the early 1990s but did not receive care nor service compensation until 2008 and 2010, respectively, primarily because she did not consider herself a veteran; she was never told this at the time of her separation.

While the VA has taken many steps to ensure smoother transition for female veterans, it seems some female veterans still experience a dissonance about whether they are truly veterans. In this particular case, after finally learning that she was indeed qualified to receive veteran benefits, her service connection claim was denied by the VA. This reinforced her former belief and led to her considering giving up on benefits that she desperately needed given that she had been homeless for many years. Additionally, numerous medical issues arose during her service. During and post service she suffered from mental health and substance abuse issues. After seeking help from a veterans representative officer, she was able to receive some compensation for service-related injuries. This glimpse into the life of one female veteran was captured in a qualitative research study of the life course experience of 14 predominantly Black homeless female veterans who discussed issues they experienced transitioning from AD to veteran status (Felder, 2019).

While preconceived notions that the feelings or experiences noted here are true of all female veterans should not be encouraged, it is important for civilian providers to be aware of the various institutional barriers to benefits, including health care. It is also critical for civilian providers to understand that the ingrained and reinforced defense mechanisms of being stoic and showing strength despite needing help were essential for survival during military service. Female veterans' experiences may lead them to be reluctant to ask for help or to acknowledge certain health or behavioral health conditions; thus, therapeutic alliance and comprehensive assessment are imperative for this population. Essentially, understanding the historical context is half the battle when caring for women veterans.

Healthcare Issues for Women Who Served in Major Conflicts

Veterans serving across different conflicts may have similar injuries resulting from service. The VA has prepared a comprehensive list of the potential ailments qualified for service connection related to conflicts beginning with World War I. The list includes health problems, injuries, and known illnesses linked to each conflict. Please refer to Appendix C for specific conflicts and the relevant healthcare issues. Please note that female veterans may have other deployments not listed.

Despite the extensive list of qualifiers, the physiological and psychological demands of AD service can lead to unique healthcare needs for female veterans of which providers need to be aware. AD service can cause some women to develop a range of reproductive health risks, including sexually transmitted illness and vaginitis, infertility, pelvic organ prolapse, and increased risk of hysterectomy (Zephyrin et al., 2014). Limited access to bathrooms in deployment environments can lead to poor vaginal hygiene and increased incidences of vaginitis. Many female veterans develop chronic urogenital problems, particularly among those who suffer from comorbid mental health conditions. Postponed urination and intentional fluid restriction can cause urinary tract infections. During service, many women are busy in uniform and find themselves holding their urine for extended periods of time. When they are out in austere environments, there are few options to relieve oneself. For example, women may have to relieve themselves in the woods or find ways to dispose of sanitary napkins. Female service members have developed kidney issues from holding urine for prolonged periods of time. Being aware of these unique healthcare problems is critical for civilian providers as these issues may not apply to care of the female civilian population (Zephyrin et al., 2014).

Integrative Health Care: Treating the Whole Person

In 2005, the Institute of Medicine (IOM) published a report noting a distinct trend toward the integration of complementary and alternative medicine (CAM) therapies into conventional medicine practices across several healthcare settings (IOM, 2005). These nonmainstream practices include the use of both natural products (herbs, vitamins, and probiotics) and/or mind-body approaches (yoga, chiropractic manipulation, meditation, and relaxation techniques) (National Center for Complementary and Integrative Health [NCCIH], 2018). The growing field of integrative health care focuses on coordinating conventional and complementary care. According to the NCCIH, CAM:

> emphasizes a holistic, patient-focused approach to health care and wellness—often including mental, emotional, functional, spiritual, social, and community aspects—and treating the whole person rather than, for example, on organ system. It aims for well-coordinated care between different providers and institutions. (2018, para 5)

Held and colleagues (2016) found that the growth in popularity of CAM services has had an impact on veterans who have been increasingly adding CAM to the VA's conventional medical care. The VA has expanded access to CAM services most commonly for the treatment of anxiety, posttraumatic stress, depression, and back pain (Held et al., 2016).

The VA Integrative Health Coordinating Center has identified and affirmed several concepts central to how integrative medicine and health is practiced within the VHA system:

- The relationship between the patient and practitioner is central to care.
- The focus is on the whole person.
- Practice must be informed by evidence.
- All appropriate therapeutic and lifestyle approaches, healthcare professionals, and disciplines contribute to the care of the veteran to achieve optimal health and healing. (VHA, n.d.)

Currently, the VA has approved acupuncture, biofeedback, clinical hypnosis, and massage therapy as complementary and integrative health approaches for treatment. For well-being, meditation, guided imagery, Tai chi, qi gong, and yoga have been approved as complementary and integrative health approaches. Local VHA facilities have a great deal of freedom as to how they will provide these services, which can include the use of volunteers, telehealth services, community partners, or the local community care network. One program offered at many VA sites is the *Whole Health Program.* The VA sees this as a cutting-edge approach that supports the veteran's health and well-being and focuses on what matters to the veteran. (For the VA's presentation, Whole Heath for Women Veterans, go to https://www.youtube.com/watch?v=UxXWf4fLbhQ.)

However, Held et al. (2016) identified several issues that the VA and any participating non-VA practitioner should consider before accessing CAM services for a veteran. Considerations included what CAM services are available and how they are accessed, how much guidance and training is needed for regular use/practice, the cost of services to the veteran, and the veteran's service preference. For example, regarding cost, even a minimal cost can be a barrier requiring extra support and advocacy and regarding service preference, some veterans may prefer to take virtual classes while others may prefer face-to-face services. Such considerations should be part of biopsychosocial-spiritual assessments.

The next sections focus on caring for the physical and emotional/mental health of female veterans that emphasizes an integrated assessment strategy leading to mutually agreed upon intervention plans. A critical part of caring for the female veteran is for providers to recognize the widespread impact of trauma on these women and the need for a trauma-informed approach to care that facilitates recovery and resilience (Substance Abuse and Mental Health Services Administration [SAMHSA], 2014). SAMHSA's (2014) guidance for developing a trauma-informed approach is worth reviewing, and providers are encouraged to reflect on how to best implement the concepts of safety; trustworthiness and transparency; peer support; collaboration and mutuality; empowerment, voice, and choice; and addressing cultural, historical, and gender issues that have disempowered and diminished the voices and agency of many women. As a first step, medical providers, social workers, and allied health providers can work to raise their own awareness of personal and cultural biases that may impede an effective collaborative approach in completing assessment of the female veteran's physical and psychological health. Providers can also advocate with the veteran to enhance her agency and expand choices for services to address her unique needs in a way that resists retraumatization and enhances resilience.

Caring for the Physical Health of Female Veterans

As stated earlier, a comprehensive assessment of female veterans' health is essential. Within this section on physical assessments, other areas are included (e.g., mental health information in this section and all domains of the female veteran's life in the integrated physical health assessment).

Women veterans face more challenges than men when maintaining their health. Women veterans deal with unique issues such as childbirth and menopause. Also, common health conditions, such as cardiovascular disease, may impact women differently than men. For example, while men have heart attacks at earlier ages, women tend to have heart attacks at older ages, and the attack may present with different symptomatology. Women also have other unique medical risk factors that men do not have such as pregnancy, endometriosis, and polycystic ovary disease. A normal, happy event, such as being pregnant, can place a mother and her child at risk due to gestational diabetes, preeclampsia and eclampsia, gestational trophoblastic disease, pregnancy-related hypertension (high blood pressure), hyperemesis gravidarum, and cholestasis of pregnancy (Papadakis et al., 2020). During the peripartum period, a woman may also be confronted with other medical complications such as mastitis and endometritis. Given these unique risks, physical assessments of the female veteran are of paramount importance.

There are two primary types of physical assessments: the comprehensive assessment and the focused assessment. A comprehensive assessment for females includes an overall assessment of the female, including breast and genitalia. At other times, a focused assessment of specific systems of the patient's body will be needed. Focused assessments are guided by a patient's complaint or need for an assessment of a particular body system. While a comprehensive assessment should include the assessment of the patient's breast and genitalia, at times these assessments may be performed during an assessment that focuses on a woman's reproductive health. When an assessment focuses only on the female's reproductive health, it is sometimes referred to as an annual well-woman visit. This section will provide a concise overview of both the well-woman exam and the comprehensive assessment.

Well-Woman Exam

The well-woman exam focuses on the breast and reproductive system, but it can also include a review and examination of other systems based on the patient's complaints or specific medical needs as deemed appropriate by the clinician. Well-woman exams are sometimes referred to as gynecologic exams, pelvic exams, or woman/female exams and typically include examination of the breasts, vaginal areas, and uterus. During the well-woman exam, it is helpful to encourage the patient to build rapport with her primary care physician.

During the exam, questions must be asked in a manner and style that builds trust between the patient and the medical provider. A direct, nonjudgmental approach is best for some questions, while other questions are best asked in a manner that moves from general to specific. For example, prior to asking questions about sexual preferences or activity, a provider may indicate that all patients are asked questions about their sexual health and functions, since some medical conditions or diseases can lead to problems in this area of their lives. The provider then can engage in general, but more focused, questions. For example, questions regarding menses can be followed up with specific questions related to menses. The provider should use the same approach to explore questions and concerns regarding sexual activities. For example, "Are you sexually active?" can be followed with questions concerning the sex of the sexual partner(s) and then specific questions such as how many sexual partners there have been in the previous 6 months followed by questions related to sexually transmitted diseases (STDs).

Remember, patients have different comfort levels as well as varying knowledge of their sexual and reproductive health. An astute clinician recognizes that the history portion of the examination provides an abundance of areas for the patient to build trust with the clinician. The clinician will also discover this part of the assessment provides opportunities to educate patients on their body and clarify any misconceptions. **Table 5-1** includes questions that may be asked during a well-woman exam.

Physical Exam

Given the challenges regarding healthcare issues, there are key areas that civilian providers should assess among female veterans. The top medical issues of female veterans 45–64 years of age, currently the largest group of VA patients, typically include cardiovascular risk, hypertension, lipid disorder, overweight/obesity, joint and spine disorders, eye and dermatologic disorders, and mental health issues such as depression. There are also those issues that may contribute to management of these health concerns, such as unresolved posttraumatic stress disorder (PTSD), subconsciously repressed sexual assaults, among others. In addition to covering these issues, the history part of the physical exam should also include:

- Routine preventive health screenings that have taken place
- Notation of all medical diagnoses and/or issues
- Immunization history and scheduling of any immunizations that require revaccinations
- Discussion of wellness areas such as healthy weight, nutrition, exercise, and smoking cessation (if applicable)
- Identification of areas that the patient would like to have or needs further education in health-related matters

During a comprehensive physical exam, it is important to cover all areas related to the veteran's overall health. **Table 5-2** displays sample questions on the veteran's medical history; the list is not intended to be all inclusive.

The purpose of the history portion of the examination is to ensure the clinician has a thorough understanding of the patient's current health as well as any risk factors that may impact the patient's future health. The history portion should include questions on personal and social history. This includes assessment of

Table 5-1 Sample Questions During the Well-Woman Exam

How are you? or How do you feel today?
Do you have any current medical concerns? If so, what are they?
Do you have any previous medical conditions? If so, what are they?
Have you been seen, assessed, or received any type of treatments by another medical provider since your last visit (if appointment is for subsequent visit)? If so, what was the reason for the visit and what was the outcome?
Have you been assessed and/or treated in an emergency room or prompt/urgent care setting since your last visit? If so, what was the reason for the visit and what was the outcome?
What medical problems do other members of your family have (i.e., family medical history)?
Do you think you might be pregnant?
Do you want to get pregnant?
Have you ever been pregnant? If so, how many times (total number, including abortions)?
Number and type of deliveries (i.e., vaginal or cesarean section)
Number of living children?
Number of abortions (spontaneous or induced)?
Any complications with previous pregnancies?
Do you or have you had any pain or discomfort in your breast? If yes, describe.
Have you noted any lumps in your breast or discharge from your nipples? If yes, describe and include if the symptoms are intermittent and if so when are they noted (i.e., associated with menstrual cycle)
Can you describe to me how you perform your breast exam and when you perform them?
Age at menarche (i.e., how old were you when you had your first period)?
When was your last period?
How often do you have periods?
How long do they last?
Do you have dysmenorrhea or painful menstruation, including abdominal cramps? If yes, what decreases the pain?
Do you take any over-the-counter medications or herbal treatments to relieve the pain?
How often do they interfere with your normal daily routine (i.e., work, recreational activity, social life, etc.)?
Do you ever bleed/spot between periods?
The following questions may be asked by a medical provider if they believe a patient is peri- or postmenopausal:
Age of menopause (12 consecutive months without a menses)?*
Any menopausal symptoms?
Any postmenopausal bleeding?
If born prior to 1971, maternal use of diethylstilbestrol (DES) during pregnancy?**
Do you have any unusual pain, itching, or discharge from your vagina or vulva?

Data from Bickley, L., & Szilagyi, P. G. (2009). Bates' guide to physical examination and history taking (10th ed., *p. 524, **p. 12). Wolters Kluwer Health.

education level, profession, family planning, homelife as well as use of tobacco products, vaping, substance abuse, and alcohol use/dependency. Finally, the history section must include a thorough review of each of the body's systems with the provider asking both general questions and specific questions based on the patient's medical conditions. Clinicians need a list of general questions they ask all of their patients and then, based on the patient and the unique medical situation, the clinician will ask more specific questions as they progress

Table 5-2 Sample Questions During the History Portion of the Physical Exam

How are you feeling today? Do you have any concerns or specific complaints?
How would you rate your overall health? Are you experiencing any medical problems that are impacting your life or satisfaction with life? Are you on medications? If so, what are they and why do you take them?
Are you allergic to any medications?
Are you allergic to anything that is not a medication?
Any previous medical diagnosis, including childhood? Any previous hospitalizations, including during childhood? If so, why, when, and where were you hospitalized? Have you ever had or been advised by a medical provider to have any surgeries? Does anyone in your family have medical conditions, including mental health and substance abuse? If so, who and what are the diagnoses?

through the review of systems. The history and system review are important, as the answers may lead the clinician to explore areas normally not noted during the exam itself. For example, a patient who reports increased thirst and urination may lead the provider to ask further questions about diabetes mellitus.

It is important for the clinician to build rapport and a trusting relation with the patient. Thus, the clinician needs to pose questions in a safe, direct, and nonjudgmental fashion that is both sensitive to the nature of the topic and takes the patient's age and level of knowledge into consideration.

After examining the female veteran's general appearance, level of alertness, and overall state of health, a head-to-toe assessment is recommended. Throughout the assessment it is important for the clinician to remain aware of nonverbal cues and if the female veteran becomes uncomfortable during the assessment. Remember parts of the examination may require touching of areas the patient is sensitive to due to past traumatic experiences. Also, be sure the physical assessment is systematic to minimize excessive touching or repositioning of the patient.

The patient has the right to consent or refuse parts or all of the assessment. It is important not to pressure or coerce the patient into complying with all or parts of the examination as this will result in barriers between the patient and the medical provider. It may also result in the healthcare provider inadvertently retraumatizing a patient during an assessment. Approaching the history and physical examination in a nonjudgmental manner and tone that permits the patient to retain control of the situation will help alleviate some of the patient's concerns and allow for a more thorough and honest examination.

The assessment should begin as soon as the clinician meets the patient and continue throughout the interaction. An observant healthcare provider can ascertain a great deal of information from the patient's verbal and nonverbal reactions to questions. Observe eye contact and body posture (i.e., holding her extremities close to her body). Does she appear tense, scared, anxious, or relaxed? Does she give clear or elusive answers to your questions? Remember, while a healthcare provider assesses the patient, the patient is assessing the healthcare provider to determine how much to trust the person who will perform the assessment. Rushing through the patient's history may provide the patient with a feeling that the information is unimportant or that the healthcare provider is not empathetic.

After completing the questions (history) portion and before beginning the physical portion of the assessment, the provider should ask the patient for questions about the examination. The healthcare provider should be ready to answer the patient's questions and explain the steps involved in the examination. A final step prior to beginning the physical portion of the assessment is to provide an examination gown and sheet to the patient, exit the room, and provide time for the patient to change into the gown.

Table 5-3 presents the elements of a comprehensive assessment of the female veteran. Remember that the veteran can refuse

Table 5-3 Elements of a Comprehensive Physical Exam

Category	Specific Assessment
General Status	Vital signs Heart rate Blood pressure Temperature Pulse oximetry Respiratory rate Pain
Appearance/Mood/Mental Health	Is the patient well groomed? Is the patient appropriately dressed? Does the patient respond appropriately to questions? What is the patient's affect? Does the patient appear anxious, nervous, restless? Does the patient express feelings of self-harm or harm to others? Are their signs of memory impairment? If so, consider performing a mini mental status examination during the exam
Head, Ears, Eyes, Nose, Throat	Observe color of lips and moistness Inspect teeth and gums Assess buccal mucosa and palate Examine tongue Examine uvula Examine tonsils Palpate nose and assess symmetry Check septum and inside nostrils Verify patency of nares Check patient's sense of smell Palpate sinuses Assess patient hearing with: Whisper test Weber's & Rinne test Assess ear canal and tympanic membrane Assess conjunctive and sclera Assess eye symmetry Assess pupils (PERRLA) Assess vision with Snellen and Allen eye charts Assess six cardinal positions of the gaze

Category	Specific Assessment
	Assess for nystagmus Fundoscopic eye exam Palpate lymph nodes Access cranial nerve, including cranial nerve XI (spinal accessory nerve (shoulder shrug)
Neck	Palpate lymph nodes Palpate thyroid gland Observe and palpate trachea and neck Assess carotid pulses Assess for jugular venous distention Range of motion (ROM)
Chest/Thorax	Assess for discoloration, symmetry, deformities, and masses Palpate for tenderness and masses
Breast	Perform a comprehensive breast examination, noting the: appearance, symmetry, color, any discoloration, nipple drainage, masses, lumps, palpable lymph nodes and tenderness
Respiratory	Auscultation of lung sounds (anterior and posterior) Assess respiratory expansion level Ask about coughing Palpate thorax Percuss lung fields
Cardiac	Auscultate heart sounds Palpate point of maximal intensity Jugular vein distention (JVD) Presence of edema Presence and grade of peripheral pulses, including radial, femoral, posterior tibial, and dorsalis pedis
Abdomen	Inspect abdomen Auscultate all four quadrants of abdomen for bowel sounds Palpate four quadrants of abdomen for pain, tenderness, and organomegaly (enlarged organs) Percuss abdomen Ask about problems with bowel or bladder
Extremities	Assess ROM and strength in all four extremities Assess sharp and dull sensation on arms/legs Check capillary refill on fingernails/toenails Palpate bony abnormalities Assess for pain with ROM or tenderness with palpation
Musculoskeletal System	Perform an assessment of the musculoskeletal system, noting strength, weakness, ROM, abnormalities in spinal curvature, deformities, etc.
Skin	Assess skin turgor Assess skin color and pallor Assess for lesions, swelling, lumps, abrasions, rashes, and discoloration Check for signs of physical injuries or abuse

(continues)

Table 5-3 Elements of a Comprehensive Physical Exam *(continued)*

Category	Specific Assessment
Neurological	Assess orientation to time, place, and person Assess cranial nerves if not previously performed with examination of the HEENT Assess gait Assess reflexes Assess fine and gross motor movement and coordination Assess presence or absence of tactile sensation (pinprick sensation and two-point discrimination tests)
Pelvic and Genitalia	Reserve for last part of exam Ensure all of the equipment you will require is available and ready. Begin with visual inspection and then proceed in a systematic manner to portions of the exam that requires touching of the patient or use medical instruments. Always inform the patient before touching her and always keep her apprised of what you are doing to prevent or decrease anxiety. Begin the exam by visualizing and palpating the external genitalia before proceeding to examine the internal genitalia. Note any discoloration, bruising, lesions, palpable lymph nodes, areas of tenderness, discharge, deformity, and signs of trauma. Collect any specimens at the time of the exam and explain what you are collecting as well as why you are collecting the specimen. Some females prefer to have a mirror placed in a manner that allows them to observe the examination. This provides the clinician the opportunity to also educate the patient on their anatomy and inquire about any abnormalities noted during the exam.

Remember, an examination must be stopped any time the patient requests it be stopped. The patient is in control of the exam, not the clinician.

permission of any element. The items listed in the table are not an all-inclusive list of possible examinations or tests performed during a comprehensive physical assessment. A medical provider adjusts examinations based on knowledge of the patient and her specific medical needs. Medical providers who conduct physical exams should refer to reference books dedicated to physical examinations for detailed guidance and instruction on performing comprehensive examinations. The following framework was taken from the nurse.org approach to conducting assessments (Nelson, 2020).

Upon completion of assessment, ensure the patient has the privacy and time to get dressed. A healthcare provider should then review the findings of the examination with the patient while giving her time to digest the information and ask questions. In addition, a provider should be prepared to review and explain any need to perform additional tests, such as laboratory tests, imaging studies, etc. If it is necessary to refer the patient for further testing or consultation with another healthcare provider, the clinician should be prepared to review the reasons for the referral.

Often, the conclusion of the assessment is considered the end of the assessment. Astute providers remain aware of the patients' reactions to negative findings and ensure their treatment plan takes the patients' reaction into consideration. For example, finding genital herpes may cause the patient to become anxious and not know how to discuss the finding with their significant others. Other findings may lead to a need for the patient to alter future family plans. A provider who continues to use nonjudgmental language and tone will facilitate a positive patient-provider relationship. The healthcare provider, on the other hand, who appears judgmental, rushed, and quickly summarizes the examination findings does not allow time for the patient to internalize the information and formulate questions. Remember, the first encounter with a healthcare provider can set the tone for a positive, long-term patient-provider relationship.

The examination is not complete until the healthcare provider documents the encounter, prescribes any follow-up testing or medication, and completes the referrals. Additionally, the provider or the staff should schedule follow-up appointments with the patient while the patient is still in the office. Finally, the office should provide a mechanism for the patient to contact the office with any additional questions.

Caring for the Emotional and Mental Health of Female Veterans: A Biopsychosocial-Spiritual Perspective

As indicted earlier, the number of women actively serving in the military continues to rise, and recent policy changes have expanded opportunities for women to serve in a variety of roles that were previously open only to men. Extrapolating from Lacks and her colleagues (2017), analysis of the biopsychosocial-spiritual needs of AD females point to the importance of providers working with female veterans to comprehend the uniqueness of the experiences of these women based on their AD service—experiences that differ from their male counterparts and from civilian women who have not served (Lacks et al., 2017). Women veterans will have been exposed to similar hazards (i.e., combat, military sexual trauma, environmental and occupational hazards) but at different rates. Though the needs are not the same, they need to be equally considered in a comprehensive assessment of the biopsychosocial-spiritual needs of each woman veteran (Mobbs, 2019).

Military social workers, social workers in the VA system, and social workers who regularly work with service members, veterans, and their families "understand the physical, psychological, social, and spiritual influences involved in military service, the adjustments that occur in multiple stages of the lifespan, and the continuum of reintegration with families and communities" (Council on Social Work Education, 2018, p. 47). The Council on Social Work Education's *Specialized Practice Curricular Guide for Military Social Work* (2018)[1] notes that dynamic and comprehensive assessments are necessary given the complex issues facing female veterans, including combat and military sexual trauma, depression, suicide, PTSD, traumatic brain injuries, and musculoskeletal injuries. In addition to gaining an understanding of military culture, providers will also need to understand that veterans live at the intersection of social identities (i.e., loss of

---

1 The Council on Social Work Education's *Specialized Practice Curricular Guide for Military Social Work* provides research and practice literature, media resources, assessment instruments, and practice assignments related to gathering and organizing data leading to developing intervention plans. It can be found at https://www.cswe.org/getattachment/Education-Resources/2015-Curricular-Guides/Military-Social-Work/MilitarySW_WEB_REV3-(002).pdf.aspx.

military identity, veteran status, civilian, professional, family, and community member). Female veterans are not often celebrated and tend to be less visible than their male peers in our society, even though they have faced many of the same challenges while on AD and in transitioning back to civilian life (Mobbs, 2019; Strong et al., 2018). An important aspect for social work and other mental health providers is the consideration of social justice issues in the assessment process. Though the VA recognizes that female veterans are the fastest growing population and has taken steps to improve access to care, female veterans do have unique health and mental health needs as well as social support needs. Identifying these needs and the unique challenges that exist for female veterans is a social justice issue, and incorporating these needs into a comprehensive assessment can empower the female veteran and support the assessment process (Dripchak, n.d.; Strong et al., 2017). Finally, the guide points to the importance of recognizing one's cultural biases and personal experiences that can either positively or negatively influence judgments during the assessment (Council on Social Work Education, 2018).

There are many frameworks for completing a biopsychosocial-spiritual assessment. While there is significant consistency in what information is being collected, there appears to be some fluidity in the spiritual domain (Saad et al., 2017). The primary goal, however, remains the same (i.e., to develop as full an understanding as possible of the unique interactions between the biological, psychological, social, and spiritual domains in the veteran's life). Central to the work of a social worker or other provider involved with a female veteran is assisting that veteran in navigating her social environment. It is important then, that the assessment also identifies institutions that have an impact on the veteran and how the veteran interacts with those institutions. Emphasizing the interactions between the veteran and her environment within the assessment will help the provider and the veteran clarify barriers to services that the veteran may experience with institutions in the service environment (Gale, 2019).

The biopsychosocial-spiritual assessment is a collaborative process between the provider and the veteran, but as the provider plans for this effort, it is important to think about the sources of relevant information. For example, there may be existing case records that can provide current and past information on health and mental health issues (i.e., treatments and medications). Other examples include military records, verbal reports from the client, standardized screening instruments, and direct observation of the client within her environment. Additionally, collateral sources (i.e., family members, friends, other professionals) can be especially useful in identifying client strengths (Gale, 2019). See the source section in Chapter 7: *Assessment in the Specialized Practice Curricular Guide for Military Social Work*. As part of the assessment process, the provider should be comfortable asking questions regarding the veterans' military service. **Table 5-4** includes screening questions recommended in the VA toolkit to gather helpful information.

The following considerations need to be kept in mind while working with female veterans:

- The client may not consider herself to be a veteran. To optimize understanding, interventions, possible referrals, benefits, and resources available, ask the client if she served in the military.
- Use the sample questions from Table 5-4 to guide your inquiry.
- Ensure that you have enough time with the service member to allow her to expand on answers if desired.
- The service member may not wish to discuss her experiences, and the provider should respect this.
- Convey a willingness to listen to the experiences if the service member wants to discuss them in the future.

Table 5-4 **Screening Questions**

Type of Question	Content
Basic Questions	Have you ever served in the military? Did you serve in the National Guard, Reserves, Coast Guard, or in any of the active duty services? Do you have a close family member who has served in the military?
Follow-up Questions	What dates did you serve? When did you separate from the military? What branch and rank were you?
Additional Questions	Where did you serve (e.g., in the U.S./where? overseas/where?) What job/roles did you have when you were serving? Were you ever deployed? If so, where and when were you deployed? Are there other things you would like to tell me about your military service?

- If a veteran has served in a combat theater, she may have experienced a range of potentially traumatic or stressful events, including being under life threat, witnessing death and dying, and experiencing the loss of a fellow comrade. It can be helpful to become familiar with events commonly experienced in combat and potential reactions to these exposures.

The VA also suggests it may be helpful in starting a conversation to give a simple indication indicating to clients an interest in knowing if they served.

In developing a biopsychosocial-spiritual assessment, it is important to have a framework to help organize the material. The University of Nevada–Reno Department of Psychiatry and Behavioral Sciences developed a framework to help students conceptualize and organize information about client problems to lead to the development of comprehensive intervention plans.[2] An edited version of the framework is presented here along with a series of prompt questions based on the university's framework. The prompt questions for gathering information in the spiritual domain are based on the work of Saguil and Phelps (2012). Some of this information may be gathered in concert with the physical exam. Providers may want to modify or add questions based on their setting and the needs of the veteran. The domains are presented in the following order: biological, psychological, social, and spiritual. Domain prompts are included in **Tables 5-5**, **5-6**, **5-7**, and **5-8** following each domain framework.

The Biological Domain: Past

Genetics:

- Consider whether any blood relatives have had psychiatric problems, substance use problems, or suicide attempts/suicides. Is there a history of close relatives who have been hospitalized for psychiatric reasons? What kind of treatments did they get? How did they respond?

2 The model can be found at https://med.unr.edu/psychiatry/education/resources/bio-psycho-social-spiritual-model.

History of Pregnancy and Birth:

- Consider pregnancy variables: Was there in utero exposure to nicotine, alcohol, medications, or substances? Anything unusual about the pregnancy?
- Note birth complications, such as prematurity, birth trauma, or extended periods of hospitalization.

Relevant Previous Illnesses:

- Consider any history of head injury, endocrine disorders (e.g., thyroid, adrenal), seizures, malignancies, or neurological illnesses.
- Consider potential lasting effects of past substance use on brain functions such as cognition, affective regulation, etc.

The Biological Domain: Present

Current Illnesses:

- Identify current illnesses and any direct impact they may have on psychiatric presentation.

Medications:

- Consider information on all current medications for both medical and psychiatric conditions and what the veteran is taking the medication for. Including information on dosage, length of time on each medication, and any side effects experienced.

Table 5-5 Prompts for the Biological Domain

Past	**Genetics:** ■ Tell me about any family history of psychiatric problems or suicide attempts. ■ Tell me about any relatives that have been hospitalized for psychiatric reasons. Tell me about any relatives that might have suffered from emotional problems. How were they treated and how did they respond to these treatments? **History of Pregnancy and Birth:** ■ Tell me about your mother's pregnancy with you. Do you know if she smoked, drank, or used any medications? ■ What have you been told about your actual birth? Were there any birth complications? **Relevant Previous Illnesses:** ■ Tell me about any major medical problems you have had in your life. Have you had any history of head injury, endocrine disorders (i.e., thyroid, adrenal), seizures, malignancies, or neurological illnesses?
Present	**Current Illnesses:** ■ Can you describe your health right now? Do you have any illnesses right now? Do you worry that you have something that has not been diagnosed? **Medications:** ■ Tell me about the prescribed and nonprescribed medications that you are taking. (Probe for medications that have psychoactive effects, such as steroids, beta blockers, pain medications, benzodiazepines, selective serotonin reuptake inhibitors (SSRIs), herbal remedies). **Substances:** ■ Tell me about your use of tobacco. Alcohol. Other drug use. Ask about vaping, over-the-counter use, and supplements.

- Also include information on any over-the-counter medications and supplements.

Substances: Ask about current and past use of

- Tobacco (cigarettes, electronic cigarettes: vaping, smokeless)
- Alcohol (wine, beer, hard liquor)
- Licit and illicit drugs, including prescription pain reliever and other opiate use, stimulant use, marijuana, etc.
- Consider the potential for withdrawal

The Psychological Domain: Past

- Consider any history of trauma (child abuse, combat, rape, serious illness), as well as resiliency (how the patient coped with trauma [e.g., friends, family, religion]).
- Consider the sources of positive self-image and positive role models.
- Comment on the patient's experience with loss.
- Comment on the patient's quality of relationships with important figures, such as grandparents, friends, significant teachers, or significant employers.
- Comment on how past medical problems, substance use, or psychiatric problems impacted the patient's development and their relevance to the patient today.

Table 5-6 Prompts for the Psychological Domain

Past	■ Tell me a bit about your childhood. (Probe for family strengths as well as evidence of trauma.) ■ Can you tell me about any trauma you might have experienced in life? (Probe for experiences of serious illnesses; verbal, physical, sexual, emotional, psychological, spiritual, and cultural violence that occurred before, during, and after service. Be especially attentive to violence related to combat and military sexual trauma.) ■ Can you describe to me any losses you have experienced in your life? How did you cope with this? ■ Tell me about your relationships with important figures, such as parents, grandparents, friends, significant teachers, or significant employers. ■ Tell me about how past medical or emotional or mental health problems influence your life today?
Present	■ Tell me about the recent events and experiences that bring you here today. ■ How have you already tried to solve your problems? (Probe for coping skills and strengths.) ■ How do you usually cope with difficult life situations? (Probe for evidence of resilience and evidence of unhealthy coping strategies.) ■ Tell me about how you are dealing with your marriage (or other relationship), divorce, birth, children leaving home, loss aging, etc. (The point here is to get a sense of what is being demanded of the person at this time, developmentally.) ■ How do current medical problems or psychiatric problems influence your life today?

The Psychological Domain: Present

- Describe the recent events and experiences that precipitated this appointment. Basically, what brings them here today?
- What current stressors are they experiencing? Do they have any symbolic meaning?
- What are the veteran's primary coping skills and defense mechanisms?
- Assess the presence or absence of cognitive distortions.
- Consider current developmental demands on the person, such as marriage, divorce, birth, children leaving home, loss, aging, etc. What stage of development is the patient at now? Is it appropriate?
- What is the developmental impact of the patient's illness?

The Social Domain

- How adequate is the patient's current support system?
- What is the status of relationships with important figures?
- What are the possible peer influences?
- What is the veteran's current housing arrangement? Previous housing arrangements?
- Is the veteran employed? Past employment?
- What was their military occupational specialty (MOS)?
- What is their current financial status?
- Do they have any legal problems?
- Consider the role of agencies (e.g., VA, Child Protective Services, Criminal Justice System, employer) in the veteran's life.
- Comment on how cultural influences might impact the veteran's current situation. How might these impact interventions?

The Spiritual Domain

- Comment on the role of spirituality in the patient's life. Is the patient affiliated with a spiritual community of some sort?
- How does spirituality contribute to the patient's ability to hope, her position on suicide if relevant, or her contact with a supportive community?

Table 5-7 Prompts for the Social Domain

- Who do you tum to when you need help? Do you have friends or family you can turn to if you need help?
- Tell me about who you rely on for company, support, and fun. Do you have friends or family that you can rely on for company, support, and fun?
- Describe your current social life. How often do you get together with people you can relate to, and do you enjoy it?
- Has there been any changes in your social life recently? Do you get together with people you could relate to or enjoy more often, less often, about the same?
- Tell me about your present housing arrangement? Are you satisfied with it?
- Tell me about previous housing arrangements. Were you satisfied with those arrangements?
- Tell me about your work life. Are you working? Is your work satisfying? Would you like some help in this area?
- Tell me about your financial circumstances.
- If not asked before, it may be a good place to ask some follow-up questions about military service.
- To help me understand you, can you tell me about cultural/family beliefs that might help me get a clear sense of your life circumstance/symptoms right now?

Emerging Issues for Female Veterans

The following section will briefly highlight military sexual trauma, homelessness, and intimate partner violence. These emerging issues, also mentioned in other chapters, should be a part of the female veteran's comprehensive evaluation.

Table 5-8 Prompts for the Spiritual Domain

- Do you have spiritual beliefs that help you cope with stress? If clients respond that they do not have any spiritual beliefs, you may want to ask: What gives your life meaning?
- Have your beliefs influenced how you take care of yourself?
- Are you part of a religious community? Is this community a support to you? How?
- How would you like to address these issues in your care?

Military Sexual Trauma

The Department of Veteran Affairs (2018) defines MST as:

> any sexual activity where someone is involved against his or her will—he or she may have been pressured into sexual activities, may have been unable to consent to sexual activities, or may have been physically forced into sexual activities. (para. 1)

This definition also includes unwanted sexual attention and gestures such as grabbing, threatening, making remarks about an individual's body or sexual activities, and unwanted sexual advances while in the military (Department of Veteran Affairs, 2018). In comparison to male veterans, female veterans are more likely to be exposed to sexual harassment and sexual assault. Recent data indicate that one of every three women (33%) in the military has reported experiencing actual or threatened physical or sexual violence during her service, a rate up from earlier findings that one in four female veterans (25%) screened by a VA provider reported experiencing MST (Benedict, 2009; Department of Veteran Affairs, 2012; VA National Center on Homelessness Among Veterans, 2016).

The VA conducted a national health study of 30,000 veterans deployed to Operation Enduring Freedom (OEF) and Operation Iraqi Freedom (OIF) and 30,000 nondeployed veterans serving elsewhere during the same time period. Of the 60,000 veterans surveyed, slightly more than one-third responded (Department of Veteran Affairs, 2015). The results indicated that 41.5% of the women respondents experienced MST compared to 4% of the men. The survey also found that female veterans in combat were 1.42 times more likely to experience sexual harassment than noncombat female veterans (Department of Veteran Affairs, 2015).

Two female veterans, participants in a study of homeless female veterans (Felder, 2019), discussed the MST they experienced during their service. These two examples highlight how MST occurs in many situations during AD and can be distinctively different. One veteran shared her experience with her recruiter, stating:

> He could tell that I was really wanting to join the Army. He would say to me, "I see where you're really worried about this. There's probably a chance they might not let you in. But I do have some influence but you gotta give me something in return." And I was required to have sex with my military recruiter to get into the military. And that became the story of my life for at least about 20 years of men just taking their liberties on me by using a fear tactic to make me give it up.

Another veteran discussed being sexually assaulted by two women colleagues due to an argument that took place earlier, stating:

> I was on the floor and she was kicking me and beating me. I fractured some ribs . . . And they pulled my pants down and one of them started [she begins to cry] stuffing in my, my

> vagina. I don't know what. I think it was probably a finger, and I don't know what she had but they had started that. And then the other girl was saying, "Quick, quick, get her up, get her pants on." And so someone had, had heard me screaming and yelling....They had to, to carry me to a stretcher, on the stretcher to the medic, to the sick bay on the base.

She had difficulty telling this story and stated that she lost her motivation after that and her career began to spiral downward. She also mentioned that she was encouraged not to report what had occurred.

These women's experiences are highlighted to demonstrate the range of abuse that can occur. Civilian providers need to be aware of the impact of MST and understand how each veteran's story is unique. Being prepared to address issues regarding MST is paramount when serving female veterans. Refer to *Understanding and Treating Victims of Military Sexual Trauma (Zaleski, 2018), for additional information and* to prepare for understanding these issues.

Homelessness Among Female Veterans

While the overall rate of veterans experiencing homelessness has decreased during the past years, the same cannot be said about female veterans who were homeless. Their numbers rose by 135% between 2006 and 2016 (Henry et al., 2017). Data also indicate that female veterans were four times more likely than male veterans to become homeless (Pavao et al., 2013; Perl, 2015; Tsai et al., 2012b; VA National Center on Homelessness Among Veterans, 2016). Furthermore, the VA National Center on Homelessness Among Veterans found, "the number of women accessing VA specialized homeless programs or with a homeless identification tripled between FY 2010 from 11,016 to 36,443 in FY 2015—1.8% of the female Veteran population" (2016, p. 6). Thus, the increased number of female veterans at risk for homelessness remains a critical issue for the VA.

While there has been a steady flow of research examining the experience of male veterans living homeless, the causes and needs of the increasing number of female veterans experiencing homelessness have only recently begun to receive attention in the literature (Perl, 2015; Tsai et al., 2014b). The VA Women Veterans Task Force (Department of Veterans Affairs, 2012) found that Black female veterans and female veterans aged 18–29 were at the highest risk for homelessness, but no detailed examination into the matter was available.

Increased interest has been directed at the various psychosocial outcomes related to homelessness among veterans (National Coalition for Homeless Veterans, n. d.; Perl, 2015; Tsai et al., 2014b). According to the VA National Center on Homelessness Among Veterans (2016), other risk factors associated with female veteran homelessness include anxiety disorder diagnosis, unmarried marital status, unemployment, and a service-connection rating of 100%. Tsai and Rosenheck (2015) called for more research into risk factors of homelessness among female veterans and increased qualitative data on how these veterans feel, their sense of agency, their regrets, their proud moments, their sense of responsibility about their lives, and their resilience. The rationale for this call for research included investigating the growing number of women serving in the military and potentially experiencing traumatic events during their service experience.

The VA expected that the number of veterans experiencing homelessness would increase with the surge of veterans returning from OIF, OEF, and Operation New Dawn (OND), all of whom were at heightened risk for homelessness. This expectation was due to the level of trauma exposure resulting from combat and the increased likelihood of PTSD. Furthermore, it was expected that the highest risk for homelessness would exist among female veterans (Department of Veteran Affairs, 2012, 2018; Perl, 2015). Findings of Tsai and colleagues (2014a) showed that 48% of female veterans who were homeless had served in OIF, OEF, and/or OND compared with 24.5% of male veterans experiencing homelessness serving in similar conflicts. Perl (2015) wrote:

> Another issue is the concern that veterans returning from Iraq and Afghanistan who are at risk of homelessness may not receive the services they need. In addition, concerns have arisen about the needs of female veterans, whose numbers are increasing. Women veterans face challenges that could contribute to their risks of homelessness. They are more likely to have experienced sexual trauma than women in the general population and are more likely than male veterans to be single parents. Historically, few homeless programs for veterans have had the facilities to provide separate accommodations for women and women with children. (para. 4)

Clearly, homelessness among female veterans remains a pressing concern and merits further inquiry into the pathways to homelessness for these women who gave their dedicated service to their country.

Intimate Partner Violence (IPV) and Domestic Violence

Intimate partner violence, also referred to as domestic violence, is prevalent among AD women, women veterans, and women in the general population. The distinction is that IPV occurs with a current or prior intimate partner, whereas domestic violence includes IPV as well as any violence that occurs within the home.

IPV is typically divided into three types: emotional IPV, physical IPV, and sexual IPV. According to Iverson et al. (2017), one-third of women veterans will experience IPV within their lifetime, in contrast to less than a quarter of civilian women. IPV can have short- and long-term consequences. Some short-term consequences of IPV include fractures, bruises, and sexually transmitted diseases. Long-term consequences include chronic pain, pregnancy complications, cardiovascular issues, and other long-term physical conditions that are typically exacerbated by stress. IPV also has critical psychological consequences. According to Iverson et al. (2017), women in the general population who experience IPV are twice as likely to commit suicide. They are also two to four times more likely to be diagnosed with depression and PTSD and to abuse substances. Additionally, IPV is a leading cause of traumatic brain injury among female veterans (Tokar, 2019). Given these statistics, recognizing the impact of IPV for female veterans is critical especially given the other psychological and physiological issues these women often face.

The VA defines emotional IPV as attempts by a person to demean and devalue a partner's self-worth. Examples of IPV provided by the Department of Veterans Affairs (2019) include:

- Name calling
- Controlling finances or spending
- Keeping a person from friends and family
- Bullying
- Stalking
- Putting a person down
- Controlling where a person goes or what the person wears
- Trying to manipulate a person's actions
- Embarrassing a person in front of others to prove a point
- Statements that a person is "crazy" or "worthless"

The VA defines physical IPV as attempts of a person to hurt a partner with physical force and provides the following examples:

- Hitting
- Shoving
- Punching
- Hair-pulling
- Choking
- Slapping
- Biting
- Kicking
- Restraining
- Pinching
- Using force in any way that intimidates

Intimate partner sexual violence can occur in all types of intimate relationships regardless of gender identities or sexual orientation. Intimate partner sexual violence is not defined by gender or sexuality, but by abusive behavior. Sexual IPV occurs when a person forces or tries to convince his/her partner to engage in sexual activities when the other partner does not want to or is unable to consent. Note the person may not be able to consent if under the influence of a substance.

Lastly, stalking is also a form of IPV. Stalking is defined as frequent or infrequent contact by a person using any of the following means when the partner does not wish to be contacted:

- Showing up at places where a person goes
- Sending mail, e-mail, texts, or pictures
- Calling or texting repeatedly
- Contacting a person or posting about a person on social networking sites (such as Facebook, Twitter, Instagram)
- Creating a website about a person
- Sending gifts
- Tracking a person via GPS devices in your phone or car
- Gaining access to a person's e-mail or social networking accounts
- Using force in any way that intimidates
- Monitoring a person's online behavior or cell phone communication (texts and phone calls)

Table 5-9 Sample Questions Regarding Intimate Partner Violence

Has a current or past partner ever:
Emotionally mistreated you (e.g., called you names, tried to embarrass or intimidate you)?
Tried to control where you go, who you talk to, what you can wear, or what you can do?
Told you that you are "crazy" or "worthless"?
Stolen or tried to control your money?
Looked at you or acted in ways that scare you?
Threatened you, your possessions, or your pets or loved ones?
Physically hurt you or tried to hurt you?
Forced you to engage in sexual activities?
Threatened to commit suicide or kill you if you left?

Given female veterans' susceptibility to IPV, it is important to assess them for IPV or domestic violence. **Table 5-9** displays questions to ask to assess whether the veteran has experienced IPV (Department of Veterans Affairs, 2019).

If the female veteran answered yes to any of these questions listed in Table 5-9, an ongoing assessment for the physical and psychological issues described earlier is warranted. Without a thorough assessment, these issues, shown to be relevant for the increasing number of female veterans, can often go undetected if thorough assessments are not completed.

Summary

This chapter presented a comprehensive integrated approach to health care as guidance for providers caring for female veterans. This approach is designed to meet the unique physical and psychological healthcare needs of the female veteran. The chapter began with a description of the female veteran and the cultural context within which she functioned during her AD service. It continued with a description of the unique healthcare needs of the female veteran. The remaining sections of the chapter focused on screenings during well-women and physical exams and guidance on how to conduct a thorough biopsychosocial-spiritual mental health examination. The chapter ended with a brief discussion of MST, homelessness, and IPV. The appendices provide additional information and pertinent resources for providers caring for female veterans and for sharing with the female veteran during her care.

References

Benedict, H. (2009). *The lonely soldier: The private war of women serving in Iraq*. Beacon Press.

Bickley, L., & Szilagyi, P. G. (2009). *Bates' guide to physical examination and history taking* (10th ed.). Wolters Kluwer Health.

Center for Women Veterans. (2019). *Messages from the center*. Department of Veterans Affairs. https://www.va.gov/womenvet/cwv/messageindex.asp

Council on Social Work Education. (2018). *Specialized practice curricular guide for military social work*. Council on Social Work Education Press.

Department of Labor. (2019). *Gender and veteran demographics*. https://www.dol.gov/agencies/vets/womenveterans/womenveterans-demographics

Department of Veterans Affairs. (n.d.). *Women veterans issues: A historical perspective*. https://www.va.gov/womenvet/docs/20yearshistoricalperspective.pdf

Department of Veterans Affairs. (2012). *Report strategies for serving our women veterans: Women veterans task force*. https://www.va.gov/opa/publications/Draft_2012_Women-Veterans_StrategicPlan.pdf

Department of Veterans Affairs. (2015). *Public health: Military sexual trauma in recent veterans*. https://www.publichealth.va.gov/epidemiology/studies/new-generation/military-sexual-trauma-infographic.asp

Department of Veterans Affairs. (2018). *Mental health: Military sexual trauma*. https://www.mentalhealth.va.gov/mentalhealth/msthome/index.asp

Department of Veterans Affairs. (2019). *Women veterans health care: Intimate partner violence*. https://www.womenshealth.va.gov/womenshealth/outreachmaterials/abuseandviolence/intimatepartnerviolence.asp

Department of Veteran Affairs. (2020). *Mission act*. https://missionact.va.gov/

Department of Veterans Affairs. (2021). *Ending veteran homelessness: A community by community tally*. https://www.va.gov/homeless/endingvetshomelessness.asp

Dripchak, V. L. (n.d.). Issues facing today's female veterans: Feeling invisible and disconnected. *Social Work Today*, *18*(6), 24. https://www.socialworktoday.com/archive/ND18p24.shtml

Felder, S. (2019). *The life course of homeless female veterans: A qualitative study*. (Doctoral dissertation). The Catholic University of America.

Frayne, S. M., Phibbs, C. S., Saechao, F., Friedman, S. A., Shaw, J. G., Romodan, Y., Berg, E., Lee, J., Ananth, L., Iqbal, S., Hayes, P. M., Haskell, S. (2018). *Sourcebook: Women veterans in the Veterans Health Administration, Volume 4: Longitudinal trends in sociodemographics, utilization, health profile, and geographic distribution*. Women's Health Evaluation Initiative, Women's Health Services, Veterans Health Administration, Department of Veterans Affairs. https://www.womenshealth.va.gov/WOMENSHEALTH/docs/WHS_Sourcebook_Vol-IV_508c.pdf

Gale, L. (2019). Biopsychosocial-spiritual assessment: An overview. CINAHL Information Systems. https://www.ebsco.com/sites/g/files/nabnos191/files/acquiadam-assets/Social-Work-Reference-Center-Skill-Biopsychosocial-Spiritual-Assessment.pdf

Hamilton, A. B., Poza, I., Hines, V., & Washington, D. (2012). Barriers to psychosocial services among homeless women veterans. *Journal of Social Work Practice in the Addictions*, *12*(1), 52–68.

Held, R. F., Santos, S., Marki, M., & Helmer, D. (2016). Veteran perceptions, interest, and use of complementary and alternative medicine. *Federal Practitioner for the Health Care Professionals of the VA, DoD, and PHS*, *33*(9), 41–47.

Henry, M., Watt, R., Rosenthal, L., & Shivji, A. (2017). *The 2017 Annual Homeless Assessment Report to Congress*. U.S. Department of Housing and Urban Development, Office of Community Planning and Development. https://www.hudexchange.info/resources/documents/2017-AHAR-Part-1.pdf

Institute of Medicine. (2005). Integration of CAM and conventional medicine. In Committee on the Use of Complementary and Alternative Medicine by the American Public (Ed.), *Complementary and alternative medicine in the United States* (pp. 196–225). National Academies Press. https://doi.org/10.17226/11182

Iverson, K. M., Dardis, C. M., & Pogoda, T. K. (2017). Traumatic brain injury and PTSD symptoms as a consequence of intimate partner violence. *Comprehensive Psychiatry, 74*, 80–87. https://doi.org/10.1016/j.comppsych.2017.01.007

Lacks, M. H., Lamson, A. L., Rappleyea, D. L., Russoniello, C. V., & Littleton, H. L. (2017). A systematic review of the biopsychosocial–spiritual health of active duty women. *Military Psychology*, *29*(6), 570–580.

Mobbs, M. C. (2019). Women veterans: Battling to be seen. [Webinar]. SAMHSA Service Members and Their Families Technical Assistance Center.

National Center for Complementary and Integrative Health (NCCIH). (2018). *Complementary, alternative, or integrative health: What's in a name?* https://www.nccih.nih.gov/health/complementary-alternative-or-integrative-health-whats-in-a-name

National Center for Veterans Analysis and Statistics. (2017). *Women veterans report: The past, present, and future of women veterans*. Department of Veterans Affairs. https://www.va.gov/vetdata/docs/SpecialReports/Women_Veterans_2015_Final.pdf

National Coalition for Homeless Veterans. (n.d.). *Homeless female veterans*. http://www.nchv.org/images/uploads/HFV%20paper.pdf

Nelson, L. (2020). How to conduct head-to-toe assessment. Nurse.org. https://nurse.org/articles/how-to-conduct-head-to-toe-assessment/

Office of the Actuary. (2011). Quick facts [PowerPoint]. Department of Veterans Affairs. https://www.va.gov/vetdata/docs/QuickFacts/population_quickfacts.pdf

Papadakis, M. A., McPhee, S. J., & Rabow, M. W. (2020). *Medical diagnosis & treatment 2020* (59th ed.). McGraw Hill Education/Medical.

Pavao, J., Turchik, T., Hyun J., Karpenko, J., Saweikis, M., McCutcheon, S., Kane, V., & Kimerling, R. (2013). Military sexual trauma among homeless veterans. *Journal of Internal Medicine*, *28*, 536. https://doi.org/10.1007/s11606-013-2341-4

Perl, L. (2015). *Veterans and homelessness*. Congressional Research Service. https://fas.org/sgp/crs/misc/RL34024.pdf

Saad, M., de Medeiros, R., & Mosini, A. C. (2017). Are we ready for a true biopsychosocial-spiritual model: The many meanings of spiritual. *Medicines*, 4(4), 79. https://doi.org/10.3390/medicines4040079

Saguil, A., & Phelps, K. (2012). The spiritual assessment. *American Family Physician*, *86*(6), 546–550.

Strong, J. D., Crowe, B. M., & Lawson, S. (2018). Female veterans: Navigating two identities. *Clinical Social Work Journal*, *46*(2), 92–99.

Substance Abuse and Mental Health Services Administration. (2014). *SAMHSA's concept of trauma and guidance for a trauma-informed approach.* https://ncsacw.samhsa.gov/userfiles/files/SAMHSA_Trauma.pdf

Tokar, S. (2019). *Women veterans confront intimate partner violence: VA Boston psychologist studies connection between domestic violence and traumatic brain injury*. https://blogs.va.gov/VAntage/63116/aboutvha-asp-index-asp/

Tsai, J., & Rosenheck, R. A. (2015). Risk factors for homelessness among US veterans. *Epidemiologic Review, 37*, 177–195. https://doi.org/10.1093/epirev/mu004

Tsai, J., Kasprow, W. J., Kane, V., & Rosenheck, R. A. (2014a). National comparison of literally homeless male and female VA service users: Entry characteristics, clinical needs, and service patterns. *Women's Health Issues, 24*, e29–e35. https://doi.org/10.1016/j.whi.013.09.007

Tsai, J., Rosenheck, R. A., & Kane, V. (2014b). Homeless female US veterans in a national supported housing program: Comparison of individual characteristics and outcomes with male veterans. *Psychological Services*, *11*(3), 309. https://doi.org/10.1037/a0036323

Tsai, J., Rosenheck, R. A., & McGuire, J. F. (2012a). Comparison of outcomes of homeless female and male veterans in transitional housing. *Community Mental Health Journal, 48*(6), 705–710. https://doi.org/10.1007/s10597-012-9482-5

Tsai, J., Rosenheck, R. A., Decker, S., Desai, R., & Harpaz–Rotem, I. (2012b). Trauma experience among homeless female veterans: Correlates and impact on housing, clinical, and psychosocial outcomes. *Journal of Traumatic Stress, 25*(6), 624–632. https://doi.org/10.1002/jts.21750

VA National Center on Homelessness Among Veterans. (2016). *Women veterans and homelessness: Homeless evidence & research* (Homeless Evidence and Research Roundtable Series). Department of Veterans Affairs. https://www.va.gov/homeless/nchav/docs/hers-womens-proceedings.pdf

Veterans Health Administration. (n.d.). *Integrative health coordinating center (IHCC)*. Department of Veterans Affairs. https://www.va.gov/WHOLEHEALTH/docs/IHCC_FactSheet_508.pdf

Women Veterans Health Care. (2012). A profile of women veterans today, rethink veterans: Who is the woman veteran? Department of Veterans Affairs. https://www.womenshealth.va.gov/womenshealth/docs/wv_profile_final.pdf

Women Veterans Health Care. (2020). *About the women veterans health care program.* Department of

Veterans Affairs. https://www.womenshealth.va.gov/WOMENSHEALTH/programoverview/about.asp#:~:text=In%201988%2C%20the%20Women%20Veterans,who%20are%20women%20is%2010%25

Zaleski, K. (2018). *Understanding and treating military sexual trauma*. Springer.

Zephyrin, L. C., Katon, J., Hoggatt, K. J., Balasubramanian, V., Saechao, F., Frayne, S. M., Mattocks, K. M., Feibus, K., Galvan, I. V., Hickman, R., Hayes, P. M., Haskell, S. G., & Yano, E. M. (2014). *State of reproductive health in women veterans: VA reproductive health diagnoses and organization of care*. Women's Health Services, Office of Patient Care Services, Veterans Health Administration, Department of Veterans Affairs. https://www.womenshealth.va.gov/docs/SRH_FINAL.pdf

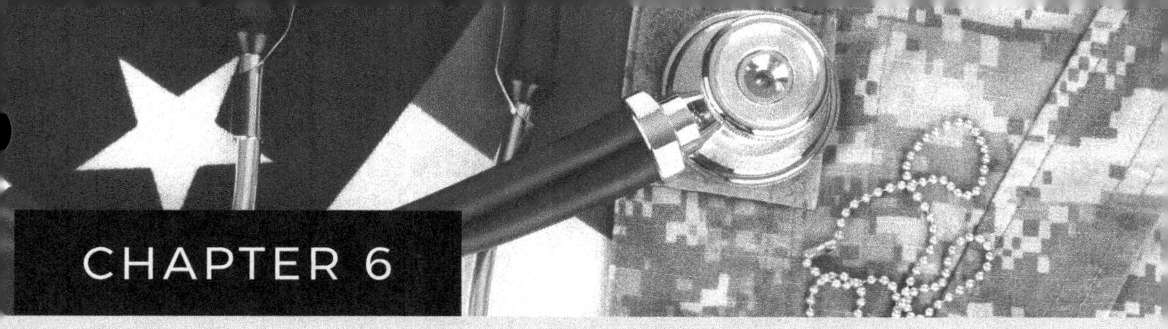

CHAPTER 6

Transition from Military to Civilian Life: Considerations for Providers

Judith Vanderryn, Ph.D.

Civilian providers treating service members (SMs) may consider the transition from military service into civilian life as a positive event. Theoretically, the SM could leave behind danger and discomfort, and return to the comfort of family life, time with friends, future career, and other life goals. Unfortunately, reintegration is not always a positive experience. The transition from military service into civilian life is often logistically complex, as it requires individuals to change almost everything about their lives: how and where they receive a variety of goods and services, who they interact with on a daily basis, and what they do for daily activities. Some of the challenges transitioning SMs may face might include the need to move out of their homes if they have lived on base; to secure employment or return to school or other training; to find new medical care, car mechanics, and other services; to find new schools for their children and help them adjust; and experiment with new modes of socializing. Navigating the sheer number of changes at the same time would be daunting for almost any individual. In addition, profound shifts in the individual's identity, sense of belonging, meaning, purpose, and even "normalcy" can be extremely taxing even when addressed directly and with significant support. It is thus not surprising that so many SMs feel lost and in some ways abandoned during this critical transition.

According to a study by the Pew Center, 27% of veterans overall stated that they had difficulty readjusting to civilian life after service—and that number increases to 44% among those who served in the years since September 11, 2001 (Morin, 2011). Providers involved in caring for veterans should have an understanding of the logistical, social, and psychospiritual aspects of this change, as the physical and psychological health consequences can be lasting for veteran patients. Difficulty reintegrating into civilian society carries increased risk of long-term problems, including premature mortality and homelessness (Boscarino, 2006; Mares & Rosenheck, 2004). Deployment and combat exposure are associated with higher levels of posttraumatic stress disorder (PTSD), anxiety disorders, alcohol abuse, depression, and suicide, both in the short and long term (Institute of Medicine, 2008; Sayer et al., 2014). Furthermore, a PTSD diagnosis was associated with higher medical mortality from a number of causes of death, including cardiovascular disease, cancer, and external causes when compared to the general population (Boscarino, 2006).

One way to conceptualize the reintegration process is by using a model of four concentric systems that must be aligned for a fully positive reintegration: individual, interpersonal, community, and societal (Elnitsky et al., 2017). In each of these areas, factors such as psychological, physical, cultural, and demographic variables play a role in a veteran's successful return to civilian life. Qualitative studies have also introduced themes using OIF/OEF (Operation Iraqi Freedom/ Operation Enduring Freedom) veterans' own words, using broad categories to understand the gestalt of their transition experiences. These categories include leaving one's chosen group ("military as family"), figuring out how to manage within civilian life ("normal is alien," "figuring out how to belong," and "searching for a new normal"), feeling alienated ("flipping the switch," "living the stress of the new normal"), and the suddenness of the transition (Ahern et al., 2015; Wands, 2013). This information received from veterans describes a profound sense of emotional vertigo while entering new and unfamiliar territory. This chapter will utilize these broad categories to provide context for the challenges veterans experience in the transition from active duty (AD) to the civilian world. Relevant themes will be presented for providers to consider when managing AD veteran patients, even those who are years away from making their transition.

Individual Considerations

Demographics

As described in the chapter in this book on military culture, veterans from the wars since September 2001 were generally older than those in previous wars upon entry to the military. In addition, more individuals who joined were married than in previous conflicts, and more women joined the all-volunteer military than ever before. Each of these characteristics implicates specific challenges as individuals return to civilian life. More married couples also means more SMs with spouses and children who were also affected. These family members may be both influenced by the veteran's return and, conversely, influence the transition by either supporting or causing increased stress on the returning SM. Reasons for this stress might be financial, logistical, and/or emotional.

Older age may certainly translate into greater maturity and resilience, but it also may mean slower recovery from physical and psychological injuries and/or greater vulnerability to long-term health issues. Older veterans may also run the risk of having difficulty "fitting in" with younger peers if returning to school or entry-level positions in the workforce. Female SMs and veterans also carry their unique challenges, as discussed in Chapters 4, 5, and 19. Other demographic variables, including urban/rural locations, race and ethnicity, and socioeconomic status both before and after the service are associated with challenges in accessing services both logistically and emotionally. Providers should be sensitive to and directly address factors that affect access to care with veteran patients. Acknowledging sociological barriers such as race, brainstorming alternative plans and problem-solving approaches, and seeking out specific resources (e.g., specific treatment programs for women veterans; accessing telehealth for veterans in rural areas) are examples of important factors that guide well-designed interventions.

Psychological Factors

Individual factors affecting the success of reintegration include overall psychological function and specific problems, including diagnosed psychological disorders and substance use. High rates of PTSD, depression, generalized anxiety disorders, panic disorders, and substance use disorders are noted in veterans from OEF and OIF (Institute of Medicine, 2010). According to the Institute of Medicine, people affected by combat-related injuries and mental health disorders tend to report poorer health and impaired function in many life activities (2010). The Pew study also reported that the probability of an "easy re-entry" dropped almost 30 percentage points for individuals who experienced a psychologically traumatic event during their service (Morin, 2011).

Even those veterans without psychological or neurological disorders such as mild traumatic brain injury (mTBI) may face challenges, such as learning to contain aggression. Anger and physical aggression are overtrained responses used in the military to help SMs focus, to act rather than "freeze" in dangerous and terrifying situations, and to push individuals past limits (e.g., sleep deprivation) to complete the mission (Hoge, 2010). When individuals return to civilian life, learned aggressiveness may clash with the behavior and values of their civilian friends, family, and coworkers, and may lead to family conflict and potential job loss. An important "side effect" of aggression for veterans is that it often leads to unhealthy risk-taking, such as reckless driving, substance use, overspending, and risky sexual behaviors (Adler et al., 2011). These behaviors provide individuals an outlet for aggressive arousal and a sense of thrill previously felt and valued in the military.

Providers need to understand that not all veterans will have the difficulties described here. Screening veteran patients for symptoms of psychological dysfunction, as well as for chronic pain, risky behaviors, and sleep issues, is critical to providing appropriate care. Asking questions about how a veteran is doing with work, finances, substances, and family life is crucial as well. Practitioners can also provide an enormous service to veterans by normalizing a variety of responses to the life changes embedded in transition, including feeling angry, helpless, lost, or confused even if an individual is not presenting symptoms of a disorder. Some patients will need to connect with specific resources (e.g., job training, social connection with other veterans) or specialized treatment. Additionally, assisting veterans in creating manageable self-care routines or structured steps to work toward identified goals, including exploring and planning for obstacles to implementing these plans, can be an extremely valuable intervention. Veterans may also need assistance in learning to regulate high levels of arousal and/or exploring other ways to feel alive or satisfied in the civilian environment.

Information/Skills

Individuals transitioning out of military service leave a highly structured system that provides for all their needs and dramatically limits choices by adhering to rigid frameworks of complicated standard operating procedures. These individuals are thrust into a life in which they will be providing for themselves and their families, and everyday decisions such as what to eat for breakfast may feel daunting. Creating their own personal daily structure is necessary to be successful. Adjusting to this "new normal" can feel overwhelming and "alien" (Ahern et al., 2015; Wands, 2013).

Some SMs who entered the service out of high school or college may not have the requisite skills or experience to make necessary decisions or to successfully apply themselves in an environment that is totally unstructured. Applying for a job is an important example. In the military, SMs are rarely given the opportunity to decide what would be most interesting or rewarding to them to pursue over a long period of time. The sheer number of skills involved in identifying potentially satisfying work, developing a résumé, making a good application, and engaging in a successful interview are not necessarily obvious to someone who has not been trained by family, education, or previous experience to engage in this complex practice. This decision is clearly crucial to veterans' satisfaction in the civilian world, and they may feel lost in how to navigate the process.

Additionally, military work skills and training may not readily transfer into the civilian world. Veterans who accept entry-level jobs may feel that their training, expertise, and overall experience of working closely with individuals toward a common goal in high-paced, high-stress situations are not valued because of this lack of carryover of specific job-related skills. If these issues are coupled with irritability and low frustration tolerance (e.g., PTSD symptoms) and/or difficulties with new learning and attention/concentration problems (as in mTBI history), finding and maintaining employment can become extremely challenging. A report in 2010 showed that at that time, almost 20% of recent veterans are unemployed, and 25% of those who are employed earn less than $21,000 per year (Institute of Medicine).

Understanding of the nature of these stressors can be crucial for civilian providers working with veteran patients. Many veterans feel both shame and anger related to being unable to provide for their families or keep a job. Naming and normalizing such difficulties can go a long way toward creating a trusting relationship that ultimately can help the veteran be more productive. As mentioned previously, helping veterans create workable external structures (including realistic goal setting and accountability) should be considered, as well as connecting with both veteran-specific and more general resources.

Purpose/Meaning

Many veterans feel a loss of meaning or purpose when they leave the service. Each branch of the military articulates its mission clearly: there is an overarching, definitive, and worthwhile purpose to one's life in the military. All activity is undertaken with the mission in mind, from the simplest act of making a bed correctly to the most complicated training routines. This value is foundational to many who join for the specific goal of serving others; when they leave the military they often find themselves floundering for purpose in the civilian world that does not necessarily revolve around the same ethos. These individuals might present with a sense of malaise or depression, aimlessness, or even contempt for civilian life and what they experience as the meaninglessness of many civilian concerns. Many veterans do look for other ways to be of service to their communities and/or families, with varying degrees of success and/or sense of fulfillment. Those veterans who are unable to find substitutes may feel a profound enough sense of loss to translate into decreased concern about their own health or life.

Belonging

In addition to potentially losing a sense of meaning, many individuals making the transition out of the military may also feel they are losing their chosen family, whether or not they have family at home. As elucidated in the chapter on military culture, when individuals join the service, they adopt their peers as family members—brothers and sisters in arms. They train with, eat and sleep with, shower with, and share their most intimate moments with members of their unit 24 hours per day. Most importantly, they understand that their lives are literally in each other's hands.

On leaving the service, SMs may be immediately bereft of their sources of entertainment, understanding, comradery, and belonging. Many people making the transition to veteran status feel they have lost the only family they have ever known, and many feel that this loss is irreplaceable. In addition to the loss of individuals who are meaningful to them, they may also feel abandoned by the institution after having "given it their all" (Wands, 2013). These factors certainly contribute to the risk for depression and loneliness, and alienation from others is also highly correlated with increased risk-taking behavior such as risky driving, unprotected sex, overspending, and substance abuse (Adler et al., 2011).

Providers sometimes hear that the only person who can truly understand is another veteran; many veterans surveyed expressed this sentiment (Ahern et al., 2015; Wands, 2013). Family relationships can become quite complicated if veterans feel as alienated from civilian family members as they do from other civilians. Veterans may feel that spouses and/or children cannot understand them, are not interested in their experiences, or that they need to protect these others from hearing about traumatic experiences (Sayers et al., 2009). Relationships with healthcare providers can be fraught with similar issues, as veterans come into treatment mistrustful of being heard, understood, or valued. Providers interested in working with veterans would be well advised to consider military cultural competency education, from written sources and/or training produced by organizations who serve veterans. Providers who understand and respect the losses veterans may feel—sometimes for the rest of their lives—are in a better position to be of help to their veteran patients, to broach sometimes painful subjects, to listen respectfully, and to more sensitively and accurately address their veteran patients' needs.

Interpersonal Considerations

Individuals often return from war stating that everything about them has changed, which may seem vividly apparent to those closest to them. Their families are often strained by the permanent return of someone they feel has become a stranger, and one who is sometimes not a very nice or predictable stranger. These families navigate the difficult waters of understanding each other's profoundly different experiences of their time apart, and of their internal and external worlds. It is no wonder that veterans and their families often report marital conflict, divorce, interpersonal violence, and parenting problems. Post-9/11 veterans who were married while they served had more difficult readjustment than either married veterans of past eras or people who were single when they served (Morin, 2011). The problem is widespread; one small study found that 75% of veterans referred for treatment reported some family readjustment issue (Sayers et al., 2009).

Returning veterans and their spouses may need to renegotiate roles within the family, particularly if the spouse has become used to running the household as the sole adult (Creech et al., 2014; Sayers et al., 2009). This is particularly true when SMs have experienced multiple deployments. They will need to become reacquainted with each other's likes and dislikes, communication styles, triggers, and/or to friends, all of which are likely to have changed at least to some degree.

Symptoms of disorders such as PTSD, depression, or mTBI can make these negotiations even harder, negatively impacting the couples' ability to communicate (Creech et al., 2014) or overall interpersonal functioning (Sayer et al., 2014). Even veterans without PTSD may have difficulty negotiating a "new normal" of communication if they have been accustomed to direct, "no nonsense" language using acronyms, or to harsh or nonemotional banter, or if they expect immediate responses to requests or "orders." Additionally, they may feel less engaged with "mundane" tasks of the household or the family if they are struggling with symptoms on either end of the arousal spectrum such as depression or high levels of sympathetic arousal.

Children react in a variety of ways to upheavals within the family system, from acting out in school to becoming anxious, depressed, or reclusive. Veterans have also reported that their children seem unfamiliar with them, may not act warmly with them, or may even be afraid of them on their return to the family (Sayers et al., 2009). One reason for these problems may be that individuals transitioning out of the highly disciplined system of the military may hold different expectations of their children's freedoms and responsibilities than their children have been accustomed to. Additionally, from the child's perspective, the parents' behavior may be unusual, difficult to understand, or frightening if the veteran is struggling with new physical or psychological symptoms.

Providers should screen for home difficulties, including parental interpersonal conflict and behavioral (e.g., school refusal or difficulty sleeping) and children's mood issues. There are several screening tools in the public domain that can help screen for children's difficulties and provide openings for conversations about problems families may be experiencing. Veterans and their spouses can benefit from parental consultation, guidance, and/or therapy to help their children navigate changes, while couples counseling may be warranted for veterans and spouses without children.

Community/Society/ System Issues

Health Care Related

One important difference relevant to the wars in Iraq and Afghanistan is that more SMs are surviving injuries than in previous conflicts as a result of improved body armor, better in-field treatment, and increased use of air evacuation to remote hospitals. Thus, more individuals are returning with combinations of TBI, amputation, spinal cord injury, chronic pain, headaches, and eye and ear injuries, among others (Institute of Medicine, 2010). Although treatment of these injuries is beyond the scope of this chapter, it is important for providers to be aware that veteran patients are likely to have experienced polytrauma rather than discrete injuries. These injuries are best treated within an integrated system, in which providers can communicate to each other quickly and directly, and treatment in one area can be informed and modified by other areas (Institute of Medicine, 2010). The following information should help providers in any area work with returning SMs and veterans more effectively.

One of the important principles in military culture is to follow the chain of command without question. While it is easy to appreciate how critical this behavior is in a high-stress, high-tempo environment in which lives are at stake, many veterans tend to generalize this principle to other areas of their lives, including health care and healthcare-related decisions. Additionally, veterans are trained to respect rank and/or education. This training may translate into veterans trusting information from others they consider to have more expertise than they do with less questioning, analysis, or even self-awareness than a provider might expect. Veterans trained to answer commanding officers with affirmatives ("yes, sir!")—whether or not they agree or even understand what is being communicated to them—may do the same in a medical provider's office.

In the military healthcare setting, SMs are rarely given choices about treatment options; instead, they are often commanded to care (that they might not seek otherwise) and directed to a specific kind of treatment. Seeking treatment on one's own is often interpreted internally as a sign of weakness, decreasing an SM's motivation to seek help from providers. In addition, seeking health care (particularly care from mental health providers) may be seen by others as proof of an SM's lack of requisite toughness or fitness for duty, and can be extremely detrimental to an SM's career. This reality may be especially true for those individuals with high security clearances or in other sensitive positions. When transitioning to civilian healthcare settings, veterans must learn how to "flip the switch" in order to report symptoms truthfully and completely and to advocate for themselves.

A number of veterans have returned home with a confusing mixture of psychological and physical conditions, as noted earlier. The combination of mTBI, sleep dysfunction, and pain from orthopedic or other injuries can interfere with function on a variety of levels. Unfortunately, veterans have often had the experience of their health complaints not being taken seriously during their time in the service. Military health care is often oriented toward returning SMs to duty or discharge as quickly as possible, which is a slightly different metric than the benchmark of optimal health that many civilian providers strive for.

In sum, SMs have been trained to do the following:

- Ignore or minimize symptoms unless they are severe
- Consider symptoms a sign of weakness that need to be overcome and/or pushed through
- Operate through pain and dysfunction
- Follow orders without question

It is important for providers working with veterans to check for understanding and ask patients to summarize what they have heard when engaging in collaborative decision making regarding health care. Veterans may also need both coaching and encouragement to ask questions in a provider's office and to advocate for themselves throughout the healthcare system. Additionally, assuring a veteran patient about confidentiality of records is important to build and maintain trusting relationships with these patients. It is equally important to be realistic about the limits to that confidentiality, as veterans are well aware that individuals who are not necessarily authorized may have access to their records, particularly in the age of electronic medical record systems. The VA healthcare system is an important example of this increased access; medical records are shared across the entire system. Providers the individual has not met can access records at any time without the individual's express consent.

Logistics of Transition

SMs who are injured in the service and thought to require rehabilitative treatment for 6 months and/or need complex medical case management before being released are assigned to a warrior transition unit (WTU) on their discharge from the service (U.S. Department of Veterans Affairs, 2020). SMs assigned to WTUs may live together on a base or they may have access to their care remotely. These units provide a range of medical, psychological, pastoral, and case management services with the goal to provide a more successful transition for wounded warriors.

Most others transitioning out of military service, no matter how long they have been in the service, are assigned to complete 3 days of transition training in the Transition Assistance Program (TAP). The program consists of five steps: (1) initial counseling, (2) preseparation briefing, (3) Department of Defense, Department of Labor, and Veterans Administration (VA) separation day briefings, (4) specialized workshops, and (5) the capstone. Counseling is designed to help the individual create a plan for the transition, while the 1-day briefing describes benefits (e.g., education assistance, employment assistance, and health care). Workshops immediately following are designed to help SMs learn more about their particular choice of "track" they will take after separation: education, finding a job, engaging in the vocational training track, or the Small Business Administration's entrepreneur track. Finally, in the capstone, SMs are asked to develop a financial plan, register with the VA benefit program, and explore available educational opportunities.

This training opportunity is designed to allow SMs to think through the variety of choices they will have to attend to on their own once separated from the military.

Unfortunately, as the Military.com website states, the final step is to make sure that the SM has "checked all the boxes." Many SMs do just that as they navigate the momentous task of leaving the organization they have relied on for years in just 3 days. A 1-day briefing full of information on a variety of programs may not provide enough processing time for an individual who is still coming to terms with trauma or chaos from a recent deployment or stress in a relationship. Veterans routinely recall their processing through the TAP as a "blur" they endured. They may later feel lost without the information needed to access benefits or services. Additionally, SMs learn from their peers that "checking the boxes" quickly and denying symptoms on these and other medically oriented transition questionnaires allows them to complete the process rapidly. Unfortunately, medical records may then remain incomplete, and they may later be denied services as a result of appearing to be symptom-free through this transition process.

Relationship with the Veterans Administration

Understanding the central role of the VA in both health care and compensation for all veterans is crucial. During active engagement in the military, health care is provided by the Military Health System (MHS) and paid for through Tricare. SMs who are retired for a medical reason or who have 20 or more years of service may continue to be covered by Tricare on leaving the service. They may also be eligible to receive medical care at VA facilities. Individuals who are not medically retired or do not have at least 20 years of military service do not have access to Tricare but may be eligible for health care with the VA system. Veterans receive low or no-cost health care from the VA for injuries that are deemed service related and are still eligible for health care from the VA for nonservice-related conditions but will be charged copayments based on a VA financial assessment.

Access to services at the VA are regulated; therefore, not all former SMs are eligible to receive health care or other VA services. Most individuals must enroll with the VA, which requires certifying their military service. Some categories of individuals can receive health care without going through the enrollment process (e.g., veterans who have experienced military sexual trauma). Finally, their injuries and/or symptoms are evaluated for eligibility for treatment and for compensation.

Individuals injured as a result of their service are eligible to receive low or no-cost medical care and monthly compensation from the VA system for what is called a "service-connected disability." This designation refers to a disability incurred during or aggravated by active military service. Service connection is rated on a percentage basis, from 0% to 100%, according to the severity of the disability. Monetary compensation is linked to the percentage of service connection. A service connection of 0% does not qualify for financial compensation but is significant in that veterans are eligible to receive low or no-cost health care for this condition.

Service-connected disability ratings are designated through a compensation and pension (C&P) process that may include assessment by a number of different providers who ascertain extent of injury/ies and whether the injury was either sustained or exacerbated in the service. Veterans are reevaluated for compensation at certain intervals and, as a result, may lose income or even their healthcare benefits if they improve. Veterans can appeal C&P adjudications, and many avail themselves of a variety of advocacy services to do so.

Service-connected disability ratings are understandably fraught with issues for the veteran community. Veterans may rely on the monthly income to provide for their family, especially if work is either hard to find or to maintain given physical, mental, or emotional challenges. However, monthly compensation, even for 100% service connected and permanent disability, may be less than what a veteran earned during AD (depending on rank) and potentially less than what a veteran could earn in the civilian world. On the other hand, the reliability of a monthly income can be a disincentive for some veterans to pursue employment, especially if such employment is less satisfying or engaging than their experience in the service. Thus, veterans often have complicated relationships with the disability rating system, their injuries, and the VA system as a whole. They may struggle with receiving legitimate lifetime pay for their service, they may have to fight for what they feel is just compensation for suffering, or they may see their rating as an obstacle to complete healing or "moving on" or even confirmation of a sense of being "broken" or "unfixable."

The VA will authorize civilian medical care in the veteran's home community in some circumstances and pay for it through the VA system through channels made available by the VA MISSION Act. This generally happens when the VA cannot provide either timely or economically feasible medical services because of where the veteran lives or because the VA cannot provide the necessary care within a timely manner. Providers should be aware that the VA will not compensate for medical care outside of the VA without such approval, except in certain emergency situations. The VA will also pay for limited civilian health care for spouses and children of veterans with total and permanent disabilities through a different program.

There are a number of other programs available to veterans through the VA, including education benefits (the "GI Bill"), vocational rehabilitation, home loan guaranty programs, and life insurance, among others. Specialized programs, such as a caregiver program for spouses who are involved in the care of veterans, also exist by application. The VA does provide case management, advisors, and care advocates to veterans with specific needs and eligibility. Providers who are interested in learning more about these programs can start at several websites the VA has constructed on healthcare programs, care management (for case management and patient advocacy), and benefits.

Community-based programs that provide a range of other supports for veterans seeking to recover, connect with fellow veterans, and access employment assistance or other services abound at the national and local levels. Providers should use caution when recommending such services without having personally vetted them, either on their own or through trusted veteran resources. Some of these programs may have limitations on who they serve (e.g., veterans from certain eras or combat-only veterans). Additionally, such programs change rapidly with the changing funding and resource environment and may or may not have the resources to offer assistance even if they have in the past.

Resilience and Growth

While it is important to note the challenges that veterans face in reintegration that may result in difficulties for themselves and for their families, mitigating factors and positive effects of reintegration have been identified. For example, commissioned officers and veterans who had graduated from college appear to have an easier time adjusting to postmilitary life (Morin, 2011). Additionally, individuals who were attached to and attended religious services of some sort were more likely to have an easier reentry, although this difference holds only for post-9/11 veterans. Reaching out for veteran support, and even becoming an "ambassador" or peer support to other veterans, has been associated with more positive reintegration for a number of individuals (Ahern et al., 2015; Falke, 2018; Wands, 2013). Additionally, those who stated they had a clear understanding of their mission while in the service were more likely to have a more successful reentry.

Veterans also routinely identify benefits of their service that should not be forgotten or undervalued. Greater sense of maturity and responsibility, the creation of lifelong friendships, sense of strength, endurance, mission, and pride in being a "protector" and member of an elite "warrior class" are among the benefits that veterans carry with them into civilian life.

There is a growing body of literature, and associated programming for veterans, exploring the idea of "posttraumatic growth," the concept that even highly stressful events can provide opportunities for individuals to change in beneficial ways (Angel, 2016; Falke, 2018; Tedeschi, 2011). Providers are encouraged to ask both recent and more seasoned veterans about the protective factors they may have experienced.

Conclusion

The transition to civilian status can be difficult for individuals for a number of reasons, some of which are under their control and some of which they will simply be required to manage. Practitioners can assist their veteran patients by being aware of the long-term effects of the transition on all levels: mental, emotional, spiritual, and physical health and the financial, emotional, and physical well-being of their families and social networks. Civilian providers working with these individuals are often in the crucial role of assisting returning veterans to address challenges at each of these levels, some of which they may not have the experience or the tendency to attend to. Tedeschi (2011) gives advice in facilitating posttraumatic growth to practitioners, including communicating respect to survivors, being a humble learner and being open to being changed by their experience, helping survivors create a coherent narrative, and encouraging the paradoxical possibility of positive change from the experience. Starting with this approach, practitioners are likely to find a number of useful avenues, including communicating openly about concerns, considering and choosing options, sharing resources, referring to appropriate programs or individuals, and teaching and modeling skills of civilian life. These interventions will assist veterans in building on their myriad skills and strengths to benefit themselves and others, and to truly and successfully return home.

References

Adler, A. B., Britt, T. W., Castro, C. A., McGurk, D., & Bliese, P. D. (2011). Effect of transition home from combat on risk-taking and health-related behaviors. *Journal of Traumatic Stress, 24*(4), 381–389. doi:10.1002/jts.20665

Ahern, J., Worthen, M., Masters, J., Lippman, S. A., Ozer, E. J., & Moos, R. (2015). The challenges of Afghanistan and Iraq veterans' transition from military to civilian Life and approaches to reconnection. *PloS One, 10*(7), e0128599. doi:10.1371/journal.pone.0128599

Angel, C. M. (2016). Resilience, post-traumatic stress, and posttraumatic growth: Veterans' and active duty military members' coping trajectories following traumatic event exposure. *Nurse Education Today, 47*, 57–60. doi:10.1016/j.nedt.2016.04.001

Boscarino, J. A. (2006). Posttraumatic stress disorder and mortality among U.S. army veterans 30 years after military service. *Annals of Epidemiology, 16*(4), 248–256. doi:10.1016/j.annepidem.2005.03.009

Creech, S. K., Hadley, W., & Borsari, B. (2014). The impact of military deployment and reintegration on children and parenting: A systematic review. *Professional Psychology, Research and Practice, 45*(6), 452. doi:10.1037/a0035055

Elnitsky, C. A., Blevins, C. L., Fisher, M. P., & Magruder, K. (2017). Military service member and veteran reintegration: A critical review and adapted ecological model. *American Journal of Orthopsychiatry, 87*(2), 114–128. doi:10.1037/ort0000244

Falke, K., Goldberg, J. (2018). *Struggle well: Thriving in the aftermath of trauma.* Lioncrest Publishing.

Hoge, C. W. (2010). *Once a warrior, always a warrior*. Lyons Press.

Institute of Medicine. (2008). Gulf war and health. In *Physiologic, psychologic, and psychosocial effects of deployment-related stress* (vol. 6). National Academies Press.

Institute of Medicine. (2010). *Returning home from Iraq and Afghanistan: Preliminary assessment of readjustment needs of veterans, service members, and their families*. National Academies Press.

Mares, A. S., & Rosenheck, R. A. (2004). Perceived relationship between military service and homelessness among homeless veterans with mental illness. *The Journal of Nervous and Mental Disease, 192*(10), 715–719. doi:10.1097/01.nmd.0000142022.08830.f4

Morin, R. (2011). The difficult transition from military to civilian life. *Social and Demographic Trends*, 1–7.

Sayer, N. A., Carlson, K. F., & Frazier, P. A. (2014). Reintegration challenges in U.S. service members and veterans following combat deployment. *Social Issues and Policy Review, 8*(1), 33–73. doi:10.1111/sipr.12001

Sayers, S. L., Farrow, V. A., Ross, J., & Oslin, D. W. (2009). Family problems among recently returned military veterans referred for a mental health evaluation. *The Journal of Clinical Psychiatry, 70*(2), 163–170. doi:10.4088/JCP.07m03863

Tedeschi, R. G. (2011). Posttraumatic growth in combat veterans. *Journal of Clinical Psychology in Medical Settings, 18*(2), 137–144. doi:10.1007/s10880-011-9255-2

U.S. Department of Veterans Affairs. (2020). *Health benefits: Veterans health benefit handbook*. Department of Veterans Affairs.

Wands, L. (2013). No one gets through it ok: The health challenge of coming home from war. *Advances in Nursing Science, 36*(3), 186–199. doi:10.1097/ANS.0b013e31829edcbe

CHAPTER 7

Veterans Health Administration

Linda Schwartz and Rita D'Aoust

"Every satisfaction which can be reasonably requested, should be given to those Veteran Troops who through almost every distress have been so long and so faithfully serving the states."

—**George Washington**, 1781

Early in the Revolutionary War, General George Washington pleaded with Congress to offer pensions for widows and orphans as well as disability payments to soldiers injured in military service. With an eye on the future, another more pragmatic thought surfaced: that future generations would view the way veterans of war were treated and appreciated by their nation. This would have a direct effect on succeeding generations and how likely they would be to volunteer to serve (Zacchea, 2013).

There are over 20 million veterans of U.S. military service living in America today (National Center for Veterans Analysis and Statistics [NCVAS], 2020]). Mistakenly, most Americans believe that all veterans are eligible to use the Department of Veterans Affairs (VA) for their health care and do so. Data indicate that of the estimated 20 million veterans only 31% (6.2 million) actually use VA health care. However, the reality that only 19% (3.8 million) of America's veterans rely exclusively on the VA for all their health care is quite significant. Even more striking, only 68% of veterans with service-connected disabilities (SCD), those with injuries and illnesses sustained as a result of military service, choose VA for their care (NCVAS, 2020).

Unquestionably, military service is an occupational hazard in and of itself. There is a myriad of physical risks, challenging missions, exposures to diseases and hazardous substances, and psychological stressors not seen or recognized in the civilian community. Some of these exposures are so complex, veterans themselves have no idea of the health risks and diseases they encountered during their military service. America's recent heavy reliance on citizen soldiers and Reserve and National Guard units has moved the focus of receiving healthcare services from military/veteran-specific sources to community health providers.

"For Those Who Have Borne the Battle"

The United States has officially been at war for 207 of the 244 years since the founding of our nation (DeBruyne, 2018). In the course of these military operations over 65.2 million men and women have served in America's armed forces and militias. Of this number, a majority of the 41,892,128 (64%) veterans served in times of war, and an estimated 23,234,000, (36%) are living today (NCVAS, 2020).

Throughout our nation's history, war and revolution have been major forces in shaping America's traditions, identity, and status in the world. In America's struggle for independence, the responsibility of caring for the casualties and fatalities of those engagements mostly fell on the shoulders of military units, their families, or even strangers. However, the magnitude of human losses and horrors of the Civil War required much more involvement and support from the federal government. Although extremely unpopular, Congress enacted legislation that imposed an obligation of military service on every citizen. The much maligned Enrollment Act of 1863 authorized conscription (mandatory enlistment) and created a draft to select recruits for military service. For the very first time in the fledgling nation's history, towns and cities nationwide were involved with providing troops for the war.

Civic and patriotic organizations in the North and South rallied to support their fighting forces and support the families left behind, forming societies to help injured soldiers and the war effort. These societies were inspired by the work of Britain's Sanitary Commissions, which brought the work of Florence Nightingale to prominence during the Crimean War. In addition to necessities and comfort items for soldiers, efforts also concentrated on measures to improve the safety, care, and welfare of the fighting forces. The active involvement of noncombatant citizens became an important factor in the evolution of care and support for those who bore the brunt of the fighting and dying on both sides.

In 1862 pensions were authorized to encourage recruitment of volunteers and later to retain and expand recruitment for the Union Army. More importantly these payments also provided subsistence for the lifetime of widows and dependent children of Union Army fatalities. This also established the custom of disability payments for soldiers with war-related injuries and their widows and children. In 2017 the VA was still paying the daughter of a Union Civil War veteran a monthly pension of $73.13 from her father's military pension (*Wall Street Journal* [WSJ], 2020).

In addition to the pensions, President Lincoln also authorized and incorporated a system of veteran asylums (Veterans Homes) located throughout the country to provide pensioners and disabled veterans a safe place to receive care, shelter, and financial assistance. Although deaths in battle and nonmortal injuries were thought to reflect the total cost of the war, a more apparent and dramatic realization surfaced—the realization that many survivors of the fighting would carry the wounds of this war throughout their entire lives.

Then, as now, the existence of these homes kept the conditions experienced by veterans and their care squarely on the congressional agenda. Along with the timing and nature of war, the Veterans Homes would move the compassionate origins of these initiatives to the political arena and ultimately become a major force in shaping VA and America's healthcare delivery systems. While there was no immediate relief for the fighting forces, Congress reasoned that these benefits would give some peace of mind and reflection to the honor and gratitude for their sacrifices and efforts (Vogt, 2015). Thus began the tradition and responsibility of the federal government to support and care for those who defend the nation in times of war and peace. The scope of those services and programs has evolved in response to the perceived and demonstrated needs of veterans and the expectations of the American people.

Over time, entitlements (including eligibility, support services, compensation, and levels of medical care and benefits) would be authorized by Congress and codified in Title 38 US Code and supporting regulations. On the surface, these veteran advantages seem to be expressions of gratitude and honor. They were seen as reasonable repayment for loss of wages, health, and opportunities forfeited by serving in defense of our nation. However, over time, the availability of these authorized entitlements has been at the mercy of public opinion and budgetary constraints. For decades, the Veterans Administration was essentially a very closed system with immense powers but very little dependability or consistency until the U.S. Department of Veterans Affairs (VA) became a Cabinet-level agency in 1989. How this system evolved is a testament to the dogged resolve of veterans and the enduring support of the American people.

Eligibility for VA Healthcare Services and Programs

When the United States entered World War I in 1917, there were high hopes among the Allied Forces that America's increased troop strength and military-industrial prowess would bring a quick victory and end to the slaughter. With the Declaration of War against Germany, once again America resorted to conscription or mandatory enlistment to meet the promise of bringing 10 million troops to the fight. In the beginning, the only benefit provided to each draftee was a life insurance policy that would be paid to a designated beneficiary in cases of death, which was directly associated with military service.

World War I was the first fully mechanized war, and as a result, soldiers were exposed to poisonous chlorine, phosgene, mustard gases, and other chemicals and fumes that required specialized care after the war. The horrors of trench warfare, incessant bombardments and incendiaries, and the scourge of the Spanish flu took a devastating toll on America's expeditionary forces. In the 17 months of America's involvement, American troops suffered 53,402 battle deaths and 204,000 wounded—it was a heavy price to pay (U.S. Department of Veterans Affairs, 2020).

In the aftermath of World War I, Congress established a new system of veterans benefits, including pensions, programs for disability compensation, insurance for service personnel, and vocational rehabilitation for the disabled. At that time there were no designated hospitals or systems of care to accommodate the tens of thousands of returning disabled veterans. Tuberculosis and neuropsychiatric hospitals opened to accommodate returning casualties with respiratory or mental health problems, which for many of the veterans lingered throughout their lifetime. The network of Veteran Homes established after the Civil War were again pressed into service and literally became America's first VA hospitals, which also included homes or domiciliary care for homeless or disenfranchised veterans.

The first consolidation of federal veteran programs took place August 9, 1921, when Congress combined all World War I veterans programs under the aegis of the Veterans Bureau. Public Health Service and Veterans Bureau hospitals were transferred to the Bureau, and an ambitious hospital construction program for World War I veterans commenced. In 1924, veterans benefits were liberalized to cover disabilities that were not service related. By 1928, admission to the National Homes was extended to ex-servicewomen, National Guard, and militia veterans (U.S. Department of Veterans Affairs, 2020).

U.S. Department of Veterans Affairs

Over time, the VA has evolved into three major divisions of services: Veterans Health

Administration (VHA), Veterans Benefits Administration (VBA), and National Cemetery Administration (NCA) (**Figure 7-1**). The VA's 2019 budget and 2020 advance appropriations request totals of $198.6 billion, an increase of $12.1 billion over 2018. This budget request is second only to the Department of Defense. The majority of this funding, $109.7 billion in mandatory funding, is used for the VBA programs with the remaining $76.5 billion in discretionary funding for veterans healthcare programs (Shane, 2018).

Also noted in Figure 7-1 is the U.S. Court of Appeals for Veterans Claims (CAVC). For almost 100 years, the nation's veterans had no power to challenge VA decisions on the levels of disabilities, compensation, pensions, or access to veteran benefits. In 1988, Congress remedied this injustice by creating an appellate body, the Board of Veteran Appeals, endowed with the power to overrule decisions made by other VA offices, including tort reform, which gave veterans and their families the right to sue for wrongful deaths and malpractice (Congressional Research Service Report, 2019). Veterans now have the right to challenge compensation and disability decisions made by the VA. This includes the right to legal representation, providing additional evidence of injury or disability while in the military, and tort reform (includes providing evidence of claims for disability challenge decisions made by the system).

The NCA, also known as Memorial Affairs, is tasked with oversight of 135 national cemeteries, 130 state veteran cemeteries, and 33 soldiers lots. Additionally, there are a variety of acknowledgments for military service, burial benefits, and headstones authorized for veterans. The VBA has 56 regional benefit offices located throughout the nation and administers the determination of levels of service-connected disabilities, disbursement of compensation payments and pensions, educational benefits, vocational rehabilitation programs, and home loan programs. The principal and best-known division is the VHA, which is responsible for the largest integrated health network in America with over 1,868 points of service, including 1,234 outpatient sites, 143 hospitals, telehealth systems, readjustment counseling centers, research facilities, and

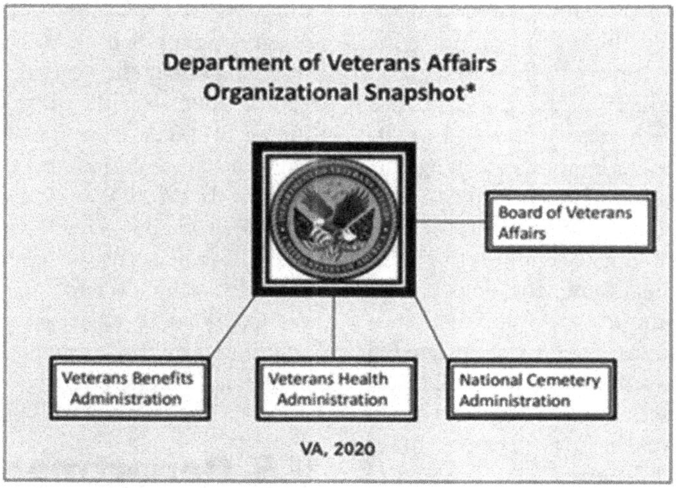

Figure 7-1 Department of Veterans Affairs organizational snapshot.

U.S. Department of Veteran Affairs. (2020). Department of Veteran Affairs Organizational Snapshot. https://fr.slideshare.net/granimal/department-of-veterans-affairs-15652856 /Veterans Affairs Organizational Snapshot

academic affiliations with most of America's major medical schools (NCVAS, 2020).

Mission of the VA Healthcare System

The VA provides health care and health-related services through the VHA, whose primary mission is to provide healthcare services to eligible veterans and some family members. The VHA is also statutorily required to conduct medical research, to train healthcare professionals, to serve as a contingency backup to the Department of Defense (DOD) medical system during a national security emergency, and to provide support to the National Disaster Medical System and the Department of Health and Human Services (HHS) as necessary (38 U.S.C. §§7301-7303; §8111A; §1785).

Eligibility and Enrollment for Care

Not all veterans are eligible to receive care, and not every eligible veteran is automatically entitled to medical care from the VHA. The system is neither designed nor funded to care for all living veterans (Jackonis et al., 2008). Eligibility for veteran health care has evolved over time, and laws governing eligibility have been amended by Congress many times. The last major eligibility amendments occurred in 1996 with enactment of the Veterans' Health Care Eligibility Reform Act of 1996 (P.L. 104-262). This law established two broad eligibility categories and required the VHA to manage the provision of hospital care and medical services through a priority enrollment system. This law also established review eligibility, determination, and appeal process.

VA Healthcare System

Once veterans are eligible and enrolled, they receive their care directly through an integrated healthcare system through the VHA. The VHA is one of the largest integrated healthcare systems in the United States, over a latticework of care sites, including hospitals, community living centers, healthcare centers, community-based outpatient clinics (CBOCs), other outpatient service sites, and dialysis centers. VHA healthcare systems are organized geographically within 18 Veterans Integrated Service Networks (VISNs). Through the VISNs (**Figure 7-2**), care is provided at 1,255 healthcare facilities, including 170 medical centers and 1,074 outpatient sites of care of varying complexity (VHA outpatient clinics). The VHA anticipates that it will provide care to 7.2 million veterans in fiscal year 2021, which is 0.1 million increase from fiscal year 2020. (U.S. Department of Veteran Affairs, 2021).

The VHA's healthcare delivery system is organized regionally, around VISNs. The VISNs were established in 1995 as a part of a strategy to decentralize VA healthcare decisions and bring decision making closer to the point of care (**Figure 7-3**). VISNs were initially designed to be the basic budgetary and planning unit of the VHA. VISN directors report to VHA's Deputy Under Secretary for Operations and Management. VISN directors have the autonomy and authority to develop and implement local management, administrative, and staffing arrangements when necessary to meet healthcare needs. Since 1995, the number of VISNs has decreased from the original 22 to 18, VISN boundaries have been realigned, and the staffing structure has changed to help support emerging VHA-wide healthcare needs (GAO, 2019a).

VISNs manage regional markets that deliver health care, social services, and support services to veterans. Each VISN is responsible for overseeing medical centers within a defined geographic area. VISNs manage the day-to-day functions of medical centers within their networks through efforts such as periodic strategic, business, and financial planning meetings. A 2019 GAO report states the

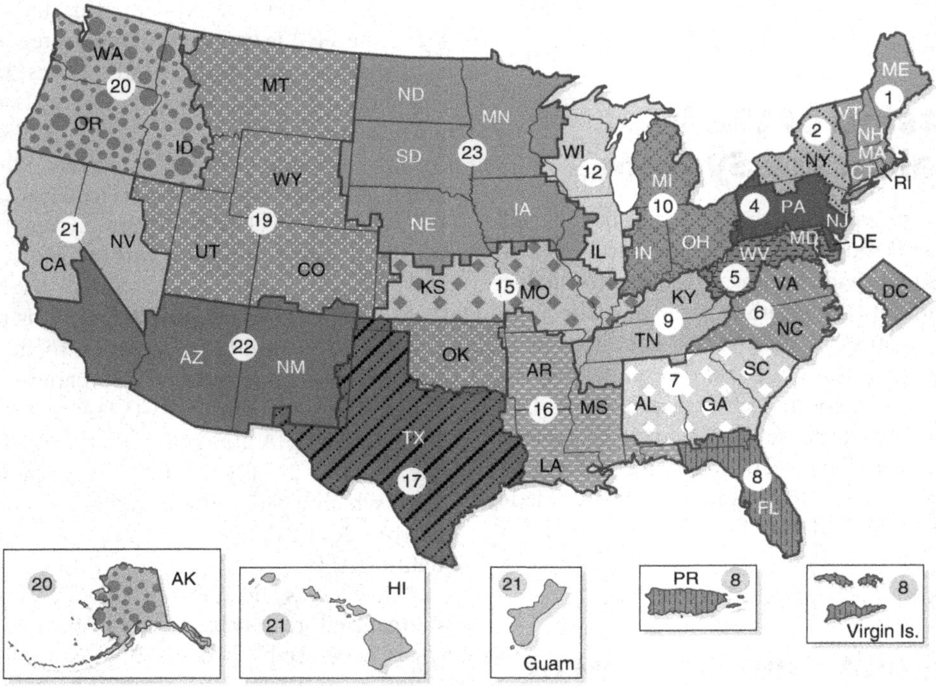

Figure 7-2 Veterans Integrated Service Network (VISN) Regions.

U.S. Department of Veterans Affairs. (n.d.). Interactive US Map. Author. https://www.va.gov/directory/guide/map.asp?dnum=1

VISN's oversight of medical centers includes the following examples:

- **Site visits.** VHA requires VISN officials to conduct site visits to medical centers at least twice a year. During these visits, VISN officials may review medical center operations or specific program areas and may make recommendations for improvement. According to VISN officials, some VISNs have tracking mechanisms to ensure medical centers take corrective actions, and others leave the responsibility for resolving site visit recommendations to medical centers.
- **Conference calls.** VISN directors and senior leadership officials hold regular conference calls with medical center staff. These calls can be used to discuss current issues of interest, including process-improvement initiatives, and challenges medical centers are experiencing, among other issues.
- **Performance reviews.** VISN officials review a dashboard of measures to assess medical center performance. The measures may include those from VHA's Strategic Analytics for Improvement and Learning (SAIL) system, which include close to 30 performance measures for quality and overall efficiency and capacity in areas such as acute care mortality, access to care, and employee satisfaction. SAIL is a diagnostic tool that allows the VHA to assess medical centers' performance relative to their peers, and determine year-to-year improvement based on relevant clinical data. SAIL includes an online performance management tool called Symphony, which tracks performance measures related to medical center access, outcomes, and productivity, and includes an early warning system to notify VISN and

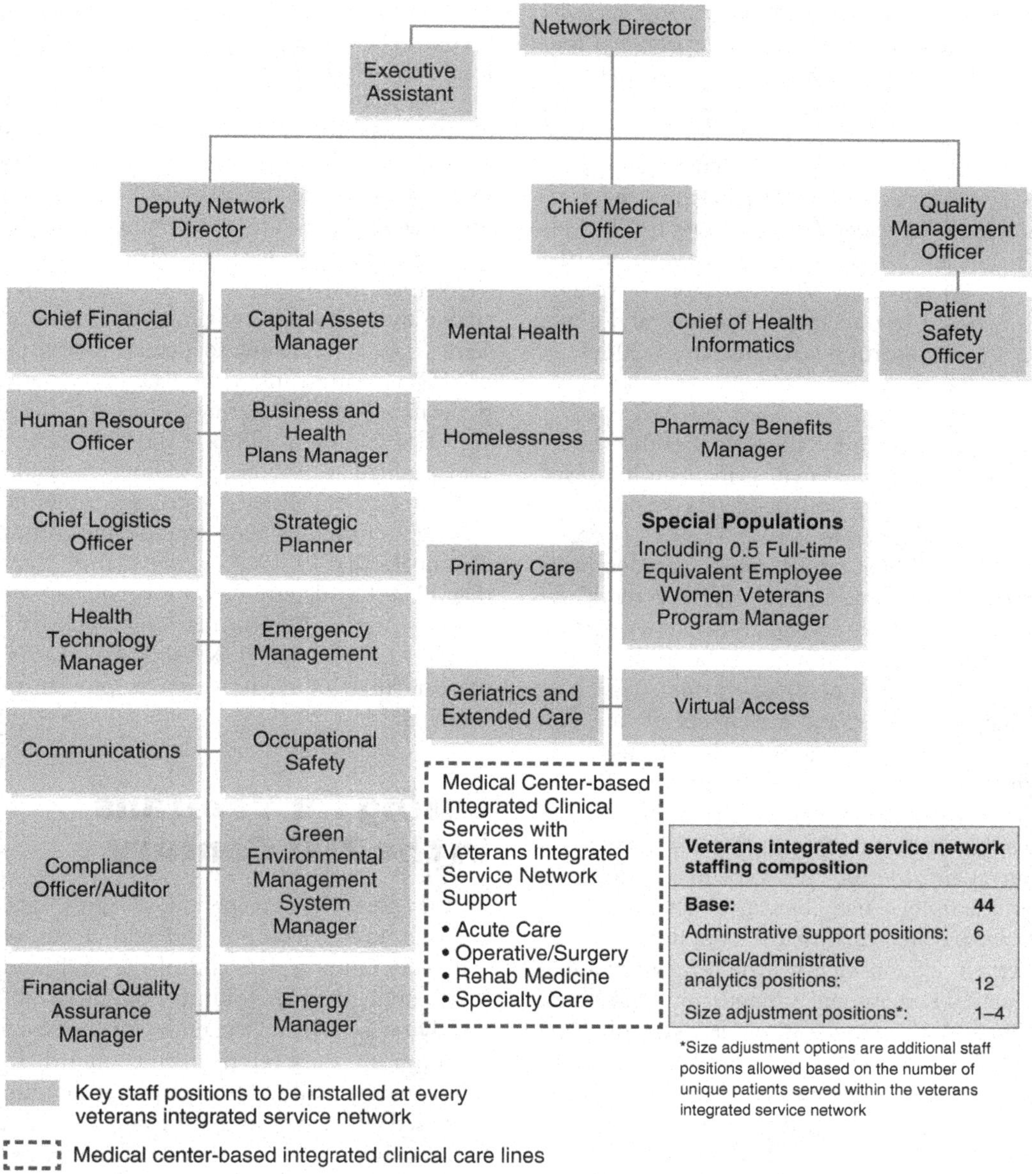

Figure 7-3 VISN Organizational Structure.

Veterans Health Administration. (2019). Regional networks need improved oversight and clearly defined roles and responsibilities. Author. https://files.gao.gov/reports/GAO-19-462/index.html

medical center officials of results that require action (GAO, 2019a).

- **Best practices and regional consortiums.** Each VISN is part of a regional consortium, which is comprised of several VISNs in a particular geographic area. Regional VISNs consortia share resources and best practices, conduct program reviews, and discuss common needs. Regional consortia were formed to foster collaboration among medical centers and to enhance operations and the delivery of health care to veterans. To accomplish these goals, the consortia use means such as regional contracts, sharing FTEs (full-time equivalents), and joint networks for referring patients and conducting telehealth, according to VISN officials. For each regional consortium, the corresponding VISN directors serve as a board of directors to approve and guide the consortium's actions (GAO, 2019a).

Policies and guidelines are developed at VA headquarters for the VHA healthcare system as a whole, and management authority for decision making and budgetary responsibilities are delegated to the VISNs. VHA operates under a different model from the predominant healthcare financing and delivery model in the United States, in which there is a payer for healthcare services (e.g., Medicare or private health insurance plan), a provider (e.g., hospital, physician), and a recipient of care (the patient). The VHA is not a health insurance financing program that provides reimbursement to providers for all or a portion of a patient's healthcare costs. VHA is primarily a direct provider of care. It owns the hospitals and employs the clinicians; however, VHA does pay for care in the community under certain circumstances. The VA Maintaining Internal Systems and Strengthening Integrated Outside Networks (MISSION) Act of 2018 (US PL 115-182) created the Veterans Community Care Program (VCCP), which applies eligibility for care in the community broadly to all enrolled veterans. For example, veterans can seek care in the community if they need a service that is unavailable at the VA, reside in a state with no full-service VA medical facility, meet certain access standards for drive or wait time, qualify under standards for previous programs, or if it is in the best medical interest of the particular veteran. While each VISN has exceeded performance measures at most civilian hospitals, the VHA does not have a comprehensive policy that defines VISNs' roles and responsibilities to manage and oversee medical centers. A recent GAO report (2019a) recommends establishing a process for assessing the overall performance of VISNs that would enable the VHA to better determine how VISNs are performing. Furthermore, a comprehensive policy clearly defining VISN roles and responsibilities would better enable the VHA to develop an effective oversight process to ensure adequate monitoring of VISN activities and a way to address poorly performing VISNs. Creating a process to oversee VISN staffing would help the VHA ensure VISNs adhere to established staffing levels and positions. By establishing a process for routine oversight of staffing, VHA would have greater assurances that VISNs have the staff in place that VHA has determined are needed to effectively operate VISNs. A lack of appropriate staffing could hinder VISNs' ability to oversee the care that VA medical centers provide to veterans.

Caring for Veterans in the 21st Century

In the post-Vietnam period, a great deal changed in the composition and needs of America's military. The end of the draft and the creation of an all-volunteer military completely revised the expectations for increased attention to duty, competence, and dedication in the ranks. More importantly with increased efficiency and professionalization of the military services, there was higher expectations for the quality of life and support of the men and women of the Armed Forces. Because of these changes. women now comprise almost 20% of the all-volunteer military, a stark contrast to the 1970s when they were limited by law to only 2% of the AD force. Another striking feature of today's military is the increased numbers of military men and women on AD who are married with children. The Department of Defense reported that 93% of career military are married, and the number of married military personnel not considered career is 58%. The American Psychiatric Association recently reported that over 700,000 children in America have had one or both parents deployed since 9/11. As a recent report by the Rand Corporation observed, "Today's military is a military of families" (Gorin, 2018).

The strategy of scaling back the size of the AD military and using citizen soldiers of the Reserve and National Guard for repeated and prolonged deployments to combat and hot zone areas was first put to the test during the Gulf War (also known as Operation Desert Shield/Desert Storm, 1990–1991). President Saddam Hussein of Iraq launched an invasion of Kuwaiti lands using the pretense that the Emir, along with Israel, United Arab Emirates, and the United States, had unfairly manipulated oil prices, which cut into his profits. Within hours, President George H.W. Bush ordered the mobilization and deployment of 694,550 U.S. military forces, mostly Reservists and National Guard, to meet the challenge. He also successfully organized 40 countries into a Coalition of the Willing, which included NATO allies, several Arab nations, and the Soviet Union. From start to finish, Desert Storm lasted only 43 days and has been called the 100-hour ground war because that was how long the fighting lasted. While this was a stunning victory, it was the first war of the all-volunteer force, which now relied on eagerness and enthusiasm of a new generation to join the military and defend the nation.

The war might have been over, but the battle for thousands of Gulf War veterans was just beginning. Although the war was brief with relatively few injuries and deaths, a substantial number of returning veterans began experiencing and reporting a variety of health problems that have persisted over time. Gulf War illness (GWI) has been designated as the signature health problem of Operation Desert Storm. Eventually, 24% to 33% of the 700,000 military and civilians who were deployed to the area, including coalition forces who served in the combat areas, also reported similar symptoms (Johnson et al., 2007). It is estimated in the United States alone, more than 100,000 cases have been reported since 1999 (Research Advisory Committee Gulf War Veterans Illnesses, 2014). GWI is a constellation of symptoms that can include headaches, joint and back pain, fatigue, indigestion, respiratory disorders, sleep problems, and cognitive dysfunction. Service members (SMs) who were deployed were exposed to many hazardous agents and situations, both known and unknown. These exposures included chemical and biological agents, mandatory vaccines, oil-well fire smoke, dust, high ambient temperatures and heat stress, pesticides, and pyridostigmine bromide (PB), which is a prophylactic agent used against potential nerve agent exposure. These toxic exposures are thought to be the etiology of this condition (Research Advisory Committee Gulf War Veterans Illnesses, 2014).

Because of the soft symptoms with no identifiable diagnostic test or treatment, there have been many sceptics who challenge the validity of the claims. In 1998, Congress tasked the Institute of Medicine (IOM) through the work of the Committee on Gulf War and Health to study the issue. There has been much controversy about the limited conclusive findings produced in the 10 years the committee has issued reports. Gulf War veterans continue to experience increased risk for chronic fatigue syndrome, functional gastrointestinal conditions, posttraumatic stress disorder (PTSD), generalized anxiety disorder, depression, and substance abuse (Sox et al., 2000). As a result of this review and their own research, the VA now accepts 10 functional disorders and 5 tropical diseases as compensable conditions associated with service of veterans deployed in the Gulf War.

Afghanistan: Operation Enduring Freedom (OEF) and Iraq: Operation Iraqi Freedom (OIF)

The attacks of 9/11 plunged the entire nation into a new defense mode and the realities that war was no longer oceans away. Since 2001, about 3 million U.S. troops have been deployed to Iraq or Afghanistan (IOM, 2010). More than 6,767 men and women have given their lives, and over 52,143 have been injured (U.S. Department of Defense, 2021). America continued to rely on Reserve and National Guard units to serve in combat. This involved multiple deployments of the same personnel with no end in sight; military families living in civilian communities; and the severity of wounds sustained. These all mark this engagement as particularly challenging. As the first casualties started to return from Iraq and Afghanistan, advances in battlefield medicine, medevac, and the sophistication of trauma care were resulting in exceptional care and high "save" rates were noted and unequalled in previous wars (U.S. Department of Defense, 2021). As heartening as this news was, the reality was that the casualties that did survive would have catastrophic injuries. The need for comprehensive support systems to ensure a suitable quality of life seemed daunting. Pictures of injured casualties with skulls half removed to reduce complications revealed the actual meaning of the mantra that traumatic brain injury (TBI) was the signature injury of this war. It conveyed that TBI was an established fact, and care issues had to be addressed (Schwartz, 2008). Problems of blunt force trauma, closed head injuries, and repeated exposures to improvised explosive devices (IED) contributed to a mounting body of evidence that TBI was indeed a factor that needed to be considered and addressed in modern battlefield medicine.

Explaining the differences between PTSD, characterized as psychological reaction to an abnormal event, and TBI, associated with actual trauma to the brain, was also problematic. Symptoms of these conditions often overlapped and were hard to distinguish without diagnostic testing and clinical interviews. Initial screenings on troops returning from combat areas often missed these conditions, which could easily be overlooked or concealed.

We have yet to know the full consequences and long-term effects of multiple deployments in relationship to family stability, successful return to the community, employment, and future recruitment potential. An entire superstructure of support systems has steadily developed to ease the problems associated with deployments and family needs. This has fueled another transformation of how healthcare programs and services are being provided to military families and veterans of the engagements in Iraq and Afghanistan.

Department of Defense reports that 1.9 million military personnel have been deployed in 3 million tours of duty (IOM, 2010). Moreover OEF/OIF together make up the longest sustained U.S. military operation since the Vietnam War and the first extended conflicts to depend on the all-volunteer military. In the rush to deploy the men and women of the Reserve and National Guard, policymakers did not take into account that this transition and the present generation's needs and expectations did not fit into the military model that has become the norm today. The self-contained military bases of the past provided a solid system of support for the men and women in uniform and their families. There were added conveniences of housing, shopping, schools, recreation, health care, and dental care located in proximity to the military members' duty station. In essence, military bases were a tight-knit enclave with a shared belief system, dedication to military service, and an atmosphere of patriotism supported by military social tradition and norms.

As a new approach to military mission readiness evolved, it became apparent that America would not return to the past tradition of creating and maintaining large bases and instillations. Reliance on Department of Defense health providers and facilities would become scarce and not as available to families of AD personnel. Because VA authority to provide services is limited by law to the military member and/or veteran only, the options for family members would become limited, perhaps even nonexistent. In reality, military and veteran health care would not be as accessible as it was in the past.

This shift away from the large Department of Defense infrastructure also challenged the resources of state and local governments to meet these new community needs. The support of family and significant others emerged as a vital dynamic in successful recruitment, retention, and reintegration of returning military from combat and deployment to civilian life. Although Congress, the Department of Defense, and the VA may identify a problem and derive solutions to these needs, the process of enacting legislation and implementing programs is years in the making. In the age of text messaging, the response time was considered by many to be out of touch and negligent as compared to what the total force generation of returning wounded warriors and heroes had come to expect in exchange for their service to the country.

For example, VA touted the fact that the national average time to process an initial disability claim for a veteran was only 136 days. Four months and 16 days is a long time to wait for a paycheck when you have no other income. Another hardship can be the real lack of financial relief, because disability compensation barely provided enough to live on. In 2020, a single veteran who is rated 100% disabled, which is a permanent and total disability rating, received $37,272.48 per year compared to the veteran rated 30% who is only entitled to $5,228.28 per year. Taking into account the addition of a spouse and one child, the benefit does increase the income of the 100% disabled veteran by $15,740.16 for a total of $53,012.64 per year and a 30% disabled veteran with spouse and child by $6,308.28 to $11,536.56 per year (U.S. Department of Veteran Affairs, 2020). America's returning veterans and their families expected a level of service and care that provided effective, efficient, and expedient responses to their needs.

A Way Forward

During the 2010 debate on the Patient Protection and Affordable Care Act, also known as the Affordable Care Act (ACA), many questions about this massive overhaul of medical care also raised interest and scrutiny of America's largest integrated health system. Heavy criticism and fear of socialized medicine, or rationing of health care, opened the door for opponents to use VA as an example of how wrong things can go. Complaints about VA's unwieldly system, lack of standardized treatments, and poor quality of care became a target for journalists, reporters, and critics. As the 2014 ACA implementation date approached, reports of negligence, misdiagnosis, and ill treatment of veterans using VA escaladed. Advertising campaigns noted, "It took the federal government longer to build a website than it did to fight World War II" (Shane, 2018). While some of these complaints were superfluous, a legitimate scandal at the Phoenix Arizona VA Medical Center (VAMC) would become a major factor in the future of care for America's veterans.

Until 2014, the VA rarely authorized or reimbursed health care for community providers. If veterans lived within 60 miles of a VA facility, they were expected to travel that distance for care. Even more troubling was the amount of time veterans were required to wait for an appointment. In some instances, appointments could take months or even years with little concern for the health status of the veterans or their capacity to travel to appointments. For millions of veterans and decades of time, this rather antiquated system was the standard of care. For the most part, veterans were very grateful for what they perceived to be "free care" for the health conditions and injuries sustained as a result of their military service. However, veterans of the Vietnam and post-9/11 generations didn't accept it and expected more.

Although America's healthcare systems had streamlined services and care, it was evident that the VA had not kept pace with the times. Traveling 60 miles to see a VA doctor and the convoluted eligibility criteria designed by Congress, as well as an influx of new veterans of Iraq and Afghanistan, created a firestorm and demands for change. With the end of the draft authority and advent of the all-volunteer force, benefits and entitlements for military service had to step up and be competitive to garner the interest of potential volunteer enlistees. Reserve and National Guard units were shouldering greater responsibilities for mission readiness and comprised 45% of the total forces deployed to Iraq and Afghanistan while sustaining almost 20% of the casualties (National Guard Bureau, 2020). This was an entirely new strategy that was changing the face, fabric, and profile of the America's veteran population.

Phoenix

In the early months of 2014, some of these antiquated policies were openly challenged in the press. Local news media reported a pervasive pattern of negligence in the treatment of the veterans receiving care at the VAMC. Investigative reporters at local news outlets found evidence that VA officials at the VAMC had been double booking and keeping secret appointment records for hundreds of veterans seeking care. This reckless disregard for their veteran patients was compounded by evidence that suggested that at least 40 veterans on the secret list died while waiting for an appointment (Lopaz, 2015). Veterans marched in the streets demanding action.

Congress and the Oversight Inspector General of the VA (VAOIG) launched immediate investigations of the appointment irregularities and the circumstances of the reported deaths. Findings indicated that the secret list was an elaborate scheme designed by the managers in Phoenix to hide the fact that 1,400 to 1,600 sick veterans were forced to wait months to see a doctor (VAOIG, 2018). Both investigations concluded that the health care of veterans in Phoenix had been compromised by delays and fraudulent record keeping. VA Secretary Shinseki ordered an immediate audit of the VA's more than 900 medical care facilities.

Subsequently, the VAOIG confirmed that similar fraudulent practices in the system and that of compromised care exposed at the Phoenix VAMC were pervasive. Inspections of at least 42 deficient VA locations ensued in rapid succession. VAOIG's systemic review found more than 120,000 veterans were left waiting or never got care and that schedulers were pressured to engage in improper practices to cover these offenses (VAOIG, 2018). Congress, the Federal Bureau of Investigation, and the White House launched additional investigations. By August 2014, 14 of the 16 presidential-appointed leaders of the VA had resigned or been removed. At the same time, conservative legislators floated the idea that privatizing VHA was the best solution for relieving the long waits and would be more convenient for veterans to use private providers than depend on the VA.

Congress acted swiftly to authorize community health care at VA expense if veterans had to wait more than 30 days for an appointment. The Veterans Access, Choice, and Accountability Act (VACAA) of 2014 (Public Law 113-146), also known as the Veterans Choice Act, required the VA to establish a temporary program known as The Choice Program to improve veterans' access to health care. VACAA authorized veterans enrolled in VA health care to use preapproved healthcare providers outside of the VA system (non-VA care) for a period of up to 3 years if (1) a VA facility was unable to schedule an appointment within 30 days, (2) the veteran lived more than 40 miles from a VA facility, or (3) the veteran had significant travel hardships. While this did provide some relief to the system, great confusion, poor dissemination of information, and the VA bureaucracy thwarted the system from attaining its full potential.

While many saw this legislation to be pragmatic given the expectations of healthcare systems in the 21st century, veterans saw this as the beginning of the end for veteran-focused health care in America. They also feared this was the beginning of the dismantling of the VA and ultimately privatization of all VA health care. The argument was not the quality, it was about access to care, which was timely, appropriate, and convenient.

In June 2018, President Trump signed the VA MISSION Act (US PL 115-182), which was designed to resolve the backlog and travel burdens for veterans using VA health care. This legislation provided options to improve VA's ability to hire healthcare providers, consolidate and improve VA community care programs, expand caregiver benefits to all veterans, and establish a process to evaluate and reform VA's aging capital infrastructure. Additionally, there was a 5-year, $55 billion commitment to expedite veterans' access to non-VA community care for clinically appropriate and preapproved care at VA expense. To continue the community health initiative, Congress modified the Choice Program termination date and appropriations limit until a more viable process could be developed.

The Way Forward

The strategy of scaling back the size of the AD military and using citizen soldiers of the Reserve and National Guard for repeated and prolonged deployments to combat and hot zone areas also precipitated health issues that had not been seen in previous conflicts. Reserve and National Guard units returning to communities directly from the combat areas brought their readjustment problems to the neighborhoods, schools, and workplaces of America. Issues that were not previously in the public eye—especially mental health conditions such as suicide, military sexual trauma, and domestic violence—quickly became headline news. Perhaps most troubling were the 2014 findings that 18 to 22 veterans a day were taking their own lives. Equally concerning were reports that women veterans were 200% more likely to take their own lives than civilian women (U.S. Department of Veteran Affairs Office of Mental Health, 2020).

The support of family and significant others also emerged as a vital dynamic in successful recruitment, retention, and reintegration of America's 21st-century military. As this new strategy for military mission readiness evolved, it become apparent that America would not return to the past tradition of creating and maintaining large bases with family-oriented housing, healthcare services, and programs. In the rush to deploy the men and women of the Reserve and National Guard, policymakers failed to realize the needs and expectations of the newly minted Total Force, which did not fit into the system that would become the norm.

This shift away from the large Department of Defense infrastructure also challenged the resources of state and local government to meet these needs. The support of family and significant others had emerged as a vital dynamic in successful recruitment, retention, and reintegration of returning military SMs from combat and deployment to civilian life. Although Congress, the Department of Defense, and the VA may have identified a problem and formulated solutions to these needs, the process of enacting legislation and implementing programs was years in the making. In the age of text messaging, the response time was considered to be out of touch and negligent compared to what returning wounded warrior and heroes had come to expect in exchange for their service to the country.

Partnerships with state governments became an effective response to the grassroots needs, which often escaped the attention of the VA. Additionally, government-based programs were augmented by thousands of private sector, community, volunteer, and faith-based initiatives to help injured SMs and their families meet a myriad of needs. Chief among the needs were housing, transportation, child care, employment, mental health, and short-term financial assistance. Consequently, patriotism and respect for the men and women in uniform became a popular focus of charitable and philanthropic attention.

References

American Academy of Nursing. (2013). *Have you ever served. Clinician pocket card.* http://www.haveyoueverserved.com/about.html

Binns, J. H., Barlow, C., Bloom, F. E., Clauw, D. J., Golomb, B. A., Graves, J. C., Hardie, A., Knox, M., Meggs Williams, J., & & Nettleman, M. D. (2008). *Gulf war illness and the health of gulf war veterans.* Research Advisory Committee on Gulf War Veterans. Department of Veterans Affairs.

Brown, J. L. (2012). The unasked question. *Journal of the American Medical Association, 308*(18), 1869–1870.

Collins, E., Wilmoth, M., & Schwartz. L., (2013). "Have you ever served in the military?" Campaign in Partnership with Joining Forces Initiative. *Nursing Outlook, 61*(5), 375–376. doi DOI:10.1016/j.outlook.2013.07.004

Congressional Research Service Report. (2019, November). The Federal Tort Claims Act (FCTA): A legal overview. *Congressional Research Service* (R45732). https://fas.org/sgp/crs/misc/R45732.pdf

DeBruyne, N. F. (2018). *American war and military operations casualties: Lists and statistics.* Congressional Research Service.

Four, M. (2020). *Leave no veteran behind the mission continues America's aging veteran population and the Covid-19 pandemic.* Vietnam Veterans of America Inc.

Gordon, S. (2018). *Wounds of war: How VA delivers health, healing and hope to the nation's veterans.* Cornell University Press.

Gorin, D. (2018). Why so many military women think about suicide. Veterans in America, RAND Corporation. https: //www.rand.org/

Gosoroski, D. M. (1996). For those who "faithfully serve." *Veterans of Foreign Wars Magazine, 84*(4), 13–16.

Gostin, L., & Wiley, L. (2016). *Public health law: Power, duty, restraint* (3rd ed.). University of California Press.

Government Accountability Office. (2019a). Veterans Health Administration: Regional networks need improved oversight and clearly defined roles and responsibilities, GAO-19-462.

Government Accountability Office. (2019b). VA Health Care: Estimating resources needed to provide community care. https://www.gao.gov/products/gao-19-478#summaryAO-19-478

Griffin, R. L. (2014). *Review of alleged patient deaths, patient waiting times and scheduling practices of VA health care systems.* Office of Inspector General. https://www.va.gov/oig/pubs/vaoig-14-02603-267.pdf

Institute of Medicine. (1977). *Report to Senate Committee on Veterans Affairs: Study of health care for American veterans.* National Academy of Health Sciences. U.S. Government Printing Office.

Institute of Medicine. (2010). *Operation Enduring Freedom and Operation Iraqi Freedom: Demographics and impact.* National Academies Press. doi:10.17226/12812

Institute of Medicine. (2013). *Returning home from Iraq and Afghanistan: Assessment of readjustment of veterans, service members and their families* (pp. 33–46). National Academies Press.

Institute of Medicine. (2016). *Update on health effects of serving in the Gulf War. Gulf War and Health* (vol. 10). National Academies Press.

Jackonis, M. J., Deyton, L., & Hess, W. J. (2008). War, its aftermath, and US health policy: Toward a comprehensive health program for America's military personnel, veterans, and their families. *The Journal of Law, Medicine & Ethics, 36*(4), 677–689.

Johnson, S. J., Sherman, M. D., Hoffman, J. S., James, L. C., Johnson, P. L., Lochman, J. E., Magee, T. N., Riggs, D., Daniel, J.H., Paolomares, R.S., Nichols-Howarth, B., & Stepney, B. (2007). *The psychological needs of US military service members and their families: A preliminary report.* American Psychological Association Presidential Task Force on Military Deployment Services for Youth, Families and Service Members. https://core.ac.uk/download/pdf/71340116.pdf

Lang, K. (2016). Facts you should know about Desert Storm. Department of Defense News Media Activity June 15, 2015. Fort Meade, MD.

Lopaz, G. (2015). *The VA scandal of 2014 explained*. https://www.vox.com/2014/9/26/18080592/va-scandal-explained; multimedia/podcasts /veterans-in-america /why-so-many-military-women-think-about-suicide .html

National Center for Veterans Analysis and Statistics, Office of Policy and Planning. (2018). *Statistics at a glance*. Department of Veteran Affairs.

National Center for Veterans Analysis and Statistics. (2020). *Veteran population*. Department of Veteran Affairs. https://www.va.gov/vetdata/veteran_population .asp

National Guard Bureau. (2020). National Guard: Service in the war on terror. Military.com. https://www .military.com/national-guard-birthday/national -guard-service-in-the-war-on-terror.html

Office of Inspector General. (2014). Review of alleged patient deaths, patient wait times and scheduling practices at Phoenix VA Health Care System. https://www .va.gov/oig/pubs/VAOIG-14-02603-267.pdf

Office of Mental Health (OMH) and Suicide Prevention. (2018). *Veteran suicide data report 2005–2016*. U.S. Department of Veteran Affairs.

Office of Public Affairs (OPA). (2018). *America's wars*. U.S. Department of Veteran Affairs.

Phillips, M. (2020, June 2). Last person to receive Civil War–era pension dies. *The Wall Street Journal*. www .wsj.com/articles/last-person-to-receive-a-civil-war -era-pension-dies-11591141193

Research Advisory Committee on Gulf War Veterans' Illnesses. (2014). *Gulf War illness and the health of Gulf War veterans: Research update and recommendations, 2009-2013*. U.S. Government Printing Office.

Schwartz, L. (2008). Testimony congressional hearing: Mental health treatment for families: Supporting those who support our veterans. House Veterans Affairs Committee 110th Congress, 2nd Session. https://archives-veterans.house.gov/witness-testimony /linda-spoonster-schwartz-rn-drph-faan

Scott, C. (2012). Veterans Affairs historical budget authority FY 1940–2012. Congressional Research Service.

Severo, R., & Milford, L. (1989). *Wages of war: When America's soldiers came home: From Valley Forge to Vietnam*. Forbidden Bookshelf Open Road Publishing.

Shane, L. (2018, February 12). VA spending up again in Trump's fiscal 2019 plan. *Military Times*. https://www .lmtonline.com/news/article/How-a-Koch-backed -veterans-group-gained-influence-12815151.php

Smith, J. (2020). Divided Koreas mark 70 years since war began, but no treaty in sight. *Emerging Markets, Reuters*. https://www.reuters.com/article/us-koreanwar -anniversary-idUSKBN23W0K5

Soucy, J. (2016). *National Guard remains a vital component of the war fight*. https://arng.ng.mil/resources/News /Pages/National-Guard-remains-a-vital-component -of-the-war-fight.aspx

Sox, H. C., Liverman, C. T., & Fulco, C. E. (Eds.). (2000). Gulf War and health. In *Depleted uranium, sarin, pyridostigmine bromide, and vaccines* (vol. 1). National Academies Press.

Title 38 U.S. Code. (1977). Section §5303(a). Authority: Section 2 of Public Law 95-126. Certain bars to benefits.

Title 38 US Code Chapter 11. (2013). *Veterans benefits compensation for service-connected disabilities or death*. Government Printing Office

Title 38 US Code Chapter 11. (2013). *Veterans benefits: Compensation for service connected disabilities or death*. U.S. Government Printing Office.

U.S. Department of Defense. (2013). "Armed Forces Strengths" Statistical Information Analysis Division. http://www.siadapp.dmdc.osd.mil/personnel /MILITARY

U.S. Department of Defense. (2021). *Casualty status*. Department of Defense. https://www.defense.gov /casualty.pdf

U.S. Department of Veteran Affairs Office of Mental Health. (2020). Office of Mental Health and Suicide Prevention annual report. https://www.mentalhealth .va.gov/docs/data-sheets/2020/2020-National-Veteran -Suicide-Prevention-Annual-Report-11-2020-508.pdf

U.S. Department of Veteran Affairs Oversight Inspector General. (2018). Comprehensive healthcare inspection program review of the Phoenix VA Health Care System Phoenix, Arizona. Report 18-00611-1180. https://www.oversight.gov/report/va/comprehensive -healthcare-inspection-program-review-phoenix-va -health-care-system-phoenix

U.S. Department of Veteran Affairs, Office of Public Affairs. (2020). *Department of Veteran Affairs organizational snapshot*. https://fr.slideshare.net/granimal /department-of-veterans-affairs-15652856

U.S. Department of Veteran Affairs. (2017). *Federal benefits for veterans, dependents and survivors*. U.S. Government Printing Office.

U.S. Department of Veteran Affairs. (2018a). *Federal benefits for veterans, dependents and survivors*. U.S. Government Printing Office.

U.S. Department of Veteran Affairs. (2018b). *VA benefits book*. Office of Public and Intergovernmental Affairs. U.S. Government Printing Office.

U.S. Department of Veteran Affairs. (2018c). Veterans compensation benefits rate table effective 12/1/18. Veterans Benefits Administration.

U.S. Department of Veteran Affairs. (2020). Veterans history office. https://www.va.gov/HISTORY/VA_History /Overview.asp

U.S. Department of Veteran Affairs. (2021). VHA Budget in Brief Fiscal Year 2021 Budget Submission https://www.va.gov/budget/docs/summary/fy2021VAbudgetInBrief.pdf

U.S. Government Accountability Office. (1982). *Actions needed to ensure that female veterans have equal access to VA benefits*, GAO/HRD-82-98. U.S. Government Printing Office. https://www.gao.gov/products/hrd-82-98#:~:text=The%20Administrator%20of%20Veterans%20Affairs,%3B%20(2)%20contracting%20with%20private

U.S. Government Accountability Office. (2019). *Veterans Health Administration: Regional networks need improved oversight and clearly defined roles and responsibilities*, GAO-19-462. Government Printing Office. https://www.gao.gov/products/gao-19-462#:~:text=GAO%2D19%2D462%20Published%3A,7%20million%20veterans%20this%20year.&text=We%20recommended%20that%20VHA%20develop,that%20they%20are%20appropriately%20staffed

U.S. Public Law 104-262. (1996). Veterans' Health Care Eligibility Reform Act of 1996. https://www.govinfo.gov/app/details/PLAW-104publ262

U.S. Public Law 113-146. (2014). Veterans Access, Choice, and Accountability Act 2014. https://www.govinfo.gov/content/pkg/PLAW-113publ146/pdf/PLAW-113publ146.pdf

U.S. Public Law 115-182. (2018). VA Maintaining Systems and Strengthening Integrated Outside Networks (MISSION) Act. https://www.congress.gov/115/plaws/publ182/PLAW-115publ182.pdf

Veterans Administration. (1967). To care for him who shall have borne the battle. U.S. Government Printing Office.

Veterans for Common Sense. (2016/02/13). *IOM Gulf War report "turns science on its head."* https://www.disabled-world.com/news/veterans/iom.php.

Vietnam Veterans of America. (2016). VVA self-help guide: Service-connected disabled compensation for exposures to Agent Orange. Agent Orange Committee, Vietnam Veterans of America. https://vva.org/wp-content/uploads/2014/12/AgentOrangeGuide.pdf

Vogt, K. S. (2015). Origins of military medical care as an essential source of morale. *Military Medicine, 180*, 604–605.

Zacchea, M. (2013). To satisfy every demand that may reasonably be requested. Entrepreneurship Bootcamp for Veterans, University of Connecticut School of Business. https://ebv.business.uconn.edu/tag/homeless-veterans/

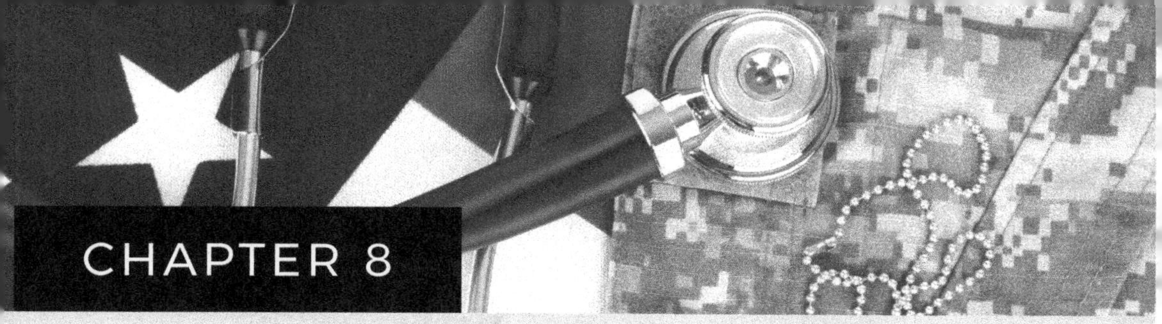

CHAPTER 8

Service-Associated Conditions and Veterans Health Administration Eligibility

Ali R. Tayyeb, Linda Schwartz, and Rita D'Aoust

"To care for him who shall have borne the battle, and for his widow, and his orphan"

—President Abraham Lincoln

As professionals in the healthcare field, it is essential to understand that all veteran benefits have a direct and generational impact on the overall health of an individual that has served in the military and on their families. Veteran benefits were established to provide ease of reintegration into the civilian population. As healthcare providers learn about veteran benefits, please keep in mind the historical and generational context and population of service members these benefits were first intended toward. Additionally, while its benefits and services may provide needed access and resources for many service members, not all service members are created equal under the Department of Veteran Affairs. Veteran benefits are not presumed, and entitlements are not automatically rendered to all prior service members.

As a healthcare team member, it is vital to understand the term *veteran*, who is considered a veteran, types of benefits, and whether a veteran is eligible for benefits. The Department of Veteran Affairs (VA) has established criteria for determination of veteran status and does not consider all service members as veterans, and not all veterans are eligible for all benefits. Not all eligibilities result in the disbursement of entitlements, making the VA system a complex network of redtape with its bureaucratic hurdles and legal language in which the service members are expected to navigate post-military service. It is essential for healthcare systems, providers, and staff to have the necessary knowledge to guide the service members, not through the VA system or process, but to the appropriate resources and individuals who are adequately trained, have the knowledge, and time to assist the service member in obtaining their benefited entitlements. It is essential to understand some terminology such as who is a veteran, what eligibility means, and how eligibility is different from entitlement. Most importantly, it is crucial to becoming comfortable asking two of the most important veteran questions. First, "Have you ever served in the military, National Guard, or the Reserve?" This should elicit the correct "yes" answer that includes everything from guard, reserve, active duty, not making it through basic training where a recruit has an undetermined classification. If the person identifies with your question, you should hear an answer such as, "Oh, yes. I was in uniform once or yes, I served with the Army or Marines. . ." It is essential because too often, post–World War II (WWII) underserved ethnic communities, women who have served, and the lesbian, gay, bisexual, trans, and queer (LGBTQ)+ communities are hesitant or unsure about their eligibility or identity as veterans. The uncertainty is sometimes due to bigotry and racism within the military service, resulting in a less than honorable discharge. So, it is important, if we want to be inclusive and get the most accurate answer as healthcare professionals, we must ask, "have you ever served in the military, National Guard, or the Reserve?"

The next question should be "Have you ever applied for VA Healthcare or other VA benefits?" This is an opportunity to gauge if the prior service member has ever sought to engage with the VA system, their knowledge of available benefits, and level of interest. Benefits other than health care such as education, housing, and job training are just as valuable to the overall health of the veteran as direct healthcare services.

The other valuable statement for every healthcare provider to feel empowered and comfortable with is the phrase, "I don't know, but here is whom you should contact." This is a powerful statement because there is no expectation of you as the care provider to know how the VA system operates. More on both of these later in the chapter. The goal is to seek understanding and provide expert resources for the prior service member. The prior service member probably has zero expectation of you knowing the VA system, so to have some working knowledge is a huge benefit to aiding your patient with much-needed resources.

Veterans

For this chapter, we will address all prior service members as veterans, regardless of their eligibility and time in service. To understand the best way to help a veteran is to gain some rudimentary knowledge of the military culture and the system available to them through the VA. First, we will look at the term *veteran*. The term *veteran* is used commonly to describe service members or those who have served in the military. The concept varies from country to country, but in the United States, the term *veteran* is very specific in order to be eligible for benefits.

The term *veteran* has several meanings. To the civilian or social community, this term in the military context depicts an individual who has served in the Armed Services of the United States at some point in their adult life, has worn a uniform, and is often stereotyped in war movies. However, the term *veteran* has varying definitions from various agencies, and sometimes even within the same agency. The U.S. Census Bureau (2017) defines veterans as,

> "Veterans are men and women who have served (even for a short time), but are not currently serving, on active duty in the US Army, Navy, Air Force, Marine Corps, or the Coast Guard, or who served in the U.S. Merchant Marine during World War II. People who served in the National Guard or Reserves are classified as veterans only if they were ever called or ordered to active duty, not counting the four to six months for initial training or yearly summer camps.

This definition may be extended to the Space Force in the future as various agencies update the definition.

The US Federal Government under Title 38—United States Code (U.S.C.), §101 (2020) Veterans Benefits Part I—General Provisions Chapter 1 defines the term *veteran* as "a person who served in the active military, naval, or air service, and who was discharged or released therefrom under conditions other than dishonorable."

States sometimes create their definitions. For example, the state of Washington only recognizes individuals that have "at the time he or she seeks the benefits has received an honorable discharge, is actively serving honorably, or received a discharge for physical reasons with an honorable record," and who meets several listed criteria that mostly include service in a period of war (Veteran, Public Employment, Civil Service, and Pensions, 2020).

Veteran Benefits

The care of soldiers injured on the battlefield has taken many shapes over several centuries. But the official role of the federal government did not emerge until the establishment of the national soldiers and sailors asylum by President Abraham Lincoln in 1865. It was the first institution of its kind set up to care for the honorably discharged veterans of the union army. However, it wasn't until World War I that Congress established what is now the largest healthcare system in the nation, the Veterans Healthcare Administration (VHA), whose sole purpose is caring for the health of American veterans (VA, 2021).

However, criteria for determining veteran status and benefits have evolved over the years. Not all veterans are eligible to receive care, and not every eligible veteran is automatically entitled to medical care from the VHA. The system is neither designed nor funded to care for all living veterans (Rothstein, 2008). Eligibility for veterans' health care has evolved over time, and laws governing eligibility have been amended by Congress many times. The last major eligibility amendments occurred in 1996 with the enactment of the Veterans' Health Care Eligibility Reform Act of 1996. (P.L. 104-262). This law established two broad eligibility categories and required the VHA to manage the provision of hospital care and medical services through a priority enrollment system. The first eligibility category includes veterans with service-connected disabilities, Medal of Honor recipients, Purple Heart recipients, former prisoners of war, veterans exposed to toxic substances and environmental hazards such as Agent Orange, and veterans whose attributable income is not greater than an amount established by a "means test." Veterans who do not meet any of the criteria in the first category compose the second eligibility category and *may* be eligible to receive care through the VHA to the extent resources permit. Once veterans are determined to be eligible for care through the VHA, most veterans are required to formally enroll in the VHA healthcare system to receive services. Once a veteran is enrolled, the veteran remains in the system and does not have to reapply for enrollment annually. Veterans are placed in one of eight priority enrollment categories. Veterans in some priority enrollment categories are required to pay co-payments for certain benefits. Enrolled veterans do not pay any premiums, deductibles, or coinsurance for their care (CRS, 2019). This is in contrast to major medical insurance plans, which typically have premiums, deductibles, and co-payments.

Under Title 38—U.S.C. §101 (2020), veterans must meet more stringent requirements for veteran benefits. Those requirements are summarized next.

Active Service

Active service is a term generally used by government agencies such as the VA as one of the determinants for benefits. To determine if a prior service member is considered eligible for benefits, active service is defined as full-time service other than for the purposes of training.

For example, a member of the Army Reserve with 20 years of Reserve duty may not be eligible for veteran benefits if they served only for training purposes. However, a person with only Reserve service may be eligible if they are injured or die in training status. At this point, VA reclassifies the person as a veteran to become eligible for VA benefits (38 U.S.C. §101, 2020).

Length of Service

For prior service members enlisted before September 8, 1980, no minimum requirements exist for the armed forces' length of service to be considered for VA benefits. However, for prior service members that served after that period of time to be considered for VA benefits eligibility, the prior service member must have served the full period for which they were called to active duty or was on 24 months of continuous active service. Exceptions to this rule as always are if the service member was injured, died, or was discharged or retired due to a disability resulting from active service.

Military Discharge

All members of the Armed Services are released from obligatory service by a process called discharge. A discharge may be issued due to various reasons such as the end of military service, retirement, various administrative reasons, medical disability, or punitive military action. (38 CFR §3.12, 2020) defines discharge as: (A) Retirement from the active military, naval, or air service, and (B) the satisfactory completion of the period of active military, naval, or air service for which a person was obligated at the time of entry into such service in the case of a person who, due to enlistment or reenlistment, was not awarded a discharge or release from such period of service at the time of such completion thereof and who, at such time, would otherwise have been eligible for the award of a discharge or release under conditions other than dishonorable.

The Department of Veteran Affairs only considers Honorable Discharges and Discharge Under Honorable Conditions as qualifying military discharges for benefits screenings and considers these individuals as eligible for benefits. The remaining characters of discharge are deemed as meeting the definition of not honorable service and are considered dishonorable and, in most cases, not eligible for most or any benefits (Szymendera, 2016).

DD Form 214 (Certificate of Release or Discharge from Active Service)

Upon discharge from the military, every service member receives a DD Form 214 (DD214), the Certificate of Release or Discharge from Active Service. This is the primary document requested by any entity for official evidence of discharge from military service. The DD214 contains within it items such as the name of the service member, start and end date of military service, any military schools attended, military awards and designation, dates and locations of deployment such as to a war zone, rank, and most importantly block 24 (Characterization of service), 26 (Separation code), 27 (Reentry code), and 28 (Narrative Reason for Separation), as these affect any future benefits eligibility for benefits along with time on active service. The information contained in the DD214 could affect the rest of a service member's life as a veteran and civilian in the form of benefits and civilian opportunities (Tayyeb, 2017).

The Character of Discharge and Associated Veteran Benefits

It is important to understand the character of the discharge as it relates to the service

SAMPLE DD 214 FORM

CERTIFICATE OF RELEASE OR DISCHARGE FROM ACTIVE DUTY

1 Name	2 Department, component, and branch		3 Social security number
4a Grade, rate, or rank	B Pay grade	5 Date of birth	6 Reserve obligation termination date

7a Place of entry into active duty

b Home at time of record

NOTE FROM THE MDHE: *This section will help determine if the veteran was a* ***Missouri resident*** *at the time he or she entered the service.*

8a Last duty assignment and major command

b Station where separated

9 Command to which transferred

10 SLGI Coverage None
Amount:

11 P

NOTE FROM THE MDHE: *This section will help determine if the veteran served* ***after September 11, 2001****.*

12 Record of service	Year(s)	Month(s)	Day(s)
a Date entered ad this period			
b Separation date this period			
c Net active service this period			
d Total prior active service			
e Total prior inactive service			
f Foreign service			
g Sea service			
h Effective date of pay grade			

13 Decorations, medals, badges, citations, and campaign ribbons awarded or authorized

NOTE FROM THE MDHE: *This section will help determine whether the veteran* ***served in armed combat****.*

14 Military education

15 a Member contributed to post-Vietnam era educational assistance program
b High school graduate or equivalent

16 Days accrued leave

17 Member was provided complete dental examination and all appropriate dental services and treatment within 90 days prior to separation

18 Remarks

NOTE FROM THE MDHE: *This section will help determine whether the veteran served* ***in armed combat****.*

This section may contain references to the geographic region where the veteran served or references to service in support of Operating Enduring Freedom ("OEF") or Operation Iraqi Freedom ("OIF").

19 a Mailing address after separation

b Nearest relative

20 Member requests copy 6 be sent to

21 Signature of member

22 Official authorized to sign

Special Additional Information

23 Type of separation

24 Character of service

NOTE FROM THE MDHE: *This section will help determine if the veteran was discharged* ***under honorable conditions****.*

25 Separation authority	26 Separation code	27 Reentry code

28 Narrative of reason for separation

NOTE FROM THE MDHE: *This section may contain information relevant to the determination of whether the veteran was discharged* ***under honorable conditions****.*

29 Dates of time lost during this period

30 Member requests copy 4

DD FORM 214

Figure 8-1 Sample Certificate of Release or Discharge from Active Duty.

Reproduced from Department of Defense. (n.d.). *DD Form 214: Certificate of release or discharge from active duty.* https://dhewd.mo.gov/ppc/documents/sampleDD214.pdf

member. Under Title 38—U.S.C., Veterans' Benefits (2020), as it defines the term *veteran*, it stipulated that a discharge must be "under conditions other than dishonorable." The characteristics of discharge are set as two general categories of Administrative (Honorable, General Discharge, and Other Than Honorable) and Punitive (Bad Conduct and Dishonorable). It is important to have a general understanding of the characterization because the VA conducts its services based on the characterization of discharge and its interpretation of the charge given to them by Congress.

Honorable Discharge

An honorable discharge is a form of administrative discharge indicating an individual has received a good to an excellent rating in the performance of their duty and has completed their contracted obligated service or is retiring from military service. This type of discharge can also be awarded to individuals who are no longer needed for their service and being separated involuntarily but still meeting high-performance ratings or are no longer able to complete their service due to various reasons such as medical or family hardships. In most cases, Medical-Under Honorable Conditions discharges are also considered honorable discharges, but due to a medical issue or disability, the service member was unable to continue with their military service. Most honorable discharges come with full VA benefits and eligibility for any other qualifying state or local benefits.

General Discharge

General discharge, also known as discharge under honorable conditions or administrative discharge, is one step below an honorable discharge and is mostly associated with having served satisfactorily and service has been less than exemplary during an obligated service. This type of discharge is awarded to individuals who may have had difficulty adjusting to a military career and often have frequent minor infractions and disciplinary action due to behavior, conduct, drug or alcohol abuse, and even some issues related to an injury and illness. The general discharge is awarded by the unit commander and is very much a subjective discharge based on the commander's discretion. Although viewed as under honorable conditions, this discharge does establish barriers to receiving full veteran benefits such as educational benefits.

A Discharge Under Other Than Honorable Conditions (OTH)

Also known as an undesirable discharge, OTH discharges are the most severe character of the administrative type of discharge that may be awarded to a service member by a unit commander without the involvement of a court martial. This type of discharge is awarded for actions that may have resulted in punishment by the civilian court system or conduct that may have discredited the military branch. Service members are allotted the benefit of an administrative discharge board and have the right to have their case heard. Service members receiving an OTH also are informed and sign an understanding of "substantial prejudice in civilian life" (Oregon Department of Veterans Affairs, n.d.). An OTH is often viewed as a less than honorable service and disqualifies the service member in many cases from enlisting in most, if not all, veteran benefits as the VA deems the OTH as not honorable service. Although the VA did place certain emergency physical and mental health provisions in place for this population of veterans in 2019, the award of an OTH in itself often acts as a barrier to seeking veteran benefits (Tayyeb, 2017)

Bad Conduct Discharge (BCD)

Also, commonly referred to in the military as the Big Chicken Dinner, the first of the punitive military characters of discharge is the BCD awarded by a special or general court martial. This punitive discharge is not awarded until the service member has had an opportunity to appeal to the court's decision and complete any military prison sentencing. The BCD is viewed as not honorable service, and in most cases, all veteran benefits are forfeited.

Dishonorable Discharge (DD)

A DD is the strongest form of punitive discharge from the US military. It is awarded only by a court martial for the most serious offenses such as murder, sexual assault, desertion, and Absent Without Leave (AWOL). A DD carries with it a lifetime of barriers and stigma. Once service members are awarded a DD, they are not considered a veteran under the law and thus lose rights to any veteran benefits. A person with a DD is also prohibited from many federal, state, and local opportunities and benefits, such as voting, owning firearms, educational loans, and grants, and are often discriminated against by employers that conduct background checks on their employees. When disclosed, these individuals cannot receive any government assistance and are unable to receive bank loans.

Bad Paper

In general, the term *bad paper* refers to the Other Than Honorable discharge. However, the term *bad paper* may be used in describing several characters of discharge. Bad papers must include discharge papers classified as Other Than Honorable, Bad Conduct, or Dishonorable discharges to be more representative of the veterans with such discharges. It should be noted based on the perceptions of the service members, a negative narrative on an honorable discharge or simply having a general discharge under honorable conditions may still be perceived as a bad paper (Tayyeb, 2017).

Taking Care of the Veteran Community

The history of taking care of "soldiers" dates back to 1636. The Plymouth Colony, which was at war with the Pequot Indians, passed a law ensuring soldiers who were disabled due to the conflict were taken care of by the colonists. Such actions were duplicated in 1776 through pensions for disabled soldiers during the Revolutionary War and enhanced through domiciliary and medical facilities for veterans in 1811 (VA, 2021).

The Civil War brought state-level benefits by establishing veterans' homes, which included some medical and hospital services. However, it wasn't until WWI that a comprehensive federal veterans program was established to aid and provide more comprehensive health and benefits services through what would become the Veterans Benefits Administration (VBA), VHA, and the National Cemetery Administration (NCA) (VA, 2021).

Today, the VHA is one of the world's largest healthcare systems and is now operating over 100 VA Medical Centers and over 1,000 outpatient sites (VA, 2021).

Eligibility for Care

The Mission of VHA-sponsored programs is primarily focused on providing medical care and treatment, first to veterans with service-connected injuries and then, under certain conditions, to other veterans whose medical needs are not directly related to their military service. The basic eligibility to qualify for VA programs and services is contingent on meeting the VA criteria for care and being placed in a VA priority group.

In the days before health insurance or Medicare, the 20 million World War II and Korean veterans relied on the VA for most healthcare. As a rule, economic status or "line of duty" connections, required by law, were not questioned. For decades, the veterans of those wars had become firmly ensconced in the system and were proficient at managing the process. However, after more than 10 years of war in Vietnam and worldwide deployments, of 8.7 million Americans, many were returning home with devastating injuries and traumatic memories. Despite this influx, Congress

Box 8-1 Am I Eligible for VA Health Care Benefits?

You may be eligible for VA healthcare benefits if you served in the active military, naval, or air service and didn't receive a dishonorable discharge.

- **If you enlisted after September 7, 1980, or entered active duty after October 16, 1981**, you must have served 24 continuous months or the full period for which you were called to active duty, unless any of the descriptions below are true for you.

The minimum duty requirement may not apply if any of these are true. You:

- Were discharged for a disability that was caused—or made worse—by your active-duty service, **or**
- Were discharged for a hardship or "early out," **or**
- Served prior to September 7, 1980

- **If you're a current or former member of the Reserves or National Guard**, you must have been called to active duty by a federal order and completed the full period for which you were called or ordered to active duty. If you had or have active duty status for training purposes only, you don't qualify for VA health care.

US Department of Veterans Affairs. (2020, August). *Disability compensation for conditions related to military sexual trauma*. https://www.benefits.va.gov/BENEFITS/factsheets/serviceconnected/MST.pdf

did not increase the VA budget. These veterans had to wait months and years to even access the system, with many never accessing the system due to distrust of the federal government and the era's anti-war movement.

It was not until 1986 that Congress enacted legislation that required a "means test" for veterans who did not have "service-connected disabilities." To address this proliferating problem, the VA set up Enrollment Priority Groups to ensure veterans with the most severe injuries or needs were given preference for care. Based on the veteran's specific eligibility status or percent of disability, they become qualified for a specific Priority Group and access to care.

Enrollment Priority Groups

(US Department of Veteran Affairs, 2017)

Priority Group 1

- Veterans with VA-rated service-connected disabilities 50% or more disabling
- Veterans determined by the VA to be unemployable due to service-connected conditions

Priority Group 2

- Veterans with VA-rated service-connected disabilities 30% or 40% disabling

Priority Group 3

- Veterans who are former prisoners of war (POWs)
- Veterans awarded the Purple Heart Medal
- Veterans whose discharge was for a disability that was incurred or aggravated in the line of duty
- Veterans with VA-rated service-connected disabilities 10% or 20% disabling
- Veterans awarded special eligibility classification under Title 38, U.S.C. §1151, "benefits for individuals disabled by treatment or vocational rehabilitation."
- Veterans awarded the Medal of Honor (MOH)

Priority Group 4

- Veterans who are receiving aid and attendance or house-bound benefits from the VA
- Veterans who have been determined by the VA to be catastrophically disabled

Priority Group 5

- Nonservice-connected veterans and noncompensable service-connected veterans rated 0% disabled by the VA with annual income and/or net worth below the VA national income limit and geographically adjusted income limit for their resident location.

- Veterans receiving VA pension benefits
- Veterans eligible for Medicaid programs

Priority Group 6

- Compensable 0% service-connected veterans
- Veterans exposed to ionizing radiation during atmospheric testing or during the occupation of Hiroshima and Nagasaki
- Project 112/SHAD participants
- Veterans who served in the Republic of Vietnam between January 9, 1962, and May 7, 1975
- Veterans of the Persian Gulf War that served in the Southwest Asia Theater of combat operations between August 2, 1990, and November 11, 1998
- *Veterans who served on active duty at Camp Lejeune for no fewer than 30 days beginning January 1, 1957, and ending December 31, 1987
- Veterans who served in a theater of combat operations after November 11, 1998, as follows: Currently enrolled veterans and new enrollees who were discharged from active duty on or after January 28, 2003, are eligible for the enhanced benefits for five years post-discharge
  Note: At the end of this enhanced enrollment priority group placement time period, veterans will be assigned to the highest Priority Group (PG) their unique eligibility status at that time qualifies for.
  *Note: While eligible for PG 6, until system changes are implemented, you would be assigned to PG 7 or 8, depending on your income.

Priority Group 7

- Veterans with gross household income below the geographically adjusted income limit (GMT) for their resident location and who agree to pay co-pays

Priority Group 8

- Veterans with gross household incomes above the VA national income limit and the geographically adjusted income limit for their resident location and who agree to pay co-pays

Veterans eligible for enrollment: Non-compensable 0% service-connected and:

- Sub-priority a: Enrolled as of January 16, 2003, and who have remained enrolled since that date and/or placed in this sub-priority due to changed eligibility status
- Sub-priority b: Enrolled on or after June 15, 2009, whose income exceeds the current VA National Income Limits or VA National Geographic Income Limits by 10% or less

Veterans eligible for enrollment: Nonservice-connected and:

- Sub-priority c: Enrolled as of January 16, 2003, and who have remained enrolled since that date and/or placed in this sub-priority due to changed eligibility status
- Sub-priority d: Enrolled on or after June 15, 2009, whose income exceeds the current VA National Income Limits or VA National Geographic Income Limits by 10% or less

Veterans eligible for enrollment: Veterans not meeting the criteria above:

- Sub-priority e: Non-compensable 0% service-connected (eligible for care of their SC condition only)
- Sub-priority f: Nonservice-connected

Veteran Benefits vs. Entitlements

The US government does not proactively help its veteran community. Although most veterans are eligible for benefits, such as housing loan assistance, education, and health care, the government does not proactively help the individual veteran. The veteran has to know the difference between benefits and entitlements. Unfortunately, most veterans are unaware of the difference, and they assume it is automatic or easily obtained. An example would be:

Paul is a veteran under Section 101 (2) and is eligible to apply for a VA Home Loan Guarantee. Paul would like to access this benefit and applies. The VA will then look to see if Paul "was on active duty," "has an honorable discharge," "Does he have a minimum of two years of service?" "Does he have the good credit?" and "does he have the right down payment?" Once Paul has met all those criteria, he becomes entitled to the benefit, and the government is obligated to pay.

Now, using that simple example, let us apply it to disability benefits. As a veteran, is Paul eligible to apply for disability benefits? Yes. Does the government tell him he is eligible? No. It is inferred. However, Paul has to apply in order to secure his entitlement. At this point, Paul is expected to fill out multiple forms and submit the evidence to show that he is entitled to collect the benefit. This process is complicated, and veterans must be encouraged to seek proper assistance (more on this in available resources). As a response to Paul's claim to his benefits, the VA will ensure that he is entitled, as it does not want to dispense compensation improperly.

When the VA makes a mistake in dispensing compensation, almost 100% of the time, the error is against the veteran. Out of 1.5 million disability claims filed per year, there are about 10 instances of fraud committed by the veteran. However, the VA may make upwards of 150,000 thousand errors where the VA improperly gave the veteran the incorrect number of benefits.

The primary reason for VA errors has to do with the veterans not submitting all of the required evidence to confirm that they are entitled to the benefit, keeping in mind the onus is really on the veteran to provide all the evidence.

Is Paul eligible for VA health care? Yes, because he is a veteran. Is Paul entitled to it? He has to apply and be approved.

Are veterans eligible for homeless assistance? As a veteran, Yes. Do they need to apply for those benefits? The answer is, again, Yes.

As you can see, although many veterans are presumed eligible for benefits, they are required to apply for those benefits, provide evidence, and await the decision of the VA to either approve or deny disbursement of entitlements.

The VHA Claims and Appeals

Claims

It is highly recommended for a veteran to seek assistance in processing their VA claim for the best outcomes. At the beginning of this chapter, we talked about a couple of phrases healthcare providers should know. Here is where one of them comes into play: "I don't know, but here is whom you should contact." Veterans receive minimal information upon discharge and often do not seek out their VA benefits. Because resources are limited, and the VA is not in every town in the country, several avenues exist for the veteran to seek assistance in starting their claims process. In general, the VA has Regional Offices in all US states, Puerto Rico, and the Philippines. These regional offices have paid trained staff to assist the veteran in developing their claim by obtaining relevant federal service records and medical evidence (Manker, 2020). The VA claims filed only require the veteran to provide evidence. The VA is not in the business of disproving the evidence provided by the veteran. They only substantiate the evidence, process the information provided, and issue their decision. Unfortunately, it does become complicated and cumbersome when the documentation and evidence are missing or incomplete, completed incorrectly, or do not support the claim. Again, this is where expert assistance is invaluable.

With the understanding that the VA regional centers are not readily accessible to all veterans, there are more accessible resources for veterans in Veteran Service Organizations (VSOs). These organizations may be more familiar to you as the American Legion, Veterans of Foreign Wars (VFW), Amvets, Vietnam Veterans of America, Disabled American Veterans (DAV), Paralyzed Veterans of America. These VSOs have both trained and accredited Veteran Service Officers who can assist and provide expertise on navigating through the VA claims system. Although many of these service officers primarily assist in VA disability benefits, they can provide information on other benefits. The veterans must end up with an accredited Service Officer.

As a healthcare provider, it is important to know the number of the VA regional center or at least the nearest VSO Service Officer, so they may provide expertise and advocacy on the veteran's behalf. So when you say, "I don't know, but here is whom you should contact. Their name is ________________ and their number is ______________________." It should be noted that although VSO memberships are exclusive and not every veteran qualifies to join, Accredited Service Officers assist ALL veterans regardless of the discharge status or membership with the organization.

It is important for the veteran to know what benefits they are asking for and to be specific. Without specificity as to what the veteran is expecting, the claim can take years to process and face multiple denials.

There are exceptions to this claims process to receive health benefits from the VHA. One of those exceptions is the Combat Veteran Eligibility (VA, 2011). On January 28, 2008, Public Law 110-181 titled the "National Defense Authorization Act of 2008" was signed into law. Section 1707 amended Title 38, U.S.C., Section 1710(e)(3), extending the period of eligibility for health care for veterans who served in a theater of combat operations after November 11, 1998, (commonly referred to as combat veterans or OEF/OIF Veterans or to the recently established Operation New Dawn Veterans). Under the "Combat Veteran" authority, the VA provides cost-free healthcare services and nursing home care for conditions possibly related to military service and enrollment in PG6, unless eligible for enrollment in a higher priority group.

Combat veterans who were discharged or released from active service on or after January 28, 2003, are now eligible to enroll in the VA healthcare system for five years from the date of discharge or release. Note: The five-year enrollment period applicable to these veterans begins on the discharge or separation date of the service member from active-duty military service, or in the case of multiple call-ups, the most recent discharge date (VA, 2011, & Title 38 U.S.C. §1710, 2020).

Additional exceptions include times a veteran may be in a mental health crisis.

Appeal Options for Disability Claims

The appeals process exists to give the veteran additional opportunities to receive benefits after the VA has denied a claim. The Board of Veteran Appeals (BVA) conducts an independent review of the claim and "must follow all applicable statutes, VA regulations, and precedent opinions of the Office of General Counsel. The BVA is responsible for making the final decision on behalf of the VA" (Manker, 2020, p. 61). The veteran may also further appeal their claim upon an unsatisfactory judgment made by the BVA to the US Court of Appeals for Veterans Claims (CAVC). "The US Court of Appeals for the Federal Circuit has exclusive limited jurisdiction to review legal (but not factual) determinations of the CAVC" (Manker, 2020, p. 613).

The Veteran Appeals Improvement and Modernization Act of 2017 became law on August 23, 2017 (Pub L. 115-55). It is also known as the Appeals Modernization Act. Specifically, the bill requires the VA to assist with a disability claim or supplemental claim up until a veteran claimant is provided notice of a decision. The bill also requires the VA to provide a notice of decision to veterans regarding decisions affecting the provision of benefits that includes specific information, such as a summary of the applicable laws and an explanation of how to obtain evidence used in making the decision. Additionally, the VA must assist a veteran during a higher-level review if an adjudicator identifies an error on the part of the agency of original jurisdiction. The new law includes three options for disagreements with decisions on a disability claim. These options include (1) higher-level review by a more senior claims adjudicator, (2) supplemental claim of new or relevant evidence to support the disability claim, and (3) direct appeal to the Board of Veteran Appeals.

Service-Connected Disability

Service-Connected Disability is an injury or illness that resulted in a disability while serving in the US Armed Forces.

> 38 CFR § 3.303. Principles Relating to Service Connection. (Legal Information Institute, n.d.-a)
> (a) General. Service connection . . . means that the facts, shown by evidence, establish that a particular illness or injury resulting in disability was incurred coincides with service in the Armed Forces, or if preexisting such service, was aggravated therein. This may be accomplished by affirmatively showing inception or aggravation during service or through the application of statutory presumptions. Each disabling condition shown by a veteran's service records, or for which he seeks a service connection must be considered based on the places, types, and circumstances of his service as shown by service records, the official history of each organization in which he served, his medical records and all pertinent medical and lay evidence. Determinations as to service connection will be based on the review of the entire evidence of record, with due consideration to the Department of Veterans Affairs policy to administer the law under a broad and liberal interpretation consistent with the facts in each individual case.

According to P. Sullivan (personal communication, November 13, 2020) and Manker (2020), to qualify for such disability compensation, a veteran must show there currently exists:

1. A current disability.
2. An illness or injury incurred or aggravated in-service.
3. A link, or nexus, between the current disability and in-service illness or injury, is shown by the evidence, or:
   a. Medical nexus opinion (private doctor/therapist).
   b. Chronicity and continuity; or
   c. Continuous symptoms since discharge.

Disability Rating and Priority Systems of Care

One of the most controversial yet essential aspects of the VA's mission has become Disability Compensation Benefits. In essence, this program is the "Workman's Compensation" component for military members. Since service members cannot sue the government for disability related to military service, this

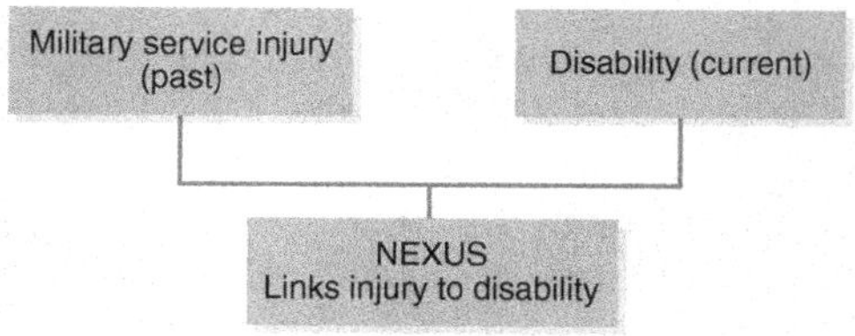

Figure 8-2 Service-connected disability.

process serves as the compensation mechanism. This process of determining eligibility can begin any time after the veteran leaves active military duty and "files a claim" with the Veterans Benefits Administration (VBA). It should be emphasized that the veteran must initiate this process and be specific about what they are seeking compensation for. Compensable service-connected disabilities range widely in severity and type. Some of the most common conditions noted are loss of limbs, hypertension, post-traumatic stress disorder, cancers, and a vast array of related conditions.

VA Criteria for Disability-Priority Treatment Groups

Specific regulations and VA policies guide claims for Disability Ratings linked to duty; compensation can also be granted for common conditions during the veteran's military service, such as hearing loss, sinusitis, and prostate cancers. All claims require physical exams, supporting evidence, and corroborative statements to assure there is an association with veterans' time in the military. The rating is linked to the clinical severity of a veteran's condition and decisions rendered to veterans with the same conditions. Rating specialists review the physical and psychological examinations and assign a composite rating, expressed as a percent of disability. Percentages are used to estimate how much the disability affects "quality of life," mastery of activities of daily living, and employability.

Additionally, the percent of disability also determines the amount of compensation provided each month. This "compensation" is meant to offset the average earnings lost due to the disabilities, whether or not a particular veteran's condition has reduced his or her earnings or interfered with their quality of life (US Department of Veteran Affairs, 2018).

Additionally, the percent of disability also determines eligibility for other VA benefits and support. For example, a veteran who sustained a head injury with residual loss of coordination and function of the left side, including upper and lower extremities, could receive a rating of 50% for that condition. If there was a loss of vision in the left eye, another 20% might be added. Seizures that require medication could add another 50%. The highest percent that can be authorized is 100% regardless of the 120% that was calculated. Veterans are required to return periodically for reassessments of their conditions. If a veteran received a 100% rating for cancers associated with Agent Orange exposure and recovers completely, the disability rating would be discontinued. Likewise, if conditions become more severe, additional assessments can also increase the percentage of disability. Once a veteran becomes 100% "Total and Permanent," the VA provides more support services commensurate with the veteran's needs. The percent of disability also determines "Priority for Treatment," which is sometimes used to allow access to care.

In addition to the disability ratings, veterans are also eligible for health care if they are financially indigent, based on Medicaid eligibility. In cases of financial difficulties, the VA also administers a "War Time Service Pension," which is a tax-free income paid to wartime veterans (or surviving spouses) who are (a) 65 years old or older (anyone over age 65 is automatically deemed disabled); (b) meet the VA limited income and asset test, and (c) served at least one day of active duty during a time of war (38 U.S.C.1513) (Legal Information Institute, n. d.-b). Payments are made in the form of monthly annuities and typically continue until death.

Other Than Honorable Discharges

Challenges to Title 38 U.S.C. and VA policy have focused on the fact that "Other-Than-Honorable" (OTH), also known as "Bad Paper" discharges, were being used to disqualify veterans from receiving any VA benefits or care. In the post-9/11 era, there are numerous instances where veterans who received an "OTH discharge, with extenuating circumstances, such as injuries or disabilities incurred while in the military, that may have contributed to the behaviors or circumstances that resulted in an OTH discharge. While the term seems fairly straightforward, it is generally applied to situations where there is a "significant departure" from expected military services that members conduct. "Acts of Omissions" could also be grounds for OTH discharges. However, this administrative characterization of discharge, often viewed by the VA as not honorable and subsequent denial of benefits, is not a dishonorable discharge.

More importantly for healthcare providers, "An individual with an *'Other than Honorable' discharge that VA has determined to be disqualifying under application of title 38 CFR §3.12 still retains eligibility for VA health care benefits for service incurred or service-aggravated disabilities unless he or she is subject to one of the statutory bars to benefits set forth in Title 38 United States Code §5303(a). Authority: Section 2 of Public Law 95-126 (October 8, 1977)*" (Department of Veterans Affairs, 2008).

The VA is charged with reviewing the entire record of a veteran and making a compassionate determination regarding access to VA healthcare programs and services. Based on reports from individuals, law firms, and advocates, claims are easily denied for the smallest errors and sometimes even with no errors. It is extremely important that the files being processed for benefits be completed with experts trained in assisting veterans with VA claims. Also, although the VA may grant benefits to the service member, it may not change the characterization of the discharge as this is a separate process, completed through a discharge review board with oversight by specific branches of the military, and not in the purview of the VA. It is important to know that many veterans in dire need do not attempt to access VA health care because of the original denial or the stigma associated with the "character of their discharge." Many service members could be eligible for benefits due to state and federal agencies' revisions of eligibility requirements to extend benefits and services to these veterans. An example of this would be service members discharged during the "don't ask, don't tell" era where over 100,000 veterans were discharged due to their sexual orientation or gender identification, subsequently ineligible for benefits. However, since the repeal of this discriminatory policy, many service members have never returned to the VA system.

Treatment for mental health conditions may be provided under VA's tentative eligibility authority (38 CFR § 17.34) to an individual with an OTH discharge who presents to the VA seeking mental health care in emergency circumstances for a condition the former service member asserts is related to military service. For non–mental health conditions, the VA may provide emergent treatment under the VA's humanitarian care authority at 38 U.S.C. 1784. In instances where a former service member's eligibility is not yet established, the former service member must sign a VA Form 119, Report of Contact, stating that if he or she is subsequently found to be NOT eligible for VA health care, they agree to pay the Humanitarian Rate for any emergent care or services provided. (VA, 2017, p. 2)

Barriers to Benefitted Entitlements

There are many reasons why a veteran may be denied benefits. Some of these barriers, such as the character of discharge, were already mentioned. The veteran simply does not meet the VA criteria to provide the veteran their entitlement due to discharge status. However, one of the largest barriers remains the veterans themselves. They insist on completing the required forms independent of expert help and simply cannot navigate the VA system effectively, resulting in missed and missing documentation, missing forms, and unawareness of their eligibility. Other factors that also play a large role is the VA will simply not meet their duty by failing to do their part in processing the claim properly and diligently. Other barriers include homelessness, rural living and unable to access the needed VA resources, poor experience during military service, mental health, post-traumatic stress disorder, traumatic brain injuries, and missing evidence or records often lead to claims not being processed or denied (P. Sullivan, personal communication, November 13, 2020).

Resources

Many resources exist for the veteran community; however, the veteran is expected to seek them out. Very few communities in the United States actively seek out veterans. For example, California developed the veteran designation on the ID or driver's license as an incentive to have more veterans meet with Service Officers.

The state of Texas has community-based benefits and free education for self-identified veterans. Also they have the Military Veterans Peer Network that proactively seeks out veterans in the community. However, such programs are not in every community and state. As a result, many veterans are expected to navigate their way to available resources.

A great place to start is the US Department of Veteran Affairs. The site is full of information that both veterans and healthcare providers will find valuable. Also every veteran must be provided with the Veteran Crisis Line 1-800-273-8255 (Press 1).

Figure 8-3 Veteran designation on a driver's license.

Other national resources should include:

- The latest edition of the *VA Federal Benefits for Veterans, Dependents, and Survivors* handbook. Available through the VA and online.
- Veteran Service Organizations
  - The American Legion
    - https://www.legion.org/
  - Veterans of Foreign Wars
    - https://www.vfw.org/
  - Amvets
    - https://amvets.org/
  - Vietnam Veterans of America
    - https://vva.org/
  - Disabled American Veterans
    - https://www.dav.org/
  - Paralyzed Veterans of America
    - https://pva.org/
- State and Local Veteran Resources
  - States, counties, and cities have veteran specific resources that are often available to assist veterans in various manners. Local information must be collected and available if you need to provide local resources to a veteran.

Military Sexual Trauma

Sexual assault and harassment remain a significant concern within the US military forces. The VA refers to military sexual trauma (MST) as "sexual assault or repeated, threatening sexual harassment experienced during their military service" (VA MST, 2020).

According to the VA MST (2020) fact sheet, 1 in 3 women and 1 in 50 men receiving

Veterans Crisis Line
1-800-273-8255 PRESS 1

Figure 8-4 Veteran's crisis line

Courtesy of U.S. Department of Veterans Affairs.

care from the VA reported having experienced MST. Considering the VA serves only about a third of the veteran population and many such incidences go unreported, the numbers of MST survivors can be significantly higher among veterans.

The VA has made great strides in removing barriers to veterans seeking care related to MST. Every VA has a designated MST Coordinator to assist veterans seeking care related to MST, has taken steps to proactively identify MST survivors during screenings and assessments, ensured care related to MST is at no cost to the veteran, able to receive this care even if not eligible for VA services, and offers both inpatient and outpatient services at some VAs.

Some barriers still exist for MST survivors within the VA system. At some VA facilities, services are not segregated by gender, leading to some MST survivors hesitant or reluctant to seek or participate in therapeutic group activities. The VA has also not been as open to granting disability benefits related to PTSD to MST survivors. With a larger number of women than men diagnosed with PTSD related to MST, women are disproportionately impacted by a higher number of denials for disability benefits. Men claiming PTSD related to MST are also more likely to be denied their claim compared to PTSD related to combat. However, the VA seems more inclined to accept diagnoses related to "major depressive disorders and anxiety disorders not otherwise specified," diagnoses related to the MST experience, to grant disability benefits (Veterans Legal Services Clinic, 2013, p. 1).

MST survivors often face barriers to disability claims because of standards in place by the VA for "service-connected" injury. Although barriers for service connection for PTSD related to combat have been significantly relaxed, PTSD related to MST remains scrutinized, and claims often denied due to lack of corroborating evidence and missing or destroyed documentation by the Department of Defense (Veterans Legal Services Clinic, 2013, p. 3).

Although the VA does encourage MST survivors with claims denied before 2018 to resubmit their claims due to new training of staff (VA, 2020), this process remains problematic, according to veteran representatives (personal communication, 2020).

Also consider that some veterans may not seek or may be hesitant to receive VA care. The VA is a reminder of the military institution and environment many MST survivors left due to their sexual assault and harassment. Also, service members may have been stigmatized and forced to leave the military due to their experience, even labeled with mental health disorders such as personality disorders or adjustment disorders after their sexual assault or harassment by the military. Such diagnosis often leads to a denial of care by the VA because it is labeled as a preexisting (pre-military) condition. (Tayyeb, 2017)

According to the VA, survivors of MST should take the following steps to file a claim related to MST.

- Apply online at https://www.va.gov.
- Appoint an accredited VSO to help file the claim.
- Complete VA Form 21-526EZ, Veteran's Application for Compensation and/or Pension. Find this form online at https://www.vba.va.gov/pubs/forms/VBA-21-526EZ-ARE.pdf.
- Contact a VBA MST Outreach Coordinator to help with the claim process.
- Female and male VBA MST Outreach Coordinators are available at all local, regional benefits offices. Veterans may visit https://www.benefits.va.gov/benefits/mstcoordinators.asp or call 1-800-827-1000 to locate one near them.

References

Authenticated U.S. Government Information. (1996). *Public Law 104-262*. https://www.congress.gov/104/plaws/publ262/PLAW-104publ262.pdf

Congressional Research Service Report. (2019, October). Introduction to Veterans Health Care. Prepared by S. Panangala & J. Sussman, *Congressional Research Service* IF 10555. https://crsreports.congress.gov

Department of Veterans Affairs. (2008). *Other than honorable discharges: Impact on eligibility for VA health care benefits*. https://www.westpalmbeach.va.gov/combat_veterans/oth_discharge_fact_sheet.pdf

Department of Veterans Affairs. (2011). *Combat veteran eligibility*. https://www.va.gov/healthbenefits/assets/documents/publications/ib-10-438_combat_veteran_eligibility.pdf

Department of Veterans Affairs. (2017, May). *Other than honorable discharge*. https://www.va.gov/healthbenefits/resources/publications/IB10-448_other_than_honorable_discharges5_17.pdf

Department of Veterans Affairs. (2018, August 6). VA history. https://www.va.gov/about_va/vahistory.asp

Legal Information Institute. (2020c, Dec 31). Character of Discharge, Title 38 CFR §3.12 https://www.law.cornell.edu/cfr/text/38/3.12

Legal Information Institute. (n.d.-b) *Veterans 65 years of age and older. Title 38 CFR §1513*. https://www.law.cornell.edu/cfr/text/38/3.303

Legal Information Institute. (n.d.). *Principles relating to service connection, Title 38 CFR §3.303*. https://www.law.cornell.edu/cfr/text/38/3.303

Manker, T. (2020). *VA handbook for veterans and advocates: How to file for VA benefits and appeal your claim*. Author House

Oregon Department of Veterans Affairs. (n.d.). *Military discharge in the United States*. http://www.oregon.gov/ODVA/docs/PDFs/Criminal_Justice_Portal/Military_discharge.pdf

Public Law No: 115-55 Veterans Appeals Improvement and Modernization Act of 2017. https://www.congress.gov/bill/115th-congress/house-bill/2288

Rothstein, M. A. (2008). Currents in contemporary ethics GINA, the ADA, and genetic discrimination in employment. *The Journal of Law, Medicine & Ethics*, *36*(4), 837–840.

Szymendera, S. D. (2016). *Who is a "Veteran"?—basic eligibility for Veterans' benefits*. https://fas.org/sgp/crs/misc/R42324.pdf.

Tayyeb, A. R. (2017). *The effect of the military character of discharge on reintegration into the civilian community: A phenomenological study* (Dissertations, 86). [Doctoral Dissertation, University of San Diego]. ProQuest Dissertations Publishing.

Title 38 US Code Chapter 11. (2013). *Veterans benefits: Compensation for service connected disabilities or death*. Government Printing Office.

US Census Bureau. (2017). *Veteran*. from https://www.census.gov/topics/population/veterans/about/glossary.html

US Department of Veteran Affairs. (2018). *VA benefits book*. DC, US Government Printing Office.

US Department of Veterans Affairs (2011). *Combat veterans' eligibility*. https://www.va.gov/healthbenefits/assets/documents/publications/ib-10-438_combat_veteran_eligibility.pdf

US Department of Veterans Affairs. (2020, August). *Disability compensation for conditions related to military sexual trauma*. https://www.benefits.va.gov/BENEFITS/factsheets/serviceconnected/MST.pdf

US Department of Veterans Affairs. (2020, November). *Military sexual trauma*. https://www.mentalhealth.va.gov/docs/mst_general_factsheet.pdf

US Department of Veterans Affairs. (2020). *VA priority groups*. https://www.va.gov/health-care/eligibility/priority-groups/

US Department of Veterans Affairs. (2021, March 26). *VA history*. https://www.va.gov/about_va/vahistory.asp

Veteran Benefits, Title 38 U.S.C. §101 et seq. (2020, December 31). https://uscode.house.gov/view.xhtml?req=granuleid:USC-prelim-title38-section101&num=0&edition=prelim#sourcecredit

Veteran Benefits, Title 38 U.S.C. §1710. (2020, December 31). https://uscode.house.gov/view.xhtml?req=(title:38%20section:1710%20edition:prelim)

Veteran, Public Employment, Civil Service, and Pensions. (2020, December 07). *Revised code of Washington*. http://apps.leg.wa.gov/RCW/default.aspx?cite=41.04.005

Veterans Legal Services Clinic. (2013). *Battle for benefits: VA discrimination against survivors of military sexual trauma*. https://www.aclu.org/sites/default/files/assets/lib13-mst-report-11062013.pdf

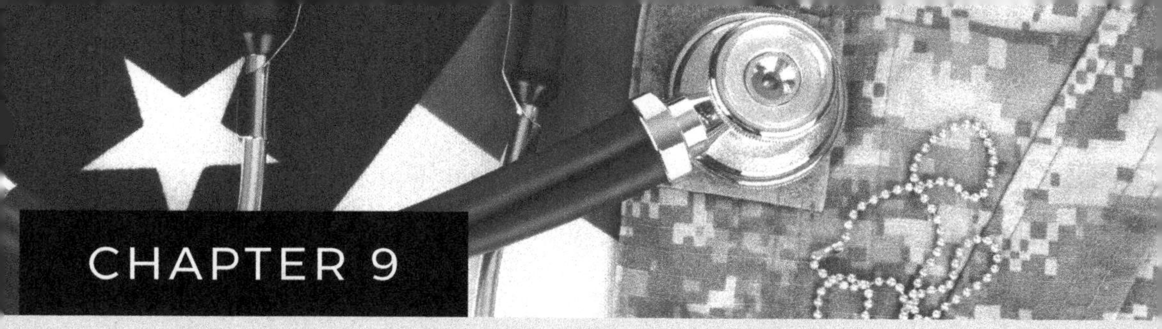

CHAPTER 9

The Use of Service, Emotional Support, and Companion Animals as a Complementary Health Approach for Military Veterans: Information for Healthcare Providers

Cheryl A. Krause-Parello, Allison E. Boyrer, S. Julianna Moreno, and Emma Meyer

"There is no psychiatrist in the world like a puppy licking your face" **—Bernard Williams**

Introduction

The use of animals for human needs dates back several millennia (Salter, 2018), with the human-animal bond being quite remarkable. During the last decade, it has become more widely accepted that pet ownership and animal assistance in therapy and education may have a multitude of positive effects on humans (Beetz et al., 2012). The social, emotional, and physical benefits of the human-animal bond is becoming more evident with research in military and veteran populations. (Krause-Parello et al., 2019; Krause-Parello & Morales, 2018; Krause-Parello, Levy et al., 2016; Owen et al., 2016) and anecdotal claims in the veteran population. More than half of the 3,000 American soldiers wounded in Iraq and Afghanistan have suffered from brain damage and, unfortunately, the trauma will have a permanent effect on their memory, mood, and behavior as well as their ability to think and work (Blech, 2006). Military veterans with post-traumatic stress disorder (PTSD) are increasingly seeking out complementary therapies such as psychiatric service dogs (LaFolette et al., 2019) to help alleviate some of these symptoms. Why is it then that the U.S. Department of the Army and the Veterans Administration support only dogs trained by an Assistance Dogs International (ADI) or International Guide Dog Federation (IGDF) accredited facility (Walther et al., 2017), organizations that focus predominantly on guide and mobility dogs? This chapter will explore service dogs, with some discussion of other support animals, such as an emotional support dog and companion animal, as alternative means of treatment, as well as defining their roles. We will also clarify the role of the healthcare provider, suggesting support of animal-assisted intervention as a complementary health approach.

Benefits of the Human-Animal Bond

The common thread between the three types of complementary therapies is the unique nature of the human-animal bond. The human-animal bond has been described as a relationship between people and animals that affects biological and psychosocial states of one another (Center for Human Animal Bond, 2019). In the case of small companion animals, this relationship likely goes back to the time of domestication of the dog some 35,000 years ago (Takashima & Day, 2014).

The common phrase *Dogs are man's best friend* comes from a long enduring history we share with our canine friends. Our relationship with domesticated companion animals has provided a long integration of attachment into our lives for generations. Over time, dogs have benefitted from us just as we have from them. Dog ownership has shown to benefit people in the aspects of psychological and physiological health (Westgarth et al., 2008). While simply owning a dog has shown a variety of health benefits for most people, specifically trained animals are capable of providing a more profound support for someone afflicted with mental and physical illnesses and disabilities. In the 19th century, animals were commonly found in mental health institutions and rehabilitation centers, and the English social reformist, statistician, and nurse Florence Nightingale advocated that the chronically ill should keep "a small pet" for an increased sense of well-being (Nightingale, 1969). The support and aid that a service animal provides is more distinct and particular to the needs of the person receiving the help than the support and companionship a pet may provide; service animals can perform tasks that are specific to the needs of the person with a disability, illness, or impairment. According to the Department of Justice of the United States, the Americans with Disabilities Act (ADA) states, "A service animal is defined as a dog that is individually trained to work or perform tasks for an individual with a disability" (U.S. Department of Justice, p. 1). Tasks that a service dog can be trained to fulfill—but are not limited to—include alerting the owner when they are having hallucinations, retrieving medications, opening doors, and comforting their owner when they are having a panic attack. By helping patients with their unique needs, service dogs provide their human owners with a supportive intervention that can help patients live a higher quality of life.

When administering care, it is essential for healthcare providers to realize the unique needs of their patients. Treatments that not only focus on the outcomes, but also rather the improvement and sustainability of a patient's health and well-being should be a significant factor in the care provided. Supplementary treatments to healthcare plans, such as the addition of a service dog, can greatly support many aspects of a patient's health. However, it is also the responsibility of the provider to consider the factors of their patients' lives to determine if the supplement of a service dog will actually benefit their health and well-being. Factors to consider can include a patient's ability to exercise, the financial means to provide for their animal's welfare, and housing accommodations. It is also important to assess whether a patient can truly benefit from owning a service dog. Patients dealing with the symptoms of depression or anxiety, such as veterans living with PTSD, may benefit from the assistance of a psychiatric service dog trained to help ease the symptoms in stressful or anxiety-inducing circumstances. Although a service dog may benefit one patient, the responsibility and obligations of being a service dog owner may not suit the needs of another. Thoughtful discussions and evaluations about the addition of a service dog should be consciously considered with care.

Service Animals: Beyond the Task

Service Animal Case Study*

U.S. Army member, First Sergeant Wilson, returned home from his first deployment overseas two months ago after being caught in an explosion due to an Improvised Explosive Device (IED). Wilson was hospitalized and treated for his injuries, but now suffers from chronic pain in his legs that makes walking for long periods of time difficult. Since returning home, First Sergeant Wilson's wife, Amanda, also noticed that he had been having moments of intense anxiety and nightmares in the middle of the night. After some encouragement from his family members, Wilson decided to attend mental health therapy. His provider diagnosed him with PTSD after a few sessions, and suggested owning a service dog to help him cope with some of the struggles he had been facing since returning home. Shortly after, First Sergeant Wilson and his wife adopted a beagle-poodle mix that they named Percy. They enrolled Percy in a service dog training course to help him learn how to assist First Sergeant Wilson in daily situations that require his support. Percy has since learned how to help alleviate some of the stress that comes with certain daily tasks for First Sergeant Wilson. Percy has also provided First Sergeant Wilson with the comfort he needs on days that feel especially difficult, whenever and wherever he may be needed.

For First Sergeant Wilson, Percy has been trained to interrupt flashbacks; helps prevent and assist during panic attacks; assists Wilson when walking, especially with stairs or other uneven levels; retrieves Wilson's pain medication when necessary; and performs a variety of other tasks that are unique to First Sergeant Wilson's needs. Percy not only acts as a reliable source of support, but he also provides a comforting sense of companionship to First Sergeant Wilson in his daily life. As a service dog, Percy also has needs that First Sergeant Wilson is expected to meet for his welfare. First Sergeant Wilson has since made more consistent efforts to go outside, exercise, and establish a day-to-day routine that also helps him care for Percy's needs, as well as his own; this beneficial relationship they share with one another has helped First Sergeant Wilson feel more fulfilled and intentional about his health choices. Percy has been able to effectively help First Sergeant Wilson live a better quality of life with his support, just as service dogs are meant to provide their human partners.

As healthcare providers, as well as veterans, the search for complementary alternative means that are effective treatment options for veterans has become increasingly sought after, and animal interventions have provided a source of support for veterans affected by the difficulties that have followed them home. Service dogs have shown that they support veterans in meeting their goals to reintegrate themselves into the civilian world, such as participating in the community or improving self-care (Crowe, 2018). This is especially helpful for veterans who suffer from the repercussions of trauma-related injuries, such as PTSD. As First Sergeant Wilson's experience with Percy revealed, service dogs can act as an intervention that helps improve the quality of life for patients suffering from combat-related wounds with unique needs. Their assistance with daily challenges provides relief and support to the aspects of life that are most affected, which provides the patient with more room to better care for themselves. The care of the service dog can also act as a means of establishing more healthy routines that encourage the welfare of both the human owner and animal, which can provide a sense of self-assurance and purpose.

Although owning a dog is clearly beneficial to a person's physiological and psychological health (Westgarth et al., 2008), attaining and maintaining a service dog comes with concomitant possible stressors, including public intrusiveness and confrontations with financial requirements and emotional travails. The ADA requires that both state and local governments provide protections that allow service dogs to access any location the general public is allowed to go. However, difficulties can still arise due to the public's general lack of awareness surrounding the law for service animals. For instance, employees of a business or entity may not ask an owner more than two specific questions about their service dog, which are (1) is the dog a service animal required because of a disability? and (2) what work or task has the dog been trained to perform? Asking the owner to demonstrate a task, for details about their disability, or for documentation of the service dog is not allowed under the ADA (U.S. Department of Justice, p. 2). Official certification and documentation does not exist for service dogs and emotional support animals (ESA) because of a lack of state- and national-level certifications, which can leave entities of the public to question the validity of an owner's need and use of a service dog. Some owners choose to buy their service animals equipment, such as vests and identification tags, to support their credibility, although it is not required by the law (U.S. Department of Justice, p. 2). There are also services that sell and provide owners with registration and certificates for their service dogs, however, the U.S. Department of Justice does not recognize, nor state, that these documents qualify as proof of a service animal. This minimal regulation was originally meant to provide owners with the ease to access acquiring a service animal, but it has created an advantage for individuals to abuse the law and register their pets as service animals to allow them to take them into any public space with them, which often invalidates the needs and use of true service animal owners with disabilities. In addition to the insufficient regulations for service animals, a service dog can be trained either by a professional training service or by the owner themselves. Although this is helpful for owners who may not be able to afford to enroll their dog into a professional training program, the lack of official certification can often foster a general sense of suspicion and doubt in the credibility of an owner's service dog among the public. Unfortunately, this uncertainty created by a lack of certification and regulation, in addition to lack of public awareness, can leave room for service dog owners with disabilities to possibly encounter discrimination and harassment from public entities that do not understand the use a service dog provides or their legal protections. The potential for public confrontation is worth considerable contemplation for those with social anxiety concerns often accompanying PTSD. At a minimum, patients utilizing service animals should be well prepared for such eventualities by their prescribing provider.

The process of attaining a service animal certainly comes with an abundance of tasks and obligations for the owner, which can be burdensome for veterans already suffering from the stress of combat-related wounds and traumatic injuries. Healthcare providers should be aware of these obligations, and whether or not it would benefit their patient. Service dogs must be trained to perform their duties and to behave in public. The type of training a dog receives is dependent on the service needed by the owner. For example, veteran patients living with PTSD may require their dog to be trained as a psychiatric service dog to support them through panic attacks and anxiety-inducing situations. Searching and paying for training classes that meet a patient's unique needs can be difficult if the owner is unable or does not know how to train their dog themselves. As a healthcare provider, it is important to note patients' needs while seeking alternative treatment options and advocate for the options that best support their health. Providers should be informed and aware of the obligations that are associated with alternative treatment options, especially when considering the ownership of a service dog. Owning a service dog can be a serious responsibility, for both the dog and owner. Thus, it is key for a healthcare provider to know their patient and evaluate whether or not they would be able to sufficiently handle that responsibility. We talk more about these responsibilities throughout this chapter.

In addition to their required training, owners must consider other aspects necessary for their service dogs. Owners must be able to provide their service dog with the appropriate living arrangements and care for the dog's general welfare. Due to the unique nature of the human-animal bond, emotional, financial, and physical stress come into play. Under the Fair Housing Act, service dog owners must be provided with reasonable accommodations to accomplish this (Humane Society of the United States, 2019) but are still held accountable for any damage to the residence caused by the dog. Because of this, some housing residencies may require service dog owners to complete paperwork that may indicate a medical need for the service dog. This can include paperwork that may ask for the approval from a medical doctor or licensed therapist for a patient's service dog, which can sometimes be difficult to attain from healthcare providers. Beyond the legal stressors, additional stressors come into play when prospective service animal owners are living communally with family or other groups. Providers should consider how the service animal could best be integrated in what may already be an emotionally charged or poor functioning home environment. With appropriate forethought to the choice and introduction of the service animal, negative consequences can be avoided and potentially the service animal can foster healing of fractured relationships.

The possible effect of stress due to the process of procuring a service dog should be a consideration for veterans suffering from combat wounds and trauma. Obtaining a service dog can be a substantial financial cost, but the stress of the process can also make it mentally and emotionally draining. Veteran patients may have to endure their symptoms for weeks or months to wait for the means of getting a service dog, although they already are in need of the support. Depending on the patient and their unique needs, some veterans may be denied financial reimbursement for dogs that provide them with assistance. Furthermore, a possible lack of resources available can prevent a veteran patient from attaining a service dog. This, along with a multitude of other factors, can make the tasks associated with service dog ownership overwhelming.

It is obvious that there are many factors to be considered in the process of attaining a service dog. There is no denying that a service dog can truly become a life-changing support for a veteran, and the costs in terms of concomitant stressors should be evaluated on a case-by-case basis for each veteran guided by their recommending provider. Owning a service dog can act as a conduit for healthy habits that also provides support in times of need. By simply owning a dog, many different areas of a person's health can benefit (Westgarth et al., 2008). By owning a service dog that is trained to meet the unique needs of a patient, the dog becomes an intervention for veterans living with traumatic injuries and combat wounds, which can help improve veteran's quality of life.

Emotional Support Animals: Salve for Hidden Wounds

Canines can provide numerous roles in the life of humans. One of the roles becoming more prevalent in society today is that of ESAs. In the first case study, Percy serves First Sergeant Wilson by performing a myriad of physical tasks such as retrieving medication and providing support while walking. The services Percy provides to First Sergeant Wilson by interrupting flashbacks and preventing/assisting during panic attacks fall into the domain of emotional support. Trauma can cause less obvious wounds to a person and ESAs can be trained to assist the person with specific emotional needs. The spectrum of support the animals provide is as broad as the symptoms that can be expressed, anything from bringing the person into the present, maintaining schedules of activity, providing a social buffer, having a vigilant partner while they sleep/stand down, and so forth. Unlike a service dog ESAs are not trained or certified to assist with a disability. Instead, these animals have the intention to build an environment of comfort and support for their owners. This can range from easing anxiety, loneliness, depression, etc. by the simple act of being present. Due to the recent arrival of ESAs throughout society, there is progress to be made in areas of education, research, and evolution. An ESA has a different route to end up in a home than a service dog or companion animal. As well, the laws, rights, and precautions in place for an ESA differ greatly from that of a service dog.

The process of obtaining an ESA begins in the office of a psychiatrist, psychologist, or even by recommendation from a family physician. While the patient may need recommendations to obtain this animal, there are no requirements for certifications or training for an ESA. Although there is no need to obtain certifications, many people spend money on fake certifications or vests and harnesses that create an official appearance. This is an unnecessary step that is considered illegal (Younggren et al., 2016) and can have disciplinary action by the state board of psychology (Younggren et al., 2016). However, this can be easily avoided with proper education and understanding of the role of an emotional support dog and due consideration to the individual patient to ameliorate the impact of stressors previously discussed.

More specifically with the lack of training and certifications, animals who are providing emotional support are not given rights of access under the Americans with Disabilities Act (ADA). While there is a lack of rights through the ADA, both the Airline Carrier Access Act (ACAA) and the Fair Housing Act (FHA) state that there must be reasonable accommodation for emotional support animals (Younggren et al., 2016). The support provided by the ACAA and FHA is dependent on a psychiatrist attesting to the need for an ESA. Most recently, many psychologists are being asked by their patients to certify their need to have a pet present in settings where the presence of the animal had previously been prohibited. This type of conduct is not without risk and can complicate psychotherapy if not properly handled. (Younggren et al., 2016). However, if an emotional support animal is beneficial to the treatment or lifestyle of their patient, it could be recommended by the psychiatrist. The treating therapist has a definitive role to provide assistance to the client along their journey to obtain an ESA and to address the potential stressors as they uniquely pertain to each client. This includes educating and informing them on the initial certification for disability, confirmation of other therapy treatments, as well as coordinating care with other healthcare providers.

Emotional Support Animals Case Study*

Airman First Class (A1C) Pete Bennet of the U.S. Air Force returns home from his six-month *deployment in Kuwait. He has been having some trouble sleeping and feels more lethargic since he has been back home. He is finding it harder to get out of bed in the morning and is on edge more than usual. After all, this is a major adjustment to experience. As he is adapting to his life back stateside he sees a post on social media for a scruffy floppy-eared dog that states, "Rescue Rocky for $25 today! Must find home by tomorrow!" He imagines life with a furry companion by his side and without a second thought drives to the shelter to pick up his new friend. Rocky comes home the next day with A1C Bennet. This is only the beginning of a blooming bond between the two. After a year goes by, A1C Bennet decides he wants to move to a bigger apartment. He dreams of a place where Rocky has more land to run on and maybe even a park nearby. He shortly finds the perfect place. The only problem is Rocky happens to be a German Shepherd, which places him on the apartment complex's list of "aggressive breeds." A1C Bennet does not know what to do; he just signed the lease yesterday. He explains to the apartment manager that Rocky serves as an emotional support dog and helps ease some of his symptoms of PTSD by acting as a measure of support. The apartment manager understands but explains he needs to fill out a form signed by a psychiatrist stating an official need for this dog. He takes a quick glance at the form and is immediately overwhelmed. The form is five pages long and he starts to worry that his need for Rocky will not be acknowledged. Hesitantly, A1C Bennet makes an appointment at the nearest psychiatrist's office. As he arrives at the psychiatrist's office he is skeptical and submerged in worry. He explains to the psychiatrist that Rocky makes him feel safe, calm, and provides a sense of relief. He is never without support when he has Rocky. The psychiatrist explains to A1C Bennet that the symptoms he is experiencing are associated with those of PTSD and anxiety. She recognizes his need for the emotional support animal and begins the process of aiding in his recovery. She recommends follow-up appointments and group therapy to assist in his process of recovery. The psychiatrist recognizes that this is a pivotal point in A1C Bennet's life and informs him of the initial certification for disability, confirmation of other treatments, and plans to work hand-in-hand with other healthcare providers to create the best plan of treatment. The psychiatrist will be A1C Bennet's greatest advocate in the future but also must remain objective to constantly reassess the necessity for an ESA. A1C Bennet receives the proper signatures on his paperwork and feels a sense of relief to begin creating a strong support system as he adjusts to life back home.*

Although ESAs have a separate process to obtain a successful relationship between the dog, owner, and clinician, it is important to acknowledge the impact this bond can create on the life of someone. A dog can play multiple healing roles throughout the life of a human, but education on the definition and background of each role can assist people in finding the right role for their needs. With proper referrals, education, coordinated care, training, and love, the addition of an ESA can be a life-changing alternative therapy.

Companion Animals: Comforting Comrades

Companion Animal Case Study*

Lt. Colonel Maverick returns home from theatre. She is greeted by her husband and teenage children. It was the second deployment overseas, and this is her last, after a career that spanned 20 years. The Maverick family decides it is time to make another "addition" to their family. They head to the local humane society and fall in love with a dachshund mix that is four years old. They bring the pup home, care for him, love him, and cuddle with him. Ultimately, they decide to name him Oscar. Lt. Colonel Maverick has been diagnosed with PTSD from her service experiences, yet Oscar seems to bring her happiness (and the rest of the family members) with his funny antics and sassy personality. Oscar travels with the family, goes for long walks with them, and even travels by car to see relatives with them. There are some places that Oscar cannot go (begrudgingly to Oscar) like the grocery store, doctor visits, and inside public buildings. However, he is quite content when he gets to go "back seat"—his cue to hop along in the car for the next adventure.

While at times, *companion animal* is used interchangeably with *ESA*; it is not, however, synonymous. Nor, should a companion animal be confused with a service animal. A companion animal, like Oscar, is better known as the family pet. While he is well-behaved in public, and may be able to roll over on command, Oscar is not individually trained to perform a specific task for the benefit of an individual with a disability (physical, sensory, psychiatric, intellectual, or other mental disability), such as a service dog is trained to do. Although Lt. Colonel Maverick would benefit from a service dog to provide deep pressure therapy for her hypervigilance, or to identify her hallucination attacks, she has not explored that option yet. Lt. Colonel Maverick has not been prescribed an ESA for her PTSD by a physician, therefore, Oscar is not considered an ESA either. Although Oscar is providing Lt. Colonel Maverick psychological support, as well as comfort when he sits on her lap, he is still classified as a companion dog. Should any of the above change, Oscar's status of companion dog may change as well.

The canine was very popular as a companion animal in late eighteenth-century English urban society. While some of these creatures were former working-class canines, others were what might be described as "professional companion animals" (i.e., creatures who had no previous work history) (Blaisdell, 2015). There are approximately 72 million companion animal dogs and 74 million companion animal cats in the United States (Komorosky et al., 2015). Most often, companion animals are dogs and cats, but horses, rabbits, goats, fish, and other species also share space in our homes. I am sure you have heard the term *man's best friend* or the saying *Dogs leave pawprints on your heart.* Companion animals are said to make the family complete and considered loyal and faithful. As we discussed in the previous sections of this chapter, pet ownership, or just being in the presence of an animal, is associated with health benefits, including improvements in mental, social, and physiologic health status (Friedmann & Son, 2009; Friedmann & Krause-Parello, 2018). Companion animals can also be a catalyst for increasing social relationships, which in turn, support mental health benefits, such as with Lt. Colonel Maverick's health challenges. Given the growing evidence for social isolation as a risk factor for mental health, and, conversely, friendships and social support as protective factors for individual and community well-being (Wood et al., 2015), companion animals may be that alternative treatment healthcare providers should consider for veterans and civilians seeking mental health wellness.

The historical trend of new recognition of populations with particular issues, such as, currently, veterans returning from the Iraq and Afghan wars, represent a challenge to nurse educators as they prepare the community to interact with patients holistically and

Figure 9-1 A Marine veteran and his companion animal—dachshund Daisy.
Courtesy of Cheryl A. Krause-Parello.

recognize their unique needs (Sharts-Hopko, 2015). Healthcare providers need to know the differences between the types of animal-assisted interventions when addressing whether an animal would be "of service" to the patient. Although most primary care providers cannot write a prescription for an emotional service dog, they can suggest a companion animal, and no prescription is needed for that. Providers need to be fully cognizant of the benefits companion animals may give a military member, and the benefits military members may give to a companion dog. There have been nearly 31 million U.S. troop deployments since 1950 (Kane, 2012), many returning with both visible and invisible wounds of war. The time is now to consider novel approaches to complementary health care, such as the value of animal companionship. These approaches are potentially more cost-effective and socially acceptable than technological solutions (Mills & Hall, 2014). In the United States alone, an estimated six to eight million dogs and cats enter shelters each year, waiting to be adopted (Humane Society of the United States, 2014).

Among the many benefits of companion animals, mostly anyone can adopt an animal. You do not need a disability or documented condition of PTSD or TBI to qualify for a dog, but you do need approval to adopt by the individual shelter based on their adoption criteria. The impact, though, that companion animals have on active-military and veterans that have a PTSD diagnosis is undeniable and life-altering. Adopting a companion dog gives veterans with PTSD, depression, and other psychological challenges a renewed sense of purpose (Colin, 2012). These animals can enhance many aspects of a person's life and daily activity, even give them a reason to live. Interestingly, yet not surprising, empirical evidence indicates that human–animal relations may not only benefit human health but may also benefit animals' health as well. For instance, the action of stroking an animal has been found to reduce the animal's heart rate (Lynch & McCarthy 1969). Since the late 1970s, scientific evidence has accumulated showing that pet ownership can have positive effects on people's physical and mental well-being (Wells, 2019). The positive therapeutic value of animal companionship continues to receive little recognition in mainstream medical literature though, and as a field of research it is grossly under supported by government funding agencies (Serpell, 2006).

Animal Welfare

Despite the increasing amounts of research suggesting a variety of benefits to applying animal-assisted intervention as a complementary approach to the conventional care supplied by healthcare providers, the needs of the veteran patient receiving care should be evaluated carefully before suggesting the assistance of an animal. While a wide range of scientific and anecdotal evidence has shown that the ownership and companionship of an animal positively supports the psychological and physiological health of an individual (Westgarth et al., 2008), the ownership of any type of animal carries a weight of responsibility that should be considered case by case. The healthcare provider must realize the influence they have in their power to suggest the supplementary treatment that comes with an animal to a patient but is not prepared to support an animal whose care and welfare should also be taken into serious consideration.

The mental health of veteran patients can be impacted by their physical and psychological wounds. Veterans with PTSD from combat, for instance, can sometimes feel isolated and anxious. The state of an animal, such as a service dog or companion dog, can impact the state of the veteran as well. Numerous studies note dogs' proficient use of humans' attentional state, as evidenced by their ability to modify their behavior to accord with where humans are visually attending (Kundey et al., 2010).

Although they are helpful, the animals that are taken in become integrated into a relationship that has a very familial dynamic. Just as with any family member, it can be difficult to maintain one's self in good spirits and a healthy state if a person knows that they are not able to fully provide their animal with the care necessary for them to live a healthy life. While living with an animal can help renew a sense of motivation and purpose for a veteran patient, it can, however, also add stress to their daily routine that can be damaging to their own well-being. Thus, engaging in thoughtful conversations with veteran patients about their mental and emotional state is especially important for the provider in order to consider if their patient is capable of taking on the responsibility associated with caring for an animal's welfare. The ownership of an animal can be stressful and emotionally taxing if a person is not prepared to care for them with as much attention as that of a family member. The needs of an animal—such as exercise, proper diet, necessary medications and veterinarian appointments, grooming, bathing, and overall well-being—is crucial to supporting an animal, such as a dog, that can help support the patient themselves. Depending on the state of a patient and their diagnosis, they may simply not be prepared to even own an animal. The stress associated with owning an animal has the potential to cause more harm than good for the patient. Thus, it is crucial for providers to evaluate if the veteran they are treating is able to withstand and live with the stress that comes with owning and caring for an animal, while still maintaining their own mental, physical, and emotional health.

In some cases, taking on the ownership of an animal, or even simply being in the presence of an animal, has shown a wide range of health benefits for the patient (Friedmann & Son, 2009). It is clear that the benefits often outweigh the difficulties associated with owning an animal for many people. In addition to other treatments for care, alternative interventions of animal-assisted therapy have helped increase health benefits and promote a better quality of life for patients (Cole & Gawlinski, 2000).

For the veterans who are able to own and support the health of an animal, it is important to assess their ability to effectively provide the care and possible training necessary for the animal's continued welfare. Providers should be aware of a veteran's lifestyle and limits in regard to their physical, mental, and emotional capabilities when caring for an animal. An animal that can live a healthy life that reflects their owner's lifestyle is most beneficial for a veteran patient seeking animal-assisted therapeutic interventions, such as owning a dog. A veteran, for instance, who may have previously owned a dog when they were younger and is seeking to own a companion dog now has trouble walking for long periods of time. Considering this, a provider should look to inform themselves on the different types of dogs that can have a friendly demeanor and do not need long walks for sufficient exercise, which is best suited for the veteran patient discussed.

In order to practically provide care for veteran patients, the aspects of their health that impact their daily lives should be considered. It is crucial to inform and educate patients of their personal role in the maintenance of owning an animal. Although companion dogs do not require any prescription from a provider, providers should still inform their veteran patients that they will be responsible for supplying their dog with any training that may be necessary for official certification as an emotional support dog or service dog. It should be noted that the ownership and welfare of an animal comes with a variety of secondary details that must be evaluated to ensure the well-being of both the patient and the animal. These details include, but are not limited to, having sufficient financial means to pay for veterinarian appointments, pet insurance, food, training, grooming supplies, and other associated costs. In addition to this, the responsibility of owning an animal, especially one that acts to provide a service that benefits the health of their owner, comes with understanding the rights and regulations for housing accommodations for people with animals that provide some form of therapeutic assistance. Some properties can have restrictions or pet fees that can prevent a patient from owning an animal. Although animals that offer helpful support and their owners do have rights to protect themselves, property owners can still enforce certain rules regarding animals living on the property (Humane Society of the United States, 2019). It is not expected that a provider understands the exact specifications of each patient's housing circumstances, but having the ability to inform the patient of the possible regulations and costs associated with animals living on a property is valuable information that can better prepare patients to navigate the obstacles that may come with owning an animal. With this in mind, it is important for a provider to follow-up and check on the health of both the animal and veteran patient as they adapt to adjustments that must be made. The well-being of one will directly affect the health of the other, so being observant of both should be consistent in helping support the therapeutic bond between the patient and their animal.

For veterans, especially with those living with PTSD, the addition of new stressors can be overwhelming. Making the choice to own an animal is a significant one that can understandably cause some anxiousness. For patients interested in but are not yet prepared to own an animal, providers can suggest alternative options for patients that can still provide them with the benefits of interacting with animals and eases them into the responsibility of caring for them without the pressure and stress of owning them. A provider can suggest volunteering at an animal shelter, or simply watching someone's dog for a few days. This can effectively introduce a patient to the responsibility that comes with owning an animal in a controlled environment that still offers the benefits of animal interaction.

During the process of suggesting an animal to support a veteran patient's health, a provider should be keen on including the necessary information regarding the maintenance of the animal's health and welfare as well. Evaluations and assessments to determine if a patient is able to own an animal may be valuable in enhancing the experience of the therapeutic animal bond to support the veteran patient's needs. Mindful consideration of the daily life and experiences of veterans during this process is critical for the provider to ensure that the key aspects of their health is positively impacted by the introduction of animal interventions.

There have been many anecdotal claims confirming that canines have helped save a military member's life, with psychiatric service dogs increasingly being sought out by military veterans as a complementary intervention (LaFollette et al., 2019) for mental health conditions, such as PTSD and TBI. As we continue to research and provide evidence to support such claims, we as a society need to be informed about the different categories of canine-assisted therapy such as was discussed in this chapter.

Research initiatives like Canines Providing Assistance to Wounded Warriors ([C-P.A.W.W.] www.nursing.fau.edu/c-paww), located in the Christine E. Lynn College of Nursing, Florida Atlantic University, Boca Raton Campus, lead the way to join with community partners to support our military, advance evidence-based practice protocols in military-related clinical settings, and promote the delivery of culturally congruent and competent care for the military members. The mission of C-P.A.W.W. is to comprehensively advance interdisciplinary research, education, and practice protocols for wounded warriors and veterans through the development of evidence-based and restorative interventions, to support military-related health initiatives by building community partnerships, to investigate therapeutic interventions—particularly those involving canine assistance—that positively influence health outcomes, and to emphasize system planning, innovative public policy making, and thorough protocols of care development for the armed forces. The C-P.A.W.W. team is committed to the evolution of nursing knowledge within the context of research, education, and practice in order to better assist the military population.

**Case studies are a work of fiction. Names, characters, businesses, places, events, locales, and incidents are either the products of the author's imagination or used in a fictitious manner. Any resemblance to actual persons, living or dead, or actual events are purely coincidental.*

Acknowledgments

The authors would like to thank all of our veterans for their service to defend our nation and freedom. We also thank the dogs who do so much for mankind.

A special thank you to Dr. Cathi Comer for her editorial assistance.

References

Beetz, A., Uvnäs-Moberg, K., Julius, H., & Kotrschal, K. (2012). Psychosocial and psychophysiological effects of human-animal interactions: The possible role of oxytocin. *Frontiers in Psychology, 3*, 234. doi:10.3389/fpsyg.2012.00234

Blaisdell, J. D. (1999). The Rise of man's best friend: The popularity of dogs as companion animals in late eighteenth-century London as reflected by the dog tax of 1796. *Anthrozoös, 12*(2), 76–87. https://doi.org/10.2752/089279399787000363.

Blech, J. (2006). Severity of injuries requires new forms of rehabilitation. *Spiegel*. http://www. spiegel.de/international/spiegel/0,1518,443754,00.html.

Center for the Human-Animal Bond, College of Veterinary Medicine, Purdue University. (n.d.). *Center for the Human-Animal Bond*. http://www.vet.purdue.edu/chab/

Cole, K., & Gawlinski, A. (2000). Animal-assisted therapy: The human-animal bond. *AACN Clinical Issues 11*(1), 139–149.

Colin C. (2012, July). How dogs can help veterans overcome PTSD. *Smithsonian Magazine*. http://www.smithsonianmag.com/science-nature/how-dogs-can-help-veterans-overcome-ptsd-137582968/?no-ist

Crowe, T. K., Sanchez, V., Howard, A., Western, B., & Barger, S. (2018). Veterans transitioning from isolation to integration: A look at veteran/service dog partnerships. *Disability and Rehabilitation, 40*(24), 2953-2961.

Friedmann, E., & Krause-Parello, C. A. (2018). Companion animals and human health: Benefits, challenges, and the road ahead of human-animal interaction and people's health. *OIE Scientific and Technical Review-Special Edition: The Contribution of Animals to Human Welfare, 37*(1), 71–82.

Friedmann, E., & Son, H. (2009). The human-companion animal bond: How humans benefit. *Veterinary Clinics of North American: Small Animal Practice, 39*(2), 293–326. https://doi.org/10.1016/j.cvsm.2008.10.015

Humane Society of the United States. (n.d.). *The Fair Housing Act and assistance animals*. https://www.humanesociety.org/resources /fair-housing-act-and-assistance-animals

Humane Society of the United States. (2019) *Pet overpopulation estimates*. http://www.humanesociety.org/issues/pet_overpopulation/facts/overpopulation_estimates.html

Kane, T. (2012). Development and US troop deployments. *Foreign Policy Analysis, 8*(3), 255–273. doi:10.1111/j.1743-8594.2011.00153.x

Komorosky, D., Rush Woods, D., & Empie, K. (2015). Considering companion animals. *Society & Animals, 23*(3), 298–315. https://doi-org.aurarialibrary.idm.oclc.org/10.1163/15685306-12341367

Krause-Parello, C. A., Friedmann, E. Blanchard, K., Payton, M., & Gee, N. (2019). Veterans and shelter dogs: Examining the impact of dog-walking intervention on physiological and post-traumatic stress symptoms. *Anthrozoos*, 225–241

Krause-Parello, C. A., Levy, C., Holman, E., & Kolassa, J. (2016). Effects of VA Facility dog on hospitalized veterans seen by a palliative care psychologist: An innovative approach to impacting stress indicators. *American Journal of Hospice and Palliative Medicine*, 1–10.

Krause-Parello, C. A., & Morales, K. (2018). Military veterans and service dogs: A qualitative inquiry using interpretive phenomenological analysis. *Anthrozoos, (31)*1, 65–75.

Kundey, S., De Los Reyes, A., Taglang, C., Allen, R., Molina, S., Royer, E., & German, R. (2010). Domesticated dogs (Canis familiaris) react to what others can and cannot hear. *Applied Animal Behaviour Science, 126*, 45–50.

LaFollette, M. R., Rodriguez, K. E., Ogata, N., & O'Haire, M. E. (2019). Military veterans and their PTSD service dogs: Associations between training methods, PTSD severity, dog behavior, and the human-animal bond. *Frontiers in Veterinary Science, 6*(23). doi:10.3389/fvets.2019.00023

Lynch, J. J., & McCarthy, J. F. (1969). Social responding in dogs: Heart rate changes to a person. *Psychophysiology, 5*(4), 389–393.

Mills, D., Hall, S. (2014) Animal-assisted interventions: making better use of the human-animal bond. *Veterinary Record, 174*, 269–273.

Nightingale, F. (1969). *Notes on Nursing*. Dover Publications.

Owen, R., Finton, B., Gibbons, S., & DeLeon, P. (2016). Canine-assisted adjunct therapy in the military: An intriguing alternative modality. *The Journal for Nurse Practitioners* 12(2), 95–101. doi:10.1016/j.nurpra.2015.09.014

Salter, C. (2018). Animals in the military. In C. Scanes & S. Toukhsati (Eds.), *Animals and Human society* (pp. 195–223). Academic Press. doi:10.1016/B978-0-12-805247-1.00013-7.

Serpell, J. (2006). Animal companions and human well-being: An historical exploration of the value of human-animal relationships. In A. Fine,(Ed.), *Handbook on animal-assisted therapy* (2nd ed., pp. 3–19). Academic Press. doi:10.1016/B978-012369484-3/50003-7

Sharts-Hopko, N. (2015). Function effectively within the organization environment and the academic community. In L. Caputi (Ed.), *Certified Nurse educator review book*. (pp. 125–139). National League for Nursing.

Takashima, G., & Day, M. (2014). Setting the one health agenda and the human-companion animal bond. *International Journal of Environmental Research and Public Health, 11*, 11110-11120. doi:10.3390/ijerph111111110

U.S. Department of Justice. (2011, July). *ADA requirements: Service dogs*. https://www.ada.gov/service_animals_2010.pdf.

U.S. Department of Justice. (2015, July 20). *Frequently asked questions about service animals and the ADA*. https://www.ada.gov/regs2010/service_animal_qa.pdf

Walther, S., Yamamoto, M., Thigpen, A. P., Garcia, A., Willits, N. H., & Hart, L. A. (2017). Assistance dogs: Historic patterns and roles of dogs placed by ADI or IGDF accredited facilities and by non-accredited U.S. facilities. *Frontiers in Veterinary Science, 4*(1). doi:10.3389/fvets.2017.00001

Wells, D. L. (2019). The state of research on human-animal relations: Implications for human health. *Anthrozoös, 32*(2), 169–181. doi:10.1080/08927936.2019.1569902

Westgarth, C., Pinchbeck, G. L., Bradshaw, J. W., Dawson, S., Gaskell, R. M., & Christley, R. M. (2008). Dog-human and dog-dog interactions of 260 dog-owning households in a community in Cheshire. *Veterinary Record, 162*(14), 436–442.

Wood, L., Martin, K., Christian, H., Nathan, A., Lauritsen, C., Houghton, S., Kawachi, I., & McCune, S. (2015). The pet factor—Companion animals as a conduit for getting to know people, friendship formation and social support. *PLoS ONE, 10*(4), e0122085. doi:10.1371/journal.pone.0122085

Younggren, J., Boisvert, J., & Boness, C. (2016). Examining emotional support animals and role conflicts in professional psychology. *Professional Psychology: Research & Practice, 47*(4), 255–260.

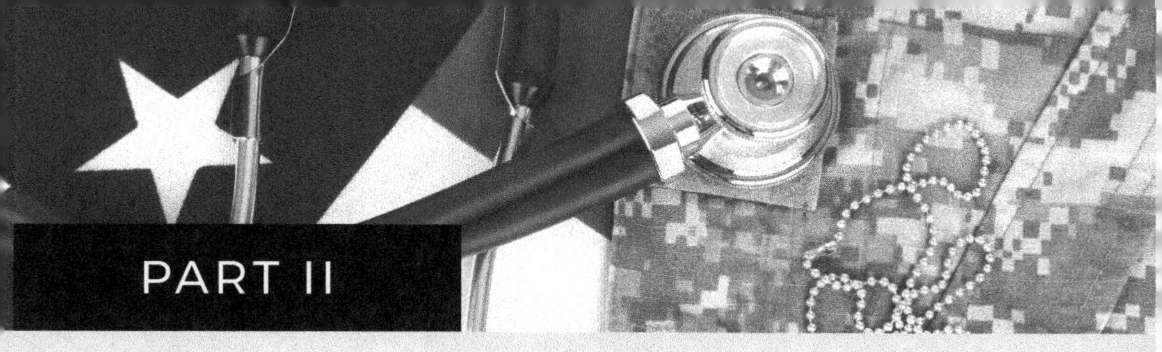

Physical Wounds of War

CHAPTER 10	Polytrauma Care Across the Continuum	155
CHAPTER 11	Military Occupational Exposures	187
CHAPTER 12	Caring for Veterans with TBI in the Private Sector	203
CHAPTER 13	Military Caregivers of Veterans and Service Members with Traumatic Brain Injury	219
CHAPTER 14	Pain and Pain Management in the Veteran	235
CHAPTER 15	Identifying the Unique Needs of Veterans That Influence End-of-Life Care	251

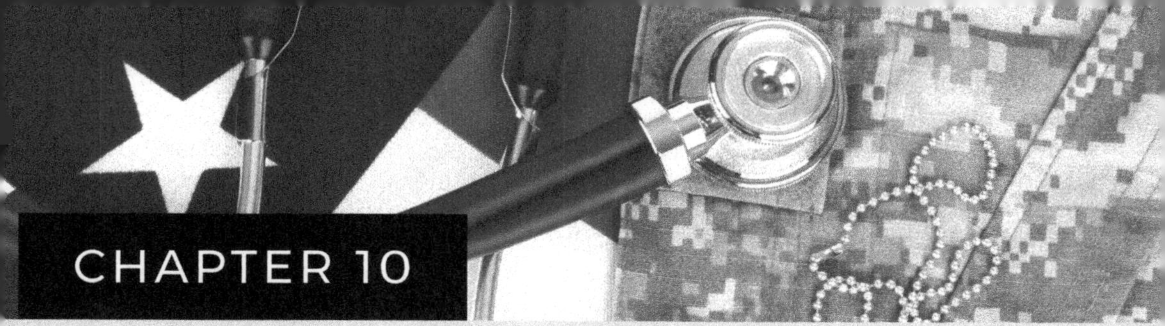

CHAPTER 10

Polytrauma Care Across the Continuum

Tanya S. Capper and Charles R. McMichael

The views presented are those of the author(s) and do not necessarily represent the views of the Department of Defense or the United States Air Force.

Introduction

This chapter will focus on providing an overview of the United States military patient movement system and how it relates to the initial care of polytrauma patients. We will define polytrauma, discuss the mechanisms of injury, and articulate the stages of care for this complex patient and how it relates to healthcare providers practicing in the civilian sector. The majority of care for the polytrauma patient is received via the Military Health System (MHS) initially, and then transitions to the Veterans Health Administration (VHA). Upon release from the Polytrauma Rehabilitation Center (PRC), continued rehabilitative support and medical services may be provided in the civilian sector.

Polytrauma Care Across the Continuum

This chapter will focus on the origination of treatment of the injured service member within a war zone and transition through the echelons of care bringing the patient all the way through the patient movement system to their disposition at a stateside medical facility and eventually the rehabilitation system within the Department of Defense (DoD) or United States (U.S.) Department of Veterans Affairs (VA). There will be discussion of training to prepare healthcare providers to treat patients in both austere (expeditionary) and definitive places of care. The process of patient movement and physiological stressors of flight will be addressed. Concepts of mechanisms of injury will be developed to include care considerations. Healthcare costs for those wounded during military service, the comorbidities that result, and the technological advancements that have recently been made will be presented. Lastly, the goals of rehabilitation and disposition to a home-care environment will be discussed. The first intent of this chapter is to prepare healthcare professionals to be able to care for veteran service members who have suffered the injuries of war that may include amputations, burns, spinal cord injuries, post-traumatic stress disorder (PTSD), and traumatic brain injury (TBI). Secondly, this chapter aims to educate medical professionals on the military healthcare system and how it is structured to meet medical needs while maintaining an economic and lethal force. Though these patients are cared for within the MHS and VHA, they will likely transition to services within the civilian sector.

Training

Trauma Combat Casualty Care Course

The Tactical Combat Casualty Care course, known as TCCC, is a DoD-developed course curriculum focusing on the care of casualties at point of injury (POI). The course focuses on care under fire, control of bleeding, and moving casualties to safety in order for triage to initiate. There are two forms of curriculum, one for medical personnel and the other for all combatants (NAEMT, 2020). Though the medical course is more in depth for medical professionals, all service members are required to be trained in the program in order to be equipped to respond to casualty incidents. The National Association of Emergency Medical Technicians (NAEMT) recognizes this course and offers a similar course for the civilian sector known as Tactical Emergency Casualty Care (TECC). TECC focuses on hemorrhage control with the use of tourniquets, surgical airway control, needle decompression, carrying patients to safety, and responding to mass casualty/active shooter events (NAEMT, 2020). Another trauma response course offered by NAEMT is Prehospital Trauma Life Support (PHTLS); the science supporting this course is founded on the elements of TCCC (NAEMT, 2020).

Clinical Practice Guidelines

The Joint Trauma System (JTS) has developed multiple clinical practice guidelines (CPGs) that are utilized by the military to provide standardized care to patients throughout the various echelons of care. The development and update of these guidelines is based on DoD Trauma Registry data, information gathered from patient records, and review of after-action reports. The implementation of these CPGs in both military and civilian sectors has shown to greatly decrease fatality rates. Guidelines are separated into four main groups: 1. JTS CPGs, 2. Prehospital/En Route CPGs, 3. Critical Care Air Transport CPGs, 4. Military Working Dog CPGs. Individuals can prepare for their deployed time by reviewing these guidelines in relation to their role (credentialed provider, registered nurse, or medic) and while focusing on the specialty where they will be working when deployed (pre-hospital, en route, or a Role 2/3 facility) (JTS, 2020). The CPGs are available online via search engine using the following key words: Joint Trauma System; Clinical Practice Guidelines.

Comprehensive Medical Readiness Program

In order for military personnel to be adequately trained on provision of care in a deployed or medical contingency environment, one must be trained on the various skills utilized and equipment available during these temporary duties. The services have developed medical readiness programs that outline training requirements for each medical military occupation specialty. For example, the Air Force has developed the Comprehensive Medical Readiness Program that outlines the skills necessary for nurses to receive training on caring for blast injuries, soft tissue injury, orthopedic injuries, and preparing for patient evacuation just to name a few. This program is supported by the CPGs discussed above as well as familiarization with equipment that will be utilized in the military contingency environment.

Civilian Sector Training Opportunities

Along with the courses presented by NAEMT described previously, other courses in the civilian sector can provide similar training opportunities outside of the military setting to include Advanced Trauma Life Support (ATLS) and the Trauma Nursing Core Course (TNCC). The American College of Surgeons (ACS) created the ATLS course and focuses on the immediate management of traumatically injured patients to include coordinating inter-hospital transport to maximize patient outcomes (ACS, 2020). TNCC was developed by the Emergency Nurses Association, and focuses on educating nurses on the identification, stabilization, and assessment of life-threatening traumatic injuries (ENA, 2020). The Stop the Bleed campaign educates the public on how to utilize tourniquets to save the lives of those suffering from a traumatic injury. The basis of this training is from the DoD Defense Health Agency and has been adopted by the ACS to train within the civilian sector (ACS, 2020). This is an important skill that the general population can learn in preparing for mass casualty situations or disaster response.

Planning and Response

As the occurrence for non-terrorist, non-military casualty events grow, it is imperative that medical facilities have contingency plans in place to respond to these types of events. The military medical community develops medical contingency response plans specific to each military treatment facility (MTF). These plans are practiced multiple times each year in response to various mass casualty events such as active shooter, aircraft incidents, or CBRN attacks. Large MTFs that have emergency, surgical, and inpatient capabilities have a massive transfusion protocol that is required to be exercised at least two times each year. A review of the data and injury patterns of combat-related injuries are used today to formulate a response to polytraumatic events in the civilian sector. Understanding these patterns and interventions allow medical professionals to research ways to increase survivability from similar traumatic events, thereby improving the national trauma care system (Janak et al., 2019).

Polytrauma

According to the VHA, polytrauma is defined as the sustainment of multiple, at least two, traumatic injuries, one of which could be considered life threatening, and are sustained during the same incident. Multiple body parts or systems may be affected and a TBI is commonly associated with the injuries. The result of these injuries can lead to various disabilities to include: physical, cognitive, psychological, and/or psychosocial impairments and/or altered functionality (Critchfield et al., 2019). Primarily, trauma results from blasts, gunshot wounds (GSW), and burns, though this is not an all-conclusive list. Secondary injuries can result from effects generated by the primary source; for example, impact injuries that result from a fall. According to Janak et al. (2019), "dismounted complex blast injuries involving traumatic amputations to lower extremities in combination with pelvic, abdominal, and genitourinary injuries are one particular injury pattern previously described as a hallmark of recent conflicts in Afghanistan and Iraq" and is a good example of a polytrauma case (p. 7).

An injury severity score (ISS) will be calculated and looks at mortality risk based off of the severity of injuries. This score utilizes the abbreviated injury scale by looking at the severity of injuries over nine regions. The ISS then generates a score from zero to 75 and categorizes injuries as no injury (0), minor injury (1–3), moderate injury (4–8), serious injury (9–15), severe injury (16–24), critical injury (25–74), and fatal injury (75). Polytraumatic injuries typically generate a score of at least 16, placing it in the severe injury category

Table 10-1 Total War-Related Injuries by Type and Characteristic

Type of Injury	Incidence by Characteristic		Total Incidence
Deaths, All	n/a		5,945
Deaths, Suicide	n/a		260
PTSD Ever Diagnosed	Deployed	66,935	88,719
	Not Deployed	21,784	
TBI Ever Diagnosed	Penetrating	3,451	202,281
	Severe	2,124	
	Moderate	34,001	
	Mild	155,623	
	Not Classifiable	7,082	
Amputations	Major Limb	1,222	1,621
	Partial	399	

Reproduced from Geiling, J., Rosen, J. M., & Edwards, R. D. (2012). Medical costs of war in 2035: Long-term care challenges for veterans of Iraq and Afghanistan. *Military Medicine, 177*(11), 1235–1244. https://doi.org/10.7205/milmed-d-12-00031

(MacGregor et al., 2020). An overview of combat-related injuries and illnesses can be found in **Table 10-1**. Of note, some statistics may pertain to service members as a whole and does not decipher between a combat and non-combat relation; for example, suicide rates.

Types of Injuries

Polytrauma mechanisms of injury are most commonly caused by explosive blasts, GSW, and motor vehicle accidents (MVA), likely leading to on average four injuries (MacGregor et al., 2020; Szuflita, et al., 2016). Plurad (2011) describes a blast as "a violent release of energy… resulting in overpressure, penetrating, blunt, and thermal insults" (p. 276). There are high and low order explosives; high-order explosions result in a larger blast which results in greater blast pressure, low-order may result in less pressure, but greater chance for a fire leading to thermal injury (Plurad, 2011). As warfare develops, explosions may contain more than just a pressurized blast. Projectiles are utilized to result in greater injury and dirty bombs may result in a CBRN event. CBRN stands for chemical, biological, radiological, nuclear; integrating one or more of these into an explosion can produce catastrophic results and add an additional layer of response for the wounded. Polytrauma injury characteristics most commonly found include the following body regions: head, neck, chest, abdomen, extremities, and other external injuries. The integration of tourniquet use, blood transfusions, and transport to care within 60 minutes has greatly decreased combat mortality, up to 44%, since the inception of modern warfare. U.S. military history was made in 2004 boasting the lowest case fatality rate (Howard et al., 2019).

Blasts

Blast injuries can be categorized into the following: primary, secondary, tertiary, quaternary,

Table 10-2 Mechanisms of Injury after Blast Exposure

Nomenclature	Mechanism	Injuries
Primary	Alternating Overpressure and Under Pressure on Tissues of Heterogeneous Densities ("Air Filled")	Tympanic Membrane Rupture, "Blast Lung," Hollow Viscous Injury, mTBI
Quaternary	Thermal, Other	Burns (Thermal, Chemical), Inhalation Injury, Other
Secondary	Fragmentation or Airborne Debris Accelerated Upon Victim	Multiple Penetrating injuries, Extensive Tissue Devastations, Traumatic Amputations
Tertiary	Structural Collapse, Violent Displacement, Entrapment	Multiple Blunt Injuries, Traumatic Asphyxiation, Crush Syndromes

Modified from U.S. Department of Defense. (2019). Blast Injury 101. Blast Injury Research Coordinating Office. https://blastinjuryresearch.amedd.army.mil/index.cfm/blast_injury_101

quinary (**Table 10-2**) (Plurad, 2011). Vast pressure differentials define primary injuries resulting in lung injury, tympanic membrane rupture, and TBI. Studies have shown that upwards of 66% of TBIs suffered in a combat setting are related to blasts (Regasa et al., 2018). Secondary injury results from fragmentation or projectiles leading to penetrating injuries that affect not only the area of impact, but can also cause cavitation. Traumatic amputations, facial injury, blindness and extensive tissue damage is also representative of a secondary injury (Plurad, 2011). Ocular injuries are most commonly caused by blasts and fragmentation from improvised explosive devices (IEDs), rocket propelled grenades (RPGs), and GSWs. Eye injuries may include open or closed globe injuries, intraocular foreign bodies, lacerations, and enucleation (Vlasov et al., 2015). Tertiary injuries result from the environment within the blast area such as building collapse, entrapment, or physical displacement such as being thrown from one point to another. Injuries seen resulting from the tertiary effects include blunt trauma, crush injuries, and asphyxiation. Whenever there is risk of a crush injury, concern for compartment syndrome must be considered. Quaternary injury results from thermal effects. Patients may present with burns from not only fire, but also from chemical components or simply inhalation injury. Lastly, quinary injuries can develop from CBRN incidents, most commonly infectious or radioactive materials (Plurad, 2011).

Penetration Injuries

Penetration injuries may result from various impacts such as GSW, projectiles present within the munition itself, such as nails or ball bearings, or debris that is catapulted as a result of the blast. Patients with penetrating injury may present with tissue damage, amputations, or internal injuries. Surgical removal of debris may be required. Traumatic amputations may have occurred at the location of impact, or limbs that may be severely damaged will result in surgical amputation (Plurad, 2011).

Soft Tissue Injury and Internal Trauma

Soft tissue injury falls under the secondary injury category. The initial blast or penetrating injury, depending on where on the body it impacts, may cause soft tissue injury alone, or fragmentation from objects may lodge themselves within soft tissue causing trauma. Unlike low-pressure or blunt-force trauma, soft tissue injury from penetrating wounds may result in more extensive trauma due to cavitation and the pressure behind the force (Plurad, 2011). As with many traumatic injuries, the potential for delayed onset of internal trauma may occur, therefore frequent assessments are vital. Focused assessments may include neurovascular checks, urine output, frequency of bowel movements, lab work to monitor kidney function and blood levels pointing to signs of internal bleeding or rhabdomyolysis, and vital signs to assess for delayed onset of shock. Exploratory surgeries may be needed to include frequent washouts and temporary closure to care for concurrent injuries, promote healing, and reduce the risk of infection (Plurad, 2011).

Orthopedic Trauma and Amputation

Multiple types of injuries may result in amputations. The amputation may occur at the POI, or result from the need to salvage life or partial limb through surgical intervention. Blasts or crush injuries are common sources of trauma resulting in amputation. If a surgical amputation is needed, the limb should be taken as distally as possible to maximize the body's ability to compensate and to promote quality of life for the patient. Intense wound care evaluation and treatment will be necessary to include debridement (Plurad, 2011). Debridement may need to be accomplished under sedation if severe enough, otherwise it may be completed at the bedside as healing progresses. Early amputation is optimal if necessary as delayed amputations over 90 days post-injury can lead to negative health outcomes as shown by both physical and psychological diagnoses. As of 2016, 10–15% of amputations related to war injuries were considered delayed amputations (Rabágo et al., 2016).

Polytrauma frequently results in bone fractures. Extremity injuries make up 80% of combat injuries, and due to the occurrence of underbody blast attacks, the majority of injuries occur to the legs and ankles (Danelson et al., 2019). Commonly, external fixation is used to set the limb and enable the safe transport of patients through the echelons of care. Neurovascular checks are highly important in order assess for compartment syndrome which must be surgically addressed with a fasciotomy as quickly as possible. To promote vascularization and perfusion, temporary vascular shunting may be an option to help salvage limbs (Plurad, 2011).

Burns

A large amount of data was collected during the height of the Iraq and Afghanistan wars; based on this data, studies showed in 2006 that 10% of casualties suffered from burns, 20% of which were considered severe, covering more than 20% of body surface area (Chung et al., 2006). Facial burns contributed to 77% of combat-related burns and 4% of these casualties passed away as a result of their injuries (Escolas, et al., 2017; Johnson et al., 2015). Burns concentrated to the head, neck, and perineal areas are related to coverage of body armor which protects the core of the body. The mechanisms of injury that commonly cause combat-related burns include IEDs, vehicle fires, and RPGs; there are also occurrences of burns resulting from aircraft crashes, flash burns from fuel, and electrical burns (Johnson et al., 2015). "Those with perineal burns were more likely to have battle-related injuries, explosive mechanisms, and severe polytrauma (Clemens et al., 2017, p. 1125).

Considerations for treating burn injuries resulting from war may include polytrauma and inhalation injury. Though evacuation times have greatly improved over the years, it still takes approximately five days for a patient to reach a burn center (Johnson et al., 2015). Fluid resuscitation is imperative and will likely require greater amounts than standard, non-war related, burn patients (Chung et al., 2006). The JTS CPG directs evaluating the burn patient using the rule of nines and then implementing burn resuscitation by calculating fluid needs using the Lund-Brower charts. Goals for a successful burn resuscitation within 24–72 hours include: alert and hemodynamically stable, urine output of 30–50 milliliters per hour, and a heart rate of 110–130 beats per minute (Driscoll et al., 2016). Combat-related burns provide a unique challenge for treatment. Those who have suffered both a burn and amputation may limit the donor sites for allografting (Johnson et al., 2015). Care by a treatment team with extensive burn training will result in improved patient outcomes (Chung et al., 2006).

Spinal Cord Injuries

The rate of spinal injuries in the modern combat setting range in occurrence from 7.4–12% (Bernstock et al., 2015). Military personnel who suffer from spinal injuries differ from non-combat injuries in that they are most commonly related to blasts, GSW, and MVA. Athletic competition is a common non-combat spinal injury source for service members (Szuflita, Neal, Rosner, Frankowski, & Grossman, 2016). According to a study completed by Szuflita et al., the most common source of spinal injury among military members is through blunt trauma (69%) and penetrating trauma (31%). Injury occurred at all levels of the spine, but the cervical(C)-spine was the most affected; thoracic(T)-spine and lumbar(L)-spine injuries were found more commonly in battle-related (78%) injuries than non-battle-related (22%) (Szuflita et al., 2016). Common combat spine injuries include lumbosacral dissociation (LSD), low lumbar burst fractures, thoracolumbar junction injury, and post-amputation scoliosis. LSD injuries are defined by sacral fractures with both horizontal and vertical findings. This type of injury has been mainly associated with IED blasts that lead to a fall or crush injury (Bernstock et al., 2015).

As modern and expeditionary medicine, as well as the improvement in protective equipment, continue to evolve, survival rates continue to improve. Research has shown that definitive fixation of spinal injuries be completed in a level IV or V facility; as transit to this type of facility takes time, there is a CPG on how to manage a spinal injury in-theater and en route (Bernstock et al., 2015). With improvement in survival and care, the chance of service members returning to duty increases. Patients who sustain spinal injuries by blunt force trauma are more likely to return to duty than those who sustain specifically a C-spine injury, or spinal injury caused by a MVA. Clinical treatment course considerations should be made for explosive energy from blasts that lead to injury of the pelvic girdle, sacrum, and L-spine as the blast energy travels up through the base of a vehicle or generates a vehicle roll-over (Szuflita et al., 2016). Head and neck injuries may be resultant from compressed head space and seating positions surrounded by equipment that are commonly found in military vehicles (Danelson et al., 2019).

Ultimately, the occurrence of spinal injuries in service members commonly results in injuries at multiple levels of the spine making spinal injuries much different when compared to non-battle-related injuries (Szufllita et al., 2016). Many patients may require operative intervention at a higher frequency for their spinal injuries and they likely have limited to no recovery of neurologic function. Evaluation of these injuries differ from the civilian sector and may be related to the rigid nature of the body armor, causing blast pressure to focus on the lower lumbar spine (Bernstock et al., 2015).

Clinical Treatment Considerations

Consideration must always be given for delayed presentation of injuries. Upon arrival to a trauma bay, the patient should receive a head-to-toe assessment that includes a bedside ultrasound exam (FAST). Airway compromise should be frequently assessed as smoke inhalation or exposure to chemicals may result in delayed inflammation. Crush injuries need to be monitored for compartment syndrome. Bowel and bladder function should be monitored for renal impairment, bowel contusion, or ischemia. Psychological considerations must also be assessed initially to evaluate for a TBI utilizing the Military Acute Concussion Evaluation (MACE) tool (Plurad, 2011). Mental health must continue to be evaluated throughout immediate care and rehabilitation of polytrauma patients as there is a high prevalence of Post-Traumatic Stress Disorder (PTSD), anxiety, depression, and suicidality. These topics are covered within their own respective sections of this textbook.

Risks to Service Members

Environmental Exposure Risks

Terrorist activities commonly have a CBRNE element involved, especially in the presence of blast events. As reviewed in a previous section, CBRNE stands for chemical, biological, radiological, nuclear, and explosives. These events do not need to contain all of the elements or occur via blast, but consideration should be given to the potential for a mix of any one of these components. Important considerations for responders to these kinds of events include awareness of potential agents, how to appropriately decontaminate the casualties, and what reversal agents may be available. For radiological components, the concept of time, distance, and shielding is imperative. Examples of hazardous chemical and toxins include: blister agents/vesicants like mustard gas; systemic agents such as cyanide; caustic acids; choking agents such as ammonia and phosgene; convulsants; nerve agents or pesticides such as sarin, soman, and tabun; biologic agents like anthrax; riot agents such as tear gas; and radiologic materials (U.S. Department of Health and Human Services, 2020).

Long-term considerations should also be given to environmental exposures that may not be CBRNE related. In many of the contingency environments, air quality does not measure up to that of developed countries. Burn pits have been heavily utilized over many years as a means of disposal. The VA has established a burn pit registry to collect information about individuals exposed to burn pits and provides a reporting system for health concerns that may be related to their exposure (VA, 2020).

Hearing loss is a common result of frequent exposure to noise. The tympanic membrane is extremely sensitive and highly susceptible to injury related to pressure injuries such as blasts (Plurad, 2011). Aside from traumatic injury though, many service members work in loud environments such as those on the flight line, on board aircraft, those working with generators, or exposure to frequent gunfire or explosions. Some career fields that have high incidents of hearing loss include, but are not limited to: pilots and aircrew; maintenance and crew chiefs; infantry; military police; and explosive ordinance technicians.

Infection Risks and Considerations

Due to the austere environment where polytrauma typically occurs for military personnel, there is a high risk of infection. To combat this potential, every casualty gets antibiotics as an early part of treatment. According to the CPG on infection prevention, patients should receive antibiotics and antifungal prophylaxis within three hours dependent on their injury. The most common medications utilized are: cefazolin, clindamycin, and metronidazole. Blast injuries can increase the risk of contracting the Hepatitis B or Hepatitis C viruses. Though low, there is also a risk of contracting the Human Immunodeficiency Virus (HIV). Patients should receive testing for these viruses at initial treatment, then again after two, four, and six months. If there is a high risk for HIV, then prophylactic treatment is recommended (Saeed et al., 2016). Secondly, infection risk can increase during the treatment and recovery process. For example, open spine injuries are susceptible to contamination and infection. These injuries are also difficult to provide surgical management on, limiting the ability to complete debridement and washouts (Bernstock et al., 2015). Those with burns have a high risk of bacteremia, increasing their risk for mortality upwards of 89%. Those with perineal burns not only have an increased incidence of bacteremia, but there is a higher chance for urinary tract infections which, left untreated, may lead to kidney injury or sepsis (Clemens et al., 2017).

Non-injury-related infections are also a risk to service members serving in austere locations. Women frequently suffer from urinary tract infections due to hygiene limitations, dehydration, and delay in the ability to urinate. Members may be exposed to infectious agents such as the following: malaria, tuberculosis, leishmaniasis causing skin infections, or diarrheal illnesses related to giardia (Spelman et al., 2012). Service members do receive various immunizations and lab tests as a part of their military service and deployment preparation. Vaccinations are received based on location of deployment and include, but are not limited to, smallpox, typhoid, and anthrax.

Emergency Response

Triage

Much like the civilian sector, the military utilizes a standardized triaging system to evaluate the severity of ones injuries. According to the Joint Theater Trauma System, patients are considered either minimal, delayed, immediate, or expectant. There are multiple levels of medical care as the casualty is evacuated from the front line through the echelons of care. At each stop the patient is re-triaged.

Minimal patients are classified as walking wounded. They can provide self-aid and need minimal medical support. Care for these patients should be carefully calculated so not to overburden the medical capabilities. Dependent on the severity of their injuries, they may be utilized to assist with other casualties ("Mass Casualty & Triage," 2018).

Delayed patients will require medical attention, most commonly surgical intervention. The delay in transport to medical care though will not limit life, limb, or eyesight. Common injuries associated with delayed patients include: blunt trauma without shock, fractures, minor GSW, soft tissue injury without excessive bleeding, and minor burns ("Mass Casualty & Triage," 2018).

Immediate patients must receive immediate medical care to prevent major disability or even death. Typical injuries are related to airway compromise, lung injury such as a tension pneumothorax, hemorrhage, amputations, or injuries to the neck, torso, and/or pelvis ("Mass Casualty & Triage," 2018).

Expectant patients present as those who have suffered injuries with no chance of survivability. The casualty may not show signs of life or have viable vital signs, they may have suffered a GSW to the head leaving them in a coma, there may be open pelvic fractures with uncontrolled bleeding, extensive burns, or spinal cord injuries occurring at a high level compromising airway management. Those considered to be expectant are retrieved from the battlefield, but no life saving measures or resources are utilized, instead comfort measures will be provided to all extent possible ("Mass Casualty & Triage," 2018). The service member must be aware of scene safety and limit placing themselves into harm way to save an expectant member. The member will still be retrieved from the battlefield with dignity.

Damage Control Resuscitation

Military conflicts around the world have paved the way for trauma care within both the military and civilian sectors. Focus on resuscitative efforts, followed by life/limb saving surgical intervention, skeletal stabilization, and later reconstruction to promote long-term function are the backbone of development of the trauma systems used at the national level (Giannoudi & Harwood, 2016). Damage control resuscitation is defined by Giannoudi and Harwood (2016) as "keeping the patient alive whilst avoiding interventions and situations that risk worsening their situation by driving the lethal triad of hypothermia, coagulopathy, and acidosis or excessively stimulating the immune-inflammatory system" (p. 273). Upon stabilization, patients must still be monitored for multi-organ dysfunction, acute lung injury, and renal, hepatic, circulatory, and immune dysfunction (Giannoudi & Harwood, 2016).

In care under fire, tourniquet use is utilized for hemorrhagic blood loss. It is placed "high and tight," meaning as proximal as possible and as tight as possible on the injured limb. If the bleeding is not controlled, an additional tourniquet can be placed next to the first one. For injuries that cannot be controlled with a tourniquet, hemostatic gauze is utilized. The use of a pelvic binder is another common intervention utilized in the field when pelvic injury is suspected. If there is an excessive loss of blood, the use of tranexamic acid (TXA) should be administered as soon as possible, but within at least three hours of injury. A second dose may be administered after initial fluid resuscitation. Fluid resuscitation is provided by using what is available, but in the following preferred order: whole blood; a 1:1:1 ratio of plasma, red blood cells, and platelets; 1:1 of plasma and red blood cells; Hextend; or a crystalloid solution (Baker, 2014; JTS, 2019). A change in practice was learned in the Iraq war. "Battlefield observations suggest improved survival of patients receiving fresh whole blood, or with packed cell transfusion augmented by fresh frozen plasma and platelets" (Baker, 2014, p. 349).

Once removed from the field and placed into an established care environment, the goals of damage control resuscitation include: permissive hypotension as tolerated, but avoided in patients presenting with head injuries; hemostatic resuscitation; rewarming; addressing acidosis; and further hemorrhage control via both surgical and non-surgical techniques (Giannoudi & Harwood, 2016). Consideration should be made to the utilization of clotting products as overtime it has been found, according to Giannoudi and Harwood (2016), that just the use of red blood cells can decrease control of hemorrhage during a massive transfusion protocol. A balance between the use of blood products, fluids, and clotting products should be closely monitored. Ultimately, the gold standard for hemorrhage control continues to be surgical intervention whether it be through open or interventional radiologic methods (Giannoudi & Harwood, 2016). Surgical interventions should be completed as quickly and in short of a time period as able to prevent the lethal triad of hypothermia, acidosis, and coagulopathy (Baker, 2014).

Pain Management

Pain control is an important facet of care during the phases of triage. According to TCCC, service members in the field will carry a medicine pack that includes meloxicam and Acetominophen that can be self-administered. In the event of a more severe injury, the combat medic can administer ketamine or provide an oral transmucosal fentanyl citrate [lollipop]. In the event of severe pain, morphine can be administered either intravenously or via intraosseous method. Due to the potential for respiratory depression, the availability of naloxone is crucial (JTS, 2019).

Introduction to Patient Movement

The DoD's Patient Movement (PM) system or en route care (ERC) capability was a major source of pride and positive press during the wars in

Iraq and Afghanistan. During these conflicts, the MHS achieved a 98% casual survival rate for those who reached a Role 3 MTF (Walrath et al., 2018). The need for a robust and expeditious PM system is validated by the fact that 87.3% of combat deaths occurred prior to arrival at a Role 3 MTF during that time (Walrath et al., 2018). The DoD considers PM as initiating movement from POI care and ending with the patient's final disposition; this definition includes all required stops or transitions that occur in the process (DoD, 2018). The PM process comes with inherent risks. The JTS CPG on interfacility theater transport states that "care capability is almost always reduced during ERC" and that "effective communication, coordination, and cooperation across the system mitigates this risk" (Walrath et al., 2018, p. 3). Therefore, PM is successfully accomplished through a joint effort of the DoD's service components.

The role system was established to standardize expeditionary care beginning at a location with limited resources and transitioning through the system in an ascending order to ensure access to increased capabilities which enhance stability and survivability. Role 1 sites act as a casualty collection point and typically have a combat medic available to provide life-saving measures, resuscitation, stability, and initiate transport to the next level of care. The goal of the Role 1 is to enact preventative measures to limit morbidity from injury or disease. The Role 2 is able to continue stabilization and resuscitative measures that were initiated at the Role 1 and may have limited lab, X-Ray, and blood product availability. They do not typically have inpatient capabilities, just a holding facility. Some Role 2 facilities are augmented with personnel (forward surgical team) to provide the capability for resuscitative damage-control surgery prior to being transported to a Role 3. The Role 3 facility has full emergency/trauma, inpatient, intensive care, and surgical services. Patients are able to receive some specialty services that may include orthopedic, thoracic, general, and neurosurgery. If a Role 3 is located within the theater of operations, then it will be the last echelon of care prior to initiating inter-theater transport. The Role 4 facility is a robust facility with definitive care. These sites are located in advanced overseas locations such as Landstuhl Regional Medical Center (LRMC) in Germany and the large MTFs located stateside ("Roles of Medical Care," 2018).

Intra-Theater and Inter-Theater Patient Movement

The PM system is a collaborative effort spanning the globe and is accomplished through the joint efforts of the military services components of the Air Force, Army, and Navy to include at times, coalition partners. Since the PM system is a global effort, the DoD establishes theaters or areas or responsibility in which military operations are conducted. The PM system is largely viewed as occurring either intra-theater or inter-theater (**Figure 10-1**). Intra-theater patient movement is the transportation of patients, in which the injury or illness occurred, to medical treatment facilities within the same theater (United States Army (USA), 2019). Inter-theater patient movement is the transportation from the theater of injury or illness to another theater or the United States with a MTF that can provide definitive care (USA, 2019). This division implies that the PM system is global, when needed, and patient hand-offs can occur numerous time throughout the process.

The phases of transportation are an important consideration that is consistent whether PM is occurring intra-theater or inter-theater. The JTS CPG on inter-facility theater transport lists the phases of transportation as (Walrath et al., 2018, p. 3):

1. Pre-movement-preparation and packaging of the patient
2. En route – provision of patient care while transportation is taking place
3. Post-movement – documentation and review of outcomes

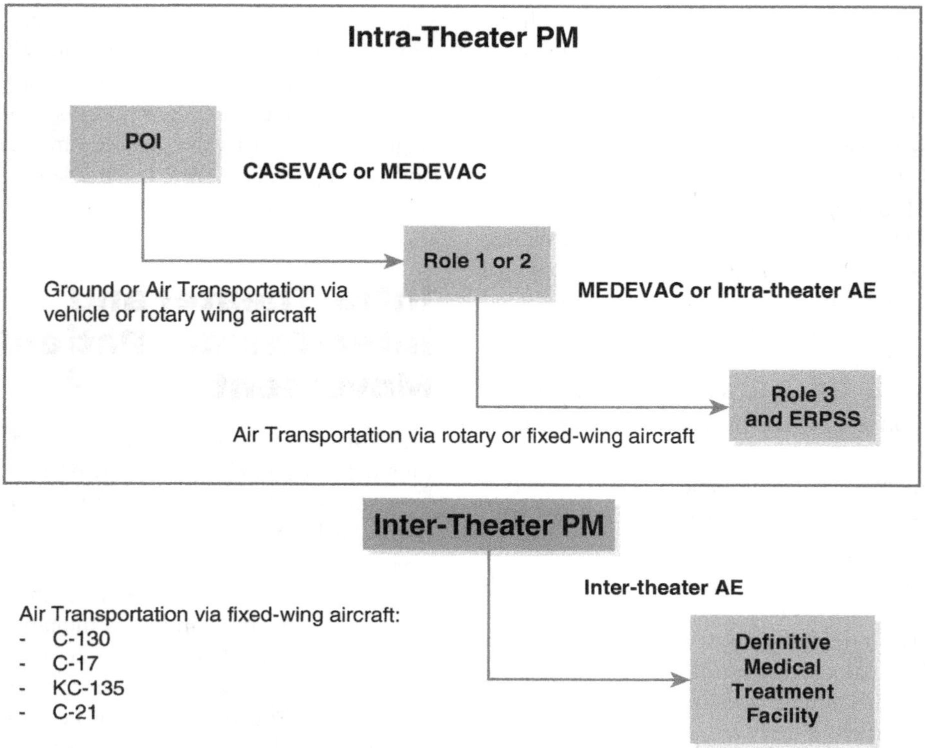

Figure 10-1 Theater Movement.

These phases are used to identify and organize tasks and safety protocols, utilizing checklists, in an effort to provide standardized and timely care.

Intra-theater PM is a highly integrated process between the military services and incorporates the distinctive cultures of the different services. Initial PM can begin as either medical evacuation (MEDEVAC) or casualty evacuation (CASEVAC). Army Techniques Publication (ATP) 4-02.2 defines MEDEVAC as being "performed by dedicated, medically equipped, and standardized MEDEVAC platforms designed especially for the MEDEVAC mission to provide en route care by trained medical professionals" (USA, 2019, pp. 1–6). MEDEVAC can occur via ground or air transportation platforms, which are designed for the evacuation and en route care of patients and must be conducted by medical professionals (USA, 2019). ATP 4-02.2 considers CASEVAC to be "the movement of casualties aboard nonmedical vehicles or aircraft without en route medical care" (USA, 2019, pp. 1–6). Whether contingency or disaster response, the decision to utilize CASEVAC would typically be made in a resource and time constrained environment as the patient may not receive medical treatment until arrival at a MTF. Thus, for the purpose of this chapter, only MEDEVAC will be addressed further.

Intra-Theater Patient Movement

MEDEVAC

MEDEVAC is the preferred initial method of PM in an effort to maximize patient outcomes. The medical condition of a patient is the determining factor for transportation platform and destination facility (USA, 2019). For the Army, the transportation platform, ground or air, can depend on the evacuation precedence. ATP 4-02.2 provides the following Priorities for evacuation precedence:

- Priority I, URGENT – assigned to patients at risk for loss of life, limb, or eyesight and should be evacuated within one hour
- Priority IA, URGENT-SURG – assigned to patients at risk for loss of life, limb, or eyesight and should be evacuated within one hour for surgical needs and stabilization
- Priority II, PRIORITY – assigned to patients needing prompt medical care and movement within four hours
- Priority III, ROUTINE – assigned to patients requiring evacuation, but condition is not likely to decline; movement should occur within 24 hours
- Priority IV, CONVENIENCE – assigned to patients whose movement is for convenience versus necessity

(USA, 2019, p. 2-2)

Once an evacuation precedence has been determined, the decision to use an air or ground asset will depend first on travel distance. Rotary-wing aircraft are commonly reserved for and tasked with urgent and priority requests. The evacuation precedence is utilized in Line 3 of the MEDEVAC 9-Line, which is addressed next. In the event a patient cannot travel via air back to the United States, transportation via the U.S. Navy will be utilized (USA, 2019).

Requests for PM via MEDEVAC begins with the 9-Line (**Table 10-3**). Designed to expedite the process, the 9-Line MEDEVAC request is an institutionalized process used for both ground and air transportation (USA, 2019). ATP 4-02.2 explains that a 9-Line is typically sent from the POI, routed through a command or dispatch center before they are received by MEDEVAC units (USA, 2019). Successful execution of MEDEVAC missions are described as requiring coordination and

Table 10-3 Line MEDEVAC

Line	Item
1	Location of pick-up site
2	Radio frequency, call sign, and suffix
3	Numbers of patients by precedence A-Urgent, B-Urgent Surgical, C- Priority, D-Routine, E-Convenience
4	Special equipment required A-None, B-Hoist, C-Extraction equipment, D-ventilator
5	Numbers of patients by type A-Litter, B-Ambulatory
6 wartime	Security of pick-up site N-No enemy troops in area, P-Possible enemy troops in area (approach with caution), E-Enemy troops in area (approach with caution), X-Enemy troops in area (armed escort required)
6 peacetime	Number and type of wound, injury, or illness
7	Method of marking pick-up site A-Panels, B-Pyrotechnic signal, C-Smoke Signal, D-None, E-Other
8	Patient nationality status A-US Military, B-US Civilian, C-Non-US Military, D-Non-US Civilian, E-Enemy Prisoner of War
9 wartime	Chemical, Biological, Radiological, and Nuclear contamination N-Nuclear, B-Biological, C-Chemical
9 peacetime	Terrain description

Modified from Army Publishing Directorate. (2019). *Medical evacuation, ATP 04-02.2* (p. C-1). Author.

integration of medical and aviation or ground assets "as well as a decentralized approval process (USA, 2019, pp. 2–3). The U.S. Army's MEDEVAC mission is typically executed via rotary wing (helicopter aircraft). During the height of the war in Afghanistan, there were numerous MEDEVAC units across the country that would transport battle-injured patients from POI to the nearest Role 2 for emergency surgery. If rotary-winged assets were in range of Craig Joint Theater Hospital, located at Bagram Airfield, Afghanistan, a Role 3 medical facility, then patients would be transferred directly to this location.

Intra-Theater Aeromedical Evacuation

The U.S. Air Force's (USAF) PM system is known as Aeromedical Evacuation (AE), which is also capable of conducting intra-theater PM. The AE system will be discussed at length momentarily, but it is important to note that inter-theater AE was used in Afghanistan to transport patients from Role 2 to Role 3 facilities that were out of range for rotary-winged assets. It is important to note that the term AE is commonly referred to as any type of patient transportation via aircraft, but for the sake of consistency, this text will refer to AE as the Air Force's PM capability (Hurd et al., 2006).

The primary goal of MEDEVAC or inter-theater AE is to transport patients to or between medical treatment facilities until the patient arrives to a medical treatment facility with the appropriate or highest level of care in the same theater that the injury or illness occurred. If patients are able to be treated within the theater, then the patient can return to duty. However, medical assets are typically limited when operations are conducted outside of the U.S. or European theater. When this occurs, inter-theater movement is required. As in the case of Afghanistan, intra-theater PM would end when the patient was transported to Craig Joint Theater Hospital and, if required, inter-theater PM would begin from this point to transport the patient outside of the area of responsibility or warzone.

Inter-Theater Patient Movement

Aeromedical Evacuation

Like MEDEVAC, AE enables the timely movement of patients to appropriate levels of care, but there are distinctive differences in the two systems. The AE system utilizes fixed-wing aircraft, which also enables timely inter-theater PM. These are opportune aircraft that are not solely designed for medical transport and must be configured for AE. This requires that the AE system be comprised of medical, support, staging, and transportation elements in order to safely deliver patients to their final destination (USAF, V1, 2017). As a result, there are multiple functions that comprise the AE system.

Patient Movement Regulation Center

The entire system begins with a patient movement request (PMR) submitted by a provider or flight surgeon, depending on the location and resources. The request places a movement precedence categorized as Urgent, Priority, or Routine (USAF, V1, 2017). A PMR can be submitted from any echelon of care and is received by a patient movement regulation center (PMRC) staffed by members from the Army, Air Force, and Navy (USA, 2019). Air Force Instruction (AFI) 48-307 states that, "The PMRC provides medical regulating services, including clinical and administrative validation, limited patient in-transit visibility, and evacuation requirement planning for intra- and inter-theater movement" (USAF, V1, 2017, p. 31). Clinical and administrative validation ensures that the right medical care will be available while en route and that the destination MTF has accepted, and can provide the appropriate care for each patient. If the patient is categorized as urgent, the transport should be initiated within 12 hours of having the PMR approved. This is used for those who require life-saving interventions. Those requiring priority movement should initiate travel within approximately 24 hours and is for those who require prompt medical intervention so to avoid deterioration. Lastly, routine movement is used for stable patients. They will be placed on the next available AE mission, ideally within seven days of the request (USAF, V1, 2017). These travel precedencies differ from that of the MEDEVAC precedencies. The validation process ensures regulated patient movement and is one of the major distinguishing factors of the AE system.

A Theater Validating Flight Surgeon (TVFS) supervises the validation process within a PMRC. Some of the roles performed by a TVFS are: validating all PMRs, ensuring compliance with practice standards, and providing medical direction for missions where a provider is not present (USAF, V1, 2017). The PMR approval generates an Air Force Form 3899 which is utilized for AE documentation throughout the duration of the patient's care both intra- and inter-theater and is placed in the permanent medical record (**Figure 10-2**) (USAF, V3, 2016). The TVFS is one of many team members working in a PMRC to ensure regulated patient movement.

En Route Patient Staging System

While patients are transiting within the AE system, the En Route Patient Staging System (ERPSS) acts as a holding facility. The ERPSS facility renders continued and supportive medical care to regulated and unregulated patients, prepares patients for flight, and provides ground transportation between aircraft and medical treatment facilities (USAF, V1, 2017). Simply put, the ERPSS acts as an intermediary between medical treatment facilities and the aeromedical evacuation crew, but may not be associated with every airfield.

Aeromedical Evacuation Crew

A basic aeromedical evacuation crew is comprised of two flight nurses (FN) and three Aeromedical Evacuation Technicians (AET). Teams can be augmented with additional FN, AETs, Flight Surgeons (FS), or attendants when needed. According to AFI 48-307 V1, this team is "specially trained to provide in-flight inpatient medical-surgical level care during air transport using medical equipment certified for use by airworthiness testing standards" (USAF, V1, 2017, p. 19). Aeromedical evacuation crew members are expected to be proficient on emergency medical and aircraft procedures in order to ensure safe transportation and appropriate clinical care. Since aircraft utilized for AE are not specifically designed for PM, aeromedical evacuation crew members must know how to configure aircraft to receive patients and set up life support systems ensuring electric and oxygen are available for use.

Critical Care Air Transport Teams

The USAF has utilized various constructs of en route critical care teams in the recent years, but the most common team is the Critical Care Air Transport Team (CCATT). CCATT is comprised of three crew members, a physician, a nurse with critical care or emergency experience, and a cardiopulmonary technician. CCATT allows for the transportation of hemodynamically unstable patients requiring critical care invasive devices such as ventilators or arterial lines.

Physiological Stressors of Flight

The environmental conditions in which en route care is provided is less than ideal as there are many considerations that must be taken into account when validating patients for aeromedical evacuation. Commonly referred to as

PATIENT MOVEMENT RECORD

DATA PROTECTED BY PRIVACY ACT OF 1974 **PERMANENT MEDICAL RECORD**

(S) - Information needed to submit patient movement record

SECTION I	**PATIENT IDENTIFICATION**					
(s) NAME (Last, First, Middle Initial)					(s) SSN	DATE OF BIRTH
(s) AGE	(s) SEX M F	(s) STATUS	(s) SERVICE	(s) GRADE	(s) UNIT OF RECORD AND PHONE NUMBER	CITE NUMBER

SECTION II	**VALIDATION INFORMATION**					
(s) Medical Treatment Facility Origination and Phone Number				(s) Ready Date (Julian Date)	APPOINTMENT DATE	NUMBER OF ATTENDANTS (s) MEDICAL (s) NON-MED
(s) Medical Treatment Facility Destination and Phone Number				(s) CLASSIFICATION 1A-5F AMBULATORY LITTER		(s) PRECEDENCE
(s) Reason Regulated	Max # Stops	Max # RONS	Altitude Restriction	(s) CCATT Required yes no	Name, sex, weight, rank of attendants:	U P R

SECTION III	**OTHER INFORMATION**			
(s) Attending Physician name, Phone Number and e-mail		(s) Attending Physician name, Phone Number and e-mail		
(s) Origination Transportation 24 Hour Phone Number		(s) Destination Transportation 24 Hour Phone Number		
(s) Insurance Company	Address	Phone #	Policy #	Relationship to policy holder
(s) Waivers (med equip, etc)				

SECTION IV **CLINICAL INFORMATION**

(s) Diagnosis	**(s) Allergies**	**LABS (Date and time drawn in Zulu)**			
		WBC	HGB	HCT	Other Labs

(s) WEIGHT:	(s) Blood type:
battle casualty	disease
non-battle injury	

Vital Signs (Date and time taken in Zulu)

Date	Time (Zulu)	B/P	Pulse	Resp	Pain Level: /10	Last Pain Med:	O2/LPM:	Route:

Baseline 02 Sat If Applicable ________ Temp ________

CLINICAL ISSUES

Infection Control Precautions: **LMP:**

Date of last bowel movement:

High Risk for Skin Breakdown yes no

Initial appropriate boxes:

Yes	No		Yes	No	
		Hearing Impaired			Hypertension
		Communication Barriers			Dizziness
		Vision impaired			Voiding difficulty
		Cardiac Hx			***Takes long-term meds**
		Diabetes			***Will sef-medicate**
		Motion Sickness			Has adequate supply of meds
		Ears/Sinus Problems			**Knows how to take meds**
		Respiratory difficulty			**(verbalized understanding)**
		***Medication listed on physician's orders**			

SPECIAL EQUIPMENT (Check all that apply) OTHER:

Suction		Traction		Orthopedic devices	
NG Tube		Monitor		Restraints	
Foley		Trach		Chest Tubes	
Incubator		IV Pumps		IV	Location:

Cast Location: ________________ Bivalved: yes no

Ventilator Ventilator Settings:

DIET INFORMATION (Check all that apply)

NPO Soft Full Liq Cl Liq Reg

Renal Gm Protein ______Gm Na ______ Meq K ______ Mag Sulfate

Tube Feeding ______ Type ______ cc/hr ______ Discontinue for Flight

Cardiac Diabetic ______ cal Infant formula: Pediatric Age:

TPN:

Other(specify):

SECTION V **PERTINENT CLINICAL HISTORY (Transfer Summary)**

Physician's Signature	Date/Time
Signature of Clearing Flight Surgeon	Date/Time

AF IMT 3899, 20060819, VI

Figure 10-2 Patient Movement Record (AF Form 3899).

Modified from U.S. Air Force. (n.d.). *AF IMT Form 3899: Aeromedical evacuation patient record.* https://www.templateroller.com/download/1900189/af-imt-form-3899-aeromedical-evacuation-patient-record .html?type=pdf&vers=main

PATIENT MOVEMENT RECORD (continuation)

DATA PROTECTED BY PRIVACY ACT OF 1974

PERMANENT MEDICAL RECORD

PATIENT MOVEMENT PHYSICIAN ORDERS (for continued care in the AE system and at enroute stops)

SECTION I. PATIENT IDENTIFICATION

1. NAME (Last, First, Middle Initial)	2. GRADE	3. SSN#
4. ALLERGIES	5. ORIGINATING MTF	6. DESTINATION MTF

SECTION II. MEDICALTION ORDERS (Drugs and IVs)	SECTION III. OTHER ORDERS (Procedures, Treatment, V/S Frequency, ETC)
[ ] yes [ ] no patient will self-medicate with the following medications:	

AF IMT 3899, 20060819, VI (*REVERSE*)

Figure 10-2 (Continued)

stresses of flight, these conditions cause stress, physiological and psychological, for both patients and aircrew. Air Force Instruction (AFI) 48-307 states, "The patients' ability to withstand physiologic effects of flight stressors will vary depending upon their underlying disease processes and their age" (USAF, V1, 2017, p. 62). The AFI lists nine stressors in total (USAF, V1, 2017).

The first, barometric pressure changes, takes into account that gas volume expands at altitude and contracts when descending. These pressure differentials can cause pain and damage to tissues and organs. Examples include sinus and ear blocks, compartment syndrome in the gastrointestinal tract, or a plethora of complications (USAF, V1, 2017). To prevent complications, the TVFS can place a cabin altitude restriction for the duration of the flight (for example 3,000 feet) in order to reduce the effects of barometric pressure changes inside the cabin. Also, patients with recent chest tube removals or surgery where air may still be present in a body cavity may be held from flights until the TVFS determines that it is safe to transport the patient. Patients flying with casts should have their cast bi-valved in order to account for the increasing pressure of altitude gain and therefore, potentially prevent compartment syndrome.

Decreased partial pressure of oxygen affects oxygen delivery and is problematic for patients with anemia, trauma, cardiac, and pulmonary disease to name a few. Due to the changes in barometric pressure, oxygen molecules move farther apart, despite oxygen concentration remaining 21% at altitude. Also, decreasing pressure makes it difficult for oxygen to cross into the bloodstream (USAF, V1, 2017). AFI 48-307 V1 refers to Dalton's Law of partial pressure when educating AECMs on this stressor of flight. Oxygen orders, standing or as needed, are commonly placed. Since Dalton's Law of partial pressure is dependent upon atmospheric pressure, a cabin altitude restriction may also be ordered in this case.

Decreased humidity at altitude causes negative effects on patients and crew aboard flights with long durations. Humidity naturally decreases with altitude as air loses its ability to hold moisture at cooler temperatures. Considerations must be made for patients in order to prevent dehydration. Renal, cardiac, or any patient with fluid balance issues are of particular concern. As a result, orders should be in place to address dehydration concerns such as oral or intravenous fluid intake, humidified oxygen, or moist dressing reinforcement (USAF, V1, 2017).

The fourth stressor is temperature variations. Ambient air temperature decreases as altitude increases and patients can experience drastic temperature changes on the flight line and upon aircraft. Patients that are of particular risk to negative effects of temperature variations are infants, elderly, patients with burns or of critical status. Patients are prepped for flight with extra blankets and clothing to mitigate associated risks (USAF, V1, 2017).

Referred to as an issue on all aircraft, high noise levels interfere with medical aircrew member's ability assess and monitor patients. Not only does the noise level add physiological stress, but it also alters the ability of the patient and caregiver to communicate. Hearing protection is provided to all patients and crew for protection (USAF, V1, 2017).

The fifth stressor, vibration, is experienced on all flights and can cause discomfort issues. Metabolic rate and oxygen requirements are increased as vibrations cause an increase in muscle activity. This metabolic increase is compared to that of gentle exercise. Mitigation strategies include padding of litters or stabilizing devices such as external fixators or casts. Pain control regime and as needed orders are typical for patients more vulnerable to the effects of vibrations (USAF, V1, 2017).

Turbulence can cause physical and physiological effect on patients and aircrew. Not only causing potential issues with motion sickness, turbulence causes body fatigue which can result in metabolic changes. Placing as needed anti-emetic orders are common practice for most patients (USAF, V1, 2017).

Gravity forces experienced during flight is the eighth stressor. AFI 48-307 V1 states, "Findings, such as increased intracranial pressure, pregnancy, unstable fractures and blood pooling are conditions to consider when examining the effects of G-Forces in AE" (USAF, V1, 2017, p. 64). An example of a mitigation strategy of G-Forces used in the AE system is loading head injury patients with their head towards the front of the aircraft as opposed to their head being toward the back of the aircraft (USAF, V1, 2017).

Finally, fatigue is listed as the ninth stressor. Fatigue is a result of the culmination of the other eight stressors and is compounded by other environmental and human factors. AFI 48-307 V1 provides the DEATH acronym to explain human system factors that also lead to fatigue: Drugs, Exhaustion, Alcohol, Tobacco, and Hypoglycemia. This acronym is utilized more for the education and awareness of aircrew members in order to promote healthy lifestyle choices (USAF, V1, 2017).

Patient Movement Summary

The PM system continues to advance as scientific research and technological advancements progress. The ablity of the services to work together to rapidly transport patients from POI to a definitive level of care continues to develop in the joint service environment. Aside from expediency, the focus on physiological altitude effects remains a facet of continued research and is closely addressed pre-, during, and post-flight. The PMRC looks at multiple considerations in order to appropriately categorize patients for urgent, priority, or routine transport with survival, patient safety, and aircrew safety at the forefront. The survival rates have drastically improved over the last 20 years of war and that is largly because of the efforts of the MHS and patient movement system.

Hospital Care

Patients receive initial care at POI, and then transition through the Role system of MTFs until they are evacuated to a Role 4 facility. Upon return to the United States, the patient will receive care from a premier MTF such as Walter Reed National Military Medical Hospital or Brooke Army Medical Center.

The patient is able to receive the most stabilizing care at a Role 3 facility. These hospitals are equipped with a trauma bay/emergency room, basic surgical capabilities, and an intensive care unit that can support the patient until they are able to be evacuated to a Role 4. Critical patients can be transported from downrange by a CCAT team typically to LRMC in less than 24 hours and commonly have received at least one exploratory laparoscopic surgery. LRMC is touted as a level II trauma center and can provide multi-disciplinary treatment and care until the patient is transported back to the United States. Patients are re-triaged and sent to the appropriate service, whether that be inpatient on a medical-surgical ward versus intensive care unit, or if they can be supported by outpatient services for minor injuries (Fang et al., 2008). Services provided stateside are similar to those provided at LRMC, but allows the patient to be surrounded by their support system.

Rehabilitation

The VA has established Polytrauma Rehabilitation Centers (PRCs) within the Polytrauma System of Care (PSC) that aim to maximize a patient's level of independence after discharge utilizing an interdisciplinary team approach. They provide lifelong management through the use of case managers and offer a vast array of resources throughout the entire VA system (Armstrong et al., 2019). The PRCs are located in Richmond, Virginia; Tampa, Florida; Minneapolis, Minnesota; Palo Alto, California; and San Antonio, Texas.

They support Polytrauma Network Sites and Polytrauma Support Clinics that are located throughout the VA system. PRCs are vital in providing coordination, leadership, and training as well as conducting research to further the care for polytrauma patients (Armstrong et al., 2019). There is also an Amputation System of Care that provides various clinical support for amputees across the United States and Puerto Rico. The DoD provides state-of-the-art rehabilitation centers located at the Military Advanced Training Center at Walter Reed National Military Medical Center, the Center for the Intrepid located at San Antonio Military Medical Center, and the Comprehensive Combat and Complex Casualty Care program at the Naval Medical Center in San Diego, California (Rabágo et al., 2016).

The PRC provides initial inpatient rehabilitative services post-injury, focusing on medical, functional, and quality-of-life needs. Inpatient services include nursing care along with at least three hours of therapy per day related to the primary condition. Other services that are implemented as needed can include assistive technology, mental health care, military liaisons, transition care management, and caregiver support (Armstrong et al., 2019).

A review of the patient's support structure is vital as the major MTFs and PRCs may not be located in close proximity to where the patient/family resides. The support system may need relocation assistance to include needs such as transportation, lodging, and childcare or schooling services. Addressing comprehensive needs of both the patient and family ties into the family-based approach to care.

Admission

Patients may be referred to a PRC via the VA system, civilian hospitals, or most commonly from the DoD Military Health System for those suffering combat-related trauma. There is a multi-disciplinary team that is a part of the admission process; these focus areas can be reviewed in **Table 10-4** (Armstrong et al., 2019).

Table 10-4 Professionals Involved in the Polytrauma Rehabilitation Center Admission Process

Responsibilities
■ Ensures that the medical admission is completed, including the history and physical, admission orders, and interim rehabilitation treatment plan
■ Facilitates the referral and admissions process for ADSMs ■ Facilitates bidirectional communication with the patient and family, PRC team, and military treatment facility ■ Helps address any transition issues that arise
■ Facilitates the referral and admissions process for ADSMs ■ Provides education to the patient and family prior to transfer ■ Collaborates with military treatment facility, PRC team and VA liaison for health care
■ Reviews clinical data with the PRC medical director ■ Monitors the patient's medical and rehabilitation status until transfer occurs ■ Informs the IDT of planned admission ■ Documents preadmission screening information in the electronic medical record ■ Confirms with referring facility that authorization for care has been provided by TRICARE or other payer as indicated ■ Helps locate appropriate setting for referred patients who are not appropriate for PRC
■ Coordinates transfers in collaboration with the admissions coordinator ■ Contacts family prior to admission to establish communication, begin orientation, and facilitate transition to PRC ■ Coordinates travel to PRC ■ Coordinate preadmission communication with Department of Defense and VA liaison to ensure smooth transition of care ■ Notifies local OEF/OIF/Operation New Dawn program manager of the admission

Modified from U.S. Department of Veterans Affairs. (2019). *Polytrauma System of Care, Veterans Health Administration Directive 1172.01*. https://www.va.gov/OPTOMETRY/docs/VHA_Directive_1172-01_Polytrauma_System_of_Care_1172_01_D_2019-01-24.pdf

Case managers are vital in communicating with the family to establish expectations and set goals. Participation by both the veteran and family member is promoted utilizing both in-person and telehealth capabilities. Support continues for post-discharge needs (Armstrong et al., 2019). Upon admission, patients are evaluated for the skills needed to promote functionality. An example of the admission criteria from the PRC in San Antonio, Texas, can be found in **Box 10-1** (Critchfield et al., 2019). Functional cognition is a focus especially for those who suffered a TBI. Cognitive rehabilitation works towards restorative and compensatory treatment. Restorative aims to improve the cognitive strengths the individual had pre-TBI and compensatory treatments train the individual to compensate for the deficits they have post-TBI. Through therapy, functional level is found to improve over time, but emotional changes post-TBI may not improve as consistently due to possible atypical presentation (Critchfield et al., 2019).

Evaluation for care needs requires extensive medication reconciliation. The interdisciplinary team should also assess common challenges such as pain control, sleep-wake cycles, bowel, and bladder changes. Skin integrity should be assessed frequently as polytrauma patients can suffer from decreased sensation, altered mobility, agitation, nutritional deficiencies, and incontinence leading to skin breakdown, which can lead to a plethora of other issues for the patient (Armstrong et al., 2019). Pain control must also be managed. It is estimated that around 85% of patients who suffered a combat related amputation suffer from a moderate to severe level of post-amputation pain (Cohen et al., 2019). Utilizing a multidisciplinary approach can lead to improved outcomes for patients.

At multiple stages throughout rehabilitation, functionality is assessed and goals are made. The PRC utilizes a standard outcome measurement for rehabilitation evaluating functional independence and rating it from dependent to fully independent. Considerations are made for cognitive components that include the ability to provide self-care, manage sphincter control, mobility, communication, and socialization. Other scales that are utilized to evaluate level of independence include: the Rancho Los Amigos Levels of Cognitive Functioning Scale, the Agitated Behavior Scale, Glasgow Outcome Scale, Disability Rating scale, JFK Coma Recovery Scale-Revised, and the Disorder of

Box 10-1 San Antonio Polytrauma Transitional Rehabilitation Program admission criteria

Residents admitted to PTRP must meet the following criteria:

1. At least 18 years of age
2. Medically stable
3. Have impairments that restrict community reintegration (impaired in areas, such as employment, school, independent living, cognition, and/or psychological adjustment secondary to TBI)
4. Have discernable goals that would benefit from a 24 hours per day, 7 days per week, structured, and supportive living setting
5. Do not exhibit behaviors posing risk/safety threat to self or others or exhibit behaviors that require alternate mental health services
6. Have the potential to successfully participate in groups and to benefit from therapy sessions
7. Need no more than supervision for basic activates of daily living
8. Can actively participate in medication self-administration program
9. Willing to participate in the program and to adhere to facility rules
10. No current substance abuses or dependence

Modified from U.S. Department of Veterans Affairs. (2016). South Texas Veteran's Healthcare System, PTRP11P-14-T011, Polytrauma Transitional Rehabilitation Program Admission Policy and Procedure.

Consciousness Scale (Armstrong et al., 2019). Patients must have an understanding of their abilities and limitations. If one becomes overconfident in their abilities, they may place themselves at a safety risk and cause re-injury (Critchfield et al., 2019).

Discharge

Though patient-centered care is on the forefront of rehabilitation, there are specific discharge criteria that must be met. Discharge planning begins from admission looking especially at the goals for functionality. In order to be discharged, rehabilitation goals need to have been met, and second, patients must achieve maximum benefit based on a plateau of subjective and objective measures. Discharge may also be considered if the patient is no longer willing to participate in rehabilitation (Armstrong et al., 2019).

To prepare for discharge, the patient, family, and caregiver should feel confident that they can manage the challenges that will continue over the long term. An assessment of the caregiver's physical, emotional, and financial capability is vital. This includes the ability to administer medications appropriately, how to use prosthetics, orthotics, and durable medical equipment correctly, and understand restrictions that may be related to swallowing, activity, or driving. The team also ensures that the family is set up with any needed resources within their home community (Armstrong et al., 2019).

Discharge from the PRC may be to various locations. The veteran may be functional enough to return home with the support of a caregiver, they may return to an MTF, return to duty, or utilize the Polytrauma Transitional Rehabilitation Program that offers residential rehab, subacute inpatient care, or outpatient services. Patients can be re-admitted to the PRC at any time in the event they need reassessment. Assessment is also offered at least annually, more frequently if necessary, to evaluate for need of continued rehabilitation services. Veterans may also be eligible for up to 30 days of respite care to allow the caregiver to recoup and the veteran to be assessed for any needs. Once the individual has been accepted to the PSC, they will receive case management and services related to TBI and polytrauma for life (Armstrong et al., 2019).

Considerations for War-Injured Service Members

Healthcare Costs

The costs of war injuries are very extensive, estimated at $984 billion for care and disability based by Congress in 2010, due to the long-term care requirements resulting from the high survival rate in today's modern war, and may be adjusted around $50 billion based on the rate of inflation by 2020. Rehabilitation care is ongoing especially for those who have prosthetics, brain injury, facial trauma, and the need for ongoing mental health care (Geiling et al., 2012). According to a review completed by Geiling et al. (2012), these high healthcare costs will begin to impact the United States around 2035.

Comorbidities surrounding war injuries must also be considered aside from the specific injury-related treatments. Amputees may develop weight gain, decreased mobility, osteoarthritis, chronic pain, coronary artery disease, and diabetes; while those with PTSD may develop obesity, depression, tobacco use, and/or substance abuse to name a few (Geiling et al., 2012). Considering those with a TBI diagnosis, regardless of severity, healthcare costs have been estimated to range from $590–910 million (Kulas & Rosenheck, 2018). Establishing interventions that can address these comorbidities early on may be helpful in decreasing healthcare costs and increasing the overall health of the veteran for the long term. A review of high-cost impacts and preventative strategies for reducing healthcare costs related to combat injuries can be found in **Table 10-5** (Geiling et al., 2012).

Multimorbidity

Rehabilitation for polytrauma patients should take into account the idea of multi-mordbidity. Multimorbidity is defined as, "a state where two or more medical conditions exist simultaneously in an individual, which can complicate treatment options and create the need for a diversity of health services" (MacGregor et al., 2020, p. 2). Utilizing this theory, the polytrauma clinical triad (PCT) has been developed and consists of post-concussion syndrome, chronic pain, and PTSD. This is very similar

Table 10-5 Healthcare Costs and Mitigating Strategies

Potential Source of Higher Medical Costs of War	Preventive Strategies to Help Mitigate Costs
Trauma and Polytrauma: Prevention	Several tactics can either prevent the trauma or reduce the level of injuries sustained and hence the costs: ■ Better preventive/protective equipment, body armor, armored vehicles, etc. ■ More ways to preventively detect or disarm IEDs
Trauma and Polytrauma: Acute Care and Treatment Surgery, transportation, medical care, rehabilitation	■ Better technology for battlefield treatment and evacuation ■ Better surgical techniques, closer to point of injury ■ Streamlined processes of moving the patient through the tiers of the medical system
Amputations	■ Improvements in prosthesis technology (may reduce time in rehabilitation or disability) ■ Improvements in care delivery that allow more amputees to return to active duty or work ■ Programs to help soldiers with polytrauma repair or regenerate their bodies for better self-image, function, cosmesis and return to work—Armed Forces Institute for Regenerative Medicine
Psychiatric and Neurological Care for PTSD, TBI, along with disability and care for comorbid illnesses, when one disease or injury begets or worsens another	Outreach, education, early detection, and treatment in primary-care clinics ■ Early identification and treatment of the "first" presenting illness, such as PTSD, to reduce the chance of the patient developing comorbidities ■ Screening for PTSD along with related comorbidities ■ PTSD decompression following deployment ■ More mental health providers in DoD/VA healthcare systems ■ The Army's protocol to "educate, train, treat and track" soldiers for TBI after concussions ■ Refined screening instruments for PTSD and TBI and ability to distinguish and treat PSTD and TBI ■ Allocating more resources for veterans' medical and mental health treatment, including Vet Centers ■ Improving processing of veterans' disability claims

(continues)

Table 10-5 Healthcare Costs and Mitigating Strategies *(continued)*

Potential Source of Higher Medical Costs of War	Preventive Strategies to Help Mitigate Costs
Additional Mental and Physical Health Impacts on the Service Member's Family ■ Anxiety over impeding deployment and family stress; unhealthy behaviors; depression ■ Cost of at-home nursing care ■ Relocation expense or lost job productivity of family members caring for the wounded ■ increased administrative and staff overhead for caring for disabled veterans ■ Stress induced by delayed response to claims	Counseling and early intervention for service members' families can treat stress and anxiety and prevent these conditions from leading to more serious issues like domestic violence ■ Military "resiliency programs" can help teach service members' families skills to cope with personal and financial problems ■ The Military Spouse Employment Partnership helps military spouses maintain portable careers ■ The VA proposed plan to compensate family members caring for wounded service members in their homes could reduce nursing-home costs ■ Some hospital programs serve veterans' families whose needs cannot be met within the VA system ■ Preventive or early-intervention programs might cure or stabilize veterans sooner and thereby mitigate the escalation of long-term extra medical or nonmedical support costs

Reproduced from Geiling, J., Rosen, J. M., & Edwards, R. D. (2012). Medical costs of war in 2035: Long-term care challenges for veterans of Iraq and Afghanistan. *Military Medicine, 177*(11), 1235–1244. https://doi.org/10.7205/milmed-d-12-00031

to chronic multi-symptom illness (CMI) that was a phenomenon developed after the Gulf War. This illness may also be apparent in Iraq and Afghanistan veterans along with the idea of post-deployment multi-symptom disorder (PMD) which references common symptoms that present in veterans, but is not related to war-related injuries. Other clusters of comorbidities found that surround the PCT include: "PCT [alone]; PCT with chronic disease; mental health and substance abuse; sleep, amputation, and chronic disease; pain and moderate PTSD; and [a] relatively healthy [individual]" (MacGregor et al., 2020, p. 2). In a study completed by MacGregor et al. (2020), the presentation of PCT with multimorbidity within the first year post-injury indicates that the quality of life continues to be affected on average six years later. Kulas and Rosenheck (2018) identified the theme of multimorbidity in a study looking at the occurrence of both PTSD and TBI. The presence of these two conditions can lead to significant social dysfunction, determines treatment options, and consistent with the previous section, greatly increases healthcare costs (Kulas & Rosenheck, 2018).

The VA completed a study looking at the use of opioids, non-pharmacologic agents, and mental health treatments within the polytrauma population. Over a quarter of the veterans cared for through the PSC filled at least one opioid prescription within the first year. Almost half of those utilized opioids for greater than 30 days within that first year of being under the PSC. The potential for unnecessary opioid use may diminish cognitive function and lead to long-term health limitations post-TBI. They found that chronic pain was the most common condition seen in the PSC (Adams et al., 2019). The presence of chronic pain, especially those with burn injuries, has shown evidence of suicidal ideation in 25–33% of patients (Escolas et al., 2017). The findings promote the use of implementing pain management tools to decrease opioid use and enhance overall improvement in rehabilitation

(Adams et al., 2019). A protective factor from suicide for burn patients with chronic pain is the presence of a strong support system (Escolas et al., 2017). Other prevalent findings within the PSC include TBI and PTSD. The recommendation was to address chronic pain with non-pharmacologic measures and implement early mental health treatment as first-line treatment to reduce the use of opioids to control pain. The most common non-pharmacologic services used within the PSC include exercise therapy, physical therapy, heat therapy, and massage. Other options that are available, but not used as frequently include manipulation/chiropractic care, lumbar support, biofeedback, traction, cold therapy, and dry needling/acupuncture. The study found that the use of non-pharmacologic methods led to a greater improvement of functioning and decreased the need to rely on opioids for chronic pain management (Adams et al., 2019).

Based on the findings of the MacGregor et al. (2020) study, it is imperative that long-term care for the polytrauma patient integrate early management of medical and psychological needs as these findings are most commonly correlated with war-associated injuries. The risk of alcohol and substance abuse in polytrauma patients is greatly increased due to various factors such as chronic pain, psychological deficiencies, and unproductive down time post-injury (Critchfield et al., 2019). A patient-centered, multi-disciplinary model should be enacted to address issues and promote high quality of life. Aside from evaluating the physical injuries of the veteran, patient-reported outcomes must also be taken into account. Considerations must be made for physical, psychological, and cognitive impairments (MacGregor et al., 2020).

Technological Advancements

As of 2015, there has been 26,000 recorded traumatic limb injuries as a result of operations in Iraq and Afghanistan. The Extremity Trauma and Amputation Center of Excellence (EACE) reports that 69% of those with extremity injuries had loss of a single limb and 31% lost more than one limb (Rabágo et al., 2016). Technology has afforded the medical community with incredible digital capabilities. Though there may be a high upfront cost, there is potential benefit of producing a fitter individual which may offset the treatment costs of comorbidities (Geiling et al., 2012). Amputees now have the highest return to duty rate, evaluated at 16.5%, than seen in previous wars (Gaunaurd et al., 2020). Due to prosthetic advancements and rehabilitation, they are able to achieve a high level of functioning and in turn, a greater quality of life. In order for the amputee to receive the most benefit from their rehabilitation and prosthetic devices, assessment and management of pain is imperative. The presence of post-amputation pain can negatively affect the ability of the patient to participate in utilizing the prosthetic or orthotic devices to maximize their functionality. Studies have shown success with reduction in post-amputation pain by the utilization of percutaneous peripheral nerve stimulation (Cohen et al., 2019).

The VA and DoD have developed a mobile rehabilitation program known as the Mobile Device Outcomes-Based Rehabilitation Program (MDORP). This program utilizes a sensor device called the Rehabilitative Lower Limb Orthopedic Analysis Device (ReLOAD) and communicates to the individual changes in gait and posture, and helps correct discrepancies to promote positive function and reduce the chance for overuse injury, pain issues, and musculoskeletal impairments. This program not only assesses and provides real-time correction, but it also provided prescripted home exercises. The research gained out of the outcome study surrounding MDORP shows that follow-up prosthetic training is highly recommended as the patient transitions from initial rehabilitation to their new active lifestyle focused on integrating back into society through work, school, and/or family time (Gaunaurd et al., 2020).

The EACE has initiated research and development of multiple rehabilitation interventions. The development of a microprocessor controlled treadmill has resulted in a 60% improvement in amputees stumbles and falls resulting in increased physical safety for amputees. Virtual reality has been utilized to develop assessments and interventions centered on identifying and correcting stability, body mechanics, cognitive, and military specific tasks. The integration of gaming technology enables service members to continue their rehabilitation at home using interactive and entertaining methods. Prosthetics and orthotics continue to improve and enhance power producing, exoskeletal, and muscle-controlled functions. There is also extensive studies occurring around the concept of regenerative medicine which aims to replace or regenerate human cells, tissues, and organs to return function to an individual. The ability to restore tissues in the limb of injury or amputation can hopefully result in even better return of function for injured service members (Rabágo et al., 2016).

Support System Considerations

Individual

Veterans of Operation Enduring Freedom (OEF) and Operation Iraqi Freedom (OIF) are eligible to VA receive care, free of cost, for five years post-separation from military service. Of those deployed in support of these operations, 57% have been discharged from the military, but only half of these have accessed the care they are afforded in the VA system (Lang et al., 2016). The VA prides itself on using a patient-centered care model to enhance the patient-care experience (Hanson et al., 2019). Based on evaluation of various research studies, pulling together the interdisciplinary team to work together towards the goals of the patient have been shown to enhance outcomes both short and long term. The Wounded Warrior Recovery Project was developed to track wounded service members over a longitudinal study. Collection of data began in 2012 and currently follows 6261 wounded warriors. Individuals are asked to complete an assessment every six months over a 15-year period to gather long-term data of their outcomes (MacGregor et al., 2020). This study looks at health outcomes related to quality of life, mental health, pain control, social support, and the use of prosthetics and orthotics (Rabágo et al., 2016).

Veterans may find that their spouse or a family member is now their caregiver which can alter the dynamic of the family unit. The veteran must be aware that too much assistance may hinder their rehabilitation growth. Involving the veteran and family throughout rehabilitation sessions will help both sides understand the level of functionality and independence to continue to promote healing and growth (Critchfield et al., 2019). Considerations must also be made for many young veterans as a barrier to care is a lack of childcare available in the medical setting and greater priorities being placed on school, employment, and family (Lang et al., 2016).

Family Members and Caregivers

Polytrauma patients require extensive support, not only from the medical team, but also from the patient's family and caregivers. Once they have completed the initial rehabilitation phase, they transition to independent care provided mainly by the designated caregiver. In a study completed by Hanson et al. (2019), the research team evaluated the satisfaction of care received from the VA PRC. It was found that overall, caregivers reported being either mostly or very satisfied with the care received during inpatient rehabilitation. The keys to gaining a high satisfaction score included caregiver social support, specific caregiver training from the VA, and feeling valued by the interdisciplinary team. The study showed that when the caregiver receives adequate training and support, it reduces the occurrence of caregiver burden and increases their mental health and quality of life. Support may be centered around navigating the VA system, managing medications and pain, supporting the patient and caregivers emotional needs, and providing education on the veteran's assistive devices. Ultimately, building rapport with the family, ensuring communication among the disciplinary team to include involving the caregiver/veteran, and valuing the veteran's support system led to high satisfaction levels (Hanson et al., 2019).

Consideration must be given to the family's ability to support the veteran both physically and mentally. Family members experience the distance caused by deployments and can also suffer invisible wounds upon learning about the traumatic injury of their loved one and transitioning through the phases of care alongside the veteran. Mental health affects the entire family unit and can be deflected onto children. Psychological support for the family and caregivers is imperative so as not to impart combat trauma throughout generations (Baker, 2014).

The VA conducted a study that looked at the relationships between veterans and their significant others in light of a TBI diagnosis. It was found that combat injuries have a significant impact on relationships. Extensive rehabilitation is typically provided in a large MTF or VA facility which does not always correlate with the place of residence for the service member and their family. This limits access to the familial support structure. Though the VA study shows positive relationship outcomes at year two post-injury, stability was commonly due to maturity, older age, length of marriage, and higher education. Those who were under mental health care for moderate to severe problems prior to injury, were more predicted to have relationship instability post-injury. Considerations for a positive relationship outcome post-injury may be attributed to financial support via VA benefits, resources, and support to manage the injury, rehabilitation, and family unit. Based on this study, recommendations for clinical care include a family-based systems approach, involving relationship counseling during polytrauma rehabilitation, identifying couples that are at risk for negative relationship outcomes, and providing caregiver training to reduce the burden of learning how to care for the veteran on their own (Stevens et al., 2017).

Resources

For Healthcare Providers

Healthcare providers can utilize resources from the VA. There are many online resources through the VA Polytrauma/TBI System of Care. These can be found on the U.S. Department of Veterans Affairs website under then Polytrauma/TBI System of Care section and delves into the system as a whole as well as specific details regarding recovery and rehabilitation (VA, 2015). The VA has also developed its own set of CPGs which can be found on their site at: https://www.healthquality.va.gov/ and information on pain management can be found at https://www.va.gov/painmanagement/ (Spelman et al., 2012).

The MHS and Defense Health Agency have developed the Psychological Health Center for Excellence. Many resources can be found on this site related to deployed health. This can be found at https://www.pdhealth.mil/ (Spelman et al., 2012). The Defense and Veterans Brain Injury Center is another resource with clinical guidance, research, and training focused on those who have suffered a TBI. The site geared towards medical providers can be found at https://dvbic.dcoe.mil/medical-providers-0 (Spelman et al., 2012).

A recommendation to implement veteran-specific screening questions is littered throughout the research. An important question that all healthcare providers should ask their patients is, "have you ever been in combat or been in

Box 10-2 Taking a Military History

- Branch: Army, Air Force, Navy, Marine Corps, and Coast Guard
- Rank/Rate: Enlisted, Warrant officer, Commissioned officer
  - Enlisted: perform specific specialties (high school diploma or GED)
  - Warrant Officer: highly trained specialist
  - Commissioned Officer (college degree), from 2nd lieutenant to a four star general
- Dates in service
- Deployments: location/dates
- What they were trained to do, what did they do

Reproduced from Spelman, J. F., Hunt, S. C., Seal, K. H., & Burgo-Black, A. L. (2012). Post deployment care for returning combat veterans, *Journal of General Internal Medicine, 27*(9), 1200–1209. https://doi.org/10.1007/s11606-012-2061-1

Box 10-3 Military Injury Focused Assessment

- Address barriers to care
- Establish a strong connection: acknowledge military service, take military history, and place this in visible, easy to access part of the chart
- Conduct a specialized review of systems:
  - Combat exposures, blast exposures/ concussive injuries
  - Illness/Injuries during deployments
  - Tinnitus, dental concerns, chronic pain, sleep disturbance, tobacco, alcohol or substance abuse, depression screen, PTSD screen, suicide assessment
- Involve all members of the healthcare team: construct an easy to follow, well sequenced and synthesized plan
- De-stigmatize mental health care
- Close follow-up is recommended
- Focus on function and reintegration
- Each VA facility has an OEF/OIF/OND program manager who acts as a community liaison and patient advocate

Reproduced from Spelman, J. F., Hunt, S. C., Seal, K. H., & Burgo-Black, A. L. (2012). Post deployment care for returning combat veterans, *Journal of General Internal Medicine, 27*(9), 1200–1209. https://doi.org/10.1007/s11606-012-2061-1

a war zone?" (Baker, 2014, p. 353). If the answer is yes, then appropriate referrals should be made to support the physical and psychological needs of this high-risk population. Providers must also consider non-military personnel who may be involved in military operations such as the civilian contractors who have worked on bases within the modern-day war zones of Iraq and Afghanistan, just to name a couple. Recommendation for taking a comprehensive military history can be reviewed in **Box 10-2** (Spelman et al., 2012). If the patient has suffered a traumatic injury as the result of their military service, a directed military history should be conducted, an example is shown in **Box 10-3** (Spelman et al., 2012).

For the Veteran or Service Member

Upon discharge from rehabilitation at the VA PRC, veterans can reach back to case managers at any time for the services they may need (Armstrong et al., 2019). These case managers have a wealth of knowledge to provide resources for the veteran and their caregiver. In today's era of modern technology, there are many smart phone applications that have been created. Some of these include PTSDCoach, Breath2Relax, and Tactical Breather (Spelman et al., 2012).

The National Resource Directory is a central repository for multiple supportive resources geared towards the veteran service member, family, and caregivers and is maintained by the Defense Health Agency's Recovery Coordination Program (National Resource Directory, 2020).

The Defense and Veterans Brain Injury Center has resources and education focused on those who have suffered a TBI. The site geared towards service members can be found at https://dvbic.dcoe.mil/service-members-and-veterans (Spelman et al., 2012).

For those with mental health concerns individuals can reach out to various sources as listed below:

Military Crisis Line 1-800-273-8255 (Press 1)

National Suicide Prevention Lifeline 1-800-273-TALK (8255)

Vet Centers Readjustment Counseling 877-WAR-VETS (927-8387) https://www.vetcenter.va.gov/

For the Caregiver and Family Members

Family members and caregivers also have multiple resources they can utilize. Military One Source provides various assistance from tax services, to health and wellness, to housing and employment assistance. These services can be accessed through https://www.militaryonesource.mil/ or by calling 800-342-9647.

Loved ones may also find that their veteran's emotional health has drastically changed since returning from their deployment or going through intense rehabilitation post-injury. Service members and family can utilize afterdeployment.org as a wellness resource and provides support for family members to include the military child. This source was established as a project under the Defense Centers of Excellence for Psychological Health and Traumatic Brain Injury (Anonymous, 2019; Spelman et al., 2012). The Defense and Veterans Brain Injury Center provides education focused on those who have suffered a TBI. The site geared towards family members can be found at https://dvbic.dcoe.mil/family-and-caregivers (Spelman et al., 2012).

Caregivers can continue to learn about how to care for their loved one by educating themselves through the Uniformed Services University Center for the Study of Traumatic Stress. This resource can be located at https://www.cstsonline.org/ (Spelman et al., 2012).

Like the veteran service member, reaching out to trained professionals can offer multiple resources to support the change in lifestyle based on polytraumatic injuries. Those who staff the VA PRC or former duty station family readiness center can be great starting points to finding the resources needed to support the veteran and family unit.

Summary

In conclusion, this chapter sought to develop the timeline from POI through rehabilitation of the polytrauma patient. The patient movement process was detailed to show the transition from the battlefield through the various echelons of care. The goal of this chapter is to better enhance the care of the veteran service member after sustaining polytraumatic injuries as a result of war. By focusing on the patients functional goals and integrating a patient/family-centered care model, outcomes for long term health may greatly improve to include potentially decreasing national healthcare costs. Recovery for polytrauma patients is a lifelong process. Long-term rehabilitative care in both the inpatient and outpatient setting continues in order to manage the patient's needs. Investment in the continued research that the DoD and VA is completing is imperative to continue improvements towards injured members functionality, quality of life, and mental health. The research being accomplished by the DoD and VA not only impacts the service members and veterans who receive their care, but also paves the way for the development of clinical discoveries that benefit the civilian sector (Rabágo et al., 2016).

References

Adams, R. S., Larson, M. J., Meerwijk, E. L., Williams, T. V., & Harris, A. H. S. (2019). Post-deployment polytrauma diagnoses among soldiers and veterans using the veterans' health affairs polytrauma system of care and receipt of opioids, nonpharmacologic, and mental health treatments. *Journal of Head Trauma Rehabilitation*, 34(3), 167-175. doi: 10.1097/HTR.0000000000000481

American College of Surgeons. (2020). Advanced trauma life support. Retrieved from https://www.facs.org/quality-programs/trauma/atls

American College of Surgeons. (2020). Stop the bleed. Retrieved from https://www.stopthebleed.org/

Anonymous. (2019). Afterdeployment.org. Retrieved from https://www.afterdeployment.org/about-us/

Armstrong, M., Champagne, J., & Mortimer, D. S. (2019). Department of Veterans Affairs polytrauma rehabilitation centers inpatient rehabilitation management of combat-related polytrauma. *Physical Medicine & Rehabilitation Clinics of North America*, 30, 13-27. doi: 10.1016/j.pmr.2018.08.013

Baker, M. S. (2014). Casualties of the Global War on Terror and their future impact on health care and society: A looming public health crisis. *Military Medicine*, 179(4), 348-355. doi: 10.7205/MILMED-D-13-00471

Bernstock, J. D., Caples, C. M, Wagner, S. C., Kang, D. G., & Lehman, R. A. (2015). Characteristics of combat-related spine injuries: A review of recent literature. *Military Medicine*, 180(5), 503-512. doi: 10.7205/MILMED-D-14-00215

Chung, K. K., Blackbourne, K. H., Wolf, S. E., White, C. E., Renz, E. M., Cancio, L. C., Holcomb, J. B., & Barillo, D. J. (2006). Evolution of burn resuscitation in Operation Iraqi Freedom. *Journal of Burn Care & Research*, 27(5), 606-611. doi: 10.1097/01.BCR.0000235466.57137.f2

Clemens, M. S., Janak, J. C., Rizzo, J. A., Graybill, J. C., Buehner, M. F., Hudak, S. J., Thompson, C. K., & Chung, K. K. (2017). Burns to the genitalia, perineum, and buttocks increase the risk of death among U.S. service members sustaining combat-related burns in Iraq and Afghanistan. *Burns*, 43, 1120-1128. doi: 10.1016/j.burns.2017.01.018

Cohen, S. P., Gilmore, C. A., Rauck, R. L., Lester, D. D., Trainer, R. J., Phan, T., Kapural, L., North, J. M., Crosby, N. D., & Boggs, J. W. (2019). Percutaneous peripheral nerve stimulation for the treatment of chronic pain following amputation. *Military Medicine*, 184(7/8), 267-274. doi: 10.1093/milmed/usz114

Congressional Research Service (CRS) Report: American War and Military Operations Casualties: Lists and Statistics. September 2010. Updated 7/29/20. Accessed at http://www.fas.org/sgp/crs/natsec/RL32492.pdf

Critchfield, E., Bain, K. M., Goudeau, C., Gillis, C. J., Gomez-Lansidel, M. T., & Eapen, B. C. (2019). *Physical Medicine & Rehabilitation Clinics of North America*, 30, 43-54. doi: 10.1016/j.pmr.2018.08.009

Danelson, K. A., Frounfelker, P., Pizzolato-Heine, K., Valentine, R., Watkins, L. C., Tegtmeyer, M., Bolte, J. H., Hardy, W. N., & Loftis, K. L. (2019). A military case review method to determine and record the mechanism of injury (BioTab) from in-theater attacks [Supplemental material]. *Military Medicine*, 184(3/4), 374-378. doi: 10.1093/milmed/usy396

Driscoll, I. R., Mann-Salinas, E. A., Boyer, N. L., Pamplin, J. C., Serio-Melvin, M. L., Salinas, J., Borgman, M. A., Sheridan, R. L., Melvin, J. J., Peterson, W. C., Graybill, J. C., Rizzo, J. A., King, B. T., Chung, K. K., Cancio, L. C., Renz, E. M., Stockinger, Z. T., & Gurney, J. (2016). Burn care. In *Joint Trauma System Clinical Practice Guidelines*. Retrieved from https://jts.amedd.army.mil/assets/docs/cpgs/JTS_Clinical_Practice_Guidelines_(CPGs)/Burn_Care_11_May_2016_ID12.pdf

Emergency Nurses Association. (2020). Trauma nursing core course. Retrieved from https://www.ena.org/education/tncc

Escolas, S. M., Archuleta, D. K., Orman, J. A., Chung, K. K., & Renz, E. M. (2017). Postdischarge cause-of-death analysis of combat-related burn patients. *Journal of Burn Care & Research*, 38(1), e158-e164. doi: 10.1097/BCR.0000000000000319

Fang, R., Pruitt, V. M., Dorlac, G. R., Silvey, S. V., Osborn, E. C., Allan, P. F, Flaherty, S. F., Perello, M. M., Wanek, S. M., & Dorlac, W. C. (2008). Critical care at Landstuhl Regional Medical Center [Supplemental material]. *Society of Critical Care Medicine*, 36(7), 383-387. doi: 10.1097/CCM.0b013e31817e3213

Gaunaurd, I., Gailey, R., Springer, B., Symsack, A., Clemens, S., Lucarevic, J., Kristal, A., Bennett, C., Isaacson, B., Agrawal, V., Applegate, B., & Pasquina, P. (2020). The effectiveness of the DoD/VA mobile device outcomes-based rehabilitation program for high functioning service members and veterans with lower limb amputation [Supplemental material]. *Military Medicine*, 185(S1), 480-489. doi: 10.1093/milmed/usz201

Geiling, J., Rosen, J. M., Edwards, R. D. (2012). Medical costs of war in 2035: Long-term care challenges for veterans of Iraq and Afghanistan. *Military Medicine*, 177(11), 1235-1244. doi: 10.7205/MILMED-D-12-00031

Giannoudi, M., & Harwood, P. (2016). Damage control resuscitation: Lessons learned. *European Journal of Trauma & Emergency Surgery*, 42, 273-282. doi: 10.1007/s00068-015-0628-3

Hanson, K. T., Carlson, K. F., Friedemann-Sanchez, G., Meis, L. A., Van Houtven, C. H., Jensen, A. C., Phelan, S. M., & Griffin, J. M. (2019). Family caregiver satisfaction with inpatient rehabilitation care. *PLoS ONE*, 14(3). doi: 10.1371/journal.pone.0213767

Howard, J. T., Kotwal, R. S., Stern, C. A., Janak, J. C., Mazuchowski, E. L., Butler, F. K., Stockinger, Z. T., Holcomb, B. R., Bono, R. C., & Smith, D. J. (2019). Use of combat casualty care data to assess the US military trauma system during the Afghanistan and Iraq conflicts, 2001-2017. *JAMA Surgery*, 154(7), 600-608. doi: 10.1001/jamasurg.2019.0151

Hurd, W. W., Montminy, R. J., De Lorenzo, R. A., Burd, L. T., Goldman, B. S., & Loftus, T. J. (2006). Physician roles in aeromedical evacuation: Current practices in USAF operations. *Aviation, Space, & Environmental Medicine*, 77(6), 631-638. Retrieved from https://pubmed.ncbi.nlm.nih.gov/16780242/

Janak, J. C., Mazuchowski, E. L., Kotwal, R. S., Stockinger, Z. T., Howard, J. T., Butler, F. K., Sosnov, J. A., Gurney, J. M., & Shackelford, S. A. (2019). Patterns of anatomic injury in critically injured combat causalities: A network analysis. *Scientific Reports*, 9(13767). doi: 10.1038/s41598-019-50272-3

Johnson, B. W., Madson, A. Q, Bong-Thakur, S., Tucker, D., Hale, R. G., & Chan, R. K. (2015). Combat-related facial burns: Analysis of strategic pitfalls. *Journal of Oral Maxillofacial Surgery*, 73, 106-111. doi: 10.1016/j.joms.2014.08.022

Joint Trauma System. (2020). Clinical Practice Guidelines. Retrieved from https://jts.amedd.army.mil/index.cfm/PI_CPGs/cpgs

Joint Trauma System. (2019). TCCC guidelines for medical personnel. In *Joint Trauma System Clinical Practice Guidelines*. Retrieved from https://jts.amedd.army.mil/assets/docs/cpgs/Prehospital_En_Route_CPGs/Tactical_Combat_Casualty_Care_Guidelines_01_Aug_2019.pdf

Kulas, J. F. & Rosenheck, R. A. (2018). A comparison of veterans with post-traumatic stress disorder, with mild traumatic brain injury and with both disorders: Understanding multimorbidity. *Military Medicine*, 183(3/4), e114-e122. doi: 10.1093/milmed/usx050

Lang, K. P., Veazey-Morris, K., Berlin, K. S., & Andrasik, F. (2016). Factors affecting health care utilizations in OEF/OIF veterans: The impact of PTSD and pain. *Military Medicine*, 181(1), 50-55. doi: 10.7205/MILMED-D-14-00444

MacGregor, A. J., Zouris, J. M., Watrous, J. R., McCabe, C. T., Dougherty, A. L., Galarneau, M. R., & Fraser, J. J. (2020). Multimorbidity and quality of life after blast-related injury among US military personnel: A cluster analysis of retrospective data. *BMC Public Health*, 20. doi: 10.1186/s12889-020-08696-4

Mass Casualty & Triage. (2018). In M. Cubano & F. K. Butler (Eds.), *Emergency War Surgery* (5th ed., pp. 23-39). Retrieved from https://www.cs.amedd.army.mil/borden/FileDownloadpublic.aspx?docid=744757d4-660d-432b-9286-9565c70f7e2b

National Association of Emergency Medical Technicians. (2020). Prehospital trauma life support. Retrieved from https://www.naemt.org/education/phtls/phtls-courses

National Association of Emergency Medical Technicians. (2020). Tactical combat casualty care. Retrieved from https://www.naemt.org/education/naemt-tccc

National Association of Emergency Medical Technicians. (2020). Tactical emergency casualty care. Retrieved from http://www.naemt.org/education/tecc

National Resource Directory. (2020). About us: National resource directory. Retrieved from https://nationalresourcedirectory.gov/About-Us

Plurad, D. S. (2011). Blast injury. *Military Medicine*, 176(3), 276-282. doi: 10.7205/milmed-d-10-00147

Psychological Health Center of Excellence. (2019). Psychological health by the numbers: Mental health disorder prevalence and incidence among active duty service members, 2005-2017. Retrieved from https://www.pdhealth.mil/sites/default/files/images/docs/20190717_Prevalence_Incidence_508FINAL_Document.pdf

Rabágo, C. A., Clouser, M., Dearth, C. L., Farrokhi, S., Calarneau, M. R., Highsmith, M. J., Wilken, J. M., Wyatt, M. P., & Hill, O. T. (2016). The extremity trauma and amputation center of excellence: Overview of the research and surveillance division [Supplemental material]. *Military Medicine*, 181(11), 3-12. doi: 10.7205/MILMED-D-16-00279

Roles of Medical Care (United States). (2018). In M. Cubano & F. K. Butler (Eds.), *Emergency War Surgery* (5th ed., pp. 19-22). Retrieved from https://www.cs.amedd.army.mil/FileDownloadpublic.aspx?docid=6f9e0685-1290-4e92-8277-c1e7b0f2fef0

Saeed, O., Tribble, D., Biever, K., Kavanaugh, M., & Crouch, H. (2016). Infection prevention in combat-related injuries. In *Joint Trauma System Clinical Practice Guidelines*. Retrieved from https://jts.amedd.army.mil/assets/docs/cpgs/JTS_Clinical_Practice_Guidelines_(CPGs)/Infection_Prevention_08_Aug_2016_ID24.pdf

Spelman, J. F., Hunt, S. C., Seal, K. H., & Burgo-Black, A. L. (2012). Post deployment care for returning combat veterans. *Journal of General Internal Medicine*, 27(9), 1200-1209. doi: 10.1007/s11606-012-2061-1

Stevens, L. F., Lapis, Y., Tang, X., Sander, A. M., Dreer, L. E., Hammond, F. M., Kreutzer, J. S., O'Neil-Pirozzi, T. M., & Nakase-Richardson, R. (2017). Relationship stability after traumatic brain injury among veterans and service members: A VA TBI model systems study. *Journal of Head Trauma Rehabilitation*, 32(4), 234-244. doi: 10.1097/HTR.0000000000000324

Szuflita, N. S., Neal, C. J., Rosner, M. K., Frankowski, R. F., & Grossman, R. G. (2016). Spine injuries sustained by U.S. military personnel in combat are different from non-combat spine injuries. *Military Medicine*, 181(10), 1314-1323. doi: 10.7205/MILMED-D-15-00332

U.S. Department of the Air Force. (2017). *En route care & aeromedical evacuation medical operations* (Air Force Instruction 48-307, Volume 1). Retrieved from https://static.e-publishing.af.mil/production/1/af_sg/publication/afi48-307v1/afi48-307v1.pdf

U.S. Department of the Air Force. (2017). *En route critical care* (Air Force Instruction 48-307, Volume 2). Retrieved from https://static.e-publishing.af.mil/production/1/af_sg/publication/afi48-307v2/afi48-307v2.pdf

U.S. Department of the Air Force. (2016). *En route care documentation* (Air Force Instruction 48-307, Volume 3). Retrieved from https://static.e-publishing.af.mil/production/1/af_sg/publication/afi48-307v3/afi48-307v3.pdf

U.S. Department of the Army. (2019). *Medical evacuation* (Army Techniques Publication No. 4-02.2). Retrieved from https://armypubs.army.mil/epubs/DR_pubs/DR_a/pdf/web/ARN17834_ATP%204-02x2%20FINAL%20WEB.pdf

U.S. Department of Defense. (2019). Blast Injury 101. Blast Injury Research Coordinating Office. Accessed at https://blastinjuryresearch.amedd.army.mil/index.cfm/blast_injury_101

U.S. Department of Defense. (2018). *Patient movement* (DoD Instruction 6000.11). Retrieved from https://www.esd.whs.mil/Portals/54/Documents/DD/issuances/dodi/600011p.pdf?ver=2017-12-01-105429-597

U.S. Department of Health & Human Services. (2020). Types and categories of hazardous chemicals and related toxidromes. Retrieved from https://chemm.nlm.nih.gov/agentcategories.htm

U.S. Department of Veterans Affairs. (2020). Burn pits. Retrievedfromhttps://www.publichealth.va.gov/exposures/burnpits/index.asp

U.S. Department of Veterans Affairs. (2019). Polytrauma System of Care, Veterans Health Administration Directive 1172.01. Retrieved from https://www.va.gov/OPTOMETRY/docs/VHA_Directive_1172-01_Polytrauma_System_of_Care_1172_01_D_2019-01-24.pdf

U.S. Department of Veterans Affairs. (2015). Polytrauma/TBI system of care. Retrieved from https://www.polytrauma.va.gov/system-of-care/index.asp

U.S. Department of Veterans Affairs. (2015). Polytrauma/TBI system of care: Recovery and Rehabilitation. Retrieved from https://www.polytrauma.va.gov/about/Recovery_and_Rehabilitation.asp

U.S. Department of Veterans Affairs. (2020). VA/DoD clinical practice guidelines. Retrieved from https://www.healthquality.va.gov/

U.S. Department of Veterans Affairs. (2016). South Texas Veteran's Healthcare System, PTRP11P-14-TO11, Polytrauma Transitional Rehabilitation Program Admission Policy and Procedure.

Vlasov, A., Ryan, D. S., Ludlow, S., Weichel, E. D., & Colyer, M. H. (2015). Causes of combat ocular trauma-related blindness from Operation Iraqi Freedom and Enduring Freedom [Supplemental material]. *Journal of Acute Care Surgery*, 79(4), S210-S215. doi: 10.1097/TA.0000000000000666

Walrath, B. D., Harper, S. A., Reno, J. L., Tobin, J. M., Davids, N., Kharod, C., Keen, D., Shackleford, S., Redman, T., Papalski, W. N., Pineda, B., Drew, B., Shinn, A., Duquette-Frame, T., Barnard, E., Selby, D., Sauer, S. W., Cunningham, C. W., & Stockinger, Z. T. (2018). Interfacility transport of patients between theater medical treatment facilities. In *Joint Trauma System Clinical Practice Guidelines*. Retrieved from https://jts.amedd.army.mil/assets/docs/cpgs/Prehospital_En_Route_CPGs/Transport_of_Patients_in_Theater_24_Apr_2018_ID27.pdf

CHAPTER 11

Military Occupational Exposures

Paul Lewis and Rich Prior

Military service members experience a wide variety of occupational exposures that can negatively affect health. Service members experience the full and broad range of occupational injuries that coexist in civilian counterparts with similar occupations. However, military service subjects members to a unique set of exposures that does not always have civilian equivalence. This chapter discusses unique toxic exposures within the military deployment environment as well as occupational health exposures that are commonly experienced by service members.

Toxic Exposures During Military Deployments

Deployments create unique exposures to known harmful and potentially harmful toxins. Some exposures are similar to comparable civilian occupations but there are many exposures that are unique to the military. Unfortunately, unlike the civilian counterpart, the tracking of toxin exposure is much more problematic in the military because the service member is part of a larger unit that is spread over a geographic location. This makes it very difficult to identify in real time exactly where a service member was on a given date, whether they were exposed to a known toxin, and how much exposure they received. The problem is further complicated by the fact that there is often a paucity of good data on the harmful effects of specific exposures. These questions only become even more difficult to answer decades later. Veterans, their families, the Department of Veterans Affairs (VA), and the military are increasingly concerned with the health effects of Agent Orange herbicide exposure during the Vietnam War; Gulf-War Illness that was experienced by veterans in the years following the Persian Gulf War; exposure to depleted uranium munitions during and after the Persian Gulf War; and the exposure to burn pits throughout contemporary military history.

The approach to a veteran with an exposure concern begins with listening to concerns and documenting deployment location, time frame, and known exposures. Providers can then explore any symptoms of illness and then recommend that the service member pursue a VA disability claim. Veterans' service organizations and advocates are extraordinarily helpful in assisting the veteran file the claim and upload any supporting documents. The VA will contact the service member to determine eligibility for continued care and compensation.

Agent Orange and Herbicidal Exposure

In an effort to stop the spread of communism throughout Southeast Asia, the United States intervened in a civil war in Vietnam in an attempt to bolster the democratic government of South Vietnam and prevent the spread of communism throughout Asia. From 1964 until the fall of Saigon on April 30, 1975, nearly 2,700,000 American troops served in Vietnam, nearly 300,000 of whom would be wounded, and 58,000 of whom would be killed (Willbanks, 2013; U.S. Department of Veterans Affairs, n.d.)

The U.S. government instituted a large-scale defoliation campaign in Vietnam from 1962 to 1971 designed to deny enemy soldiers concealment in the jungles and crops to feed their armies. Deemed "Operation Ranch Hand," the Air Force sprayed over 9,000 miles of terrain with over 19 million gallons of herbicidal exfoliants, dispersing 3 gallons of product per acre or about .009 of an ounce per square foot. The program also included additional spraying by helicopter and by hand (Boyne, 2000). The exfoliants were shipped to Vietnam in 55-gallon drums, which were color-coded orange to identify their contents. "Agent Orange contained 2,3,7,8-tetrachlorodibenzo-p-dioxin (TCDD), the dioxin that is accused of causing the morbidity associated with Agent Orange. The compound was also used in the United States in commercially available herbicides until the 1970s when it was banned due to suspicions of causing birth defects" (Stellman & Stellman, 2018).

Little is known about how large a population of military service members were exposed to Agent Orange. Individuals who directly participated in Operation Ranch Hand as well as those in the Army who handled the herbicide had particularly high levels of exposure, and some studies showed as much as three times higher levels of dioxin as the civilian population. Studies have attempted to determine whether ground troops who served in Vietnam have higher serum dioxin levels than those veterans who served elsewhere during the same period but found no discernable difference. It is acknowledged that some Navy veterans who served on rivers in Vietnam (known as the "Brown Water Navy") may have had exposure, while little is known about exposures to those sailors on ships offshore ("Blue Water Navy") (National Academies of Sciences, Engineering, and Medicine, 2018a).

In 1991, Congress passed the Agent Orange Act of 1991, which required the Department of Veterans Affairs and the National Academies of Sciences, Engineering, and Medicine to cooperate in evaluating scientific and statistical data to determine associations of disease with exposure to Agent Orange and other herbicides. The first report was published in 1994 and as of this writing, has been updated 11 times. The report is publicly available and is free of charge.

The conclusions in the 11th edition of the report state there is sufficient evidence of a positive association between exposure to Agent Orange and hypertension as well as several soft tissue cancers. A large cohort study of 3,086 Vietnam Veteran Army Chemical Corps soldiers found that those soldiers who had sprayed TCDD in Vietnam had a significantly higher rate of a self-reported diagnosis of hypertension compared to those who had neither sprayed TCDD nor been in Vietnam (adjusted odds ratio of 2.21). There was also a strong association of hypertension when comparing those who had sprayed TCDD compared to those who have not (adjust odds ratio of 1.74) regardless of service in Vietnam (Cypel et al., 2016). A strong association was also found to exist between Agent Orange and non-Hodgkin's lymphoma, chronic lymphocytic leukemia, and Hodgkin's lymphoma. While studies of Vietnam veterans have not found significant increases in rates of soft-tissue cancers, several case-control studies of chemical and industrial workers exposed to TCDD suggest associations between exposure and cancer (National Academies of Sciences, Engineering, and Medicine, 2018a).

The latest version of the veterans and Agent Orange report finds limited evidence of associations between TCDD exposure and other disorders to include laryngeal cancer, lung cancer, prostate cancer, bladder cancer, multiple myeloma, peripheral neuropathy, Parkinson's disease, polyphira cutanea tarda, ischemic heart disease, stroke, and hypothyroidism.

The Department of Veterans Administration takes a liberal approach to disability compensation and exposure to TCDD. Initial criteria for a VA disability requires service between 1962 and 1975 for any length of time in the Republic of Vietnam, aboard a U.S. military vessel that operated inside the waterways of Vietnam, on a vessel operating within 12 nautical miles of Vietnam or Cambodia, on regular perimeter duty of a fenced-in area on the U.S. Army installation in Thailand or a Royal Thai Air Force base, or were involved with handling Agent Orange during their military service (U.S. Department of Veterans Affairs, 2020a). The Blue Water Navy Veterans Act of 2019 formally presumes that military service members who served within 12 nautical miles of the Republic of Vietnam between January 1962 and May 1965 were exposed to herbicidal agents and are entitled to submit or resubmit VA claims for any associated illness.

Those who meet service requirements can be considered for disability with a cancer diagnosis of chronic-B cell leukemia, Hodgkin's lymphoma, multiple myeloma, non-Hodgkin's lymphoma, prostate cancer, pulmonary cancers, soft-tissue sarcomas. Other disorders that qualify include amyloid light chain amyloidosis, acne-form diseases, type II diabetes mellitus, ischemic heart disease, Parkinson's disease, early onset peripheral neuropathy, and porphyria cutanea tarda (U.S. Department of Veterans Affairs, 2020a).

Gulf War Illness

In August 1990, 100,000 Iraqi Soldiers invaded the small nation of Kuwait to annex its substantial oil fields and improve its financial status. In response, the United States deployed over 600,000 service members to neighboring Saudi Arabia and commenced a war that began on January 17, 1991, and lasted until March 1991 (U.S. Army Center of Military History, 2010). An estimated 25%–32% of Gulf War veterans suffer from a broad range of unexplained health problems most recently known as Gulf War Illness–previously referred to as Gulf War Syndrome (Mawson & Croft, 2019).

Concerns developed in the early 1990s when veterans of the Persian Gulf War seemed to develop a diffuse constellation of symptoms and disorders. A VA survey conducted in 1995 of 15,000 Gulf War veterans and 15,000 non-deployed veterans found higher rates of unexplained health problems in the Gulf War population than the non-deployed population. A follow-up study in 2012 found higher rates of several disorders in a Gulf-War veteran cohort that included chronic multi-symptom illness (43.9% vs 20.3%, adjust odds ratio 2.36), chronic fatigue syndrome (11.8% vs 5.3%, adjusted odds ratio 2.36), neuralgias (9.4% vs 6.3%, adjusted odds ratio 1.65), gastritis (20.2% vs 14.3%, adjusted odds ratio 1.59), chronic obstructive pulmonary disease (8.4% vs 6.3%, adjusted odds ratio 1.48), fibromyalgia (3.7% vs 2.9%, adjusted odds ratio 1.48%), and a host of other disorders with less strong associations (Mawson & Croft, 2019).

The cause of Gulf War Illness is unknown. Many theories suggest an interplay of exposures that could include local parasitic diseases such as schistosomiasis and leishmaniasis; deployment-specific vaccines such as anthrax; insecticides; exposures to Iraqi chemical weapons such as sarin or mustard gasses; pollutants from oil fires and the administration of pyridostigmine bromide as prophylaxis against sarin nerve gas (Nettleman, 2015).

Like the work done for Agent Orange, the National Academies of Sciences, Engineering, and Medicine has collaborated with the Department of Veterans Affairs since 1998 in evaluating scientific and medical literature regarding the effects of exposure. The committee finds no direct causal relationship, but there is sufficient evidence to identify an association between the Gulf War exposures and adverse pregnancy outcomes. The committee found sufficient evidence of an association with leishmaniasis infection and adverse pregnancy outcomes; hexavalent chromium exposure (an anti-corrosive chemical found at a water treatment plant in Basrah, Iraq) and reproductive effects in men; of prenatal exposure to hexavalent chromium exposure and developmental effects in women; of prenatal exposure and to certain pesticides and neurodevelopmental effects, to certain pesticides and reproductive effects in men; to prenatal exposure to particulate matter and adverse pregnancy effects in women, and prenatal exposure to benzene and childhood leukemia (National Academies of Sciences, Engineering, and Medicine, 2018b).

The Department of Veterans Affairs grants disability to veterans who have served in the Southwest Asia theater of military operations who have demonstrated a history of myalgic encephalomyelitis/chronic fatigue syndrome, fibromyalgia, functional gastrointestinal disorders such as irritable bowel disease, and undiagnosed illnesses such as abnormal weight loss, fatigue, cardiovascular disease, muscle and joint pain, headaches, menstrual disorders, neurological and psychological problems, skin conditions, respiratory disorders, and sleep disturbances. Veterans must have these symptoms for six or more months (U.S. Department of Veterans Affairs, n.d.-b)

Depleted Uranium

The U.S. military uses depleted uranium (DU) as a core component of munitions, which adds density and therefore lethality to ammunition. Depleted uranium is a by-product of the uranium enrichment process and is 40% less radioactive than naturally occurring uranium.

Depleted uranium munitions were used by the U.S. military for the first time during the Persian Gulf War. Exposure to DU can occur through being wounded by shrapnel containing DU, by internalizing DU through inhalations of contaminated dust, contaminated open wounds, or by drinking water/eating foods that are contaminated. Retained shrapnel fragments oxidize over time and result in chronic exposure within body fluids with blood and urine levels remaining elevated for years (Bleise et al., 2003; Corredor et al., 2019). When DU is ingested, as much as 98% is eliminated in the stool or filtered by the kidneys. A small portion of DU can be absorbed into bone where it remains potentially for years.

The long-term effects of DU exposure are still being evaluated. In animal models, DU has been shown to cause soft-tissue cancers and leukemia. In humans, acute high-level exposure to DU has been shown to lead to nephrotoxicity, but U.S. soldiers who had an acute high-level exposure demonstrated normal renal function years later (Shaki et al., 2019). Some researchers view exposure to depleted uranium as a possible cause of Gulf War Illness (Bjorklund et al., 2019). A cohort of 36 Gulf War veterans with known DU exposure is followed at the Baltimore Veteran's Affairs Medical Center. At the 25-year anniversary of their exposure, researchers conducted a cohort study monitoring for uranium levels in urine, pulmonary function, and the long-term medical effects of exposure. The participants showed no uranium-related long-term health effects (McDiarmid et al., 2017).

The VA decides disability compensation claims for health problems related to DU on a case-by-case basis. The VA maintains a screening program for those veterans exposed to DU in the Persian Gulf War, Bosnia, Iraq, and Afghanistan. Care includes monitoring, assessment, and continuous evaluation of retained fragments for removal (U.S. Department of Veterans Affairs, 2020b).

Burn Pits

The term "burn pits" applies to the military practice of open air burning of human waste, food, equipment, and other garbage in forward-deployed areas outside of the United States. It is estimated that as much as 250 tons of garbage per day were burned in Iraq and Afghanistan using jet fuel in pits that were as close as a mile from service members' barracks. The use of burn pits is considered a practice of last resort to be used when preferred methods of refuse disposal are absent or impractical. However, as late as 2019 the Department of Defense continued to operate several burn pits in the Middle East, several of which are operated by contractors as opposed to service members (Myers, 2019).

To better understand the health effects of burn-pit exposure, Congress passed Public Law 112-260 in 2013, which called for the establishment of a registry that is open to those who have served in the Persian Gulf War, operations in Iraq or Afghanistan, or in Djibouti, Africa, on or after September 11, 2001. To date, over 200,000 veterans have participated. Over 92% of the survey participants reported exposure during deployment, and 60% of the participants reported duties involving burn pits. Thirty-four percent of respondents sought care from a provider due to respiratory issues associated with air quality. The most commonly self-reported medical conditions among respondents included insomnia (81.9%), neurological problems (72.4%), allergies (39.8%), and hypertension (37.2%) (U.S. Department of Veterans Affairs, 2020c). A 2017 report from the National Academies of Sciences, Engineering, and Medicine praised the efforts of the VA while offering suggestions for improvement in the design of the survey.

To date, there has been a lack of strong evidence associating burn-pit exposure to health consequences. A 2018 retrospective cohort study comparing 200 service members with known burn-pit exposures to 200 non-deployed service members found that there was a slight increased risk for respiratory disease in service members deployed to Bagram Air Force Base in Iraq (adjusted relative risk: 1.259) and there was a slightly increased risk of cardiovascular disease in a group deployed to Balad, Iraq (adjusted relative risk: 1.072), but neither increase was considered significant (Rohrbeck et al., 2016). A second study conducted by the Armed Forces Health Surveillance Center followed a cohort of active duty service members known to have been deployed to locations operating burn pits. A 36-month follow-up found no evidence that service members assigned to bases with burn pits had an increased risk of respiratory disease when compared to service members who reported no burn-pit exposure (Sharkey et al., 2015).

The VA does not view exposure to burn pits as a long-term risk at this time. Veterans who believe that they have a disability are invited to file claims for disability, which is decided on a case-by-case basis.

Toxic Exposures in the United States

Not all of a military member's toxic exposures are the result of combat. The military is a relatively closed system in that service members tend to live on the military bases where they work and train. Each military base is its own community with housing, stores, and recreational facilities and military members will often go to and from work while never leaving the military installation. This makes the DoD responsible for insuring a safe living environment for military members and their families. Through the years, there have been many instances where the DoD has failed in this responsibility. The military is an occupation that handles many toxic substances from simple motor oil from the numerous vehicles, to other more serious chemicals such as volatile organic compounds and heavy metals. Prior to 1976, many of these dangerous substances were not adequately tracked or disposed of and many ended up in the soil and groundwater. In 1976, Congress passed the Resource Conservation and Recovery Act, which was aimed at tracking and managing the disposal of toxic wastes. This brought to light the many areas in the military, as well as the United States overall, that had inadequate disposal of toxic substances. Congress then passed the Comprehensive Environmental Response Compensation and Liability Act, more commonly known as the Superfund Act. This provided the framework for mandating and resourcing the cleanup of these sites. Today there are currently over 126 DoD sites that are on the National Priority List under the Superfund Act. These include all services from Air Force sites such as Wright Patterson AFB and Andrews AFB, to the Army posts of Fort McClellan and Aberdeen Proving Grounds and the Navy at Camp Lejeune and Camp Pendleton. These sites have soil contamination and some have water contamination from substances such as heavy metals, arsenic, benzene, or volatile organic compounds like tetracholorethene due to previous spills or inadequate disposal. These chemicals are known to cause many health effects including neurological disorders, diabetes, cancer, and possibly birth defects in children.

While many DoD sites are on the NPL, only one site to date has been recognized by the VA as a clear and present danger to service members. The VA has recognized that between 1953 to 1987 service members stationed at Camp Lejeune were exposed to dangerous chemicals such as thrichlorothylene, benzene, perchloroethylene, and other compounds in the drinking water. There are 15 conditions that the VA specifies as possible compensable illnesses for service members exposed to these substances, which include bladder cancer, breast cancer, lung cancer, multiple myeloma, and others. This situation gained significant national attention and prompted the Congress to pass the Honoring America's Veterans and Caring for Camp Lejeune Families Act, which also extended medical benefits to the family members who were also stationed at Camp Lejeune during that period.

Military-Specific Occupational Exposures

The military has unique occupational risks and potential exposures associated with deployments as stated previously. However, with an all-volunteer military that numbers about 1.3 million, there are many other occupational exposures in the normal day-to-day mission. Many aspects of military duty are considered dangerous due to operating in and around heavy machinery, handling dangerous substances, increased physical activity while bearing weight, and working in noisy environments. Unlike the exposures seen during deployments, most of the occupational exposures during regular duty are cumulative in nature. These exposures result in injury and illness, which may eventually cause the military member to be discharged from duty. This section will evaluate the occupational risks to which military members are exposed by significant body system.

Eyes

Military Background

Maintaining good eyesight in the military is not just a priority but is essential to carry out the mission of the military. The military requires all members to undergo routine examinations and to have 20/20 vision or vision corrected to 20/20. Military service is inherently dangerous and recent conflicts have found that eye trauma has become increasingly more common. Historical data shows the incidence of ocular injuries is increasing in both number and severity with each subsequent war (Cho &

Savitsky, 2012) with the vast majority (78%) of eye injuries occurring as a result of blast injuries. Eye injuries in this population can also be part of larger overall combat trauma. Research from the wars in Iraq and Afghanistan found that up to 10%–15% of combat injuries also included eye injuries (Cho & Savitsky, 2012).

Military Ocular Health and Injury Prevention Programs

Due to both the importance of acute vision and the increasing incidence of serious injuries, the military has established a specific program that monitors and strives to conserve the vision of military members. Initially, each service was separately monitoring their service members' vision. However, during the Persian Gulf War, it was found that 23% of the troops deployed either did not have 20/20 vision or did not have appropriate eyewear that corrected the vision to 20/20. As a result, in 1996 the program called Tri-Service Vision Conservation and Readiness Program with the motto "Preserve the Sight to Fight!" was developed. The mission of this organization is to "optimize visual performance, promote ocular health and reduce the rate of ocular injuries." The program continues to serve as a central guiding force for military vision conservation and readiness. Service members are closely monitored to ensure each has a recent visual exam and at least two sets of glasses prior to a deployment. A recent initiative also requires ballistic eyewear protection as a standard issue item. A second entity focused on military ocular care is the Department of Defense/Veterans Affairs Vision Center of Excellence, which was established by Congress under the 2008 National Defense Authorization Act. The goal of this organization is the prevention, diagnosis, mitigation, treatment, and rehabilitation of military eye injuries (Public Law 110-181, Section 1623, 2008). This Center of Excellence also develops Clinical Practice Guidelines for urgent ocular treatment.

Veteran Ocular Health Assessment

Routine medical visits for eye complaints among veterans are not dissimilar than those seen among civilian providers. A study conducted in 2018 found that the top three reasons military members received ocular care was for refractive error (51.1%), conjunctival disorders (13.3%), and corneal disorders (7.5%) (Reynolds et al., 2019) with the top three most frequent conditions diagnoses of myopia, astigmatism, and acute conjunctivitis.

Military members have an increased risk for eye injuries, which is not dissimilar to other industrial occupations that work with heavy machinery or in dusty, windy environments. Foreign bodies or corneal abrasions are not uncommon among service members. Among the young population, these injures are usually treated quickly with little long-term sequela. Military members, however, are at a uniquely elevated risk for two specific injuries: penetrating eye injuries and ocular laser injuries.

Box 11-1 Quick Notes: Eye Assessment

Most common diagnoses:*

- Myopia
- Astigmatism
- Acute Conjunctivitis

Highest likelihood of traumatic eye injury:**

- Ambulatory visit: enlisted, healthcare profession and over 40 years old
- Hospitalization: young (20- to 24-year-old), female enlisted combat arms Marine

Military specific considerations:

- Penetrating injury
- Laser injury

*(Reynolds et al., 2019)
**(Hilber, 2011)
Data from Reynolds, M. E., Williams, V. F., Taubman, S. B., & Stahlman, S. (2019). Absolute and relative morbidity burdens attributable to ocular and vision-related conditions, active component. *U.S. Armed Forces. Medical Surveillance Monthly Report, 26*(9), 4–11; and Hilber, D. (2011). Eye injuries, active component, U.S. Armed Forces, 2000–2010. *Medical Surveillance Monthly Report, 18*(5), 2–11.

The military risk of ocular-penetrating injury is a result of close proximity exposure to a blast and subsequent shrapnel. A study by Fatih et al. (2016) found that among service members who suffered a combat-related ocular injury, 56% were open globe injuries with 95% of those having a foreign body present. The majority (58.3%) of blast injures are the result of improvised explosive devices (Fatih et al., 2016) and up to 66% may also have concomitant traumatic brain injury (Eric et al., 2009).

The second specific risk is the new and developing risk of injuries by directed energy or lasers. The military uses lasers for both combat applications such as target illumination, radar warning systems, range finders, and "smart" bomb guidance as well as for training purposes such as on the multiple integrated laser engagement system (MILES) used to train realistic combat maneuvers without using live ammunition (similar to the recreational laser tag). The lasers employed by the military are typically grade 3 (MILES equipment) to grade 4 (range finders, target illumination). Both of these types of lasers are capable of producing ocular retinal injury when viewed either directly or from a reflection (Thompson 1993). The DoD has published an instruction titled "DoD Laser Protection Program," which provides a DoD-wide risk mitigation and monitoring platform. Designated within that instruction is the establishment of the Laser Accident and Incident Registry, which tracks and analyzes all reported laser injuries with the additional role of developing safety, protection, and treatment programs (Department of Defense, 2007). In response to the growing risk of ocular laser injuries, a clinical practice guideline has been developed to assist military practitioners in evaluating and treating ocular-laser injuries.

Ears

Military Background

Hearing loss has been called the "single most injurious hazard in terms of cost and frequency of occurrence for active duty military" (Mallon, 2019). Historically males are about twice as likely to have hearing issues as compared to females (Frayne et al., 2010). Service members who deploy to combat settings have shown a higher incidence of noise-induced hearing loss (Helfer, 2011) with returning veterans 1.63 times more likely to experience new onset hearing loss (Wells et al., 2015). Military members are particularly susceptible to acoustic trauma with resultant sensorineural hearing loss (SNHL) from high-level impulse noise as experienced with exposure to improvised explosive devices (Joseph et al., 2020) or weapons such as shoulder-fired rockets (Ohlin et al., 2019). Research into combat-related hearing loss is also finding a significant relationship between SNHL and concomitant traumatic brain injury (Karch, et al., 2016) and PTSD (MacGregor et al., 2020).

Military Hearing Conservation Programs

Recognition of the need for hearing conservation in the military began back as early as 1944 when it was recommended that personnel regularly exposed to gunfire should be issued hearing protection (Ohlin et al., 2019). The Air Force published the first regulation on noise in 1949 (Department of the Air Force, 1949). In 1950, the Army established the U.S. Army Environmental Hygiene Agency, which focused on noise hazard identification and hearing conservation (Ohlin, et al., 2019). The framework for an official DoD hearing conservation program was laid out in the 1987 DoD Instruction 6055.12 titled "Hearing Conservation" (Department of Defense, 1987). This DoD Instruction has been updated through the years with the most recent update completed in 2019 (Department of Defense, 2019). The Occupational Safety and Health Administration requires employers to maintain accurate records of workers' noise exposure and audiometric testing data. To meet this requirement, the DOD established the Defense Occupational and Environmental

Health Readiness System-Hearing Conservation Data Repository. This system captures the audiograms of service members and DoD personnel wherever they are in the world and consolidates it to allow for centralized monitoring (Batchelor et al., 2020).

Veteran Auditory Health Assessment

Hearing loss along with tinnitus are the most prevalent service-related disabilities among U.S. veterans with over 1.3 million having hearing loss and over 2.1 million experiencing tinnitus. Combined tinnitus and hearing loss account for more service-connected disability than the next three categories combined (Veterans Benefits Administration, 2019). Sensory-neural hearing loss with or without tinnitus is a very common finding among previous military members. A good history will reveal risk factors such as chronic exposure to loud machinery or close proximity to an explosion. Each service carries unique exposures, but the higher hearing deficits have been found with veterans who have worked on the flight line in either the Air Force or Navy, and Army veterans who were close to louds weapons such as tanks or field artillery. A clinical exam may reveal significant hearing loss, but audiogram testing is the best way to establish a baseline and to allow tracking of any changes over time. The veteran may also have been evaluated by the VA and given a service-related hearing disability. Establishing a baseline is an important assessment so any future changes can be tracked.

Box 11-2 Quick Notes: Hearing Assessment

Highest likelihood of hearing loss: *

- Men > Women
- Caucasian
- Guard/ Reserve
- Blast exposure**

Other considerations for hearing loss:

- Being a Marine
  - Years of service
  - Number of deployments***
- mTBI
- PTSD

*(Swan et al., 2017)
**(Joseph et al., 2020)
***(Gordon, Griest et al., 2017)

Data from Swan, A. A., Nelson, J. T., Swiger, B., Jaramillo, C. A., Eapen, B. C., Packer, M., & Pugh, M. (2017). Prevalence of hearing loss and tinnitus in Iraq and Afghanistan veterans: A chronic effects of neurotrauma consortium study. *Hearing Research, 349*, 4–12; Joseph, A. R., Shaw, J. L., Clouser, M. C., MacGregor, A. J., Dougherty, A. L., & Galarneau, M. R. (2020). Clinical audiometric patterns of hearing loss following blast-related injury in U.S. military personnel. *International Journal of Audiology, 59*(10), 772–779; and Gordon, J. S., Griest, S. E., Thielman, E. J., Carlson, K. F., Helt, W. J., Lewis, M. S., Blankenship, C., Austin, D., Theodoroff, S. M., & Henry, J. A. (2017). Audiologic characteristics in a sample of recently-separated military veterans: The Noise Outcomes in Servicemembers Epidemiology Study (NOISE Study). *Hearing Research, 349*, 21–30.

Pulmonary

Military Background

Respiratory illnesses are common in the military population. In 2018, respiratory illnesses accounted for 350,000 medical visits with over 500 hospitalized-bed days. Of particular interest to the military are the adenoviruses which, prior to vaccines, caused an attack rate in this population as high as 80% with a hospitalization rate about 33 times higher for recruits than non-recruits. With the return of the vaccine in 2011, these rates have dramatically reduced (Sanchez et al., 2015).

The military is particularly vulnerable to respiratory transmission of illnesses due to the close proximity in which military members work and live. This is especially true for the military recruits who live in barracks and Navy seaman that serve aboard ships. Military recruits tend to train in close proximity, are physically and psychologically stressed, and have interrupted sleep cycles. Among this group, respiratory infections are the most common diagnosis resulting in approximately 100,000 medical encounters with between

Box 11-3 Quick Notes: Pulmonary Assessment

Common Pulmonary Diagnoses

- COPD (9.4% of patients seen at VA)*
- Asthma (2.5% of patients seen at VA)*

Considerations for Pulmonary Assessment:

- Deployment history
- Burn-pit exposure
- Exposure to man-made and geologic particulate matter on deployment
- Current or past tobacco use

*(Yu et al., 2003)

Data from Yu, W., Ravelo, A., Wagner, T. H., Phibbs, C. S., Bhandari, A., Chen, S., & Barnett, P. G. (2003). Prevalence and costs of chronic conditions in the VA Health Care System. *Medical Care Research and Review, 60*(3), 146S–167S.

12,000 to 27,000 lost days of training each year. The incidence of hospitalizations for respiratory illnesses among military recruits is about three to four times that which is seen in the civilian sector and accounts for about 25% of infectious disease hospitalizations. The risk of pulmonary infections among Navy seaman was made very clear during an outbreak of COVID-19 aboard the USS *Theodore Roosevelt*. The virus rapidly spread through the ship with an estimated 1,000 of the 1,400-person crew becoming infected, which forced the aircraft carrier to abandon its current mission and put in at Guam to treat the sick (Payne et al., 2020).

Service members who return from deployment in the Middle East have a higher rate of respiratory symptoms when compared to service members who do not deploy. There is growing evidence that this is due to exposure to elevated levels of particulate matter (PM) from a number of sources both geologic (blowing sand, dust) and man-made (combustion of fossil fuels, fires). There have been numerous health effects associated with elevated PM exposure to include respiratory and cardiopulmonary effects, increased hospitalizations, and even increased mortality. It has been shown that deployed service members have been exposed to particulate matter from two to five times the EPA's recommended 24-hour exposure levels. While burn-pit exposure has received much attention, an Institute of Medicine (IOM) report tasked with investigating burn-pit exposures concluded that high ambient concentrations of particulate matter outside of the burn-pit contribution might be associated with long-term health effects (Institute of Medicine, 2011). A series of studies called the STAMPEDE studies (Morris et al., 2014, Morris et al. (2020) which evaluated service members who had recently returned from a deployment and were complaining of new-onset pulmonary symptoms found that between 14%–22% of service members had new onset asthma upon returning from deployment and an additional 15% had elevated airway hyperreactivity with normal spirometry.

Veteran Pulmonary Health Assessment

The three most common pulmonary diagnoses of veterans seen at the VA, which effects over 430,000 veterans, are COPD, asthma, and lung cancer. Veterans are three times more likely to develop COPD than the general population, and it affects about 15% of veterans who get care at the VA. The cause for the elevated incidence of COPD in this population is not clear, but smoking and environmental exposures are likely causes. Deployments have been shown to increase the incidence of asthma among veterans with those who have deployed being 1.5 times more likely to develop asthma when compared to veterans who did not deploy (Szema et al., 2010). While the exact cause is still under investigation, repeated deployments do not seem to increase the risk (Abraham et al., 2012).

Smoking remains a significant health risk for veterans and contributes to both the increased incidence of COPD and lung cancer. Almost 30% of veterans use tobacco with cigarettes being the most common (21.6%) followed by cigars (6.2%). The prevalence was highest among those aged 18–25 (56.8%), Hispanic (34.0%), with less than a high school education (37.9%), and making less than $20,000 per year (44.3%) (Odani et al., 2018). The prevalence of current tobacco use is particularly high among young male veterans (50.2%) compared to male non-veterans of a similar age (35.3%). It is important to note that 40% of these tobacco users also report having serious psychological distress (Odani et al., 2018). Tobacco use among veterans carries a significant healthcare burden. A study conducted in 2015 estimated that about $2.7 billion, or 7.6%, of the annual healthcare expenditures by the VA were attributable to the effects of smoking (Barnett et al., 2015).

Musculoskeletal

Military Background

Even though the military is a relatively young and a very active population, there are a significant number of jobs in the military that are demanding and cause stress on the musculoskeletal system, from infantrymen carrying packs over 50 pounds, to prolonged riding in a vehicle or aircraft, to parachute jumps from aircraft. Musculoskeletal system disorders are the number one diagnostic category for ambulatory care visits among the military accounting for 36.7% of the overall visits to outpatient care or over 4.4 million visits. The top two unique diagnoses found for those being seen for musculoskeletal system disorders was pain in joints (40.5%) and low back pain (18.1%) (Armed Forces Health Surveillance Branch, 2020). Over 50% of military members who had work limitations were due to musculoskeletal issues (Armed Forces Health Surveillance Branch, 2020). Musculoskeletal pain is so common that in 2014 over 80% of active duty service members received a prescription for a nonsteroidal anti-inflammatory drug for musculoskeletal injuries. (Walker et al., 2017). Women experience musculoskeletal injures at almost twice the rate of male service members (Springer & Ross, 2011).

Musculoskeletal pain in this population is partly a function of the high physical activity required as well as the heavy loads carried by service members. Working in austere environments with uncertain support means a military member must carry on his or her back all the essential supplies for both combat and survival. This is called the combat load. The combat load is divided into the fighting load (when enemy contact is likely) and approach load (included extra supplies such as sleeping and hygiene supplies). Current U.S. Army doctrine recommends 22 kg or 30% of body weight for the fighting load and 33 kg or 45% of body weight for the approach load. This weight is in addition to the body armor worn in combat environments, which can weigh in excess of 13 kg (26 lbs). The physical toll required to carry this load results in many musculoskeletal injuries that include knee and back injuries as well as stress fractures.

Box 11-4 Quick Notes: Musculoskeletal Assessment

Most Common Complaint:

- Arthritis (predominantly lower extremity)
- Low back pain

Highest likelihood of musculoskeletal pain:*

- Women > Men
- Army
- Enlisted personnel

Other considerations for musculoskeletal pain:

- Amount of time in vehicle
- Prolonged wearing of body armor
- Smoking**

*(Bader et al., 2018)

**(Cowan et al., 2003)

Data from Bader, C. E., Giordano, N. A., McDonald, C. C., Meghani, S. H., & Polomano, R. C. (2018). Musculoskeletal pain and headache in the active duty military population: An Integrative review. *Worldviews on Evidence-Based Nursing, 15*(4), 264–271; Cowan, D. N., Jones, B. H., & Shaffer, R. A. (2003). Musculoskeletal injuries in the military training environment. In P. W. Kelley (Ed.), *Military preventive medicine, mobilization and deployment* (Vol. 1). Borden Institute.

This burden on the musculoskeletal system is only worsened during conflict. In the combat environment, up to 50% of non-battle injuries and 43% of battle injuries involved musculoskeletal problems (Owens & Cameron 2016). Over a quarter of all injuries in Iraq and Afghanistan were due to musculoskeletal injuries (Hauret et al., 2010) and the more general category of extremity injuries were responsible for 65% of hospitalizations, 64% of those deemed "unfit for duty," and 64% of the projected disability benefit costs as a result of injury (Masini et al., 2009). The top five most common reasons to visit a physical therapist in the combat theater was mechanical low back pain, ankle sprains, retro-patellar pain syndrome, contusions, and plantar fasciitis (Roy, 2011). The most common musculoskeletal injury seen in a combat environment was an overuse injury. Medical evacuations due to musculoskeletal injuries out of the combat zone was primarily due to sports activities or physical training.

Veteran Musculoskeletal Health Assessment

Complaints of musculoskeletal disorders are common among veterans. A review in 2011 found that 70% of service members discharged for medical reasons was due to orthopedic conditions with degenerative arthritis being the most common (Cross et al., 2011). About 26% of women and 29% of men present to the VA medical system with musculoskeletal complaints (Haskell et al., 2020). Of the top five common conditions seen in the VA, osteoarthritis is number three and low back pain is number five.

While degenerative arthritis becomes more prevalent with age, the incidence of arthritis is higher in military veterans at an earlier age. The incidence can be as high as 12% among veterans in their forties. This elevated prevalence has been hypothesized to be due to post-traumatic arthritis as a result of the numerous injuries sustained to the joints as a result of military service (Rivera et al., 2017).

A special population of veterans with unique musculoskeletal concerns are the veterans who have experienced a limb amputation as a consequence of military service. While this population requires specialized care outside the focus of this chapter, it bears mentioning the long-term musculoskeletal impact. These veterans, predominantly younger men, have numerous musculoskeletal complaints. Over half of amputees report low back pain, which they attribute to their amputation (Ehde, et al., 2001). There is also a higher incidence of knee pain, knee arthritis, hip pain, and hip arthritis, and about two thirds are likely to develop a musculoskeletal overuse injury in the first year after the amputation. This population is twice as likely to develop a lumbar injury and two to four times more likely to develop an upper limb overuse injury (Farrokhi et al., 2018).

Neurological

Military Background

Casualties from war have historically been the result of ballistic injuries from projectile weapons. The Iraq and Afghanistan Wars are the first wars the United States has been involved in which the improvised explosive device (IED) is the preferred offensive weapon of choice. This close proximity exposure to explosions produces significant soft tissue damage but also results in what has come to be known as the signature injury of these wars—traumatic brain injury (TBI). While it is not the purpose of this chapter to discuss the details of a TBI, it is worth noting the occupational risks and outcomes as a result of that exposure. Over 300,000 service members have received a diagnosis of TBI since 2000, which ranges from mild to severe, and it has been estimated that 65% of the casualties from the Iraq and Afghanistan wars involve blast exposure (Wojcik et al., 2010). Soldiers who have been exposed to a blast while deployed return with a higher severity of post-deployment symptoms when compared to those not exposed to a blast (Quigley et al., 2012). With increased interest in the impact of TBI, it has come to light that this problem is not unique to combat. The Armed Forces Health Surveillance Center conducted a 10-year study (1997–2006), which found 110,392 military members experienced a TBI with over 15,000 hospitalizations predominantly as the result of falls or motor vehicle accidents (Army Medical Surveillance Activity, 2007). Recent research has also begun to explore the repetitive minor blast exposures military members experience during training while firing heavy weapons such as artillery, shoulder-launched rockets, and recoilless rifles. The people affected have dubbed it "breachers brain" as it was first noted in personnel using low-level explosives to breach building entrances (Kamimori et al., 2017). Reported symptoms include headache, fatigue, memory difficulties, and slowed thought processes (Tate et al., 2013).

Veteran Neurological Health Assessment

The long-term effects of blast exposure are categorized under post-concussive symptoms but the true long-term effect of being exposed to a blast is still being investigated. The three main outcomes to consider for veterans if they were exposed to blast trauma are neurocognitive, neurologic, and psychiatric. There is consistent evidence that severe brain injury results in neurocognitive deficits to include deficits in memory, attention, processing speed, and executive functions. Due to the lack of definitive distinction between moderate and mild brain injury however, the literature is mixed on the neurocognitive effects of these two categories of TBI (Institute of Medicine, 2011). Common neurologic symptoms after a TBI include the cluster of post-concussive symptoms of memory problems, dizziness, and irritability. The development of unprovoked seizures is also possible. Compared to uninjured individuals, unprovoked seizures were 2.9–6.6 times higher in moderate TBI and 1.5 times higher in mild TBI. Evidence is beginning to emerge that mild TBI may also be associated with the development of ocular and visual motor deterioration (Institute of Medicine, 2011). Possible psychiatric outcomes associated with TBI are less clear. There is stronger evidence to suggest military members who have experienced a TBI will also experience depression and display aggressive behaviors. There is limited but suggestive evidence that PTSD and completed (but not attempted) suicides are associated with suffering a TBI (Institute of Medicine, 2011).

Box 11-5 Quick Notes: Neurological Assessment

Questions regarding explosion exposure:

- Exposure to:
  - IEDs
  - Large weapons systems
- Breaching exposure
- Number of exposures
- Distance from explosion
- Mild/moderate/severe TBI

Potential neurological effects:

- Strong Evidence:
- Memory issues
- Dizziness (up to 80% of TBI patients)
- Irritability
- Insomnia
- Seizures (greatest in first year)

Evidence of Associations (mod/severe TBI):

- Vestibular injury
- Neurodegenerative diseases (dementia, parkinsonism)
- Chronic Traumatic Encephalopathy
- Depression
- Aggression
- PTSD
- Impaired social functioning
- Endocrine dysfunction (hypopituitarism, growth hormone insufficiency)

*(Institute of Medicine, 2009)

Data from Institute of Medicine. (2009). *Gulf war and health: Long-term consequences of traumatic brain injury* (Vol. 7). The National Academies Press.

Conclusion

Military veterans, recruited from the general public, enter military service with the same physical and mental vulnerabilities as typically seen in the citizens of the United States. But once they enter service, they are no longer typical. The physical demands placed on them are more intense and require a high level of physical fitness and resilience. The locations where they are required to conduct their work is far from their home environment and carry risks still not clearly understood. The occupational exposures they experience are very broad extending from those that are immediately life-threatening to more subtle exposures, which are only beginning to be understood decades later. The occupational risks may be a one-time exposure during a military deployment or they may be cumulative over the course of their military career. Regardless of the job or location in which the military member served, there is a high likelihood they experienced occupational exposures, which make them a unique population when being evaluated medically. This chapter explained some of the occupational exposures that are common to most veterans. While this chapter is not all-inclusive of every potential occupational exposure, it did highlight health consequences of common exposures for which the veteran may seek treatment once they leave military service. While medical care tends to look for typical explanations to common problems, with 1.3 million military members spread across the world doing hundreds of different jobs with thousands of potential occupational risks, there is not really any such thing as a typical military veteran.

References

Bjorklund, G., Pivina, L., Dadar, N., Semenova, Y., Rahman, M. M., Chirumbolo, S., & Aaseth, J. (2019). Depleted uranium and Gulf War Illness: Updates and comments on possible mechanisms behind the syndrome. *Environmental Research, 181*, 1–5.

Bleise, A., Danesi, P. R., & Burkart, W. (2003). Properties, use, and health effects of depleted uranium (DU): A general overview. *Journal of Environmental Radioactivity, 64*(2003), 93–112.

Boyne, W. J. (2000). Ranch Hand. https://www.airforcemag.com/article/0800ranch/

Corredor, C. E., Goodison, S., Barrickman, D., Alberth, D., Bower, M. W., Jones, C., Muller, M. W., Edge, H., & Dunston, S. G. (2019). Ioninizing radiation. In T. M. Mallon (Ed.), *Occupational health and the service member* (pp. 434–436). Borden Institute.

Cypel, Y. S., Kress, A. M., Eber, S. M., Schneiderman, A. I., & Davey, V. J. (2016). Herbicide exposure, Vietnam service, and hyptertension risk in Army Chemical Corps veterans. *JOEM, 58*(11), 1127–1136.

Kennedy, K. (2020). *We're better than this: Jon Stewart, veterans advocates rally for bipartisan burn pit legislation.* https://www.military.com/dailynews/2020/11/03/were-better-jon-stewart-veterans-advocates-rally-bipartisan-burn-pit-legislation.html

Mawson, A. R., & Croft, A. M. (2019). Gulf War Illness: Unifying hypothesis for a continuing health problem. *International Journal of Environmental Research and Public Health, 16*(111), 1–16.

McDiarmid, M. A., Gaitens, J. M., Hines, S., Condon, M., Roth, T., Oliver, M., Gucer, P., Brown, L., Centeno, J. A., Dux, M., & Squibb, K. S. (2017). The U.S. Department of Veterans' Affairs depleted uranium exposed cohort at 25 years: Longitudinal surveillance results. *Environmental Research, 152*(2017), 175–184.

Myers, M. (2019). *Why DoD is still using burn pits, even while acknowledging their danger.* https://militarytimes.com/news/your-military/2019/07/12/why-dod-is-still-using-burn-pits-even-while-now-acknowledging-their-danger/

National Academies of Sciences, Engineering, and Medicine. (2018a). *Agent Orange: Update 11*. National Academies Press.

National Academies of Sciences, Engineering, and Medicine. (2018b). *Gulf War and health: Generational health effects of serving in the Gulf War (Vol. 11)*. National Academies Press.

Nettleman, M. (2015). Gulf War Illness: Challenges persist. *Transactions of the American Clinical and Climatological Association, 126*, 237–247.

Rohrbeck, P., Hu, Z., & Mallon, T. M. (2016). Assessing health outcomes after environmental exposures associated with open put burning in deployed U.S. servce members. *Journal of Occupational and Environmental Medicine, 58*(8), S104–S110.

Shaki, F., Zamani, E., Arjmand, A., & Pourahmad, J. (2019). A review on toxoicodynamics of depleted uranium. *Iranian Journal of Pharmaceutical Research, 18*(Supp. 1), 90–100.

Sharkey, J., Baird, C., Eick-Cost, A., Clark, L., Hu, Z., Ludwig, S., & Abraham, J. (2015). Review of epidemiological analyses of respiratory health outcomes after military deployment to burn pit locations with respect to feasibility and design issues highlighted by the Institute of Medicine. In C. P. Baird & D. K. Harkins (Eds.), *Airborne hazards related to deployment* (pp. 291–296). Borden Institute.

Stellman, J. M., & Stellman, S. D. (2018). Agent Orange during the Vietnam War: The lingering issue of its civilian and military impact. *AJPH, 108*(6), 726–728.

U.S. Army Center of Military History. (2010). *War in the Persian Gulf: Operations Desert Shield and Desert Storm August 1990–March 1991.* U.S. Army Center of Military History.

U.S. Department of Veterans Affairs. (n.d.-a). *Military health history pocket card.* https://www.va.gov/OAA/pocketcard/m-vietnam.asp

U.S. Department of Veterans Affairs. (2020a). *Agent Orange exposure and VA disability compensation.* https://www.va.gov/disability/eligibility/hazardous-materials-exposure/agent-orange/

U.S. Department of Veterans Affairs. (2020b). *Depleted uranium follow-up program.* https://www.publichealth.va.gov/exposures/depleted_uranium/followup_program.asp

U.S. Department of Veterans Affairs. (2020c). *Self-reported health information from the airborne hazards and open burn pit registry: Cumulative from June 2014 through December 31, 2019.* https://www.publichealth.va.gov/docs/exposures/va-ahobp-registry-data-report-dec2019.pdf#

U.S. Department of Veterans Affairs. (n.d.). *Gulf War veterans' medically unexplained illnesses.* https://www.publichealth.va.gov/exposures/gulfwar/medically-unexplained-illness.asp

Willbanks, J. H. (2013). Overview of the Vietnam War. In J. H. Willbanks (Ed.), *Vietnam War: The essential reference guide.* ABC-CLIO.

(2008). National Defense Authorization Act for Fiscal Year 2008. t. Congress.

Abraham, J. H., et al. (2012). "Does Deployment to Iraq and Afghanistan Affect Respiratory Health of US Military Personnel?" *Journal of Occupational and Environmental Medicine 54*(6), 740–745.

Armed Forces Health Surveillance Branch (2020). "Ambulatory Visits, Active Component, U.S. Armed Forces, 2019." *MSMR 27*(5), 18–24.

Army Medical Surveillance Activity (2007). "Traumatic Brain Injury Among Military Members of Active Components, U.S. Armed Forces, 1997–2006." *Medical Surveillance Monthly Report 15*(1), 2–8.

Bader, C. E., et al. (2018). "Musculoskeletal Pain and Headache in the Active Duty Military Population: An Integrative Review." *Worldviews on Evidence-Based Nursing 15*(4), 264–271.

Barnett, P. G., et al. (2015). "Health Care Expenditures Attributable to Smoking in Military Veterans." *Nicotine & Tobacco Research 17*(5), 586–591.

Batchelor, E., et al. (2020). "Hearing conservation measures of effectiveness across the Department of Defense." *MSMR 27*(7), 2–6.

Cho, R. I., & Savitsky, E. (2012). Ocular trauma. Combat casualty care: Lessons learned from OEF and OIF. E. Savitsky & B. Eastridge. Borden Institute.

Cowan, D. N., et al. (2003). Musculoskeletal Injuries in the Military Training Program. Military Preventive Medicine, Mobilization and Deployment, Vol 1. P. W. Kelley. Borden Institute.

Cross, J. D., et al. (2011). "Battlefield Orthopaedic Injuries Cause the Majority of Long-term Disabilities." *Journal of the American Academy of Orthopaedic Surgeons 19*, S1–S7.

Department of Defense. (1987). Hearing Conservation. DoD Instruction 6055.12.

Department of Defense. (2007). Laser Protection Program. DOD Instruction 6055.15.

Department of Defense. (2019). Hearing Conservation Pro DoD Instruction 6055.12.

Department of the Air Force. (1949, August 31). Air Force Regulation No. 160-3.

Ehde, D. M., et al. (2001). "Back Pain as a Secondary Disability in Persons With Lower Limb Amputations." *Archives of Physical Medicine and Rehabilitation 82*(6), 731–734.

Eric, W., et al. (2009). "Traumatic Brain Injury Associated with Combat Ocular Trauma." *Journal of Head Trauma Rehabilitation 24*, 41–50.

Farrokhi, S., et al. (2018). "Incidence of Overuse Musculoskeletal Injuries in Military Service Members with Traumatic Lower Limb Amputation." *Archives of Physical Medicine and Rehabilitation 99*, 348–354.

Fatih, G., et al. (2016). "Ocular blast injuries related to explosive military ammunition." *BMJ Military Health 162*, 39–43.

Frayne, S., et al. (2010). "Medical care needs of returning veterans with PTSD: Their other burden." *Journal of General Internal Medicine 26*(1), 33–39.

Gordon, J., et al. (2017). "Audiologic characteristics in a sample of recently-separated military veterans: The Noise Outcomes in Servicemembers Epidemiology Study (NOISE Study)." *Hearing Research 349*, 21–30.

Haskell, S. G., et al. (2020). "Incident Musculoskeletal Conditions Among Men and Women Veterans Returning from Deployment." *Medical Care 00*(00), 1–9.

Hauret, K. G., et al. (2010). "Frequency and Causes of Nonbattle Injuries Air Evacuated from Operations Iraqi Freedom and Enduring Freedom, U.S. Army,

2001-2006." *American Journal of Preventative Medicine 38*(1S), S94–S107.

Helfer, T. (2011). "Noise-induced hearing injuries, active component, U.S. Armed Forces, 2007-2010." *MSMR 18*, 7–10.

Hilber, D. (2011). "Eye injuries, active component, U.S. Armed Forces, 2000-2010." *Medical Surveillance Monthly Report 18*(5), 2–11.

Institute of Medicine. (2009). *Gulf War and health: Long-term consequences of traumatic brain injury* (Vol. 7). National Academies Press.

Institute of Medicine (2011). *Long-term health consequences of exposure to burn pits in Iraq and Afghanistan. C. o. t. L.-T. H. C. o. E. t. B. P. i. I. a. Afghanistan*. National Academies Press.

Joseph, A. R., et al. (2020). "Clinical audiometric patterns of hearing loss following blast-related injury in U.S. military personnel." *International journal of audiology 59*(10), 772–779.

Kamimori, G. H., et al. (2017). "Occupational overpressure exposure of breachers and military personnel." *Shock Waves 27*, 837–847.

Karch, S. J., et al. (2016). "Hearing Loss and Tinnitus in Military Personnel with Deployment-Related Mild Traumatic Brain Injury." *U.S. Army Medical Department Journal*, 52–63.

MacGregor, A. J., et al. (2020). "Co-occurence of hearing loss and posttraumatic stress disorder among injured military personnel: a retrospective study." *BMC Public Health 20*, 1076.

Mallon, T. M. N., C J.; Deeter, D P.; Ruff, J M. (2019). Medical Surveillance. Occupational Health and the Service Member. M. T. M. Fort Sam Houston TX, Borden Institute.

Masini, B. D., et al. (2009). "Resource Utilization and Disability Outcome Assessment of Combat Casualties From Operation Iraqi Freedom and Operation Enduring Freedom." *Journal of Orthopedic Trauma 23*(4), 261–266.

Morris, M. J., et al. (2014). "Study of Active Duty Military for Pulmonary Disease Related to Environmental Deployment Exposures (STAMPEDE)." *American Journal Respiratory Critical Care Medicine 190*(1), 77–84.

Morris, M. J., et al. (2020). "Clinical Evaluation of Deployed Military Personnel with Chronic Respiratory Symptoms" *Chest 157*(6), 1559–1567.

Odani, S., et al. (2018). "Tobacco Product Use Among Military Veterans - United States, 2010–2015." *MMWR 67*, 7–12.

Ohlin, D., et al. (2019). Army Hearing Program. Occupational Health and the Service Member. M. Timothy. Borden Institute.

Owens, B. D. and K. L. Cameron (2016). The Burden of Musculoskeletal Injuries in the Military. Musculoskeletal Injuries in the Military. K. L. Cameron and B. D. Owens. New York, NY, Springer New York: 3-10.

Payne, D. C., et al. (2020). "SARS-CoV-2 Infections and Serologic Responses from a Sample of U.S. Navy Service Members - USS Theodore Roosevelt, April 2020." *MMWR 69*(23), 714–721.

Quigley, K. S., et al. (2012). "Prevalence of Environmental and Other Military Exposure Concerns in Operation Enduring Freedom and Operation Iraqi Freedom Veterans." *Journal of Occupational and Environmental Medicine 54*(6), 259–264.

Reynolds, M. E., et al. (2019). "Absolute and relative morbidity burdens attributable to ocular and vision-related conditions, active component, U.S. Armed Forces, 2018." *MSMR 26*(9), 4–11.

Rivera, J. C., et al. (2017). "Arthritis, Comorbidities, and Care Utilization in Veterans of Operations Enduring and Iraqi Freedom." *Journal of Orthopedic Research 35*, 682–687.

Roy, T. C. (2011). "Diagnoses and Mechanisms of Musculoskeletal Injuries in an Infantry Brigade Combat Team Deployed to Afghanistan Evaluated by the Brigade Physical Therapist." *Military Medicine 176*(8), 903–908.

Sanchez, J. L., et al. (2015). "Respiratory Infections in the U.S. Military: Recent Experience and Control." *Clinical Microbiology Reviews 28*(3), 743–798.

Springer, B. A. and A. E. Ross (2011). Muskuloskeletal injuries in military women. Borden Institute.

Swan, A. A., et al. (2017). "Prevalence of hearing loss and tinnitus in Iraq and Afghanistan veterans: A chronic effecs of neurotrauma consortium study." *Hearing research 349*, 4–12.

Szema, A. M., et al. (2010). "New-onset Asthma Among Soldiers Serving in Iraq and Afghanistan." *Allergy Ashtma Proceedings 31*, e67–e71.

Tate, C. M., et al. (2013). "Serum Brain Biomarker Level, Neurocognitive Performance, and Self-Reported Symptom Changes in Soldiers Repeatedly Exposed to Low-Level Blast: A Breacher Pilot Study." *Journal of Neurotrauma 30*(19), 1620–1630.

Thompson, A. K. (1993). Conserving vision. Occupational Health: The Soldier and the Industrial Base. E. A. Lindeke. Fort Sam Houston, TX, Borden Institute.

Veterans Benefits Administration. (2019). *VBA annual benefits report fiscal year 2019*. https://benefits.va.gov/REPORTS/abr/docs/2019-compensation.pdf.

Walker, L. A., et al. (2017). "Widespread Use of Prescription Nonsteroidal Anti-Inflammatory Drugs Among U.S. Army Active Duty Soldiers." *Military Medicine 182*(e1709–e1712).

Wells, T., et al. (2015). "Hearing loss associated with US military combat deployment." *Noise & health 17*(74), 34–42.

Wojcik, B. E., et al. (2010). "Traumatic Brain Injury Hospitalizations of U.S. Army Soldiers Deployed to Afghanistan and Iraq." *American Journal of Preventative Medicine 38*(1S), S108–S116.

Yu, W., et al. (2003). "Prevalence and Costs of Chronic Conditions in the VA Health Care System." *Medical Care Research and Review 60*(3), 146S–167S.

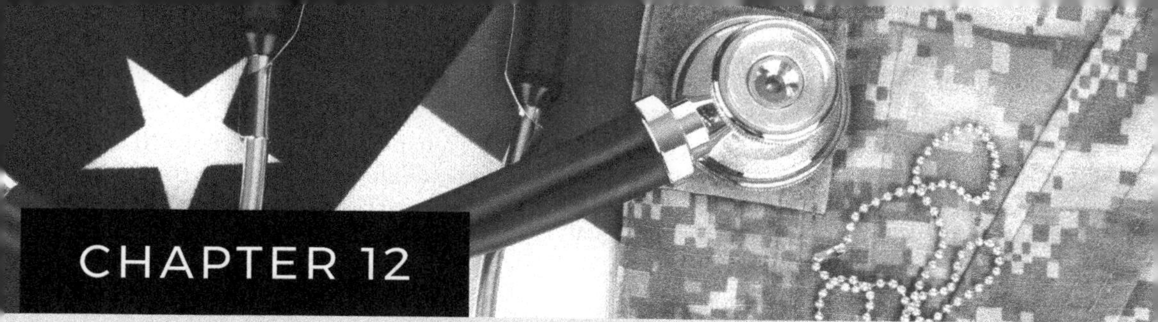

CHAPTER 12

Caring for Veterans with TBI in the Private Sector

Alison M. Cogan, Christina Dillahunt-Aspillaga, and Joel Scholten

Introduction

In this chapter, we provide an overview of issues that impact military veterans and active duty service members (V/SM) with a history of traumatic brain injury (TBI). We present incidence data, describe differences between military and civilian injuries, review TBI severity levels as defined by the Departments of Veterans Affairs and Defense, and review typical associated symptoms and challenges with community reintegration (CR) unique to V/SMs. At the end of this chapter, we provide a list of resources for healthcare providers who may encounter V/SMs with TBI in their practices.

TBI Reintegration: The Military/Civilian Divide

Traumatic brain injury (TBI) is a major public health concern. The Centers for Disease Control (CDC) report 2.87 million emergency department visits, hospitalizations, or deaths from TBI in the United States during 2014 alone (CDC, n.d.). The Department of Defense (DoD) records TBI incidence separately and has identified more than 380,000 service members with TBI from 2000 to 2018 across all military branches (Defense and Veterans Brain Injury Center, 2018). In the military population, more than 80% of injuries are classified as mild, which is similar to estimates of TBI injury severity in civilians (Tagliaferri et al., 2006).

Key distinctions between military and civilian TBI include combat exposure, injury by an improvised explosive device (IED) blast, prevalence of psychiatric comorbidities, and the influence of military culture on healthcare usage (Armistead-Jehle et al., 2017). Mild TBI (mTBI) is labeled the "signature injury" of the wars in Iraq and Afghanistan (Tanielian et al., 2008) Advances in protective equipment as well as medical technology have resulted in service members surviving events that may have been fatal in prior eras. As a result of this higher survival rate in the wars in Iraq and Afghanistan, prevalence of mTBI among deployed service members is estimated to be between 15% and 20% (Tanielian et al., 2008; Hoge et al., 2008), approximately half of which are related to blasts (Benzinger, 2009). Overall, however, only about 20% of mTBIs among active duty service members occur during combat deployments; the vast majority happen in the continental United States (CONUS) where they may occur during training exercises or typical life activities (e.g., falls, motor vehicle accidents) (Cameron et al., 2019)

Definition of Community Reintegration

Community reintegration (CR), a Department of Veterans Affairs (VA) priority, is defined as participation in community life, including employment or other productive activities, independent living, and social relationships (Department of Veterans Affairs, 2018). A substantial proportion of veterans report difficulties with CR following discharge from military service (Sayer et al., 2010). These difficulties are associated with poor social and family relationships, unemployment, financial strain, homelessness, and poor physical and mental health (Romaniuk & Kidd, 2018). CR difficulties are compounded for veterans with disabilities, including TBI (Department of Veterans Affairs, 2019). Coupling problems related to TBI with the transition from military to civilian worlds puts V/SM with TBI at high risk for a myriad of CR problems. Approximately 4.6 million veterans have a service-connected disability (Department of Veterans Affairs, 2019), not including those living with functional limitations from chronic medical conditions. The number of veterans with disabilities is expected to increase as the veteran population ages (Hale-Gallardo et al., 2017).

In 2012, the VA convened a state-of-the-art (SOTA) working group to advance the science and measurement of CR for injured service members. This group adopted the International Classification of Functioning (ICF) domain of participation as a theoretical framework and identified the following key areas of relevance for V/SM: social, work, education, parental, spouse/significant other, spiritual/religious, leisure, domestic life, civic, self-care, and economic life (Resnik et al., 2012). Reintegration difficulties are experienced by about half of service members after returning from deployment including participating in community activities, relationships with intimate partners and children, work or school tasks, maintaining non-military friendships (Sayer et al., 2010). Multiple problems are associated with history of TBI (Sayer et al., 2014), including decreased leisure participation, concerns/problems with work, and understanding one's role in the family (Daggett et al., 2013).

TBI Definition and Severity Levels

The VA/DoD guidelines define TBI as:

> A traumatically induced structural injury or physiological disruption of brain function, as a result of an external force, that is indicated by new onset or worsening of at least one of the following clinical signs immediately after the event:

- Any alteration in mental status (e.g., confusion, disorientation, slowed thinking, etc.)
- Any loss of memory for events immediately before or after the injury
- Any period of loss of or a decreased level of consciousness, observed or self-reported (Department of Veterans Affairs and Defense, 2016)

External forces include the head striking or being struck by an object, acceleration/deceleration movement without direct trauma to the head, and forces generated from a blast or explosion including penetrating injuries. Common mechanisms of injury among V/SMs are falls, motor vehicle accidents, assault, and blast exposure (Hoge et al., 2008; Helmick et al., 2015). Importantly, TBI severity is based on clinical presentation at the time of the injury event. Long-term prognosis varies at all severity levels (Carroll et al., 2014; Maas et al., 2008).

Table 12-1 Traumatic Brain Injury Severity Definitions

Criterion	Mild	Moderate	Severe
Structural imaging	Imaging is not indicated for mild injuries. Normal findings if done.	Normal or abnormal findings	Normal or abnormal findings
Loss of consciousness (LOC)	0–30 minutes	> 30 minutes and < 24 hours	> 24 hours
Alteration of consciousness* (AOC)	A moment, up to 24 hours	> 24 hours	> 24 hours
Post-traumatic amnesia (PTA)	0–1 day	> 1 day and < 7 days	> 7 days
Glasgow Coma Scale (GCS)[2] (Teasdale et al., 2014).	13–15	9–12	< 9

*Alteration of consciousness is not sufficient criteria to diagnose moderate or severe injuries
From VA/DoD Clinical Practice Guideline
Departments of Veterans Affairs and Defense. (2016). *Management of concussion-mild traumatic brain injury (MTBI)*. Author. https://www.healthquality.va.gov/guidelines/Rehab/mtbi/mTBICPGFullCPG50821816.pdf

Mild TBI

The diagnosis of mTBI does not require loss of consciousness; rather, a brief alteration of consciousness may meet the diagnostic criteria is described as "seeing stars or having one's bell rung" (Department of Veterans Affairs and Defense, 2016). Additionally, for an injury to be classified as mild, structural damage cannot be visible in brain imaging studies, such as computerized tomography (CT) or magnetic resonance imaging (MRI) (Department of Veterans Affairs and Defense, 2016). Military service members often do not seek care immediately, requiring clinicians to rely on self-report about loss of consciousness, post-traumatic amnesia (PTA), and alteration of consciousness (AOC) (Brenner et al., 2009).

Table 12-2 Traumatic Brain Injury Symptoms

Category	Possible Symptoms
Physical	Headache, dizziness, balance disorders, nausea, fatigue, sleep disturbance, blurred vision, sensitivity to light, hearing difficulty/loss, tinnitus, sensitivity to noise, seizure, transient neurological abnormalities, numbness, tingling
Cognitive	Problems with attention, concentration, memory, speed of processing, judgment, executive control
Emotional	Depression, anxiety, agitation, irritability, impulsivity, aggression

Departments of Veterans Affairs and Defense. (2016). *Management of concussion-mild traumatic brain injury (MTBI)*. Author. https://www.healthquality.va.gov/guidelines/Rehab/mtbi/mTBICPGFullCPG50821816.pdf

Symptoms

After an injury event, a person may experience a variety of physical, cognitive, and emotional symptoms (see **Table 12-2**). Typically, symptoms resolve without treatment within 90 days of the injury (Carroll et al., 2014). Some people, however, report symptoms that persist or worsen after 90 days (see the "Common Post-concussion Symptoms" section).

Moderate and Severe TBI

As indicated in Table 12-1, moderate and severe TBI are designated by the length of loss of consciousness at the time of injury, a period of post-traumatic amnesia, and impaired responsiveness as measured by the GCS (Teasdale et al., 2014). Moderate and severe TBI often result in abnormal findings on brain imaging studies, although that is not required for diagnosis. Depending on the cause of injury, moderate to severe TBI may be accompanied by other physical injuries (Maddry et al., 2019). Moderate and severe TBI make up less than 20% of those experienced by active duty SM (Defense and Veterans Brain Injury Center, 2018). V/SM who incur these injuries in combat are likely to be evacuated to receive immediate medical treatment (Maddry et al., 2019).

TBI Screening

TBI screening and assessment systems are established within the DoD and VA to identify TBI at multiple time points throughout the system of care. Screening occurs pre-deployment in CONUS, post-deployment, and periodically dependent on the health and duties of the V/SM. First responders use the Mild Acute Concussion Evaluation (MACE) (French et al., 2008). This assessment tool includes the Standardized Assessment of Concussion (SAC). In combination with information about loss of consciousness (LOC) and post-traumatic amnesia (PTA), the MACE Score may include cognitive performance scores and indicate the need for medical evacuation (Girard et al., 2016). A concise algorithm is used to provide triage, field management, and evacuation guidance for more serious brain injuries (moderate to severe) (Girard et al., 2016). V/SM who experience ongoing cognitive symptoms may undergo comprehensive neuropsychological evaluations (e.g., computer testing) to guide prescribed rest or return to duty (McLay et al., 2010). Examples of neuropsychological assessment used in military medical facilities include the Neurobehavioral Symptom Inventory (NSI), the State-Trait Anxiety Inventory (STAI), Automated Neuropsychological Assessment Metrics (ANAM), and the Repeatable Battery for the Assessment of Neuropsychological Status (RBANS) (Girard et al., 2016).

All veterans with a service separation date after September 11, 2001, receive a four-question TBI screen upon entry into the VA healthcare system. Veterans answering yes to all four questions, indicating a history of a traumatic event with immediate symptoms and ongoing symptoms, are referred for a comprehensive TBI evaluation (CTBIE) for a definitive diagnosis and individualized treatment plan (Department of Veterans Affairs, 2017).

Environments of Care

TBI occurs in a myriad of environments and SMs may be treated in military medical facilities in the United States in non-deployed settings. If injuries during deployment are severe, SM may be evacuated from theater for treatment elsewhere. In some cases, TBI—usually mild—may not be identified until after the deployment has ended. The deployed setting Clinical Practice Guidelines (CPG) guide course of care and treatment recommendations (Helmick et al., 2015). The Post-Deployment-Health Assessment (PDHA) helps screen and manage TBI symptoms in primary care settings (Drake et al., 2010). When a V/SM is deemed unfit for duty, they may separate or retire for medical reasons. This determination is made by the Medical Evaluation Board (MEB) and the Physical Evaluation Board (PEB). The PEB is the formal board that determines fitness for duty and disability ratings. The VA schedule for rating disabilities is 0%–100% (Department of Veterans Affairs, 2019).

Polytrauma System of Care

The VA implemented the Polytrauma System of Care to provide expert TBI care for V/SMs with TBI and complex co-occurring injuries. Polytrauma is defined as "two or more injuries, one of which may be life-threatening, sustained in the same incident that affect multiple body parts or organ systems and result in physical, cognitive, psychological, or psychosocial impairments and functional disabilities. Traumatic brain injuries frequently occur in polytrauma in combination with other disabling conditions, such as: traumatic amputations, open wounds, musculoskeletal injuries, burns, pain, auditory and visual impairments, posttraumatic stress disorder (PTSD), and other mental health problems" (Department of Veterans Affairs, 2019).

In 2008, the Department of VA Polytrauma Rehabilitation Centers (PRCs) partnered with the National Institute on Disability, Independent Living, and Rehabilitation Research (formerly National Institute on Disability and Rehabilitation Research) to establish a Model Systems program of research that closely mirrors the civilian Traumatic Brain Injury Model Systems (TBIMS) Centers Program established in 1987 (Lamberty et al., 2014). The five VA PRC sites provide comprehensive inpatient, residential, and outpatient TBI care within the VA system. The PRCs are regional hubs in the Polytrauma System of Care's nationwide model of care. Multiple levels of care from acute rehabilitation to residential and outpatient programming are provided in facilities accredited by the Commission on the Accreditation of Rehabilitation Facilities. See Nakase-Richardson et al. (2017) for a comparison of Civilian and VA TBIMS cohorts.

Blast Injuries

Blast injuries are exceptionally rare in the civilian population and differ from brain injury via other mechanisms due to the overpressure of blast waves, which can result in systemic injuries. In addition, blasts often include impact

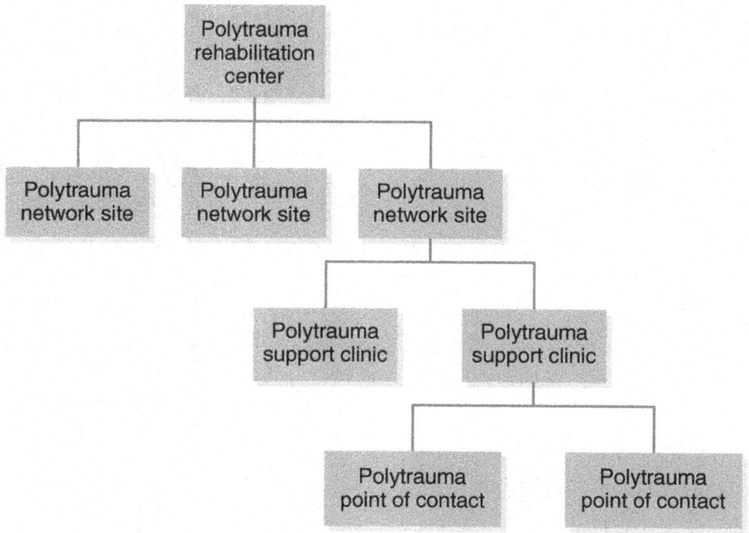

Figure 12-1 Schematic of the Polytrauma System of Care of the Veterans Health Administration.[33]

Reproduced from U.S. Department of Veterans Affairs. (n.d.). *Polytrauma/TBI system of care*. https://www.polytrauma.va.gov/system-of-care/index.asp

injuries from projectiles or from the body being thrown into objects (Finkel, 2006; Hicks et al., 2010; Wolf et al., 2009; Institute of Medicine, 2014). **Table 12-3** contains a summary of mechanisms of blast injury.

During active duty, service members may experience repeated blast exposure in training exercises as well as during deployment. This exposure may result in mTBI-like symptoms over time even if no single exposure meets the strict criteria for mTBI (Wilk et al., 2010; Quigley et al., 2012; Spelman et al., 2012). Certain military operational specialties (jobs), such as infantry or explosive ordinance disposal, are more likely to experience low-level blasts regularly throughout their careers. Similar rates of symptom reporting in blast and non-blast groups are reported, but results are inconclusive due to a paucity of studies examining outcomes by mechanism of injury (Greer et al., 2018).

In combat settings, service members are frequently sleep-deprived and operate under significant levels of stress (Rigg et al., 2011). In the immediate post-injury period, V/SM may not immediately recognize symptoms of mTBI as different from those of stress or sleep disruptions. They are also less likely to seek

Table 12-3 Mechanisms of Blast Injury

Category	Characteristics	Body Part Affected	Types of Injuries
Primary	Unique to high-order explosives, results from the impact of the overpressure wave with body surfaces	Gas-filled structures are most susceptible: lungs, GI tract, middle ear	■ Blast lung (pulmonary barotrauma) ■ Tympanic membrane rupture and middle ear damage ■ Abdominal hemorrhage and perforation ■ Globe (eye) rupture ■ Concussion (TBI without physical signs of head injury)
Secondary	Results from flying debris and bomb fragments	Any body part may be affected	■ Penetrating ballistic (fragmentation) or blunt injuries ■ Eye penetration (can be occult)
Tertiary	Results from individuals being thrown by the blast wind	Any body part may be affected	■ Fracture and traumatic amputation ■ Closed and open brain injury
Quarternary	All explosion-related injuries, illnesses, or diseases not due to primary, secondary, or tertiary mechanisms; includes exacerbation or complications of existing conditions	Any body part may be affected	■ Burns (flash, partial, and full thickness) ■ Crush injuries ■ Closed and open brain injury ■ Asthma, COPD, or other breathing problems from dust, smoke, or toxic fumes ■ Angina ■ Hyperglycemia, hypertension

Centers for Disease Control and Prevention. (n.d.). *Explosions and blast injuries: A primer for clinicians*. https://www.cdc.gov/masstrauma/preparedness/primer.pdf

help or leave duty to pursue medical attention unless they undergo mandatory field screening and are required to go for evaluation by a superior (MACE) (French et al., 2008).

TBI as a Chronic Condition

Although TBI is often thought of as an event, many healthcare professionals now consider it a chronic condition (Corrigan & Hammond, 2013; Malec et al., 2013; Masel & De Witt, 2010; Wilson et al., 2017). After a TBI, people are at greater risk for psychiatric diagnoses (Masel & De Witt, 2010), neurodegenerative conditions (Institute of Medicine, 2009), and shorter life expectancy (Wilson et al, 2017). Not all individuals who experience a TBI will develop chronic (Corrigan & Hammond, 2013); however, healthcare practitioners should monitor changes in their patients with a history of TBI. Recent evidence has shown that V/SM with a history of TBI are at higher risk of dying of suicide by firearm compared to V/SM without TBI (Hostetter et al., 2019), therefore screening for suicidal ideation and lethal means safety is recommended.

Common Post-Concussion Symptoms

Although mTBI symptoms frequently resolve without intervention (Carroll et al., 2014). an estimated 15%–20% of people experience physical, cognitive, and emotional symptoms that persist beyond 90 days post-injury. The symptoms that are attributed to mTBI are common to many other conditions and are often reported by adults with no injury history or medical diagnosis (Iverson et al., 2010; Lange et al., 2010). Despite many studies, the relationship of TBI symptoms to an mTBI event remains unclear (Brenner et al., 2009; Lange et al., 2010; Brenner et al., 2010; O'Neil et al., 2014). Further complicating matters, many service members with mTBI have concurrent diagnoses of sleep, anxiety, depressive, and other disorders, including PTSD, making it impractical to conclusively connect the presence of a symptom with any single diagnosis (Brenner et al., 2009; Brenner et al., Carlson et al., 2011; Nelson et al., 2012; Yeh et al., 2014). V/SMs experience higher rates of mental health comorbidities after TBI compared to civilians (CHapman & Diaz-Arrastia, 2014). Several factors predict persistent post-concussion symptoms, including prior head injuries, stress levels, and LOC at time of injury (Stein et al., 2016).

Sleep disorders

Sleep disorders are common among V/SM (Plumb et al., 2016). and are worse for those with a history of TBI (Lu et al., 2019). Problems with sleep exacerbate other symptoms, making participation in daily life even more challenging (Ishak et al., 2012). Sleep quality was predictive of cognitive function in combat veterans independently of mTBI or PTSD diagnoses (Martindale et al., 2017). Screening for and treatment of sleep problems is a high priority among veterans with a possible history of TBI. High rates of obstructive sleep apnea, insomnia, or both occur among previously deployed military personnel (Mysliwiec et al., 2013). These conditions are frequently comorbid with mTBI, PTSD, depression, pain, or a combination of these diagnoses (Mysliwiec et al., 2013). Hypersomnia and daytime somnolence have also been reported (Collen et al., 2012). There is a positive correlation between rates of insomnia and exposure to multiple mTBI events among SMs (Bryan, 2013).

Cognitive symptoms

V/SM often report memory impairment after mTBI (Larson et al., 2013). Limited evidence suggests that lower premorbid cognitive ability, based on the Wechsler Test of Adult Reading, increases risk for post-concussion symptoms after mTBI (Larson et al., 2013). Other cognitive symptoms may include impaired attention, processing speed, and executive function (Helmik & Members of Consensus Conference, 2010). Treatment for cognitive impairment does not vary based on mechanism of injury. A combination of remedial and compensatory strategies is often appropriate (Defense and Veterans Brain Injury Center, 2019).

Visual symptoms

Visual symptoms after mTBI may include deficits in reading, saccades, pursuits, and vergence, as well as photosensitivity (Capó-Aponte et al., 2012). Prevalence of visual impairments after mTBI does not appear to differ based on mechanism of injury (Capó-Aponte et al., 2012; Capó-Aponte et al., 2017). Visual screening with appropriate referrals for services may be warranted for persistent complaints (Radomski et al., 2014).

Chronic pain

Musculoskeletal pain and headaches are highly prevalent among V/SM (Bader et al., 2018). Mild TBI, depression, and PTSD symptoms are significantly correlated with presence of pain (Stratton et al., 2014) and pain intensity (Stojanovic et al., 2016). Anxiety and sleep disorders also contribute to pain, (Hoot et al., 2018). therefore it is important to assess and treat these contributing factors. Pain treatment can include pharmacological and non-pharmacological approaches (Departments of Veterans Affairs and Defense, 2017a). In general, opioid therapy should be used according to VA/DoD clinical practice guidelines (Departments of Veterans Affairs and Defense, 2017b).

Behavioral/Mental health diagnoses

TBI is associated with increased risk for mental health diagnoses such as depression, anxiety, and PTSD (Kontos et al., 2013; Vanderploeg et al., 2012). TBI exposure has been positively correlated with the number of symptoms that V/SM report (Kontos et al., 2013). Female veterans with TBI are more likely to be diagnosed with depression and non-PTSD anxiety disorders (Iverson et al., 2011).

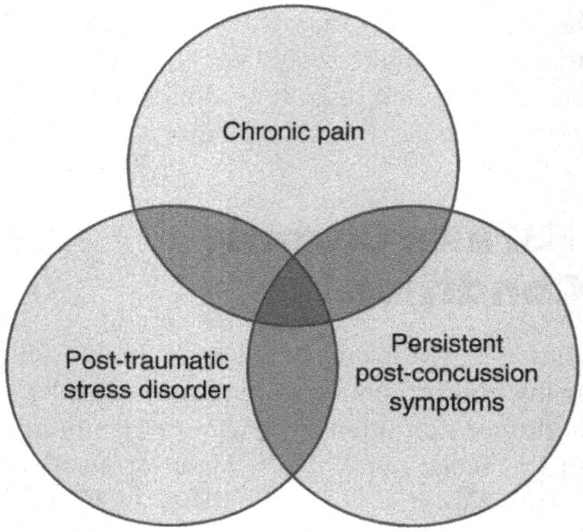

Figure 12-2 Polytrauma clinical triad.

Polytrauma clinical triad

The polytrauma clinical triad (PCT) is defined as co-occurring chronic persistent post-concussion symptoms, chronic pain, and PTSD (Lew et al., 2009). Lew and colleagues reported that more than 40% of the veterans who were receiving care at a VA Polytrauma Network Site (PNS) presented with all three conditions. The most common locations of pain were back and head (Lew et al., 2009). The high prevalence of PCT among V/SM with TBI highlights the complexity of caring for this patient population. Less is known about V/SM with PCT who do not seek care in the VA system.

Treatment Considerations and Resources

Treatment of deployment and combat-related TBI involves a myriad of professionals and components. Rehabilitation and treatment needs of combat-injured service members are complex and require specialized training, skill, and care (Sayer et al., 2009). Initial treatment typically involves, but is not limited to, an interdisciplinary team who work together to provide emergency care, surgeries, various therapies (e.g., speech, occupational, vision, physical, recreational), orthotics, prosthetics, education, symptom management, vocational rehabilitation (VR), and assistive technology. Despite the considerable resources that have been allocated to studying and improving treatment in this cohort, many V/SMs may not receive the care that they need (Sayer et al., 2010). A comprehensive treatment approach that includes public and private partnerships is needed (Sayer et al., 2010). Research is lacking on V/SMs who do not use VA healthcare and it is likely that private-sector healthcare systems and providers are not consistently prepared to understand and address unique V/SM needs (Sayer et al., 2014). It is recommended that providers in the private sector screen for veteran status and be able to provide patients with information about the VA and how to access VA services (Sayer et al., 2014). With the implementation of the MISSION Act (Isakson, 2018), private sector health care professionals can anticipate an increase in the number of veterans they see in their practice. VA Clinical Practice Guidelines (CPG) for mTBI may be useful in guiding treatment decisions (Departments of Veterans Affairs and Defense, 2016).

In addition to the VA CPG for mTBI (Departments of Veterans Affairs and Defense, 2016), there are additional resources available to support treatment of specific symptoms and concerns. VA has CPGs for low back pain (Departments of Veterans Affairs and Defense, 2017a), opioid therapy for chronic pain (Departments of Veterans Affairs and Defense, 2017b), and mental health conditions including PTSD (Departments of Veterans Affairs and Defense, 2017c) and depression (Departments of Veterans Affairs and Defense, 2016). The Defense and Veterans Brain Injury Center updated clinical recommendations for cognitive rehabilitation in 2019 (Defense and Veterans Brain Injury Center, 2019). There is a freely available online Cognitive Behavioral Therapy

Table 12-4 Delineation of Community-Integrated Rehabilitation (CIR) Models

Model	Participant Characteristics	Description
Neurobehavioral	Severe behavioral disturbances; require 24-hour supervision	Residential setting; intense behavioral management
Residential Community	Cannot participate as outpatients; require 24-hour supervision or support	Residential setting with full community integration; comprehensive clinical team treatment
Comprehensive Holistic	Need for intensive services; benefit from improved awareness	Day treatment programs; integrated, multimodal rehabilitation
Home-Based Program	Able to reside at home; able to self-direct care	Education and advisement; telephonic and Web-based support and services; home-based therapeutic activity; availability of outpatient supplemental services; highly variable

Trudel, T. M., Nidiffer, F. D., & Barth, J. T. (2007). Community-integrated brain injury rehabilitation: Treatment models and challenges for civilian, military, and veteran populations. *Journal of Rehabilitation Research & Development, 44*(7), 1007–1016.

for Insomnia (CBT-I) program as well. Apps such as Concussion Coach (Department of Veterans Affairs, n.d.) may be useful to V/SM for tracking symptoms. The Concussion Coach app also includes educational content, strategies for symptom management, planning tools, and links to crisis resources.

Community-Integrated Rehabilitation (CIR) is an umbrella term that envelops a variety of approaches and treatments (hospital, home, day programs, neurobehavioral, and residential settings) that enhances rehabilitation after acute rehabilitation is completed (Trudel et al., 2007). The Defense and Veterans Brain Injury Center (DVBIC) is an example of a military program that provides CIR services. CIR models include (a) neurobehavioral, (b) residential community, (c) comprehensive holistic, and (d) home based (Trudel et al., 2007). Research on the CIR program shows improvements in social and functional outcomes, vocational outcomes, and self-efficacy and productivity (Ben-Yishay et al., 1987, pp. 90–95).

Conclusion

A myriad of issues impact V/SMs' reintegration into the community including accessing healthcare services. TBI is common among V/SM, with most being classified as mild. Most V/SM with mTBI will experience a complete recovery within a few months of the injury event, yet some experience persistent and ongoing symptoms. TBI is best understood as a chronic condition. The implementation of the MISSION Act in 2019 will likely increase the number of veterans seeking care in their civilian communities. It is therefore essential that private sector healthcare providers become aware of the unique needs of V/SMs with TBI and have access to appropriate resources for training and referral. Ultimately, the goal of treatment and rehabilitation for V/SMs with TBI and their families is engagement in meaningful, healthy, productive activity. Healthcare providers are uniquely positioned to meet the health and CR needs of this important cohort.

Training and Resources for Private Sector Providers

1. Community care provider resources: https://www.va.gov/COMMUNITYCARE/providers/index.asp
2. Community provider took kit: https://www.mentalhealth.va.gov/communityproviders/
3. VHA TRAIN: https://www.train.org/vha/welcome
4. Military Culture Training: https://www.va.gov/COMMUNITYCARE/docs/providers/VA-FS_Military-Culture-Training.pdf#
5. VA/DoD Clinical Practice Guideline for mTBI: https://www.healthquality.va.gov/guidelines/Rehab/mtbi/mTBICPGFullCPG50821816.pdf
6. Concussion Coach app: https://www.polytrauma.va.gov/ConcussionCoach.asp
7. VA/DoD Clinical Practice Guidelines for Pain
   - Low Back Pain: https://www.healthquality.va.gov/guidelines/Pain/lbp/
   - Opioid Use: https://www.healthquality.va.gov/guidelines/Pain/cot/
8. Cognitive behavioral therapy for insomnia (CBT-I): https://www.veterantraining.va.gov/insomnia/index.asp
9. Defense and Veterans Brain Injury Center Cognitive Rehabilitation clinical recommendations: https://dvbic.dcoe.mil/cogrehab/index.html

Mission Act Resources

1. Official source—VA web landing page for the MISSION Act: www.missionact.VA.gov
2. *Providence (RI) Journal* article: https://www.providencejournal.com/news/20190616/veterans-journal-new-mission-act-offers-enhanced-health-care-coverage
3. Military.com: https://www.military.com/benefits/veterans-health-care/va-will-now-let-you-go-civilian-urgent-care-doctors.html
4. Military.com: https://www.military.com/daily-news/2019/05/24/va-ready-roll-out-mission-act-program-june-6-expect-glitches-officials.html

Resources for the Military Family/Caregiver

1. Veterans Crisis Line: https://www.veteranscrisisline.net/ and 1-800-273-TALK (8255) option 1; text 838255
2. The Defense and Veterans Brain Injury Center: https://dvbic.dcoe.mil/
3. Support for caregivers: https://veterancaregiver.com
4. The Elizabeth Dole Foundation: https://www.elizabethdolefoundation.org/
5. Resource Locator to find the contact information for VA locations in your community: https://www.veteranscrisisline.net/GetHelp/ResourceLocator.aspx
6. Blue Star Families: http://www.bluestarfam.org/resources/deployments/deployment-resources/
7. Military.com: http://www.military.com/spouse/military-life/military-resources/family-support-services.html
8. Military One Source: http://www.militaryonesource.mil
9. National Military Family Association: http://www.militaryfamily.org
10. The Biden Foundation: https://bidenfoundation.org/about/
11. Military Network Radio: https://militarynetworkradio.com
12. Brainline: https://www.brainline.org/
13. Brain Injury Association of America: https://www.biausa.org/
14. Brain Injury Alliance: https://usbia.org/

References

Armistead-Jehle, P., Soble, J. R., Cooper, D. B., & Belanger, H. G. (2017). Unique aspects of traumatic brain injury in military and veteran populations. *Physical Medicine and Rehabilitation Clinics of North America, 28*(2), 323–337. doi:10.1016/j.pmr.2016.12.008

Bader, C. E., Giordano, N. A., McDonald, C. C., Meghani, S. H., & Polomano, R. C. (2018). Musculoskeletal pain and headache in the active duty military population: An integrative review. *Worldviews on Evidence-Based Nursing, 15*(4), 264–271. doi:10.1111/wvn.12301

Ben-Yishay, Y., Silver, S. M., Piasetsky, E., & Rattok, J. (1987). Relationship between employability and vocational outcome after intensive holistic cognitive rehabilitation. *Journal of Head Trauma Rehabilitation, 2*(1), 35–48. doi:10.1097/00001199-198703000-00007

Benzinger, T. L. S., Brody, D., Cardin, S., Curley, K. C., Mintun, M. A., Mun, S. K., Wong, K. H., & Wrathall, J. R. (2009). Blast-related brain injury: Imaging for clinical and research applications: Report of the 2008 St. Louis Workshop. *Journal of Neurotrauma, 26*(12), 2127–2144. doi:10.1089/neu.2009.0885

Brenner, L. A., Ivins, B. J., Schwab, K., Warden, D., Nelson, L. A., Jaffee, M., & Terrio, H. (2010). Traumatic brain injury, posttraumatic stress disorder, and postconcussive symptom reporting among troops returning from Iraq. *The Journal of Head Trauma Rehabilitation, 25*(5), 307–312. doi:10.1097/HTR.0b013e3181cada03

Brenner, L. A., Vanderploeg, R. D., & Terrio, H. (2009). Assessment and diagnosis of mild traumatic brain injury, posttraumatic stress disorder, and other polytrauma conditions: Burden of adversity hypothesis. *Rehabilitation Psychology, 54*(3), 239–246. doi:10.1037/a0016908

Bryan, C. J. (2013). Repetitive traumatic brain injury (or concussion) increases severity of sleep disturbance among deployed military personnel. *Sleep, 36*(6), 941–946. doi:10.5665/sleep.2730

Cameron, K. L., Sturdivant, R. X., & Baker, S. P. (2019). Trends in the incidence of physician-diagnosed posttraumatic stress disorder among active-duty U.S. military personnel between 1999 and 2008. *Military Medical Research, 6*(1), 8. doi:10.1186/s40779-019-0198-5

Capó-Aponte, J. E., Jorgensen-Wagers, K. L., Sosa, J. A., Walsh, D. V., Goodrich, G. L., Temme, L. A., & Riggs, D. W. (2017). Visual dysfunctions at different stages after blast and non-blast mild traumatic brain injury. *Optometry and Vision Science: Official Publication of the American Academy of Optometry, 94*(1), 7–15. doi:10.1097/OPX.0000000000000825

Capó-Aponte, J. E., Urosevich, T. G., Temme, L. A., Tarbett, A. K., & Sanghera, N. K. (2012). Visual dysfunctions and symptoms during the subacute stage of blast-induced mild traumatic brain injury. *Military Medicine, 177*(7), 804–813. doi:10.7205/milmed-d-12-00061

Carlson, K. F., Kehle, S. M., Meis, L. A., Greer, N., Macdonald, R., Rutks, I., Sayer, N. A., Dobscha, S. K., & Wilt, T. J. (2011). Prevalence, assessment, and treatment of mild traumatic brain injury and posttraumatic stress disorder: A systematic review of the evidence. *The Journal of Head Trauma Rehabilitation, 26*(2), 103–115. doi:10.1097/HTR.0b013e3181e50ef1

Carroll, L. J., Cassidy, J. D., Cancelliere, C., Côté, P., Hincapié, C. A., Kristman, V. L., Holm, L. W., Borg, J., Nygren-de Boussard, C., & Hartvigsen, J. (2014). Systematic review of the prognosis after mild traumatic brain injury in adults: cognitive, psychiatric, and mortality outcomes: results of the International Collaboration on Mild Traumatic Brain Injury Prognosis. *Archives of Physical Medicine and Rehabilitation, 95*(3 Suppl), S152–S173. doi:10.1016/j.apmr.2013.08.300

Centers for Disease Control and Prevention. (2019). *TBI-related emergency department visits, hospitalizations, and deaths (EDHDs)*. Retrieved July 11, 2019, from https://www.cdc.gov/traumaticbraininjury/data/tbi-edhd.html

Centers for Disease Control and Prevention. (n.d.). *Explosions and blast injuries: A primer for clinicians*. https://www.cdc.gov/masstrauma/preparedness/primer.pdf

Chapman, J. C., & Diaz-Arrastia, R. (2014). Military traumatic brain injury: A review. *Alzheimer's & Dementia, 10*(3 Suppl), S97–S104. doi:10.1016/j.jalz.2014.04.012

Cicerone, K. D., Mott, T., Azulay, J., & Friel, J. C. (2004). Community integration and satisfaction with functioning after intensive cognitive rehabilitation for traumatic brain injury. *Archives of Physical Medicine and Rehabilitation, 85*(6), 943–950.

Collen, J., Orr, N., Lettieri, C. J., Carter, K., & Holley, A. B. (2012). Sleep disturbances among soldiers with combat-related traumatic brain injury. *Chest, 142*(3), 622–630. doi:10.1378/chest.11-1603

Corrigan, J. D., & Hammond, F. M. (2013). Traumatic brain injury as a chronic health condition. *Archives of Physical Medicine and Rehabilitation, 94*(6), 1199–1201. doi:10.1016/j.apmr.2013.01.023

Daggett, V. S., Bakas, T., Buelow, J., Habermann, B., & Murray, L. L. (2013). Needs and concerns of male combat Veterans with mild traumatic brain injury. *Journal of Rehabilitation Research and Development, 50*(3), 327–340.

Defense and Veterans Brain Injury Center. (2018). *DoD numbers for traumatic brain injury: Worldwide totals*. Retrieved August 5, 2019, from https://dvbic.dcoe.mil/system/files/tbi-numbers/worldwide-totals-2000-2018Q1-total_jun-21-2018_v1.0_2018-07-26_0.pdf

Defense and Veterans Brain Injury Center. (2019). *Cognitive rehabilitation clinical recommendations*. Retrieved August 6, 2019, from https://dvbic.dcoe.mil/cogrehab/index.html

Department of Veterans Affairs. (2017). *Screening and evaluation of Traumatic Brain Injury (TBI) in Operation Enduring Freedom (OEF), Operation Iraqi Freedom (OIF), and Operation New Dawn (OND) Veterans*. https://www.va.gov/vhapublications/ViewPublication.asp?pub_ID=5376

Department of Veterans Affairs. (2018). *Health care services for women veterans*. https://www.va.gov/vhapublications/ViewPublication.asp?pub_ID=5332

Department of Veterans Affairs. (2019a). 38 *CFR Book C, schedule for rating disabilities*. https://www.benefits.va.gov/WARMS/bookc.asp

Department of Veterans Affairs. (2019b). *Department of Veterans Affairs FY 2018–2024 strategic plan*. https://www.va.gov/oei/docs/VA2018-2024strategicPlan.pdf

Department of Veterans Affairs. (2019c). *VHA Directive 1172.01: Polytrauma System of Care*. https://www.va.gov/OPTOMETRY/docs/VHA_Directive_1172-01_Polytrauma_System_of_Care_1172_01_D_2019-01-24.pdf

Department of Veterans Affairs. (n.d.). *Concussion coach mobile app*. Retrieved September 15, 2019, from https://www.polytrauma.va.gov/ConcussionCoach.asp

Departments of Veterans Affairs and Defense. (2016a). *Management of concussion-mild traumatic brain injury (MTBI)*. https://www.healthquality.va.gov/guidelines/Rehab/mtbi/mTBICPGFullCPG50821816.pdf

Departments of Veterans Affairs and Defense. (2016b). *Management of major depressive disorder (MDD) 2016*. Retrieved September 15, 2019, from https://www.healthquality.va.gov/guidelines/MH/mdd/

Departments of Veterans Affairs and Defense. (2017a). *Diagnosis and treatment of low back pain (LBP)*. https://www.healthquality.va.gov/guidelines/Pain/lbp/

Departments of Veterans Affairs and Defense. (2017b). *Management of opioid therapy for chronic pain*. https://www.healthquality.va.gov/guidelines/Pain/cot/VADoDOTCPG022717.pdf

Departments of Veterans Affairs and Defense. (2017c). *Management of posttraumatic stress disorder and acute stress reaction 2017*. Retrieved September 15, 2019, from https://www.healthquality.va.gov/guidelines/MH/ptsd/

Drake, A. I., Meyer, K. S., Cessante, L. M., Cheung, C. R., Cullen, M. A., McDonald, E. C., & Holland, M. C. (2010). Routine TBI screening following combat deployments. *NeuroRehabilitation, 26*(3), 183–189. doi:10.3233/NRE-2010-0554

Finkel, M. F. (2006). The neurological consequences of explosives. *Journal of the Neurological Sciences, 249*(1), 63–67. doi:10.1016/j.jns.2006.06.005

French, L., McCrea, M., & Baggett, M. (2008). The military acute concussion evaluation (MACE). *Journal of Special Operations Medicine, 8*, 11.

Girard, P., Meyer, K., & Schneider, J. (2016). Military populations. In *The essential brain injury guide* (5th ed., pp. 376–394). Brain Injury Association of America.

Greer, N., Sayer, N., Koeller, E., Velasquez, T., & Wilt, T. J. (2018). Outcomes associated with blast versus nonblast-related traumatic brain injury in US military service members and Veterans: A systematic review. *The Journal of Head Trauma Rehabilitation, 33*(2), E16–E29. doi:10.1097/HTR.0000000000000304

Hale-Gallardo, J., Jia, H., Delisle, T., Levy, C. E., Osorio, V., Smith, J. A., & Hannold, E. M. (2017). Enhancing health and independent living for veterans with disabilities by leveraging community-based resources. *Journal of Multidisciplinary Healthcare, 10*, 41–47. doi:10.2147/JMDH.S118706

Helmick, K., & Members of Consensus Conference. (2010). Cognitive rehabilitation for military personnel with mild traumatic brain injury and chronic post-concussional disorder: Results of April 2009 Consensus Conference. *NeuroRehabilitation, 26*(3), 239–255. doi:10.3233/NRE-2010-0560

Helmick, K. M., Spells, C. A., Malik, S. Z., Davies, C. A., Marion, D. W., & Hinds, S. R. (2015). Traumatic brain injury in the US military: Epidemiology and key clinical and research programs. *Brain Imaging and Behavior, 9*(3), 358–366. doi:10.1007/s11682-015-9399-z

Hicks, R. R., Fertig, S. J., Desrocher, R. E., Koroshetz, W. J., & Pancrazio, J. J. (2010). Neurological effects of blast injury. *The Journal of Trauma, 68*(5), 1257–1263. doi:10.1097/TA.0b013e3181d8956d

Hoge, C. W., McGurk, D., Thomas, J. L., Cox, A. L., Engel, C. C., & Castro, C. A. (2008). Mild traumatic brain injury in U.S. soldiers returning from Iraq. *New England Journal of Medicine, 358*(5), 453–463. doi:10.1056/NEJMoa072972

Hoot, M. R., Levin, H. S., Smith, A. N., Goldberg, G., Wilde, E. A., Walker, W. C., Eapen, B. C., Nolen, T., & Pugh, N. L. (2018). Pain and chronic mild traumatic brain injury in the US military population: A Chronic Effects of Neurotrauma Consortium study. *Brain Injury, 32*(10), 1169–1177. doi:10.1080/02699052.2018.1482427

Hostetter, T. A., Hoffmire, C. A., Forster, J. E., Adams, R. S., Stearns-Yoder, K. A., & Brenner, L. A. (2019). Suicide and traumatic brain injury among individuals seeking Veterans Health Administration services between fiscal years 2006 and 2015. *The Journal of Head Trauma Rehabilitation, 34*(5), E1–E9. doi:10.1097/HTR.0000000000000489

Institute of Medicine. (2009). *Long-term consequences of traumatic brain injury* (Vol. 7). National Academies Press.

Institute of Medicine. (2014). *Long-term effects of blast exposures* (Vol. 9). National Academies Press. https://www.nap.edu/read/18253/chapter/1

Isakson, J. (2018). *VA Mission Act of 2018*. https://www.congress.gov/bill/115th-congress/senate-bill/2372/text

Ishak, W. W., Bagot, K., Thomas, S., Magakian, N., Bedwani, D., Larson, D., Brownstein, A., & Zaky, C. (2012). Quality of life in patients suffering from insomnia. *Innovations in Clinical Neuroscience, 9*(10), 13–26.

Iverson, G. L., Lange, R. T., Brooks, B. L., & Rennison, V. L. A. (2010). "Good old days" bias following mild traumatic brain injury. *The Clinical Neuropsychologist, 24*(1), 17–37. doi:10.1080/13854040903190797

Iverson, K. M., Hendricks, A. M., Kimerling, R., Krengel, M., Meterko, M., Stolzmann, K. L., Baker, E., Pogoda, T. K., Vasterling, J. J., & Lew, H. L. (2011). Psychiatric diagnoses and neurobehavioral symptom severity among OEF/OIF VA patients with deployment-related traumatic brain injury: A gender comparison. *Women's Health Issues: Official Publication of the Jacobs Institute of Women's Health, 21*(4 Suppl), S210–S217. doi:10.1016/j.whi.2011.04.019

Kontos, A. P., Kotwal, R. S., Elbin, R. J., Lutz, R. H., Forsten, R. D., Benson, P. J., & Guskiewicz, K. M. (2013). Residual effects of combat-related mild traumatic brain injury. *Journal of Neurotrauma, 30*(8), 680–686. doi:10.1089/neu.2012.2506

Lamberty, G. J., Nakase-Richardson, R., Farrell-Carnahan, L., McGarity, S., Bidelspach, D., Harrison-Felix, C., & Cifu, D. X. (2014). Development of a traumatic brain injury model system within the Department of Veterans Affairs Polytrauma System of Care. *The Journal of Head Trauma Rehabilitation, 29*(3), E1–E7. doi:10.1097/HTR.0b013e31829a64d1

Lange, R. T., Iverson, G. L., & Rose, A. (2010). Post-concussion symptom reporting and the "good-old-days" bias following mild traumatic brain injury. *Archives of Clinical Neuropsychology, 25*(5), 442–450. doi:10.1093/arclin/acq031

Larson, E., Zollman, F., Kondiles, B., & Starr, C. (2013). Memory deficits, postconcussive complaints, and posttraumatic stress disorder in a volunteer sample of veterans. *Rehabilitation psychology, 58*(3), 245–252. doi:10.1037/a0032953

Lew, H. L., Otis, J. D., Tun, C., Kerns, R. D., Clark, M. E., & Cifu, D. X. (2009). Prevalence of chronic pain, posttraumatic stress disorder, and persistent postconcussive symptoms in OIF/OEF veterans: polytrauma clinical triad. *Journal of Rehabilitation Research and Development, 46*(6), 697–702.

Lu, L. H., Reid, M. W., Cooper, D. B., & Kennedy, J. E. (2019). Sleep problems contribute to post-concussive symptoms in service members with a history of mild traumatic brain injury without posttraumatic stress disorder or major depressive disorder. *NeuroRehabilitation, 44*(4), 511–521. doi:10.3233/NRE-192702

Maas, A. I., Stocchetti, N., & Bullock, R. (2008). Moderate and severe traumatic brain injury in adults. *The Lancet: Neurology, 7*(8), 728–741. doi:10.1016/S1474-4422(08)70164-9

Maddry, J. K., Arana, A. A., Perez, C. A., Medellin, K. L., Paciocco, J. A., Mora, A. G., Holder, W. G., Davis, W. T., Herson, P. S., & Bebarta, V. S. (2019). Influence of time to transport to a higher level facility on the clinical outcomes of US combat casualties with TBI: A multicenter 7-year study. *Military Medicine, 185*(1–2), e138–e145. doi:10.1093/milmed/usz178

Malec, J. F. (2001). Impact of comprehensive day treatment on societal participation for persons with acquired brain injury. *Archives of Physical Medicine and Rehabilitation, 82*(7), 885–895. doi:10.1053/apmr.2001.23895

Malec, J. F., & Basford, J. S. (1996). Postacute brain injury rehabilitation. *Archives of Physical Medicine and Rehabilitation, 77*(2), 198–207.

Malec, J. F., Hammond, F. M., Flanagan, S., Kean, J., Sander, A., Sherer, M., & Masel, B. E. (2013). Recommendations from the 2013 Galveston Brain Injury Conference for implementation of a chronic care model in brain injury. *The Journal of Head Trauma Rehabilitation, 28*(6), 476–483. doi:10.1097/HTR.0000000000000003

Martindale, S. L., Morissette, S. B., Rowland, J. A., & Dolan, S. L. (2017). Sleep quality affects cognitive functioning in returning combat veterans beyond combat exposure, PTSD, and mild TBI history. *Neuropsychology, 31*(1), 93–104. doi:10.1037/neu0000312

Masel, B. E., & DeWitt, D. S. (2010). Traumatic brain injury: A disease process, not an event. *Journal of Neurotrauma, 27*(8), 1529–1540. doi:10.1089/neu.2010.1358

McLay, R., Spira, J., & Reeves, D. (2010). Use of computerized neuropsychological testing to help determine fitness to return to combat operations when taking medication that can influence cognitive function. *Military Medicine, 175*(12), 945–946. doi:10.7205/milmed-d-09-00237

Mysliwiec, V., Gill, J., Lee, H., Baxter, T., Pierce, R., Barr, T. L., Krakow, B., & Roth, B. J. (2013). Sleep disorders in US military personnel: A high rate of comorbid insomnia and obstructive sleep apnea. *Chest, 144*(2), 549–557. doi:10.1378/chest.13-0088

Nakase-Richardson, R., Stevens, L. F., Tang, X., Lamberty, G. J., Sherer, M., Walker, W. C., Pugh, M. J., Eapen, B. C., Finn, J. A., Saylors, M., Dillahunt-Aspillaga, C., Adams, R. S., & Garofano, J. S. (2017). Comparison of the VA and NIDILRR TBI model system cohorts. *The Journal of Head Trauma Rehabilitation, 32*(4), 221–233. doi:10.1097/HTR.0000000000000334

Nelson, N. W., Hoelzle, J. B., Doane, B. M., McGuire, K. A., Ferrier-Auerbach, A. G., Charlesworth, M. J., Lamberty, G. J., Polusny, M. A., Arbisi, P. A., & Sponheim, S. R. (2012). Neuropsychological outcomes of U.S. Veterans with report of remote blast-related concussion and current psychopathology. *Journal of the International Neuropsychological Society: JINS, 18*(5), 845–855. doi:10.1017/S1355617712000616

O'Neil, M. E., Carlson, K. F., Storzbach, D., Brenner, L. A., Freeman, M., Quiñones, A. R., Motu'apuaka, M., & Kansagara, D. (2014). Factors associated with mild traumatic brain injury in Veterans and military personnel: A systematic review. *Journal of the International Neuropsychological Society,* 1–13. doi:10.1017/S135561771300146X

Ottomanelli, L., Bakken, S., Dillahunt-Aspillaga, C., Pastorek, N., & Young, C. (2019). Vocational rehabilitation in the Veterans Health Administration Polytrauma System of Care: Current practices, unique challenges, and future directions. *The Journal of Head Trauma Rehabilitation, 34*(3), 158–166. doi:10.1097/HTR.0000000000000493

Plumb, T. R., Peachey, J. T., & Zelman, D. C. (2014). Sleep disturbance is common among servicemembers and veterans of Operations Enduring Freedom and Iraqi Freedom. *Psychological Services, 11*(2), 209–219. doi:10.1037/a0034958

Quigley, K. S., McAndrew, L. M., Almeida, L., D'Andrea, E. A., Engel, C. C., Hamtil, H., & Ackerman, A. J. (2012). Prevalence of environmental and other military exposure concerns in Operation Enduring Freedom and Operation Iraqi Freedom veterans. *Journal of Occupational and Environmental Medicine, 54*(6), 659–664. doi:10.1097/JOM.0b013e3182570506

Radomski, M. V., Finkelstein, M., Llanos, I., Scheiman, M., & Wagener, S. G. (2014). Composition of a vision screen for servicemembers with traumatic brain injury: Consensus using a modified nominal group technique. *The American Journal of Occupational Therapy: Official Publication of the American Occupational Therapy Association, 68*(4), 422–429. doi:10.5014/ajot.2014.011445

Resnik, L., Bradford, D. W., Glynn, S. M., Jette, A. M., Hernandez, C. J., & Wills, S. (2012). Issues in defining and measuring veteran community reintegration: Proceedings of the Working Group on Community Reintegration, VA Rehabilitation Outcomes Conference, Miami, Florida. *Journal of Rehabilitation Research and Development, 49*(1), 87. doi:10.1682/JRRD.2010.06.0107

Rigg, J. L., & Mooney, S. R. (2011). Concussions and the military: Issues specific to service members. *PM & R: the Journal of Injury, Function, and Rehabilitation, 3*(10 Suppl 2), S380–S386. doi:10.1016/j.pmrj.2011.08.005

Romaniuk, M., & Kidd, C. (2018). The psychological adjustment experience of reintegration following discharge from military service: A systemic review. *Journal of Military and Veterans Health, 26*(2), 60.

Sander, A. M., Roebuck, T. M., Struchen, M. A., Sherer, M., & High, W. M., Jr. (2001). Long-term maintenance of gains obtained in postacute rehabilitation by persons with traumatic brain injury. *The Journal of Head Trauma Rehabilitation, 16*(4), 356–373.

Sarajuuri, J. M., Kaipio, M. L., Koskinen, S. K., Niemelä, M. R., Servo, A. R., & Vilkki, J. S. (2005). Outcome of a comprehensive neurorehabilitation program for patients with traumatic brain injury. *Archives of Physical Medicine and Rehabilitation, 86*(12), 2296–2302. doi:10.1016/j.apmr.2005.06.018

Sayer, N. A., Carlson, K. F., & Frazier, P. A. (2014). Reintegration challenges in U.S. service members and veterans following combat deployment: Postdeployment reintegration challenges. *Social Issues and Policy Review, 8*(1), 33–73. doi:10.1111/sipr.12001

Sayer, N. A., Cifu, D. X., McNamee, S., Chiros, C. E., Sigford, B. J., Scott, S., & Lew, H. L. (2009).Rehabilitation needs of combat-injured service members admitted to the VA Polytrauma Rehabilitation Centers: The role of PM&R in the care of wounded warriors. *PM & R: The Journal of Injury, Function, and Rehabilitation, 1*(1), 23–28. doi:10.1016/j.pmrj.2008.10.003

Sayer, N. A., Noorbaloochi, S., Frazier, P., Carlson, K., Gravely, A., & Murdoch, M. (2010). Reintegration problems and treatment interests among Iraq and Afghanistan combat veterans receiving VA medical care. *Psychiatric Services (Washington, D.C.), 61*(6), 589–597. doi:10.1176/ps.2010.61.6.589

Spelman, J. F., Hunt, S. C., Seal, K. H., & Burgo-Black, A. L. (2012). Post deployment care for returning combat veterans. *Journal of General Internal Medicine, 27*(9), 1200–1209. doi:10.1007/s11606-012-2061-1

Stein, M. B., Ursano, R. J., Campbell-Sills, L., Colpe, L. J., Fullerton, C. S., Heeringa, S. G., Nock, M. K., Sampson, N. A., Schoenbaum, M., Sun, X., Jain, S., & Kessler, R. C. (2016). Prognostic indicators of persistent post-concussive symptoms after deployment-related mild traumatic brain injury: A prospective longitudinal study in U.S. Army soldiers. *Journal of Neurotrauma, 33*(23), 2125–2132. doi:10.1089/neu.2015.4320

Stojanovic, M. P., Fonda, J., Fortier, C. B., Higgins, D. M., Rudolph, J. L., Milberg, W. P., & McGlinchey, R. E. (2016). Influence of mild traumatic brain injury (TBI) and posttraumatic stress disorder (PTSD) on pain intensity levels in OEF/OIF/OND veterans. *Pain Medicine (Malden, Mass.), 17*(11), 2017–2025. doi:10.1093/pm/pnw042

Stratton, K. J., Hawn, S. E., Amstadter, A. B., Cifu, D. X., & Walker, W. C. (2014). Correlates of pain symptoms among Iraq and Afghanistan military personnel following combat-related blast exposure. *Journal of Rehabilitation Research and Development, 51*(8), 1189–1202.

Tagliaferri, F., Compagnone, C., Korsic, M., Servadei, F., & Kraus, J. (2006). A systematic review of brain injury epidemiology in Europe. *Acta Neurochirgica (Wien), 148*(3), 255–268. doi:10.1007/s00701-005-0651-y

Tanielian, T., Jaycox, L. H., Adamson, D. M., Burnam, M. A., Burns, R. M., Caldarone, L. B., Cox, R. A., D'Amico, E. J., Diaz, C., Eibner, C., Fisher, G., Helmus, T. C., Karney, B., Kilmer, B., Marshall, G. N., Martin, L. T., Meredith, L. S., Metscher, K. N., Osilla, K. C., … Yochelson, M. R. (2008). *Invisible wounds of war*. RAND Corporation https://www.rand.org/pubs/monographs/MG720.html

Teasdale, G., Maas, A., Lecky, F., Manley, G., Stocchetti, N., & Murray, G. (2014). The Glasgow Coma Scale at 40 years: Standing the test of time. *The Lancet: Neurology, 13*(8), 844–854. doi:10.1016/S1474-4422(14)70120-6

Trudel, T. M., Nidiffer, F. D., & Barth, J. T. (2007). Community-integrated brain injury rehabilitation: Treatment models and challenges for civilian, military, and veteran populations. *Journal of Rehabilitation Research and Development, 44*(7), 1007–1016.

VA Polytrauma System of Care. (n.d.). *Polytrauma/TBI System of Care*. https://www.polytrauma.va.gov/system-of-care/index.asp

Vanderploeg, R. D., Belanger, H. G., Horner, R. D., Spehar, A. M., Powell-Cope, G., Luther, S. L., & Scott, S. G. (2012). Health outcomes associated with military deployment: Mild traumatic brain injury, blast, trauma, and combat associations in the Florida National Guard. *Archives of Physical Medicine and Rehabilitation, 93*(11), 1887–1895. doi:10.1016/j.apmr.2012.05.024

Wilk, J. E., Thomas, J. L., McGurk, D. M., Riviere, L. A., Castro, C. A., & Hoge, C. W. (2010). Mild traumatic brain injury (concussion) during combat: Lack of association of blast mechanism with persistent postconcussive symptoms. *The Journal of Head Trauma Rehabilitation, 25*(1), 9–14. doi:10.1097/HTR.0b013e3181bd090f

Wilson, L., Stewart, W., Dams-O'Connor, K., Diaz-Arrastia, R., Horton, L., Menon, D. K., & Polinder, S. (2017). The chronic and evolving neurological consequences of traumatic brain injury. *The Lancet: Neurology, 16*(10), 813–825. doi:10.1016/S1474-4422(17)30279-X

Wolf, S. J., Bebarta, V. S., Bonnett, C. J., Pons, P. T., & Cantrill, S. V. (2009). Blast injuries. *Lancet (London England), 374*(9687), 405–415. doi:10.1016/S0140-6736(09)60257-9

Wood, R., & Worthington, A. (1999). Outcome in community rehabilitation: Measuring the social impact of disability. *Neuropsychological Rehabilitation, 9*(3–4), 505–516.

Yeh, P.-H., Wang, B., Oakes, T. R., French, L. M., Pan, H., Graner, J., Liu, W., & Riedy, G. (2014). Post-concussional disorder and PTSD symptoms of military-related traumatic brain injury associated with compromised neurocircuitry. *Human Brain Mapping, 35*(6), 2652–2673. doi:10.1002/hbm.22358

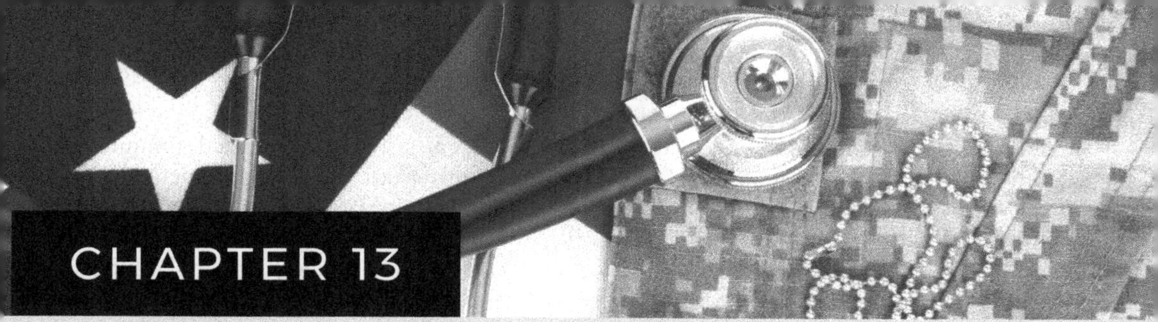

CHAPTER 13

Military Caregivers of Veterans and Service Members with Traumatic Brain Injury

Lillian Flores Stevens, Angelle M. Sander, and Noelle E. Carlozzi

Incidence of TBI

The incidence rate of traumatic brain injury (TBI) in civilian populations is estimated to be 1.4 million per year, with approximately 90,000 individuals experiencing long-term impairments and disabilities (Sosin et al., 1995; Thurman et al., 2007). TBI is among the most common injuries experienced during military training and combat operations (Thurman et al., 2007; Okie, 2005) and is considered the signature injury of the Operation Enduring Freedom (OEF), Operation Iraqi Freedom (OIF), and Operation New Dawn (OND) U.S. military conflicts (Okie, 2005). According to the Defense and Veterans Brain Injury Center (Department of Defense, 2017). 383,947 medical diagnoses of TBI have occurred in the military from 2000 through the first quarter of 2018, with the majority (82.3%) of mild severity.

TBI is considered a long-term condition. Approximately one-third of persons with TBI have moderate to severe disability (Langlois et al., 1997), with persistent and often devastating physical (Basford et al., 2003; Kapoor & Ciuffreda, 2002; Krauss, 2016), mental (Osborn et al., 2016; Osborn et al., 2014), behavioral (Sabaz et al., 2014; Simpson et al., 2013), and cognitive (Rabinowitz & Levin, 2014) impairments. These impairments necessitate supervision at one year post-injury in about one-third of persons with TBI (Hart et al., 2003), and over one-fourth still require assistance two to nine years post-injury (Hall et al., 2001). By five years post-injury, it has been estimated that 22% of individuals with TBI have died and 30% have worsened (Corrigan et al., 2014). Unemployment is another major problem for individuals with TBI; only about 30–40% are working at one year post-injury (Doctor et al., 2005; Malec & Moessner, 2006; Murphy et al., 2006; Dillahunt-Aspillaga et al., 2017). Given these chronic sequalae, one or more family members are often required to assume a care-partner role, bearing primary responsibility for assisting the person with TBI in physical, mental, financial, and leisure activities (Verhaeghe et al., 2005). For the rest of this chapter, these family member care partners will be referred to as caregivers.

Impact of TBI on Caregivers

It is well understood that caregiving for an individual with TBI can come with frequent negative impacts. Caregivers of persons with TBI commonly report problems with physical (Saban et al., 2016; Carlozzi et al., 2016; Knight et al., 1998; Marsh et al., 2002; Marsh et al., 1998; Arrango-Lasprilla et al., 2011; McPHerson, 2000; Morin et al., 1994; Montgomery & Dennis, 2003; Carlozzi et al., 2015), mental (Marsh et al., 1998; Kreutzer et al., 1994; Hall et al., 1994; Panting, et al., 1972; Livingston et al., 1985). and social health (Kreutzer et al., 1994; Livingston et al., 1985; Peters et al., 1990; Wood et al., 1997; Jacobs, 1988; Kozloff, 1987), as well as compromised health-related quality of life (HRQoL) (Verhaeghe et al., 2005; Carlozzi et al., 2016; Carlozzi et al., 2015; Griffin et al., 2017; Chronister et al., 2010). Additionally, caregivers experience increased financial strain and higher likelihood of leaving the labor force, increased family and marital strain, decreased family communication, disruption of family roles, and inattention to their own physical and mental health needs (Malec et al., 2017). Caring for an individual with TBI can have a profound negative impact on family relationships (Carlozzi et al., 2015; Griffin et al., 2017; Carlozzi et al., 2018; Qadeer et al., 2017). and there are a number of unmet family and spousal needs that these caregivers report (Misra-Hebert et al., 2015; Lewy et al., 2014; Verdeli et al., 2011; Gorman et al., 2011; Eaton et al., 2008). Negative outcomes include decreased communication (Kreutzer et al., 1994), and increased marital strain and divorce (especially for spousal caregivers) (Gosling & Oddy, 1999). In addition, families with unhealthy family functioning prior to the injury are at even higher risk for poor outcomes (Sander et al., 2003; Sander et al., 2002).

Furthermore, unique factors exist in providing care for persons with TBI that may place caregivers at increased risk for compromised physical and mental health relative to those providing care in other clinical populations. For example, caregivers of persons with TBI are typically caring for persons who are younger than those in other populations; as a result, these caregivers are in the caregiving role longer, which may increase their risk for negative physical and mental health outcomes. In fact, mental health, caregiver burden, and HRQoL are reportedly worse for caregivers of younger adults with brain injury relative to caregivers of older adults with dementia or of persons with cancer (Harding et al., 2015; Jackson et al., 2009). Additionally, it has long been documented that behavioral changes associated with TBI, such as impulsivity and disinhibition, are the most stressful to caregivers (Marsh et al., 1998; Griffin et al., 2017; Norup et al., 2012; Ponsford et al., 2003; Kinsella et al., 1991; Oddy et al., 1978; Kreutzer & Gervasio, 1994). These challenges may lead to poor physical and psychological health in the caregiver, causing reduced capacity to perform the care needed by the person with TBI. Given that caregivers' well-being and functioning affect both their own personal health outcomes as well as the functional and rehabilitation outcomes of the person with TBI (Sander et al., 2002; Anderson et al., 2001; TEmple et al., 2016; Holland & Schmidt, 2015; Shonberger et al., 2010; Ramkumar & Elliott, 2010; Kreutzer et al., 2010; Vangel et al., 2011; Sander et al., 2012; Smith & Schwirian, 1998), there is an urgent need to improve HRQOL for these caregivers.

Unique Characteristics of Military Caregivers of Individuals with TBI

Most of the literature on caregivers of individuals with TBI is based on civilians. While there are several commonalities between caregivers of civilians and caregivers of service members and veterans (SMVs) with TBI, military caregivers differ from civilian caregivers in several important ways, including managing increased medical complexity of injuries, family strain and deployment-related changes, and navigation of complex medical systems.

Increased Medical Complexity

In addition to TBI, service members are also likely to experience comorbid injuries (pain, amputation, repeat injuries), and psychological comorbidities (Langlois et al., 2003; Basford et al., 2003; Kapoor & Ciuffreda, 2002; Krauss, 2015). In particular, SMVs frequently experience post-traumatic stress disorder (PTSD), which affects up to 44% of SMVs with mild TBI and 42% of SMVs with a moderate or severe TBI (Hoge et al., 2008; Schneiderman et al., 2008; Lange et al., n.d.; Hines et al., 2014; Yurgil et al., 2014). Given the polytraumatic nature of injuries, military families have to cope with a much more uncontrollable and unpredictable medical treatment course (Collins & Kennedy, 2008). Families of polytrauma patients also tend to be more distressed than families of patients who sustain a TBI with no other injuries (Friedemann-Sánchez et al., 2008).

As many TBIs are sustained during combat situations (which are associated with intense psychological stress (Dausch & Saliman, 2009; Hoge et al., 2004; Sammons & Batten, 2008; Seal et al., 2008; Kennedy et al., 2010; French et al., 2012)), it is not surprising, that caregivers of SMVs with TBI commonly report that a large part of the caregiver role is focused on the management of emotional problems of the person with TBI (regardless of other cognitive or physical problems) (Osborn et al., 2016). This is especially important given general caregiver literature that indicates the presence of PTSD and other mental health symptoms is related to worse caregiver outcomes (Morin et al., 1994; Montgomery & Dennis, 2003; Carlozzi et al., 2015). Although worse emotional adjustment among the individuals with TBI is associated with greater caregiver burden for caregivers of both civilians and SMVs, this relationship is even more pronounced among caregivers of SMVs (Keatley et al., 2019).

Family Strain and Deployment-Related Changes

Many injured service members are young with relatively recent marriages and young children, rendering them more vulnerable to strain. Military families also undergo strain and role changes due to the service member's deployment. Family members may have emotionally prepared themselves for death and injury of their loved one, but most have not prepared for long-lasting personality or neurobehavioral changes resulting from injury. Caregivers of SMVs are also more likely to experience additional deployment-related stressors (Hoge et al., 2004; Renshaw et al., 2009; Sammons & Batten, 2008; Tanielian & Jacox, 2008) related to frequent relocations, deployment, and reintegration. Such stressors frequently persist several years post-deployment placing an undue strain on reintegration and family functioning (Sausch & Saliman, 2009; Sayers et al., 2009; McNulty, 2013; McNulty, 2010; McFarlane, 2009; Gironda et al., 2009; Hyatt et al., 2014; Chandra & Martin, 2010).

The road to recovery for the SMV can be complicated. Seriously injured service members often require intensive long-term treatment (both inpatient and outpatient). Often, acute medical stabilization and inpatient care occurs at foreign or military-designated hospitals around the world. Once the service member is stable enough for transport, they are transferred to a stateside regional hospital managed by the Department of Defense (DoD) or the Department of Veterans Affairs (VA). Throughout this process, families may temporarily or permanently relocate in order to engage with their loved one's care. Therefore, families of injured service members typically spend long periods of time with their loved one at rehabilitation settings far from home, resulting in prolonged limited accessibility to familiar support networks (Collins & Kennedy, 2008). Although acute and subacute care is typically provided during the active duty phase for a service member, as these individuals with TBI are transitioned to outpatient care and/or medically discharged from the military, family members are commonly faced with the burden of care (Osborn & Mathias, 2016). Like their civilian counterparts, caregivers of SMVs commonly experience problems with social health (financial strain, social isolation, and disrupted social roles) and emotional health (anger, depression, and anxiety) (Osborn & Mathias, 2016; Hart et al., 2003; Hart et al., 2001).

Navigation of Complex Healthcare Systems

The DoD and VA Health Care Systems include specialized TBI programs with dedicated providers (including neurologists, neuropsychologist, physiatrists, psychiatrists, and rehabilitation providers) and case management networks designed to guide patients through the care continuum. In most cases, active duty service members initially receive their health care through the DoD and VA care systems until separation from the military. Upon this separation, the veteran typically receives their care from the VA system or civilian-based healthcare system. Some veterans will continue to receive services through the DoD if the services that they need are not available at their local VA.

A number of potential barriers to care have been identified within the military healthcare system. Common complaints across SMVs include access to care (e.g., long wait times, geographic distance, and difficulties scheduling appointments) (Misra-Hebert et al., 2015; Lewy et al., 2014; Gorman et al., 2011; Eaton et al., 2008; Chokshi, 2014; Schall et al., 2004; Elnitsky et al., 2013; Kim et al., 2010; Hoge et al., 2008; Fletcher et al., 2016) as well as unmet family/spousal needs (Misra-Hebert et al., 2015; Lewy & Oliver, 2014; Verdeli et al., 2011; Gorman et al., 2011; Eaton et al., 2008), and a general lack of knowledge about where to get services (Lewy & Oliver, 2014; Gorman et al., 2011; Eaton et al., 2008). These complaints have been established in caregivers of SMVs with TBI; common complaints include difficulty navigating the healthcare system, qualifying and accessing appropriate benefits, paperwork burden, getting timely appointments, disruption of financial benefits (for the SMV), and a perceived lack of coordinated care for the caregiver and/or other family members (Carlozzi et al., 2018; Carlozzi et al., 2016).

How Military Caregiver Outcomes Differ from Civilian Caregivers

Qualitative work within the past five years has shed light on the differential psychosocial impact of caregiving between military versus civilian caregivers. Generally, there are a lot of commonalities between the two groups, but military caregivers experience specific additional challenges or symptoms with various domains, including financial, mental health, HRQoL, and sleep.

Financial

Caregivers of both civilians and SMVs frequently report changes in social roles and activities and increased financial strain. However, caregivers of SMVs frequently raised concerns related to losing caregiver compensation benefits (i.e., healthcare benefits that are specific to the military healthcare system), whereas discussion for caregivers of civilians focused more on loss of income (for both the caregiver and individuals with the TBI) and overall medical expenses related to TBI (Carlozzi et al., 2016; Carlozzi et al., 2015).

Mental Health

Caregivers of both SMVs and civilians also report several common mental health concerns, including feelings of burden and loss, depression, and anxiety (Carlozzi et al., 2016; Carlozzi et al., 2015). However, caregivers of SMVs also frequently discussed hypervigilance and emotional suppression topics, which were rarely initiated among caregivers of civilians (Carlozzi et al., 2016; Carlozzi et al., 2015). In a series of focus groups conducted with caregivers of veterans, Carlozzi and colleagues found that many caregivers described hypervigilance (or the need to constantly monitor and control their own behavior and the behavior of other individuals to avoid upsetting the person with TBI) (Carlozzi et al., 2016). Consequences of not being able to control the environment could range from minor emotional upset in the person with TBI to verbal and/or physical abuse perpetrated by the person with TBI (commonly directed at the caregiver or other family members) (Carlozzi et al., 2016). These concerns appear to be associated with the unpredictable behaviors of the person with the TBI (for both caregivers of civilians and SMVs), as well as the high prevalence of comorbid PTSD among SMVs (Hoge et al., 2008; Schneiderman et al., 2008; Lange et al., n.d.). In the same series of focus groups, caregivers described feeling the need to present a brave face to others, even when they were feeling stressed or sad. These attempts to hide one's feelings in order to appear okay can be termed emotional suppression. Emotional suppression has been shown to be associated with negative physical and mental health consequences in normal people. Negative physiological impacts include increased cardiovascular and sympathetic nervous system activity (Gross & Levenson, 1993; Roberts et al., 2008). Emotional suppression has also been shown to be related to decreased positive affect in normal people (Abler et al., 2010; Kwon & Kim, 2018; Gross & John, 2003). In a recent study, Sander and colleagues (2019) showed that emotional suppression was associated with greater negative affect and less positive affect in a sample of 165 caregivers of SMVs with TBI. The authors postulated that these findings likely reflect unique aspects of military culture (Hall, 2011; Meyer, 2015). an environment in which any admitted or perceived weakness may result in a significant reduction in duties and/or responsibilities (Meyer, 2015).

HRQoL

There is also quantitative data suggesting that caregivers of SMVs appear to have worse outcomes relative to their civilian counterparts. For example, a study in nonequivalent samples reported that caregivers of SMVs are more likely to report worse emotional and social HRQoL, and greater levels of feeling trapped by the caregiver role than their civilian counterparts (Keatley et al., 2019). Caregivers of SMVs also report poorer HRQoL compared to their civilian counterparts across a variety of domains Carlozzi, Kallen, Hanks et al., 2019), including mental (anxiety [Carlozzi, Hanks et al., 2019], depression [Carlozzi, Hanks et al., 2019], anger [Carlozzi, Hanks et al., 2019],), physical (sleep disturbance (Carlozzi, Ianni, et al., 2019; Carlozzi et al., n.d.), sleep-related impairment (Carlozzi et al., n.d.), and fatigue (Carlozzi, Ianni, et al., 2019)), and social (emotional support (Carlozzi, Ianni, Lange et al., 2019), informational support (Carlozzi, Ianni, Lange et al., 2019), social isolation (Carlozzi, Ianni, Lange et al., 2019), social participation (Carlozzi, Ianni, Lange et al., 2019), and social satisfaction (Carlozzi, Ianni, Lange et al.,

2019)). Additional caregiver-specific domains also demonstrated poorer HRQoL, including caregiver strain (Carlozzi, Kallen, Hanks et al., 2019; Carlozzi, Kallen, Ianni et al., 2019), caregiver-specific anxiety (Carlozzi, Kallen, Hanks et al., 2019; Carlozzi, Kallen, Sander et al., 2019), feelings of being trapped (Carlozzi, Kallen, Hanks et al., 2019; Carlozzi, Kallen, Hanks et al., 2019), feelings of loss related to themselves and the person with TBI (Carlozzi, Kallen, Hanks et al., 2019), family disruption (Carlozzi et al., n.d.), emotional suppression (Carlozzi, Kalen, Brickell et al., n.d.), and vigilance (Carlozzi, Lange et al., n.d.). Although these findings are for nonequivalent samples, findings indicate that caregivers of SMVs with TBI are reporting negative HRQoL outcomes that warrant further exploration.

Sleep

More than half of persons with TBI experience sleep disturbances (Marsh et al., 2002; Marsh et al., 1998) and persons with TBI are at increased risk for sleep disorders (Mathias & Alvaro, 2012; Castriotta & Murthy, 2011). In addition, the literature would suggest that ~50–60% of caregivers of persons with TBI report sleep disturbances (Saban et al., 2016; Carlozzi et al., 2016; Knight et al., 1998; Marsh et al., 2002; Marsh et al., 1998; Arango-Lasprilla et al., 2011; McPherson et al., 2000; Morin et al., 1994; Montgomery & Dennis, 2003; Carlozzi et al., 2015), although actual rates of sleep disorders in these caregivers is unknown. Such disturbances are associated with increased risk for negative health outcomes including obesity, cardiovascular disease (including stroke), prolonged recovery times from illness, and worsening of mood disorders (Wells et al., 2005; Javaheri & Redline, 2017; Sofi et al., 2014; Hsu et al., 2012; Chen et al., 2015; Li et al., 2014; Potter et al., 2016; Denner et al., 2014; Levy et al., 2009; Jun et al., 2009; Mullington et al., 2009; Van Cauter et al., 2008; Farrell & Richards, 2017; Duss et al., 2018; Wickwire et al., 2016; McCurry et al., 2015). The relationship between sleep disturbance in persons with TBI and that of their caregivers has not been investigated, but these have the potential to be related, as caregivers' sleep may be disrupted by activity of the person with TBI at night.

Recent work in caregivers of persons with TBI (a combined sample of caregivers of civilians and caregivers of SMVs) indicates that sleep-related impairment is associated with worse HRQoL, but that this relationship is moderated by the functional status of the person with TBI. For caregivers of persons with TBI and low functional independence, caregivers' sleep impairment was associated with poor HRQoL outcomes, including depression, fatigue, poor participation in social roles and activities, greater social isolation, greater caregiver strain/burden, higher caregiver vigilance, and increased feelings of being trapped. Sleep-related impairment was not associated with HRQoL for caregivers who were caring for individuals with greater functional independence (Carlozzi et al., n.d.).

Interestingly, additional work comparing caregivers of SMVs to caregivers of civilians with TBI found that military status was a very strong predictor of caregiver sleep-related impairment. Caregivers of SMVs reported much higher levels of sleep-related impairment compared to caregivers of civilians (Kratz et al., n.d.). In addition, for caregivers of SMVs, sleep-related impairment in the person with TBI contributes to caregivers' sleep impairment more than does the functional dependence of the person with injury. This is different from the pattern found among caregivers of civilians with TBI and suggests that different factors may impact sleep in caregivers of SMVs.

Clinical Recommendations

The existing research on military caregivers has implications for the kinds of services from which they may benefit. The services can generally be classified into one of three categories: assistance managing cognitive and emotional difficulties in the SMV for whom they provide care; assistance managing their own emotions and stress; and assistance with obtaining needed services for the SMV for whom they provide care and everyday needs.

Assistance with Managing Cognitive and Emotional Difficulties for the SMV

A variety of studies have shown that caregivers of persons with TBI consistently rate the need to receive education on the physical, cognitive, and emotional/behavioral changes in the person with TBI as their top need following injury (Kreutzer et al., 1994; Serio et al., 1995; Witol et al., 1996). Caregivers express the desire to have this information presented honestly and in a language they can understand. They wish to be told not only what to expect regarding cognitive and emotional changes, but also what they can do to help. While many caregivers may receive this information in the rehabilitation setting, the chaos and information overload associated with the early stages of recovery may prevent them from hearing the information at that time and/or from remembering it. Many caregivers of SMVs with TBI may not have heard this information previously before they present to community providers, since many have co-occurring bodily injuries that were the main focus during initial medical treatment, and some may not have received rehabilitation. This may particularly be the case for persons with mild TBI.

There are several sources that exist to help with educating caregivers about the cognitive and emotional sequelae of injury and how they can help. The use of these written materials is recommended because they can be turned to when caregivers no longer have contact with medical professionals. Some recommended sources are:

- A series of brief fact sheets has been developed by the Traumatic Brain Injury Models Systems investigators, funded by the National Institute on Disability, Independent Living, and Rehabilitation Research. Examples of fact sheet topics include memory, depression, sexuality, sleep disturbance, and driving ability. These can be printed and distributed to persons with injury and family members at no cost from http://www.msktc.org/tbi/factsheets.
- Another set of resources has been developed by the Defense and Veterans Brain Injury Center (DVBIC) that provides fact sheets for patients and families as well as clinical tools for providers. These can be downloaded or ordered at no cost from https://dvbic.dcoe.mil/resources.

It is important to remember that caregivers may require assistance in implementing the strategies described in these materials. It is also important to remember that these materials were developed largely for caregivers of civilians with TBI. While many of the problems faced by SMV caregivers are the same, they may have unique needs not covered in these materials, such as coping with symptoms of PTSD in their SMV. Separate educational materials may be required for this.

Assistance with Self-Management of Emotions and Stress

Caregivers of SMVs with TBI may benefit from stress management training and psychotherapy services that have utility for reducing emotional distress and/or the perceived burden in caregivers of civilians with TBI. These include cognitive-behavioral therapy (Sander, 2005), and holistic family intervention (including psychoeducation, skill building, and support) (Kreutzer et al., 2015; Niemeier et al., 2018). However, therapists providing this treatment should be aware of the military culture that may impact the willingness of caregivers of SMVs to seek help and/or to express emotion within a treatment setting. This may be particularly important for caregivers of persons in rural areas, as persons in rural areas may avoid seeking professional health care. Problem-solving training has been shown to be useful for assisting caregivers in self-managing stress in a variety of injury populations, including TBI (Powell et al., 2016; Rivera et al., 2008). Problem-solving training can be successfully provided by phone, as well as in person, which increases its utility for caregivers living in rural areas. The more educational approach to problem-solving training, as well as its applicability to a variety of life situations, may increase acceptability by persons who are more uncomfortable with traditional healthcare approaches.

Based on the research described in an earlier section, many caregivers of SMVs with TBI report frequent use of emotional suppression (Carlozzi et al., 2016). These caregivers may need permission to experience their emotions and assistance with relating to them in a nonjudgmental way. Psychotherapies that focus on nonjudgmental experience of emotions, such as Acceptance Commitment Therapy (ACT) and mindfulness-based therapies, may have benefit for these caregivers.

Hypervigilance, or a heightened state of alertness and sensitivity to one's surroundings, has also been verbalized by many caregivers of SMVs with TBI (Carlozzi et al., 2016). Hypervigilance can be a symptom of emotional distress, including anxiety, and it can result in misperception of neutral situations (Kimble et al., 2014). The therapies recommended previously that emphasize nonjudgmental experience of emotions, may also assist with hypervigilance. Caregivers can learn to acknowledge when they are experiencing thoughts and/or feelings associated with hypervigilance, but can be taught to not always act on them. For example, if they notice themselves feeling fearful or anxious, or thinking that they must do something to prevent triggering an explosion in their SMV, they can be taught to stop, take a breath, and mindfully notice what is happening inside them and in the surrounding environment. This practice of being mindful of their thoughts, feelings, and surroundings in a nonjudgmental and nonreactive way may combat hypervigilance and lead them to more fully appreciate possibilities for action. They may begin to see that they often anticipate situations that do not occur. Alternatively, they may be able to perceive their SMV's behavior from a new perspective and discern more possibilities for helping.

Assistance with Obtaining Needed Services and with Everyday Needs

There are several initiatives within the current military system that caregivers of SMVs can turn to for finding a variety of services for themselves and their SMV. Several educational opportunities exist for families, and indeed VA policy mandates documentation of efforts to prepare family members for changes associated with injury (Department of Veterans Affairs, 2013). On a national scale, the Polytrauma System of Care has developed an information guide, *Traumatic Brain Injury: A Guide for Caregivers of Service Members and Veterans*, that outlines general information about the structure and functioning of the brain, how TBI can affect brain functioning, the possible physical, cognitive, communication, behavioral, and emotional sequalae of TBI, support and information for family caregivers, and information on the services and benefits available. The Caregivers and Veterans Omnibus Health Service Act of 2010 authorizes VA's Comprehensive Caregiver Program to provide financial stipends, health care, respite, counseling, and travel reimbursement to eligible caregivers of veterans injured in OEF/OIF (Caregivers and Veterans Omnibus Health Act, 2010).

It should be noted that in spite of the availability of these services, many caregivers report substantial anger and frustration over the lack of services to assist them and their SMV (Schneiderman et al., 2008; Sammons &

Batten, 2008). Non-military health providers may be treating these caregivers and should be aware of this potential frustration and/or anger. The reasons for lack of knowledge about existing resources are complex, but caregivers may need assistance with accessing services. It is important for non-military health providers to familiarize themselves with the resources that are available within the military, which are typically provided at no cost. Providers can encourage caregivers to access these resources, which may provide an important supplement to services being provided by the non-military professionals. For example, a caregiver who is overwhelmed may be able to have a home health worker to assist. Caregivers who are unable to work due to caring for the SMV may be able to apply for a paid caregiver role, which may reduce financial stress.

Summary and Conclusion

Caregivers of SMVs with TBI face unique challenges and stress that can impact their physical, cognitive, emotional, and social health. While resources are available for these caregivers within the DoD and VA systems, they may not have knowledge of these resources and may perceive few choices for assistance. Many SMVs end up being treated in the civilian healthcare system, and their special needs may not be understood by these healthcare providers. Civilian healthcare providers should familiarize themselves with the military culture and how it may impact caregivers' willingness to seek help and to express their needs. They should also become familiar with military resources available that could supplement their existing health care.

References

Abler, B., Hofer, C., Walter, H., Erk, S., Hoffmann, H., Traue, H. C., & Kessler, H. (2010). Habitual emotion regulation strategies and depressive symptoms in healthy subjects predict fMRI brain activation patterns related to major depression. *Psychiatry Research, 183*(2), 105–113.

Anderson, V., Catroppa, C., Haritou, F., Morse, S., Pentland, L., Rosenfeld, J., & Stargatt, R. (2001). Predictors of acute child and family outcome following traumatic brain injury in children. *Pediatric Neurosurgery, 34*(3), 138–148.

Arango-Lasprilla, J. C., Nicholls, E., Villaseñor Cabrera, T., Drew, A., Jimenez-Maldonado, M., & Martinez-Cortes, M. L. (2011). Health-related quality of life in caregivers of individuals with traumatic brain injury from Guadalajara, Mexico. *Journal of Rehabilitation Medicine, 43*(11), 983–986.

Basford, J. R., Chou, L. S., Kaufman, K. R., Brey, R. H., Walker, A., Malec, J. F., Moessner, A. M., & Brown, A. W. (2003). An assessment of gait and balance deficits after traumatic brain injury. *Archives of Physical Medicine and Rehabilitation, 84*(3), 343–349.

Caregivers and Veterans Omnibus Health Service Act of 2010. In. *Pub. L No. 111-163 101 U.S.C.*

Carlozzi, N. E., Boileau, N. R., Ianni, P. A., et al. Reliability and validity data to support the clinical utility of the TBI-CareQOL measurement system. *Rehabilitation Psychology*. In Press.

Carlozzi, N. E., Brickell, T. A., French, L. M., Sander, A., Kratz, A. L., Tulsky, D. S., Chiaravalloti, N. D., Hahn, E. A., Kallen, M., Austin, A. M., Miner, J. A., & Lange, R. T. (2016). Caring for our wounded warriors: A qualitative examination of health-related quality of life in caregivers of individuals with military-related traumatic brain injury. *Journal of Rehabilitation Research and Development, 53*(6), 669–680.

Carlozzi, N. E., Brickell, T. A., French, L. M., Sander, A., Kratz, A. L., Tulsky, D. S., Chiaravalloti, N. D., Hahn, E. A., Kallen, M., Austin, A. M., Miner, J. A., & Lange, R. T. (2016). Caring for our wounded warriors: A qualitative examination of health-related quality of life in caregivers of individuals with military-related traumatic brain injury. *Journal of Rehabilitation Research and Development, 53*(6), 669–680.

Carlozzi, N. E., Hanks, R., Lange, R. T., Brickell, T. A., Ianni, P. A., Miner, J. A., French, L. M., Kallen, M. A., & Sander, A. M. (2019). Understanding health-related quality of life in caregivers of civilians and service members/veterans with traumatic brain injury: Establishing the reliability and validity of PROMIS mental health measures. *Archives of Physical Medicine and Rehabilitation, 100*(4S), S94–S101.

Carlozzi, N. E., Ianni, P. A., Lange, R. T., Brickell, T. A., Kallen, M. A., Hahn, E. A., French, L. M., Cella, D., Miner, J. A., & Tulsky, D. S. (2019). Understanding health-related quality of life of caregivers of civilians and service members/veterans with traumatic brain injury: Establishing the reliability and validity of PROMIS social health measures. *Archives of Physical Medicine and Rehabilitation, 100*(4S), S110–S118.

Carlozzi, N. E., Ianni, P. A., Tulsky, D. S., Brickell, T. A., Lange, R. T., French, L. M., Cella, D., Kallen, M. A., Miner, J. A., & Kratz, A. L. (2019). Understanding health-related quality of life in caregivers of civilians and service members/veterans with traumatic brain injury: Establishing the reliability and validity of PROMIS fatigue and sleep disturbance item banks. *Archives of Physical Medicine and Rehabilitation, 100*(4S), S102–S109.

Carlozzi, N. E., Kallen, M. A., Brickell, T. A., Lange, R. T., Boileau, N. R., Tulsky, D., Hanks, R. A., Massengale, J. P., Nakase-Richardson, R., Ianni, P. A., Miner, J. A., French, L. M., & Sander, A. M. (2020). Measuring emotional suppression in caregivers of adults with traumatic brain injury. *Rehabilitation Psychology, 65*(4), 455–470.

Carlozzi, N. E., Kallen, M. A., Hanks, R., Hahn, E. A., Brickell, T. A., Lange, R. T., French, L. M., Kratz, A. L., Tulsky, D. S., Cella, D., Miner, J. A., Ianni, P. A., & Sander, A. M. (2019). The TBI-CareQOL Measurement System: Development and preliminary validation of health-related quality of life measures for caregivers of civilians and service members/veterans with traumatic brain injury. *Archives of Physical Medicine and Rehabilitation, 100*(4S), S1–S12.

Carlozzi, N. E., Kallen, M. A., Hanks, R., Kratz, A. L., Hahn, E. A., Brickell, T. A., Lange, R. T., French, L. M., Ianni, P. A., Miner, J. A., & Sander, A. M. (2019). The development of a new computer adaptive test to evaluate feelings of being trapped in caregivers of individuals with traumatic brain injury: TBI-CareQOL Feeling Trapped item bank. *Archives of Physical Medicine and Rehabilitation, 100*(4S), S43–S51.

Carlozzi, N. E., Kallen, M. A., Ianni, P. A., Hahn, E. A., French, L. M., Lange, R. T., Brickell, T. A., Hanks, R., & Sander, A. M. (2019). The development of a new computer-adaptive test to evaluate strain in caregivers of individuals with TBI: TBI-CareQOL Caregiver Strain. *Archives of Physical Medicine and Rehabilitation, 100*(4S), S13–S21.

Carlozzi, N. E., Kallen, M. A., Ianni, P. A., Sander, A. M., Hahn, E. A., Lange, R. T., Brickell, T. A., French, L. M., Miner, J. A., & Hanks, R. (2019). The development of two new computer adaptive tests to evaluate feelings of loss in caregivers of individuals with traumatic brain injury: TBI-CareQOL Feelings of Loss-Self and Feelings of Loss-Person With Traumatic Brain Injury. *Archives of Physical Medicine and Rehabilitation, 100*(4S), S31–S42.

Carlozzi, N. E., Kallen, M. A., Sander, A. M., Brickell, T. A., Lange, R. T., French, L. M., Ianni, P. A., Miner, J. A., & Hanks, R. (2019). The development of a new computer adaptive test to evaluate anxiety in caregivers of individuals with traumatic brain injury: TBI-CareQOL Caregiver-Specific Anxiety. *Archives of Physical Medicine and Rehabilitation, 100*(4S), S22–S30.

Carlozzi, N. E., Kratz, A. L., Sander, A. M., Chiaravalloti, N. D., Brickell, T. A., Lange, R. T., Hahn, E. A., Austin, A., Miner, J. A., & Tulsky, D. S. (2015). Health-related quality of life in caregivers of individuals with traumatic brain injury: Development of a conceptual model. *Archives of Physical Medicine and Rehabilitation, 96*(1), 105–113.

Carlozzi, N. E., Kratz, A. L., Sander, A. M., Chiaravalloti, N. D., Brickell, T. A., Lange, R. T., Hahn, E. A., Austin, A., Miner, J. A., & Tulsky, D. S. (2015). Health-related quality of life in caregivers of individuals with traumatic brain injury: Development of a conceptual model. *Archives of Physical Medicine and Rehabilitation, 96*(1), 105–113.

Carlozzi, N. E., Lange, R. T., Boileau, N. R., Kallen, M. A., Sander, A. M., Hanks, R. A., Nakase-Richardson, R., Tulsky, D. S., Massengale, J. P., French, L. M., & Brickell, T. A. (2020). TBI-CareQOL family disruption: Family disruption in caregivers of persons with TBI. *Rehabilitation Psychology, 65*(4), 390–400.

Carlozzi, N. E., Lange, R. T., French, L. M., Sander, A. M., Freedman, J., & Brickell, T. A. (2018). A latent content analysis of barriers and supports to healthcare: Perspectives from caregivers of service members and veterans with military-related traumatic brain injury. *The Journal of Head Trauma Rehabilitation, 33*(5), 342–353.

Carlozzi, N. E., Lange, R. T., Kallen, M. A., Boileau, N. R., Sander, A. M., Massengale, J. P., Nakase-Richardson, R., Tulsky, D. S., French, L. M., Hahn, E. A., Ianni, P. A., Miner, J. A., Hanks, R., & Brickell, T. A. (2020). Assessing vigilance in caregivers after traumatic brain injury: TBI-CareQOL Caregiver Vigilance. *Rehabilitation Psychology*, 65(4), 418–431.

Castriotta, R. J., & Murthy, J. N. (2011). Sleep disorders in patients with traumatic brain injury: A review. *CNS Drugs*, 25(3), 175–185.

Chandra, A., Martin, L. T., Hawkins, S. A., & Richardson, A. (2010). The impact of parental deployment on child social and emotional functioning: Perspectives of school staff. *The Journal of Adolescent Medicine*, 46(3), 218–223.

Chen, Y., & Lu, Y. (2015). The association between insomnia symptoms and mortality: A prospective study of US men. *Journal of the American Geriatrics Society, 63*, S365–S365.

Chokshi D. A. (2014). Improving health care for veterans--a watershed moment for the VA. *The New England Journal of Medicine*, 371(4), 297–299.

Chronister, J., Chan, F., Sasson-Gelman, E. J., & Chiu, C. Y. (2010). The association of stress-coping variables to quality of life among caregivers of individuals with traumatic brain injury. *NeuroRehabilitation, 27*(1), 49–62.

Collins, R. C., & Kennedy, M. C. (2008). Serving families who have served: Providing family therapy and support in interdisciplinary polytrauma rehabilitation. *Journal of Clinical Psychology, 64*(8), 993–1003.

Corrigan, J. D., Cuthbert, J. P., Harrison-Felix, C., Whiteneck, G. G., Bell, J. M., Miller, A. C., Coronado, V. G., & Pretz, C. R. (2014). US population estimates of health and social outcomes 5 years after rehabilitation for traumatic brain injury. *The Journal of Head Trauma Rehabilitation, 29*(6), E1–E9.

Dausch, B. M., & Saliman, S. (2009). Use of family focused therapy in rehabilitation for veterans with traumatic brain injury. *Rehabilitation Psychology, 54*(3), 279–287.

Department of Veterans Affairs. (2013). *VHA handbook 1172.01: Polytrauma system of care.* Veterans Health Administrtaion.

Depner, C. M., Stothard, E. R., & Wright, K. P., Jr. (2014). Metabolic consequences of sleep and circadian disorders. *Current Diabetes Reports, 14*(7):507.

Dillahunt-Aspillaga, C., Nakase-Richardson, R., Hart, T., Powell-Cope, G., Dreer, L. E., Eapen, B. C., Barnett, S. D., Mellick, D., Haskin, A., & Silva, M. A. (2017). Predictors of employment outcomes in veterans with traumatic brain injury: A VA traumatic brain injury model systems study. *The Journal of Head Trauma Rehabilitation, 32*(4), 271–282.

Doctor, J. N., Castro, J., Temkin, N. R., Fraser, R. T., Machamer, J. E., & Dikmen, S. S. (2005). Workers' risk of unemployment after traumatic brain injury: A normed comparison. *Journal of the International Neuropsychological Society, 11*(6), 747–752.

DoD Worldwide Numbers. (2017). http://dvbic.dcoe.mil/files/tbi-numbers/DoD-TBI-Worldwide-Totals_2000-2016_Feb-17-2017_v1.0_2017-04-06.pdf

Duss, S. B., Brill, A. K., Bargiotas, P., Facchin, L., Alexiev, F., Manconi, M., & Bassetti, C. L. (2018). Sleep-wake disorders in stroke-increased stroke risk and deteriorated recovery? An evaluation on the necessity for prevention and treatment. *Current Neurology and Neuroscience Reports, 18*(10), 72.

Eaton, K. M., Hoge, C. W., Messer, S. C., Whitt, A. A., Cabrera, O. A., McGurk, D., Cox, A., & Castro, C. A. (2008). Prevalence of mental health problems, treatment need, and barriers to care among primary care-seeking spouses of military service members involved in Iraq and Afghanistan deployments. *Military medicine, 173*(11), 1051–1056.

Elnitsky, C. A., Andresen, E. M., Clark, M. E., McGarity, S., Hall, C. G., & Kerns, R. D. (2013). Access to the US Department of Veterans Affairs health system: Self-reported barriers to care among returnees of Operations Enduring Freedom and Iraqi Freedom. *BMC Health Services Research, 13*, 498.

Farrell, P. C., & Richards, G. (2017). Recognition and treatment of sleep-disordered breathing: An important component of chronic disease management. *Journal of Translational Medicine, 15*(1), 114.

Fletcher, C. E., Mitchinson, A. R., Trumble, E., Hinshaw, D. B., & Dusek, J. A. (2017). Providers' and administrators' perceptions of complementary and integrative health practices across the Veterans Health Administration. *Journal of Alternative and Complementary Medicine (New York, N.Y.), 23*(1), 26–34.

French, L. M., Iverson, G. L., Lange, R. T., & Bryant, R. A. (2012). Neuropsychological consequences of injury in military personnel. In S. S. Bush, G. L. Iverson, B. L. Brooks, R. A. Bryant, & K. E. Ferguson (Eds.), *Neuropsychological assessment of work-related injuries* (pp. 127–160). Guilford Press.

Friedemann-Sánchez, G., Griffin, J. M., Rettmann, N. A., Rittman, M., & Partin, M. R. (2008). Communicating information to families of polytrauma patients: A narrative literature review. *Rehabilitation Nursing, 33*(5), 206–213.

Gironda, R. J., Clark, M. E., Ruff, R. L., Chait, S., Craine, M., Walker, R., & Scholten, J. (2009). Traumatic brain injury, polytrauma, and pain: Challenges and treatment strategies for the polytrauma rehabilitation. *Rehabilitation Psychology, 54*(3), 247–258.

Gorman, L. A., Blow, A. J., Ames, B. D., & Reed, P. L. (2011). National guard families after combat: Mental health, use of mental health services, and perceived treatment barriers. *Psychiatric Services (Washington, D.C.), 62*(1), 28–34.

Gosling J, Oddy M. (1999). Rearranged marriages: Marital relationships after head injury. *Brain Injury, 13*(10), 785–796.

Griffin, J. M., Lee, M. K., Bangerter, L. R., Van Houtven, C. H., Friedemann-Sánchez, G., Phelan, S. M., Carlson, K. F., & Meis, L. A. (2017). Burden and mental health among caregivers of veterans with traumatic brain injury/polytrauma. *The American Journal of Orthopsychiatry, 87*(2), 139–148.

Gross, J. J., & John, O. P. (2003). Individual differences in two emotion regulation processes: Implications for affect, relationships, and well-being. *Journal of Personality and Social Psychology, 85*(2), 348–362.

Gross, J. J., & Levenson, R. W. (1993). Emotional suppression: Physiology, self-report, and expressive behavior. *Journal of Personality and Social Psychology, 64*(6), 970–986.

Hall, K. M., Bushnik, T., Lakisic-Kazazic, B., Wright, J., & Cantagallo, A. (2001). Assessing traumatic brain injury outcome measures for long-term follow-up of community-based individuals. *Archives of Physical Medicine and Rehabilitation, 82*(3), 367–374.

Hall, K. M., Karzmark, P., Stevens, M., Englander, J., O'Hare, P., & Wright, J. (1994). Family stressors in traumatic brain injury: A two-year follow-up. *Archives of Physical Medicine and Rehabilitation, 75*(8), 876–884.

Hall, L. K. (2011). The importance of understanding military culture. *Social Work in Health Care, 50*(1), 4–18.

Harding, R., Gao, W., Jackson, D., Pearson, C., Murray, J., & Higginson, I. J. (2015). comparative analysis of informal caregiver burden in advanced cancer, dementia, and acquired brain injury. *Journal of Pain and Symptom Management, 50*(4), 445–452.

Hart, T., Millis, S., Novack, T., Englander, J., Fidler-Sheppard, R., & Bell, K. R. (2003). The relationship between neuropsychologic function and level of caregiver supervision at 1 year after traumatic brain injury. *Archives of Physical Medicine and Rehabilitation, 84*(2), 221–230.

Hines, L. A., Sundin, J., Rona, R. J., Wessely, S., & Fear, N. T. (2014). Posttraumatic stress disorder post Iraq and Afghanistan: Prevalence among military subgroups. *Canadian Journal of Psychiatry, 59*(9), 468–479.

Hoge, C. W., Castro, C. A., Messer, S. C., McGurk, D., Cotting, D. I., & Koffman, R. L. (2004). Combat duty in Iraq and Afghanistan, mental health problems, and barriers to care. *The New England Journal of Medicine, 351*(1), 13–22.

Hoge, C. W., Castro, C. A., Messer, S. C., McGurk, D., Cotting, D. I., & Koffman, R. L. (2008). Combat duty in Iraq and Afghanistan, mental health problems and barriers to care. *United States Army Medical Department Journal*, 7–17.

Hoge, C. W., McGurk, D., Thomas, J. L., Cox, A. L., Engel, C. C., & Castro, C. A. (2008). Mild traumatic brain injury in U.S. Soldiers returning from Iraq. *The New England Journal of Medicine, 358*(5), 453–463.

Holcomb, E. M., Schwartz, D. J., McCarthy, M., Thomas, B., Barnett, S. D., & Nakase-Richardson, R. (2016). Incidence, characterization, and predictors of sleep apnea in consecutive brain injury rehabilitation admissions. *The Journal of Head Trauma Rehabilitation, 31*(2), 82–100.

Holland, J. N., & Schmidt, A. T. (2015). Static and dynamic factors promoting resilience following traumatic brain injury: A brief review. *Neural Plasticity, 2015*, 902802.

Hsu, C. Y., Huang, C. C., Huang, P. H., Chiang, C. H., & Leu, H. B. (2012). Insomnia and risk of cardiovascular disease. *Circulation, 126*(21).

Hyatt, K., Davis, L. L., & Barroso, J. (2014). Chasing the care: Soldiers experience following combat-related mild traumatic brain injury. *Military Medicine, 179*(8), 849–855.

Jackson, D., Turner-Stokes, L., Murray, J., Leese, M., & McPherson, K. M. (2009). Acquired brain injury and dementia: A comparison of carer experiences. *Brain Injury, 23*(5), 433–444.

Jacobs, H. E. (1988). The Los Angeles Head Injury Survey: Procedures and initial findings. *Archives of Physical Medicine and Rehabilitation, 69*(6), 425–431.Javaheri, S., & Redline, S. (2017). Insomnia and risk of cardiovascular disease. *Chest, 152*(2), 435–444.

Jun, J., & Polotsky, V. Y. (2009). Metabolic consequences of sleep-disordered breathing. *ILAR Journal, 50*(3), 289–306.

Kapoor, N., & Ciuffreda, K. J. (2002). Vision Disturbances Following Traumatic Brain Injury. *Current Treatment Options in Neurology, 4*(4), 271–280.

Keatley, E., Hanks, R., Sander, A. M., Kratz, A. L., Tulsky, D. S., Ianni, P., Miner, J., & Carlozzi, N. E. (2019). Group differences among caregivers of civilians and service members or veterans with traumatic brain injury. *Archives of Physical Medicine and Rehabilitation, 100*(4S), S52–S57.

Kennedy, J. E., Leal, F. O., Lewis, J. D., Cullen, M. A., & Amador, R. R. (2010). Posttraumatic stress symptoms in OIF/OEF service members with blast-related and non-blast-related mild TBI. *NeuroRehabilitation, 26*(3), 223–231.

Kim, P. Y., Thomas, J. L., Wilk, J. E., Castro, C. A., & Hoge, C. W. (2010). Stigma, barriers to care, and use of mental health services among active duty and National Guard soldiers after combat. *Psychiatric Services (Washington, D.C.), 61*(6), 582–588.

Kimble, M., Boxwala, M., Bean, W., Maletsky, K., Halper, J., Spollen, K., & Fleming, K. (2014). The impact of hypervigilance: Evidence for a forward feedback loop. *Journal of Anxiety Disorders, 28*(2), 241–245.

Kinsella, G., Packer, S., & Olver, J. (1991). Maternal reporting of behaviour following very severe blunt head injury. *Journal of Neurology, Neurosurgery, and Psychiatry, 54*(5), 422–426.

Knight, R. G., Devereux, R., & Godfrey, H. (1998). Caring for a family member with a traumatic brain injury. *Brain Injury, 12*(6), 467–481.

Kozloff, R. (1987). Networks of social support and the outcome from severe head injury. *Journal of Head Trauma Rehabilitation*, 2, 14–23.

Krauss, J. K. (2015). Movement disorders secondary to craniocerebral trauma. *Handbook of Clinical Neurology, 128*, 475–496.

Kreutzer, J. S., Gervasio, A. H., & Camplair, P. S. (1994). Patient correlates of caregivers' distress and family functioning after traumatic brain injury. *Brain Injury, 8*(3), 211–230.

Kreutzer, J. S., Gervasio, A. H., & Camplair, P. S. (1994). Primary caregivers' psychological status and family functioning after traumatic brain injury. *Brain Injury, 8*(3), 197–210.

Kreutzer, J. S., Marwitz, J. H., Godwin, E. E., & Arango-Lasprilla, J. C. (2010). Practical approaches to effective family intervention after brain injury. *The Journal of Head Trauma Rehabilitation, 25*(2), 113–120.

Kreutzer, J. S., Marwitz, J. H., Sima, A. P., & Godwin, E. E. (2015). Efficacy of the brain injury family intervention: Impact on family members. *The Journal of Head Trauma Rehabilitation, 30*(4), 249–260.

Kreutzer, J., Serio, C., & Bergquist, S. (1994). Family needs after brain injury: A quantitative analysis. *The Journal of Head Trauma Rehabilitation, 9*(3), 104–115.

Kwon, H., & Kim, Y. H. (2018). Perceived emotion suppression and culture: Effects on psychological well-being. *International Journal of Psychology, 54*(4), 448–453.

Lange, R. T., French, L. M., Lippa, S. M., Bailie, J. M., & Brickell, T. A. (2020). Posttraumatic stress disorder is a stronger predictor of long-term neurobehavioral outcomes than traumatic brain injury severity. *Journal of Traumatic Stress, 33*(3), 318–329.

Langlois, J. A., Kegler, S. R., Butler, J. A., Gotsch, K. E., Johnson, R. L., Reichard, A. A., Webb, K. W., Coronado, V. G., Selassie, A. W., & Thurman, D. J. (2003). Traumatic brain injury-related hospital discharges. Results from a 14-state surveillance system, 1997. *Morbidity and Mortality Weekly Report. Surveillance Summaries (Washington, D.C. : 2002), 52*(4), 1–20.

Levy, P., Bonsignore, M. R., & Eckel J. (2009). Sleep, sleep-disordered breathing and metabolic consequences. *The European Respiratory Journal, 34*(1), 243–260.

Lewy, C. S., Oliver, C. M., & McFarland, B. H. (2014). Barriers to mental health treatment for military wives. *Psychiatric Services (Washington, D.C.), 65*(9), 1170–1173.

Li, Y., Zhang, X., Winkelman, J. W., Redline, S., Hu, F. B., Stampfer, M., Ma, J., & Gao, X. (2014). Association between insomnia symptoms and mortality: A prospective study of U.S. men. *Circulation, 129*(7), 737–746.

Livingston, M. G., Brooks, D. N., & Bond, M. R. (1985). Patient outcome in the year following severe head injury and relatives' psychiatric and social functioning. *Journal of Neurology, Neurosurgery, and Psychiatry, 48*(9), 876–881.

Malec, J. F., & Moessner, A. M. (2006). Replicated positive results for the VCC model of vocational intervention after ABI within the social model of disability. *Brain Injury, 20*(3), 227–236.

Malec, J. F., Van Houtven, C. H., Tanielian, T., Atizado, A., & Dorn, M. C. (2017). Impact of TBI on caregivers of veterans with TBI: Burden and interventions. *Brain Injury, 31*(9), 1235–1245.

Marsh, N. V., Kersel, D. A., Havill, J. A., & Sleigh, J. W. (2002). Caregiver burden during the year following severe traumatic brain injury. *Journal of Clinical and Experimental Neuropsychology, 24*(4), 434–447.

Marsh, N. V., Kersel, D. A., Havill, J. H., & Sleigh, J. W. (1998). Caregiver burden at 6 months following severe traumatic brain injury. *Brain Injury, 12*(3), 225–238.

Mathias, J. L., & Alvaro, P. K. (2012). Prevalence of sleep disturbances, disorders, and problems following traumatic brain injury: A meta-analysis. *Sleep Medicine, 13*(7), 898–905.

McCurry, S. M., Song, Y., & Martin, J. L. (2015). Sleep in caregivers: What we know and what we need to learn. *Current Opinion in Psychiatry, 28*(6), 497–503.

McFarlane, A. C. (2009). Military deployment: The impact on children and family adjustment and the need for care. *Current Opinion in Psychiatry*, 22(4), 369–373.

McNulty, P. A. (2010). Adaptability and resiliency of army families during reunification: Initial results of a longitudinal study. *Federal Practitioner, 27*(3), 18–27.

McNulty, P. A. (2013). Adaptability and resiliency of military families during reunification: Results of a longitudinal study. *Federal Practitioner, 30*(8), 14–22.

McPherson, K. M., Pentland, B., & McNaughton, H. K. (2000). Brain injury - The perceived health of carers. *Disability and Rehabilitation, 22*(15), 683–689.

Meyer, E. G. (2015). The importance of understanding military culture. *Academic Psychiatry: The Journal of the American Association of Directors of Psychiatric Residency Training and the Association for Academic Psychiatry, 39*(4), 416–418.

Misra-Hebert, A. D., Santurri, L., DeChant, R., Watts, B., Rothberg, M., Sehgal, A. R., & Aron, D. C. (2015). Understanding the health needs and barriers to seeking health care of veteran students in the community. *Southern Medical Journal, 108*(8), 488–493.

Montgomery, P., & Dennis, J. (2003). Cognitive behavioural interventions for sleep problems in adults aged 60+. *The Cochrane Database of Systematic Reviews*, (1), CD003161.

Morin, C. M., Culbert, J. P., & Schwartz, S. M. (1994). Nonpharmacological interventions for insomnia: A meta-analysis of treatment efficacy. *The American Journal of Psychiatry, 151*(8), 1172–1180.

Mullington, J. M., Haack, M., Toth, M., Serrador, J. M., & Meier-Ewert, H. K. (2009). Cardiovascular, inflammatory, and metabolic consequences of sleep deprivation. *Progress in Cardiovascular Diseases, 51*(4), 294–302.

Murphy, L., Chamberlain, E., Weir, J., Berry, A., Nathaniel-James, D., & Agnew, R. (2006). Effectiveness of vocational rehabilitation following acquired brain injury: Preliminary evaluation of a UK specialist rehabilitation programme. *Brain Injury, 20*(11), 1119–1129.

Niemeier, J. P., Kreutzer, J. S., Marwitz, J. H., & Sima, A. P. (2019). A randomized controlled pilot study of a manualized intervention for caregivers of patients with traumatic brain injury in inpatient rehabilitation. *Archives of Physical Medicine and Rehabilitation, 100*(4S), S65–S75.

Norup, A., Welling, K. L., Qvist, J., Siert, L., & Mortensen, E. L. (2012). Depression, anxiety and quality-of-life among relatives of patients with severe brain injury: The acute phase. *Brain Injury, 26*(10), 1192–1200.

Oddy, M., Humphrey, M., & Uttley, D. (1978). Stresses upon the relatives of head-injured patients. *The British Journal of Psychiatry: The Journal of Mental Science, 133*, 507–513.

Okie S. (2005). Traumatic brain injury in the war zone. *The New England Journal of Medicine, 352*(20), 2043–2047.

Osborn, A. J., Mathias, J. L., & Fairweather-Schmidt, A. K. (2014). Depression following adult, non-penetrating traumatic brain injury: A meta-analysis examining methodological variables and sample characteristics. *Neuroscience and Biobehavioral Reviews, 47*, 1–15.

Osborn, A. J., Mathias, J. L., & Fairweather-Schmidt, A. K. (2016). Prevalence of anxiety following adult traumatic brain injury: A meta-analysis comparing measures, samples and postinjury intervals. *Neuropsychology, 30*(2), 247–261.

Panting, A., & Merry, P. (1972). The long term rehabilitation of severe head injuries with particular reference to the need for social and medical support for the patient's family. *Rehabilitation*, 38, 33–37.

Peters, L. C., Stambrook, M., Moore, A. D., & Esses, L. (1990). Psychosocial sequelae of closed head injury: Effects on the marital relationship. *Brain Injury, 4*(1), 39–47.

Ponsford, J., Olver, J., Ponsford, M., & Nelms, R. (2003). Long-term adjustment of families following traumatic brain injury where comprehensive rehabilitation has been provided. *Brain Injury, 17*(6), 453–468.

Potter, G. D., Skene, D. J., Arendt, J., Cade, J. E., Grant, P. J., & Hardie, L. J. (2016). Circadian rhythm and sleep disruption: Causes, metabolic consequences, and countermeasures. *Endocrine Reviews, 37*(6), 584–608.

Powell, J. M., Fraser, R., Brockway, J. A., Temkin, N., & Bell, K. R. (2016). A telehealth approach to caregiver self-management following traumatic brain injury: A randomized controlled trial. *The Journal of Head Trauma Rehabilitation, 31*(3), 180–190.

Qadeer, A., Khalid, U., Amin, M., Murtaza, S., Khaliq, M. F., & Shoaib, M. (2017). Caregiver's burden of the patients with traumatic brain injury. *Cureus, 9*(8), e1590.

Rabinowitz, A. R., & Levin, H. S. (2014). Cognitive sequelae of traumatic brain injury. *The Psychiatric Clinics of North America, 37*(1), 1–11.

Ramkumar, N. A., & Elliott, T. R. (2010). Family caregiving of persons following neurotrauma: Issues in research, service and policy. *Neurorehabilitation, 27*(1), 105–112.

Renshaw, K. D., Rodrigues, C. S., & Jones, D. H. (2009). Combat exposure, psychological symptoms, and marital satisfaction in National Guard soldiers who served in Operation Iraqi Freedom from 2005 to 2006. *Anxiety, Stress & Coping: An International Journal*, 22(1), 101–115.

Rivera, P. A., Elliott, T. R., Berry, J. W., & Grant, J. S. (2008). Problem-solving training for family caregivers of persons with traumatic brain injuries: A randomized controlled trial. *Archives of Physical Medicine and Rehabilitation, 89*(5), 931–941.

Roberts, N. A., Levenson, R. W., & Gross, J. J. (2008). Cardiovascular costs of emotion suppression cross ethnic lines. *International Journal of Psychophysiology : Official Journal of the International Organization of Psychophysiology, 70*(1), 82–87.

Saban, K. L., Griffin, J. M., Urban, A., Janusek, M. A., Pape, T. L., & Collins, E. (2016). Perceived health, caregiver burden, and quality of life in women partners providing care to Veterans with traumatic brain injury. *Journal of Rehabilitation Research and Development, 53*(6), 681–692.

Sabaz, M., Simpson, G. K., Walker, A. J., Rogers, J. M., Gillis, I., & Strettles, B. (2014). Prevalence, comorbidities, and correlates of challenging behavior among community-dwelling adults with severe traumatic brain injury: A multicenter study. *The Journal of Head Trauma Rehabilitation, 29*(2), E19–E30.

Sammons, M. T., & Batten, S. V. (2008). Psychological services for returning veterans and their families: Evolving conceptualizations of the sequelae of warzone experiences. *Journal of Clinical Psychology, 64*(8), 921–927.

Sander, A. M. (2005). A cognitive-behavioral intervention for family members of persons with traumtic brian injury. In N. Zasler, R. Zafonte, & D. Katz (Eds.), *Brain injury medicine* (pp. 1117–1130). Demos Publishing.

Sander, A. M., Boileau, N. R., Hanks, R. A., Tulsky, D. S., & Carlozzi, N. E. (2020). Emotional suppression and hypervigilance in military caregivers: Relationship to negative and positive affect. *The Journal of Head Trauma Rehabilitation, 35*(1), E10–E20.

Sander, A. M., Caroselli, J. S., High, W. M., Becker, C., Neese, L., & Scheibel, R. (2002). Relationship of family functioning to progress in a post-acute rehabilitation programme following traumatic brain injury. *Brain Injury, 16*(8), 649–657.

Sander, A. M., Maestas, K. L., Sherer, M., Malec, J. F., & Nakase-Richardson, R. (2012). Relationship of caregiver and family functioning to participation outcomes after postacute rehabilitation for traumatic brain injury: A multicenter investigation. *Archives of Physical Medicine and Rehabilitation*, 93(5), 842–848.

Sander, A. M., Sherer, M., Malec, J. F. , High, W. M., Jr, Thompson, R. N., Moessner, A. M., & Josey, J. (2003). Preinjury emotional and family functioning in caregivers of persons with traumatic brain injury. *Archives of Physical Medicine & Rehabilitation, 84*(2), 197–203.

Sayers, S. L., Farrow, V. A., Ross, J., & Oslin, D. W. (2009). Family problems among recently returned military veterans referred for a mental health evaluation. *The Journal of Clinical Psychiatry, 70*(2), 163–170.

Schall, M. W., Duffy, T., Krishnamurthy, A., Levesque, O., Mehta, P., Murray, M., Parlier, R., Petzel, R., &

Sanderson, J. (2004). Improving patient access to the Veterans Health Administration's primary care and specialty clinics. *Joint Commission Journal on Quality and Safety*, *30*(8), 415–423.

Schneiderman, A. I., Braver, E. R., & Kang, H. K. (2008). Understanding sequelae of injury mechanisms and mild traumatic brain injury incurred during the conflicts in Iraq and Afghanistan: Persistent post-concussive symptoms and posttraumatic stress disorder. *American Journal of Epidemiology*, *167*(12), 1446–1452.

Schonberger, M., Ponsford, J., Olver, J., & Ponsford, M. (2010). A longitudinal study of family functioning after TBI and relatives' emotional status. *Neuropsychological Rehabilitation*, *20*(6), 813–829.

Seal, K. H., Bertenthal, D., Maguen, S., Gima, K., Chu, A., & Marmar, C. R. (2008). Getting beyond "Don't ask; don't tell": An evaluation of US Veterans Administration postdeployment mental health screening of veterans returning from Iraq and Afghanistan. *American Journal of Public Health*, *98*(4), 714–720.

Serio, C., Kreutzer, J., & Gervasio, A. (1995). Predicting family needs after traumatic brain injury: Implications for intervention. *The Journal of Head Trauma Rehabilitation*, *10*(2), 32–45.

Simpson, G. K., Sabaz, M., & Daher, M. (2013). Prevalence, clinical features, and correlates of inappropriate sexual behavior after traumatic brain injury: A multicenter study. *The Journal of Head Trauma Rehabilitation*, *28*(3), 202–210.

Smith, A. M., & Schwirian, P. M. (1998). The relationship between caregiver burden and TBI survivors' cognition and functional ability after discharge. *Rehabilitation Nursing*, *23*(5), 252–257.

Sofi, F., Cesari, F., Casini, A., Macchi, C., Abbate, R., & Gensini, G. F. (2014). Insomnia and risk of cardiovascular disease: A meta-analysis. *European Journal of Preventive Cardiology*, *21*(1), 57–64.

Sosin, D. M., Sniezek, J. E., & Waxweiler, R. J. (1995). Trends in death associated with traumatic brain injury, 1979 through 1992. Success and failure. *JAMA*, *273*(22), 1778–1780.

Taft, C. T., Schumm, J. A., Panuzio, J., & Proctor, S. P. (2008). An examination of family adjustment among Operation Desert Storm veterans. *Journal of consulting and clinical psychology*, *76*(4), 648–656.

Tanielian, T. L., Jaycox, L., Rand Corporation, California Community Foundation, RAND Health, Rand Corporation. National Security Research Division. (2008). *Invisible wounds of war: Psychological and cognitive injuries, their consequences, and services to assist recovery*. RAND Center for Military Health Policy Research.

Temple, J. L., Struchen, M. A., & Pappadis, M. R. (2016). Impact of pre-injury family functioning and resources on self-reported post-concussive symptoms and functional outcomes in persons with mild TBI. *Brain Injury*, *30*(13-14), 1672–1682.

Thurman, D., Coronado, V., & Selassie, A. W. (2007). Epidemiology of traumatic brain injury. In N. D. Zasler, D. I. Katz, & R. D. Zafonte (Eds.), *Brain injury medicine : Principles and practice* (2nd ed., pp. 373–405). Demos.

Van Cauter, E., Spiegel, K., Tasali, E., & Leproult R. (2008). Metabolic consequences of sleep and sleep loss. *Sleep Medicine*, *9*(Suppl 1), S23–S28.

Vangel, S. J., Jr, Rapport, L. J., & Hanks, R. A. (2011). Effects of family and caregiver psychosocial functioning on outcomes in persons with traumatic brain injury. *The Journal of Head Trauma Rehabilitation*, *26*(1), 20–29.

Verdeli, H., Baily, C., Vousoura, E., Belser, A., Singla, D., & Manos, G. (2011). The case for treating depression in military spouses. *Journal of Family Psychology*, *25*(4), 488–496.

Verhaeghe, S., Defloor, T., & Grypdonck, M. (2005). Stress and coping among families of patients with traumatic brain injury: A review of the literature. *Journal of Clinical Nursing*, *14*(8), 1004–1012.

Webster, J. B., Bell, K. R., Hussey, J. D., Natale, T. K., & Lakshminarayan, S. (2001). Sleep apnea in adults with traumatic brain injury: A preliminary investigation. *Archives of Physical Medicine and Rehabilitation*, *82*(3), 316–321.

Wells, R., Dywan, J., & Dumas, J. (2005). Life satisfaction and distress in family caregivers as related to specific behavioural changes after traumatic brain injury. *Brain Injury*, *19*(13), 1105–1115.

Wickwire, E. M., Shaya, F. T., & Scharf, S. M. (2016). Health economics of insomnia treatments: The return on investment for a good night's sleep. *Sleep Medicine Reviews*, *30*, 72–82.

Witol, A. D., Sander, A. M., & Kreutzer, J. S. (1996). A longitudinal analysis of family needs following traumatic brain injury. *Neurorehabilitation*, *7*(3), 175–187.

Wood, R. L., & Yurdakul, L. K. (1997). Change in relationship status following traumatic brain injury. *Brain Injury*, *11*(7), 491–501.

Yurgil, K. A., Barkauskas, D. A., Vasterling, J. J., Nievergelt, C. M., Larson, G. E., Schork, N. J., Litz, B. T., Nash, W. P., Baker, D. G., & Marine Resiliency Study Team (2014). Association between traumatic brain injury and risk of posttraumatic stress disorder in active-duty Marines. *JAMA Psychiatry*, *71*(2), 149–157.

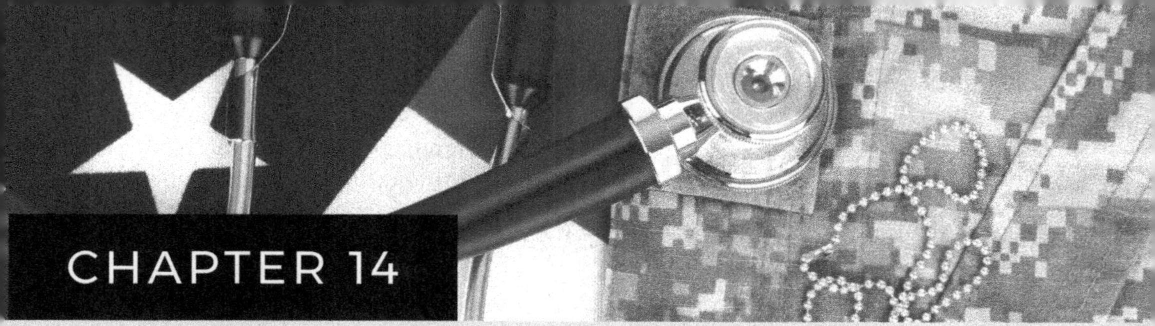

CHAPTER 14

Pain and Pain Management in the Veteran

Renee Holleran

Introduction

Pain continues to be one of the primary reasons that cause patients to seek health care. It is estimated that about 30% of the population in the United States experience chronic pain (Ahluwalia et al., 2018; Gallagher, 2016). However, in contrast, approximately 50% of military veterans experience chronic pain. Chronic pain has particularly become more common in veterans who have participated in Operation Enduring Freedom (OEF), Operation Iraqi Freedom (OIF), and Operation New Dawn (OND) (Gallagher, 2016; Blakely et al., 2018).

In 2015 (Gallagher, 2016), the U.S. Department of Veterans Affairs identified six steps to good chronic pain care. These include:

- Educate veterans and their families about pain and promote self-efficacy
- Educate and train all team members who provide care for veterans
- Develop nonpharmacologic modalities for pain management
- Institute safe medication prescribing, including safe opioid use (universal precautions)
- Develop approaches to bringing the veteran's expanded team together (virtual pain consulting and education as well as ongoing communication between team members)
- Establish metrics to monitor pain care

The focus of this chapter includes:

- The current definitions of pain
- Definition of acute and chronic pain.
- Causes and associated factors related to pain in veterans
- Multimodal treatments for chronic pain
- The effects of traumatic brain injury (TBI) and post-traumatic stress disorder (PTSD) on a veteran's pain
- The use of an interdisciplinary team to manage pain
- Veterans Health Administration Opioid Safety Initiative
- The role of the family in caring for the veteran with chronic pain

Definitions of Pain

Pain is defined by the International Association for the Study of Pain (IASP) (https://www.iasp-pain.org/terminology?navItemNumber=576#Pain) as a negative emotional or sensory experience associated with actual or potential tissue damage, or described in terms of such damage. It is important to remember that pain is not only a physiological process but also involves a complex emotional experience influenced by multiple factors, particularly to the veteran depending on the causes and situations they may encounter as a part of their service.

As the concept of pain and its management has "expanded," new definitions of pain are being explored. For example, a recent paper that was published in *Neuroscience Letters* describes pain as the "detection/evaluation perception of *failure* to protect the body from injury (actual or potential" (Apkarin, 2019, p. 1). This description of pain may help explain why and how many veterans experience pain because it includes the perception of pain, not just the physiological components. It may also explain the success or failure of pharmacological or non-pharmacological pain-management interventions.

In 2019, the IASP added an additional pain descriptor to help explain the pain from such diseases as fibromyalgia, nonspecific back pain, nonspecific peripheral joint pain, and complex regional pain syndrome. The term is *nociplastic pain*. The definition that has been put forward for nociplastic pain describes pain that arises from altered nociception despite no clear evidence of actual or threatened tissue damage that has caused activation of the body's nociceptors or evidence of a disease of lesion of the somatosensory system that may have initiated the pain response.

Pain Descriptors and Pain Physiology

Traditionally, pain has been identified as either acute or chronic. The transition of acute to chronic pain continues to be a challenge to understand. In the veteran population, especially older veterans, it has been estimated that over 50% suffer from chronic pain (Ahluwalia et al., 2018). This emphasizes, again, that pain is a major problem among veterans. It is important to understand the pain descriptors and physiology of pain.

Acute Pain

Acute pain is the result of nociception or the process of interpreting a noxious stimulus to body such as an injury. Acute pain is provoked by a specific disease or injury. It generally is considered to have a "warning" and protective role to prevent further damage to the affected area of the body. The pain should decrease and subside as the healing process takes place (Ellison, 2017; McCormick & Frampton, 2019; Hudspith, 2019; Aronoff, 2016).

Pain signals travel from receptors located in specific areas of the body. Somatic pain receptors are in the skin, subcutaneous tissues, fascia, connective tissues, periosteum, and joint capsules. Visceral pain receptors are located in most of the body viscera and the surrounding connective tissue (Ellison, 2017; McCormick & Frampton, 2019; Hudspith, 2019; Aronoff, 2016). Somatic pain is described as sharp or dull. The pain is generally localized to the injured area (Ellison, 2017; McCormick & Frampton, 2019; Hudspith, 2019; Aronoff, 2016). Visceral pain is described as a deep or cramping type of pain depending on what area of the body has been affected by injury or infection. It can radiate (Ellison, 2017; McCormick & Frampton, 2019; Hudspith, 2019; Aronoff, 2016).

Pain signals are transmitted to the brain through nociception. This process starts when nociceptive nerve fibers are triggered by inflammation, chemicals, thermal stimuli, or by injuries such as a physical event such as a fall injuring a limb. Pain itself involves the perception of nociception that occurs in the brain (Ellison, 2017; McCormick & Frampton, 2019; Hudspith, 2019; Aronoff, 2016). **Table 14-1**

Table 14-1 Brief Summary of Nociception

Transduction	Conversion of a noxious stimuli such as a chemical, mechanical, or thermal stimulus, into electrical activity in the peripheral terminals of the nociceptor fibers. A delta fibers and C fibers are the two types of nociceptors that transmit the electrical impulses to the spinal cord, brainstem, thalamus, and cortex
Transmission	Conduction of pain impulses travel along the A and C fibers to the dorsal horn of the spinal cord and form synapses (excitatory and inhibitory interneurons) in the substantia gelatinosa. Pain control takes place when neurotransmitters release opioids, which block pain transmission at the spinal level. The pain impulse will then synapse with projection neurons, cross the midline of the spinal cord, and ascend to the brain. This occurs over two tracts. One is the spinothalamic, which carries fast impulses that result in sharp pain. The other—paleo spinothalamic tract—are slower and produce dull or chronic pain. These tracts connect to the thalamus, hypothalamus, and limbic system (relay centers in the brain). These centers send the impulses for interpretation of the pain.
Perception	Perception involves interpretation of the afferent input. This leads to the conscious awareness of pain. Many factors can influence the perception of pain including the patient's gender, culture, and previous experiences with pain.

contains a summary of this physiological process (Ellison, 2017; McCormick & Frampton, 2019; Hudspith, 2019; Aronoff, 2016).

Chronic Pain

Chronic pain is defined as "persistent pain" lasting over three months. It has been noted that chronic pain is the pain that lasts beyond the time of "healing" from the illness or injury (Ellison, 2017; McCormick & Frampton, 2019; Hudspith, 2019; Aronoff, 2016; Schonebroom et al., 2016).

Chronic pain results from persistent pain that initiates a cascade of cellular, molecular, and neuronal events that cause enhanced neurotransmission between neurons and pathways within the nociceptive system, which results in central sensitization. Central sensitization results in an inability within the peripheral and central nervous system to appropriately interpret the pain signal. Central sensitization causes an increase in responsiveness of the nociceptive neurons in the central nervous system. In other words, the patient is more sensitive to pain impulses. This can give rise to continuous pain complaints such as burning, itching, numbing, and "skin crawling." These symptoms continue despite treatment (Trouvinm & Perrot, 2019; Schonebroom et al., 2016). Clinical conditions involving central sensitization include neuropathic pain; migraines; Complex Regional Pain Syndrome (CRPS); post-surgical pain; fibromyalgia; temporomandibular disorders; central post-stroke pain; and irritable bowel syndrome (Aronoff, 2016).

Chronic pain not only involves physiological changes, but also because of its impact on people's lives, may include emotional and psychological components. Chronic pain is further complicated in veterans due to the "polytrauma clinical triad." This is composed of combat-associated physical and psychological injuries such as traumatic brain injury (TBI) and post-traumatic stress disorder (PTSD) (Schonebroom et al., 2016).

Cancer Pain

Cancer pain may involve nociceptive or neuropathic sources or both. The pain can be nociceptive-somatic or visceral-inflammatory or ischemic (Gallagher, 2016; McCormick & Frampton, 2019). The pain can be the result of the cancer itself or the treatments used to manage it.

Veterans are at risk of multiple cancers including prostate and breast cancers. Cancer pain can be a combination of nociceptive and neuropathic pain from the disease as well as the treatments required to manage the cancer. In addition, the cause of the cancer such as chemical exposures can contribute the emotional experience the vet is suffering. Chronic cancer pain can continue in the veteran even after the treatment has stopped and the patient considered cancer free.

Acute or Chronic Pain

Acute or chronic pain occurs when the veteran who is being treated for a chronic pain condition experiences an acute injury such as a fractured limb or an intervention such as a surgical procedure.

If the veteran is being treated for chronic pain, acute pain management needs to be appropriately assessed and managed by experienced clinicians so that the veteran's pain is appropriately managed. Inadequate pain management can trigger physiological, psychological, and behavioral problems. It is important that all members of the pain management team are involved in the veteran's care.

Veterans and Pain

It is estimated that 50% of US military veterans suffer from some sort of chronic pain (Blakely, 2018). Veterans may suffer from combat-related injuries or unrelated physical injuries. Soldiers are also exposed to environmental and mental stressors (Nahin, 2017). The pain experienced by veterans is also influenced by factors specific to veterans including TBI, post-concussive syndrome, PTSD, and behavioral health disorders (Schonebroom et al., 2016). Reports have also documented a high prevalence of pain-related conditions including abdominal pain, arthritis, musculoskeletal—especially low back pain, fibromyalgia, headaches, and joint pain (Nahin, 2017).

The war or area of conflict the veteran participated in has contributed to their source of pain. During the Vietnam War, many soldiers were exposed to Agent Orange. This has resulted in such diseases as diabetes and cancers requiring therapies resulting in peripheral neuropathies (U.S. Department of Veterans Affairs, n.d.). **Box 14-1** and **Box 14-2** list a

Box 14-1 Sources of Chronic Pain in Veterans

- Pain from service-related and battlefield injuries
- Chronic musculoskeletal injuries
- Pain from exposure to toxins and diseases
- Pain from previous surgeries that did not relieve pain (i.e., placement of rods, screws, fusions)
- Pain from diseases: diabetes, CAD, cancer
- Pain from aging
- Psychological: PTSD

Box 14-2 Sources of Chronic Pain Related to the Vietnam War

- Agent Orange Exposure
- Al amyloidosis
- Chronic B-cell leukemia
- Chloracne (or similar acneiform skin conditions)
- Diabetes Type II
- Hodgkin's disease
- Ischemic heart disease
- Multiple myeloma
- Non-Hodgkin's disease
- Prostate cancer
- Respiratory cancers and skin and soft tissue sarcomas

U.S. Department of Veterans Affairs. (n.d.). Veterans diseases associated with agent Orange. https://www.publichealth.va.gov/exposures/agentorange/conditions/index.asp

summary of some of the sources of chronic pain in veterans based on the eras of service.

Since the start of Operations Iraqi Freedom in 2003, improvised explosive devices (IEDs) and other types of devices have caused serious injuries including loss of limbs and TBI. The risk of developing chronic pain related to a TBI was higher in veterans with higher to moderate to severe pain. Acute and post-traumatic headaches frequently occur and contribute to the development of chronic pain. In addition, many veterans who sustained a TBI also complain of musculoskeletal pain (Thompson et al., 2019; Khoury & Benavides, 2018).

Along with the chronic pain from injury or exposure to combat, many veterans suffer from PTSD (Blakely et al., 2018; Schonebroom et al., 2016; Domenichiello & Ramsden, 2019; Nahin, 2017; Thompson et al., 2019; Khoury & Benavides, 2018; Giordano et al., 2018). This has been described as a polytrauma clinical triad, which includes pain, PTSD, and a TBI. In addition, many mental illnesses such as depression and anxiety occur making pain management even more challenging (Giordano et al., 2018).

Exposure to combat, environmental toxins, and other physical and psychological stressors leave the veteran at greater risk for the development of chronic pain. The prevalence of severe pain is greater in the veteran from back pain, sciatica, jaw pain, joint pain, migraine, and neck pain (Nahin, 2017; Buttner et al., 2017).

Gender may play a role in chronic pain in veterans as well. In one study, female veterans were at greater risk of increased pain intensity and somatic pain and depression when exposed to combat (Nahin, 2017; Buttner et al., 2017). As more soldiers return from the current deployments and seek care in the Veterans Healthcare Administration (VHA), more research and attention needs to be paid to chronic pain, PTSD, and depression and their effects on chronic pain (Nahin, 2017; Buttner et al., 2017).

Veterans make up a significant percentage of the growing number of aging Americans (Aronoff, 2016). In 2018, approximately 46% of veterans were over the age of 75. (Source: https://www.statista.com/statistics/250267/us-veterans-by-age-and-gender/. Accessed: February 23, 2020).

Chronic pain is common in older adults. It can cause problems leading to a premature death (Schonebroom et al., 2016; Domenichiello & Ramsden, 2019; Nahin, 2017). Pain may be further complicated in the older veteran as previously noted by PTSD and depression.

Pain is a significant problem in veterans. Pain complaints in veterans include abdominal pain, arthritis, musculoskeletal pain—especially in the back, and headaches. Just as chronic pain is a multifaceted issue, so is its management.

Management of Pain in the Veterans Health Administration (VHA)

As previously noted, it has been estimated over 50% of veterans suffer from some type of chronic pain (Gallagher, 2016; Blakely et al., 2018). Additionally, approximately 60% of veterans from the recent Middle Eastern wars enrolling in the VHA have had musculoskeletal problems such as low back pain, spinal cord injuries, amputations, and other somatic sources of pain (Gallagher, 2016). Chronic pain in veterans is also complicated by physical injuries such as TBI and other psychological problems such as PTSD and depression (Blakely et al., 2018).

In 2015, the VHA proposed six steps to managing chronic pain. These steps are summarized in **Box 14-3**. They serve as a foundation to developing a care plan for the veteran with chronic pain.

The VHA uses a primary, secondary, and tertiary model to prevent chronic pain (Gallagher, 2016). Primary prevention encompasses the deterrence of pain-causing injuries

Box 14-3 The Six Essentials Elements of Good Pain Care

1. Educate veterans/families to promote self-efficacy and shared decision-making; provide access to all relevant resources.
2. Educate/Train all team members to their discipline specific competencies, including team-based care.
3. Develop and integrate non-pharmacological modalities into care plans.
4. Institute evidence-based medication prescribing, use of pain procedures, and safe opioid use (universal precautions).
5. Implement approaches for bringing the veteran's whole team together such as virtual pain consulting (SCAN-ECHO, e-consults, tele-health, clinical video tele-consultation, and education) and for maintaining ongoing communication between team members.
6. Establish metrics to monitor pain care and outcomes at both the individual level and the population level.

U.S. Department of Veterans Affairs. (2020). *VHA pain management.* https://www.va.gov/painmanagement/

and illnesses. Healthy lifestyles including nutrition and exercise and the use of protective devices such as body armor and seat belts are examples of this.

Secondary prevention focuses on effective pain care. For example, identifying the sources of pain through a comprehensive history and physical examination. It is also helpful to correctly list the pain diagnoses including the sources of the pain and the complicating factors that impact the pain and pain management. **Box 14-4** contains an example of pain diagnoses.

Tertiary prevention concentrates on restoring function in the veteran when a painful condition persists (Gallagher, 2016). Chronic pain can cause the veteran to become "conditioned" to pain and methods of pain relief including medications. Pain perception is not

Box 14-4 Examples of Chronic Pain Diagnoses

1. Low back pain somatic nociceptive related to degenerative joint disease as seen on imaging
2. Bilateral leg pain related to small fiber neuropathy related to diabetes mellitus
3. Case complicated by age over 65, diabetes not well managed, frequent homelessness, PTSD, and depression

only centered on the pathology of persistent pain, particularly in the brain and spinal cord, but also is influenced by emotions, cognition, and risk of maladaptive behaviors, particularly substance abuse (Gallagher, 2016; Dobscha et al., 2016).

The management of chronic pain requires a multimodal approach. Chronic pain management is affected by the complexity of the chronic pain itself. Chronic pain treatments do not always work and are influenced by a veteran's comorbidities. These might include the type of injury caused during military service, presence of social issues such as homelessness, age, limited financial support, and risk of inappropriate medication use such as Opioid Use Disorder (OUD) or Substance Abuse Disorder (SUD).

The management of chronic pain requires a multimodal approach. These modalities include pharmacotherapy, psychotherapies such as (CBT-P) cognitive behavioral therapy for pain, interventions such as surgery and injections, and complementary and alternative modalities (Dale & Stacey, 2016). The following is a summary of some of the practices used to manage chronic pain in the VHA.

Pharmacological Pain Management

Medication is one of the common approaches to manage chronic pain. Ironically, many of the medications used to treat chronic pain have side effects that may contribute to complications in coping with chronic pain. In addition, there may be multiple sources of the chronic pain, for example, somatic and neuropathic. Each of type of pain may need to be treated with different medications that focus on the specific pain. It has been found that the management of chronic pain can be more effective with an appropriate combination of medications (Dale & Stacey, 2016). However, combinations of medications place the patient at risk for more side effects (Dale & Stacey, 2016; Nisbet & Sehgal, 2019; Rosenburg et al., 2018; Yarmanaka & Miller, 2019; Li, 2019; Pascual et al., 2018; Harbaugh & Suwanabol, 2019).

It is imperative that the veteran receive a comprehensive physical, psychological, and social assessment before medications are prescribed. A step-wise approach (see Box 14-3) should be used when prescribing medications to manage chronic pain (Harbaugh & Suwanabol, 2019).

The prescriber should address the veteran's pain using a holistic approach that focuses on the source of the pain and what are the goals such as improved physical or psychological function. In addition, other approaches to chronic pain management need to be incorporated in the veteran's care plan from the beginning and modified as needed. The VHA has devoted multiple resources to support this. **Table 14-2** presents some examples of medications used for chronic pain management (Dale & Stacey, 2016; Nisbet & Sehgal, 2019; Rosenburg et al., 2018; Yarmanaka & Miller, 2019; Li, 2019; Pascual et al., 2018; Harbaugh & Suwanabol, 2019). Side effects are included, which must always be considered before starting medications and frequently assessed while the veteran is using these medications. Opioid safety is discussed later in this chapter.

It is important to mention the use of cannabinoids in the management of chronic pain even though currently their use is not legal within the VHA (Nisbet & Sehgal, 2019; Li, 2019). There are cannabinoid receptors found in both the central nervous system and immune cells. Research continues in the use of cannabinoids for treatment of many diseases that cause chronic pain including fibromyalgia, migraine headache, neuropathic pain, and cancer pain (Li, 2019).

Medical marijuana is legal in 33 states and Washington DC, California, Arizona, Oregon, Alaska, and Washington were some of the first states to legalize medical marijuana. Utah and Missouri voted to legalize medical marijuana in the 2018 midterm elections. However, the use of marijuana is classified by federal law as a schedule 1 drug (U.S. Department of Veterans Affairs, 2017).

The VHA has published a document for both veterans and healthcare providers who practice in the VHA, which outlines the use of medical marijuana for veterans who live in states where it is legal. **Box 14-5** contains a summary of these guidelines. It is important to note that veterans who participate in state marijuana programs to manage chronic pain will not lose their benefits. However, it is essential that the veteran and their healthcare provider discuss the use of marijuana, especially related to the other medications that are being used to manage the veteran's chronic pain.

Opioid therapy has been a part pain management for over 30 years. A paper written by Portney (1990) discussed the use of opioids in chronic pain. He noted that the available evidence at that time suggested that in a selected subpopulation of patients with chronic nonmalignant pain may obtain sustained partial analgesia without developing toxicity or the physiological and behavioral characteristics of addiction. In the year 2000, the VHA released a document as a part of *Pain as the 5th Vital Sign* (U.S. Department of Veterans Affairs, 2000). The focus was on managing all pain, including chronic pain. Unfortunately, it laid the groundwork for many of the challenges faced today in the management of chronic pain, especially related to the use of opioids in the management of chronic pain and veterans who have been treated for many decades with opioids for their chronic pain (Jay & Barkin, 2018; Demidenko et al., 2017).

Table 14-2 Medications and Side Effects for Chronic Pain Management

(Please note that this is not a comprehensive source of all medications that may be used for the management of chronic pain.)

Medication	Chronic Pain	Side Effects
Acetaminophen	Low back pain	Hepatotoxicity Decreased renal function
Nonsteroidal Anti-inflammatory Drugs Ibuprofen Naproxen Celecoxib	Useful for mild to moderate pain, osteoarthritis, low back pain, useful as a topical agent for inflammatory pain	GI upset, risk of GI bleed, decreased renal function, dangerous interaction with some medications, for example, warfarin
Anticonvulsants Gabapentin Pregabalin Topiramate Oxcarbazepine	Postherpetic neuralgia, diabetic peripheral neuropathy, neuropathy associated with Agent Orange exposure	Somnolence, dizziness, increased risk of falls, fatigue, "fogginess," lower extremity swelling
Antidepressants Tricyclic Antidepressants Serotonin-norepinephrine reuptake inhibitors (SSNRI)	Neuropathic pain May decrease occurrence of post-herpetic neuralgia if used early in the disease, some efficacy in fibromyalgia. Osteoarthritis of the knee	Cardiotoxicity, orthostatic hypotension, somnolence, altered mental status, dry mouth, blurred vision, and urinary retention
Opioids Morphine Hydromorphone Methadone Oxycodone Tramadol APAP/Hydrocodone Fentanyl Buprenorphine	Neuropathic pain Functional pain control, impact of pain on veteran's family, work, and life; family history of chronic pain, psychological factors influenced by pain such as TBI and PTSD	Respiratory depression, constipation, endocrine dysfunction, opioid tolerance, withdrawal, Opioid Use Disorder (OUD), social stresses that may put the patient and family at risk for diversion or risk of maltreatment
Topical agents Lidocaine cream and patches Diclofenac gel Capsaicin	Neuropathic pain Chronic joint pain	Local skin irritation
Ketamine	Neuropathic pain, particularly Complex Regional Pain Syndrome	Cognitive disturbances, psychological addiction, severe and persistent urinary disease, hepatic dysfunction, hyperventilation

Box 14-5 VA and Marijuana: What Veterans Need to Know

- Veterans will not be denied VA benefits because of marijuana use.
- Veterans are encouraged to discuss marijuana use with their VA providers.
- VA healthcare providers will record marijuana use in the veteran's VA medical record in order to have the information available in treatment planning. As with all clinical information, this is part of the confidential medical record and protected under patient privacy and confidentiality laws and regulations.
- VA clinicians may not recommend medical marijuana.
- VA clinicians may only prescribe medications that have been approved by the U.S. Food and Drug Administration (FDA) for medical use. At present, most products containing tetrahydrocannabinol (THC), cannabidiol (CBD), or other cannabinoids are not approved for this purpose by the FDA.
- VA clinicians may not complete paperwork/forms required for veteran patients to participate in state-approved marijuana programs.
- VA pharmacies may not fill prescriptions for medical marijuana.
- VA will not pay for medical marijuana prescriptions from any source.
- VA scientists may conduct research on marijuana benefits and risks, and potential for abuse, under regulatory approval.
- The use or possession of marijuana is prohibited at all VA medical centers, locations, and grounds. When you are on VA grounds, it is federal law that is in force, not the laws of the state.
- Veterans who are VA employees are subject to drug testing under the terms of employment.

U.S. Department of Veterans Affairs. (n.d.). *VA and marijuana—what veterans need to know*. https://www.publichealth.va.gov/marijuana.asp

The VHA provides a comprehensive guideline for the initiation of Opioid Therapy for Veterans who suffer from chronic pain. 23 Long-term Opioid Therapy should be considered when potential small benefits do not outweigh the risks (Card, 2017).

Opioid Therapy for chronic pain begins with education. The VHA has developed a booklet that contains key information about safe and responsible use of opioids in chronic pain. This document is available with Card, P. (2017). VA/DoD Clinical Practice Guideline for Opioid Therapy for Chronic Pain. Department Veterans Aff Department Defense, 3.

An important part of the assessment related to starting opioid therapy for chronic pain must include risk mitigation related to the use of opioids. The components of risk mitigation should include ongoing random urine drug testing, including confirmation. It is important that the provider interpreting the confirmation be educated about what it means. Unfortunately, some veterans have been inappropriately denied or taken off opioid therapy because of this. The suicidal ideology must be assessed and monitored at each visit. Naloxone education and naloxone use must also be included not just for the veteran, but their family as well.

Prescribing opioid therapy for chronic pain requires education, monitoring, and the development of trust between their healthcare provider and the veteran. Chronic opioid use today is particularly challenging in the atmosphere of the opioid crisis (Jay & Barkin, 2018; Demidenko et al., 2017; Huygen et al., 2019). The reduction or stopping of chronic opioid therapy has resulted in increased pain, which has led to suicidal ideation or suicide or seeking illicit substances for pain management. Persistent pain has also been associated with decreased physical function, memory loss, and increased risk of dementia.

In summary, the role of opioids continues to be uncertain, but many veterans have been started on opioids for several reasons. When opioids are prescribed, the veteran must be educated, monitored, and continuously encouraged to participate in the use of non-opioid and other non-pharmacological methods to manage chronic pain. The healthcare provider prescribing has an obligation to keep the veteran safe and assist in exploring other approaches to chronic pain management, which are discussed in the following sections.

Interventions for the Management of Pain in Veterans

A multi-modal approach has been found to improve the management of chronic pain in the veteran (Gallagher, 2016; Schonebroom et al., 2016; Dale & Stacey, 2016; Harbaugh & Suwanabol, 2019; Huygen et al., 2019; Lyons & Koneti, 2019; Brooks & Udoji, 2016; Malhotra et al., 2019). One approach that has been used for several years is interventional therapy. Examples of the types of chronic pain that have treated with interventional pain management include trigeminal neuralgia, headaches, thoracic and lumbar radicular pain, and complex regional pain syndrome (Huygen et al., 2019; Cheng et al., 2019; Brooks & Udoji, 2016; Malhotra et al., 2019).

Interventional pain management techniques target specific nociceptive transmission sites (Brooks & Udoji, 2016; Malhotra et al., 2019). A combination of a local anesthetic along with a corticosteroid is the most common medication used in selective interventions such as an epidural injection. Other interventions include microvascular nerve decompression, pulse radiofrequency, radiofrequency of selected nerves, and direct nerve blocks such as an intercostal nerve block. Botulinum toxin injections may be used for certain types of headaches and neuropathic pain (Huygen et al., 2019; Lyons & Koneti, 2019; Cheng et al., 2019; Brooks & Udoji, 2016; Malhotra et al., 2019).

There are contraindications to injections including anticoagulation use; infection near the injections site, elevated hemoglobin A1C, allergies to medications, anatomical changes that may interfere with the procedure, and immunosuppression. Complications related to interventions used for chronic pain include anaphylaxis, accidental injection into other spaces, side effects of steroids including osteoporosis, and avascular necrosis. Other complications include local skin irritation and infections, injury from needle insertion, and inadvertent injection into vascular structure (Huygen et al., 2019; Lyons & Koneti, 2019; Cheng et al., 2019; Brooks & Udoji, 2016; Malhotra et al., 2019).

Interventional chronic pain management continues to grow. It is one of the common methods used in the VHA for the management of both acute and chronic pain and should be included in the veteran's chronic pain management plan.

Integrative Medicine and Complementary Therapies for Chronic Pain Management

Integrative medicine (IM) promotes a "whole person" approach to chronic pain management. It includes both conventional and nonconventional treatments for chronic pain management (Madsen et al., 2017; Williams et al., 2020; Groessl et al., 2016; Highland et al., 2018; You et al., 2019; Madsen et al., 2018; Walker et al., 2016). IM includes five areas: patient-provider partnership, considering all factors that influence a patient's health, wellness, and disease, including physical, mental, spiritual elements; facilitating the body's innate ability to heal with using both conventional and nonconventional methods; use of less invasive and less harmful treatments whenever possible; treat the whole patient instead of just the disease; and the "ideal" of medicine as science-based, but willing to give critical considerations to new ideas (Madsen et al., 2017).

Complementary therapies are described as nonconventional modalities when replacing mainstream therapies and complementary when used as an adjunct to mainstream therapies (Madsen et al., 2017).

The VHA uses an IM focus involving the use of complementary therapies in the management of chronic pain. For the veteran, this an important advantage for the management of chronic pain because generally outside of the VHA and Department of Defense (DoD) many health insurance companies do not provide or cover these modalities. However, there is a movement to change this point of view particularly in the management of chronic pain and the issues surrounding the use of pharmacological management of pain in general (Madsen et al., 2017; Williams et al., 2020; Groessl et al., 2016; Highland et al., 2018; You et al., 2019; Madsen et al., 2018; Walker et al., 2016).

Research has found that some of the following modalities have been effective for the management of chronic pain in veterans (Madsen et al., 2017; Williams et al., 2020; Groessl et al., 2016; Highland et al., 2018; You et al., 2019; Madsen et al., 2018; Walker et al., 2016). It is important to mention that since PTSD and depression frequently are a part of chronic pain, these modalities have also been found to be effective methods in managing these other complex problems.

- Acupuncture: An originally Chinese practice of inserting fine needles through the skin at specific points especially to cure disease or relieve pain (as in surgery); a method of relieving pain or curing illness by placing needles into a person's skin at particular points on the body.
- Alpha Stim Therapy: The Alpha-Stim AID is a drug-free cranial electrotherapy stimulation (CES) medical device that uses low-level electrical current to safely and effectively treat anxiety, depression, and insomnia. CES was cleared by the FDA in 1992 as a prescriptive, noninvasive treatment. Improving a patient's sleep will also help with the management of chronic pain (Alpha-Stim, n.d.).
- Battlefield acupuncture: Auricular acupuncture (You et al., 2019; Walker et al., 2016).
- Biofeedback (Madsen, 2017): Using sensors that help the veteran to detect and learn to control autonomous functions.
- Chronic Behavioral Therapies (Madsen, 2017): A standard set of tools that focus on changing patterns of thoughts to change behaviors or emotions related to the thoughts
- Hypnosis (Williams et al., 2020): A trancelike state that resembles sleep but is induced by a person whose suggestions are readily accepted by the subject.
- Manual Medicine: Chiropractic care
- Massage Therapy (Madsen, 2017): Soft tissue manipulation.
- Meditation (Williams et al., 2020): Focus one's mind on an object, thought, or activity to clear one's mind and achieve an emotionally stable state.
- Mindfulness (Williams et al., 2020): Use techniques to focus on the present moment without one's judgment.
- Qigong: Roots in Chinese medicine involving coordinated body posture movements, breathing, and meditation.
- Tai Chi: Internal Chinese martial arts related to the forces of yin and yang related to the moves as well as meditation.
- Thermotherapy: Use of cold and heat for painful musculoskeletal areas of the body
- Yoga (Madsen et al., 2017; Groessl et al., 2016; Highland et al., 2018): Hindu spiritual discipline including postures and breathing

Chronic Pain and Its Impact on Veterans and Their Families

The chronic pain experienced by veterans is complex. Many veterans suffer from polytrauma, which may include PTSD, a TBI, depression, and chronic pain. The veteran may be irritable, easily become angry, have mood changes, and be unable to participate in family activities. In most cases, the veteran's family is affected by the chronic pain as well as the other challenges that may be present (Merritt et al., 2019).

Including the veteran's family in his or her chronic pain management is an important intervention. Family members need to be educated about what chronic pain is and how it is different from acute pain. Many family members, particularly children, may not understand why their mother or father is unable to be involved or participate in the family Compton & Blacher, 2020).

The veteran and his or her family need to be encouraged to actively become educated about the cause of the veteran's pain, how it is being managed, and what effect this may have on them. The VHA has some useful resources for both veterans and their families. One resource is *Chronic Pain 101*, which can be found at https://www.va.gov/PAINMANAGEMENT/Veteran_Public/index.asp Accessed March 8, 2020.

When the veteran has been prescribed medications, especially opioids, the safe storage of all medications needs to be discussed. The *Safe and Responsible Use of Opioids for Chronic Pain: A Patient Information Guide* contains important information about drug storage and can be found at https://www.va.gov/PAINMANAGEMENT/Opioid_Safety/OSI_docs/10-791-Safe_and_Responsible_Use_508.pdf#.

The veteran and pertinent family members should receive Naloxone use education. Naloxone kits need to be dispensed and if used or expire be quickly replaced.

Chronic pain has been found to place a veteran at an increased risk of suicide. Family members should be made aware of the warning signs of the veteran being at risk or considering or attempting suicide, which include hopelessness, withdrawing from family and friends, talking about killing themselves, having a suicidal plan, or displaying self-destructive behavior such as taking too many medications or having access to a weapon. Additional information including the current Suicide Crisis Line number is available at https://www.mentalhealth.va.gov/MENTALHEALTH/suicide_prevention/index.asp. Family members should be strongly encouraged to keep all this information easily accessible.

Abuse Disorders Related to Chronic Pain

Chronification of pain, tapering off opioids, or sudden stopping of opioid medications can be driving forces to the development of an OUD or an SUD (Compton & Blacher, 2020; Manhapra & Becker, 2018; Murray et al., 2019; Farrar et al., 2017). Chronification of pain is influenced by psychological factors, comorbidities like PTSD, depression,medication dependence, or a history of substance or opioid abuse disorder (SUD or OUD) (Manhapra & Becker, 2018). Behaviors that may be indicative of SUD or OUD are inappropriate use of prescribed medications (taking more than prescribed), running out of mediations early, or obtaining and using illegal substances.

This needs to be recognized quickly and the veteran referred to the proper resources as soon as possible (see https://www.mentalhealth.va.gov/mentalhealth/substance-abuse/index.asp). This can be a very difficult situation for the veteran, his or her family, and the provider who has been managing the veteran's chronic pain. However, the focus must always be on patient safety.

Summary

Chronic pain is a significant problem for veterans. It can be complicated by multiple medical and psychological factors. It requires a multidisciplinary team including the veteran's primary care provider (PCP), mental health provider, pharmacist, pain medicine specialist, PDMP, integrative medicine, complementary therapies, and especially the veteran and his or her family.

Pain management requires a holistic approach. Healthcare providers have an ethical and a moral duty to manage a veteran's pain. Fears of drug addiction, myths about the use of opioids in pain management, and the unfounded biases that have been created from inadequate information has produced unnecessary pain for veterans who have served. We owe them an informed and compassionate pain management plan.

References

Ahluwalia, S., Guannitrapani, K., Dobscha, S., Cromer, R., & Lorenz, K. (2018). "It encourages them to complain": A qualitative study of the unintended consequences of assessing patient-reported pain. *Journal of Pain, 19*(5), 562–568.

Alpha-Stim. (n.d.). Treating mood conditions. https://www.alpha-stim.com/healthcare-professionals/treating-mood-conditions

Apkarin, A. (2019). Definitions of nociception, pain, and chronic pain with implications regarding science and society. *Neuroscience Letters, 702*, 1–2.

Aronoff, G. M. (2016). What do we know about the pathophysiology of chronic pain? *Medical Clinics of North America, 100*, 31–42.

Ashrafioun, L., Allen, K., & Pigeon, W. (2018). Utilization of complementary and integrative health services and opioid therapy by patients receiving Veterans Health Administration pain care. *Complimentary Therapies in Medicine, 39*, 8–13.

Blakely, S., Wagner, H. R., Naylor, J., Brancu, M., Lane, I., Sallee, M., Kimbrel, N., VA Mid-Atlantic MIRECC Workgroup, & Elbogen, E. (2018). Chronic pain, TBI, and PTSD in military veterans: A link to suicidal ideation and violent impulses? *Journal of Pain, 19*(7), 797–806.

Brooks, A., & Udoji, M. (2016). Interventional techniques for management of pain in older adults. *Clinical Geriatric Medicine, 32*, 773–785.

Buttner, M., Godfrey, K., Floto, E., Pittman, J., Lindmar, L., & Afari, N. (2017). Combat exposure and pain in male and female Afghanistan and Iraq veterans: The role of mediators and moderators. *Psychiatry Research, 257*, 7–13.

Carroll, C. P. (2020). Opioid treatment for acute and chronic pain in patients with sickle cell disease. *Neuroscience Letters, 714*, 135434.

Cheng, J., Salmasi, V., You, J., Grille, M., Yang, D., Mascha, E., Cheng, O., Zhao, F., & Rosenquist, R. (2019). Outcomes of sympathetic blocks in the management of complex regional pain syndrome: A retrospective cohort study. *Anesthesiology, 131*(4), 883–893.

Compton, P., & Blacher, S. (2020). Nursing education in the midst of the opioid crisis. *Pain Management Nursing, 21*(1), 35–42.

Dale, R., & Stacey, B. (2016). Multimodal treatment of chronic pain. *Medical Clinics of North America, 100*, 55–64.

Demidenko, M., Dobscha, S., Morasco, B., Meath, T., & Ilgen, M. (2017). Suicidal ideation and suicidal self-directed violence following clinician-initiated prescription opioid discontinuation among long-term opioid users. *General Hospital Psychiatry, 47*, 29–35.

Dobscha, S., Lovejoy, T., Morasco, B., Kovas, A., Peters, D., Hart, K., Williams, J., & McFarland, B. (2016). Predictors of improvements in pain intensity in a national cohort of older veterans with chronic pain. *Journal of Pain, 17*(7), 834–835.

Domenichiello, A., & Ramsden, C. (2019). The silent epidemic of chronic pain in older adults. *Progress in Neuro-Psychopharmacology & Biological Psychiatry, 93*, 284–290.

Ellison, D. (2017). Physiology of pain. *Critical Care Nursing Clinics of North America, 29*(4), 397–406.

Farrar, F., White, D., & Darnell, L. (2017). Pharmacologic interventions for pain management. *Critical Care Clinics of North America, 29*, 427–447.

Gallagher, R. M. (2016). Advancing the pain agenda in the veteran population. *Anesthesiology Clinics, 34*, 357–378.

Giordano, N., Bader, C., Richmond, T., & Polomano, R. (2018). Complexity of the relationships of pain, post-traumatic stress, and depression in combat-injured populations: An integrative review to inform evidence-based practice. *Worldviews on Evidenced-Based Nursing, 15*(2), 113–126.

Groessl, E., Schmalzl, L., Maiya, M., Liu, L., Goodman, D., Chang, D., Wetherell, J., Bormann, J., Atkinson, J., & Baxi, S. (2016). Yoga for veterans with chronic low back pain: Design and methods of a randomized clinical trial. *Contemporary Clinical Trails, 48*, 110–118.

Harbaugh, C., & Suwanabol, P. (2019). Optimizing pain control during the opioid epidemic. *Surgical Clinics of North America, 99*, 867–883.

Highland, K., Schoomaker, A., Rojas, W., Suen, J., Ahmed, A., Zhang, Z., Carlin, S., Calilung, C., Kent, M., McDonough, C., & Buckenmaier, C. (2018). Benefits of the restorative exercise and strength training for operational resilience and excellence yoga program for chronic low back pain in service members: A pilot randomized controlled trail. *Archives of Physical Medicine and Rehabilitation, 99*, 91–98.

Hudspith, M. (2019). Anatomy, physiology and pharmacology of pain. *Anesthesia & Intensive Care Medicine, 20*, 419–425.

Huygen, F., Kallewaard, J., Tulder, M., Boxem, K., Vissers, K., Kleef, M., & Zundert, J. (2019). Evidence-based interventional pain medicine according to clinical diagnoses: Update 2018. *Pain Practice, 19*(6), 664–675.

Jay, G., & Barkin, R. (2018). Perspectives on the opioid crisis from pain medicine clinicians. *Disease a Month, 64*, 451–466.

Khoury, S., & Benavides, R. (2018). Pain with traumatic brain injury and psychological disorders. *Progress in Neuropsychopharmacology & Biological Psychiatry, 87*, 224–233.

Li, J.-X. (2019). Combining opioids and non-opioids for pain management: Current status. *Neuropharmacology, 158*, 1–7.

Lyons, R., & Koneti, K. (2019). Surgical management for chronic pain. *Surgery, 37*(8), 472–477.

Madsen, C., Patel, A., Vaughan, M., & Kochlmoos, T. (2018). Use of acupuncture in the United States Military Healthcare System. *Medical Acupuncture, 30*(1), 33–38.

Madsen, C., Vaughan, M., & Koehlmoos, T. (2017). Use of integrative medicine in the United States Military Health System. *Evidenced Based Complementary and Alternative Medicine*. doi:10.1155/2017/9529257

Malhotra, A., Shehebar, M., & Khelemsky, Y. (2019). Anesthesia and chronic pain management. *Otolaryngologic Clinics of North America, 52*(6), 1083–1094.

Manhapra, A., & Becker, W. (2018). Pain and addiction. *Medical Clinics of North America, 102*, 745–763.

McCormick, T., & Frampton, C. (2019). Assessment of acute and chronic pain. *Anesthesia & Intensive Care Medicine, 20*, 405–409.

Merritt, B., Kretzmer, T., McKenzie-Hartman, T., & Gootman, P. (2019). Neurobehavioral management of the polytrauma veteran. *Physical Medicine and Rehabilitation Clinics of North America, 30*, 133–154.

Montgomery, P., Shank, B., & Black, A. (2017). The role of pain classification systems in pain management. *Critical Care Nursing Clinics of North America, 29*, 407–418.

Murray, M., Stone, A., Pearson, V., & Treisman, G. (2019). Clinical solutions to chronic pain and the opiate epidemic. *Preventive Medicine, 118*, 171–175.

Nahin, R. (2017). Severe pain in veterans: The effects of age, sex, and comparisons with the general population. *Journal of Pain, 18*(3), 247–254.

Nisbet, G., & Sehgal, A. (2019). Pharmacology management of chronic pain. *Anesthesia and Intensive Care Medicine, 20*(10), 555–558.

Pascual, D., Sanchex-Robles, E., Garcia, M., & Goicoechea, C. (2018). Chronic pain and cannabinoids. Great expectations or a christmas carol. *Biochemical Pharmacology, 157*, 33–42.

Portney, R. K. (1990). Chronic opioid therapy in nonmalignant pain. *Journal of Pain Symptom Management, 5*(1 Suppl), S46–S62.

Rosenburg, J. M., Bilka, B. M., Wilson, S. M., & Spevak, C. (2018). Opioid therapy for chronic pain: Overview of the 2017 US Department of Veterans Affairs and US Department of Defense clinical practice guideline. *Pain Medicine (Malden, Mass.), 19*(5), 928–941. https://doi.org/10.1093/pm/pnx203

Russo, M. M., & Sundaramurthi, T. (2019). An overview of cancer pain: Epidemiology and pathophysiology. *Seminars in Oncology Nursing, 35*, 223–228.

Schonebroom, B., Perry, S., Barnhill, W., Giordano, N., Nicely, K., & Poloman, R. (2016). Answering the call to address chronic pain in military service members and veterans: Progress is improving pain care and restoring health. *Nursing Outlook, 64*, 459–484.

Thompson, K. B., Krispinsky, L., & Stark, R. (2019). Late immune consequences if combat trauma: A review of trauma-related immune dysfunction and potential therapies. *Military Medical Research, 6*(11), 1–13.

Trouvinm, A. P., & Perrot, S. (2019). New concepts of pain. *Best Practice & Research Clinical Rheumatology, 33*(3), 101415.

Walker, P., Pock, A., Ling, C., Kwon, K., & Vaughn, M. (2016). Battlefield acupuncture: Opening the door for acupuncture in Department of Defense/Veteran's Administration health care. *Nursing Outlook, 64*(5), 491–498.

Williams, R. D., Ehde, D., Day, M., Turner, A., Hakimian, S., Gertz, K., Ciol, M., McCall, A., Kincaid, C., Pettet,

M., Patterson, D., Suri, P., & Jensen, M. (2020). The chronic pain skills study: Protocol for a randomized controlled trial comparing hypnosis, mindfulness meditation and pain education in Veterans. *Contemporary Clinical Trials, 90*, 105935.

U.S. Department of Veterans Affairs. (n.d.). *Veterans' diseases associated with Agent Orange*. https://www.publichealth.va.gov/exposures/agentorange/conditions/index.asp

U.S. Department of Veterans Affairs. 2017. VA and marijuana—what veterans need to know. https://www.publichealth.va.gov/marijuana.asp

U.S. Department of Veterans Affairs. (2000). *Pain as the 5th vital sign*. https://www.va.gov/PAINMANAGEMENT/docs/Pain_As_the_5th_Vital_Sign_Toolkit.pdf

Yarmanaka, S., & Miller, L. (2019). Opioids in the management of persistent non-cancer 46.

You, E., Kim, D., Harris, R., & D'Alonzo, K. (2019). Effects of auricular acupressure on pain management: A systematic review. *Pain Management Nursing, 20*, 17–26.

CHAPTER 15

Identifying the Unique Needs of Veterans That Influence End-of-Life Care

Deborah L. Grassman and Katherine G. Kemp

Military experiences change veterans in fundamental ways that shape the rest of their lives, including the *end* of their lives (Grassman, 2012). This chapter will identify some of the military influences impacting hospice and palliative care healthcare delivery, as well as provide resources that the National Hospice and Palliative Care Organization (NHPCO) provides healthcare providers to support veterans and their families at the end of life.

Stoicism: A Help and a Hindrance

The dictionary defines stoicism as: showing indifference to joy, grief, pleasure, pain (*Webster's New World Dictionary*, 1995). The value of stoicism so necessarily indoctrinated in young soldiers might interfere with peaceful deaths for all veterans, depending on the degree to which stoicism permeated their later lives. Stoicism is necessary on the battlefield, even essential. After discharge from military service, stoicism continues to be helpful because it allows veterans to overcome hardships and provides protection from untrustworthy influences. "Sucking it up" and "biting the bullet" are important self-mastery skills to achieve goals without getting diverted by every fleeting emotion.

Ironically, veterans also report that stoic walls sometimes create problems, especially at the end of their lives. Perspectives shift when death is near. Things that seemed important yesterday fade in priority today; things that were not previously important seem urgent to now complete. Regrets surface; opportunities for healing emerge. Stoicism, however, sometimes interferes with these opportunities. Stoicism might prevent veterans from experiencing feelings, expressing love and connection with others, or asking for help. Physical limitations and emotional displays might embarrass veterans and create fears that others will perceive them as weak. They may view "letting go" as an admission of defeat or an act of surrender, something "good soldiers" do not do. Stoic control can prevent them from acknowledging failing health, weakness, or other changes. Anything threatening control or independence might incite anger and defensive responses. Fear of being at the mercy of others also causes resistance. Yet, mature mental health includes identifying needs and asking for help when it is needed. Stoicism often keeps veterans from saying what they need or allowing others to meet their needs because it requires the veteran to be vulnerable. This attitude can cause frustration for their families or professional caregivers who want to provide support.

Healthcare Practice Tips for Stoic Veterans

Veterans sometimes describe themselves as "stubbornly independent." Aging is a humbling experience that challenges independence and control (Tucci & Doka, 2013). Pride often takes a blow as independence wanes. Sooner or later, the stoic wall has to crumble. Later means fighting to the bitter end; sooner means a weary soldier is finally able to surrender to hope for a peaceful death. This takes courage, and it is as heroic as facing any enemy in battle. Caregivers can help veterans recognize that courage is not about covering up or "grinning and bearing it" nor is it about "being strong" by hiding behind stoic walls.

Serious illness changes everything. Ask veterans to consider using different coping mechanisms to deal with this new situation. Rather than erecting a stoic wall that might shut them off from others (and even themselves), have them consider using stoicism like a door they can open or close at will. Help them realize that there is no shame in being human, and there is freedom in being able to acknowledge and fully experience their humanity, especially the grief they might feel right now. This is not weakness; rather it requires strength and courage.

Asking for help is not easy for a veteran. Pave the way by teaching them the value of doing so: "You've given to your country; you've given to your family; you've given to your community. Now is the cycle in life to learn how to receive—to learn how to receive *graciously*."

PTSD At-Risk Environments: Dangerous Duty Military Assignments

Stoicism permeates military culture, whether a veteran served in combat or not. Those who have served in combat or other dangerous-duty assignments may also have traumatic memories. For some, the memories crystallize into a constellation of symptoms known as post-traumatic stress disorder (PTSD; see **Box 15-1**) (American Psychiatric Association, 2013).

Veterans deal with PTSD in different ways. (Van der Kolk, 2014). Many have successfully suffered war experiences by learning lessons that helped them live their lives, deal with trauma, reckon with PTSD, and face aging issues. They know what eases their symptoms. They might have a network of friends with PTSD who provide support. Family members often know how to respond to episodes of PTSD because it is familiar territory for them. On the other hand, the veteran may not have integrated the trauma into their life experience, compartmentalizing the trauma by banishing it into unconsciousness or using a stoic wall to try to shield symptoms. The symptoms, however, usually leak out: hollowness, aloofness, workaholism or its opposite (job-hopping or joblessness), or addictions. As veterans age, however, it may be harder to "white knuckle" the symptoms.

Healthcare Practice Tips for Veterans with PTSD

Helplessness commonly occurs during trauma. This can subsequently incite overly controlling behaviors in order to ward off experiencing helpless feelings again. As illness progresses, the veteran's diminished ability to exert their will acts as a trigger for the original helplessness they felt when traumatized. This often causes anxiety and, if close to death, agitation. The agitation

Box 15-1 Post-Traumatic Stress Disorder (American Psychiatric Association, 2013).

A. Exposure to actual or threatened death, serious injury, or sexual violence in at least one of the following ways:
   1. Direct experience
   2. In-person witnessing of others being traumatized
   3. Learning about a loved one's traumatic event
B. At least one intrusive symptom that began after the trauma:
   1. Recurrent, intrusive memories of the trauma
   2. Distressing dreams related to the trauma
   3. Dissociative reactions (e.g., flashbacks)
   4. Psychological distress to cues that trigger traumatic memories
   5. Physiological reactions caused by traumatic memories
C. Avoidance of stimuli associated with the trauma as evidenced by at least one of the following:
   1. Avoiding memories, thoughts, or feelings associated with the trauma
   2. Avoiding external reminders of the trauma (people, places, activities, etc.)
D. Adverse changes in cognitions and mood related to the trauma, as evidenced by at least two of the following:
   1. Inability to remember an important aspect of the trauma
   2. Exaggerated negative beliefs about self and others
   3. Distorted beliefs that cause blame of self or others
   4. Persistent negative emotional state
   5. Marked disinterest in significant activities
   6. Feelings of detachment or estrangement from others
   7. Inability to experience positive emotions
E. Marked reactivity associated with the trauma, as evidenced by at least two of the following:
   1. Irritable and angry outbursts
   2. Reckless or self-destructive behavior
   3. Hypervigilance
   4. Exaggerated startle reflex
   5. Difficulty concentrating
   6. Sleep disturbances
F. Duration of the symptoms last at least one month
G. Symptoms cause significant functional impairment
H. Symptoms cannot be attributed to the effects of a substance or medical condition

might not respond to benzodiazepine-type medications. In fact, anti-anxiety medications sometimes cause a paradoxical reaction (instead of decreasing anxiety, they increase anxiety). A chain reaction might be initiated in which the medication causes loss of control, which increases feelings of helplessness, which acts as a trigger for the original helplessness, which causes them to fight even harder to counteract the effect of the medication so they can regain control, which is manifested as agitation.

One of the secrets for cultivating a "good" death is to make peace with the helplessness that occurs as weakness and loss of independence arise. This usually requires the caregiver to initiate the conversation: "You probably feel helpless with many of the things that you are experiencing right now. Helplessness is not easy for anyone to experience, but it is especially difficult for veterans." Veterans are used to protecting, fixing, and controlling. Ironically, helping them to *feel* the helplessness rather than trying to *not* feel it can increase peacefulness: "Rather than trying to control or to fight feelings of helplessness, consider letting yourself *feel* helpless because, indeed, there are many things that are happening that you have no control over. The task now is to learn to let go—to make peace with what is happening."

Guilt and Shame: Emotions That Might Surface as Veterans Prepare to "Meet Their Maker"

Forgiveness can bring peace with a painful past. Although the past cannot be changed, the *relationship to* the past can. Forgiveness is the means to that end. Making peace with unpeaceful memories begins by acknowledging guilt without trying to gloss over it or pretend it away. If the guilt is *irrational* because the veteran is accepting responsibility for something he/she had no control over, then they were helpless; they may be using *irrational* guilt to give them the illusion that they had control, which numbs the helpless feeling they are avoiding.

Guilt takes many forms. Although some veterans feel guilty about the killing they had to do, others feel guilty for *not* killing: "They had to take me off the front lines. I was such a coward." Some non-combat veterans feel guilty because they think their sacrifice was not enough. For example, one veteran was a talented trumpeter assigned to the Navy band, playing as ships left harbor for Vietnam: "Here I was with this cushy job playing an instrument I loved to play. It wasn't fair." Military nurses and medics can also experience guilt about the life and death decisions they made. One nurse said she was not afraid of hell: "I've already been there. I have to live every day with the faces of those soldiers who didn't have a chance during mass casualties. The doctor left it up to me, a 21-year-old nurse, to decide which ones got surgery and which ones were left to die." Survivor's guilt is common. One World War II veteran said, "When I landed on the beach, there were all these dead bodies. The sand underneath them was pink with their blood." Then he tearfully added, "They didn't get to have grandkids the way I did. It's not fair that I should have this enjoyment when they can't."

Some Vietnam veterans struggle with forgiving the government for using and betraying them. Korean and Vietnam veterans might have to forgive the American public for ignoring or scorning them. Soldiers may have to forgive the world for being unfair and for having cruelty and war in it; they have to forgive God for allowing the world to be like it is with war in it.

Veterans sometimes reveal a wound that is different than the PTSD that many of them have. Some veterans call it a "Soul Injury." Whereas PTSD affects a person's brain (especially the amygdala, the part of the brain that reacts to real or perceived threats), a soul injury affects a person's sense of being. The term *Soul Injury*, introduced here, and to be further described in the next chapter, was first described by Deborah Grassman and the four VA hospice nurses of Opus Peace. They define Soul Injury as:

- A wound to our sense of self—our *real* self behind the facade
- A wound that stifles full potential, separating a person from who they are meant to be

Soul Injury might accompany PTSD in veterans if the trauma changed how they perceive themselves. For example, a veteran's action or non-action harms a comrade, causing feelings of shame and worthlessness. Less apparent is "insidious soul injury," which occurs more gradually and becomes chronic before it becomes obvious. For example, a veteran has an unfair military administrative action taken against him/her or is labeled as "weak" when unable to maintain a stoic façade. Over time, this might cause the veteran to feel defective or inadequate—hallmarks of Soul Injury. Unmourned loss/hurt and unforgiven guilt/shame often keep the Soul Injury alive throughout a lifetime.

Moral injuries (Grassman, 2017) can further develop into a Soul Injury. The VA and the Department of Defense have adopted the term *moral injury* and define it as events that are considered morally injurious if they transgress deeply held moral beliefs and expectations (U.S. Department of Veterans Affairs, 2016). This chapter further describes moral injury, comparing and contrasting it with Soul Injury.

Unburdening moral injury at the end of life is captured by a poem entitled "Atoning," by Ron Mann displayed in the National Vietnam Veterans Art Museum in Chicago:

> *Hoping and wishing*
>
> *you can settle*
>
> *this whole thing in your mind*
>
> *about this war*
>
> *resolving it within yourself*
>
> *before the time of atonement comes,*
>
> *weeping and crying at the end of your life.*

If a veteran has not been able to achieve forgiveness, they might arrive at the end of life filled with bitterness. Stockpiling transgressions of others (blame) or self (shame) is the recipe for making bitterness. Bitterness is a poison that can complicate peaceful dying. Visiting veteran memorial monuments can be a catalyst for healing bitterness because the monuments often serve as a repository for shame, precipitating the courage to seek forgiveness. *Honor Flight* is a program that offers healing to veterans by flying them to Washington, D.C., to see their memorials. Many community hospices have programs to support this program so that healing can be precipitated. A photo of a young North Vietnamese soldier and his daughter was left at the Vietnam Veterans Memorial by the American GI who had killed him. This note was attached to the photo:

> Dear Sir, for 22 years I have carried your picture in my wallet. I was only 18 years old that day we faced one another. . . Why you didn't take my life I'll never know. You stared at me so long, armed with your AK-47, and yet you did not fire. Forgive me for taking your life. So many times over the years I have stared at your picture and your daughter, I suspect. Each time my heart and guts would burn with the pain of guilt. . . . Forgive me, Sir. (Grassman, 2009)

Guilt, Shame, and Soul Injury Practice Considerations

If harm was done during military assignment, a veteran may or may not have already come to terms with what happened. If the memory still triggers guilt, however, it might be helpful to consider bringing it out in the open. Soul Injury interventions focus on learning how to mourn losses and hurts, forgive self and others, and cultivate love and self-compassion. These interventions are not routinely taught in healthcare or trauma curricula. However, providing these interventions at the end of life when Soul Injuries tend to surface can have a dramatic impact on a dying person's quality of life, as well as their family (Tucci & Doka, 2019).

It is essential that clinicians know how to create a safe emotional environment that allows Soul Injuries to surface. This includes not dismissing or minimizing guilt with well-intentioned platitudes such as: "You were following orders" or "You were being a good soldier; we have our freedom because of you." Even though these things are true, delivering these kinds of messages essentially communicates to the veteran: "Don't tell me about your guilt and shame. Keep it buried behind that stoic wall." Instead, caregivers can learn how to create a safe emotional environment so guilt and shame can be revealed *if the veteran so chooses*. However, this needs to be done cautiously. At no time, should the clinician overtly, covertly, or subtly convey that the veteran "needs to forgive," for example, saying: "You need to forgive so you can have peace." This can actually add another layer of damage by causing additional guilt about their inability to forgive themselves or others. Rather, the clinician should simply offer the consideration of forgiveness and invite the veteran to stay open to its possibility. "Now is a time to look back over your life. Is there anything that might still be troubling you? Anything about the war that might still haunt you?" Then, sit quietly. These are not the kind of answers that can be hurried.

A tool has been preliminarily developed to screen for soul injuries (Ferrell & Paice, 2019; Soul Injury Inventory, n.d.). The Soul Injury Self-Awareness Inventory can be used to open a meaningful dialogue. Some agencies have developed a team of chaplains and social workers who can follow up with soul-injury assessment and intervention using the Soul Injury Self-Awareness Inventory. (See Chapter for details about the Soul Injury Self-Awareness Inventory.)

"Thank You" Is Not Enough: Helping Veterans UNBURDEN

Attaining a peaceful death is the aim of most hospice interventions. Learning how to create safe emotional environments for untold military stories to emerge is a skill set that veteran caregivers need to cultivate because *untold* stories often conceal unforgiven guilt and shame that might complicate peaceful dying. For example, one veteran expressed regret to his hospice nurse for a wrong decision that caused harm to his unit. "I did the right thing 99 times out of 100. But it's that ONE mistake, that ONE wrong decision that continues to haunt me." He expressed relief after revealing his story. Sadly, he said that it was the first time someone listened to his mistake rather than trying to reframe his error into an unavoidable act that he had no control over. "Nobody wanted to hear this part of my story until I came to hospice." Well-intentioned platitudes, minimizing guilt and shame, and attempts to make them not feel what they are feeling leaves the veteran isolated and alone with their personal reality.

Military personnel are not the only ones who demand perfection. The idealized image that civilians often maintain about soldiers never making a mistake, never making a wrong decision, always acting honorably is simply not true. Soldiers, sailors, marines, and airmen are human beings who act good, bad, and indifferent just like everyone else. Inadvertently, the public's patriotic projection of the "ideal" warrior discourages that warrior from telling stories that run counter to that image; opportunities for healing "untold" stories are then missed.

Case Example: Exert Care That "Image" Does Not Inadvertently Silence the Untold Story

Larry is a veteran who experienced severe childhood physical, emotional, and sexual abuse at the hands of his parents. He used drugs to numb the pain and was in and out of jail: "I actually slept better in jail because I had a locked door with someone outside making sure I was safe." A judge offered him the option of prison or the Armed Forces enlistment station so at age 17 Larry joined the Navy. "My father always told me I was not 'good enough.' The judge told me I was a 'lost cause.' Joining the Navy was my only hope." Larry had learned survival skills early in life, so he did well in boot camp: "My soul started to reappear although parts of it would not reattach for decades."

The rest of Larry's story remained untold for decades. Larry explains his rationale:

> I have never told ALL of my story. There are two reasons for this. One: my military service does not fit the "image" the public wants to have about their soldiers and sailors. Secondly: I have feared being judged—judged for not fitting that image. But, I have changed my mind because after I left military service, I worked for the

> Department of Corrections for 30 years. I occasionally shared a piece of my story to a prisoner or another officer. It seemed to help them, and they didn't judge me. Now, I work for a veterans organization and I listen to veterans tell *their* stories. Many of their stories are similar to mine. And do you know what? My story helps them. This has given me the courage to tell my *whole* story.

Larry's "whole" story includes excelling in the Navy. He stayed away from drugs, but drinking was a problem: "Binge drinking, I discovered, is a huge part of a sailor hitting port for liberty calls after 40 days out to sea without a glimpse of land." He was in a fighter squadron attached to the USS *Kitty Hawk*. Workdays were 12 hours on and 12 off and commonly extended for 30 to 40 days before he got a day off: "But I would never claim to have anything close to the experience of most military personnel who served as 'boots on the ground.'"

Ports were Larry's biggest struggle: "Many of the sailors behaved honorably and many did not. I am sick to my stomach to this day because of the way that some of us behaved with women. I tried to participate but I felt the pain of sexual abuse as an adolescent myself. I couldn't do it. I felt guilt and shame for what I had done." Larry stopped participating and spoke up about what was happening, but he was threatened to be thrown off the ship: "So I resumed my use of drugs. It was how I was used to keeping the family secrets."

He began to have other moral dilemmas. "I loaded bombs on planes and they returned without them. I long pondered the thought that the bombs had to be landing somewhere. I will never forget the day I stood on the flight deck and wondered why we were doing what we were doing."

Larry was honorably discharged from the service and he kept the "ugly" part of his story under wraps: "I don't want to dishonor the many honorable men and women I served with because most sailors I served with are proud veterans. No doubt they would be disgusted by my story. Part of my fear of telling my story is that it could tarnish those who serve with such honor and integrity."

It was a hospice nurse who convinced Larry to speak up:

> Deborah Grassman told me she had heard hundreds of these types of stories from other veterans—veterans who were dying. She said that the truth is the truth and we should not be afraid of the truth. So I am willing to tell my story even though it is my perception that there are parts of my military experience that the world doesn't want to even acknowledge. What gives me the courage is it is an untold truth that many of my comrades also share.
>
> I also tell my story because it is a story about healing—healing my heart. It's about sitting in my pain without numbing out. It's about working a 12-step recovery program. It's about being grateful for the life experiences that I have not wasted. I am able to sit comfortably with homeless veterans. I can be the safe space where I witness others find their own truth. They don't need to be fixed. They need HOPE. We all need hope.
>
> Hi, my name is Larry. I am a veteran, and I refuse to be a "hopeless case" and I am not willing to be a "lost cause". (Larry, personal communication, [date])

Specialized Consideration: Vietnam Veterans

There is scant research on what is needed when providing care at the end of life to Vietnam Veterans. Through the partnership with the VA, a pilot project was started in 2018 using qualitative research to provide a better understanding of the mindset of Vietnam Veterans as they enter hospice care, identify meaningful experiences related to their service in Vietnam, and identify other needs among Vietnam Veterans and their caregivers related to end-of-life care beyond "the basics" (pain management, medications, etc.), see **Box 15-2**.

Vietnam-era veterans are the largest veterans population utilizing hospice services at this time. Unlike World War II veterans who were welcomed home with open arms and parades, Vietnam veterans were often vilified. They were spit on and called "baby killers" or "murderers" right in the airports as they came stateside. Their stories of trauma quickly went underground because the truth is the American public did not want to hear them. This often caused what is now known as "secondary wounding."

Secondary wounding occurs when someone who has been traumatized is not supported or, worse, blamed for the trauma. It adds insult to injury. For example, it is not unusual for adults who were molested as children to report that it is harder to forgive the parent who protected the abuser than it was to forgive the abuser. Vietnam veterans provide similar reports. They experienced the betrayal of secondary wounding on multiple levels from both the government and the American public: "What happened to me in Vietnam was bad, but what happened when I got home was worse." Some vets report that they could forgive the North Vietnamese for shooting them "because they were doing what they were supposed to do," but forgiving the American public was different: "We needed their support and instead we got their hate."

Box 15-2 Key Findings from Preliminary Research about Caring for Vietnam Veterans at End of Life (StrategyGen, 2019)

1. Vietnam-era veterans are likely to be skeptical of social and health services, including hospice.
2. More than veterans of other wars, Vietnam veterans are likely to have avoided discussing, reflecting on, and processing their service trauma. Leaving their experiences unprocessed can create a barrier to finding peace as they near end of life.
3. Hospice teams must be prepared to help Vietnam veterans reflect on their service in unexpected, unpredictable, and even aggressive ways.
4. Vietnam veterans have unique conditions and needs, including substance abuse, PTSD, service-connected illnesses, emotional distress, and abandonment.
5. The need for some form of mental health services is great among veterans War veterans in end-of-life care.
6. Resources available to Vietnam veterans are underutilized. Some Vietnam veterans and their caregivers report having to proactively seek out resources; others share difficulty accessing resources including counseling.
7. Existing training and resources for serving veterans are extremely well received (particularly resources that come with the We Honor Veterans Partner Levels), but nurses are asking for more tools and training specific to Vietnam veterans.
8. While there is a distinct culture among Vietnam War veterans, it is important to understand that there are different population segments within this population, each with their unique needs for services and specific protocols.

Case Example: "Welcoming Home" Vietnam Veterans

It is not too late to welcome home Vietnam veterans. Deborah Grassman reports the following:

> In the early 1990s, the Persian Gulf War Veterans were returning home victorious, greeted as heroes. For some of our Vietnam vets, this was a bitter reminder of how differently *they* had been greeted. "No one ever welcomed us home like that,"

Bryan told me. "They didn't want to see 'Nam vets or hear what *we* had to say." He was glad that new veterans didn't have to suffer what he had suffered. "But it still hurts," he added.

I could feel the bitterness that was still poisoning his life thirty years later. Then he said something that was heartbreaking. "All that for nothing. My buddies killed for nothing. The government duped us. It was all just politics and money. Our nation is sinful. All I've been through these past years since the war . . . for nothing."

I let myself feel his bitterness, then I rose slowly and knelt before his chair. I took his hands in mine, forced my gaze to meet his hung head and downcast eyes. I felt the shame of our nation's shabby treatment of vets like Bryan. I let myself feel the bitterness of suffering in vain, the emptiness of suffering without meaning. Then I spoke words he needed to hear. "Bryan, I am so sorry for how we treated you. I am so sorry for the indignities you've had to suffer because of our ignorance. I don't know if that war was an unjust one or not. If it was, then you've had to bear the 'sins' of our nation. What I *do* know, is that you were treated unjustly. I want you to know that you *are* a hero. And *unsung* heroes are the *most* worthy kind."

His eyes never diverted from mine, then he slumped forward in my arms and sobbed. (Grassman, 2009)

Often Forgotten: Women Veterans

Traditional veteran "images" do not automatically elicit a woman in the public mind. Yet, women have long marched off to join the ranks and not in small numbers either. More than 400,000 women served during World War II (Holm, 1998). These women are often cast from a different mold that does not conform to societal expectations. They have sometimes had to defy family cultural values to enlist in a nontraditional female career.

Once in the military, a woman's role was not always easily accepted by their male counterparts. They were often put in a position of having to "prove" themselves as having the mental, emotional, and physical strength to achieve the mission. Promotions sometimes caused conflict about a woman's ability to supervise or give orders to men. Sexual assault is high in the military: one out of five women have endured assault, prompting the VA to provide specialized Military Sexual Trauma (MST) programs to deal with the aftermath. These issues sometimes resurface as death approaches.

Resources and Support for Veteran Healthcare Providers

In 2002, hospice-veteran partnerships were created to provide hospice services to veterans. Regional teams were organized to identify patients who were veterans, educate staff on how to provide veteran-centric care, and honor veterans and their families for their sacrifices. In-home ceremonies attended by staff, veteran volunteers, and the veteran's family were designed to create a safe emotional environment that invites the veteran's military stories, assess any "unfinished business" that might still be troublesome, and honor the veteran—often with a pin or other symbol of gratitude. These ceremonies are often received with tears of humble gratitude for the recognition. More importantly, the ceremony often prompts "untold" stories that tend to surface at the end of life when the conscious mind is becoming weaker and the unconscious mind becomes stronger. This sometimes causes unbidden memories that had been previously suppressed to emerge. "I never heard that before," is commonly heard from family members as they bear witness to the previously untold story.

The success of the regional Hospice Veterans Partnership programs led to the development of the We Honor Veterans program by the National Hospice and Palliative Care Organization (NHPCO). While the official launch of the We Honor Veterans program occurred in 2010, work with the Department of Veterans Affairs (VA) surrounding end-of-life care began years before with a project entitled: Reaching Out: Quality Hospice and Palliative Care for Rural and Homeless Veterans. One result of this increased awareness included increased utilization of the Military History Checklist by hospice providers (**Box 15-3**).

We Honor Veterans (WHV) Partners focus on "serving those who first served us." This pioneering program facilitates respectful inquiry, compassionate listening, and grateful acknowledgment. The program provides educational tools and resources that promote veteran-centric educational activities, increase organizational capacity to serve veterans, support development of strategic partnerships, and increase access and improve quality. It provides tiered recognition to organizations who demonstrate a systematic commitment to improving care for veterans. Partner organizations assess their ability to serve veterans and integrate best practices for providing end-of-life care (see **Box 15-4**) (We Honor Veterans, n.d.-a).

Box 15-3 Military History Checklist

Helps staff identify who is a veteran, evaluate the impact of the experience, and determine if there are benefits to which the veteran and surviving dependents may be entitled by asking:

- Did you (or your spouse or family member) serve in the military?
- In which branch of the military did you serve?
- In which war era or period of service did you serve?
- Overall, how do you view your experience in the military?
- If available would you like your hospice staff/volunteer to have military experience?
- Are you enrolled in the VA?

U.S. Department of Veterans Affairs. (n.d.). *Military history checklist*. https://www.wehonorveterans.org/wp-content/uploads/2020/02/Veterans_Military_History_Checklist.pdf

Box 15-4 We Honor Veterans Partner Levels

Level 1: Provide veteran-centric education by conducting veteran-specific presentations, reviewing the Military History Checklist, and identifying and connecting with the contact person at the closest VA Medical Center and/or Community-Based Outpatient Clinic (We Honor Veterans, n.d.-g).

Level 2: Build organizational capacity through more veteran-specific in-services and integrating content into staff and volunteer orientation, community outreach presentations, and identifying an established Hospice-Veteran Partnership (HVP) in the area (We Honor Veterans, n.d.-i).

Level 3: Develop and strengthen relationships by developing a veteran-to-veteran volunteer program, continuing outreach presentations, reviewing NHPCO's Standards of Practice for Hospice Programs, conducting an annual evaluation of the Military History Checklist, developing procedures for assisting accessing VA benefits, and active participation in an HVP (We Honor Veterans, n.d.-h).

Level 4: Increase access and improve quality by providing an annual review of veteran-specific examples from NHPCO's Standards, monitor demographics using the Military History Checklist, developing procedures for transitioning veterans across venues of care, implementing veteran-specific questions or similar survey within the organization, and develop a Performance Improvement Project (We Honor Veterans, n.d.-f).

Level 5: Newly developed. By working with a diverse pilot group of established Level 4 WHV hospice partners, a Level 5 partner was recently created. Level 5 goes beyond raising awareness within community hospices to ensuring holistic hospice strategies for "unburdening" veterans if regrets surface at the end of life. Level 5 partners become recertified on an annual basis and complete activities both within their organizations and in partnership with their community coalitions. They hold annual Welcome Home Vietnam Veterans Day events, serve as regional mentors to other WHV partners, and track best practices for all pinning and honor ceremonies provided to veteran patients under their care. Most importantly, an outlined Plan of Care requires that staff screen for PTSD, Soul Injury, and relevant military rituals (We Honor Veterans, 2018a).

- **VA Fact Sheet for Hospice Partners** (We Honor Veterans, 2018b) is a template for VA staff to share with community partners to provide vital information such as VAMC and Regional (VISN) office contact information, after-hours contacts, service area covered, process for expedited enrollment and approval of VA-paid hospice services, billing issues contact, PTSD and Homeless resource coordinator information, and further resources.
- **NHPCO's Veteran-Related Standards of Practice for Hospice Programs** (We Honor Veterans, 2019b) set benchmarks for hospice organizations to assess the quality they provide. They are organized around the 10 components of quality in hospice care and provide standards and practice examples surrounding Patient and Family-Centered Care, Clinical Excellence and Safety, Inclusion and Access, Workforce Excellence, Compliance with Laws and Regulations, and Performance Measurement.
- **Veterans-Specific Questions** (National Hospice and Palliative Care Organization, n.d.). is a post-death survey to help hospices evaluate the care they have delivered to their veteran-patients and is designed to yield actionable information that reflects the quality of hospice-care delivery from the perspective of family caregivers. Questions include:
  1. Did someone ask the patient about his/her military service and experiences? (For example, which branch of the military he/she served in or his/her dates of service?)
  2. How often did the hospice staff take the time to listen to the patient's stories and/or concerns related to his/her military experience?
  3. Some veterans near the end of life reexperience the stress and emotions that they had when they were in combat. Did this happen to the patient?
  4. Would it have been helpful to have more information about VA benefits for surviving spouses and dependents?
  5. Would it have been helpful to have more information about VA burial and memorial benefits?
  6. Did the patient receive health care from the VA?
- **Educational resources** (We Honor Veterans, n.d.-b) include the End-of-Life Nursing Education Consortium (ELNEC) (We Honor Veterans, 2017)—for Veterans curricula and webinars and PowerPoint presentations for on-demand viewing covering topics such as Suicide Prevention in Vietnam Veterans (We Honor Veterans, 2019a), Soul Injury (Grassman, 2018), Moral Injury (U.S. Department of Veterans Affairs & We Honor Veterans, 2019b), Hospice-Veteran Partnerships 101 (We Honor Veterans, 2019a), and VA Benefits (We Honor Veterans, n.d.-b).
- **Other Partner Resources include:**
  - Templates and guidelines for honoring and pinning veteran patients and their spouses (We Honor Veterans, n.d.-e)
  - Grief and Bereavement (We Honor Veterans, n.d.-d)
  - Volunteer program tools including training videos based on the "No Veteran Dies Alone" training manual (PsychArmor Institute, n.d.)
  - Event planning (We Honor Veterans, n.d.-c) and advocacy templates (Hospice Action Network (n.d.)
  - Communications, marketing, and social media tools (We Honor Veterans, n.d.-j)

A Final Word to a Dying Veteran from a Hospice Nurse

You have had many great adventures in the past. Remember when you were recruited and inducted into the military? You were probably filled with both dread and excitement. You dreaded leaving the comfort and familiarity of your family and friends as you headed to far-off lands in unknown territory. You may have had some anxiety about leaving the security of your home and town; but there may have also been a bit of adventure that sparked interest and anticipation about what you would be encountering. In many ways, facing death is like that. It is the next big adventure scheduled on your transfer orders. Open up to it. There is a still small voice inside you that whispers peace and wisdom to you. Trust it. Summon the honesty, humility, and courage to listen to that deeper part of yourself. It knew how to bring you into this world, and it knows how to carry you out of it.

References

American Psychiatric Association. (2013). *Diagnostic and statistical manual of mental disorders* (5th ed.). Author.

Ferrell, B. R., & Paice, J. A. (Eds.). (2019). *Oxford textbook of palliative nursing*. Oxford University Press.

Grassman D. (2019). *"Thank You" is not enough: Helping veterans UNBURDEN*. Opus Peace. https://wehonorveterans.org/thank-you-not-enough-helping-veterans-unburden-end-life-webinar

Grassman, D. (2009). *Peace at last: Stories of hope and healing for veterans and their families*. Vandamere Press.

Grassman, D. (2012). *The hero within: redeeming the destiny we were born to fulfill*. Vandamere Press.

Grassman, D. (2017). PTSD and soul injury: The aftermath of war that complicates peaceful dying. *Journal of Arizona Geriatrics Society*, *24*(2). https://azgsjournal.scholasticahq.com/article/3188

Grassman, D. (2018). *Soul Injury. Opus Peace*. https://www.wehonorveterans.org/soul-injury-and-opus-peace-tools-deborah-grassman

Holm, J. (1998). *In defense of a nation: Servicewomen in World War II*. Vandamere Press.

Hospice Action Network & We Honor Veterans. (n.d.). *Advocacy templates*. https://www.wehonorveterans.org/advocacy-toolkit

National Hospice and Palliative Care Organization. (n.d.). *Veteran specific questions and evaluation for hospice care*. https://www.wehonorveterans.org /get-practical-resources/resources-topic/veteran-specfic-questions-vsq-evaluation-hospice-care

PsychArmor Institute & We Honor Veterans. (n.d.). *No Veteran Dies Alone*. https://www.wehonorveterans.org/get-practical-resources/resources-topic/volunteer -programs

Soul Injury Inventory. (n.d.). *Soul Injury inventory instructions*. https://opuspeace.org/BlankSite/media/Documents/Soul-Injury-Inventory-Instructions.pdf

StrategyGen & We Honor Veterans . (2019). *Market research for Vietnam veterans in hospice care*. https://www.wehonorveterans.org/reports

Tucci, A., & Doka, K. (Eds.). (2013). *Improving care for veterans: Facing illness and death*. Hospice Foundation of America.

Tucci, A., & Doka, K. (Eds.). (2019). *Aging America: Coping with loss, dying, and death in later life*. Hospice Foundation of America.

U.S. Department of Veterans Affairs. (2016). *Moral injury in the context of war*. National Center for PTSD.

U.S. Department of Veterans Affairs & We Honor Veterans. (2019a). *Moral injury in Vietnam veterans*. https:// www.wehonorveterans.org/moral-injury-vietnam-veterans-webinar

U.S. Department of Veterans Affairs & We Honor Veterans (2019b). *Suicide prevention in Vietnam veterans*. https://www.wehonorveterans.org/suicide-prevention-vietnam-veterans-webinar

U.S. Department of Veterans Affairs & We Honor Veterans (n.d.-a). *Military history checklist*.

U.S. Department of Veterans Affairs & We Honor Veterans. (n.d.-b). *VAbenefits*. https://www.wehonorveterans.org/va-veteran-organizations/veteran-benefits

Van der Kolk, B. (2014). *The body keeps the score*. Viking Press.

We Honor Veterans. (2017). *End of Life Nursing Education Consortium*. https://www.wehonorveterans.org/elnec-%E2%80%93-veterans-updated-curriculum

We Honor Veterans. (2018a). *Level Five*. https://www.wehonorveterans.org/partner-level-5-overview-and-activities

We Honor Veterans. (2018b). *VA fact sheet for hospice partners*. https://www.wehonorveterans.org/sites/default/files/public/VA-FactSheet_Hospice_Partners.pdf

We Honor Veterans. (2019a). *Hospice Veteran Partnership 101webinar.* https://www.wehonorveterans.org/hvp-101-webinar-2019

We Honor Veterans. (2019b). *Standards of practice for hospice programs, veteran-related standards.* https://www.wehonorveterans.org/sites/default/files/Vet_Related_Standards_Practice_0.pdf

We Honor Veterans. (n.d.-a). *About Us.* https://www.wehonorveterans.org/about-us

We Honor Veterans. (n.d.-b). *Educational resources.* https://www.wehonorveterans.org/education-offerings

We Honor Veterans. (n.d.-c). *Event planning.* https://www.wehonorveterans.org/event-planning

We Honor Veterans. (n.d.-d). *Grief and bereavement.* https://www.wehonorveterans.org/get-practical-resources/resources-topic/grief-bereavement

We Honor Veterans. (n.d.-e). *Honoring veterans.* https://www.wehonorveterans.org/get-practical-resources/resources-topic/honoring-veterans

We Honor Veterans. (n.d.-f). *Level Four.* https://www.wehonorveterans.org/partner-level-four

We Honor Veterans. (n.d.-g). *Level One.* https://www.wehonorveterans.org/partner-level-one

We Honor Veterans. (n.d.-h). *Level Three.* https://www.wehonorveterans.org/partner-level-three

We Honor Veterans. (n.d.-i). *Level Two.* https://www.wehonorveterans.org/partner-level-two

We Honor Veterans. (n.d.-j). *Marketing materials.* https://www.wehonorveterans.org/we-honor-veterans-whv-marketing-materials

Webster's New World Dictionary. (1995). Simon & Schuster.

PART III

Psychological Wounds of War

CHAPTER 16	PTSD in Military Veterans: What Civilian Providers Should Know	267
CHAPTER 17	Suicide Risk Evaluation and Management Among Veterans Receiving Community-Based Care	295
CHAPTER 18	Caring for Veterans with Substance Use Disorders (SUD)	319
CHAPTER 19	Treating Victims of Military Sexual Trauma	335
CHAPTER 20	Assessing and Addressing Health Care for Veterans Experiencing Homelessness	351
CHAPTER 21	Identifying Soul Injury: A Self-Awareness Inventory	375
CHAPTER 22	Moral Stress and Injury in the Military and Veterans	387

CHAPTER 16

PTSD in Military Veterans: What Civilian Providers Should Know

Catharine Johnston-Brooks and Judith Vanderryn

Civilian healthcare providers know the importance of understanding the physical, emotional, and psychiatric history of patients and how this information reveals risk or protection factors for physical and/or mental illness. While veterans are similar to civilian patients in that they may have psychologically traumatic life experiences prior to and following their military service, the events of military service and associated traumatic experiences are unique. Therefore, civilian providers should understand how mental health conditions, including post-traumatic stress disorder (PTSD), present uniquely in their veteran patients. This chapter will cover the expected course and likely outcomes of PTSD treatment in military veterans.

PTSD commonly occurs among civilians and veterans alike. The lifetime prevalence of PTSD in civilian populations is 6.8%, 9.7% for females and 3.6% for males (National Comorbidity Survey (NCS), 2005). The prevalence of PTSD in veteran populations tends to be greater than in civilian populations and varies depending upon the era in which the veteran served. For example, for Vietnam-era veterans, the estimated lifetime prevalence of PTSD is 30.9% for men and 26.9% for women (Kulka, 1990). Among Gulf War veterans, PTSD prevalence is estimated to be 10.1% (Kang et al., 2003). Finally, the prevalence of PTSD among post-9/11 veterans differs depending on the population sampled (e.g., veterans seeking care in the VA, or active duty service members a week before deployment), and the conditions of their combat. In a population-based study of 1,965 previously deployed service members, 13% were diagnosed with "probable PTSD" based on responses to a PTSD survey (Ramchand et al., 2008). Furthermore, a review of 29 studies of PTSD prevalence among service members deployed to Iraq and Afghanistan found prevalence estimates ranging from 5–20% among those not seeking treatment, and up to 50% among those who were (Ramchand et al., 2010).

In addition to PTSD, veterans often have higher rates of other comorbid conditions such as depression and substance misuse (Hoggatt et al., 2017). Furthermore, suicide rates among service members and veterans is 1.5 times greater than in the general population (U.S. Department of Veterans Affairs, 2019). In light of these realities, it is important for providers to screen their veteran patients for depression, substance use, and suicidality in addition to PTSD. Offering education, support, and treatment options for these disorders is crucial; chapters on suicidality and substance use in veteran populations appear elsewhere in this book.

Understanding veterans' mental health conditions will allow providers to target appropriate interventions more effectively. For example, patients' beliefs about their health, including chronic conditions, can shape health behaviors, engagement in treatment, and ultimately their recovery (Michie et al., 2018). For veterans specifically, it has been demonstrated that PTSD symptom severity amplifies their negative perceptions and beliefs about injuries (Bahraini et al., 2017). Therefore, understanding the emotional backdrop of our patients helps inform how best to target interventions, and may alert providers to focus on injury and health perceptions (attitudes) as part of the treatment plan. An important point to keep in mind is that veterans can be reluctant to seek care in behavioral health settings (Maguen et al., 2012; Possemato et al., 2018).

Finally, military and veteran cultural competence (Tam-Seto et al., 2020) should be blended with an understanding of individual veteran patients. Providers should begin with asking questions and careful listening, recognizing that each veteran has had a unique experience leading to contact with the medical system. Use of a patient-centered approach, including understanding the emotional contours of our patients' histories and present complaints, may help alert providers to focus on injury and health perceptions as part of the treatment plan and more effectively target interventions. This approach is likely to lead to better rapport with patients and ultimately more efficacious treatment (Butler et al., 2015; Vest et al., 2019).

What is Post-Traumatic Stress Disorder?

Understanding the natural human response to stress will help put symptoms of PTSD into context. Essentially, humans experience a range of physiological, psychological, and behavioral changes in response to frightening, threatening, and/or horrifying experiences. If these consequences continue for more than a month and negatively impact a person's quality of life, the person may meet criteria for a diagnosis of PTSD. It is important to emphasize that while initial, and sometimes even lasting, responses to traumatic events are not in themselves *disordered*, sometimes the ongoing effects of the trauma create disruptions in a person's life that develop into the disorder of PTSD.

In this chapter, two terms will appear depending on the context of the section: post-traumatic stress (PTS) and PTSD. Implicit in this distinction is the idea that conceptualizing PTS as a disorder is in itself, paradoxical; the symptoms veterans experience following traumatic events are more often functional rather than disordered (Hoge, 2010). The normal human responses to such events are usually appropriate in context, and the ongoing experiences following the event may also be quite normal and adaptive. Thus, veterans can exhibit symptoms of PTS without meeting criteria for the disorder known as PTSD. The thoughts, behaviors, and feelings of PTS become a "disorder" when they interfere with a veteran being able to live life to the fullest. For the purposes of this chapter, the term *PTSD* will be used when referring to formulating a diagnosis and conducting formal mental health treatment. In contrast, PTS will be used in more general discussions of the veteran's symptoms associated with experiencing emotional, physical, or spiritual trauma. The approaches and information discussed in this chapter will be useful for working with veterans who have either PTS or PTSD.

The American Psychiatric Association (APA) has long used a diagnostic classification system as a means of categorizing behavioral patterns into groups. Such classification is essentially a means of shorthand communication between professionals in an effort to efficiently describe phenomena and target appropriate treatment. The most updated system in the APA's *Diagnostic and Statistical Manual of Mental Disorders*, Fifth Edition (DSM-5) (2013), lists five essential clinical criteria for PTSD: experience of a traumatic event, intrusive experiences with physiological arousal, avoidance behavior, negative alterations in thoughts and mood, and alterations in emotional and behavioral reactivity. Symptoms must be present for at least one month, can cause significant distress or impairment in functioning, and cannot be solely the result of substance (medication, alcohol) use or another medical condition.

Criterion A: Traumatic Experience

Experiencing a psychologically traumatic event is the first criterion for the diagnosis of PTSD. To better understand what constitutes trauma, it is important to appreciate the physiological and psychological elements of the human stress response. Humans take information in through the senses: sight, hearing, smell, touch, and taste. The brain evaluates this information and reacts accordingly. In some circumstances, information is carefully and thoughtfully evaluated before a person decides what actions to take. For example, when feeling hungry, one may *think* about healthy choices or what one has eaten earlier that day and may also check in with the accompanying *feelings*, (e.g., hunger, cravings). In theory, one analyzes both *thoughts* ("I need to watch my salt intake.") and *feelings* (craving salty food) to consciously determine a *behavior* (choosing what to eat).

In other circumstances, the brain takes in information through the senses and immediately interprets threat, without much conscious awareness or rational processing. When the limbic system (particularly the amygdala) receives input interpreted as threatening, it activates the sympathetic nervous system via the hypothalamus-pituitary axis, resulting in a flood of adrenaline throughout the body (Koolhaas et al., 2011). Blood pressure and heart rate increases, triggering a fight-or-flight response. As awareness of the threat emerges, the brain becomes focused on the information judged as necessary for survival, and disregards details regarded as unimportant. In addition, some individuals experience a "freeze" or engage in dissociation, an involuntary response in which one mentally separates one's self from the actual events that are taking place (Lensvelt-Mulders et al., 2008). These automatic, unconscious reactions may help explain why survivors of trauma are often unable to report the details of the event in a coherent narrative.

Our brains are built to recognize patterns and categorize information for efficiency. Therefore, if a person has previously experienced threat and danger, that individual may be "primed" to perceive similar experiences as threatening, and reactions may be more automatic, rapid, and intense. Additionally, people may be primed by earlier experiences to respond to threat with defenses previously used, including dissociative "distancing" from the situation. It is important to understand that even when danger is subjectively perceived, the brain may engage in the threat response. In this situation, the threat does not need to be "real" by any objective standards, and others experiencing the same event may have no adverse response. This phenomenon explains why it is difficult to understand why a veteran with PTSD has a strong reaction to stimuli in the civilian world (e.g., trash on the side of the road) typically perceived by others as innocuous.

Criterion B: Intrusive Symptoms

Following a traumatic event, distressing memories of past events can spontaneously occur, both while awake and in the form of dreams. These experiences may occur because of exposure to an internal or external cue that symbolizes or resembles an aspect of the traumatic event, which are known as triggers. Sometimes, the memories of traumatic events can alter perception of reality, and, in more extreme cases, the veteran feels or acts as if the traumatic event is recurring (this experience is sometimes called a flashback). Memories of past events are often accompanied by psychological distress (e.g., fear, anxiety, sadness, anger) along with physiological reactions (e.g., increased heart rate, sweating, fight-or-flight responses). Intrusive experiences may also occur without obvious triggers. Unfortunately, as long as the impaired nervous system goes untreated, triggers often increase. For example, the initial fear associated with a specific assailant could become a more generalized fear of all tall bearded men.

Criterion C: Avoidance and Numbing

Avoidance is a natural and understandable pattern of behavior that reflects the veteran's attempts to reduce exposure to triggers or potential triggers and neutralize physiological and psychological responses. People suffering with PTSD may avoid a number of settings and experiences, including public or crowded places, certain people or types of people, situations in which they will be exposed to noise, or even intimacy. Avoidance thus may lead to emotional distance between themselves and others. People with PTSD also often cope by numbing their feelings and/or compartmentalizing thoughts and emotions, coping mechanisms that are valued in the military. Individuals who compartmentalize often describe this coping strategy as "just not thinking about it," which may lead to numbing behavior. Some examples of numbing include the use of substances, gambling, compulsive sex/pornography, eating, spending money, and excessive use of exercise. These, or other methods, serve to decrease or distract from negative internal experiences.

While avoidance and numbing may seem like logical, reasonable coping responses, some of these behaviors can become problematic, creating additional layers of distress (e.g., depression, substance misuse, relationship conflict). In addition, by engaging in avoidance and numbing, veterans paradoxically increase (rather than decrease) their sensitivity to triggers. A good metaphor for this concept is the increased sensitivity our eyes have to sunlight if we have spent a few hours in a dark room. Finally, use of avoidance and numbing can also lead to a decrease in healthy coping skills, and may reinforce the perceived danger of the trigger.

Criterion D: Negative Cognitive and Mood Symptoms

Following a traumatic event, a veteran's mind begins the process of trying to make sense of what happened. These events can be difficult to process if aspects of the events have not been properly encoded in memory and/or are altered by the acute state of emotional and physiological stress under which they were perceived. Additionally, traumatic events from military experiences can be horrifying, and involve dead or dismembered bodies, loss of close friends, witnessing the death of civilians and/or children, or killing another person. It is common for survivors of trauma to experience ongoing horror, shame, or guilt about the event(s) or about themselves, even when they do not readily admit to such feelings. Understandably, these types of experiences can shape a veteran's worldview and self-concept. For example, a veteran may develop a belief that the world is not a safe place, that others cannot be trusted, or that a successful, happy future is not possible. The individual may become emotionally detached, have difficulty experiencing positive feelings, and lose interest in participating in life activities.

Criterion E: Marked alterations in arousal and reactivity

Long-term triggering of the fight-or-flight response can result in chronic sympathetic nervous system arousal. Symptoms of such over-arousal may include irritability, angry outbursts (sometimes with little to no provocation), difficulty sleeping, and/or relaxing, and even verbal or physical aggression toward other people or objects. Sometimes individuals with chronic over-arousal engage in reckless or self-destructive behavior to maintain the high level of intensity and/or excitement experienced during military service. The positive feelings of intensity and excitement, combined with the horrific experiences of suffering and death, often lead veterans to remember combat experiences as "the best of times and the worst of times" (Hoge, 2010). It may be difficult as civilians to understand the longing to return to the thrill and excitement of combat, which is like no other "rush" in the world (Yehuda et al., 2014).

Other symptoms in this category fit with the experience of the trauma and activation of the survival instinct. For example, hypervigilance, a state of increased awareness, is common and may be presented in several ways. Service members are extensively drilled in situational awareness, scanning the environment for threats or potential threats, and making contingency plans for action in the event of threat. Veterans on combat deployments must be constantly vigilant as life-threatening events can be an everyday occurrence. Hypervigilance becomes innate and unconscious, and veterans may always be automatically scanning the environment for danger. Veterans often feel more comfortable sitting where others cannot be behind them, and where entrances and exits are clearly visible and accessible. Exaggerated startle responses to unexpected stimuli (e.g., loud noises) are another symptom of nervous system over-arousal that may manifest as elevated heart rate, palpitations, or other physical symptoms of anxiety. A later section in this chapter explains other common behavioral manifestations that providers may observe in a treatment setting, with guidance on how to manage these events.

As might be imagined, these symptoms consume a great deal of attention and energy, and often veterans with PTSD report difficulty with memory and concentration as well as high levels of fatigue. Veterans may experience difficulty focusing in the therapeutic environment. Such difficulty can present on a continuum, from mild forms such as not tracking for short periods of conversation to a more serious inability to remember an entire conversation or action. Similarly, veterans or their family members may report memory lapses ranging from mild to more significant loss of memory or awareness. A veteran with a history of either documented or suspected traumatic brain injury (TBI) may find these episodes particularly worrisome if interpreted as signs of brain damage or loss of functioning. If the individual has not been evaluated for TBI, it could be helpful to suggest or facilitate such evaluation. Educating patients about normal attention and memory function as an initial intervention may also be helpful, providing assurance that these types of memory problems are common and expected given the attentional demand that PTSD symptoms impose. The provider must again find the balance between listening to and validating the patient's experience and providing assurance and education about common symptoms while thoughtfully considering referral given the information later in this chapter on mild TBI.

Military Sexual Trauma

Military sexual trauma (MST) encompasses any sexual activity that occurs against a service member's will. MST can encompass sexual assault, unwanted touching, explicit sexual comments, or innuendo, deprecating comments of a sexual nature, and threats.

While sexual harassment and sexual assault certainly occur in civilian populations, these issues present unique challenges in a military environment. The military is a hierarchical system where orders are given and expected to be obeyed without question. In such a system, abuses of power that occur can be devastating to the individual on the receiving end. Furthermore, service members are trained to work and fight as a collective; when trust is breached within that collective, the victims become especially vulnerable to the many other stressors in their environment. Victims are often blamed as being the source of disruption in the collective, particularly when pursuing justice, which might include disciplinary action against the perpetrator.

Reactions to MST can vary depending on a variety of factors. Some are related to the event itself including type of abuse, the presence of violence, and whether the event was one instance or repeated over time. Other factors include prior trauma or sexual abuse, reactions of others, and institutional betrayal when the victim discloses the event (Andresen et al., 2019). It is important to realize that MST is an event, not a diagnosis. Some individuals recover without treatment, while others develop symptoms that require intervention. While MST can contribute to PTSD, diagnoses of depression and substance misuse are just as common (Calhoun et al., 2018; Goldberg et al., 2019). A recent meta-analysis of both VA and non-VA healthcare settings found 15.7% of military personnel and veterans report MST (3.9% of men, 38.4% of women) when the measure includes both harassment and assault. Additionally, 13.9% report MST (1.9% of men, 23.6% of women) when the measure assesses only assault, and 31.2% report MST (8.9% of men, 52.5% of women) when the measure assesses only harassment. MST is clearly a pervasive problem, and while women are most often the targets, men are also victims at a concerning rate (Wilson, 2018). Survivors of MST sometimes require specialized therapies to combat their symptoms, and for those who require more intensive treatment, there are several national VA treatment programs oriented specifically toward treating veterans with MST.

Moral Injury

Some veterans have engaged in or witnessed events that defy a personal, moral sense of right and wrong, in combat or even in training. Litz and colleagues named this construct moral injury and hypothesized that such acts can be emotionally, psychologically, behaviorally, spiritually, and socially deleterious in the long-term (Litz et al., 2009). Examples can include different types of betrayals (i.e., by peers, leadership, trusted civilians, or self), and acts of disproportionate violence in the war zone (e.g., acts of revenge and/or retribution, unnecessary destruction of civilian property). Further examples include incidents involving death/harm to civilians, acts of violence committed within military ranks (i.e., friendly fire incidents), inability to prevent death/suffering, and ethical dilemmas or moral conflicts from deployment-related decisions/actions such as violating rules of engagement to save the life of a comrade or a civilian (Currier et al., 2015). Veterans often do not bring up these events because of overwhelming feelings of shame and fear of repercussions or being misunderstood, which can lead to multiple symptoms, including social isolation, depression, and suicidality. While moral injury is not included in the definition of PTSD in the DSM-5, emerging literature suggests that traditional PTSD treatments do not sufficiently redress moral injury (Currier et al., 2015; Litz et al., 2009) and moral injury may be one reason for the intractability of PTSD symptoms in a subset of the military population. Treatment modalities for moral injury must address the need for self-forgiveness, social reintegration, and acceptance (Burkman et al., 2019).

What Is Unique About PTSD in Veterans

The context of the events that lead to trauma for military veterans is important to understand. Some factors may not be intuitive or familiar to civilian providers.

Training and Culture

As discussed elsewhere in this book, military culture, a sense of unity, and a focus on mission are instilled into veterans' identities. Furthermore, veterans have been specifically prepared to encounter horrifying and life-threatening situations. Many veterans have encountered life-threatening situations and experienced trauma without a combat deployment. Training accidents, mass shootings on base, physical assault, and sexual assault are just a few of the possible ways in which our veterans may have experienced trauma stateside.

Conditions of Deployments

Common experiences among deployed service members include disrupted sleep routines, stress from separation from families, and overall unpleasant living conditions. However, not all deployments are created equal. First, some deployments are designated as combat, while others are non-combat and/or humanitarian. Furthermore, some combat deployments do not include actual combat or life-threatening situations for certain veterans. Some deployments are extremely kinetic (engaging in active warfare and use of lethal force), while others are less so. It is important to note that PTSD can arise from traumatic experiences in any location (e.g., the U.S. Military humanitarian earthquake response to Haiti in 2010 or in the Battle of Ramadi, Iraq, in 2006). Trauma can even occur in training events and training accidents. To best understand the nature of the PTSD symptoms, providers should resist the temptation to assume that a combat veteran has PTSD and that a non-combat veteran does not and instead ask about the nature and quality of deployments.

Military Occupational Specialty

Exposure to traumatic events is often related to the type of work a veteran performed while in the service. Asking in detail about the experiences of your patient is important. For example, an explosion ordinance disposal (EOD) technician has likely been exposed to many concussive blast waves, witnessed multiple deaths, and handled human remains of both fellow soldiers and the enemy. Knowledge of military occupational specialty (MOS) can provide insight into the kind of training a veteran has had, and since physical and psychological trauma can occur in the context of training, this information can be vital. For example, Special Forces training includes hostage and torture training and brutal combative (fighting). Some veterans have even witnessed or known a fellow service member killed in training events. Finally, in addition to MOS, it is important to know the highest rank achieved by a veteran, as it provides insight into elements of their traumatic experiences. Officers and NCOs have held positions of leadership. This added role and its responsibilities can alter the landscape of a veteran's combat experiences.

Frequency of Deployment and Dwell Time

In the post-9/11 era, individual military service members have been deployed more frequently than in previous military practice, with shorter lengths of recovery time between deployments (known as dwell time). It is estimated that 28% of service members have deployed twice and an additional 25% have deployed three or more times (Armed Forces Health Surveillance Center, 2011). These rates are notably higher than during any other era of military service and are related to increased exposure to physical and psychological traumas, including TBI (Varga et al., 2018). Reduced time between deployments has also led to adverse psychological outcomes (Macgregor et al., 2014).

Traumatic Brain Injury

Traumatic brain injury (TBI), a major health problem around the world, has been termed a "signature wound" of recent military conflicts in the Middle East (Snell & Halter, 2010). Between 2000 and 2019, over 413,000 U.S. service members were identified as having at least one service-related TBI, the vast majority of which (82%) are considered mild or mTBI (Defense and Veterans Brain Injury Center, 2020). These injuries can occur by the impact of a head striking a fixed object, an object striking the head with or without skull penetration, whiplash, or blast. Blast events are unique in that in addition to the injuries of the primary force of the decompression wave, there can be secondary (airborne debris), as well as tertiary (transposition of the body or structural collapse) injuries (Przekwas et al., 2019). As there are currently no biomarkers that can reliably identify mTBI, the diagnosis is founded on report or observation of the injury event. Typical post-concussive symptoms (PCS) following mTBI include:

- *Physical symptoms* (e.g., nausea, vomiting, dizziness, headache, blurred vision, sleep disturbance, quickness to fatigue, lethargy, or other sensory loss)
- *Cognitive deficits* (e.g., involving attention, concentration, perception, memory, speech/ language, or executive functions)
- *Behavioral change(s)* and/or alterations in degree of emotional responsivity (e.g., irritability, quickness to anger, disinhibition, or emotional lability)

Recovery rates from mTBI are typically reported as 80–90% (Katz et al., 2015) and the prescription for a positive recovery trajectory includes reduced stimulation (auditory and visual) and physical and mental rest immediately following the injury with gradual return to life activities as symptoms subside. However, mTBI in military populations is unique in that patients may not report the injury or seek treatment and, even if they do, treatment may not be available. Furthermore, there is often no opportunity for a full recovery period because of the tempo of combat operations, need of the military unit, unavailability of personnel to fill in for a service member, or other considerations. In addition, it is quite common for veterans to have multiple mTBI events, sometimes in very close temporal proximity. These types of injuries certainly occur while on deployment, and many more happen in training.

There is evidence to suggest that veterans who have comorbid PTSD and mTBI experience greater PCS and PTSD symptoms than either condition alone, or even among those that have moderate/severe TBI (Bahraini et al., 2014). There is consensus in the field that psychotherapy that addresses PTS in a non-brain-injured population can also be effectively used to treat PTS in veterans with mTBI (Scholten et al., 2017). However, if a patient has a history of mTBI, providers are encouraged to screen for PCS with an instrument such as the Neurobehavioral Symptom Inventory (Cicerone & Kalmar, 1995). Some symptoms (e.g., vestibular and ocular motor disruption, headache, sleep disorders) can interfere with the efficacy of the psychotherapy and may require intervention from other specialties (e.g., vestibular physical therapy, as well as headache and sleep specialists) for the therapy to progress.

Polytrauma

Major advances in protective gear and medical technology allow for survival of injuries that would have previously been fatal (Tanielian, 2008). Veterans are now surviving with polytrauma. which includes significant physical injuries and chronic pain in addition to the persistent PCS and psychiatric comorbidities.

Veterans with polytrauma present with needs that are unique and challenging in the treatment setting (Sayer et al., 2009; Waszak & Holmes, 2017). Specifically, the polytrauma triad of PTSD, chronic pain and TBI with persistent post-concussive symptoms (Lew et al., 2009) has been linked to sleep disturbances (Lew et al., 2010) as well as healthcare utilization and adverse events (Pugh et al., 2014). Furthermore, providers should be aware that when this triad is present with substance use and/or depression, suicidal risk increases significantly (Finley et al., 2015).

Risk and Protective Factors for Developing PTSD

Among veterans, factors such as lower levels of education, younger age, and being single or unmarried appear to be associated with a higher risk for development of PTSD (Ramchand et al., 2015). In addition, childhood adverse experiences (ACEs) also place veterans at a higher risk of developing PTSD and other comorbid psychiatric disorders. One study demonstrated that of 162 service members who sought behavioral health treatment while in a combat zone, 83% had at least one ACE and 40% experienced four or more ACEs (Applewhite et al., 2016). In another community-based survey of 8,360 active duty service members, exposure to ACEs was significantly associated with past-year mood or anxiety disorder among men and women even after controlling for deployment-related trauma exposure (DRTE). Importantly, participants exposed to both ACEs and DRTEs had the highest prevalence of past-year mood or anxiety disorder in comparison to those who were exposed to either ACEs or DRTEs alone, or no exposure (Sareen et al., 2013).

Military and deployment risk factors appear to increase risk for PTSD and include combat exposure (Ramchand et al., 2015; Ramchand et al., 2010), perceptions of being prepared for deployment, leadership during deployment, concerns about family during deployment (Renshaw, 2011; Vogt et al., 2013) and injury in theater (Brenner et al., 2009). Some studies have found that deployment conditions and combat exposure are the strongest predictors of mental and behavioral health disturbances. Further work is needed to control for such exposure, to better understand the role of gender, age, branch, marital status, education, and ACEs and determine highest risk groups. Finally, as time since returning from deployment increases, veterans are more likely to develop symptoms of PTSD.

It is also important to understand the mitigating factors that protect against the development of PTSD in veterans, some of which have been found to moderate the relationship between combat exposure and PTSD symptoms. These include strong unit leadership (Han et al., 2014), a sense of unit cohesion (Nevarez et al., 2017) and high unit morale (Britt et al., 2013). In addition, social support before and after deployment, community integration, engagement in private religious/spiritual activities, and dispositional optimism have also been found to mitigate the effects of trauma and development of PTSD symptoms (Nichter et al., 2020).

Screening for PTSD

There are several different approaches to the screening and assessment of PTSD. Defining the question being asked and the purpose of the assessment when deciding which measure to use is important. In a primary care office, a quick screen might be warranted to determine if further evaluation is needed. In a mental health provider's office, a reliable diagnosis is critical. Details for each of the measures discussed next can be found in **Table 16-1**.

The Primary Care PTSD screen (PC-PTSD) is a quick five-question instrument that provides information on whether a veteran has experienced a traumatic event and is experiencing symptoms of PTSD (Prins et al., 2016). This instrument does not contain enough

Table 16-1 Suggested Measures for PTSD Screening and Diagnosis

Construct	Measure	Scores
Basic Screen in Primary Care Setting	**Primary Care PTSD Screen for DSM-5** ■ https://www.ptsd.va.gov/professional/assessment/screens/pc-ptsd.asp ■ https://www.ptsd.va.gov/professional/assessment/documents/pc-ptsd5-screen.pdf ■ Prins, A., Bovin, M. J., Smolenski, D. J., Mark, B. P., Kimerling, R., Jenkins-Guarnieri, M. A., Kaloupek, D. G., Schnurr, P. P., Pless Kaiser, A., Leyva, Y. E., & Tiet, Q. Q. (2016). The Primary Care PTSD Screen for DSM-5 (PC-PTSD-5): Development and evaluation within a Veteran primary care sample. *Journal of General Internal Medicine, 31,* 1206–1211. doi:10.1007/s11606-016-3703-5	A cut-point of 3 on the PC-PTSD-5 (e.g., respondent answers "yes" to any three of five questions about how the traumatic event(s) have affected them over the past month) is optimally sensitive to probable PTSD.
PTSD Symptoms	**PTSD Checklist for DSM-5 (PCL-5)** ■ https://www.ptsd.va.gov/professional/assessment/adult-sr/ptsd-checklist.asp ■ Blevins, C. A., Weathers, F. W., Davis, M. T., Witte, T. K., & Domino, J. L. (2015). The Posttraumatic Stress Disorder Checklist for *DSM-5* (PCL-5): Development and initial psychometric evaluation. *Journal of Trauma Stress, 28,*489–498.	A PCL-5 cut-point between 31–33 is a positive screen for PTSD.
PTSD Diagnosis	**Clinician Administered PTSD Scale for DSM-V (CAPS)** ■ https://www.ptsd.va.gov/professional/assessment/adult-int/caps.asp ■ Weathers, F. W., et al., (2018). The Clinician-Administered PTSD Scale for DSM-5 (CAPS-5): Development and initial psychometric evaluation in military veterans. *Psychological Assessment, 30*(3), 383. Available from www.ptsd.va.gov.	**Full training and scoring can be found at:** https://www.ptsd.va.gov/professional/assessment/adult-int/caps.asp#training

detail for a full diagnosis but can be helpful in deciding whether a referral is necessary for a more comprehensive evaluation.

PTSD Checklist for DSM-5 (PCL-5) is a 20-item measure that allows a clinician to screen for PTSD and make a provisional PTSD diagnosis using the cut-off scores, and monitor symptom change (Blevins et al., 2015). Mental health providers can use this measure to inform a clinical diagnostic process that includes more comprehensive interview and assessment.

The Clinician Administered PTSD Scale for DSM-5 (CAPS-5) is considered the gold standard for diagnosis of PTSD (Weathers et al., 2018). This is a 30-item structured interview that requires comprehensive administrator training for reliability and validity. The materials and trainings are all available in the public domain. The CAPS-5 scale allows the clinician to make a current (past month) diagnosis of PTSD, a lifetime diagnosis of PTSD, and PTSD symptoms over the past week. The full interview can take 45–60 minutes to administer.

Behaviors Encountered in a Clinical Setting

Veterans may exhibit behaviors related to PTS or PTSD, even if diagnostic criteria for the diagnoses are not met. Such issues may include autonomic over-reactivity, difficulty focusing, irritability, and suicidal thoughts. This section is intended to introduce a variety of responses that may be helpful in patient care.

Not all behaviors exhibited by veterans diagnosed with PTS or PTSD can be ascribed to these syndromes. Many circumstances may contribute to increased irritability, including sleep deprivation, grief and loss, depression, or immediate life stressors. Providers must find the balance between understanding behaviors resulting from PTSD and assuming that all veterans with the syndrome will be presenting with symptoms at any given time. Communicating openness to learning and collaborative problem solving are keys to maintaining the ongoing relationship with the veteran and creating positive resolution of any specific issue that arises.

Autonomic Reactivity

One important action that addresses autonomic over reactivity such as hypervigilance is to make sure the patients perceive a sense of control over their environment. This intervention starts with an awareness that veteran patients likely do not take safety for granted in any situation regardless of how "safe" it might seem to others. Individuals should be assured that they are free to move around, and even to leave for some period if they become too uncomfortable. At the same time, it is not helpful to reinforce veterans' avoidant behavior, as explained previously in this chapter. Expressing a willingness to talk through a veteran's discomfort and encouraging the use of skills or techniques learned in behavioral health settings designed to decrease autonomic over-arousal, could be key in these moments. A few such skills are listed below.

Skills to decrease over-arousal:

- Diaphragmatic breathing—individual is coached to breathe from belly rather than chest; slowing breath to 4-second inhale, 5-second exhale.
- Grounding—increasing physical awareness, orienting to the present moment, and taking conscious control and slowing system down by:
  - Feeling feet on ground
  - Being aware of specific parts of body (e.g., feet, lower legs, hands) and/or specific items in the surrounding area
  - Energy techniques such as Cook's hookup or acupressure techniques
- Self-talk—consciously using internal dialogue to assess and control internal experience
  - orienting to specific surroundings
  - self-coaching in challenging threat-assessing thoughts

Inattention and Distraction

Veterans may struggle with difficulty focusing in the therapeutic environment. As noted in the section on Criterion E, veterans' cognitive difficulties present with a range of severity. Interventions for periods of inattention/distraction in session should vary with the length of time and/or seriousness of the incident. Mild distraction may simply recede organically without intervention, although respectfully noting a moment of distraction may be useful. Veterans can be encouraged to take notes or otherwise actively engage to help maintain focus during the appointment. More significant or longer periods of distraction or dissociation generally require direct intervention using techniques such as those described next. If these experiences occur frequently, further psychological treatment is usually necessary.

Skills for inattention/distraction

- Using other modes of learning (e.g., kinesthetic, visual) to increase participation in any interaction.
- Self-guiding through present-focus by connecting to content (e.g., "what is she saying now; what does it mean?").
- Orienting: focusing on specific present stimuli, such as color, sound, shape in the immediate environment. Sometimes the person will need to describe these out loud (e.g., "I am seeing a blue square; I hear a bird singing behind me").
- Moving head and neck while orienting can help to trigger a vagus nerve response
- Using the PPP technique: **pause** to regulate breathing, **pressure** of feet against floor, slowly moving weight side-to-side (**pendulating**).
- Using energy techniques such as Cook's hookup or acupressure techniques

Irritability and Anger

Irritability is related to autonomic over-arousal and can be conceptualized as lower threshold and/or greater sensitivity to react to internal or external stimuli. The symptom may be observed as physical jumpiness, general difficulty with noises or other sensations (e.g., touch), overall mood dysregulation, decrease in motivation, or in varying degrees of anger. Behavioral manifestations requiring intervention may range from mild peevishness to dramatic experiences of rage. A veteran may appear touchier than others or may report overreactions at home or in the workplace, causing the patient deep concern or even shame. In rare instances, the veteran's behavior or potential behavior may instill fear in the healthcare provider or others. Interventions focused on anger are similar in scope to those addressing other PTS symptoms, starting with provider awareness and openness to addressing the behavior directly. It is important to remember that sleep deprivation, chronic pain, and a variety of stressors can contribute substantially to irritability. Exploring these areas with the patient and considering specific treatment to address such issues are important interventions.

If a veteran patient is expressing concern about anger, either with family members or in other settings, (such as road rage incidents), this admission could be an important opening into movement toward further treatment. The patient should be acknowledged for addressing an issue that might be a source of shame, guilt, or other self-judgments. Helping the individual understand that anger is a normal emotion that often arises in response to situations in which more difficult and/or unacceptable emotions (e.g., fear, pain) are triggered is often useful. Therapies that increase patients' internal awareness of these other emotions may be helpful resources.

De-escalation might be necessary in an office situation. Professional training in de-escalation may be useful; some basic de-escalation skills are listed next.

De-escalation techniques

- Directly addressing an increase in arousal, including raised voice, aggressive tone or behavior (e.g., "I noticed your voice increased in volume; are you angry right now?")
- Asking the veteran what he or she needs to calm down and if he or she can use skills to do so. It is important to communicate the validity of the veteran's concern (e.g., "I understand you are angry that I am not comfortable renewing your medication") while also stating that the specific behavior is unacceptable.
- Give the veteran time and space to use tools. You might leave the room, or ask if the veteran needs to take a short break.

If one of you leaves, set a time to return and check in.

- If the veteran does not identify his or her own calming techniques, specifically state what you need the individual to do (e.g., "I need you to sit down.")
- Suggest separation if necessary and set a time to reconvene.

Any concern for the safety of providers must be addressed directly and immediately. Workplace policies on disruptive behaviors and on firearms should be familiar to all office staff and communicated to the patient. Veteran patients are typically comfortable with firearms and often possess them. Questions about possession of firearms and other weapons should be routinely asked, including whether firearms are in the home and what safety measures are taken to prevent accessibility to children or others.

Suicidal Thoughts

Suicidal thoughts or intention (SI) should also be directly addressed. SI can range from occasional thoughts tied to specific painful incidents (e.g., "I wish this pain was over") to the creation of concrete plans with specific means to follow through. Suicidal thoughts should be explored with any patient, especially with veterans considering high rates of suicide in this population, military training in lethal means, and general access to weapons. Another chapter in this book is devoted entirely to this topic.

Treatment for PTSD

Veterans can seek out a number of effective, evidence-based psychotherapeutic treatments for PTSD as well as several emerging forms of psychotherapy, all of which should be conducted by trained mental health clinicians. The DOD/VA working group (Ostacher & Cifu, 2019), the American Psychological Association (Guideline Development Panel for the Treatment of PTSD in Adults, 2019), the United Kingdom's National Institute for Health and Clinical Excellence (Megnin-Viggars et al., 2019) and the International Society for Traumatic Stress Studies (Bisson et al., 2019), among others, have conducted exhaustive reviews of the research literature. Each of these groups has published clinical practice guidelines documenting the research and their recommendations for treatment with both adults and children/adolescents with PTSD. These resources are available in the public domain.

Most clinical practice guidelines clearly recommend individual, manualized, trauma-focused psychological treatments that include a cognitive restructuring component over other forms of treatment. When such therapy is not available, or the patient is not willing to engage in this therapy, it is recommended that pharmacotherapy or individual non-trauma-focused therapy be used over no therapy. The International Society for Traumatic Stress includes additional recommendations for treating complex trauma including: sequencing treatment with an initial emphasis placed on personal safety, emotional regulation skills, creating overall stability in life arenas, and creating the therapeutic relationship before starting trauma-focused therapy (Bisson et al., 2019). Some therapy is better than none, but the working groups and other meta-analyses of the treatment outcome literature (Cusack et al., 2016) consistently report insufficient evidence to consistently or reliably recommend one mode of psychotherapeutic treatment over another.

Even though effective treatment for PTSD is available, several problems emerge from a careful reading of the literature. Engaging veterans in treatment initially has been noted to be problematic, and dropout levels are often high. A 2010 study found that only 66% of a group of over 20,000 veterans diagnosed with PTSD initiated any type of mental health treatment; of these, only 25% attended a "minimally adequate dose" of eight or more sessions (Spoont et al., 2010). Other studies point to less than 10% of veterans with PTSD having received or completed an evidenced-based treatment (EBT) protocol (Mott et al., 2014). Veterans' lack of knowledge about the overall effectiveness of treatment has been identified as one barrier to seeking care (Deviva et al., 2016).

Steenkamp and her colleagues also note that studies conducted with both active duty service members (SMs) and veterans do not necessarily show the same overall rates of recovery from PTSD as members of the general population, for whom many of these therapies were first developed. These researchers raise the alarm that outcomes in the reviewed studies appear to be highly individualized and that both dropout and treatment nonresponse rates were high. The authors also point out that, though a number of RCTs have reported large effect size for several EBTs, many veterans (up to 60% in some trials) experience symptom reduction but still retain the diagnosis of PTSD (Steenkamp et al., 2020). Longer-term personalized approaches are more likely to be effective with the "complex clinical reality of managing military-related PTSD" (Steenkamp et al., 2020). These findings may reflect the complexity of veterans' experiences as compared to most civilian sufferers with PTSD, including multiple traumatic experiences over a sustained time, potential unaddressed moral injury, and associated changes in identity, as described earlier in this chapter.

Clearly, high numbers of veterans suffer with PTSD for which they have received inadequate—if any—treatment. Having at least a basic knowledge of treatment choices and encouraging patients to seek treatment is imperative. Treatment may also be important for those veterans who are not necessarily diagnosed with the full-blown syndrome but still experience enough symptoms to feel their lives are disrupted (e.g., PTS). Considering other therapies, such as meditation, art therapy, mind-body modalities such as yoga and tai chi, and animal-assisted therapies shown to be effective adjuncts for treating a variety of symptoms of PTSD (Lobban & Murphy, 2019; Sornborger et al., 2017) may also be in order. In addition to providing therapeutic benefit, these therapies could assist in increasing the individualization of treatment that Steenkamp and her colleagues recommend (2020). While these therapies have not been shown to have significant treatment effects on PTSD when used alone, they do provide important avenues to healing and may evoke less resistance than exposure-based trauma psychotherapies.

In considering how to make the decision of one treatment versus another, clinicians must be aware of the low utilization of effective tools and the fact that effect sizes and treatment outcomes are similar across the various evidence-based modalities. Shared decision-making (SDM) is an approach that provides information on treatments and engages patients in choosing an effective treatment modality. SDM supports patient buy-in and honors the individual's belief system, two important components of effective care.

The shared-decision making (SDM) approach consists of three elements: "choice talk" provides awareness that treatment choices exist; "option talk" provides detailed information regarding available options, and "decision talk" identifies personal preferences, helping patients make informed decisions about treatment (Hessinger et al., 2018). Several studies researching the use of SDM have shown that patients who have engaged in SDM were more likely to choose an EBT, to initiate treatment quickly, and to complete the chosen treatment (Hessinger et al., 2018; Mott et al., 2014). Techniques derived from motivational interviewing (Miller, 1991), an approach that encourages people to explore and resolve ambivalence, may also be very helpful in engaging patients in the exploration of options and understanding unique, personal needs and values in this decision.

Both the patient and the provider need a basic understanding of different treatment options in order to engage in a conversation about which options are best suited for the individual. The National Center for PTSD website provides detailed descriptions of CPT, PE, and EMDR (www.ptsd.va.gov/decisionaid). Unfortunately, few studies have examined factors that predict patient success in one trauma-based treatment relative to another, which increases the challenge for both providers and patients in deciding which treatment is best (Harick, 2018). Recognizing that any treatment is preferable to none, the veteran's preferences, as well as the availability of the different treatment modalities, should be considered in making the final decision. Considering multimodal treatment, particularly for those veterans who have complex medical and psychological presentations as a result of the factors listed in this chapter, may be useful. The next section will provide a brief explanation of the enumerated treatments as well as some expectations of what the patient might experience in this treatment modality.

All the EBTs and several of the emerging psychotherapies use exposure to traumatic content as a central component; thus one common "side effect" patients might experience is temporary increase of symptoms while processing traumatic experiences. It can be helpful to remind patients—and family members—of the temporary nature of this symptom exacerbation. Encouraging patients and family members to make increased use of self-care strategies may be important during these times, as can monitoring potential destructive behaviors and consultation with their individual therapists.

Evidence-Based Psychotherapies

Cognitive Processing Therapy (CPT) focuses on how the traumatic event is construed by a person trying to regain a sense of mastery and control (Resick et al., 2008). Patients learn about the connections among thoughts, emotions, and behaviors, and to identify automatic patterns of thought that may be maintaining symptoms. The patient writes a detailed account of an identified trauma, reads the account in session, and engages with the therapist in questioning or challenging unhelpful thoughts—also known as "stuck points." The therapist helps the patient use this process to monitor and change reactions to present-day events and function.

Prolonged Exposure Therapy (PE) helps the patient learn to gradually approach trauma-related memories, feelings, and situations to decrease avoidance and physiological symptoms of trauma (Foa et al., 2007; Hembree et al., 2003). Treatment begins with psychoeducation about avoidance and exposure as well as learning diaphragmatic breathing to develop a basic sense of safety and control. The therapist assists the patient in constructing a hierarchical list of feared situations after which the patient engages in *imaginal exposure*, describing the event in detail in the present tense with the therapist in session and processing emotion. Sessions are recorded and the patient is assigned to listen to the recording between sessions. Patients are also assigned *in vivo exposure*, in which they expose themselves to items from their hierarchical list in a graduated, controlled fashion, as homework.

In Eye Movement Desensitization and Reprocessing (EMDR), the patient is instructed to focus on both a disturbing memory and on the cognitive/emotional components of the memory while following a series of bilateral stimulation (BLS) methods introduced by the therapist (Shapiro, 1995). Traumatic experiences are posited to have been stored within the nervous system essentially in raw form. These traumas are then activated and replayed in the presence of any triggering stimulus. The method originally used eye movements for the BLS, but many therapists now use bilateral audio or kinesthetic (handheld "buzzers" or light tapping on the body) stimuli. Others have recommended specific modifications in the manualized treatment and EMDR treatment protocol to treat both veterans and active duty personnel successfully (Russell & Figley, 2013).

Brief Eclectic Psychotherapy (BEP) combines elements from psychodynamic, directive psychotherapy and cognitive-behavioral therapy, and shares components of psychoeducation, exposure, and structured writing tasks with other methods. BEP emphasizes finding meaning in patients' experience, acknowledging that their view of the world is often changed by the experience(s). Increased sense of vulnerability is often emphasized. A final farewell ritual is incorporated into the treatment (Gersons & Schnyder, 2013).

Narrative Exposure Therapy (NET) embeds trauma exposure in an autobiographical context. The therapist and patient create a timeline of the patient's life and then work together to develop a coherent narrative of the patient's life (Lely et al., 2019). The method was originally developed for use with people who have histories of multiple traumatic events over long periods (Mørkved et al., 2014).

Emerging and Adjunctive Therapies

Several emerging psychotherapies appear promising for the treatment of PTSD in adults, but do not yet have the research base to be considered evidence-based or evidence-supported. The following are some examples of these more recently developed psychotherapeutic innovations.

ART is a variant of EMDR developed to be a shorter and more directive version of EMDR, which identifies and treats the "major" traumas while helping patients generalize lessons learned to other areas of their lives. The treatment takes less time than other PTSD therapies and the limited research available is promising in that effect sizes appear similar to those of EBT's (Kip et al., 2015).

Virtual reality exposure therapy (VRET) has been used as both an adjunct to other exposure therapies and as a primary therapy especially for those patients who have a difficult time using their imaginations to engage with the emotional content that exposure therapy generally requires. A limited number of available studies have shown VRET to be efficacious. The method may be useful for patients who are resistant to traditional exposure (Gonçalves et al., 2012).

Present-centered therapy (PCT), interpersonal therapy (IT), and stress inoculation training (SIT) all have the patient's current function as the target of treatment, and do not specifically process past traumatic material. The trauma is acknowledged as one reason why a patient may be having difficulty presently, but the focus is more on the impact on current problems (PCT), relationships (IT), or stress responses in everyday life (SIT). There is very little evidence for the efficacy of other modalities, such as DBT, ACT, or supportive counseling in the specific treatment of PTSD, although these modalities have been effective for other psychiatric disorders.

Mindfulness-based interventions have been shown to improve psychological stress, anxiety, and depression in a variety of subjects and settings (Sornborger et al., 2017). Researchers point out that there are two components of mindfulness practice that may have a positive effect: self-regulation of attention, and the qualities a practitioner brings to the patient's attention, such as curiosity, kindness, and acceptance (Bishop et al., 2004). Mindfulness sessions taught by a trained teacher may assist veteran-patients with engagement in treatment, including making the decision to adhere to difficult treatment, and in developing the ability to tolerate strong emotions accessed in trauma-focused psychotherapies (Sornborger et al., 2017).

Yoga practice is an effective tool that can enhance interceptive awareness, which has been linked to improvements in emotional regulation. Yoga also provides a movement-based practice of mindfulness (Sornborger et al., 2017). Some veterans may find yoga, a body-based, action-oriented approach, more palatable than a sitting-based meditation practice. Trauma-sensitive and trauma-informed versions of yoga have been developed, as have variations in which patients are not required to engage in strenuous physical activity (e.g., chair yoga). Another form of movement to consider is Tai Chi, which includes both contemplation, building balance, and strength. Acupuncture has been found to reduce headaches and chronic pain, anxiety, sleep disturbance, and PTSD in some individuals in small clinical trials (Engel et al., 2014; Kim et al., 2013).

Art therapy was first introduced as a therapeutic tool with wounded soldiers in 1941 (Lobban & Murphy, 2019). Making visual art can assist veterans in self-expression that may be less challenging than putting their experience into words (which may be coded more in images and emotions as elucidated earlier in this chapter), and may reveal some aspects of their internal landscape that were previously unavailable. "The creative process has been seen to help veterans access, express, and make sense of hitherto unconscious, avoided, or suppressed material" (Lobban & Murphy, 2019, p. 41).

Finally, exercise and nutrition are part of a comprehensive plan for any patient's health, and veterans are no exception. As with any of the therapies described in this section, engagement in exercise and in changes in nutrition/diet should be conducted under the supervision of a licensed clinician who has some specialized training in working with patients with PSTD.

Specific guidelines for pharmacologic treatment of PTSD have been developed for both recommended agents and those not considered effective. These guidelines are beyond the scope of this work, but can be found in several of the well-regarded clinical practice guidelines cited (Ostacher & Cifu, 2019).

Table 16-2 may be useful for both providers and veterans considering the important question of which treatment to pursue. As stated previously in this chapter, the research on what type of treatment is more efficacious for particular individuals is not robust enough to guide this decision (Cusack et al., 2016; Harick, 2018). Therefore, other factors, such as availability of trained practitioners, previous experience in treatment, and overall preferences must be considered when choosing a modality.

As part of this process, providers may find it useful to use Shared Decision Making (SDM) and/or elements of Motivational Interviewing (MI) to assist patients who have previously engaged unsuccessfully with one type of treatment to identify the problematic components of that treatment experience. For example, patients who had difficulty completing "homework" assignments crucial for PE and CPT may find EMDR or ART better suited to their preference. Alternatively, a veteran may prefer group over individual treatment for the social support and normalizing inherent in the modality.

All of the treatment modalities in the table that follows have research evidence to support their use for PTSD treatment specifically, either at the level considered "evidence-based" (e.g., larger body of research) or "emerging" (research is supportive but not yet conclusive). Adjunct treatments such as Art Therapy or trauma-informed yoga are not included in the table but may be helpful for individuals seeking holistic approaches to treatment. **Table 16-3** discusses different diagnostic criteria for PTSD.

Family Considerations

A veteran's family members can be challenged to live with the litany of disruptions associated with PTSD, including sleep issues, irritability, emotional withdrawal and overreactions, substance use, and problems at work. Clearly, the veteran is suffering, but PTSD is deleterious to families as well.

The term *secondary traumatization* has been used to describe the phenomenon in

Table 16-2 **Treatment Options**

Therapy type	Theoretical Basis	Treatment Modality	Typical # of Weeks	Targets of Treatment	Homework?	Mode	About Trauma During Therapy?
CPT	Traumatic memory is "locked" into thought and behavior patterns	Writing and reading trauma experience habituates and allows for restructuring cognition	Twelve	Trauma-related thoughts/beliefs about world and self; avoidant behaviors	Yes	Group or individual	yes
PE	Arousal during trauma teaches that anything associated with trauma is "dangerous"	Exposure to graded list of feared experiences habituates	Eight to twelve sessions may last 120 minutes	Avoidance of discomfort	Yes	individual	yes
EMDR	Trauma memories are stored differently/ not processed and are triggered in a number of situations	Imaginal exposure coupled with bilateral stimulation in eight phase process	Varies	Trauma memories that translate into symptoms and beliefs about self	No	individual	Not necessarily
BEP	Strong emotions need to be brought to surface and processed within emotionally safe environment; meaning needs to be re-created	Exposure is a necessary element; exploration of new meaning is central	Up to sixteen	Processing memories to fully engage emotional content	No	individual	yes
NET	Traumatic experiences form fear networks that lack information; leaving blanks in patient's sense of self	Imaginary exposure and reorganization of memories; focus on life span	Four to twelve 90-minute sessions	Coherent/Rebuilt autobiographic memory ("life story")	No	individual	yes

Table 16-3 **DSM-5 Diagnostic Criteria for Post-Traumatic Stress Disorder**

Criterion A: *Exposure to actual or threatened death, serious injury, or sexual violence in one (or more) of the following ways:*
1. Directly experiencing the traumatic event(s).
2. Witnessing, in person, the event(s) as it occurred to others.
3. Learning that the traumatic event(s) occurred to a close family member or close friend. In cases of actual or threatened death of a family member or friend, the event(s) must have been violent or accidental.
4. Experiencing repeated or extreme exposure to aversive details of the traumatic event(s) (e.g., first responders collecting human remains; police officers repeatedly exposed to details of child abuse).
Criterion B: *Presence of one (or more) of the following intrusion symptoms associated with the traumatic event(s), beginning after the traumatic event(s) occurred:*
1. Recurrent, involuntary, and intrusive distressing memories of the traumatic event(s).
2. Recurrent distressing dreams in which the content and/or effect of the dream are related to the traumatic event(s).
3. Dissociative reactions (e.g., flashbacks) in which the individual feels or acts as if the traumatic event(s) were recurring. (Such reactions may occur on a continuum, with the most extreme expression being a complete loss of awareness of present surroundings.)
4. Intense or prolonged psychological distress at exposure to internal or external cues that symbolize or resemble an aspect of the traumatic event(s).
5. Marked physiological reactions to internal or external cues that symbolize or resemble an aspect of the traumatic event(s).
Criterion C: *Persistent avoidance of stimuli associated with the traumatic event(s), beginning after the traumatic event(s) occurred, as evidenced by one or both of the following:*
1. Avoidance of or efforts to avoid distressing memories, thoughts, or feelings about or closely associated with the traumatic event(s).
2. Avoidance of or efforts to avoid external reminders (people, places, conversations, activities, objects, situations) that arouse distressing memories, thoughts, or feelings about or closely associated with the traumatic event(s).
Criterion D: *Negative alterations in cognitions and mood associated with the traumatic event(s), beginning or worsening after the traumatic event(s) occurred, as evidenced by two (or more) of the following:*
1. Inability to remember an important aspect of the traumatic event(s) (typically due to dissociative amnesia and not to other factors such as head injury, alcohol, or drugs).
2. Persistent and exaggerated negative beliefs or expectations about oneself, others, or the world (e.g., "I am bad," "No one can be trusted," "The world is completely dangerous," "My whole nervous system is permanently ruined").
3. Persistent negative emotional state (e.g., fear, horror, anger, guilt, or shame).
4. Markedly diminished interest or participation in significant activities.
5. Feelings of detachment or estrangement from others.
6. Persistent inability to experience positive emotions (e.g., inability to experience happiness, satisfaction, or loving feelings).

(continues)

Table 16-3 DSM-5 Diagnostic Criteria for Post-Traumatic Stress Disorder *(continued)*

Criterion E: *Marked alterations in arousal and reactivity associated with the traumatic event(s), beginning or worsening after the traumatic event(s) occurred, as evidenced by two (or more) of the following:*
1. Irritable behavior and angry outbursts (with little or no provocation) typically expressed as verbal or physical aggression toward people or objects
2. Reckless or self-destructive behavior
3. Hypervigilance
4. Exaggerated startle response
5. Problems with concentration
6. Sleep disturbance (e.g., difficulty falling or staying asleep or restless sleep)
Criterion F: *The duration of the disturbance (Criteria B, C, D, and E) is more than one month.*
Criterion G: *The disturbance causes clinically significant distress or impairment in social, occupational, or other important areas of functioning.*
Criterion H: *The disturbance is not attributable to the physiological effects of a substance (e.g., medication, alcohol) or another medical condition.*

which people living with traumatized partners or family members become traumatized themselves (Figley, 1988). The phrase has been applied in two ways. The first has to do with transmission of the actual trauma—in which the family member who did not witness the event(s) subsequently develops symptoms specific to trauma exposure. The broader meaning of the term describes transmission of stress from the traumatized individual to family members or other close individuals. This usage does not necessarily make a distinction between PTSD symptoms and other generalized symptoms of distress in the affected individual, but does recognize the impact of living closely with people suffering from mental health challenges (Galovski & Lyons, 2004).

There is robust literature documenting reports of increased spousal anxiety, depression, and caregiver burden among partners of veterans diagnosed with PTSD even years after military service. (Blow et al., 2015; Knobloch-Fedders et al., 2017; O'Toole et al., 2010). A literature review on the effect of PTSD on veteran parenting and family distress concluded that a veteran's diagnosis of PTSD predicts spouse's distress and poor psychological well-being over and above other factors such as financial stress or quality of the relationship before deployment. Two factors—angry outbursts and emotional withdrawal or numbing—appeared to be particularly problematic (Galovski & Lyons, 2004). In one of the few direct observational studies found, military couples with a PTSD diagnosis showed more interpersonal hostility and need for control, with fewer connecting and affirming behaviors than couples in which neither member suffered from PTSD (Knobloch-Fedders et al., 2017).

Evidence also suggests that incidents of spousal violence are generally higher in military and veteran populations than among the US civilian population (Blow et al., 2015), although higher interpersonal violence may also be associated with higher rates of psychopathology, including PTSD (Jones, 2012). Several research studies have concluded that veterans diagnosed with PTSD have higher levels of family violence than civilians or veterans without PTSD. In a 1983 study of reports of domestic violence, PTSD—but not combat exposure by itself—predicted higher levels of marital violence. Anger and aggression are more likely to be reported by parents with PTSD than those without the disorder (Leen-Feldner et al., 2011; Sherman et al., 2016). Interestingly, emotional numbing symptoms were predictive of parent-child aggression in at least one study (Lauterbach et al., 2007).

Fewer studies have examined the link between PTSD and specific disruption for children in veteran families. One review of the literature on the effect of deployment and reintegration on active-duty families concluded that: (1) the number of children receiving mental health services as a result of parental deployment has increased; (2) school performance does appear to decline during deployment for at least some military children; (3) rates of increased child maltreatment do not appear to be greater than in the civilian population (except when alcohol and drug use was present, a higher incidence was observed). The authors proposed that children's developmental stage is an important variable when considering parental impact (Alfano et al., 2016). While this information pertains to active duty military, the conclusions are similar to effects posited for families of veterans suffering with PTSD.

Studies using veterans' self-reports have shown avoidance symptoms to be associated with decreased participation in children's activities, while alterations in cognition and mood were described as influencing self-worth as a parent, family engagement, and attachment (Brockman et al., 2016). Many of these studies relied on respondents' self-report, which is somewhat problematic in that negative self-evaluations common in individuals with PSTD may artificially inflate reports of aggression and overall family dysfunction. However, several small observational studies of veteran parents with PTSD showed less positive engagement with children (Brockman et al., 2016) and an increase in children's internalizing symptoms (Herzog et al., 2011).

Given this body of research, family members may need assistance from providers in three areas: (1) finding or helping their veteran find appropriate assistance; (2) receiving support themselves; and (3) managing and helping children. Each of these issues will be addressed in the following section.

Helping Veterans Seek Assistance

Sometimes family members realize that a veteran needs help before the veteran does. Some veterans are more comfortable talking with close friends or family members; others may believe "burdening" family members is unacceptable. Thus, partners or other family members may also need some coaching in how to safely and effectively approach and communicate with their veteran.

Directly identifying a concerning behavior (e.g., "I've noticed that your anger incidents have been increasing lately"; or "You've seemed sadder than normal recently") is a good general approach. Next, asking for a description of what the veteran has noticed, and what steps are possible to take in order to move in a positive direction, are more likely to be successful than a more confrontational approach. Family members should be encouraged to communicate what action they would like the veteran to take (e.g., "I would appreciate it if you would call the veteran help line") and what the family member would be willing to do as well ("I'll be happy to be on the call if you think that would be helpful").

It is important to ask family members what they notice in the veteran's actions or communications and to gauge any imminently dangerous behavior—either suicidality or homicidality—directly and clearly. Family members often feel relief at being asked about subjects deemed unacceptable, to open discussions with other contacts. Behaviors such as reckless driving or other high-risk activities may also be concerning to veteran family members, particularly if children are involved. These potential issues should be queried and directly addressed in a similar manner. See Chapter 17 on suicidality to find specific resources on how to address danger to self and others.

Supporting Family Members

Family members may feel hurt, alienated, angry, sad, discouraged, or other emotions as a consequence of living with someone with PTSD. In addition, family members may devote themselves totally to those they care for, out of love, a sense of duty, or even the fear of the consequences if they do not do so. Thus, they often neglect their own needs.

Family members should be validated and counseled that emotional reactions to a veteran with PTSD are normal and that help is available. Unfortunately, many spouses or other family members hesitate to reach out because of busy schedules, believing assistance is not necessary, worry about their partner's reactions, feeling their needs are not as important as the veteran's or concern about receiving unhelpful or unacceptable advice. Family members often have the experience that others—particularly those with minimal experience with military culture—offer solutions that are untenable (e.g., "You should just leave him") instead of understanding and support. The clinician's role could be to gauge the family member's openness to engaging in support systems, such as networks of military/veteran family members and/or individual counseling. Exploring barriers to using either of these avenues, referring, and even reaching out to make the original contacts are also important services to offer.

Family members should also be assisted in identifying small actions to take toward self-care. Education about how stress can manifest in a variety of ways such as not sleeping, feeling increasingly irritable or less patient, crying or not feeling anything, or eating too much or too little is important. Identifying some of these symptoms of stress can be helpful in building self-awareness. Some family members resist the idea of self-care because of lack of time and/or because of the fear of being "selfish." Active listening and patient support are key in assisting overburdened caregivers to acknowledge emotional wear and tear, and to allow for moments of restoration. At times, setting boundaries with loved ones can be difficult for caregivers. If this is an area of particular challenge, individual counseling may be a helpful suggestion.

Managing and Helping Children

Adults in the caregiver role—both veteran and non-veteran—may notice the consequences for children in their families with little sense of how to help. Shielding children from the effects of PTSD can unwittingly exacerbate the problem by trying to hide, deny, or minimize symptoms. Unfortunately, this response generally teaches children to deny or mistrust their own experiences, rather than being reassuring.

Family members should be counseled to share information about the effects of PTSD and the efforts the adults are taking to address the issues with children in an age-appropriate manner. Children need help in understanding that blame for the parent's behavior does not belong to the child. Parents or other family members can also teach self-soothing, relaxation, or stress reduction skills to children, and/or practice these skills as a family. Psychotherapy for the child or for the family may also be important; therapists need to create a safe, supportive space for children to express feelings. The VA is one important repository of resources for parents of children of all ages (see Resources).

Resources for Family Members of Veterans

- Coaching into Care (888-823-6458) at the VA provides coaches to choose effective communication strategies and help veterans access care if needed. Representatives answer questions about the type of services available at the VA and arrange for a specialist to speak with the provider on the phone about how to talk with the veteran.

- Cohen Veterans Network Clinics provide confidential therapy service to post-911 veterans, family members, and loved ones regardless of discharge status. Telehealth is available. https://www.cohenveterans network.org/clinics/
- PTSD Family Coach app provides support for concerned family members. This app provides family members with education to learn about the syndrome, how to implement self-care, and how to manage relationships with loved ones or children.
- Guide: *Understanding PTSD: A Guide for Family and Friends*
- Online Course: Help with PTSD. Self-paced online course on how to help a loved one get into treatment
- Community Reinforcement and Family Training (CRAFT-PTSD)
- Military One Source: https://www.military onesource.mil/
- National Center for Posttraumatic Stress Disorder: https://www.ptsd.va.gov
- National Alliance on Mental Illness (NAMI): http:// www.nami.org/Veterans
- https://www.mirecc.va.gov/visn19/talk2 kids/preschooler.asp
- https://www.ptsd.va.gov/professional /treat/specific/parent_ptsd.asp
- https://www.mirecc.va.gov/VISN16/docs /Talking_with_Kids_about_PTSD.pdf

References

Alfano, C. A., Lau, S., Balderas, J., Bunnell, B. E., & Beidel, D. C. (2016). The impact of military deployment on children: Placing developmental risk in context. *Clinical Psychology Review, 43*, 17–29. doi:10.1016/j .cpr.2015.11.003

American Psychiatric Association (2013). *Diagnostic and Statistical Manual of Mental Disorders* (5th ed.). Author.

Andresen, F. J., Monteith, L. L., Kugler, J., Cruz, R. A., & Blais, R. K. (2019). Institutional betrayal following military sexual trauma is associated with more severe depression and specific posttraumatic stress disorder symptom clusters. *Journal of Clinical Psychology, 75*(7), 1305-1319. doi:10.1002/jclp.22773

Applewhite, L., Arincorayan, D., & Adams, B. (2016). Exploring the prevalence of adverse childhood experiences in soldiers seeking behavioral health care during a combat deployment. *Military Medicine, 181*(10), 1275–1280. doi:10.7205/milmed-d-15-00460

Armed Forces Health Surveillance Center. (2011). *Associations between repeated deployments to Iraq (OIF/OND) and Afghanistan (OEF) and post-deployment illnesses and injuries, Active Component, U.S. Armed Forces, 2003–2010.*

Bahraini, N. H., Breshears, R. E., Hernandez, T. D., Schneider, A. L., Forster, J. E., & Brenner, L. A. (2014). Traumatic brain injury and posttraumatic stress disorder. *Psychiatric Clinics of North America, 37*(1), 55–75. doi:10.1016/j.psc.2013.11.002

Bahraini, N. H., Monteith, L. L., Gerber, H. R., Forster, J. E., Hostetter, T. A., & Brenner, L. A. (2017). The association between posttraumatic stress disorder and perceptions of deployment-related injury in veterans-veterans with and without mild traumatic brain injury. *Journal of Head Trauma Rehabilitation*. doi:10.1097/ HTR.0000000000000307

Bishop, S. R., Lau, M., Shapiro, S., Carlson, L., Anderson, N. D., Carmody, J., . . . Devins, G. (2004). Mindfulness: A proposed operational definition. *Clinical Psychology: Science and Practice, 11*(3), 230–241. doi:10.1093 /clipsy.bph077

Bisson, J. I., Berliner, L., Cloitre, M., Forbes, D., Jensen, T. K., Lewis, C., . . . Shapiro, F. (2019). The International Society for Traumatic Stress Studies New Guidelines for the Prevention and Treatment of Posttraumatic Stress Disorder: Methodology and development process. *Journal of Traumatic Stress, 32*(4), 475–483. doi:10.1002/jts.22421

Blevins, C. A., Weathers, F. W., Davis, M. T., Witte, T. K., & Domino, J. L. (2015). The Posttraumatic Stress Disorder Checklist for DSM-5 (PCL-5): Development and initial psychometric evaluation. *Journal of Traumatic Stress, 28*(6), 489–498. doi:10.1002/jts.22059

Blow, A., Curtis, A., Wittenborn, A., & Gorman, L. (2015). Relationship problems and military related PTSD: The case for using emotionally focused therapy for couples. *Contemporary Family Therapy, 37*(3), 261–270. doi:10.1007/s10591-015-9345-7

Brenner, L. A., Vanderploeg, R. D., & Terrio, H. (2009). Assessment and diagnosis of mild traumatic brain injury, posttraumatic stress disorder, and other polytrauma conditions: Burden of adversity hypothesis. *Rehabilitation Psychology, 54*(3), 239–246. doi:10.1037/a0016908

Britt, T. W., Adler, A. B., Bliese, P. D., & Moore, D. (2013). Morale as a moderator of the combat exposure-ptsd symptom relationship. *Journal of Traumatic Stress, 26*(1), 94–101. doi:10.1002/jts.21775

Brockman, C., Snyder, J., Gewirtz, A., Gird, S. R., Quattlebaum, J., Schmidt, N., . . . Degarmo, D. (2016). Relationship of service members' deployment trauma, PTSD symptoms, and experiential avoidance to post-deployment family reengagement. *Journal of Family Psychology, 30*(1), 52. doi:10.1037/fam0000152

Burkman, K., Purcell, N., & Maguen, S. (2019). Provider perspectives on a novel moral injury treatment for veteransveterans: Initial assessment of acceptability and feasibility of the Impact of Killing treatment materials. *Journal of Clinical Psychology, 75*(1), 79–94. doi:10.1002/jclp.22702

Butler, L. D., Linn, B. K., Meeker, M. A., McClain-Meeder, K., & Nochajski, T. H. (2015). "We Don't Complain About Little Things": Views of veterans and military family members on health care gaps and needs. *Military Behavioral Health, 3*(2), 116–124. doi:10.1080/21635781.2015.1009209

Calhoun, P. S., Schry, A. R., Dennis, P. A., Wagner, H. R., Kimbrel, N. A., Bastian, L. A., . . . Straits-Tröster, K. (2018). The association between military sexual trauma and use of VA and non-VA health care services among female veterans with military service in Iraq or Afghanistan. *Journal of Interpersonal Violence, 33*(15), 2439–2464. doi:10.1177/0886260515625909

Cicerone, K. D., & Kalmar, K. (1995). Persistent postconcussion syndrome: The structure of subjective complaints after mild traumatic brain injury. *The Journal of Head Trauma Rehabilitation, 10*(3), 1–17.

Currier, J. M., Holland, J. M., Drescher, K., & Foy, D. (2015). Initial psychometric evaluation of the Moral Injury Questionnaire—Military Version. *Clinical Psychology & Psychotherapy, 22*(1), 54–63. doi:10.1002/cpp.1866

Currier, J. M., Holland, J. M., & Malott, J. (2015). Moral injury, meaning making, and mental health in returning veterans. *Journal of Clinical Psychology, 71*(3), 229–240. doi:10.1002/jclp.22134

Cusack, K., Jonas, D. E., Forneris, C. A., Wines, C., Sonis, J., Middleton, J. C., . . . Gaynes, B. N. (2016). Psychological treatments for adults with posttraumatic stress disorder: A systematic review and meta-analysis. *Clinical Psychology Review, 43*, 128–141. doi:10.1016/j.cpr.2015.10.003

Defense and VeteransVeterans Brain Injury Center. (2020, 2019). DoD worldwide numbers for TBI. https://dvbic.dcoe.mil/dod-worldwide-numbers-tbi

Deviva, J. C., Sheerin, C. M., Southwick, S. M., Roy, A. M., Pietrzak, R. H., & Harpaz-Rotem, I. (2016). Correlates of VA mental health treatment utilization among OEF/OIF/OND veteransveterans: Resilience, stigma, social support, personality, and beliefs about treatment. *Psychological Trauma: Theory, Research, Practice and Policy, 8*(3), 310. doi:10.1037/tra0000075

Engel, C. C., Cordova, H. E., Benedek, M. D., Liu, L. X., Gore, C. K., Goertz, B. C., . . . Ursano, J. R. (2014). Randomized effectiveness trial of a brief course of acupuncture for posttraumatic stress disorder. *Medical Care, 52*(12 Suppl 5), S57–S64. doi:10.1097/MLR.0000000000000237

Figley, C. R. (1988). Victimization, trauma, and traumatic stress. *The Counseling Psychologist, 16*(4), 635–641. doi:10.1177/0011000088164005

Finley, E. P., Bollinger, M., Noël, P. H., Amuan, M. E., Copeland, L. A., Pugh, J. A., . . . Pugh, M. J. V. (2015). A National Cohort Study of the Association Between the Polytrauma Clinical Triad and Suicide-Related Behavior Among US VeteransVeterans Who Served in Iraq and Afghanistan. *American Journal of Public Health (1971), 105*(2), 380–387. doi:10.2105/ajph.2014.301957

Foa, E. B., Hembree, E. A., & Rothbaum, B. O. (2007). *Prolonged Exposure Therapy for PTSD: Emotional processing of traumatic experinces therapist guide*. Oxford University Press.

Galovski, T., & Lyons, J. A. (2004). Psychological sequelae of combat violence: A review of the impact of PTSD on the veteranveteran's family and possible interventions. *Aggression and Violent Behavior, 9*(5), 477–501. doi:10.1016/S1359-1789(03)00045-4

Gersons, B. P. R., & Schnyder, U. (2013). Learning from traumatic experiences with brief eclectic psychotherapy for PTSD. *European Journal of Psychotraumatology, 4*(1). doi:10.3402/ejpt.v4i0.21369

Goldberg, S. B., Livingston, W. S., Blais, R. K., Brignone, E., Suo, Y., Lehavot, K., . . . Gundlapalli, A. V. (2019). A positive screen for military sexual trauma is associated with greater risk for substance use disorders in women veteransveterans. *Psychology of Addictive Behaviors: Journal of the Society of Psychologists in Addictive Behaviors, 33*(5), 477. doi:10.1037/adb0000486

Gonçalves, R., Pedrozo, A. L., Coutinho, E. S. F., Figueira, I., Ventura, P., & Slater, M. (2012). Efficacy of virtual reality exposure therapy in the treatment of PTSD: A systematic review. *PLoS ONE, 7*(12). doi:10.1371/journal.pone.0048469

Guideline Development Panel for the Treatment of PTSD in Adults, A. P. A. (2019). Summary of the clinical practice guideline for the treatment of posttraumatic stress disorder (PTSD) in adults. *The American Psychologist, 74*(5), 596–607. doi:10.1037/amp0000473

Han, S. C., Castro, F., Lee, L. O., Charney, M. E., Marx, B. P., Brailey, K., . . . Vasterling, J. J. (2014). Military unit support, postdeployment social support, and PTSD symptoms among active duty and National Guard soldiers deployed to Iraq. *Journal of Anxiety Disorders, 28*(5), 446–453. doi:10.1016/j.janxdis.2014.04.004

Harick, J. (2018). Shared decision-making for PTSD. *PTSD Research Quarterly, 29*(1), 1–9.

Hembree, E. A., Rauch, S. A. M., & Foa, E. B. (2003). Beyond the manual: The insider's guide to Prolonged Exposure therapy for PTSD. *Cognitive and Behavioral Practice, 10*(1), 22–30. doi:10.1016/S1077-7229(03)80005-6

Herzog, J., Everson, R., & Whitworth, J. (2011). Do secondary trauma symptoms in spouses of combat-exposed national guard soldiers mediate impacts of soldiers' trauma exposure on their children? *Child and Adolescent Social Work Journal, 28*(6), 459–473. doi:10.1007/s10560-011-0243-z

Hessinger, J. D., London, M. J., & Baer, S. M. (2018). Evaluation of a shared decision-making intervention on the utilization of evidence-based psychotherapy in a VA outpatient PTSD clinic. *Psychological services, 15*(4), 437. doi:10.1037/ser0000141

Hoge, C. W. (2010). *Once a warrior always a warrier: Navigating the transition from combat to home*. Lyons Press.

Hoggatt, K., Levahot, K., Krenenk, M., Schweizer, C. A., & Simpson, T. (2017). Prevalence of substance misuse among US veterans in the general population. *The American Journal on Addictions, 26*, 357–365.

Jones, A. D. (2012). Intimate partner violence in military couples: A review of the literature. *Aggression and Violent Behavior, 17*(2), 147–157. doi:10.1016/j.avb.2011.12.002

Kang, H. K., Natelson, B. H., Mahan, C. M., Lee, K. Y., & Murphy, F. M. (2003). Post-Traumatic stress disorder and chronic fatigue syndrome-like illness among Gulf War Veterans: A population-based survey of 30,000 veterans. *American Journal of Epidemiology, 157*(2), 141–148. doi:10.1093/aje/kwf187

Katz, D.I., Cohen, S.I., & Alexander, M. P. (2015). Mild traumatic brain injury. In: Handbook of Clinical Neurology, pp. 131–156. Edited by Grafman, A, Salazar, A. M.: Amsterdam, Elsevier.

Kim, Y.-D., Heo, I., Shin, B.-C., Crawford, C., Kang, H.-W., & Lim, J.-H. (2013). Acupuncture for posttraumatic stress disorder: A systematic review of randomized controlled trials and prospective clinical trials. *Evidence-Based Complementary and Alternative Medicine, 2013*. doi:10.1155/2013/615857

Kip, K. E., Hernandez, D. F., Shuman, A., Witt, A., Diamond, D. M., Davis, S., . . . Rosenzweig, L. (2015). Comparison of accelerated resolution therapy (ART) for treatment of symptoms of PTSD and sexual trauma between civilian and military adults. *Military Medicine, 180*(9), 964. doi:10.7205/MILMED-D-14-00307

Knobloch-Fedders, L. M., Caska-Wallace, C., Smith, T. W., & Renshaw, K. (2017). Battling on the home front: Posttraumatic stress disorder and conflict behavior among military couples. *Behavior Therapy, 48*(2), 247–261. doi:10.1016/j.beth.2016.08.014

Koolhaas, J. M., Bartolomucci, A., Buwalda, B., De Boer, S. F., Flügge, G., Korte, S. M., . . . Fuchs, E. (2011). Stress revisited: A critical evaluation of the stress concept. *Neuroscience & Biobehavioral Reviews, 35*(5), 1291–1301. doi:10.1016/j.neubiorev.2011.02.003

Kulka, R. A. (1990). *Trauma and the Vietnam War generation: Report of findings from the National Vietnam VeteransVeterans Readjustment Study*. Brunner/Mazel.

Lauterbach, D., Bak, C., Reiland, S., Mason, S., Lute, M. R., & Earls, L. (2007). Quality of parental relationships among persons with a lifetime history of posttraumatic stress disorder. *Journal of Traumatic Stress, 20*(2), 161–172. doi:10.1002/jts.20194

Leen-Feldner, E. W., Feldner, M. T., Bunaciu, L., & Blumenthal, H. (2011). Associations between parental posttraumatic stress disorder and both offspring internalizing problems and parental aggression within the National Comorbidity Survey-Replication. *Journal of Anxiety Disorders, 25*(2), 169–175. doi:10.1016/j.janxdis.2010.08.017

Lely, J. C. G., Smid, G. E., Jongedijk, R. A., W. Knipscheer, J., & Kleber, R. J. (2019). The effectiveness of narrative exposure therapy: A review, meta-analysis and meta-regression analysis. *European Journal of Psychotraumatology, 10*(1), 1550344. doi:10.1080/20008198.2018.1550344

Lensvelt-Mulders, G., van der Hart, O., van Ochten, J., van Son, M., Steele, K., & Breeman, L. (2008). Relations among peritraumatic dissociation and posttraumatic stress: A meta-analysis. *Clinical Psychology Review, 28*(7), 1138–1151.

Lew, H. L., Otis, J. D., Tun, C., Kerns, R. D., Clark, M. E., & Cifu, D. X. (2009). Prevalence of chronic pain, posttraumatic stress disorder, and persistent postconcussive symptoms in OIF/OEF veterans: Polytrauma clinical triad. *The Journal of Rehabilitation Research and Development, 46*(6), 697. doi:10.1682/jrrd.2009.01.0006

Lew, H. L., Pogoda, T. K., Hsu, P.-T., Cohen, S., Amick, M. M., Baker, E., . . . Vanderploeg, R. D. (2010). Impact of the "polytrauma clinical triad" on sleep disturbance in a department of veterans affairs outpatient rehabilitation setting. *American Journal of Physical Medicine & Rehabilitation, 89*(6), 437–445. doi:10.1097/phm.0b013e3181ddd301

Litz, B. T., Stein, N., Delaney, E., Lebowitz, L., Nash, W. P., Silva, C., & Maguen, S. (2009). Moral injury and moral repair in war veteransveterans: A preliminary model and intervention strategy. *Clinical Psychology Review, 29*(8), 695–706. doi:10.1016/j.cpr.2009.07.003

Lobban, J., & Murphy, D. (2019). Understanding the role art therapy can take in treating veterans with chronic post-traumatic stress disorder. *The Arts in Psychotherapy, 62*, 37–44. doi:10.1016/j.aip.2018.11.011

Macgregor, A. J., Heltemes, K. J., Clouser, M. C., Han, P. P., & Galarneau, M. R. (2014). Dwell time and psychological screening outcomes among military service members with multiple combat deployments. *Military Medicine, 179*(4), 381–387. doi:10.7205/milmed-d-13-00314

Maguen, S., Lau, K. M., Madden, E., & Seal, K. (2012). Relationship of screen-based symptoms for mild traumatic brain injury and mental health problems in Iraq and Afghanistan veteransveterans: Distinct or overlapping symptoms? *Journal of Rehabilitation Research & Development, 49*(7), 1115–1126. Retrieved from https://www.ncbi.nlm.nih.gov/pubmed/23341283

Megnin-Viggars, O., Mavranezouli, I., Greenberg, N., Hajioff, S., & Leach, J. (2019). Post-traumatic stress disorder: what does NICE guidance mean for primary care? *British journal of general practice, 69*(684), 328–329. doi:10.3399/bjgp19X704189

Michie, S., Marques, M. M., Norris, E., & Johnston, M. (2018). Theories and Interventions in Health Behavior Change. In T. A. Revenson & R. Grurung (Eds.), *Handbook of health psychology.* Taylor and Francis Group.

Miller, W. R. (1991). *Motivational interviewing: Preparing people to change addictive behavior*. Guilford Press.

Mørkved, N., Hartmann, K., Aarsheim, L. M., Holen, D., Milde, A. M., Bomyea, J., & Thorp, S. R. (2014). A comparison of narrative exposure therapy and prolonged exposure therapy for PTSD. *Clinical Psychology Review, 34*(6), 453–467. doi:10.1016/j.cpr.2014.06.005

Mott, J. M., Stanley, M. A., Street, R. L., Grady, R. H., & Teng, E. J. (2014). Increasing engagement in evidence-based PTSD treatment through shared decision-making: A pilot study. *Military Medicine, 179*(2), 143. doi:10.7205/MILMED-D-13-00363

National Comorbidity Survey (NCS). (2005). https://www.hcp.med.harvard.edu/ncs/index.php https://www.hcp.med.harvard.edu/ncs/index.php

Nevarez, M. D., Yee, H. M., & Waldinger, R. J. (2017). Friendship in war: Camaraderie and prevention of posttraumatic stress disorder prevention. *Journal of Traumatic Stress, 30*(5), 512–520. doi:10.1002/jts.22224

Nichter, B., Haller, M., Norman, S., & Pietrzak, R. H. (2020). Risk and protective factors associated with comorbid PTSD and depression in U.S. military veterans: Results from the National Health and Resilience in Veterans Study. *Journal of Psychiatric Research, 121*, 56–61. doi:10.1016/j.jpsychires.2019.11.008

Ostacher, M. J., & Cifu, A. S. (2019). Management of posttraumatic stress disorder. *JAMA, 321*(2), 200. doi:10.1001/jama.2018.19290

O'toole, I. B., Outram, V. S., Catts, R. S., & Pierse, R. K. (2010). The mental health of partners of australian vietnam veterans three decades after the war and its relation to veteran military service, combat, and PTSD. *The Journal of Nervous and Mental Disease, 198*(11), 841–845. doi:10.1097/NMD.0b013e3181f98037

Possemato, K., Wray, L. O., Johnson, E., Webster, B., & Beehler, G. P. (2018). Facilitators and barriers to seeking mental health care among primary care veterans with posttraumatic stress disorder. *Journal of Traumatic Stress, 31*(5), 742–752. doi:10.1002/jts.22327

Prins, A., Bovin, M. J., Smolenski, D. J., Marx, B. P., Kimerling, R., Jenkins-Guarnieri, M. A., . . . Tiet, Q. Q. (2016). The Primary Care PTSD Screen for DSM-5 (PC-PTSD-5): Development and evaluation within a veteran primary care sample. *Journal of General Internal Medicine, 31*(10), 1206–1211. doi:10.1007/s11606-016-3703-5

Przekwas, A., Garimella, H. T., Tan, X. G., Chen, Z. J., Miao, Y., Harrand, V., . . . Gupta, R. K. (2019). Biomechanics of Blast TBI with time-resolved consecutive primary, secondary, and tertiary loads. *Military Medicine, 184*(Supp 1), 195–205. doi:10.1093/milmed/usy344

Pugh, M. J., V., Finley, E., P., Copeland, L., A., Wang, C.-P., Noel, P., H., Amuan, M., E., . . . Pugh, J., A. (2014). Complex comorbidity clusters in OEF/OIF veterans: The polytrauma clinical triad and beyond. *Medical Care, 52*(2), 172–181. doi:10.1097/MLR.0000000000000059

Ramchand, R., Karney, B. R., Osilla, K. C., Burns, R. M., & Caldarone, L. B. (2008). Prevalence of PTSD, depression, and TBI among returning servicemembers. In T. Tanielian & L. H. Jaycox (Eds.), *Invisible wounds of war* (pp. 35–86). RAND Corporation.

Ramchand, R., Rudavsky, R., Grant, S., Tanielian, T., & Jaycox, L. (2015). Prevalence of, risk factors for, and consequences of posttraumatic stress disorder and other mental health problems in military populations deployed to Iraq and Afghanistan. *Current Psychiatry Reports, 17*(5). doi:10.1007/s11920-015-0575-z

Ramchand, R., Schell, T. L., Karney, B. R., Osilla, K. C., Burns, R. M., & Caldarone, L. B. (2010). Disparate prevalence estimates of PTSD among service members who served in Iraq and Afghanistan: Possible explanations. *Journal of Traumatic Stress.* doi:10.1002/jts.20486

Renshaw, K. D. (2011). An integrated model of risk and protective factors for post-deployment PTSD symptoms in OEF/OIF era combat veterans. *Journal of Affective Disorders, 128*(3), 321–326. doi:10.1016/j.jad.2010.07.022

Resick, P. A., Monson, C. M., & Chard, K. M. (2008). *Cognitive processing therapy veteran/military version.*

Russell, M. C., & Figley, C. R. (2013). *Treating traumatic stress injuries in military personnel: An EMDR practitioner's guide*. Routledge.

Sareen, J., Henriksen, C. A., Bolton, S. L., Afifi, T. O., Stein, M. B., & Asmundson, G. J. G. (2013). Adverse childhood experiences in relation to mood and anxiety disorders in a population-based sample of active military personnel. *Psychological Medicine, 43*(1), 73–84. doi:10.1017/s003329171200102x

Sayer, N. A., Rettmann, N. A., Carlson, K. F., Bernardy, N., Sigford, B. J., Hamblen, J. L., & Friedman, M. J. (2009). Veterans with history of mild traumatic brain injury and posttraumatic stress disorder: challenges from provider perspective. *Journal of Rehabilitation Research & Development, 46*(6), 703–716. https://www.ncbi.nlm.nih.gov/pubmed/20104400

Scholten, J., Vasterling, J. J., & Grimes, J. B. (2017). Traumatic brain injury clinical practice guidelines and best practices from the VA state of the art conference. *Brain Injury, 31*(9), 1246–1251. doi:10.1080/02699052.2016.1274780

Shapiro, F. (1995). *Eye movement desensitization and reprocessing : Basic principles, protocols, and procedures.* Guilford Press.

Sherman, M. D., Gress Smith, J. L., Straits-Troster, K., Larsen, J. L., & Gewirtz, A. (2016). Veterans' perceptions of the impact of PTSD on their parenting and children. *Psychological Services, 13*(4), 401.

Snell, F. I., & Halter, M. J. (2010). A signature wound of war: Mild traumatic brain injury. *Journal of Psychosocial Nursing and Mental Health Services, 48*(2), 22–28. doi:10.3928/02793695-20100107-01

Sornborger, J., Fann, A., Serpa, J. G., Ventrelle, J., R.D.N, M. S., Ming Foynes, M., . . . Sylvia, L. G. (2017). Integrative therapy approaches for posttraumatic stress disorder: A special focus on treating veterans. *FOCUS, 15*(4), 390–398. doi:10.1176/appi.focus.20170026

Spoont, M. R., Murdoch, M., Hodges, J., & Nugent, S. (2010). Treatment receipt by veterans after a PTSD diagnosis in PTSD, mental health, or general medical clinics. *Psychiatric Services, 61*(1), 58–63. doi:10.1176/ps.2010.61.1.58

Steenkamp, M. M., Litz, B. T., & Marmar, C. R. (2020). First-line psychotherapies for military-related PTSD. *JAMA, 323*(7). doi:10.1001/jama.2019.20825

Tam-Seto, L., Krupa, T., Stuart, H., Lingley-Pottie, P., Aiken, A., & Cramm, H. (2020). The validation of the military and veteran family cultural competency model (MVF-CCM). *Military Behavioral Health, 8*(1), 96–108. doi:10.1080/21635781.2019.1689875

Tanielian, T. L. (2008). *Invisible wounds of war psychological and cognitive injuries, their consequences, and services to assist recovery.* RAND.

U.S. Department of Veterans Affairs. (2019). *National Veteran Suicide Prevention Annual Report.*

Varga, C. M., Haibach, M. A., Rowan, A. B., & Haibach, J. P. (2018). Psychiatric history, deployments, and potential impacts of mental health care in a combat theater. *Military Medicine, 183*(1–2), e77–e82. doi:10.1093/milmed/usx012

Vest, B. M., Kulak, J. A., & Homish, G. G. (2019). Caring for veterans in US civilian primary care: Qualitative interviews with primary care providers. *Family Practice, 36*(3), 343-350. doi:10.1093/fampra/cmy078

Vogt, D., Smith, B. N., King, L. A., King, D. W., Knight, J., & Vasterling, J. J. (2013). Deployment Risk and Resilience Inventory-2 (DRRI-2): An updated tool for assessing psychosocial risk and resilience factors among service members and veterans. *Journal of Traumatic Stress, 26*(6), 710–717. doi:10.1002/jts.21868

Waszak, D. L., & Holmes, A. M. (2017). The unique health needs of post-9/11 U.S. veterans. *Workplace Health & Safety, 65*(9), 430–444. doi:10.1177/2165079916682524

Weathers, F. W., Bovin, M. J., Lee, D. J., Sloan, D. M., Schnurr, P. P., Kaloupek, D. G., . . . Marx, B. P. (2018). The Clinician-Administered PTSD Scale for DSM-5 (CAPS-5): Development and initial psychometric evaluation in military veterans. *Psychological Assessment, 30*(3), 383. doi:10.1037/pas0000486

Wilson, L. C. (2018). The prevalence of military sexual trauma: A meta-analysis. *Trauma, Violence, & Abuse, 19*(5), 584–597. doi:10.1177/1524838016683459

Yehuda, R., Vermetten, E., McFarlane, A. C., & Lehrner, A. (2014). PTSD in the military: Special considerations for understanding prevalence, pathophysiology and treatment following deployment. *European Journal of Psychotraumatology, 5*(1), 25322. doi:10.3402/ejpt.v5.25322

CHAPTER 17

Suicide Risk Evaluation and Management Among Veterans Receiving Community-Based Care

Morgan Nance, Spencer Young, Lisa A. Brenner, and Adam R. Kinney

This material is based upon work supported in part by the Department of Veterans Affairs (VA) and the Rocky Mountain MIRECC for Suicide Prevention. The views expressed are those of the authors and do not necessarily represent the views or policy of the VA or the United States Government.

Suicide is a public health crisis in America, affecting both the general population and Veterans at staggering rates. It is the 10th leading cause of death in the United States, with 132 deaths by suicide occurring each day (American Foundation for Suicide Prevention, 2020). Between 2005 and 2017, suicide deaths in the United States increased from 31,610 to 45,390 per year, representing a 43.6% increase over 12 years (U.S. Department of Veterans Affairs, 2019).

Compared to the general population, veterans experience an especially high risk for suicide. According to the *2019 National Veteran Suicide Prevention Annual Report* (U.S. Department of Veterans Affairs, 2019), veterans are 1.5 times more likely to die by suicide compared to non-veteran adults, and the rate continues to rise. From 2005 to 2017, veteran suicides increased from 5,787 to 6,139 per year. This translates to an age- and sex-adjusted rate increase from 18.5 per 100,000 in 2005 to 27.7 per 100,000 in 2017 (U.S. Department of Veterans Affairs, 2019).

In response to the troubling trend of increased rates of veteran suicide, there has been considerable scientific investment in identifying and mitigating suicide risk factors in this population. To date, research suggests that veterans may be at a uniquely high risk for suicide due to the high prevalence and co-occurrence of several risk factors for suicide. For example, traumatic brain injuries and chronic pain are associated with heightened suicide risk (Ashrafioun et al., 2019; Hostetter et al., 2019), and both are more common among veterans relative to the general population (McCarthy et al., 2015; Spelman et al., 2012). Moreover, veterans are more likely to have access to firearms (Cleveland et al., 2017) and are more likely to act on suicidal thoughts than non-veterans (Sher et al., 2012). While these risk factors tend to be predictive of suicidal behaviors, it bears noting there is no universal path to suicide, and relatedly, no universally effective suicide prevention strategy (U.S. Department of Veterans Affairs, 2019). Each veteran will present with their own set of unique risk factors, and treatment should be individualized with sensitivity to the sociocultural context in which they live. Given the complex nature of veteran suicide risk, it is imperative that community-based providers are equipped with evidence-based approaches to identifying and managing such risk among this population.

While there is variation in the probability of veterans receiving community-based care, there is a growing need for community providers to be knowledgeable regarding evidence-based approaches for identifying, managing, and preventing suicide risk among veterans. Younger veterans both utilize VHA care and die by suicide at higher rates compared to other cohorts (Office of Suicide Prevention, 2016). Despite this VHA care utilization, younger veterans tend to believe that VHA care is for older and sicker patients, thus discouraging them from seeking VHA care (Tanielian & Jaycox, 2008). Further, providers need to be aware of the unique military culture veterans are a part of, and the values and norms that shape how they communicate and interact with others; namely, honor, integrity, and commitment (Coll et al., 2011). Veterans who recently served tend to be adapted to a life with rigid structure, regimentation, and conformity, as well as frequent family separations and household relocations (Hall, 2011). Thus, many veterans struggle returning to civilian life, faced with more autonomy and less connection to a community. Understanding this important cultural shift is imperative for community providers so they can offer informed suicide risk care. Accordingly, the VA's National Strategy for Preventing Veteran Suicide (2018) emphasizes the need for community provider knowledge of the VA/DoD Clinical Practice Guidelines (Department of Veterans Affairs & Department of Defense, 2019) for veteran suicide prevention.

This chapter will seek to enhance community providers' understanding of evidence-based approaches to preventing veteran suicide. To do so, we will describe best practices for suicide prevention, as informed by the VA/DoD CPG (Department of Veterans Affairs & Department of Defense, 2019), as well as additional evidence-based and -informed best practices. We will focus primarily on suicide risk identification, evaluation, stratification, and management.

Suicide Risk Identification, Evaluation, Stratification, and Management

Screening, evaluating, stratifying, and managing suicide risk are critical components of any evidence-based suicide prevention strategy. Each of these components should be achieved using principles of patient-centered care, which emphasizes aligning treatment with patient needs and preferences (Robinson et al., & Dearing, 2008). Patient-centered care is best achieved using shared decision making. Shared decision making is the collaborative process between clinicians and patients, facilitated by clinicians' provision of accurate and ample information to the patient, that enables patients to make informed decisions about their care (Department of Veterans Affairs & Department of Defense, 2019). Suicide prevention should also be addressed using a multidisciplinary approach, allowing the care team to evaluate and manage diverse comorbidities to ensure greater coverage of suicide risk factors (Department of Veterans Affairs & Department of Defense, 2019). A suicide prevention approach that reflects the previously mentioned principles increases the likelihood of success by effectively capturing a complete picture of a patient's history and current suicidality, thus informing the best care plan for their needs. Sources and links for more in-depth information about patient-centered care and shared decision making will be provided at the end of this chapter.

In general, suicide prevention strategies in community-based healthcare settings should include suicide risk: (1) screening; (2) evaluation; and, (3) stratification and management to address relevant acute and chronic factors. See Figures **17-1 through 17-5** for an overview of the screening, evaluation, and risk stratification and management processes from the Veterans Affairs/Department of Defense CPG (Department of Veterans Affairs & Department of Defense, 2019).

Suicide Risk Screening

Suicidal ideation is a robust predictor of both chronic and acute suicide risk (Britton et al., & Conner, 2012; Brown et al., 2000), making universal screening procedures designed to detect suicidal ideation a critical component of veteran suicide prevention efforts. However, screening can be challenging because many veterans at risk of suicide are not engaged in mental health care treatment, and primary care physicians do not frequently screen for suicide as part of the standard of care, even when a patient is diagnosed with depression (McDowell et al., 2011). Studies have found that only 32–45.2% of individuals who died by suicide received any type of mental health care within a year prior to their deaths (Ahmedani et al., 2014; Luoma et al., 2002). However, most individuals who die by suicide received some type of non–mental health care within a year of their deaths. In a 2015 retrospective review of over 22,000 suicide attempts, Ahmedani et al. (2015) found that 38% of individuals who attempted suicide had been seen by a healthcare provider in the week prior. That number increased to 95% when they examined the year before the suicide attempt. These findings underscore the importance of universal suicide risk screening, regardless of clinical setting and patient population.

The Columbia-Suicide Severity Rating Scale Screener (C-SSRS) is recommended as a universal screening tool for suicide risk identification (Department of Veterans Affairs & Department of Defense, 2019; Viguera et al., 2015). The C-SSRS is an evidence-based measure and is widely used due to its ability to detect the nature of risk (e.g., the presence of suicidal intent and/or a plan) with an acceptable degree of specificity (Viguera et al., 2015). It has good convergent and divergent validity as well as high interrater reliability (Mundt et al., 2010; Posner et al., 2011). Posner et al. (2011) also found that the C-SSRS demonstrated sensitivity to detecting change in suicidal behavior over time. Importantly, studies of civilian (Mundt et al., 2010) and veteran populations (Matarazzo, Brown, et al., 2019) support its utility in identifying risk for future suicide attempts.

There exist common misconceptions regarding the safety and feasibility of universal screening for suicide. A common concern among clinicians and institutional review boards is that universal suicide screening may increase suicidal ideation in patients (Dazzi et al., 2014). However, this concern lacks supporting evidence, as several studies examining the effects of repeated suicide screening over time have found no iatrogenic effects of screening protocols (Harris & Goh, 2017; Mathias et al., 2012). Indeed, these studies observed a decrease in suicidal ideation resulting from the screening procedures. Similarly, a recent meta-analysis of 13 studies found that suicide screening did not increase suicidality, and that universal screening for suicide risk is appropriate (DeCou & Schumann, 2018).

Concerns regarding the feasibility of implementing universal screening procedures similarly lack evidence. In 2018, two research teams studied the implementation of the C-SSRS Screener at Parkland Health and Hospital System in Dallas, Texas, a safety-net hospital system serving several surrounding counties. Roaten et al. (2018) observed 328,064 suicide screens and found that screening procedures did not overwhelm the system's resources. Similarly, Imran et al. (2018) found that only 4% screened positive for suicide risk, and because of the relatively low rate of positive screens, universal screening using the C-SSRS was feasible and manageable at a system level.

See **Figure 17-1** for an algorithm that illustrates a best practice for suicide risk screening. This algorithm can be used in conjunction with clinical judgment to assist

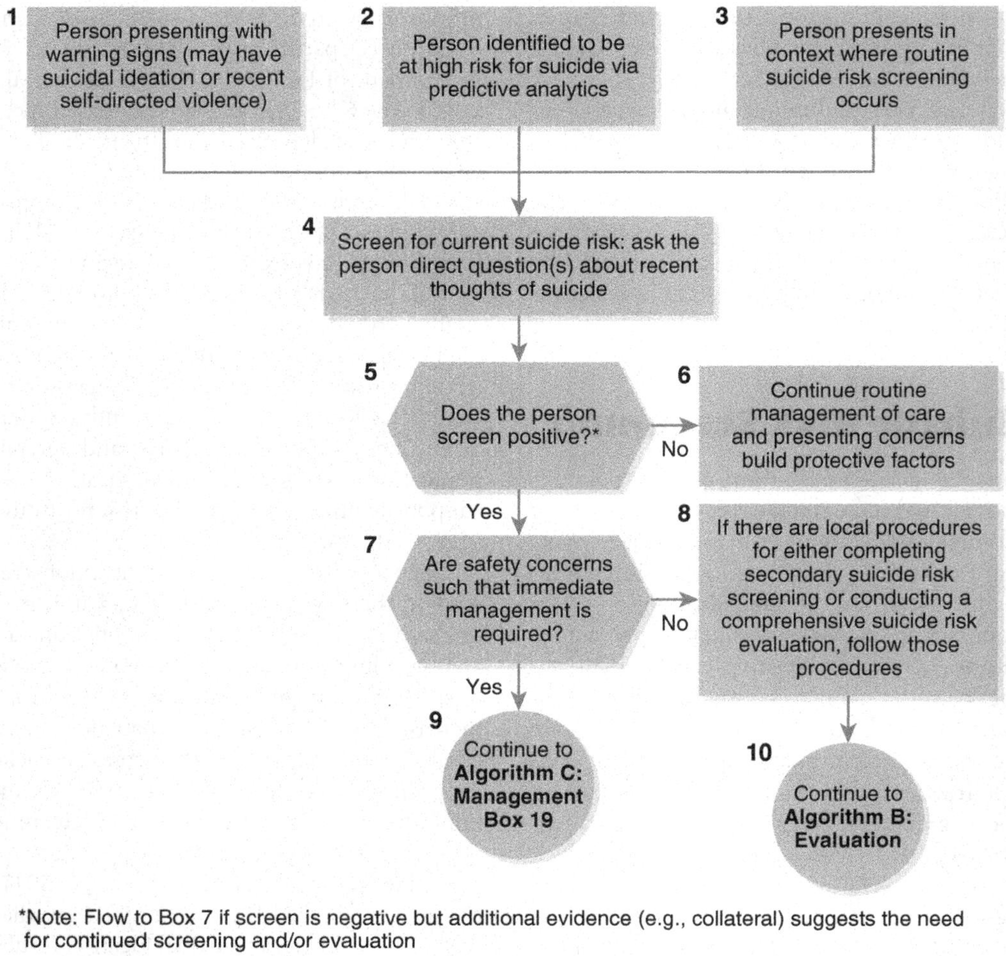

Figure 17-1 Algorithm A: Clinical algorithm illustrating the process of suicide risk screening.

Department of Veterans Affairs and Department of Defense. (2019). *VA/DoD clinical practice guideline for the assessment and management of patients at risk for suicide*. Author. https://www.healthquality.va.gov/guidelines/MH/srb/VADoDSuicideRiskFullCPGFinal5088212019.pdf

clinical decision making. The referenced Algorithm B and Algorithm C are included later in this chapter.

Evaluation of Suicide Risk

In the event of a positive screening for suicidal ideation or intent, a more complete evaluation is recommended (Department of Veterans Affairs & Department of Defense, 2019). Risk evaluation is a highly individualized and collaborative effort that utilizes an assessment tool and clinical interview to inform and facilitate appropriate risk management (Department of Veterans Affairs & Department of Defense, 2019). A comprehensive evaluation is critical to fully assess the presence of specific risk factors such as suicidal ideation, history of self-directed violence (SDV), psychiatric conditions, access to lethal means, individual warning signs of crisis (e.g., anger, increased isolation, recklessness), and protective factors. Collecting information regarding the presence of the above factors informs clinicians' appraisal of the nature of patients' risk (e.g., severity or chronicity). However, knowledge of the presence of suicide-related factors alone is insufficient for adequately informing the clinician of suicide risk. Individual history and needs should be central to suicide risk evaluation and management. Many veterans will have several compounding risk factors, each of which will affect individuals differently.

What follows is a discussion of salient predictors of suicidal behavior for inclusion in risk evaluations for the veteran population, including a description of recommended practices for stratifying risk to inform subsequent treatment. This discussion is not intended as an exhaustive list of factors relevant to suicide risk. Rather, we present those factors with the strongest supportive evidence and those most germane to the veteran population.

Demographic Characteristics

Risk factors among veterans often mirror those of non-veterans. For instance, sex and age contribute to suicide risk among both the general (National Institute of Mental Health, 2019) and veteran population (U.S. Department of Veterans Affairs, 2019). Male veterans are at an increased risk for suicide, with an age-adjusted suicide rate of 39.1 per 100,000, compared to 16.8 per 100,000 among female veterans. These numbers show that, among veterans, men are more than twice as likely to die by suicide, as are women. However, women veterans are also at an increased risk, and die by suicide 2.2 times more often than non-veteran women (U.S. Department of Veterans Affairs, 2019). With respect to age, veterans aged 18–34 are at the highest risk for suicide with a suicide rate of 44.5 per 100,000 in 2017. However, the absolute number of suicide deaths was the highest among veterans aged 55–74, representing 38% of all veteran suicides in 2017 (U.S. Department of Veterans Affairs, 2019).

History of SDV Thoughts and Behaviors

It is critical that an evaluation of suicide risk includes an assessment of recent SDV, prior suicide attempts, and current suicidal ideation, all of which are robust predictors of suicide (Franklin et al., 2017; Nock et al., 2018). Non-suicidal self-injury (NSSI), where one injures oneself without intent to die (e.g., cutting, burning), is an example of SDV strongly associated with suicide risk (Baer et al., 2018). Andover and Gibb (2010) found that among psychiatric inpatients, a history of NSSI was more strongly linked with suicide attempts than other risk factors such as depressive symptoms and hopelessness. They also found that those with a history of both NSSI and suicide attempts reported greater lethal intent for their most severe attempt (Andover & Gibb, 2010). Further, a study conducted by Turner et al. (2019) found a 6.3% lifetime prevalence of NSSI among active-duty soldiers, and that soldiers with NSSI were more likely to have attempted suicide multiple times.

A history of suicidal thoughts and behaviors also tends to be predictive of future suicidality (Park et al., 2017) and thus should also be included in evaluations of suicide risk. Moreover, prior suicide attempts are a strong predictor of death by suicide, primarily when the nature of the index attempt (i.e., the first lifetime suicide attempt needing medical attention) is considered (Bostwick et al., 2016). Fedyszyn et al. (2016) found that those who were hospitalized for an index attempt of hanging or strangling were at increased risk for suicide compared to other attempts such as self-poisoning and cutting. Suicide risk evaluations should thus consider the occurrence of, and circumstances surrounding, a prior suicide attempt. This is particularly relevant for the veteran population, who attempt suicide with more lethal means (e.g., firearms) (Anglemyer et al., 2014).

Psychiatric Conditions and Symptoms

Nonetheless, psychiatric history is strongly connected with suicide risk. For example, prior psychiatric hospitalization is a particularly strong predictor of risk for suicide and should be included in comprehensive risk evaluations. Franklin et al. (2017) found that prior psychiatric hospitalization was the greatest overall predictor of suicide, even when compared to robust suicide risk factors such as history of suicide attempts and suicidal ideation.

Similarly, the presence of psychiatric conditions tends to be predictive of suicidal behaviors. Mood disorders, such as major depressive disorder (MDD) and bipolar disorder, are associated with higher suicide risk (Ilgen et al., 2016; Lee et al., 2018; Yoshimasu et al., 2008). Anxiety and anxiety sensitivity (i.e., anxiety-related sensations) are also predictors of both suicidal ideation and suicide attempts (Franklin et al., 2017; Stanley et al., 2018). Psychosis and related disorders are also significantly associated with suicidal ideation and attempts, with positive psychotic symptoms (e.g., hallucinations, delusions) consistently contributing to the risk (Huang et al., 2018). For instance, studies report patients with schizophrenia die by suicide more than eight times more often than the general population, with up to 50% of individuals with this condition experiencing suicidal ideation and attempting suicide at some point in their lifetime (Kasckow et al., 2011). Personality disorders may also pose a risk for suicidal behaviors. In particular, patients with borderline personality disorder (BPD) are at heightened risk for suicide; about 10% of individuals with a BPD diagnosis die by suicide, and about 75% report lifetime suicide attempts (Black et al., 2004). Last, substance use disorders (SUDs) are significantly linked to suicide risk, especially among veterans (Bohnert et al., 2017; Lee et al., 2018). Symptoms associated with psychiatric diagnoses may sometimes occur independent of a formal psychiatric diagnosis but may nonetheless increase suicide risk. For example, hopelessness, depressed mood, anxiety, insomnia, problem-solving difficulties, agitation, and rumination increase suicide risk (Franklin et al., 2017; Glenn et al., 2018), and should also be considered in risk evaluations. Risk evaluations should also account for the co-morbidity of multiple psychiatric conditions because the co-occurrence of such conditions may exacerbate risk for suicide in the veteran population. For example, patients with BPD and comorbid MDD or SUDs are at especially high risk for suicide (Black et al., 2004). Additionally, comorbid PTSD and depression are common among the veteran population, and their co-occurrence has been linked to suicidal behaviors (Kimbrel et al., 2016).

Physical Health Conditions

Additionally, certain physical health conditions may also place veterans at increased risk for suicide, namely moderate to severe traumatic brain injuries (TBIs) (Hostetter et al., 2019; McCarthy et al., 2015). TBIs are prevalent among veterans, with over 185,000 veterans with TBI receiving VHA care (Whiteneck et al., 2015). Those with a TBI have more than two times the suicide risk than those who do not have a history of TBI (Hostetter et al., 2019). Further, one study found that nearly 90% of veterans with a TBI had a co-occurring psychiatric diagnosis (e.g., PTSD), and 70% had a pain diagnosis (Taylor et al., 2012); both of these conditions are associated with suicide risk (Ashrafioun et al., 2019; Ilgen et al., 2010). These findings emphasize the patterns of comorbid health conditions that veterans often face, which put them at an alarmingly high risk for suicide.

Pain is a prevalent and robust risk factor for suicidal behavior among veterans, and thus warrants attention during evaluation of suicide risk. About two-thirds of veterans report feeling bodily pain, and veterans are much more likely to experience severe pain than non-veterans (Nahin, 2017). Veterans' experience of pain also tends to be more long-lasting; combat veterans are more likely to develop chronic pain conditions (i.e., pain lasting more than 12 weeks) than the general population (Spelman et al., 2012). In turn, bodily pain heightens veterans' risk for suicidality; a recent study of over 220,000 veterans revealed that, even after adjusting for other factors like past suicide attempts and opioid prescriptions, pain increased risk for suicide (Ashrafioun et al., 2019). Other studies have linked chronic pain with higher rates of suicidal ideation and suicide attempts (Edwards et al., 2006; Smith et al., 2004). Evidence indicates that potential mechanisms through which bodily pain increases suicidality include hopelessness, helplessness (Tang & Crane, 2006), and catastrophic thinking (Legarreta et al., 2018).

Biopsychosocial Stressors

Biopsychosocial stressors heighten risk for suicide and should also be included in suicide risk evaluations. Stressors like exposure to suicide, homelessness, job loss, loss of a relationship (e.g., death, divorce), and traumatic exposure (e.g., witnessing death of a family member) can all place veterans at increased risk for suicide (Franklin et al., 2017; Hom et al., 2017; Kimbrel et al., 2016). Such stressors may put veterans at risk for suicide, and highlight the importance of assessing person-specific, co-occurring stressors (Hom et al., 2017; Kimerling et al., 2016).

Deployment and Combat-Related Experiences

The evidence underlying the relationship between combat deployments and suicidality is mixed, but given that deployment experiences are especially germane to the veteran population, they warrant discussion. In a retrospective study of veteran mortality, Kang et al. (2015) found that veterans had a significantly higher risk of suicide compared to the general U.S. adult population. Surprisingly, they also found that veterans who had deployed to a war zone were at a lower risk of suicide (41% higher than the general population) than veterans who never deployed (61% higher than the general population). Additionally, Ursano et al. (2016) found that among enlisted soldiers who had previously attempted suicide, over 60% had never been deployed. However, recent research suggests that certain combat experiences (e.g., witnessing death or serious injury) heighten veterans' risk for suicide (Nichter et al., 2020). While further research is needed, the specific nature of potential combat experiences may be worthy of inclusion in a comprehensive evaluation of veteran suicide risk.

Access to Lethal Means

One of the most crucial suicide risk factors to assess for is access to lethal means for suicide (e.g., firearms). Access to firearms is associated with increased risk of death by suicide and is especially relevant among the veteran population (Anglemyer et al., 2014). A 2016 systematic review of nearly 1,800 studies found that having firearms in the home was correlated with significantly higher rates of suicide (Zalsman et al., 2016). Nearly half of all veterans own at least one firearm, with 33% storing one firearm loaded, and unlocked (Cleveland et al., 2017; Simonetti et al., 2018). Further, firearms are the most used means of suicide among veterans, with over 70% of male and 43% of female veterans suicides occurring by firearm (U.S. Department of Veterans Affairs, 2019).

Suicide by poisoning, which includes overdose of medications, is also a common method among veterans, accounting for nearly 10% of male and almost 30% of female veteran suicides (U.S. Department of Veterans Affairs, 2019). Poisoning by medications is particularly pertinent considering the prevalence of pain in the veteran population. While the VA has successfully decreased prescription opioid use by 64% over the past several years, there are still nearly a quarter million veterans prescribed opiates (U.S. Department of Veterans Affairs, 2019). A recent VA study found that increased doses of opioids were associated with increased suicide risk, not just from intentional overdoses but from all methods (Ilgen et al., 2016). Those with opioid use disorder (OUD) are at even greater risk; those with OUD are up to 13 times more likely to die by suicide than those without OUD (Wilcox et al., 2004).

Warning Signs

Warning signs are observable changes in a patient's thoughts or behaviors that may indicate higher intent to die by suicide in the short-term (Rudd, 2008; Rudd et al., 2006). Unlike risk factors that may persist over a patient's lifetime (e.g., psychiatric diagnosis, history of SDV), warning signs are episodic, fluctuate, and can help both the patient and the clinician identify when the patient is at elevated risk for suicide (Rudd et al., 2006). Warning signs are helpful in suicide risk evaluation because they can help the clinician determine when a patient is at more imminent risk. This is often done by reviewing thoughts and behaviors that were exhibited before past episodes of suicidal ideation or behavior. Salient warning signs are: (1) speaking or writing about suicide; (2) seeking access to lethal means (e.g., buying a gun or collecting pills); and (3) suicide preparatory behavior (e.g., giving away valuables or writing a suicide note) (Department of Veterans Affairs & Department of Defense, 2019). Other examples of warning signs, which may vary between patients, include increased hopelessness; disengagement from treatment; increased anger or aggression; increased social isolation; recklessness; and drastic changes in sleep or appetite (Rudd, 2008; Rudd et al., 2006). Clinicians and patients should collaboratively identify individual warning signs and include them in any safety plan.

Protective Factors

Last, there is emerging, yet limited evidence that certain factors may protect against suicidal behavior. As such, a suicide risk evaluation should include the collaborative identification of protective factors such as social support, coping skills, reasons for living, and spiritual or religious beliefs (Department of Veterans Affairs & Department of Defense, 2019). While the presence of protective factors may not completely eliminate risk for suicide, a patient's protective resources may help mitigate the influence of suicide risk factors. For example, individuals with high levels of social support, whether from friends or relatives, may be almost one-third less likely to attempt suicide than those with low levels of social support (Kleiman & Liu, 2013). Among patients with MDD, those who had more reasons for living (e.g., feeling responsible for family) and those who possessed greater coping skills were less likely to attempt suicide than those with fewer reasons for living and those with lesser coping skills (Malone et al., 2000). Religious affiliation is also associated with lower levels of suicidal behaviors and higher levels of moral objection to suicide, while those without religious affiliation report more lifetime suicide attempts (Dervic et al., 2005). Assessing the presence of relevant protective factors among veterans can assist in discerning a comprehensive understanding of suicide risk.

Risk Stratification

Upon completion of a comprehensive suicide-risk evaluation, a clinician may complete a risk stratification, which categorizes level of risk according to the severity and chronicity of risk (Wortzel et al., 2013). Though risk stratification should not be the only element of a clinical assessment, it can help inform risk mitigation strategies and treatment options for suicidal behavior. Risk stratification is also useful because it provides clinicians with a common language with which they can consider and communicate risk (Department of Veterans Affairs & Department of Defense, 2019). While definitive evidence in support of risk stratification remains elusive, this lack of support may be explained by methodological limitations rather than a lack of clinical benefit (Department of Veterans Affairs & Department of Defense, 2019). As such, risk stratification is still considered best practice for suicide prevention (Department of Veterans Affairs & Department of Defense, 2019).

Suicide risk is stratified according to two criteria: (1) acute or chronic risk; and (2) low, intermediate, or high risk. Patients with low-acute risk typically present with suicidal ideation but with no intent or plan to die by suicide. Those with low-chronic risk may have mental illness or SUD but will typically have no history of SDV or suicidal ideation. Both subgroups of low-risk patients may be effectively treated in outpatient mental health settings or by primary care providers, depending on individual risk factors and coping skills. Patients with high-acute risk express suicidal ideation with a plan and intent to die. These patients are generally unable to keep themselves safe and often require hospitalization until they are stabilized. In contrast, individuals with high-chronic risk may have chronic mental or physical illnesses, histories of SDV, and/or unstable relationships. They are at risk for becoming high-acute risk and often require routine mental health visits to encourage coping skills, develop a safety plan, and manage risk factors. Those considered to be at intermediate risk, whether acute or chronic, share many features of those at high risk but generally have more protective factors. Those at intermediate-chronic risk may respond well to outpatient mental health appointments and a safety plan, while patients at intermediate-acute risk may, in some circumstances, require hospitalization if they are not able to independently engage in strategies to maintain safety. As may be apparent from the previous discussion, the stratification of suicide risk can help inform risk mitigation strategies and treatment options for suicidal behavior. See **Figures 17-2** and **17-3** for more specific guidance on risk stratification.

See **Figure 17-4** for an algorithm depicting suicide risk evaluation steps, which includes a collaborative risk evaluation and risk stratification completed by the provider. This algorithm can be used to help the clinician determine next steps. The referenced Algorithm C is included later in this chapter.

Suicide Risk Management

Depending on the level of risk determined through risk evaluation and stratification, there are several available treatments that may mitigate suicide risk. Options include both non-pharmacologic as well as pharmacologic treatments, and vary according to setting

ACUTE Therapeutic Risk Management – ***Risk Stratification Table*** ROCKY MOUNTAIN MIRECC

HIGH CHRONIC RISK

Essential Features

- **Suicidal ideation with intent to die by suicide**
- **Inability to maintain safety independent external support/help**

Common Warning Signs

- A plan for suicide
- Recent attempt and/or ongoing preparatory behaviors
- Acute major mental illness (e.g., MD episode, acute mania, acute psychosis, recent/current drug relapse)
- Exacerbation of personality disorder (e.g., increased borderline symptomatology)

Common Risk Factors

- Access to means
- Acute psychosocial stressors (e.g., job loss, relationship dissolution, relapse on alcohol)

Action

Typically requires psychiatric hospitalization to maintain safety and aggressively target modifiable factors.

These individuals need to be directly observed until on a secure unit and kept in an environment with limited access to lethal means (e.g., keep away from sharps, cord/tubing, toxic substances).

During hospitalization co-occurring psychiatric symptoms should also be addressed.

INTERMEDIATE ACUTE RISK

Essential Features

- **Suicide ideation to die by suicide**
- **Ability to maintain safety, independent of external support/help**

These individuals may present similarly to those at high acute risk, sharing many of the features. The only difference may be lack of intent, based upon an identified reason for living (e.g., children), and ability to abide by a safety plan and maintain their own safety. Preparatory behaviors are likely to be absent.

Action

Consider psychiatric hospitalization, if related factors driving risk are responsive to inpatient treatment (e.g., acute psychosis).

Outpatient management of suicidal thoughts and/or behaviors should be intensive and include:

- Frequent contact,
- Regular re-assessment of risk, and
- A well-articulated safety plan

Mental health treatment should also address co-occurring psychiatric symptoms.

LOW ACUTE RISK

Essential Features

- **No current suicidal intent AND**
- **No specific and current suicidal plan AND**
- **No preparatory behaviors AND**
- **Collective high confidence**y (e.g., patient, care provider, family member) in the ability of the patient to independently maintain safety

Individuals may have suicidal ideation, but it will be **with little or no intent or specific current plan.** If a plan is present, the plan is general and/or vague, and without any associated preparatory behaviors (e.g., "I'd shoot myself if things got bad enough, but I don't have a gun"). These patients will be capable of engaging appropriate coping strategies, and willing and able to utilize a safety plan in a crisis situation.

Action

Can be managed in primary care.

Outpatient mental health treatment may also be indicated, particularly if suicidal ideation and psychiatric symptoms are co-occurring.

*Overall level of individual risk may be increased or decreased based upon warning signs, risk factors and **protective factors**

Figure 17-2 Risk Stratification Table—Acute Risk

Rocky Mountain MIRECC, VA Office of Mental Health and Suicide Prevention, & VA Office of Emergency Medicine. (2020). *Safety planning in the emergency department.*. https://www.mirecc.va.gov/visn19/trm

CHRONIC Therapeutic Risk Management – *Risk Stratification Table*

ROCKY MOUNTAIN MIRECC

HIGH CHRONIC RISK

Essential Features

Common Warning sign

- Chronic Suicidal ideation

Common Risk Factors

- Chronic major mental illness and/or personality disorder
- History of prior suicide attempt(s)
- History of substance abuse/dependence
- Chronic pain
- Chronic medical condition'
- Limited coping skills
- Unstable or turbulent psychosocial status (e.g., unstable housing, erratic relationship, marginal employment)
- Limited ability to identify reasons for living

Action

These individual are considered to be at chronic risk for becoming acutely suicidal, often in the context of unpredictable situational contingencies (e.g., job loss, loss of relationships, and relapse on drugs).

These individuals typically require:

- routine mental health follow-up
- a well-articulated safety plan, including means safety (e.g., no access to guns, limited medication supply)
- routine suicide risk screening
- coping skills building
- management of co-occurring psychiatric symptoms

INTERMEDIATE CHRONIC RISK

Essential Features

These individuals may feature similar chronicity as those at high chronic risk with respect to psychiatric, substance abuse, medical and painful conditions.

Protective factors, coping skill, reason for living, and relative psychosocial stability suggest enhances ability to endure future crisis without resorting to self-directed violence.

Action

These individuals typically require:

- routine mental health care to optimize psychiatric condition and maintain/enhance coping skills and protective factors.
- a well articulated safety plan, including means safety (e.g., no access to guns, limited medication supply)
- management of co-occurring psychiatric symptoms

LOW CHRONIC RISK

Essential Features

These individuals may range from persons with no or little in the way of mental health or substance abuse problems, to persons with significant mental illness that is associated with relatively abundant strengths/resources.

Stressors historically have typically been endured absent suicidal ideation.

The following factors will generally be missing

- history of self-directed violence
- chronic suicidal ideation
- tendency towards being highly impulsive
- risky behaviors
- marginal psychosocial functioning

Action

Appropriate for mental health care on an as needed basis, some may be managed in primary care settings. Others may require mental health follow-up to continue successful treatments.

Figure 17-3 Risk Stratification Table—Chronic Risk

Rocky Mountain MIRECC, VA Office of Mental Health and Suicide Prevention, & VA Office of Emergency Medicine. (2020). *Safety planning in the emergency department.* https://www.mirecc.va.gov/visn19/trm

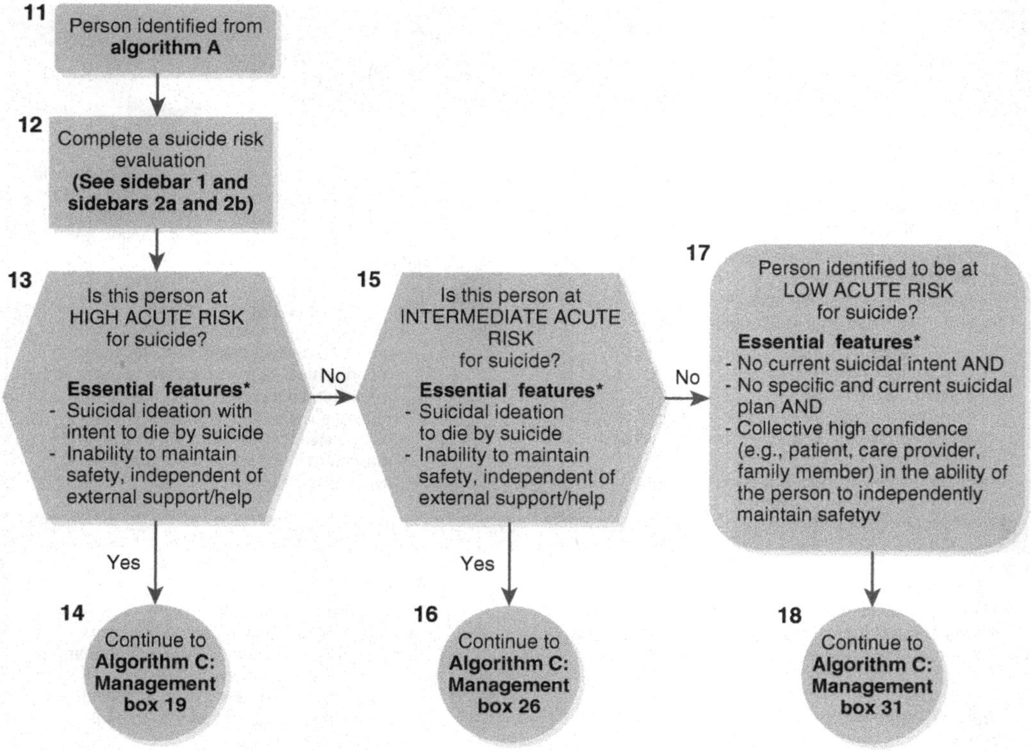

Figure 17-4 Algorithm B: Clinical algorithm illustrating the evaluation of suicide risk

Department of Veterans Affairs and Department of Defense. (2019). *VA/DoD clinical practice guideline for the assessment and management of patients at risk for suicide.* Author. https://www.healthquality.va.gov/guidelines/MH/srb/VADoDSuicideRiskFullCPGFinal5088212019.pdf

(e.g., post-acute care) and modality (e.g., technology-based modalities). Many patients may benefit from a combination of treatments and appropriate follow-up. Treatments should be selected collaboratively between providers and patients and should be informed by veterans' values and preferences (Department of Veterans Affairs & Department of Defense, 2019). What follows is a summary of available evidence-based approaches for suicide risk mitigation in the veteran population that should be considered in any community-based healthcare setting. Additional resources for suicide risk assessment and management are provided later for further information and review.

Non-pharmacologic Treatments

Safety Planning Interventions

Safety plans are a collaborative effort between patients and the provider, during which they review recent suicidal thoughts or behavior and identify individual warning signs of crisis (Department of Veterans Affairs & Department of Defense, 2019). Additionally, patients and clinicians identify self-management and coping skills they can use when needed (e.g., go for a walk, watch a favorite TV show); the availability of social support systems (e.g., specific family members or friends); reasons for living (e.g., children, things to look forward to); crisis resources (e.g., therapist; crisis and suicide hotlines); and strategies to limit access to lethal means like firearms or medications (Department of Veterans Affairs & Department of Defense, 2019).

Research supports the effectiveness of safety planning interventions in reducing suicidal behavior and in increasing follow-up treatment after suicidal behavior. For example, researchers at the VA compared a safety planning intervention combined with structured outreach to treatment as usual among veterans admitted to the VHA Emergency Department with suicide-related concerns (Stanley et al., 2018). They found that veterans who received the safety planning intervention were about half as likely to exhibit suicidal behaviors and about twice as likely to attend a mental health follow-up visit as those in the control group. Based on this research, the VA implemented the Safety Planning in the Emergency Department (SPED) initiative. SPED mandates that patients who are being discharged from the emergency department and are determined to be at intermediate or high acute or chronic risk should receive a safety planning intervention as well as follow-up outreach from VA staff (Rocky Mountain MIRECC, VA Office of Mental Health and Suicide Prevention, & VA Office of Emergency Medicine, 2020).

Cognitive Behavioral Therapy for Suicide Prevention (CBT-SP)

Cognitive Behavioral Therapy for Suicide Prevention (CBT-SP) is a type of structured psychotherapy that tailors the fundamental principles of Cognitive Behavioral Therapy (CBT) to those at risk for suicide (Bryan, 2019). CBT-SP sessions are organized sequentially and are designed to help patients challenge negative thinking patterns and learn coping skills (Department of Veterans Affairs & Department of Defense, 2019). Clinicians may help suicidal patients develop a safety plan and identify thoughts and feelings present during suicidal behaviors, as well as conditions that precipitate these thoughts (Department of Veterans Affairs & Department of Defense, 2019). Clinicians then help the patient develop strategies to mitigate these thoughts and feelings (Department of Veterans Affairs & Department of Defense, 2019). Importantly, CBT is relatively brief; patients usually receive 12 sessions or fewer (Department of Veterans Affairs & Department of Defense, 2019), which can be easier to implement than other longer recommended treatments. The current body of evidence indicates that CBT-SP reduces suicide-related outcomes among patients with a recent history of suicidal behaviors more than treatment-as-usual (Bryan, 2019). For instance, a 2005 randomized control trial (RCT) that enrolled patients within 48 hours of a suicide attempt found that those who received CBT were 50% less likely to re-attempt suicide than those in the control group (Brown et al., 2005). Another RCT in active duty soldiers with recent suicidality found that soldiers receiving CBT-SP were 60% less likely to attempt suicide than those in the control group (Rudd et al., 2015).

Problem-Solving Therapy

Problem-Solving Therapy (PST) is a type of CBT that focuses on the development of problem-solving skills to help patients cope with life stressors (Department of Veterans Affairs & Department of Defense, 2019). There is evidence that PST may be a useful treatment in patients who have a history of repeated SDV. A large randomized trial in New Zealand found that PST reduced SDV in those who had a history of repeated SDV by nearly 40% within the one-year follow-up period compared to the control group (Hatcher et al., 2011). Moreover, a 2001 meta-analysis of PST in patients with a history of SDV found significant reductions in hopelessness and depression compared to the control group (Townsend et al., 2001). Emerging evidence indicates that PST may be beneficial to other populations at risk for suicide. For example, Brenner et al. (2018) observed reductions in hopelessness after veterans with TBI received Window to Hope, a group therapy intervention based on principles of PST.

Pharmacologic Treatments

Pharmacological agents may also help mitigate suicide risk. A growing body of literature suggests that ketamine may be effective in reducing suicidal behaviors. A recent meta-analysis (Wilkinson et al., 2018) revealed that those receiving ketamine experienced rapid reductions in suicidal thoughts. In a recent study of patients with MDD and suicidal ideation, receipt of ketamine similarly reduced depressive symptoms and suicidal thoughts, with effects exhibiting promising durability (i.e., up to six weeks) (Grunebaum et al., 2018). Ample research has also been conducted on the use of lithium in patients with mood disorders. Meta-analytic studies of patients with mood disorders (Baldessarini et al., 2006; Cipriani et al., 2013) reveal that lithium reduces suicide risk and deaths compared to those receiving a placebo. Both ketamine and lithium may result in serious side effects, and their use should be weighed against potential benefits and patient preferences, while taking precautions to prevent overdose (Department of Veterans Affairs & Department of Defense, 2019).

Treatment Options for Suicidal Behavior in Individuals with Specific Psychiatric Conditions

Evidence indicates that suicide risk among patients with certain psychiatric conditions may be amenable to specific treatments. For example, Dialectical Behavior Therapy (DBT) has demonstrated promising results among patients with BPD. DBT is a type of CBT, which builds on the foundations of CBT by adding mindfulness principles and skills development to improve emotional regulation and interpersonal relationships (Department of Veterans Affairs & Department of Defense, 2019). DBT was developed to treat patients with Borderline Personality Disorder (BPD), who, as discussed earlier, are at high risk for suicidal behavior (Department of Veterans Affairs & Department of Defense, 2019). Emerging evidence indicates that implementing DBT among patients with BPD results in significant reductions of SDV (Hawton et al., 2016; Mann et al., 2005; McMain et al., 2017). Further, clozapine may also be an effective pharmacological treatment for suicide risk mitigation in patients with schizophrenia. A meta-analysis found that long-term treatment using clozapine was more effective at reducing suicide attempts and deaths among patients with schizophrenia than other treatments (Hennen & Baldessarini, 2005). While there may be serious adverse health consequences of clozapine, clozapine should be considered for patients with schizophrenia and suicidal behaviors when other treatments have been ineffective (Department of Veterans Affairs & Department of Defense, 2019).

Post-Acute Care

Following acute inpatient treatment for suicidal behaviors, evidence supports the efficacy of implementing several post-acute treatments for suicide risk as adjunctive treatments in addition to usual care. First, caring communications, or postcards and letters sent to patients following psychiatric hospitalizations for suicidality, have promising effects. Studies suggest that multiple communications sent at set intervals can help reduce suicidal ideation and attempts (Hassanian-Moghaddam et al., 2017; Motto & Bostrom, 2001). The delivery of frequent communications appears to produce particular benefit; sending a single communication may have no effect on suicidal behavior (Chen et al., 2013). Further, caring communications are a low-cost, adaptable method to assist with reducing subsequent suicidal behavior (Department of Veterans Affairs & Department of Defense, 2019).

Second, offering in-home visits after a suicide attempt to support outpatient care among patients not attending their appointments may be beneficial. For example, Matarazzo et al. (2019) examined the impact of the Home-Based Mental Health Evaluation (HOME) Program, which supports veterans through phone- and home-based contact after a psychiatric hospitalization. They found that veterans in the HOME Program were 1.33 times more likely to engage with treatment and attended 55% more individual appointments compared to those receiving care as usual (Matarazzo, Forster, et al., 2019). Not only did researchers support the efficacy of HOME with respect to treatment adherence, but also patients reported high levels of satisfaction with the program (Matarazzo et al., 2017). These findings are consistent with the research of similar programs delivered to civilian populations (Gibbons et al., & Gibbons 1978; Matarazzo et al., 2017; Van Heeringen et al., 1995), and may be indicated for veterans discharged from community-based inpatient settings.

Third, the World Health Organization Brief Intervention and Contact (WHO BIC) treatment is an effective follow-up tool after a suicide attempt, and consists of a one-hour information session with nine follow-up points, for up to 18 months after discharge (Fleisch-mann et al., 2008). Studies of the efficacy of the WHO BIC indicate that it significantly decreases suicide among those with a history of suicide attempts (Fleischmann et al., 2008; Riblet et al., 2017). While the VA/DoD CPG cautions against the generalizability of the WHO BIC because most studies have been conducted in low- to middle-income countries, the results are encouraging regarding the benefit of longer-term contact upon suicide-related outcomes. Such adjunct care methods, delivered along with usual care, may be effective approaches in reducing veteran suicides in community settings.

Technology-Based Modalities

While current evidence is relatively sparse, technology-based treatment modalities for suicide risk, both user-directed and provider-delivered, offer a promising approach to overcoming treatment barriers such as distance, stigma of arriving in-person to a facility, and rurality (Department of Veterans Affairs & Department of Defense, 2019). Moreover, technology-based approaches can offer patients greater autonomy and access to manage their own treatment, aligning treatment with patient preferences. Crucially, such adjunctive treatments can make it easier for providers to monitor patients' progress and treatment engagement. For example, Beating the Blues (BtB) is a computerized Cognitive Behavioral Therapy (cCBT) intervention designed to treat mild to moderate depression symptoms. BtB has demonstrated acceptability in primary care settings and effectively reduces suicide risk factors such as symptoms of depression and anxiety (Cavanagh et al., 2011; Ormrod et al., 2010). Available studies also support the feasibility and acceptability of technology-based mental health care support, with such options revealing significant improvement in coping abilities (Bush et al., 2017; Kasckow et al., 2016). For example, Bush et al. (2017) developed a phone application called Virtual Hope Box (VHB), where individuals can store personalized content such as pictures and music. Researchers found that the VHB improved one's ability to cope with negative feelings and thoughts, indicating that such interventions may bolster protective resources and mitigate risk for suicide.

Means Safety Counseling

Limiting patients' access to lethal means, such as firearms and medications, may help mitigate death by suicide among at-risk veterans. Means safety counseling is an emerging and promising approach to limiting lethal means access among at-risk populations (Department of Veterans Affairs & Department of Defense, 2019). This intervention is not simply removal of firearms and potentially dangerous medications; rather, it involves clinicians and patients collaborating to identify actions that the patient can take to reduce their risk of suicide (Department of Veterans Affairs & Department of Defense, 2019). Regarding firearms, this might include safely storing guns through the use of gun safes, cabinets, or cases, gunlocks, firing pin removal, and/or voluntary and temporarily transferring firearms to a trusted family member or friend (Department of Veterans Affairs & Department of Defense, 2019). Preliminary studies suggest that safety intervention initiatives, like giving out firearm safety devices, increases the proportion of firearms that are stored safely (Rowhani-Rahbar et al., 2016; Simonetti et al., 2018).

Reducing access to medications may also be helpful in reducing suicide deaths. The VA has initiated the VA Center for Medication Safety (VA MedSAFE), a program designed to prevent adverse effects of medications, including suicide, through tracking high-risk medications, improving safety measures, and delivering community education (U.S. Department of Veterans Affairs, 2020). As part of the MedSAFE program, VHAs now offer receptacles and pre-paid envelopes so patients can return unused and unwanted medications to be disposed of safely. While no research has examined the impact of VA MedSAFE on suicide-related outcomes specifically, research indicates that limiting access to medication can reduce overall death rates, suggesting that such an intervention can similarly assist in prevention of intentional medication overdoses. For instance, one study found that legislation limiting the package size of paracetamol, a non-opioid pain medication, was associated with a significantly lower rate of accidental and intentional overdoses (Hawton et al., 2013). Initiatives designed to limit non-essential access to harmful medications among at-risk veterans may play an important role in reducing suicide risk in this population.

See **Figure 17-5** for an illustration of best practice for suicide-risk management among patients at acute risk. This algorithm can be used in conjunction with other clinical tools to help most effectively treat patients at risk for suicide.

Challenges in Veteran Suicide Prevention

It should be noted that suicide prevention efforts still face many barriers, especially in community settings. First, there is an inherent challenge to providing necessary care to those who do not seek help or disclose suicidal thoughts and behaviors, perhaps to avoid hospitalization or to be discharged from the hospital sooner (Oquendo & Bernanke, 2017). Second, there is often a lack of adequate resources for robust suicide-prevention efforts. For example, training and staff with expertise in suicide-prevention care, especially in emergency departments, are lacking (Asarnow et al., 2017). Healthcare system difficulties such as a lack of financial resources and a shortage of psychiatric staff and inpatient beds also present barriers to suicide care (Asarnow et al., 2017).

Further, while much progress has been made with regard to the development of evidence-based models for suicide risk management, challenges persist (Cramer & Kapusta, 2017). For example, a systematic review by Chan et al. (2016) found that while identifiable suicide risk factors exist (e.g., previous self-harm, suicidal intent), they are common in clinical populations, undermining their utility for identifying at-risk patients. Many in the field argue that a move to a multi-level suicide prevention models would be more effective (Cramer & Kapusta, 2017; van der Feltz-Cornelis et al., 2011). Cramer and Kapusta (2017) advocate for a social-ecological model of suicide risk identification, in which

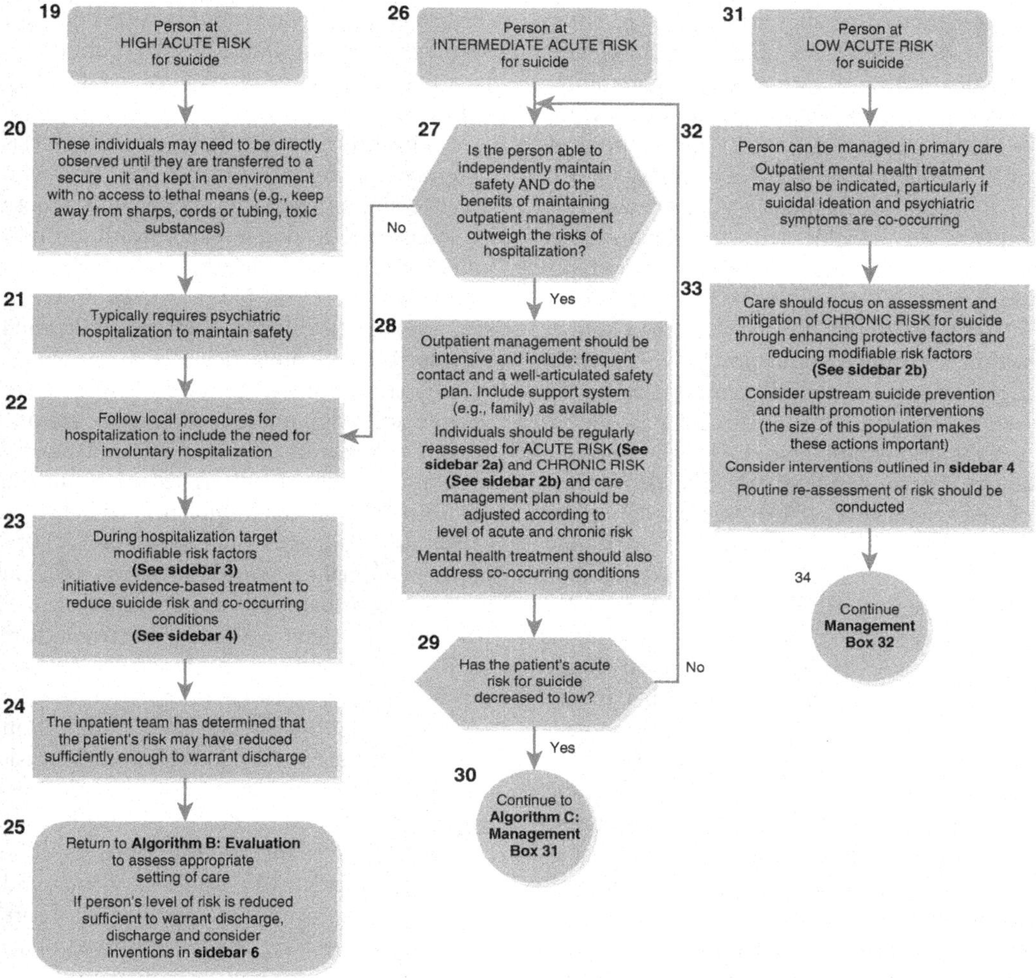

Figure 17-5 Algorithm C: Clinical algorithm illustrating the management of patients at acute risk for suicide

Department of Veterans Affairs and Department of Defense. (2019). *VA/DoD clinical practice guideline for the assessment and management of patients at risk for suicide*. Author. https://www.healthquality.va.gov/guidelines/MH/srb/VADoDSuicideRiskFullCPGFinal5088212019.pdf

four levels of risk should be assessed: societal (e.g., cultural norms, public policy), community (e.g., workplaces, schools, available healthcare providers), relational (e.g., available social support networks, friends and family), and individual (e.g., demographics, attitudes, individual risk factors). They argue that, while several suicide prevention strategies have been identified as effective, they typically address only one or two of these domains at a time, overlooking important contributors to suicide risk (Cramer & Kapusta, 2017). Suicide-risk assessments that attend to all four risk levels may be more successful (Cramer & Kapusta, 2017), and may have important implications for risk mitigation. For example, Hofstra et al. (2020)

suggest innovative approaches capable of targeting multiple levels of risk, such as integrated systems of care, training community workers (e.g., teachers and pastors) to identify people at elevated risk, and training the press on how to report on suicides responsibly.

The previously mentioned challenges may explain why suicide rates continue to rise among both the general population and veterans (U.S. Department of Veterans Affairs, 2019). Importantly, however, rates of suicide within the general population have risen more rapidly relative to the veteran population. Between 2005 and 2017, suicide rates among the general population rose 43%, while veteran suicide rates rose only 6.1% (U.S. Department of Veterans Affairs, 2019). Interestingly, those who accessed VHA care had even better outcomes. Between 2016 and 2017, suicide rates among veterans with recent VHA use rose 1.3%, compared to 11.8% among veterans who did not access VHA care. Encouragingly, rates of suicide among veterans with a depression diagnosis who received VHA care actually decreased between 2005 and 2017 (U.S. Department of Veterans Affairs, 2019). Favorable data among those seeking VHA care suggests that while suicide prevention remains a challenge, the VHA's investment in the evidence-based strategies outlined in this chapter (e.g., universal screening) (Matarazzo et al., 2020) has produced beneficial outcomes. With a similar level of prioritization, comparable outcomes may be achieved among community settings.

Conclusion

With veterans' heightened risk for suicide, combined with the influx of veterans seeking community-based care, it is critical that community providers are prepared to address veteran suicide risk using best practices. Evidence-based approaches have been developed to reduce and prevent the public health crisis concerning suicide among the veteran population. As presented throughout this chapter, evidence-based best practices for suicide prevention should inform community-based efforts to identify, evaluate, stratify, and manage veteran suicide.

Universal screening for suicide risk has potential for detecting at-risk veterans who access community-based care, including those who seek care in non–mental health settings, where suicide risk screening is less frequent (McDowell et al., 2011). Next, comprehensive evaluations further elucidate individual suicide risk and protective factors through a collaborative clinical process. While every veteran will have unique suicide-risk factors, certain risk factors must be assessed due to the strong evidence linking them to suicide, including self-directed violence, psychiatric conditions and associated symptoms, TBIs, biopsychosocial stressors, and access to lethal means (Department of Veterans Affairs & Department of Defense, 2019). Protective factors such as social support, coping skills, reasons for living, and spiritual or religious beliefs should also be considered. Risk stratification can help further understanding of suicide risk and may inform treatment options by classifying the severity and chronicity of suicide risk.

Treatment plans are informed by the nature of suicide risk, veterans' values and preferences, and clinical judgment. There are several promising, evidenced-based treatments for suicide risk. Among these are non-pharmacological options, including safety plans, CBT, DBT, and PST, all of which are designed to help patients develop skills that address suicidal thoughts and behaviors. There are also pharmacological options such as ketamine and lithium, which reduce risk among patients with MDD and mood disorders, respectively. Further, post-acute care treatments, such as caring communications and in-home visits, may also be effective adjunctive options, while means safety counseling can both remove access to lethal means and help patients identify self-directed actions for reducing suicide risk. Finally, technology-based treatments (e.g., computerized interventions;

Resources for Community-Based Suicide Prevention for Veterans

Resource	Description	Link
VA Clinical Practice Guidelines	Clinical practice guidelines for veteran suicide prevention and related provider pocket guides	https://www.healthquality.va.gov/guidelines/MH/srb
Suicide Risk Management Consultation Program (SRM)	Free consultation, support, and resources for providers working with veterans at risk of suicide	https://www.mirecc.va.gov/visn19/consult/index.asp
Community Provider Toolkit: Military Culture Training	Free courses about military culture, structure, and values for community providers	https://www.mentalhealth.va.gov/communityproviders/military_culture.asp
Means Safety Messaging for Clinical Staff	Guide for how to talk to patients about means safety, including firearms and medications	https://www.mentalhealth.va.gov/suicide_prevention/docs/Means_safety_messaging_for_clinical_staff.pdf
VA Assessment and Management of Patients at Risk for Suicide (2019) Webpage	Patient-provider tools, including crisis response and safety response plan guidance	https://www.healthquality.va.gov/guidelines/MH/srb/
Community Provider Toolkit: Suicide Prevention	Suicide prevention information, training, and resources for community providers	https://www.mentalhealth.va.gov/communityproviders/clinic_suicideprevention.asp

phone applications) are promising options for suicide-risk management and warrant continued consideration. Community-based settings represent a critical front in national veteran suicide prevention efforts (Department of Veterans Affairs, 2018). Greater knowledge and utilization of the previously mentioned best practices by community providers can enhance the detection, evaluation, and management of suicide risk among veterans accessing community-based care, thereby reducing the likelihood of veteran suicide.

References

Ahmedani, B. K., Simon, G. E., Stewart, C., Beck, A., Waitzfelder, B. E., Rossom, R., . . . Solberg, L. I. (2014). Health care contacts in the year before suicide death. *Journal of General Internal Medicine, 29*(6), 870–877. doi:10.1007/s11606-014-2767-3

Ahmedani, B. K., Stewart, C., Simon, G. E., Lynch, F., Lu, C. Y., Waitzfelder, B. E., . . . Williams, K. (2015). Racial/Ethnic differences in health care visits made before suicide attempt across the United States. *Med Care, 53*(5), 430–435. doi:10.1097/mlr.0000000000000335

American Foundation for Suicide Prevention. (2020). *Suicide facts & figures: United States 2020*. https://chapterland.org/wp-content/uploads/sites/13/2017/11/US_FactsFigures_Flyer.pdf

Andover, M. S., & Gibb, B. E. (2010). Non-suicidal self-injury, attempted suicide, and suicidal intent among psychiatric inpatients. *Psychiatry Res, 178*(1), 101–105. doi:10.1016/j.psychres.2010.03.019

Anglemyer, A., Horvath, T., & Rutherford, G. (2014). The accessibility of firearms and risk for suicide and homicide victimization among household members: a systematic review and meta-analysis. *Annals of Internal Medicine, 160*(2), 101–110. doi:10.7326/m13-1301

Asarnow, J. R., Babeva, K., & Horstmann, E. (2017). The emergency department: Challenges and opportunities for suicide prevention. *Child and Adolescent Psychiatric Clinics of North America, 26*(4), 771–783. doi:10.1016/j.chc.2017.05.002

Ashrafioun, L., Kane, C., Bishop, T. M., Britton, P. C., & Pigeon, W. R. (2019). The association of pain intensity and suicide attempts among patients initiating pain specialty services. *The Journal of Pain, 20*(7), 852–859. doi:10.1016/j.jpain.2019.01.012

Baer, M. M., LaCroix, J. M., Browne, J. C., Hassen, H. O., Perera, K. U., Weaver, J., . . . Ghahramanlou-Holloway, M. (2018). Non-Suicidal self-injury elevates suicide risk among United States military personnel with lifetime attempted suicide. *Arch Suicide Res, 22*(3), 453–464. doi:10.1080/13811118.2017.1358225

Baldessarini, R. J., Tondo, L., Davis, P., Pompili, M., Goodwin, F. K., & Hennen, J. (2006). Decreased risk of suicides and attempts during long-term lithium treatment: A meta-analytic review. *Bipolar Disord, 8*(5 Pt 2), 625–639. doi:10.1111/j.1399-5618.2006.00344.x

Black, D. W., Blum, N., Pfohl, B., & Hale, N. (2004). Suicidal behavior in borderline personality disorder: Prevalence, risk factors, prediction, and prevention. *J Pers Disord, 18*(3), 226–239. doi:10.1521/pedi.18.3.226.35445

Bohnert, K. M., Ilgen, M. A., Louzon, S., McCarthy, J. F., & Katz, I. R. (2017). Substance use disorders and the risk of suicide mortality among men and women in the US Veterans Health Administration. *Addiction, 112*(7), 1193–1201. doi:10.1111/add.13774

Bostwick, J. M., Pabbati, C., Geske, J. R., & McKean, A. J. (2016). Suicide attempt as a risk factor for completed suicide: Even more lethal than we knew. *Am J Psychiatry, 173*(11), 1094–1100. doi:10.1176/appi.ajp.2016.15070854

Brenner, L. A., Forster, J. E., Hoffberg, A. S., Matarazzo, B. B., Hostetter, T. A., Signoracci, G., & Simpson, G. K. (2018). Window to hope: A randomized controlled trial of a psychological intervention for the treatment of hopelessness among veterans with moderate to severe traumatic brain injury. *J Head Trauma Rehabil, 33*(2), E64–e73. doi:10.1097/htr.0000000000000351

Britton, P. C., Ilgen, M. A., Rudd, M. D., & Conner, K. R. (2012). Warning signs for suicide within a week of healthcare contact in Veteran decedents. *Psychiatry Res, 200*(2-3), 395–399. doi:10.1016/j.psychres.2012.06.036

Brown, G. K., Beck, A. T., Steer, R. A., & Grisham, J. R. (2000). Risk factors for suicide in psychiatric outpatients: A 20-year prospective study. *Journal of Consulting and Clinical Psychology, 68*(3), 371–377. doi:10.1037/0022-006X.68.3.371

Brown, G. K., Ten Have, T., Henriques, G. R., Xie, S. X., Hollander, J. E., & Beck, A. T. (2005). Cognitive therapy for the prevention of suicide attempts: A randomized controlled trial. *JAMA, 294*(5), 563–570. doi:10.1001/jama.294.5.563

Bryan, C. J. (2019). Cognitive behavioral therapy for suicide prevention (CBT-SP): Implications for meeting standard of care expectations with suicidal patients. *Behav Sci Law, 37*(3), 247–258. doi:10.1002/bsl.2411

Bush, N. E., Smolenski, D. J., Denneson, L. M., Williams, H. B., Thomas, E. K., & Dobscha, S. K. (2017). A virtual hope box: Randomized controlled trial of a smartphone app for emotional regulation and coping with distress. *Psychiatr Serv, 68*(4), 330–336. doi:10.1176/appi.ps.201600283

Cavanagh, K., Seccombe, N., & Lidbetter, N. (2011). The implementation of computerized cognitive behavioural therapies in a service user-led, third sector self help clinic. *Behav Cogn Psychother, 39*(4), 427–442. doi:10.1017/s1352465810000858

Chen, W. J., Ho, C. K., Shyu, S. S., Chen, C. C., Lin, G. G., Chou, L. S., . . . Chou, F. H. (2013). Employing crisis postcards with case management in Kaohsiung, Taiwan: 6-month outcomes of a randomised controlled trial for suicide attempters. *BMC Psychiatry, 13*, 191. doi:10.1186/1471-244x-13-191

Cipriani, A., Hawton, K., Stockton, S., & Geddes, J. R. (2013). Lithium in the prevention of suicide in mood disorders: Updated systematic review and meta-analysis. *BMJ : British Medical Journal, 346*, f3646. doi:10.1136/bmj.f3646

Cleveland, E. C., Azrael, D., Simonetti, J. A., & Miller, M. (2017). Firearm ownership among American veterans: Findings from the 2015 National Firearm Survey. *Inj Epidemiol, 4*(1), 33. doi:10.1186/s40621-017-0130-y

Coll, J. E., Weiss, E. L., & Yarvis, J. S. (2011). No one leaves unchanged: Insights for civilian mental health care professionals into the military experience and culture. *Soc Work Health Care, 50*(7), 487–500. doi:10.1080/00981389.2010.528727

Cramer, R. J., & Kapusta, N. D. (2017). A social-ecological framework of theory, assessment, and prevention of suicide. *Frontiers in Psychology, 8*(1756). doi:10.3389/fpsyg.2017.01756

Dazzi, T., Gribble, R., Wessely, S., & Fear, N. T. (2014). Does asking about suicide and related behaviours induce suicidal ideation? What is the evidence? *Psychological Medicine, 44*(16), 3361–3363. doi:10.1017/S0033291714001299

DeCou, C. R., & Schumann, M. E. (2018). On the iatrogenic risk of assessing suicidality: A meta-analysis. *Suicide Life Threat Behav, 48*(5), 531–543. doi:10.1111/sltb.12368

Department of Veterans Affairs. (2018). National strategy for preventing veteran suicide: 2018–2028. Author.

Department of Veterans Affairs, & Department of Defense. (2019). *VA/DoD clinical practice guideline for the assessment and management of patients at risk for suicide*. https://www.healthquality.va.gov/guidelines/MH/srb/VADoDSuicideRiskFullCPGFinal5088212019.pdf

Dervic, K., Oquendo, M., Grunebaum, M., Ellis, S., Burke, A., & Mann, J. (2005). Religious affiliation and suicide attempt. *The American Journal of Psychiatry, 161*, 2303–2308. doi:10.1176/appi.ajp.161.12.2303

Edwards, R. R., Smith, M. T., Kudel, I., & Haythornthwaite, J. (2006). Pain-related catastrophizing as a risk factor for suicidal ideation in chronic pain. *Pain, 126*(1-3), 272–279. doi:10.1016/j.pain.2006.07.004

Fedyszyn, I. E., Erlangsen, A., Hjorthøj, C., Madsen, T., & Nordentoft, M. (2016). Repeated suicide attempts and suicide among individuals with a first emergency department contact for attempted suicide: A prospective, nationwide, Danish register-based study. *J Clin Psychiatry, 77*(6), 832–840. doi:10.4088/JCP.15m09793

Fleischmann, A., Bertolote, J. M., Wasserman, D., De Leo, D., Bolhari, J., Botega, N. J., . . . Thanh, H. T. (2008). Effectiveness of brief intervention and contact for suicide attempters: A randomized controlled trial in five countries. *Bull World Health Organization, 86*(9), 703–709. doi:10.2471/blt.07.046995

Franklin, J. C., Ribeiro, J. D., Fox, K. R., Bentley, K. H., Kleiman, E. M., Huang, X., . . . Nock, M. K. (2017). Risk factors for suicidal thoughts and behaviors: A meta-analysis of 50 years of research. *Psychol Bulletin, 143*(2), 187–232. doi:10.1037/bul0000084

Gibbons, J. S., Butler, J., Urwin, P., & Gibbons, J. L. (1978). Evaluation of a social work service for self-poisoning patients. *Br J Psychiatry, 133*, 111–118. doi:10.1192/bjp.133.2.111

Glenn, C. R., Kleiman, E. M., Cha, C. B., Deming, C. A., Franklin, J. C., & Nock, M. K. (2018). Understanding suicide risk within the Research Domain Criteria (RDoC) framework: A meta-analytic review. *Depress Anxiety, 35*(1), 65–88. doi:10.1002/da.22686

Grunebaum, M. F., Galfalvy, H. C., Choo, T., Keilp, J. G., Moitra, V. K., Parris, M. S., . . . Mann, J. J. (2018). Ketamine for rapid reduction of suicidal thoughts in major depression: A midazolam-controlled randomized clinical trial. *American Journal of Psychiatry, 175*(4), 327–335. doi:10.1176/appi.ajp.2017.17060647

Hall, L. K. (2011). The importance of understanding military culture. *Soc Work Health Care, 50*(1), 4–18. doi:10.1080/00981389.2010.513914

Harris, K. M., & Goh, M. T. (2017). Is suicide assessment harmful to participants? Findings from a randomized controlled trial. *Int J Ment Health Nurs, 26*(2), 181–190. doi:10.1111/inm.12223

Hassanian-Moghaddam, H., Sarjami, S., Kolahi, A. A., Lewin, T., & Carter, G. (2017). Postcards in Persia: A twelve to twenty-four month follow-up of a randomized controlled trial for hospital-treated deliberate self-poisoning. *Arch Suicide Res, 21*(1), 138–154. doi:10.1080/13811118.2015.1004473

Hatcher, S., Sharon, C., Parag, V., & Collins, N. (2011). Problem-solving therapy for people who present to hospital with self-harm: Zelen randomised controlled trial. *Br J Psychiatry, 199*(4), 310–316. doi:10.1192/bjp.bp.110.090126

Hawton, K., Bergen, H., Simkin, S., Dodd, S., Pocock, P., Bernal, W., . . . Kapur, N. (2013). Long term effect of reduced pack sizes of paracetamol on poisoning deaths and liver transplant activity in England and Wales: Interrupted time series analyses. *BMJ : British Medical Journal, 346*, f403. doi:10.1136/bmj.f403

Hawton, K., Witt, K. G., Taylor Salisbury, T. L., Arensman, E., Gunnell, D., Hazell, P., . . . van Heeringen, K. (2016). Psychosocial interventions for self-harm in adults. *Cochrane Database Syst Rev*(5), CD012189. doi:10.1002/14651858.CD012189

Hennen, J., & Baldessarini, R. J. (2005). Suicidal risk during treatment with clozapine: A meta-analysis. *Schizophrenia Research, 73*(2), 139–145. doi:10.1016/j.schres.2004.05.015

Hofstra, E., van Nieuwenhuizen, C., Bakker, M., Özgül, D., Elfeddali, I., de Jong, S. J., & van der Feltz-Cornelis, C. M. (2020). Effectiveness of suicide prevention interventions: A systematic review and meta-analysis. *General Hospital Psychiatry, 63*, 127–140. doi:10.1016/j.genhosppsych.2019.04.011

Hom, M. A., Stanley, I. H., Gutierrez, P. M., & Joiner, T. E., Jr. (2017). Exploring the association between exposure to suicide and suicide risk among military service members and veterans. *J Affect Disord, 207*, 327–335. doi:10.1016/j.jad.2016.09.043

Hostetter, T. A., Hoffmire, C. A., Forster, J. E., Adams, R. S., Stearns-Yoder, K. A., & Brenner, L. A. (2019). Suicide and traumatic brain injury among individuals seeking Veterans Health Administration services between fiscal years 2006 and 2015. *J Head Trauma Rehabil, 34*(5), E1–E9. doi:10.1097/HTR.0000000000000489

Huang, X., Fox, K. R., Ribeiro, J. D., & Franklin, J. C. (2018). Psychosis as a risk factor for suicidal thoughts and behaviors: A meta-analysis of longitudinal studies. *Psychol Med, 48*(5), 765–776. doi:10.1017/s0033291717002136

Hubers, A. A. M., Moaddine, S., Peersmann, S. H. M., Stijnen, T., van Duijn, E., van der Mast, R. C., . . . Giltay, E. J. (2018). Suicidal ideation and subsequent completed suicide in both psychiatric and non-psychiatric populations: A meta-analysis. *Epidemiol Psychiatr Sci, 27*(2), 186–198. doi:10.1017/s2045796016001049

Ilgen, M. A., Bohnert, A. S. B., Ganoczy, D., Bair, M. J., McCarthy, J. F., & Blow, F. C. (2016). Opioid dose and risk of suicide. *Pain, 157*(5), 1079–1084. doi:10.1097/j.pain.0000000000000484

Ilgen, M. A., Bohnert, A. S. B., Ignacio, R. V., McCarthy, J. F., Valenstein, M. M., Kim, H. M., & Blow, F. C. (2010). Psychiatric diagnoses and risk of suicide in veterans. *Archives of General Psychiatry, 67*(11), 1152–1158. doi:10.1001/archgenpsychiatry.2010.129

Imran, J. B., Richmond, R. E., Madni, T. D., Roaten, K., Clark, A. T., Huang, E. Y., . . . Eastman, A. L. (2018). Determining suicide risk in trauma patients using a universal screening program. *Journal of Trauma and Acute Care Surgery, 85*(1), 182–186. doi:10.1097/ta.0000000000001899

Kang, H. K., Bullman, T. A., Smolenski, D. J., Skopp, N. A., Gahm, G. A., & Reger, M. A. (2015). Suicide risk among 1.3 million veterans who were on active duty during the Iraq and Afghanistan wars. *Ann Epidemiol, 25*(2), 96–100. doi:10.1016/j.annepidem.2014.11.020

Kasckow, J., Felmet, K., & Zisook, S. (2011). Managing suicide risk in patients with schizophrenia. *CNS Drugs, 25*(2), 129–143. doi:10.2165/11586450-000000000-00000

Kasckow, J., Zickmund, S., Gurklis, J., Luther, J., Fox, L., Taylor, M., . . . Haas, G. L. (2016). Using telehealth to augment an intensive case monitoring program in veterans with schizophrenia and suicidal ideation: A pilot trial. *Psychiatry Res, 239*, 111–116. doi:10.1016/j.psychres.2016.02.049

Kimbrel, N. A., Meyer, E. C., DeBeer, B. B., Gulliver, S. B., & Morissette, S. B. (2016). A 12-month prospective study of the effects of PTSD-depression comorbidity on suicidal behavior in Iraq/Afghanistan-era veterans. *Psychiatry Res, 243*, 97–99. doi:10.1016/j.psychres.2016.06.011

Kimerling, R., Makin-Byrd, K., Louzon, S., Ignacio, R. V., & McCarthy, J. F. (2016). Military sexual trauma and suicide mortality. *Am J Prev Med, 50*(6), 684–691. doi:10.1016/j.amepre.2015.10.019

Kleiman, E. M., & Liu, R. T. (2013). Social support as a protective factor in suicide: Findings from two nationally representative samples. *Journal of affective disorders, 150*(2), 540–545. doi:10.1016/j.jad.2013.01.033

Lee, D. J., Kearns, J. C., Wisco, B. E., Green, J. D., Gradus, J. L., Sloan, D. M., . . . Marx, B. P. (2018). A longitudinal study of risk factors for suicide attempts among Operation Enduring Freedom and Operation Iraqi Freedom veterans. *Depress Anxiety, 35*(7), 609–618. doi:10.1002/da.22736

Legarreta, M., Bueler, E., DiMuzio, J., McGlade, E., & Yurgelun-Todd, D. (2018). Suicide behavior and chronic pain: An exploration of pain-related catastrophic thinking, disability, and descriptions of the pain experience. *The Journal of Nervous and Mental Disease, 206*(3), 217–222. doi:10.1097/nmd.0000000000000799

Luoma, J. B., Martin, C. E., & Pearson, J. L. (2002). Contact with mental health and primary care providers before suicide: a review of the evidence. *Am J Psychiatry, 159*(6), 909–916. doi:10.1176/appi.ajp.159.6.909

Malone, K., Oquendo, M. A., Haas, A., Ellis, S., Li, S., & Mann, J. (2000). Protective factors against suicidal acts in major depression: Reasons for living. *American Journal of Psychiatry, 157*(7), 1084–1088. doi:10.1176/appi.ajp.157.7.1084

Mann, J. J., Apter, A., Bertolote, J., Beautrais, A., Currier, D., Haas, A., . . . Hendin, H. (2005). Suicide prevention strategies: A systematic review. *JAMA, 294*(16), 2064–2074. doi:10.1001/jama.294.16.2064

Matarazzo, B. B., Brenner, L. A., Wortzel, H. S., & Bahraini, N. H. (2020). Balancing scientific evidence, clinical expertise, and patient preferences: VHA's suicide risk identification strategy. *Psychiatric Services, 0*(0). doi:10.1176/appi.ps.202000109

Matarazzo, B. B., Brown, G. K., Stanley, B., Forster, J. E., Billera, M., Currier, G. W., . . . Brenner, L. A. (2019). Predictive validity of the Columbia-Suicide Severity Rating Scale among a cohort of at-risk veterans. *Suicide Life Threat Behav, 49*(5), 1255–1265. doi:10.1111/sltb.12515

Matarazzo, B. B., Farro, S. A., Billera, M., Forster, J. E., Kemp, J. E., & Brenner, L. A. (2017). Connecting veterans at risk for suicide to care through the HOME program. *Suicide Life Threat Behav, 47*(6), 709–717. doi:10.1111/sltb.12334

Matarazzo, B. B., Forster, J. E., Hostetter, T. A., Billera, M., Adler, G., Ganzini, L. K., . . . Brenner, L. A. (2019). Efficacy of the Home-Based Mental Health Evaluation (HOME) Program for engaging patients in care after hospitalization. *Psychiatr Serv, 70*(12), 1094–1100. doi:10.1176/appi.ps.201900002

Mathias, C. W., Michael Furr, R., Sheftall, A. H., Hill-Kapturczak, N., Crum, P., & Dougherty, D. M. (2012). What's the harm in asking about suicidal ideation? *Suicide Life Threat Behav, 42*(3), 341–351. doi:10.1111/j.1943-278X.2012.0095.x

McCarthy, J. F., Bossarte, R. M., Katz, I. R., Thompson, C., Kemp, J., Hannemann, C. M., . . . Schoenbaum, M. (2015). Predictive modeling and concentration of the risk of suicide: Implications for preventive interventions in the US Department of Veterans Affairs. *Am J Public Health, 105*(9), 1935–1942. doi:10.2105/AJPH.2015.302737

McDowell, A. K., Lineberry, T. W., & Bostwick, J. M. (2011). Practical suicide-risk management for the busy primary care physician. *Mayo Clin Proc, 86*(8), 792–800. doi:10.4065/mcp.2011.0076

McMain, S. F., Guimond, T., Barnhart, R., Habinski, L., & Streiner, D. L. (2017). A randomized trial of brief dialectical behaviour therapy skills training in suicidal patients suffering from borderline disorder.

Acta Psychiatr Scand, 135(2), 138–148. doi:10.1111/acps.12664

Motto, J. A., & Bostrom, A. G. (2001). A randomized controlled trial of postcrisis suicide prevention. *Psychiatr Serv, 52*(6), 828–833. doi:10.1176/appi.ps.52.6.828

Mundt, J. C., Greist, J. H., Gelenberg, A. J., Katzelnick, D. J., Jefferson, J. W., & Modell, J. G. (2010). Feasibility and validation of a computer-automated Columbia-Suicide Severity Rating Scale using interactive voice response technology. *J Psychiatr Res, 44*(16), 1224–1228. doi:10.1016/j.jpsychires.2010.04.025

Nahin, R. L. (2017). Severe pain in veterans: The effect of age and sex, and comparisons with the general population. *J Pain, 18*(3), 247–254. doi:10.1016/j.jpain.2016.10.021

National Institute of Mental Health. (2019, April 2019). Suicide. https://www.nimh.nih.gov/health/statistics/suicide.shtml#part_155143

Nichter, B., Hill, M., Norman, S., Haller, M., & Pietrzak, R. H. (2020). Associations of childhood abuse and combat exposure with suicidal ideation and suicide attempt in U.S. military veterans: a nationally representative study. *J Affect Disord, 276*, 1102–1108. doi:10.1016/j.jad.2020.07.120

Nock, M. K., Millner, A. J., Joiner, T. E., Gutierrez, P. M., Han, G., Hwang, I., . . . Kessler, R. C. (2018). Risk factors for the transition from suicide ideation to suicide attempt: Results from the Army Study to Assess Risk and Resilience in Servicemembers (Army STARRS). *J Abnorm Psychol, 127*(2), 139–149. doi:10.1037/abn0000317

Office of Suicide Prevention. (2016). *Suicide among veterans and other americans 2001–2014*. https://www.mentalhealth.va.gov/docs/2016suicidedatareport.pdf

Oquendo, M. A., & Bernanke, J. A. (2017). Suicide risk assessment: Tools and challenges. *World Psychiatry: Official Journal of the World Psychiatric Association (WPA), 16*(1), 28–29. doi:10.1002/wps.20396

Ormrod, J. A., Kennedy, L., Scott, J., & Cavanagh, K. (2010). Computerised cognitive behavioural therapy in an adult mental health service: A pilot study of outcomes and alliance. *Cogn Behav Ther, 39*(3), 188–192. doi:10.1080/16506071003675614

Park, E. H., Hong, N., Jon, D. I., Hong, H. J., & Jung, M. H. (2017). Past suicidal ideation as an independent risk factor for suicide behaviours in patients with depression. *Int J Psychiatry Clin Pract, 21*(1), 24–28. doi:10.1080/13651501.2016.1249489

Posner, K., Brown, G. K., Stanley, B., Brent, D. A., Yershova, K. V., Oquendo, M. A., . . . Mann, J. J. (2011). The Columbia-Suicide Severity Rating Scale: Initial validity and internal consistency findings from three multisite studies with adolescents and adults. *Am J Psychiatry, 168*(12), 1266–1277. doi:10.1176/appi.ajp.2011.10111704

Riblet, N. B. V., Shiner, B., Young-Xu, Y., & Watts, B. V. (2017). Strategies to prevent death by suicide: Meta-analysis of randomised controlled trials. *Br J Psychiatry, 210*(6), 396–402. doi:10.1192/bjp.bp.116.187799

Roaten, K., Johnson, C., Genzel, R., Khan, F., & North, C. S. (2018). Development and implementation of a universal suicide risk screening program in a safety-net hospital system. *The Joint Commission Journal on Quality and Patient Safety, 44*(1), 4–11. doi:https://doi.org/10.1016/j.jcjq.2017.07.006

Rocky Mountain MIRECC, VA Office of Mental Health and Suicide Prevention, & VA Office of Emergency Medicine. (2020). *Safety planning in the emergency department*. https://dvagov.sharepoint.com/sites/ECH/srsa/Shared%20Documents/Forms/AllItems.aspx?id=%2Fsites%2FECH%2Fsrsa%2FShared%20Documents%2FSPED%2FSPED%20Flow%20Map%2Epdf&parent=%2Fsites%2FECH%2Fsrsa%2FShared%20Documents%2FSPED

Rowhani-Rahbar, A., Simonetti, J. A., & Rivara, F. P. (2016). Effectiveness of interventions to promote safe firearm storage. *Epidemiol Rev, 38*(1), 111–124. doi:10.1093/epirev/mxv006

Rudd, M. D. (2008). Suicide warning signs in clinical practice. *Curr Psychiatry Rep, 10*(1), 87–90. doi:10.1007/s11920-008-0015-4

Rudd, M. D., Berman, A. L., Joiner, T. E., Jr., Nock, M. K., Silverman, M. M., Mandrusiak, M., . . . Witte, T. (2006). Warning signs for suicide: theory, research, and clinical applications. *Suicide Life Threat Behav, 36*(3), 255–262. doi:10.1521/suli.2006.36.3.255

Rudd, M. D., Bryan, C. J., Wertenberger, E. G., Peterson, A. L., Young-McCaughan, S., Mintz, J., . . . Bruce, T. O. (2015). Brief cognitive-behavioral therapy effects on post-treatment suicide attempts in a military sample: Results of a randomized clinical trial with 2-year follow-up. *Am J Psychiatry, 172*(5), 441–449. doi:10.1176/appi.ajp.2014.14070843

Sher, L., Braquehais, M. D., & Casas, M. (2012). Posttraumatic stress disorder, depression, and suicide in veterans. *Cleveland Clinic Journal of Medicine, 79*(2), 92–97. doi:10.3949/ccjm.79a.11069

Simonetti, J. A., Azrael, D., Rowhani-Rahbar, A., & Miller, M. (2018). Firearm storage practices among American veterans. *Am J Prev Med, 55*(4), 445–454. doi:10.1016/j.amepre.2018.04.014

Smith, M. T., Edwards, R. R., Robinson, R. C., & Dworkin, R. H. (2004). Suicidal ideation, plans, and attempts in chronic pain patients: Factors associated with increased risk. *Pain, 111*(1-2), 201–208. doi:10.1016/j.pain.2004.06.016

Spelman, J. F., Hunt, S. C., Seal, K. H., & Burgo-Black, A. L. (2012). Post deployment care for returning combat veterans. *J Gen Intern Med, 27*(9), 1200–1209. doi:10.1007/s11606-012-2061-1

Stanley, B., Brown, G. K., Brenner, L. A., Galfalvy, H. C., Currier, G. W., Knox, K. L., . . . Green, K. L. (2018). Comparison of the safety planning intervention with follow-up vs usual care of suicidal patients treated in the emergency department. *JAMA Psychiatry, 75*(9), 894–900. doi:10.1001/jamapsychiatry.2018.1776

Tang, N. K., & Crane, C. (2006). Suicidality in chronic pain: A review of the prevalence, risk factors and psychological links. *Psychol Med, 36*(5), 575–586. doi:10.1017/s0033291705006859

Tanielian, T., & Jaycox, L. (2008). *Invisible wounds of war: Psychological and cognitive injuries, their consequences, and services to assist recovery* (Vol. 1): Rand Corporation.

Taylor, B. C., Hagel, E. M., Carlson, K. F., Cifu, D. X., Cutting, A., Bidelspach, D. E., & Sayer, N. A. (2012). Prevalence and costs of co-occurring traumatic brain injury with and without psychiatric disturbance and pain among Afghanistan and Iraq War Veteran V.A. users. *Med Care, 50*(4), 342–346. doi:10.1097/MLR.0b013e318245a558

Townsend, E., Hawton, K., Altman, D. G., Arensman, E., Gunnell, D., Hazell, P., . . . Van Heeringen, K. (2001). The efficacy of problem-solving treatments after deliberate self-harm: meta-analysis of randomized controlled trials with respect to depression, hopelessness and improvement in problems. *Psychological Medicine, 31*(6), 979–988. doi:10.1017/S0033291701004238

Turner, B. J., Kleiman, E. M., & Nock, M. K. (2019). Non-suicidal self-injury prevalence, course, and association with suicidal thoughts and behaviors in two large, representative samples of US Army soldiers. *Psychol Med, 49*(9), 1470–1480. doi:10.1017/s0033291718002015

U.S. Department of Veterans Affairs. (2019). *National veteran suicide prevention annual report*. https://www.mentalhealth.va.gov/docs/data-sheets/2019/2019_National_Veteran_Suicide_Prevention_Annual_Report_508.pdf

U.S. Department of Veterans Affairs. (2020, February 18, 2020). *VA Center for Medication Safety (VA MedSAFE)*. https://www.pbm.va.gov/PBM/vacenterformedicationsafety/vacenterformedicationsafetyaboutus.asp

Ursano, R. J., Kessler, R. C., Stein, M. B., Naifeh, J. A., Aliaga, P. A., Fullerton, C. S., . . . Army, S. C. (2016). Risk factors, methods, and timing of suicide attempts among US army soldiers. *JAMA Psychiatry, 73*(7), 741–749. doi:10.1001/jamapsychiatry.2016.0600

Van der Feltz-Cornelis, C. M., Sarchiapone, M., Postuvan, V., Volker, D., Roskar, S., Grum, A. T., . . . Hegerl, U. (2011). Best practice elements of multilevel suicide prevention strategies: A review of systematic reviews. *Crisis, 32*(6), 319–333. doi:10.1027/0227-5910/a000109

Van Heeringen, C., Jannes, S., Buylaert, W., Henderick, H., De Bacquer, D., & Van Remoortel, J. (1995). The management of non-compliance with referral to out-patient after-care among attempted suicide patients: A controlled intervention study. *Psychol Med, 25*(5), 963–970. doi:10.1017/s0033291700037454

Viguera, A. C., Milano, N., Laurel, R., Thompson, N. R., Griffith, S. D., Baldessarini, R. J., & Katzan, I. L. (2015). Comparison of electronic screening for suicidal risk with the Patient Health Questionnaire Item 9 and the Columbia Suicide Severity Rating Scale in an outpatient psychiatric clinic. *Psychosomatics, 56*(5), 460–469. doi:https://doi.org/10.1016/j.psym.2015.04.005

Whiteneck, G., Cutherbert, J., & Mellick, D. (2015). *VA Traumatic brain injury report*. https://www.publichealth.va.gov/docs/epidemiology/TBI-report-fy2013-qtr4.pdf

Wilcox, H. C., Conner, K. R., & Caine, E. D. (2004). Association of alcohol and drug use disorders and completed suicide: An empirical review of cohort studies. *Drug and Alcohol Dependence, 76*, S11–S19. doi:https://doi.org/10.1016/j.drugalcdep.2004.08.003

Wilkinson, S. T., Ballard, E. D., Bloch, M. H., Mathew, S. J., Murrough, J. W., Feder, A., . . . Sanacora, G. (2018). The effect of a single dose of intravenous ketamine on suicidal ideation: A systematic review and individual participant data meta-analysis. *The American Journal of Psychiatry, 175*(2), 150–158. doi:10.1176/appi.ajp.2017.17040472

Wortzel, H. S., Matarazzo, B., & Homaifar, B. (2013). A Model for Therapeutic Risk Management of the Suicidal Patient. *Journal of Psychiatric Practice, 19*(4). https://journals.lww.com/practicalpsychiatry/Fulltext/2013/07000/A_Model_for_Therapeutic_Risk_Management_of_the.10.aspx

Yoshimasu, K., Kiyohara, C., & Miyashita, K. (2008). Suicidal risk factors and completed suicide: Meta-analyses based on psychological autopsy studies. *Environ Health Prev Med, 13*(5), 243–256. doi:10.1007/s12199-008-0037-x

Zalsman, G., Hawton, K., Wasserman, D., van Heeringen, K., Arensman, E., Sarchiapone, M., . . . Zohar, J. (2016). Suicide prevention strategies revisited: 10-year systematic review. *The Lancet Psychiatry, 3*(7), 646–659. doi:10.1016/s2215-0366(16)30030-x

CHAPTER 18

Caring for Veterans with Substance Use Disorders (SUD)

Connie Braybrook

Substance Use Disorders (SUD)

Substance use disorders (SUD) have been well documented and researched within the military and veteran population. Early identification of SUD is paramount within the military to prevent mission impact, while continued identification and treatment for veterans is paramount due to this being a potential consequence from their service (maladaptive coping from the effects of war). This chapter will discuss the prevalence and risk factors for SUD among the active duty and veteran population, differentiate between low-risk to high-risk drinking behaviors, discuss in detail the early intervention approach of Screening, Brief Intervention, and Referral to Treatment (SBIRT), and understand withdrawal and delirium tremens, family involvement, and implications with trauma.

Prevalence and Risk Factors

SUD is defined in the fifth edition of *The Diagnostic and Statistical Manual of Mental Disorders* (DSM-5) as a "pattern of use that results in marked distress and/or impairment, with two or more symptoms occurring in the past year" (American Psychiatric Association [APA], 2013). See **Table 18-1** for diagnostic criteria for SUD. SUD among veterans continue to rise despite efforts from the Veterans Administration (VA) (Teeters et al., 2017). The following prevalence data may have some selection bias due to limitations, such as not all veterans seeking treatment through the VA. Heavy episodic drinking and daily cigarette smoking were the most prevalent types of substance misuse among men and women veterans (Hoggatt et al., 2017). Approximately 11% of veterans meet the criteria for a

Table 18-1 DSM-5 Alcohol Use Disorders Diagnostic Criteria

A. A Problematic pattern of alcohol use leading to clinically significant impairment of distress, as manifested by at least two of the following, occurring within a 12-month period:
   1. Alcohol is often taken in larger amounts or over a longer period than was intended.
   2. There is a persistent desire or unsuccessful efforts to cut down or control alcohol use.
   3. A great deal of time is spent in activities necessary to obtain alcohol, use alcohol, or recover from its effects.
   4. Craving, or a strong desire or urge to use alcohol.
   5. Recurrent alcohol use resulting in a failure to fulfill major role obligations at work, school, or home.
   6. Continued alcohol use despite having persistent or recurrent social or interpersonal problems caused or exacerbated by the effects of alcohol.
   7. Important social, occupational, or recreational activities are given up or reduced because of alcohol use.
   8. Recurrent alcohol use in situations in which it is physically hazardous.
   9. Alcohol use is continued despite knowledge of having a persistent or recurrent physical or psychological problem that is likely to have been caused or exacerbated by alcohol.
   10. Tolerance, as defined by either of the following:
       a. A need for markedly increased amounts of alcohol to achieve intoxication or desired effect.
       b. A markedly diminished effect with continued use of the same amount of alcohol.
   11. Withdrawal, as manifested by either of the following:
       a. The characteristic withdrawal syndrome for alcohol (refer to Criteria A and B of the criteria set for alcohol withdrawal)
       b. Alcohol (or a closely related substance, such as a benzodiazepine) is taken to relieve or avoid withdrawal symptoms.

Modified from American Psychiatric Association. (2013). Substance use disorders. In *Diagnostic and statistical manual of mental disorders* (5th ed.). Author.

substance use disorder; alcohol and drug use disorders are more common among male veterans (10.5% and 4.8% respectively; female veteran alcohol use disorders are 4.8% and drug use disorders are 2.4%) (Teeters et al., 2017). Veterans are diagnosed with SUD more than the general population; one in ten veterans have an SUD (*Drug facts*, 2019). Veterans and military personnel have unique stressors that contribute to SUD, which include deployment, combat exposure, and post-deployment civilian reintegration challenges, in addition to mental health conditions such as post-traumatic stress disorder or depression (Teeters et al., 2017).

Illicit drug use among the active duty personnel has decreased in years from 2015 in comparison to 2011 according to the Health Related Behaviors Survey (HRBS) (*Drug facts*, 2019). Less than 1% of service members reported drug use, however, rates increase once active duty personnel leave military service (*Drug facts*, 2019). Cannabis accounts for the most common illicit drug use, while 10.7% of veteran admissions to substance treatment centers were for heroin and 6% were for cocaine (*Drug facts*, 2019).

Alcohol is the most prevalent SUD among military personnel accounting for 5.4% of active duty service members being heavy drinkers according to the HRBS (*Drug facts*, 2019). In 2015, approximately 30% of service members were considered binge drinkers, with one in three personnel meeting criteria for hazardous drinking with rates higher among men (*Drug facts*, 2019). According to a 2017 study, 56.6% of veterans are more likely to use alcohol, and 65% of veterans who enter a treatment program are enrolled for an alcohol-use disorder (*Drug facts*, 2019).

Military and veterans are not immune to the risk factors of substance use disorders of

Table 18-2 Alcoholic Drink Equivalents of Select Beverages

Drink Description	Drink Equivalent
Beer, beer coolers, and malt beverages	
12 fl oz at 4.2% alcohol	0.8
12 fl oz at 5% alcohol (reference beverage)	1.0
16 fl oz at 5% alcohol	1.3
12 fl oz at 7% alcohol	1.4
12 fl oz at 9% alcohol	1.8
Wine	
5 fl oz at 12% alcohol (reference beverage)	1.0
9 fl oz at 12% alcohol	1.8
5 fl oz at 15% alcohol	1.3
5 fl oz at 17% alcohol	1.4
Distilled spirits	
1.5 fl oz 80 proof distilled spirits (40% alcohol) (reference beverage)	1
Mixed drink with more than 1.5 fl oz 80 proof distilled spirits (40% alcohol)	>1

Olson, R., Casavale, K., Rihane, C., Stoody, E. E., Britten, P., Reedy, J., Rahavi, E., de Jesus, J., Piercy, K., Mosher, A., Fu, S., Larson, J., & Rodgers, A. B. (2015). *2015–2020 dietary guidelines*. U.S. Department of Health and Human Services and U.S. Department of Agriculture. https://health.gov/sites/default/files/2019-09/2015-2020_Dietary_Guidelines.pdf

biologic, psychological, and early exposure, and socioeconomic status as every population; in fact, they have additional risk factors. Biological factors include gender, ethnicity, and other medical comorbidities. Service culture and combat operations have been found to contribute to military and veteran substance use disorders (Sirratt et al., 2012). Within the military population, SUD is commonly a co-occurring disorder among those diagnosed with post-traumatic stress disorder (PTSD) (The Management of Substance Use Disorders Work Group, 2015).

Drinking Behaviors

Dietary guidelines determine risky drinking behaviors. The healthiest drinking behavior is to consume alcohol in moderation, which is defined by one drink per day for women and two drinks per day for men (Olson et al., 2015). To determine standard drinks, or drink equivalents, see **Table 18-2**.

High-risk drinking is defined as consuming four or more drinks in one day or eight or more drinks in one week for women and five or more drinks in one day or fifteen or more drinks in one week for men (Olson et al., 2015). When women consume four or more drinks or men consume five or more drinks in a two-hour period, this is considered binge drinking (Olson et al., 2015). This consumption typically brings the blood alcohol concentration to 0.08% or higher during this timeframe (National Institutes of Health, n.d.). Excessive drinking can increase the risk for harmful consequences to include alcohol-use disorders and is a significant cause for mortality and morbidity. High-risk drinking is considered eight or more drinks a week for women and fifteen or more drinks a week for men (Olson et al., 2015).

Early Intervention

Early intervention is paramount to identifying at-risk substance users before more severe consequences occur. A comprehensive approach that is applicable in all settings (emergency room, primary care, community health) is called SBIRT: Screening, Brief Intervention, and Referral to Treatment (Substance Abuse and Mental Health Services Administration, n.d.). "The main goal for SBIRT is to improve community health by reducing the prevalence of adverse consequences of substance misuse, including SUDs through early intervention and, when needed, referral to treatment" (Agerwala & McCance-Katz, 2012, p. 307). A large SBIRT study revealed six-month follow-up outcomes of 68% illicit lower drug use and 39% decrease in heavy alcohol consumption in positive screenings (Agerwala & McCance-Katz, 2012). The VA/DoD Clinical Practice Guideline (CPG) designed an algorithm to assist with the clinical decision-making process in managing SUD patients. CPGs are based on a systematic review of evidence available at the time of publication and developed by a panel of multidisciplinary experts (The Management of Substance Use Disorders Work Group, 2015). Each category of SBIRT is explained using the evidence from the VA/DoD CPG.

Screening

VA/DoD CPGs recommend annual screening for unhealthy alcohol use; evidence demonstrates screenings followed by alcohol counseling decreases risky drinking behaviors (The Management of Substance Use Disorders Work Group, 2015). The recommended screening tool is the three-item Alcohol Use Disorder Identification Test-Consumption (AUDIT-C) or Single Item Alcohol Screening Questionnaire (SASQ) (**Table 18-3**). The AUDIT-C and SASQ are validated, self-report instruments that are quick and efficient to screen for unhealthy alcohol consumption. Screening for an alcohol-use disorder can be conducted prior to any medical examination; however, it is especially important in the following patients:

- Are pregnant or trying to conceive.
- Are at risk for binge drinking or heaving drinking.
- Have health problems that may be induced or exacerbated by alcohol (e.g., cardiac arrhythmia, depression or anxiety, dyspepsia, insomnia, liver disease, a history of traumatic injury).
- Have one or more chronic health problems (e.g., diabetes, heart disease, hypertension, gastrointestinal [GI] disorders, chronic pain) that are not responding to treatment.
- Have social or legal problems that may be caused or worsened by alcohol use (e.g., marital/family issues, driving-while-under-the-influence convictions).

(Substance Abuse and Mental Health Services Administration and National Institute on Alcohol Abuse and Alcoholism [SAMHSA/NIAAA], 2015, p. 7)

Brief Intervention

After a positive screening is identified, and the individual does not have an identified alcohol-use disorder, brief intervention is recommended (The Management of Substance Use Disorders Work Group, 2015). The evidence studied for the CPGs revealed brief intervention reduces consumption outcomes and improves health outcomes for those that do not meet the criteria for an alcohol-use disorder (The Management of Substance Use Disorders Work Group, 2015). Brief intervention can occur in any clinical setting that alcohol screenings occur, such as emergency rooms, primary care clinics, specialty clinics, and hospital settings. There is no set time determination on the brief intervention given (5, 10, 20 minutes); evidence shows there is no difference in efficacy between time and components of brief intervention (The Management of Substance Use Disorders Work Group, 2015). The two elements that research has shown to be most often

Table 18-3 Screening Tools for Unhealthy Alcohol Use

	Alcohol-Use Disorders Identification Test-Consumption (AUDIT-C)	Single Item Alcohol Screening Questionnaire (SASQ)
Items	1. How often did you have a drink containing alcohol in the past year? Never — 0 point Monthly or less — 1 point 2-4 times per month — 2 points 2-3 times per week — 3 points 4 or more times per week — 4 points 2. On days in the past year when you drank, alcohol how many drinks did you typically drink? 0, 1, or 2 — 0 point 3 or 4 — 1 point 5 or 6 — 2 points 7-9 — 3 points 10 or more — 4 points 3. How often did you have six or more drinks on an occasion in the past year? Never — 0 point Less than monthly — 1 point Monthly — 2 points Weekly — 3 points Daily or almost daily — 4 points	4. Do you sometimes drink beer, wine, or other alcoholic beverages? (Followed by the screening question) 5. How many times in the past year have you had . . . Men: 5 or more drinks in a day Women: 4 or more drinks in a day
Scoring	The minimum score (for non-drinkers) is 0 and the maximum possible score is 12. Consider a screen positive for unhealthy alcohol use if AUDIT-C score is ≥ 4 points for men or ≥ 3 points for women. Note: For VA, documentation of brief alcohol counseling is required for those with AUDIT-C ≥ 5 points, for both men and women. This higher score for follow-up was selected to minimize the false-positive rate and to target implementation efforts. Follow-up of lower screening scores < 5 is left to provider discretion.	A positive screen is any report of drinking 5 or more (men) or 4 or more (women) drinks on an occasion in the past year.

The Management of Substance Use Disorders Work Group. (2015). *VA/DoD clinical practice guidelines for the management of substance use disorders* (VA/DoD Version 3.0). Department of Veterans Affairs and Department of Defense. https://www.healthquality.va.gov/guidelines/MH/sud/VADODSUDCPGRevised22216.pdf

provided are feedback regarding an individual's level of alcohol-related risk coupled with any alcohol-related adverse effects and brief advice regarding abstinence or drinking within recommended gender limits (The Management of Substance Use Disorders Work Group, 2015). Additional components of brief intervention can include why cutting down will benefit the individual and local resources to assist if necessary. It is important to remember, brief intervention is not indicated for individuals that are identified to have a substance-use disorder.

Specialty Care. Those identified as having a substance-use disorder are recommended to be referred to specialty care for treatment.

Specialty care treatment assists the patient to address the problems/issues contributing to their substance use. "A referral to specialty SUD care should be offered if the patient has at least one of the following:

- May benefit from additional evaluation of his/her substance use and related problems
- Has been diagnosed as having an SUD
- Is willing to engage in specialty care"

(The Management of Substance Use Disorders Work Group, 2015, p. 32)

There are different levels of SUD treatment to include Outpatient, Intensive Outpatient, Residential, and Detoxification. "The American Society of Addiction Medicine Patient Placement Criteria (The ASAM Criteria, 2013) have been widely promulgated as a system to determine level of care based on assessment of six dimensions (acute intoxication and/or withdrawal potential; biomedical conditions and complications; emotional, behavioral or cognitive conditions and complications; readiness to change; relapse, continued use, or continued problem potential; and recovery/living environment)" (The Management of Substance Use Disorders Work Group, 2015, p. 33). Once the patient is referred to the specialty care facility, the specialist will determine the level of treatment indicated.

Signs and Symptoms of Withdrawal and Delirium Tremens

Alcohol withdrawal can be fatal if not medically managed. Alcohol withdrawal typically begins 24–48 hours after the individual's last drink and the withdrawal symptoms can continue for 5 to 7 days (SAMHSA/NIAAA, 2015). Withdrawal symptoms can vary in intensity from mild tremors to delirium tremens to death if symptoms are not treated. The intensity of withdrawal symptoms varies from each individual dependent on their duration of having an alcohol-use disorder and the volume of alcohol consumption (Newman et al., 2020). See **Table 18-4** for a breakdown of withdrawal symptoms.

Table 18-4 Range of Withdrawal Symptoms

Mild Withdrawal Symptoms (within 6 hours from last drink)	Insomnia, tremulousness, hyperreflexia, anxiety, gastrointestinal upset, headache, palpitations.
Moderate Withdrawal Symptoms (12–24 hours after last drink)	All the mild symptoms plus generalized seizures.
Delirium Tremens (can last up to 7 days after last drink)	Altered sensorium with autonomic dysfunction and vital sign abnormalities. Visual hallucinations, tachycardia, hypertension, hyperthermia, agitation, diaphoresis.

Data from Newman, R. K., Stobart Gallagher, M. A., & Gomez, A. E. (2020). *Alcohol withdrawal*. https://www.ncbi.nlm.nih.gov/books/NBK441882/

Withdrawal Interventions and Safety

The goal of managing withdrawal symptoms is to prevent worsening progression. The range of treatment, based on severity of withdrawals symptoms, includes rehydration to benzodiazepines. Continuous symptom re-assessment is imperative to determine withdrawal severity, which determines treatment.

All members of the healthcare team need to be familiar with the symptoms of alcohol withdrawal and management. Assessment of symptoms is conducted utilizing the Clinical Institute for Withdrawal Assessment for Alcohol revised scale (CIWA-Ar). This tool allows clinicians to determine the severity of withdrawal symptoms and when to initiate medical therapeutic interventions (Newman et al., 2020). The CIWA-Ar monitors nausea/vomiting, headache, auditory disturbances, agitation, paroxysmal sweating, visual disturbances, tremor, clouding of sensorium, orientation, and anxiety (Newman et al., 2020).

Ideally, patients should be managed in a controlled environment due to the life-threatening risks of withdrawal. Patients with mild symptoms can be managed as outpatients, however, patients with suicidal ideations, polysubstance abuse, co-morbid psychiatric conditions, history of withdrawal seizures, high risk of delirium tremens, abnormal laboratory results, and absence of a support system should be admitted (Newman et al., 2020). Patients experiencing mild to moderate symptoms receive intravenous rehydration and correction of electrolyte abnormalities (Newman et al., 2020). Management of severe withdrawal symptoms is the use of long-acting benzodiazepines. Typical benzodiazepines used intravenously for withdrawal symptom management are lorazepam (Ativan) or diazepam (Valium) (Newman et al., 2020). Other medications can be added, such as anticonvulsants for severe seizures. In addition, "propofol is used to manage refractory cases of delirium tremens, and baclofen can be used to treat muscle spasms" (Newman et al., 2020, Section 7). Delirium tremens is a medical emergency and needs to be managed in an inpatient or intensive care setting (Grover & Ghosh, 2018). Regular monitoring of vital signs, fluid and electrolyte imbalance, and nutritional issues is necessary (Grover & Ghosh, 2018). Patients should be in a calm, comfortable, and quiet environment to minimize agitation.

After detoxification is complete, patients are encouraged to participate in therapeutic or mutual-help programs to promote long-term recovery. Offering one or more of the following therapeutic treatments is recommended: behavioral couples therapy for AUD, cognitive behavioral therapy for SUD, community reinforcement approach, motivational enhancement therapy, or 12-step facilitation (The Management of Substance Use Disorders Work Group, 2015). "Recovery is a process of change through which people improve their health and wellness, live self-directed lives, and strive to reach their full potential" (Substance Abuse and Mental Health Service Administration [SAMHSA], 2020, para. 1). The process of recovery involves support of peers, social networks, and families. Understanding the benefits of mutual help groups and other recovery-oriented support is important to be able to discuss with patients to discuss the benefits for their recovery (The Management of Substance Use Disorders Work Group, 2015).

Family Involvement

Family involvement is cardinal to recovery but can also be complex for both the patient and family. Patients with SUD will have individualized treatment plans, where families are encouraged to be aware of these goals. Family-involved therapy helps the family to understand their relationship patterns contributing to their loved ones' continued substance use (SAMHSA, 2004). Most treatment facilities provide families with psychoeducation to help them gain an understanding of their loved one's substance abuse, behaviors, and psychological consequences of use (SAMHSA, 2004). Families who engage in family therapy will develop ways to live without substances of abuse, which brings the families' strengths together to improve the support system and the impact the substance dependence had (SAMHSA, 2004).

Trauma and Substance Abuse

Service members and veterans with SUD often have co-occurring disorders such as post-traumatic stress disorder (PTSD). Research has shown that 82%–93% of veterans diagnosed with SUD were three to four times more likely to have a PTSD or depression diagnosis (Teeters et al., 2017). Of veterans who served in Operation Enduring Freedom (OEF) and Operation Iraqi Freedom (OIF) and were diagnosed with SUD, 63% had a diagnosis for PTSD (Teeters et al., 2017). Co-occurring disorder treatment decreases substance use when implementing the trauma-focused interventions (Teeters et al., 2017). Veterans who received SUD-only treatment result in leaving with untreated PTSD and may potentially relapse (Teeters et al., 2017). There are many different approaches to trauma treatment, which include trauma-informed therapy and trauma-focused interventions.

Trauma-informed care focuses on clinicians to acknowledge and understand a patient's life experience to deliver effective care to improve patient outcomes through increased engagement, adherence, and rapport (Menschner & Maul, 2016). Trauma-focused interventions directly address the trauma impact on a patient's life to focus on recovery. **Table 18-5** discusses research regarding different integrated treatments. The most studied integrated treatment program for SUD and PTSD is Seeking Safety. Seeking Safety is a manualized therapy that does not expose the patient to their trauma, however, it utilizes cognitive behavioral techniques to prioritize safety. Overall, integrated treatments have promising findings due to being tolerated by patients, demonstrating the ability to reduce symptoms of PTSD, SUD, and other pathology such as depression or anxiety (McCauley et al., 2012).

Suicide

"Suicide is the 10th leading cause of death for all ages in the United States" (Hedegaard et al., 2020, p. 1). Suicide is associated with a combination of individual, societal, relationship, and community factors (CDC, 2019). Risk factors include:

- Family history of suicide
- Family history of child maltreatment
- Previous suicide attempt(s)
- History of mental disorders, particularly clinical depression
- History of alcohol and substance abuse
- Feelings of hopelessness
- Impulsive or aggressive tendencies
- Cultural and religious beliefs (e.g., belief that suicide is a noble resolution of a personal dilemma)
- Local epidemics of suicide
- Isolation, a feeling of being cut off from other people
- Barriers to accessing mental health treatment
- Loss (relational, social, work, or financial)
- Physical illness
- Easy access to lethal methods
- Unwillingness to seek help because of the stigma attached to mental health and substance abuse disorders or to suicidal thoughts

(CDC, 2019, p. 1)

A meta-analysis was conducted by Poorolajal et al. (2015) to determine the association between SUD and suicide outcomes. After reviewing 12,413 references and 43 studies and a total of 870,967 participants, the authors concluded there is a strong association between SUD and suicide outcomes (Poorolajal et al., 2015). "Heavy alcohol consumers had a five-fold higher risk of suicide than social drinkers" (Pompili et al., 2010, p. 1396). Individuals who are diagnosed with a SUD typically have other risk factors of suicide to include financial problems and/or being cut-off from others. "Substance use and abuse can be common among persons prone to be impulsive, and among persons who engage in many types of high-risk behaviors that result in self-harm" (Digital Communications Division, 2008). Ultimately, alcohol consumption and drug use can exacerbate extreme moods or symptoms of a disorder resulting in disinhibition and impulsivity. This can lead to actions resulting in an unintentional suicide due to being under the influence of alcohol/drugs. In addition, individuals have a significant risk of death when combining alcohol with illicit or prescription drugs.

Table 18-5 Integrated Treatments for Comorbid PTSD and SUD

Treatment	Exposure	Trial Design	Sample	Outcomes	References
TREM Trauma Exposure and Empowerment Model	None	**Quasi- Experimental, Non-Equivalent Group** TREM as part of a larger comprehensive treatment model v. TAU at community substance use treatment program; 6- and 12-month follow-up	342 women with a trauma history and SUD, presenting for SUD treatment	Significantly greater reduction in drug use and PTSD symptoms among integrated treatment (including TREM) group compared to TAU.	Harris, 1998; Amaro et al., 2007
CBT for PTSD	None	**Open Pilot Trial** Post-treatment and 3-month follow-up	11 patients in community addictions treatment	Significant impact on PTSD symptoms and substance use; demonstrated feasibility of delivery in community addictions treatment facility.	McGovern et al., 2009
Transcend	None	**Open Pilot Trial** 6- and 12-month follow-up	46 male Vietnam veterans with PTSD and SUDs, presenting in partial hospitalization program	Significant improvements in PTSD symptoms across all follow-ups; Decreased substance use at follow-up.	Donovan et al., 2001
Seeking Safety	None	**Uncontrolled Trial** 3-month follow-up	27 females with trauma history and SUD, recruited from the community	Among completers ($n = 17$), significant improvements in substance use, trauma-related symptoms, suicide risk, depression, social adjustment, problem solving, family functioning, and cognitions about substance use.	Najavits, 1998

(continues)

Table 18-5 Integrated Treatments for Comorbid PTSD and SUD *(continued)*

Treatment	Exposure	Trial Design	Sample	Outcomes	References
		Uncontrolled Trial 3-month follow-up	17 females with PTSD and SUD, incarcerated sample	Significant improvement in PTSD symptoms (53% no longer met criteria at post-treatment); improvement in PTSD maintained at follow-up; significant reductions in SUD symptoms, with only 35% reporting use within 3 months of prison release.	Zlotnick et al., 2003
		Uncontrolled Trial Pre and post only	25 male and female veterans with PTSD and SUD, presenting in outpatient Veterans Administration clinic	Significant improvements in self-reported PTSD symptoms, quality of life, communication, problem-solving skills and abstinence at post-treatment.	Cook et al., 2006
		RCT SS and standard community care v. relapse prevention and standard community care; 6- and 9-month follow-ups	107 females with PTSD or sub-threshold PTSD and SUD, presenting in community clinic	Significant reductions in SUDs and PTSD for both groups; PTSD symptoms still in moderate severity range; no group differences at follow-up.	Hien et al., 2004
		Uncontrolled Pilot SS plus prolonged exposure	5 men with comorbid PTSD and substance dependence presenting at outpatient clinic	Significant improvements in drug use, trauma symptoms, psychosocial functioning, anxiety, and feelings/thoughts related to safety.	Najavits et al., 2005

		RCT SS and standard community care v. standard community care; 3-month follow-up	33 adolescent girls with PTSD and SUD, recruited from community and community clinics	Significantly improved outcomes among SS group regarding attitudes toward substance use, some trauma-related symptoms, and associated pathology.	Najavits et al., 2006
		Quasi-Experimental SS v. wait list control	107 females with PTSD or sub-threshold PTSD and SUD, low-income sample	Significant reductions in PTSD symptoms and alcohol use among SS v. wait list control; trend toward significant decrease in drug use for SS group.	Cohen et al., 2006
		Quasi-Experimental SS group v. TAU	313 women with trauma history, SUD and comorbid Axis I or Axis II disorder	SS group showed greater treatment retention over 3 months and greater improvement in PTSD symptoms and coping skills than TAU.	Gatz et al., 2007
		RCT SS and TAU v. TAU	49 females with PTSD or sub-threshold PTSD and SUD, incarcerated sample	No significant differences between groups on all key domains; both conditions showed significant improvements in PTSD and SUD symptoms across time.	Zlotnick et al., 2009
		RCT SS v. Women's Health Education; 6-, 9-, and 12-month follow-up	353 females with PTSD or sub-threshold PTSD and SUD, from national, multi-site community sample	Significant reduction in PTSD for both groups; no group differences on PTSD outcomes; no significant impact on abstinence at follow-up.	Hien et al., 2009

(continues)

Table 18-5 **Integrated Treatments for Comorbid PTSD and SUD** *(continued)*

Treatment	Exposure	Trial Design	Sample	Outcomes	References
		Uncontrolled Pilot	14 male OEF/OIF veterans	Preliminary findings show significant reductions in PTSD symptoms and alcohol use.	Norman et al., 2010
		Controlled Trial SS v. wait list control	114 incarcerated women reporting trauma history, history of SUD, and at least moderate PTSD symptoms	SS group demonstrated decreased depression, improved interpersonal functioning, and decreased maladaptive coping compared to control group.	Lynch et al., 2012
		RCT SS v. TAU; 3-month follow-up	98 male veterans with PTSD and SUD (treatment as usual did not have to meet criteria for PTSD), presenting in outpatient Veterans Administration clinic	Significantly better drug use outcomes among SS than TAU; no differences between groups in alcohol use or PTSD symptom improvement.	Boden et al., 2012
		RCT SDPT v. 12-Step Facilitation; 1-month follow-up	19 men and women with PTSD or sub-threshold PTSD and SUD, presenting in methadone clinic	Significant improvement in SUD and PTSD severity for both groups; no differences between groups.	Triffleman et al., 2000

SDPT Substance Dependence PTSD Therapy	In vivo	**Open Pilot Trial** 6-month follow-up	39 men and women with PTSD and cocaine dependence, presenting for SUD treatment	Significant improvement in PTSD and cocaine dependence symptoms for completers; improvements maintained at follow-up.	Back et al., 2001; Brady et al., 2001
COPE Concurrent treatment of PTSD and SUD using Prolonged Exposure	In vivo and Imaginal	**RCT** COPE plus TAU v. TAU; 3- and 9-month follow-up	103 men and women with PTSD and drug dependence, presenting for SUD treatment in Australia	Significant improvement in SUD and PTSD severity for both groups; Greater reduction in PTSD among treatment group.	Mills et al., in press
		Case Study 3- and 6-month follow-up	OEF/OIF male veteran with PTSD and alcohol dependence	Preliminary findings show significant improvement in SUD and PTSD at end of treatment and both follow-up time points.	Back et al., 2012

McCauley, J. L., Killeen, T., Gros, D. F., Brady, K. T., & Back, S. E. (2012, September 1). Posttraumatic stress disorder and co-occurring substance use disorders: Advances in assessment and treatment. *Clinical Psychology, 19*(3). https://doi.org/10.1111/cpsp.12006

Clinicians can assist patients to minimize the risk of overdose when prescribing opioids by also prescribing Naloxone. In response to our nation's opioid crisis, the U.S. Surgeon General called to action for clinician's to prescribe Naloxone for high opioid utilizers and for individuals who are using illicit drugs to ask their clinician to prescribe them Naloxone (U.S. Health and Human Services, 2018). Evidence has shown that Naloxone has saved lives from opioid overdoses. Clinicians should prescribe Naloxone to:

- Patients prescribed opioids who:
  - Are receiving opioids at a dosage of 50 morphine milligram equivalents (MME) per day or greater (the CDC's MME calculator can be accessed here).
  - Have respiratory conditions such as chronic obstructive pulmonary disease (COPD) or obstructive sleep apnea (regardless of opioid dose).
  - Have been prescribed benzodiazepines (regardless of opioid dose). o Have a non-opioid substance use disorder, report excessive alcohol use, or have a mental health disorder (regardless of opioid dose).
- Patients at high risk for experiencing or responding to an opioid overdose, including individuals:
  - Using heroin, illicit synthetic opioids or misusing prescription opioids.
  - Using other illicit drugs such as stimulants, including methamphetamine and cocaine, which could potentially be contaminated with illicit synthetic opioids like fentanyl.
  - Receiving treatment for opioid use disorder, including medication-assisted treatment with methadone, buprenorphine, or naltrexone.
  - With a history of opioid misuse that were recently released from incarceration or other controlled settings where tolerance to opioids has been lost.(U.S. Health and Human Services, 2018, p. 2)

Conclusion

High-risk drinking behaviors are common within the military and veteran population. Early intervention utilizing the SBIRT method will help identify patients early and reduce high-risk drinking behaviors. SBIRT can be utilized by all healthcare practitioners in all settings to provide early intervention to as many patients as possible. There are different treatment modalities to include medications and co-occurring programs to address underlying mental health conditions. There is a strong association between suicide and heavy alcohol consumption. Individuals with substance use disorders have multiple suicide risk factors to be aware of. One life-saving technique is to prescribe Naloxone to individuals who are prescribed opioids to prevent overdose.

References

Agerwala, S. M., & McCance-Katz, E. F. (2012). Integrating screening, brief intervention, and referral to treatment (SBIRT) into clinical practice settings: A brief review. *Journal of Psychoactive Drugs*, *44*, 307–317.

American Psychiatric Association. (2013). Substance use disorders. In *Diagnostic and statistical manual of mental disorders* (5th ed.). Government Printing Office.

CDC. (2019). *Suicide: Risk and protective factors.* https://www.cdc.gov/violenceprevention/suicide/riskprotectivefactors.html

Digital Communications Division. (2008). *Does alcohol and other drug abuse increase the risk for suicide?* https://www.hhs.gov/answers/mental-health-and-substance-abuse/does-alcohol-increase-risk-of-suicide/index.html

Drug facts: Substance use and military life. (2019). *National Institute on Drug Abuse*, 1–11.

Grover, S., & Ghosh, A. (2018). Delirium tremens: Assessment and management. *Journal of Clinical and Experimental Hepatology*, *8*, 460–470.

Hedegaard, H., Curtin, S. C., & Warner, M. (2020, April). *Increase in suicide mortality in the United States, 1999-2018* [Press release]. Centers for Disease Control and Prevention National Center for Health Statistics: https://www.cdc.gov/nchs/products/index.htm

Hoggatt, K. J., Lehavot, K., Krenek, M., Schweizer, C. A., & Simpson, T. (2017, March 29). Prevalence of substance misuse among US veterans in the general population. *The American Journal on Addictions, 26*, 357–365. doi:10.1111/ajad.12534

McCauley, J. L., Killeen, T., Gros, D. F., Brady, K. T., & Back, S. E. (2012, September 1). Posttraumatic stress disorder and co-occurring substance use disorders: Advances in assessment and treatment. *Clinical Psychology, 19*(3). doi:10.1111/cpsp.12006

Menschner, C., & Maul, A. (2016,). April. *Center for Health Care Strategies*. https://www.samhsa.gov/sites/default/files/programs_campaigns/childrens_mental_health/atc-whitepaper-040616.pdf

National Institutes of Health. (n.d.). Rethinking drinking: Alcohol & your health. https://www.rethinkingdrinking.niaaa.nih.gov/How-much-is-too-much/Is-your-drinking-pattern-risky/Drinking-Levels.aspx

Newman, R. K., Stobart Gallagher, M. A., & Gomez, A. E. (2020). *Alcohol withdrawal*. https://www.ncbi.nlm.nih.gov/books/NBK441882/

Olson, R., Casavale, K., Rihane, C., Stoody, E. E., Britten, P., Reedy, J., ... Rodgers, A. B. (2015). *2015–2020 dietary guidelines*. Retrieved from Office of Disease Prevention and Health Promotion: https://health.gov/our-work/food-nutrition/2015-2020-dietary-guidelines/guidelines/appendix-9/

Pompili, M., Serafini, G., Innamorati, M., Dominici, G., Ferracuti, S., Kotzalidis, G. D., ... Lester, D. (2010, March 29). Suicidal behavior and alcohol abuse. *International Journal of Environmental Research and Public Health, 7*, 1392–1431. doi:10.3390/ijerph7041392

Poorolajal, J., Haghtalab, T., Farhadi, M., & Darvishi, N. (2015). Substance use disorder and risk of suicidal ideation, suicide attempt and suicide death: A meta-analysis. *Journal of Public Health, 38*, 282–291. https://doi.org/10.1093/pubmed/fdv148

Sirratt, D., Ozanian, A., & Traenkner, B. (2012). Epidemiology and prevention of substance use disorders in the military. *Military Medicine, 177*, 21–28.

Substance Abuse and Mental Health Services Administration. (2004). Substance abuse treatment and family therapy. In *Center for Substance Abuse Treatment: Treatment improvement protocol (TIP) series No. 39*. https://www.ncbi.nlm.nih.gov/books/NBK64265/?report=reader

Substance Abuse and Mental Health Service Administration. *Recovery and recovery support*. (2020). https://www samhsa.gov/find-help/recovery

Substance Abuse and Mental Health Services Administration website. (n.d.). https://www.samhsa.gov/sbirt/about

Substance Abuse and Mental Health Services Administration and National Institute on Alcohol Abuse and Alcoholism. (2015). *Medication for the treatment of alcohol use disorder: A brief guide* [HHS Publication No. (SMA) 15-4907]. Substance Abuse and Mental Health Services Administration.

Teeters, J. B., Lancaster, C. L., Brown, D. G., & Back, S. E. (2017, August 30). Substance use disorders in military veterans: Prevalence and treatment challenges. *Substance Abuse and Rehabilitation*, 69–77. doi:10.2147/SAR.SI16720

The Management of Substance Use Disorders Work Group. (2015). *VA/DoD clinical practice guidelines for the management of substance use disorders* (VA/DoD Version 3.0). Government Printing Office.

U.S. Health and Human Services. (2018). *Naloxone: The opioid reversal drug that saves lives*. https://www.hhs.gov/opioids/sites/default/files/2018-12/naloxone-coprescribing-guidance.pdf

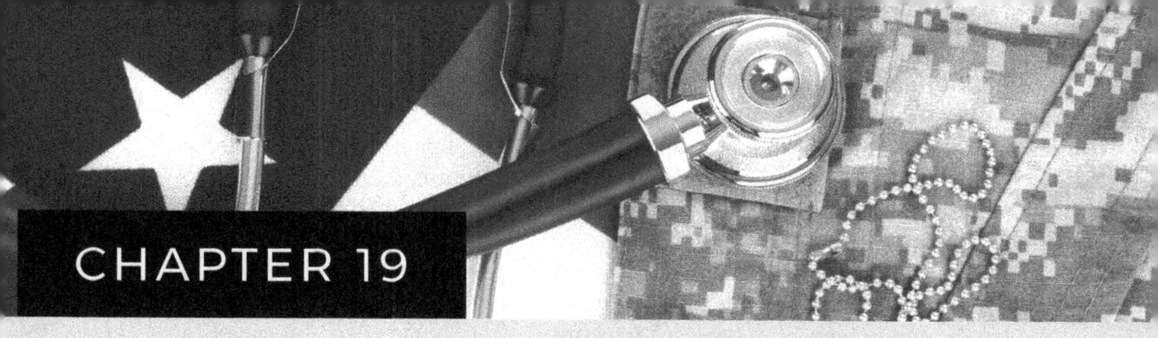

CHAPTER 19

Treating Victims of Military Sexual Trauma

Jennifer Korkosz and Wendy Lee

It is crucial that civilian healthcare professionals be prepared to treat victims of trauma caused by a sexual assault (SA) experienced while serving in the military. Therefore, the purpose of this chapter is to inform and prepare civilian healthcare providers with the discernment needed to care for victims of military sexual trauma (MST). While this chapter is focused on the female veteran population and MST, it is important to keep in mind that males can also experience MST—it is estimated that 4% of servicemen in the OIF/OEF era have acknowledged experiencing some event that meets the accepted definition of sexual trauma (Barth et al., 2016). Because of this, it is important that universally both men and women be asked about sexual harassment and assault.

Why Prepare for MST Patients?

MST victims often present to civilian healthcare providers for various ailments whose cause could originate from a sexual assault. Sexual assault (SA) occurs at lower rates in the military than in civilian life, at about 1.5% per person per year in the military compared to an estimated one in five women and one in seventy-one men in civilian lifetime rates (Black, 2011; Rees et al., 2011; Defense Manpower Data Center [DMDC], 2018). However, this 1.5% rate in the military translates to more than 20,000 cases per year. Approximately one-third of the victims are male and two-thirds female (DMDC, 2018). Although the SA rate is relatively lower in the military than in the civilian population, the absolute MST numbers are substantial.

Victims who have experienced sexual harassment are more prone to be sexually assaulted. Researchers reported out of 901 adults in the U.S., 32.7% adults reported sexual harassment and 24.6% reported sexual assault (Mumford et al., 2020). Out of those who were sexually harassed, respondents were 20 times more likely to report sexual assault (Mumford et al., 2020). Earlier research on military populations evaluating risk factors for sexual assault found that when sexual harassment was escalated, physical assaults were more common (Sadler et al., 2001).

In addition to logistical constraints, MST victims may report to civilian healthcare facilities because they would prefer to avoid reporting an SA to their military superiors out of fear of stigma or concerns of reprisal. Additionally, some MST patients who are no longer military members present to civilian healthcare facilities to avoid the Veterans Administration (VA), either to receive prompt care, or to avoid VA hassles and to prevent possible VA tracking regarding this sensitive personal issue.

Furthermore, providers in general may lack appropriate training and may be uneasy in conducting sexual assault examinations and providing appropriate care (Lee et al., 2019). While the Association of American Medical Colleges recommends that academic institutions incorporate instruction to overcome these barriers (Agency for Healthcare, Research, and Quality [AHRQ], 2003; American Association of Colleges for Nursing [AACN], 2015a; Association of American Medical Colleges, 2014), medical professional education lags in implementing SA education and training (Koo et al., 2013). Worse, training rates may be declining. A 2014 Association of American Medical Colleges report found that only 38% of graduating U.S. physicians participated in sexual assault care education, a decrease of 7% from 2010 (Solymos et al., 2015). For these reasons, civilian healthcare providers need to properly prepare to care for MST victims.

Defining MST and Sexual Assault and Sexual Harassment

Sexual trauma follows an SA. That is, an SA is an experience, not a stand-alone diagnosis (Scott & Philpott, 2014). In the context of this chapter, MST refers to trauma that results from sexual activities that are unwanted or forced against the wishes of a military victim. According to the U.S. Commission on Civil Rights (2014), these acts may be provoked by pressure and abuse of authority for favors, such as promotions or improved circumstances that the assaulted person may have been unable to refuse.

According to the Department of Defense (DOD) Directive 6495.01, Sexual Assault Prevention and Response (SAPR) Program, sexual assault is defined as "Intentional sexual contact characterized by use of force, threats, intimidation, or abuse of authority or when the victim does not or cannot consent. Sexual assault includes rape, forcible sodomy (oral or anal sex), and other unwanted sexual contact that is aggravated, abusive, or wrongful (including unwanted and inappropriate sexual contact), or attempts to commit these acts."

Briefly, the military defines sexual harassment as unwelcomed "offensive comments and gestures of a sexual nature" that are "severe or pervasive," and if overlooked or submitted to, can impact career decisions or career situation (e.g., job status, pay, DoD, 2018, p. 9). The military does not require a demonstration of "concrete psychological harm," but merely that "a reasonable person would perceive, and the victim [complainant] does perceive, the environment as hostile or offensive," whether this behavior occurs in person, through electronic communications, or through social media (DoD, 2018, p.9). Further, supervisors are explicitly responsible to address, (and not overlook) sexual harassment in any form.

However, these definitions are not identical to civilian definitions, which vary from jurisdiction to jurisdiction. For clarity, differences between civilian and military definitions, laws, and guidelines are provided in Appendix A.

Traumatic Effects of SA

The experience by men and women of sexual assault/sexual trauma can have lifelong detrimental effects physically and emotionally. Sexual assaults have a range of trauma effects beyond the immediate injuries, including physical and mental anguish. Victims often have unpredictable levels of reactions, thoughts of detachment, and difficulty sleeping. They also have trouble remembering or focusing. Problems with coping can often lead to alcohol or drug abuse.

Daily events can trigger a traumatic memory of the abuse. They find it difficult to establish and maintain personal friendships or long-term relationships. Other residual physical health problems can include headaches, pain, reduced or absent sexual libido, and gastrointestinal problems (Wolff & Mills, 2016).

Comorbidities

Effective treatment is important because SA patients often experience a combination of physical injuries and psychological symptoms, which may lead to long-term health problems and the development of associated comorbidities, such as asthma, bowel disorders, diabetes, chronic pain, headaches, and difficulty sleeping (Black et al., 2011; DeLahunta, 1997; Molnar et al., 2001; Planty et al., 2013; Rees et al., 2011). The quality of these patients' lives may suffer, and without identification and adequate treatment, they may develop depression, anxiety, or suicidal tendencies. Female veterans with a history of MST had more pain diagnoses—headache, chronic pelvic pain, chronic back pain, non-specific joint pain, fibromyalgia, generalized abdominal pain, dyspareunia, and irritable bowel syndrome—in comparison to those without a history of MST (Cichowski et al., 2017).

SA patients might also be at increased risk of developing psychiatric disorders, such as phobias, aggression, alienation, and sexual dysfunction (Black et al., 2011; DeLahunta, 1997; Molnar et al., 2001; Planty et al., 2013; Rees et al., 2011). Patients who have experienced SA have also been noted to be at increased risk for tobacco use, alcohol and drug use, and disordered eating habits (Santaularia et al., 2014). It is important that we identify their history to better help them manage the sequelae that may affect them individually.

Symptoms of post-traumatic stress disorder (PTSD) are also common in SA victims. Military women seem to show higher rates and levels of PTSD following an SA than victims experiencing the same crime in civilian life. For example, PTSD is nine times higher for those who experienced MST than for military members who did not experience sexual trauma, and five times higher for those with MST than for those with civilian trauma (Fayazrad, 2013).

Barriers to Reporting SA

Both military and civilian SA victims face significant barriers to reporting, including blame, disbelief, inaction, retaliation, humiliation, ostracism, and damage to one's career and reputation (Bergman et al., 2002; Cortina & Berdahl, 2008).

Fear of reporting also includes assumptions that the process of reporting would be costly to the victim and not render many benefits (Cortina & Berdahl, 2008; Cortina & Magley, 2003; Nelson, 2018).

Many victims instead choose to evade the person who attacked them and separate themselves mentally from the situation. They continue to suffer without attempting to settle the situation, or they attempt to appease their offender by formulating excuse justifications to explain the perpetrator's behavior (Magley, 2002).

SA victims may therefore overlook the event or placate the harasser in an effort to maintain the relationship (Magley, 2002). While victims may seek support from peers, friends, or family, only one third report the harassment to management (Cortina & Berdahl, 2008; Cortina & Magley, 2003; Magley, 2002).

This low level of reporting may be due to military culture, as military members believe that they need to be strong and handle situations on their own. Due to this belief, they may not report an SA because they are afraid that no one would take them seriously, fear that their military careers might be ruined, or fear the stigma often associated with SA. This is compounded by the fear of retaliation from the perpetrator or others who know about the incident; therefore, they blame themselves instead of taking action (Fayazrad, 2013).

Fear of retaliation is perhaps the most insidious reason for not reporting an assault. Retaliation may take the form of work-related actions that have negative effects on the employee. Retaliation may take a social form with verbal and nonverbal acts such as name calling, ostracism, blame, threats, or the "silent treatment" (Cortina & Magley, 2003). Consequently, some SA victims simply consider leaving their profession/military altogether (National Academies of Sciences, Engineering, and Medicine, 2018; Nelson, 2018).

MST Victims Are Reluctant Patients

Treating MST patients is particularly challenging because victims are often reluctant patients. This reluctance is revealed in multiple ways.

First, they are hesitant to seek medical treatment, so it is important for civilian providers to recognize that MST victims may delay presentation for days, months, or years after their assault.

Second, many MST victims have low levels of disclosure because they are not comfortable talking about the sexual assault (Berry & Rutledge 2016).

Third, MST victims often present with a chief complaint that is not directly related to their assault, so it is perhaps not surprising that only roughly one quarter of victims are screened for SA by their healthcare providers.

It is therefore crucial for civilian healthcare providers to ask the right questions, get complete answers, and take appropriate steps to help MST victims.

Most are not going to present themselves with their chief complaint directly related to their assault. It is up to the provider to ask the questions, get the answers, and be able to appropriately help them. Berry and Rutledge (2016) found that most of the 143 women included in their cross-sectional descriptive survey (n = 103, 72.5%) agreed that they felt comfortable with being asked about sexual assault, but there were only 41 (28.7%) who had been screened for sexual assault by their healthcare providers. Some may disclose on their own; however, unless asked by the health provider, most victims would not raise the subject on their own.

How to Prepare for Sexual Assault Patients

First, Be Aware

Be aware that MST victims may be male or female.

Be aware that MST victims are reluctant patients.

Be aware that many MST victims therefore delay before presenting.

Be aware that many MST victims present for something other than sexual trauma.

Be aware that many MST victims do not feel comfortable talking about their assault. The patient will not truthfully answer the screening questions until they have established a relationship with a provider in the civilian healthcare setting. Therefore, the first action toward treating a MST victim is establishing a supportive relationship that fosters clear, comprehensive, and honest communication.

Communication guidance comes from the Concept of Trauma and Guidance for a trauma-informed approach (2014) of the Substance Abuse and Mental Health Services Administration (SAMHSA). They provide six key principles:

1. Safety
2. Trustworthiness and Transparency
3. Peer Support
4. Collaboration and Mutuality
5. Empowerment, Voice, and Choice
6. Cultural, Historical, and Gender Issues

Following these principles is fundamental to providing an ethical and effective relationship with the MST patient.

Second, Prepare

Education and training are necessary when preparing to act. There are multiple ways to build professional competency and comfort with the possible presentations and sequelae associated with patients who survive sexual trauma.

Whether through professional conferences, online educational offerings, staying current with the literature, or continuing education presentations, on-point information is readily available and can bring with it the confidence patients count on their providers to possess. In this context, all members of the healthcare team should be educated and trained to ask appropriate questions, recognize MST, and provide the foundation for appropriate care.

Practice can greatly assist in preparing for MST patients. This is crucial, because MST patients are reluctant patients, with low levels of divulgence regarding their SA. They delay in seeking treatment, presenting with primary complaints other than those related to the SA. Assault victims may experience shame, guilt, self-blame, or PTSD symptoms. They may fear that revealing their assault could jeopardize their privacy or ruin their careers. Further, SA is a sensitive topic, so providers may be generally uneasy about discussing SA with a patient.

Simulation events provide a useful practice method to prepare to treat MST patients. Simulation events are becoming increasingly common in health care because simulation events allow healthcare providers the opportunity to practice the steps involved in interviewing, assessing, and developing treatment plans for patients without exposing actual patients to risk (Lee et al., 2019).

Formal simulation events often involve the use of a standardized patient who is trained to play the role of the MST patient. This realism fosters interview skills, effective communication, and confidence in treating MST victims (Lee et al., 2019).

For treating MST patients, simulations can be particularly effective because sexual-trauma patients are reticent to divulge information about the assault and because the topic of sexual assault and trauma is often an uncomfortable topic for healthcare providers.

Practicing in preparation for MST patients can potentially make the provider more relaxed and more confident, thereby building a foundation for providing quality care. To prepare for MST patients, we therefore recommend practicing the interview, assessment, and treatment plan, either with a standardized patient or with role-playing exercises using colleagues as the faux MST victim.

Third, Act

Civilian providers must take action with MST victims. Whether by preparation, by screening and diagnosing, by treating, or by providing follow-up, civilian providers are responsible to provide high levels of care for MST patients.

Diagnosing MST

The first step in diagnosing MST is looking beyond the primary-patient complaint at presentation. While it is possible that an MST victim will present for problems directly related to the assault, it is likely more common that the primary complaint will be unrelated to the assault.

Providers must therefore look beyond common complaints of, for example, somatic issues, genitourinary/gynecological issues, or psychological issues. **Table 19-1** provides examples of common primary complaints of MST victims unrelated to their assault (WHO, 2017, Wolff & Mills, 2016).

It is also important to realize that the primary complaint may not be clearly expressed by the reluctant MST patient. Helping the MST victim to peel back the layers can take

Table 19-1 Common Primary Complaints of MST Victims Unrelated to their Assault

Category	Complaints
Somatic	Abdominal pain, gastrointestinal disorders, headaches, back pain, limited mobility, or overall poor health
Genitourinary/ Gynecological	Sexually transmitted infections, or unwanted pregnancy
Psychological	Depression, anxiety, or post-traumatic stress disorder

Data from World Health Organization. (2017). *Violence against women fact sheet.* https://www.who.int/en/news-room/fact-sheets/detail/violence-against-women; Wolff, K. B., & Mills, P. D. (2016). Reporting military sexual trauma: A mixed-methods study of women veterans' experiences who served from World War II to the war in Afghanistan. *Military Medicine*, 181(8), 840–848. https://doi.org/10.7205/milmed-d-15-00404

Table 19-2 Sample Sexual Assault Screening Questions

Item Question
1. Did you have any unwanted sexual experiences in the military? For example, threatening or repeated sexual attention, comments or touching?
2. Did you have any sexual contact against your will or when unable to say no, such as being forced, or when asleep or intoxicated?

Reproduced from U.S. Department of Veterans Affairs. (2019). *Military health history.* https://www.va.gov/OAA/archive/Military-Health-History-Card-for-print.pdf

time, patience, supportive compassion, and careful and diplomatic wordings.

The consultation is likely to involve uncomfortable questions—uncomfortable for both the patient and the provider, which is why preparation and practice are so important to diagnosing the MST victim.

Table 19-2 displays sample sexual assault screening questions from the ACOG Committee Opinion No 777 (2019).

The MST diagnosis may not be clearly visible, so multiple appointments may be necessary, to compile lab results, radiologic reports, and other exam components, as well as to coax the victim into revealing that they were sexually assaulted. Persistence is key. Appropriate questions should be asked at every visit. As Moore (2015) noted, "If we exclude patients for any reason, for example, we know the patient or the patient doesn't look like someone we think would have experienced a sexual assault, we will miss the chance to intervene for a number of patients in need" (p. 1).

Treating MST

Appropriately treating MST depends on the individual situation. Treating the immediate medical issues is primary, but because of the extensive list of possibilities, exhaustive treatment protocols will not be detailed here. However, it is crucial to provide compassionate and effective care, as well as appropriate follow-up and referrals. A Post-Assault Clinical Flow Sheet is provided in Appendix B.

If a patient acknowledges being a sexual assault survivor, the first step is to determine whether they currently feel safe or have safety concerns (Moore, 2015). Next, the provider should ask when the incident happened and if they have sought any other care. "If more than 7 days have elapsed since the alleged incident, the likelihood of obtaining DNA evidence is extremely low and forensic swabs and samples are usually not obtained" (Kennedy & White, 2015, p. 43).

Whether presentation is immediate or delayed, MST victims can be offered the same counseling regarding their treatment options. If within 72 hours of possible exposure, then initiating HIV post-prophylaxis is recommended (CDC, 2015).

Consideration for emergency contraception or pregnancy testing should be evaluated in female survivors. Depending on the injuries suffered, a tetanus booster may be warranted and, in some cases, serum testing for HIV, hepatitis B, and syphilis infections are necessary.

Once the survivor is 2–3 weeks from their sexual assault, screening for chlamydia and gonorrhea for both males and females is recommended. If symptomatic, screening is appropriate for vaginal infections (bacterial vaginosis, trichomonas, and candidiasis) for females. HPV vaccination may be appropriate for both male and female survivors.

The CDC 2015 Sexually Transmitted Diseases Treatment Guidelines state, "There could be an indication for post-exposure hepatitis B vaccination (without Hepatitis B immunoglobulin) if the hepatitis status of the assailant is unknown and the survivor has not been previously vaccinated." (p. 1)

Follow-up and Referrals

If an acute exam was completed and it included initial testing, a follow-up visit roughly one week later can provide an opportunity to review any results, provide essential treatments, and plan for any further follow-ups. If the initial tests are negative and prophylactic treatment was not provided, then repeat STD testing can either reaffirm the negative results or reveal a positive test that perhaps had initial levels that were too low.

An additional exam at 1–2 months can allow for a physical exam for symptoms not apparent in prior visits, such as the development of genital warts. The CDC guidance also advocates laboratory testing for syphilis to be repeated at 4–6 weeks and 3 months, and HIV testing to be repeated at 6 weeks, 3 months, and 6 months.

The MST survivor's mental healthcare needs should be assessed at every visit and referred to appropriate experts when the physician considers it necessary for the patient's mental state. Ensuring "that they are receiving adequate psychological support is vital, as sexual violence is a leading cause of post-traumatic stress disorder" (Kennedy & White, 2015, p. 44).

Importance of Documentation

Documentation is crucial. For the continuity of their care, it is important to document the interventions that have been taken and what procedures should be followed during subsequent follow-up exams.

Provide enough information so the next provider or professional doesn't have to repeat the same question pathway; avoiding redundancy is of great benefit toward reducing survivor frustration. Please emphasize that confidentiality will be protected and the MST survivor will not have additional suffering because their story was shared inappropriately.

Know the Law, Follow the Law

It is crucial that medical professionals know the law and follow the law regarding sexual assault. Sexual assault is a crime under federal law (10 U.S. Code 920, Art. 120) (**Table 19-3**). Some states require mandatory reporting, some states do not require reporting, and some states require consent of the victim before health providers can report sexual assault to legal authorities. The Victim Rights Law Center tracks state-by-state laws and mandatory reporting requirements (https://www.victimrights.org/resources-professionals). Other legal and support resources are provided in Appendix C.

Table 19-3 ICD-10 Sampling of codes related to sexual assault (CMS, 2019)

ICD-10-CM Diagnosis Code	Description
T74.2	Sexual abuse, confirmed
T74.21XA	Adult sexual abuse, confirmed, initial encounter
S00-T88	Injury, poisoning, and certain other consequences of external causes
Z04.41	Encounter for examination and observation following alleged adult rape

Centers for Medicare & Medicaid Services. (2019). *ICD-10-CM official guidelines for coding and reporting*. https://www.cms.gov/Medicare/Coding/ICD10/Downloads/2020-Coding-Guidelines.pdf

References

10 U.S.C. § 920—U.S. Code—Unannotated Title 10. Armed Forces § 920. Art. 120. *Rape and sexual assault generally on Westlaw*. https://codes.findlaw.com/us/title-10-armed-forces/10-usc-sect-920.html.

Agency for Healthcare Research and Quality (AHRQ) (2003). Health professions training programs, professional standards, and guidelines. http://archive.ahrq.gov/research/victsexual/victsex2.htm.

American Association of Colleges for Nursing. (2015) Violence as a public health problem 2015. http://www.aacn.nche.edu/publications/position/violence-problem.

American College of Obstetricians and Gynecologists. (2019). ACOG Committee Opinion Number 777. Committee on Health Care for Underserved Women. Sexual assault. *Obstetrics and Gynecology*, *133*, e296–e302. DOI: 10.3399/bjgp15X683305

Association of American Medical Colleges. (2014) Medical School Graduation Questionnaire: 2014 all schools summary report 2014. https://www.aamc.org/download/397432/data/2014gqallschoolssummaryreport.pdf.

Barth, S. K., Kimerling, R. E., Pavao, J., McCutcheon, S. J., Batten, S. V., Dursa, E. et al. (2016). Military sexual trauma among recent veterans: Correlates of sexual assault and sexual harassment. *American Journal of Preventive Medicine*, *50*(1), 77–86. doi:10.1016/j.amepre.2015.06.012

Bergman, M. E., Langhout, R. D., Palmieri, P. A., Cortina, L. M., & Fitzgerald, L. F. (2002). The (un) reasonableness of reporting: Antecedents and consequences of reporting sexual harassment. *Journal of Applied Psychology*, *87*(2), 230.

Berry, K. M., & Rutledge, C. M. (2016). Factors that influence women to disclose sexual assault history to health care providers. *Journal of Obstetric, Gynecologic & Neonatal Nursing*, *45*(4), 553–564.

Black, M. C., Basile, K. C., Breiding, M. J., Smith, S. G., Walters, M. L., Merrick, M. T., . . Stevens, M. R. (2011). *National intimate partner and sexual violence survey: 2010 summary report*. National Center for Injury Prevention and Control of the Centers for Disease Control and Prevention.

Centers for Disease Control and Prevention. (2015). Sexual assault and abuse and STDs. *2015 sexually transmitted diseases treatment guidelines*. https://www.cdc.gov/std/tg2015/sexual-assault.htm.

Centers for Medicare & Medicaid Services. (2019). ICD-10-CM Official Guidelines for Coding and Reporting. Available at: https://www.cms.gov/Medicare/Coding/ICD10/Downloads/2020-Coding-Guidelines.pdf

Cichowski, S. B., Rogers, R. G., Clark, E. A., Murata, E., Murata, A., & Murata, G. (2017). Military sexual trauma in female veterans is associated with chronic pain conditions. Military medicine, 182(9-10), e1895–e1899. doi: 10.7205/MILMED-D-16-00393

Cortina, L. M., & Berdahl, J. L. (2008). Sexual harassment in organizations: A decade of research in review. *Handbook of Organizational Behavior*, *1*, 469–497.

Cortina, L. M., & Magley, V. J. (2003). Raising voice, risking retaliation: Events following interpersonal mistreatment in the workplace. *Journal of Occupational Health Psychology*, *8*(4), 247.

Defense Manpower Data Center (DMDC). (2018), *DoD personnel, workforce reports & publications*. Retrieved from https://www.dmdc.osd.mil/appj/dwp/dwp_reports.jsp

DeLahunta, E. & Tulsky, A. (1996). Personal exposure of faculty and medical students to family violence. *JAMA* 275(24), 1903–1906.

DeLahunta, E. (1997). Sexual assault. *Clinical Obstetrics and Gynecology, 40*(3): 648–660

Department of Defense. (2018). *DoD Instruction 1020.03—Harassment prevention and response in the Armed Forces*. (1020.03). https://www.documentcloud.org/documents/4375091-DOD-INSTRUCTION-1020-03-HARASSMENT-PREVENTION.html.

Department of Defense Office of Inspector General. (2019). Audit of DoD efforts to consult with victims of sexual assault committed by military personnel in the United States regarding the victim's preference for prosecution DODIG-2019-064. Retrieved Nov 10, 2019 from https://www.dodig.mil/reports.html/Article/1792879/audit-of-dod-efforts-to-consult-with-victims-of-sexual-assault-committed-by-mil/

Fayazrad, A. D. (2013). *Females in the military and military sexual trauma*. Alliant International University.

Giardino, A. P., Faugno, D. K., Spencer, M. J., Weaver, M. L. & Speck, P. M. (2017). Sexual assault—victimization across the life space: Investigation, diagnosis and the multidisciplinary team. http://ebookcentral.proquest.com

Gilberd, K. (2017). Challenging military sexual violence: a guide to sexual assault and sexual harassment policies in the US armed forces for service members, msv survivors and their advocates. Retrieved https://nlgmltf.org/military-law-library/publications/memos/military-sexual-violence/.

Holland, K., Rabelo, V., & Cortina, L. (2016). Collateral damage: Military sexual trauma and help-seeking barriers. *Psychology of Violence, 6*(2), 253–261. doi:10.1037/a0039467

Kennedy, K. M., & White, C. (2015). What can GPs do for adult patients disclosing recent sexual violence? *British Journal of General Practice, 65*(630), 42–44.

Koo,. W., Idzik, S. R., Hammersla, M. B., & Windemuth, B. F. (2013). Developing standardized patient clinical simulations to apply concepts of interdisciplinary collaboration. *Journal of Nursing Education*, 52(12), 705–708. doi:10.3928/01484834-20131121-04

Lee, W. J., Clark, L., Wortmann, K., Taylor, L. A., & Pock, A.R. (2019). interprofessional healthcare student training in the care of sexual assault patients utilizing standardized patient methodology. *Simulation in Healthcare*, *14*(1), 10–17. PMID: 30407955.

Magley, V. J. (2002). Coping with sexual harassment: Reconceptualizing women's resistance. *Journal of Personality and Social Psychology*, 83(4), 930.

Milone, J. M., Burg, M. A., Duerson, M. C., Hagen, M. G., & Pauly, R. R. (2010). The effect of lecture and a standardized patient encounter on medical student rape myth acceptance and attitudes toward screening patients for a history of sexual assault. *Teaching and Learning in Medicine*, 22(1), 37–44. doi: 10.1080/10401330903446321

Molnar, B. E., Buka, S. L., & Kessler, R. C. (2001). Child sexual abuse and subsequent psychopathology: Results from the national comorbidity survey. *American Journal of Public Health, 91*(5), 753–760.

Moore, G. (2015). Sexual assault screening in the outpatient setting. *American Nurse Today, 10*(8). https://www.americannursetoday.com/sexual-assault-screening-outpatient-setting/

Mumford, E. A., Potter, S. P., Taylor, B. G., & Stapleton, J. (2020). Sexual harassment and sexual assault in early adulthood: National estimates for college and non-college students. *Public Health Reports, 35*(5), 555–559.

Munro-Kramer, M. L., Dulin, A. C., & Gaither, C. (2017). What survivors want: Understanding the needs of sexual assault survivors. *Journal of American College Health, 65*(5), 297–305.

National Academies of Sciences, Engineering, and Medicine. (2018). Job and health outcomes of sexual harassment and how women respond to sexual harassment. https://www.ncbi.nlm.nih.gov/books/NBK519461/%22%20%5Ct%20%22_blank

National District Attorneys Association. (2010). Mandatory reporting of domestic violence and sexual assault statutes. https://www.evawintl.org/images/uploads/NDAA_Mandatory%20Reporting%20Compilation_2010.pdf.

Nelson, R. (2018). Sexual harassment in nursing: a long-standing, but rarely studied problem. *AJN The American Journal of Nursing, 118*(5), 19–20.

Planty, M., Berzofsyk, M., Krebs, C., Langton, L., & Smiley-McDonald, H. (2013). Female victims of sexual violence, 1994–2010. http://www.bjs.gov/content/pub/pdf/fvsv9410.pdf.

Rape and sexual assault generally. (2017). 10 U.S. Code § 920. Art. 120. https://www.law.cornell.edu/uscode/text/10/920

Rees, S., Silove, D., Chey, T., Ivancie, L., Steel, Z., Creamer, M., . . . Forbes, D. (2011). Lifetime prevalence of gender-based violence in women and the relationship with mental disorders and psychosocial function. *JAMA, 306*(5), 513–521.

Sadler, A. G., Booth, B. M., Cook, B. L., Torner, J. C., & Doebbeling, B.N. (2001). The military environment: Risk factors for women's non-fatal assaults. *Journal of Occupational and Environmental Medicine/American College of Occupational and Environmental Medicine,* 43(4), 325–334.

Santaularia, J., Johnson, M., Hart, L., Haskett, L., Welsh, E. & Faseru, B. (2014). Relationships between sexual violence and chronic disease: A cross-sectional study. *BMC*

Public Health, 14(1286). http://www.biomedcentral.com/1471-2458/14/1286

Scalzo, T. (2007). *Rape and sexual assault reporting requirements for competent adult victims.* Department of Defense Sexual Assault Prevention and Response Office. https://www.sapr.mil/public/docs/laws/lawsummary.pdf.

Scott, J., & Philpott, S.C. (2014). *Sexual assault in the military: A guide for victims and families.* Rowman & Littlefield.

Sexual assault. ACOG Committee Opinion No, 777. American College of Obstetricians and Gynecologists. Obstet Gynecol 2019;133:e296-302. DOI:10.3399/bjgp15X683305

Solymos, O., O'Kelly, P., & Walshe, C. M. (2015). Pilot study comparing simulation-based and didactic lecture-based critical care teaching for final-year medical students. *BMC Anesthesiology, 15,* 153. doi: 10.1186/s12871-015-0109-6

Substance Abuse and Mental Health Services Administration. (2014). SAMHSA's concept of trauma and guidance for a trauma-informed approach. HHS Publication No.(SMA) 14-4884. SAMHSA. https://store.samhsa.gov/shin/contenet/SMA14-4884/SMA14-4884.pdf.

The Marshall Project. (2019). A unique military program helps sexual assault survivors. But not all of them. https://www.themarshallproject.org/2019/07/30/a-unique-military-program-helps-sexual-assault-survivors-but-not-all-of-them.

U.S. Department of Defense. (2013, April). Sexual Assault Prevention and Response (SAPR) Program. Department of Defense Directive 6495.01. https://www.sapr.mil/public/docs/instructions/DoDI_649501_20130430.pdf

U.S. Equal Employment Opportunity Commission. (1997). Fact sheet: Sexual harassment discrimination. https://www.eeoc.gov/publications/facts-about-sexual-harassment.

Witt, J. S., Carlson, K., Colbert, S., Cordle, C., Hitchcock, K., & Kelly, P. J. (2015). SANE-A-PALOOZA: A clinical immersion experience to close the gap for new sexual assault nurse examiners. *J Forensic Nurs 11*(2), 101–106. doi:10.1097/JFN.0000000000000069

Wolff, K. B., & Mills, P. D. (2016). Reporting military sexual trauma: A mixed-methods study of women veterans' experiences who served from World War II to the war in Afghanistan. *Military Medicine, 181*(8), 840–848. DOI: 10.7205/MILMED-D-15-00404

World Health Organization. (2017). Violence against women fact sheet. https://www.who.int/en/news-room/fact-sheets/detail/violence-against-women

Appendix A

Differences between Military and Civilian Sexual Assault Definitions, Laws, and Guidelines

Issue	Military	Civilian
Sexual Assault Definition	Sexual Assault is clearly defined in military wide policy: 10 U.S.C. § 920—U.S. Code—of Justice.	In the United States, the definition of sexual assault varies widely among the individual states. However, in most states sexual assault occurs when there is lack of consent from one of the individuals involved. Consent must take place between two adults who are not incapacitated and can change during any time during the sexual act.
Sexual Harassment Definition	The military definition of sexual harassment is outlined in Section 3.3 of DoD Instruction 1020.03	The EEOC defines the offense as follows: *"Unwelcome sexual advances, requests for sexual favors, and other verbal or physical conduct of a sexual nature constitutes sexual harassment when submission to or rejection of this conduct explicitly or implicitly affects an individual's employment, unreasonably interferes with an individual's work performance or creates an intimidating, hostile or offensive work environment."* (US Equal Employment Opportunity Commission, 1997)

(continues)

Issue	Military	Civilian
Law Enforcement	The victim makes the decision to report the incident to the law. The victim receives medical care, treatment, and counseling without notifying their command or law enforcement officers.	Except in situations covered by mandatory reporting laws (child, elderly, vulnerable dependent adults), patients, not healthcare workers, make the decision to report a sexual assault to law enforcement.
Legal Representation	Since 2013, the military has used special victims' counsels to advocate on behalf of survivors of sexual assault. During investigations, the lawyers accompany victims and defend the victim's rights.	In civilian courts, crime victims don't have personal lawyers to guide them through an investigation or trial, unless they can afford one.
Levels of Reporting	All sexual assaults across the military are reported as either Restricted reporting or Unrestricted reporting.	States vary on the level of reporting requirements. For instance, some states do not require health providers report patients who have assault-related injuries. Other states have reporting requirements for injuries resulting from crimes. Several states have statutes that specifically require health providers to report injuries resulting from domestic violence.
Payment of a forensic examination		States have statutes that may require a rape to be reported before a forensic examination is covered by the state and not the patient.

Appendix B

Post-Assault Clinical Flow Sheet

Clinical Flow Sheet Post-Sexual Assault© Developed by Jennifer A. Korkosz, DNP, WHNP			1 week post-assault	2 weeks post-assault	1–2 months post-assault	4–6 months post-assault
Patient name (Last, First, MI)	**SAFE exam conducted? Yes ❐ No ❐ (If no, call SANE for an appointment)**	**Legal plan in place? Yes ❐ No ❐ Resources needed? Yes ❐ No ❐**				
Height:	**Weight:**	**DOB:**				
Physical examination						
Physical injuries: Continue to follow until completely healed						
Signs and symptoms (e.g., discharge, rash, odor, itching): Evaluate						
Persistent symptoms (e.g., joint/muscle pain, lack of appetite, pelvic or abdominal pain): Note development and evaluate						
Laboratory tests						
Previous tests: Review results from previously tested samples						
Pregnancy testing: Administer if no menstrual cycle since assault						
N. gonorrhoeae and *Chlamydia trachomatis* testing: Check for infection if antibiotic prophylaxis was not previously completed and if symptoms are present						
Syphilis and HIV testing: Repeat at 6 weeks and at 3–6 months						

(continues)

Clinical Flow Sheet Post-Sexual Assault© Developed by Jennifer A. Korkosz, DNP, WHNP			**1 week post-assault**	**2 weeks post-assault**	**1–2 months post-assault**	**4–6 months post-assault**
Patient name (Last, First, MI)	**SAFE exam conducted? Yes ❐ No ❐ (If no, call SANE for an appointment)**	**Legal plan in place? Yes ❐ No ❐ Resources needed? Yes ❐ No ❐**				
Height:	**Weight:**	**DOB:**				
Medications						
Previous medication(s): Ask whether patient has completed course(s)						
Hepatitis B vaccination: Administer at 1–2 months and 4–6 months following first dose						
Antidepressant or anti-anxiety medications: Consider prescribing as needed						
History						
Safety: Ask patient, "Do you feel safe at home? Do you feel safe with friends? Do you feel safe at school? Do you feel safe at your job?"						
Sleeping habits: Ask patient, "Do you have difficulty falling or staying asleep?"						
Substance use/misuse: Ask patient, "Do you need to use alcohol or drugs to help you function or sleep? Have you found it necessary to self-medicate?"						
Relationship status: Ask patient, "How are you doing with your partner? Have you begun counseling?"						
Intrusive thoughts, nightmares, flashbacks: Ask patient, "Do you find yourself having a difficult time dismissing memories or find that you are reliving events?"						
Return to previous habits, lifestyle, relationships: Ask patient, "Do you find yourself avoiding activities that used to bring you pleasure? Have you returned to the activities in which you used to participate?"						

Clinical Flow Sheet Post-Sexual Assault© Developed by Jennifer A. Korkosz, DNP, WHNP			1 week post-assault	2 weeks post-assault	1–2 months post-assault	4–6 months post-assault
Patient name (Last, First, MI)	**SAFE exam conducted? Yes ❒ No ❒ (If no, call SANE for an appointment)**	**Legal plan in place? Yes ❒ No ❒ Resources needed? Yes ❒ No ❒**				
Height:	**Weight:**	**DOB:**				
Psychological status						
Ongoing support/referrals: Provide as needed						
Post-traumatic stress disorder: Screen patient utilizing clinical resources available						
Depression: Screen patient utilizing clinical resources available						
Anxiety: Screen patient utilizing clinical resources available						
Coping methods: Ensure that coping is adequate and counseling has been thorough						

Appendix C

MST Resources for Civilian Providers

VA and Vet Center facility locators (www.va.gov; www.vetcenter.va.gov)

U.S. Department of Veterans' Affairs.

Military Sexual Trauma Resources (www.mentalhealth.va.gov/msthome/index.asp)

Centers for Disease Control and Prevention

2015 STD Treatment Guidelines (www.cdc.gov/std/tg2015/default.htm)

Violence Prevention (www.cdc.gov/violence prevention/sexualviolence/)

National Center on Domestic and Sexual Violence (www.ncdsv.org)

Rape, Abuse & Incest National Network (RAINN) (www.rainn.org)

National Domestic Violence Hotline: 1-800-799- SAFE

National Sexual Assault Hotline: 1-800-656-HOPE

The Victim Rights Law Center (www.victimrights.org)

Resource for Professionals

Mandatory Reporting of Non-Accidental Injuries: A State-by-State Guide

CHAPTER 20

Assessing and Addressing Health Care for Veterans Experiencing Homelessness

Susan K. Lee, Pamela Willson, and Catherine G. Ling

Soldier's Creed
I am an American Soldier.
I am a warrior and a member of a team.
I serve the people of the United States and live the Army Values.
I will always place the mission first.
I will never accept defeat.
I will never quit.
I will never leave a fallen comrade.
I am disciplined, physically and mentally tough, trained and proficient in my warrior tasks and drills.
I always maintain my arms, my equipment and myself.
I am an expert and I am a professional.
I stand ready to deploy, engage, and destroy the enemies of the United States of America in close combat.
I am a guardian of freedom and the American way of life.
I am an American Soldier. https://www.army.mil/e2/downloads/rv7/values/posters/creed.pdf

Introduction

In the United States, homelessness in the general population is a grave problem with estimates of more than 40,000 of the homeless adult population being veterans (U.S. Department of Housing and Urban Development [HUD], 2020). For the 68% of homeless veterans who live in principal cities (like Los Angeles, New York City, or Washington, DC), the price of housing, poverty, availability of housing substitutes and homeless shelters, and the ability to live unsheltered in temperate climates contribute to homelessness (HUD, 2020). About a third (32%) of homeless veterans live in suburban or rural areas (National Coalition for Homeless Veterans [NCHV], 2020), such as the Gulf Coast region of the United States.

Veterans are significantly represented among people experiencing homelessness. One in five (20%) homeless males are veterans and one in eleven (9%) is female. These women are often living alone in urban areas with mental illnesses, substance use disorders, or debilitating ailments. More than half of homeless veterans have physical disabilities (51%); serious mental illnesses (50%); or substance abuse problems (70%), including illegal drugs and/or alcohol (NCHV, 2020). Of the veteran adult male homeless population, 57% are White and 45% African American or Hispanic. African Americans account for 10.4% of the U.S. veteran population and 3.4% identify as Hispanic. Homeless veterans are younger than the total veteran populations, with 9% between 18 and 30 years of age, and 41% between 31 and 50 years of age. The incidence of young homeless veterans is increasing (NCHV, 2020). Additional complexity in discussing homelessness lies in the differences between urban and rural populations. Unemployment rates are higher and incomes are lower in rural areas. Housing quality and housing instability along with residential mobility barriers are common in these areas (VA National Center on Homelessness Among Veterans, 2017). Rurality has been identified as a significant contributor of health disparities with lack of access to services. See **Figure 20-1** for demographic summary.

Homeless veterans have served in every era and conflict; World War II, the Korean War, the Cold War, Vietnam, Grenada, Panama, Lebanon, the Persian Gulf War, Afghanistan, Iraq, and in anti-drug efforts in South America. Nearly half served during Vietnam with one third of those serving in combat (HUD, 2020). Additionally, 1.4 million veterans are at risk of becoming homeless because of poverty, lack of social support, overcrowded or substandard housing (HUD, 2020), and incarceration. Veterans experiencing mental health issues and/or substance use disorders or who have experienced family dissolution are also at increased risk.

Despite these risks and due to significant efforts on the part of the Veterans Administration and Congress, veteran homelessness has significantly decreased even though it is unclear if there is a concurrent decrease in homelessness in the general population. This lack of clarity can be attributed to inconsistent definitions of homelessness and inadequate documentation of unsheltered homeless people (Council of Economic Advisers [CEA], 2019). HUD defines a homeless person as someone who does not have a regular, adequate nighttime residence (HUD 2020). Veterans are classified as homeless when any VA homeless services are accessed, when veterans are assigned an International Classification of Diseases (ICD) Lack of Housing code, or when they receive any specialty bed section codes designated by the VA for homeless veterans (Metraux et al., 2013). Veterans are not identified as homeless during the first year they are homeless. Instead, new cases are identified and counted during the follow-up year.

As of 2020, 79 communities and three states have reported effectively ending veteran homelessness (U.S. Department of Veterans Affairs [VA], 2020) through the collaborative efforts of the VA, HUD, and the U.S. Interagency Council on Homelessness (USICH). Homelessness is the only social problem in the United States that has reported a decline in incidence. "Functional zero" is a term used when all homeless veterans who choose to be housed are placed. Functional zero does not prevent veteran homelessness from occurring or end homelessness for all veterans. Those veterans who choose to not be placed

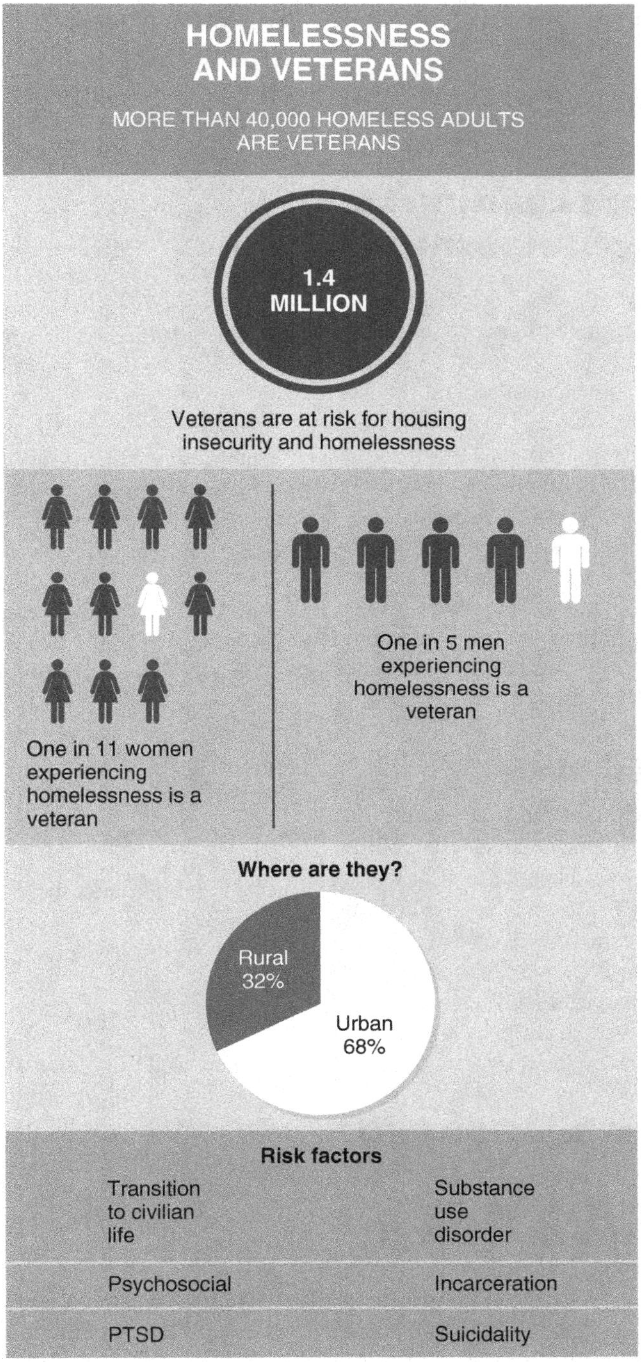

Figure 20-1 Demographic characteristics of veterans experiencing homelessness.

National Coalition for Homeless Veterans. (2020). *Background and statistics.* http://nchv.org/index.php/news/media/background_and_statistics/

in housing are not counted, thereby allowing communities to report ending homelessness. However, new cases of veteran homelessness continue to appear.

Risk Factors Leading to Veteran Homelessness

The circumstances that lead a person into homelessness can be a single event (e.g., national disaster), but more often is a cascade of several situations or factors. Mental illness, substance use, incarceration, low income and poverty, weak social connections, family dissolution, and lack of available housing increase an individual's risk of homelessness (CEA, 2019). Veterans also experience difficulty when separating from the Department of Defense (DoD) and moving to VA services. This transition involves finding adequate employment and reintegrating with family and social circles.

Psychosocial Risks

Mental health conditions can lead to and are exacerbated by homelessness. These conditions include chronic and latent post-traumatic stress disorder (PTSD), major depression (see Chapter 16 for further discussion), psychotic disorders such as schizophrenia (see Chapter 17 for further discussion), acute and chronic substance use disorders (SUD), and suicide ideation and suicide attempts.

Post-Traumatic Stress Disorder

PTSD is one of the "signature wounds of war" among veterans who served in the conflicts in Afghanistan and Iraq (Cooper et al., 2020, p. 1). The estimated lifetime prevalence of PTSD among veterans is 11% to 20% (VA Posttraumatic Stress Disorder Fact Sheet, 2020). This is nearly double that of the general adult population in the United States, which is 6% to 8% (Cooper et al., 2020).

Substance Use Disorders

Veterans with physical and emotional challenges, PTSD, depression, or suicidal ideation sometimes turn to alcohol and/or drugs as self-treatment to relieve stress. Between 2004 and 2006, 7.1% of veterans showed signs of SUD, with 25% between 18 to 25 years of age (American Addiction Centers, 2020). Factors that place veterans at risk of developing SUDs include trauma exposure, sexual trauma, availability of prescription medications, homelessness, stigma, and reluctance to seek treatment.

For service members involved in Iraq and Afghanistan conflicts, 10–18.5% have PTSD, SUDs, and depression, while 20% of veterans with PTSD also have an SUD. This is of particular concern with veterans who served after 9/11. A large number of Operation Enduring Freedom (OEF) and Operation Iraqi Freedom (OIF) veterans (82–93%) diagnosed with SUD also have a co-occurring mental health disorder (American Addiction Centers, 2020).

The majority of SUDs involve prescription opioids, such as oxycodone and hydrocodone. Alcohol use, particularly binge drinking, is prevalent among service members. This poses significant threats to physical and mental health. Service members with higher rates of combat exposure reported higher rates of binge drinking (American Addiction Centers, 2020).

The symptoms of SUD include:

- Increased tolerance (the need to drink more alcohol or use greater quantities of drugs to get the desired effect).
- An inability to stop drinking or using drugs despite negative consequences.
- Feeling sick when drinking or drug use stops.

SUDs are diagnosable conditions involving compulsive alcohol or drug use. The resultant physical, social, and psychological harm often leads to health, relationship, employment, legal difficulties, and homelessness.

Incarceration

A substantial proportion of U.S. military veterans experience mental health and/or substance use disorders, which unfortunately can lead to incarceration. It is estimated that 140,000 veterans are imprisoned, with 127,500 in state prisons, and 12,500 in federal prisons. Veterans who are in prison are almost exclusively male (99%). Yet, male veterans are less likely to be incarcerated (0.63%) than their civilian counterparts (1.39%). Some estimates indicate that as many as half of all veterans experiencing homelessness are in the criminal justice system (NCHV, 2020).

Given the substantial risk of homelessness associated with incarceration, strategies to end veteran homelessness must incorporate justice system involvement. A starting point is to include criminal justice services in locations where veterans experiencing and at-risk of homelessness are identified and engaged. These services should involve all stages of the criminal justice process, from arrest to reintegration into society.

VA Justice Programs (VJP) partner with the criminal justice system to identify veterans who could benefit from treatment as an alternative to incarceration. VJP ensures access to care that is tailored to meet the veteran's needs by linking each veteran to VA and community services that prevent homelessness, improve social and clinical outcomes, and facilitate recovery. Key primary, secondary, and tertiary prevention approaches include: (1) jail-based, in-reach efforts as communities identify and engage all veterans who are experiencing or at risk of homelessness, (2) working with corrections departments to prevent the homelessness of veterans who are re-entering the community from prison or jail, and (3) building collaborations with law enforcement agencies and courts to divert veterans from jail to advance alternatives to incarceration (DVA, 2020c).

The Sequential Intercept Model is a framework used when interfacing between the criminal justice and mental health systems. The model has five interception points for preventive strategies (Munetz & Griffin, 2006). The connections occur with law enforcement, initial detention and hearing, jail and courts, reentry, and community corrections, which are outlined below with best practices prevention.

1. Law Enforcement—911, Local Law Enforcement
   - Adopt policies and implement practices that avoid criminalizing behaviors associated with homelessness.
   - Partner with law enforcement and emergency services to create a systematic response to ensure that veterans and all people experiencing homelessness are connected with housing assistance and supportive services, rather than being unnecessarily arrested.
2. Initial Detention/Initial Hearing—Arrest, Initial Detention, First Court Appearance
   - Identify veterans entering the criminal justice system.
   - Screen for housing status and homelessness.
   - Maximize opportunities for pre-trial release.
   - Formulate an action plan, which addresses the veteran's housing and service delivery needs.
3. Jails and Courts—Jail, Specialty Court, Dispositional Court
   - Divert veterans to problem-solving courts, such as Veterans Treatment Courts.
4. Reentry—Jail/Reentry, Prison/Reentry
   - Build strong and collaborative reentry support systems to assist veterans as they leave prison or jail, reenter society, and follow their reentry plan.
5. Community Corrections—Probation/Parole
   - Collaborate with corrections departments and VJO Program for legal, housing, and supportive services,

including employment and training supports to achieve positive primary, secondary, and tertiary outcomes (Munetz & Griffin, 2006). See **Table 20-1** for resource information.

Transition to Civilian Life

Difficulty transitioning between active duty and civilian life affects more than half (54%) of veterans, and symptoms of these issues

Table 20-1 Quick Resource Guide for Veterans Experiencing Homelessness by Service Need, Resource Agency, and Contact Information

Service Need	Resource Agency	Contact Information
Homeless or Imminent Risk for Homelessness	National Call Center for Homeless Veterans	Phone: (877) 4AID-VET (877-424-3838) https://www.va.gov/homeless/ Health Care and Mental Health Services Fact sheet: https://www.va.gov/HOMELESS/docs/HCHV-Fact-Sheet-508.pdf *Note: VA registration nor enrollment in VA health care is required to use services*
Health Care	Health Care for Homeless Veterans (HCHV) Program	https://www.va.gov/homeless/hchv.asp Call, Chat Online, and VA Medical Center (VAMC) Locator *Note: Ask about Contract Residential Treatment programs in your location.*
Telehealth care Sites	VA's Office of Connected Care	https://connectedcare.va.gov/partners/atlas
Military Sexual Trauma	VA's	https://www.va.gov/health-care/health-needs-conditions/military-sexual-trauma/
Legal Services	Veterans Justice Outreach (VJO) Program	Main website: https://www.va.gov/HOMELESS/VJO.asp VJO program specialists by state: https://www.va.gov/homeless/vjo.asp#contacts
Employment Services	VA Employment Programs for Homeless Veterans Veteran and Military Transition Center	https://www.va.gov/homeless/employment_programs.asp Career Center: https://www.careeronestop.org/Veterans/default.aspx *Note: Skills, Job Search, School, Benefits and Assistance, Toolkit* Unemployment benefits: https://www.careeronestop.org/Veterans/BenefitsAndAssistance/unemployment-benefits.aspx *Note: Federal government options for states, unemployment insurance benefits related to COVID-19*

Service Need	Resource Agency	Contact Information
COVID-19 Homeless Prevention & Treatment	Information for individuals, providers, agencies who serve homeless persons	https://www.va.gov/HOMELESS/coronavirus.asp *Note: Webinar slides available—COVID-19 Future Planning for Homelessness Response System: Lessons Learned from Seattle & King County, Los Angeles, and Houston. June 17, 2020.*
PTSD Assessment Tools	VA: National PTSD Center	https://www.ptsd.va.gov/professional/assessment/list_measures.asp

are often overlooked by healthcare providers (Sayer et al., 2014). Service members transition from a highly structured and hierarchical environment with daily guidance, rules, and commands. While in the military, they experience strong bonds of camaraderie that develop through service, being told where to go, what to wear, what to do, when and with whom to take action. Rejoining civilian life involves reintegrating with family, civilian or previous employment, and societal roles with different responsibilities. Additionally, service men and women are trained for occupations that do not readily translate to civilian careers, leaving veterans vulnerable without financial means to support themselves and their families. Many find themselves with limited resources, in search of stability and purpose, such as employment and income (Elnitsky, et al., 2017). Inability to transition leads to lack of employment, poverty, issues with personal relationships and the breakdown of family, all of which increase the risk of homelessness.

Transitioning to civilian life is an emotional process as well as administrative. It is not uncommon for the veteran to exhibit restlessness or frustration upon separation from active duty (Elnitsky et al., 2017) or to experience chronic fatigue due to an inability to relax due to hypervigilance (NCHV, 2020). Veterans may need assistance to find housing, employment, food, health care, and treatment for substance use disorders and mental health issues (NCHV, 2020). Veterans may not know of available resources to keep them housed or offer employment, thus, becoming homeless.

Federal Policies to Reduce Veteran Homelessness

Homelessness among veterans decreased 48% between 2009 and 2018, and by 5% (N = 37,878) in 2017 and 2018, which is the lowest total on record. The incidence of homelessness in sheltered (46%) and unsheltered (51%) veterans has decreased substantially since 2009 (CEA, 2019). The VA provides a range of services, including mental health and SUD programs to assist in efforts to prevent and mitigate homelessness. These include HUD-VA Supported Housing (VASH); Support Services for Veteran Families (SSVF); VA Grant and Per Diem (GPD); and Health Care for Homeless Veterans (HCHV). Supplementary programs are Veterans Justice Outreach (VJO); Homeless Veterans Employment Coordinators (HVEC); Compensated Work Therapy (CWT); Community Resource and Referral Centers (CRRC); and Homeless Patient Aligned Care Teams (HPACT).

These programs are critical in preventing and ending homelessness among veterans and require coordinated efforts for a seamless Continuum of Care (CoC) to initiate change, innovation, and implementation of best practices in addressing the complex factors associated with homelessness. CoCs coordinate community resources to integrate shelters, services, and housing programs. The U.S. Department of Health and Human Services, the U.S. Department of Education, and the U.S. Department of Labor also provide services (CEA, 2019).

Veterans Administration

At the Veterans Administration (VA), transition/homeless programs are more reactive and situation-focused than preventative. The VA has a Veteran Homelessness Demonstration Program and the Supportive Services for Veteran Families Program, which address veteran homelessness from impending homelessness rather than taking proactive, preventative measures. VA homelessness programs provide health care to almost 150,000 homeless veterans and additional services to more than 112,000 veterans. More than 40,000 homeless veterans receive compensation or pension benefits each month (NCHV, 2020). Eligibility for VA benefits is based on discharge from active military service under honorable or generable conditions. Benefits vary according to factors connected with the type and length of military service (NCHV, 2020), such as serving during the Vietnam War. Although there is an overwhelming amount of information and support for separating service members, choosing to receive VA benefits is seen as a sign of weakness for many veterans.

The VA, HUD, and the USICH partner to provide housing for veterans who are homeless. These agencies share a common mission to ensure veterans, regardless of gender, age, race, or disability are provided with resources and assistance to prevent homelessness, to rehabilitate and reintegrate into society by providing immediate and long-term assistance to facilitate the return to civilian life. The Housing First Model facilitates rapid placement of veterans who are homeless into Permanent Supportive Housing. SSVF and HUD-Veterans Affairs Supportive Housing (VASH) combines housing assistance with supportive VA services (CEA, 2019). HUD-VASH has been successful in reducing veteran homelessness (Evans et al., 2019).

In addition to the myriad of VA programs, the reduction of incidences of veteran homelessness might be attributed to fewer homeless veterans between the ages of 18 and 65 (O'Flaherty, 2019). Another explanation could be semantic as the term "transitional housing," which defines veterans as homeless, was replaced with SSVF, which does not label veterans as homeless. Since 2014, fewer veterans are living in transitional housing, representing a 71% decline in sheltered veteran homelessness between 2014 and 2018 (CEA, 2019).

Other-Than-Honorable Discharge

Veterans are eligible for VA health care if they actively served in and separated from the military with an honorable discharge. Traditionally, veterans with "other-than-honorable" discharges have not been eligible to participate in VA healthcare services, the HUD-VASH program, or services that provide access to stable housing. The National Coalition for Homeless Veterans (NCHV) (2021) reports that 25% of veterans who experience homelessness have other-than-honorable discharges, and in some urban communities that percentage may be higher (NCHV, 2021). Currently, other-than-honorable discharged veterans are eligible for benefits, such as SSVF, GPD, and the Department of Labor Veterans' Employment and Training Service (DOL VETS). They are still not eligible for HU-VASH or VA healthcare services. Key components to health care may be missing if the veteran lives in a state without a Medicaid expansion program or a Continuum of Care designed for the general homeless population. For states that have expanded Medicaid programs, all people with household incomes below a certain level are eligible. Thirty-nine states, including Washington, DC, have adopted Medicaid expansion (Kaiser Family Foundation, 2021).

For veterans who receive other-than-honorable, bad conduct, or dishonorable discharges, benefit eligibility may be changed upon applying for and receiving a discharge upgrade or correction. With an upgrade, veterans are eligible for VA benefits earned during the period of service. Discharge upgrades may result if the discharge was related to mental health conditions, such as PTSD; traumatic brain injury; military sexual trauma (MST); or sexual orientation (Don't Ask, Don't Tell). Even with other-than-honorable discharges, veterans may request a Character of Discharge review to determine if the service was "honorable for VA purposes." This review may take a year to complete. If denied, veterans may reapply following a process specific to their situations, providing additional evidence or because the DoD has changed the rules related to discharge upgrade conditions. The probability of success with the second application is high. When the DoD upgrades a veteran's discharge, it usually issues a DD215 showing corrections to the DD214. DD Form 214 is a certificate of release or discharge from active duty and is referred to as a DD214. This is issued to service members on retirement, separation, or discharge from active military duty (DVA, 2021). An easy method to identify homeless veterans is to ask for their DD214. Even if they do not have it, they know what it is.

The Decision-Making Process Used by Homeless Veterans in Accessing Health Care

For veterans experiencing homelessness, healthcare decision-making can be impacted by a combination of effects from military experiences; substance use; communication that occurs via the grapevine; and access issues that stem from difficulty with mobility, convenience, quality, and system inefficiencies. For the homeless, convenience in accessing health care becomes more important than quality, as barriers create insurmountable barriers. While none of these factors in isolation appear to be a primary driver of healthcare decision making in homeless veterans, healthcare decision making certainly occurs within the collective of these (Lee & Willson, 2017).

Symbolic Interactionism

Symbolic Interactionism (SI) uses a social psychology approach, changing analysis based on how people act and interact while concentrating on exchanges with other people. Individuals respond to other people based on social exchanges and interpretations that lead to behavior changes (Blumer, 1969). SI has three foundational principles. The first is meaning, which denotes that human behavior is a response to things or signs. The second is thought, which is based on a continual process of deriving meaning from things. The third is language, which is thought about or developed, and used to describe meanings (Blumer, 1969). Even though behavior may be influenced by situations, history, and social patterns, these symbols do not govern behavior.

The spirit of SI is how people infer situations or use thought processes to apply meaning and choose a course of action. For example, there are three truths in all circumstances: my understanding of what happened, your understanding of what happened, and what actually happened. Thus, the relationship between a person and a symbol allows for various social interpretations. As people develop, important individuals and social mores influence reference groups and learned roles (Blumer, 1969).

SI is considered to be a means to understand human complexity as it provides an understanding of how people apply meaning to situations where programmed responses are insufficient. For instance, for people who have little or no wealth, relationships with other people are important; there is symbolism in those relationships (Payne, 2019). For veterans, including those who are homeless, rank and position at the group and individual level have meaning. Lab coats, scrubs, stethoscopes, and identification badges imply knowledge and roles that healthcare professionals hold. Military rank, such as lieutenant or sergeant, are recognized and understood, as the interactive process is influenced and impacted. Healthcare professionals, including doctors, nurses, social workers, and therapists, may be assigned professional status as diagnoses, treatment, and prognoses are delivered.

Meanings that form our sense of who we are emerge from these interactions, which may include discussions and ideas. It is important to the person to be part of social interactions, having a role, such as those that develop from military experiences. After serving in the military, possibly as a leader, homelessness and/or illness may lead to feelings of vulnerability and weakness. Personal networks and interpretations become gauges for mutual interaction, influencing decision making. The social framework of military life affects interactions with others, while utilizing language and symbols. There is a military hierarchy that is respected long after veterans separate from active duty. To compound vulnerability, homeless veterans may be identified by health conditions rather than as individuals.

Homeless Vietnam Veteran (HVV) Healthcare Utilization Theory

When homeless veterans enter the healthcare environment, especially when using VA facilities, they experience more burden than benefit because of access issues (e.g., long wait times, inconvenient locations, lost records). As the homeless veteran is determining whether or not to access health care, factors such as substance use, the lack of shelter, and past military experiences influence the outcome. Military experiences are not modifiable—unlike the other factors, they cannot be changed. Camaraderie is important as informal information sharing occurs, as through the grapevine, to gather information about which healthcare providers to see or avoid. The Homeless Vietnam Veteran (HVV) Healthcare Utilization Theory is based on the premise that homeless veterans have alternative views of wellness and health. Being homeless intensifies weakened or compromised health where health is not the absence of disease; it is surviving with disease. For healthcare providers, it is important for veterans to be recognized as people who were shaped by their military service, and who then made additional contributions. Following social norms and mores, such as making eye contact, showing respect, and speaking English clearly become very important for the homeless veteran. See **Figure 20-2** to visualize this complex interplay.

Healthcare Needs

The Veterans Health Administration's (VHA) mission is to provide veterans with world-class benefits and services, while at the same time striving to maintain high standards. Because of VHA benefits, homeless veterans are significantly more likely than homeless non-veterans to have health insurance. Even so, there are many veterans who do not utilize VHA services.

For homeless veterans, especially those who are older, there are many challenges that affect health status and quality of life. These challenges involve decreased social supports, including separation from or death of family members and friends; depression; and becoming dependent on others because of illnesses, such as dementia or cerebrovascular accidents. Medical concerns of homeless veterans include dental health, pulmonary, endocrine, orthopedic, cardiac, oncology, optometry, audiology, and podiatry (DVA, 2020b). Psychiatric needs include suicide prevention, PTSD,

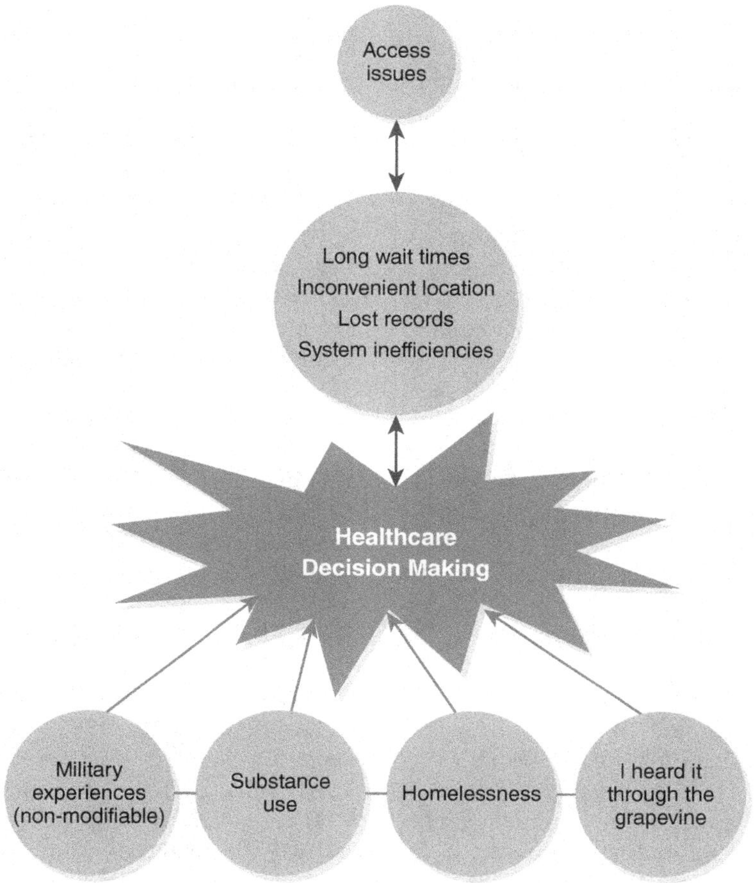

Figure 20-2 HVV healthcare utilization theory.

Modified from Lee, S., & Willson, P. (2017). Soldiers on the streets: How homeless Vietnam veterans decide to seek healthcare. *The Internet Journal of Advanced Nursing Practice, 16*(1). https://ispub.com/doi/10.5580/IJANP.47907

anger issues, anxiety, schizophrenia, bipolar disorder, substance use, and sleep disorders. As veterans age, health status becomes more fragile and geriatric issues arise. Homeless veterans who were involved in combat have substantial needs, especially those associated with physical injury, psychiatric issues, substance abuse, and medical illnesses. Identifying, recognizing, correcting, and limiting barriers that fragment healthcare delivery among multiple specialists and systems can improve overall health and well-being of homeless veterans.

When self-reporting, homeless veterans describe their health status as fair or poor, and indicate they have a multitude of health concerns that include physical and psychological medical problems, PTSD or anxiety, and alcohol or drug dependencies. Malnutrition, skin disorders, and injuries related to violence are major health issues that often are untreated. Homeless veterans were found to be less likely to utilize community healthcare clinics even though they had medical and psychiatric healthcare needs. Homeless veterans were also found to be frustrated and experienced high stress levels with the VHA, partly because veterans' benefits are needed to receive VA healthcare services. For homeless veterans, signing up for VHA benefits can be difficult and time-consuming, though more than half of homeless veterans have a chronic medical condition, and two-thirds have a chronic psychiatric condition, many of which are untreated. Prompt attention to health care may improve the prognosis; however, homeless veterans tend to delay seeking medical attention.

Access to quality health care is associated with a care-giving environment and social interaction between healthcare provider and client. When homeless veterans attempt to access health care, barriers may be difficult to overcome; this impacts the decision-making process as to whether or not to access healthcare services. When starting a discussion with a veteran who is homeless, one suggestion is to ask about changes that occurred upon returning home from deployment. Subtopics in this conversation include family, employment, and community, changes that may be concerning or frustrating. For veterans struggling to reintegrate into family and community life, isolation and feeling misunderstood can occur. By attempting to understand the life experiences of clients, healthcare providers can offer reassurance, access to resources, such as support groups, and medication, if warranted (Kranke et al., 2018).

Psychiatric Needs

Post-Traumatic Stress Disorder

Epidemiological studies find that 80% of individuals with PTSD meet the criteria for another lifetime psychological disorder, the most common comorbidity being major depression (Fonda et al, 2019). PTSD and depression are closely linked to drug and alcohol use, with 20% of veterans experiencing both PTSD and drug addiction, a situation known as a dual diagnosis (American Addiction Centers, 2020). Veterans may use substances in an attempt to alleviate their PTSD symptoms. Drugs and alcohol may serve as a means of avoiding intrusive thoughts, memories, or nightmares of a previous trauma (American Addiction Centers, 2020). Addictive behaviors may ease short-term pain and discomfort. However, over time, drug and alcohol use can actually intensify mental health symptoms. Drug and alcohol use can increase negative feelings and sleeping problems and make it more difficult to work through trauma in treatment. Dealing with substance use while experiencing symptoms of PTSD can be difficult. Fortunately, treatment programs are available that specialize in treating veterans with dual diagnosis disorders simultaneously treating concurrent illnesses, which can hasten long-term recovery. See Table 20-1 for dual diagnosis resources.

PTSD is associated with an increased risk of morbidity and mortality (Meier et al., 2016). In a longitudinal cohort of post-9/11 veterans, 71% of veterans reported pain, 64% had a diagnosis of PTSD, 48% had at least one deployment-related traumatic brain injury, and 28% had a diagnosis of a mood disorder; 58% had three or more current psychiatric and somatic conditions (Fonda et al., 2019). PTSD differs from acute stress reaction (ASR), which is a transient normal reaction to a traumatic stress. ASR symptoms may occur during or following the event and resolve rapidly with reassurance, rest, and ensuring safety.

Combat and Operational Stress Reaction

Combat and Operational Stress Reaction (COSR) is the military equivalent of ASR and reflects a normal, transient, acute reaction to a high-stress operational or combat-related traumatic event in a military occupational setting (VA/DOD, 2017). ASR/COSR clinical presentation involves a broad array of physical, mental, behavioral, and emotional symptoms and signs (e.g., depression, fatigue, anxiety, panic, decreased concentration/memory, hyperarousal, dissociation). Veterans presenting with COSR should receive a comprehensive assessment of symptoms for onset, frequency, severity, and functional impairment. When ASR/COSR with persistent limitations of functioning extends beyond three days, acute stress disorder (ASD) development with impaired functioning is possible, which if untreated, progresses to persistent PTSD (VA/DOD, 2017). PTSD's traumatic event or series of events is defined by the *Diagnostic and Statistical Manual of Mental Disorders, Fifth Edition* (DSM-5), which is where an individual has been personally or indirectly exposed to an actual or threatened death, serious injury, or sexual violence. Among veterans, PTSD is associated with increased impairment in psychosocial functioning, decreased health-associated quality of life, and increased mortality. PTSD patients usually exhibit at least one symptom from each of the following categories:

- Intrusive symptoms—reexperiencing the traumatic event (e.g., nightmare, flashback, or sudden vivid memories accompanied by painful emotions)
- Avoidance symptoms—avoidance of activity or situation that might revive memories of the trauma (e.g., strained relationships with family, friends because of their inclusion with avoidance situations)
- Hyperarousal symptoms—hypersensitive or on edge (e.g., being easily startled by unexpected sounds or encounters, concentration difficulties, angry outbursts, and terrifying nightmares, which may lead to insomnia)

DSM-5 criteria for a diagnosis of PTSD is based on symptoms being persistent for more than one month and causing a clinically significant amount of distress in social, occupational, or other areas of function. PTSD is termed acute if symptoms have persisted for less than three months, chronic if symptom duration is for more than three months and delayed if symptom onset begins six months or longer after the trauma (Dunphy et al., 2015).

Suicide Ideation and Suicide Attempt

Veteran suicide is currently at the highest recorded level in U.S. history and was 1.5 times the rate for non-veterans (Department of Veteran Affairs [DVA], 2020a). Suicide is a leading cause of death among service members and veterans who suffer from PTSD. In a longitudinal study, Glenn and colleagues (2020) found that the effects of combat exposure on suicidal ideation are mediated by PTSD symptom severity, which highlights the importance of targeting such symptoms in treatment to mitigate suicide risk among veterans with combat exposure. Suicide risk often persists through civilian reintegration. Furthermore, suicide rates have increased more than twofold since engagement in Iraq and Afghanistan, and suicide is the second leading cause of death in U.S. military personnel (Carroll et al., 2020). In addition to the veteran suicides, there were 919 suicides among never federally activated former National Guard and Reserve members in 2017, for an average daily suicide rate of 2.5 persons (DVA, 2020a). Suicide deaths have also risen in the general population. From 2005 to 2017, there was a 43.6% increase in the number of deaths and for the veteran population a 6.1% increase in suicide deaths. In 2017, an average of 16.8 veterans versus 86.6 non-veteran adults died by suicide each day (DVA, 2020a). Suicide rates among veteran users of VHA services have been found "to be affected by economic disparities, homelessness, unemployment, level of military service-connected disability status, community connection, and personal health and well-being" (DVA, 2020a, p. 6).

Using data from the National Health and Resilience in Veterans Study, Nichter et al. (2020) found that overall combat exposure had a weak positive associated with suicide ideation and suicide attempts, after adjusting for sociodemographic characteristics and lifetime trauma burden [odds ratios

Box 20-1 **EBP: PTSD Screen Is Predictive of Veteran Suicide**

Article: Cooper, A. A., Szymanski, B. R., Bohnert, K. M., Sripada, R. K., & McCarthy, J. F. (2020). Association between positive results on the Primary Care-Posttraumatic Stress Disorder (PC-PTSD) Screen and suicide mortality among U.S. veterans. *JAMA Network Open, 3*(9), e2015707. doi:10.1001/jamanetworkopen.2020.15707

Summary: A total of 1,693,449 PC-PTSDs were completed by 1,552,581 individual veteran patients in 2014. Most of the patients were White (73.9%), married (52.2%), male (91.1%), 55 years or older (62.5%), and had completed only 1 PC-PTSD (92.1%). In multivariable analyses, positive PC-PTSD results were associated with a 58% increase in the risk of suicide mortality at 1 day after screening (hazard ratio [HR], 1.58; 95% CI, 1.19–2.10) and a 26% increase in the risk of suicide mortality at 1 year after screening (HR, 1.26; 95% CI, 1.07–1.48). A positive response on item 4 ("felt numb or detached from others, activities, or your surroundings") of the PC-PTSD was associated with a 70% increase in suicide mortality risk at 1 day after screening (HR, 1.70; 95% CI, 1.27–2.28).

(ORs) = 1.02–1.03]. However, combat experiences involving direct exposure to death, killing, or grave injury were independently associated with suicide ideation and suicide attempts (ORs = 1.46–1.70), while several general combat experiences (e.g., combat patrols) were negatively associated with suicide ideation and suicide attempts (ORs = 0.44–0.65). Results indicate that U.S. combat veterans who have witnessed others being killed or wounded in combat are at substantially higher risk for suicide ideation and suicide attempts as compared to those without such histories (Nichter et al., 2020).

In 2017, the U.S. Department of Housing and Urban Development Point-in-Time Count estimated that 40,000 veterans were homeless and just over 15,300 were living on the street or unsheltered on any given night (HUD, 2018). Homelessness appears to play a role in suicide for VHA patients, as those who were homeless and or received homelessness-related services had higher rates of suicide than other VHA patients (McCarthy et al, 2015).

Military Sexual Trauma

Military sexual trauma (MST) is a form of sexual assault and sexual harassment that occurs during service in the U.S. Armed Forces and can lead to adverse health outcomes, such as PTSD, depression, and suicidal ideation (Livingston et al., 2020; Lofgreen et al., 2020). Kim et al. (2019) found that 20–48% of homeless female veterans were diagnosed with MST. Homeless female veterans were found to be younger, non-White, and single, with a service-connected disability, and to have served in OEF/OIF/OND compared to homeless male veterans (Kim et al., 2019). A meta-analysis by Wilson and colleagues (2018) determined that 15.7% of veterans, 38.4% women and 3.9% men reported MST when asked about military sexual harassment and military sexual assault. MST includes any sexual activity during military service where there is unwilling pressure into sexual activities, unconsented sexual activities, or physically forced sexual activities. Other MST experiences include unwanted sexual touching or grabbing, threatening or offensive remarks, and unwelcomed sexual advances. When screening 435,690 Iraq/Afghanistan VHA veteran medical records from 2004–2014, suicide and intentional self-inflicted injury were observed in 16,149 (3.71%) veterans (Livingston et al., 2020). Positive screening for MST was highest among veterans with comorbid PTSD and depression diagnoses (indirect effect = 3.18%, 95%

Box 20-2 EBP: Mediators of Military Sexual Trauma and Suicidal Ideation

Article: Blais, R. K., & Geiser, C. (2019). Depression and PTSD-related anhedonia mediate the association of military sexual trauma and suicidal ideation in female service members/veterans. *Psychiatry Research, 279*, 148–154. doi:10.1016/j.psychres.2018.12.148

Summary: Female service members/veterans (N=1,190) were examined for PTSD symptom clusters and depression mediated by military sexual trauma (MST) (none, harassment-only, assault) and suicidal ideation (SI). Structural equation modeling revealed an association of MST, particularly assault, with SI when mediated by depression severity and PTSD-related anhedonia. SI was significantly positively related to depression severity ($\beta = 0.40$, $p < .001$) and anhedonia ($\beta = 0.17$, $p = .03$). Clinical interventions to reducing PTSD-related anhedonia and depression symptoms may mitigate suicide risk in those with histories of assault MST.

confidence interval [CI] [3.01%, 3.32%]), with smaller probabilities observed for both PTSD-only (indirect effect = −0.18%, 95% CI [−0.20%, −0.14%]) and depression-only (indirect effect = 0.56%, 95% CI [0.51%, 0.62%]) (Livingston et al., 2020).

MST is a more common experience for both male and female service members than previously recognized. Consequently, the military and VHA are expanding services for victims of MST, including universal screening, increasing treatment options, and the use of victims' advocates (Wilson, 2020). Veteran resources are available regardless of discharge status (honorable, dishonorable, etc.). Table 20-1 shows an MST resource link.

Transgender Veterans

In the United States, transgender individuals are twice as likely as those who identify with their birth sex to serve in the military. Transgender individuals assigned female at birth are three times more likely to serve while transgender individuals assigned male at birth are 1.6 times more likely to serve (Gates & Herman, 2014). Of the 134,300 identified transgender veterans, 21% are likely to experience homelessness (Harrison-Quintana & Herman, 2013). Transgender civilians who are homeless were sexually assaulted in 33% of cases (Grant et al., 2011). Given the rates of transgender veterans who experience homelessness and incidences of trauma, implementation of accommodations for transgender women should be made considering the expressed and experienced gender of the individual (Kim et al., 2019).

Street Medicine/Health Care

For those unhoused veterans making do with cardboard/tarps or tent shelters in the woods ("camps"), underpasses, and on city sidewalks, street medicine or street healthcare may be their only accessible care options. Street medicine/health care is simply defined as delivery of healthcare services to persons sleeping outside. To overcome the lack of access to health care, providers take their services to the people, via walking teams or mobile units (cars, vans, bicycles, and horseback) (National Health Care for the Homeless Council [NHCHC], 2019). Since 1992, Jim Withers has been regarded as the father of the street medicine movement. Partnering with a formerly homeless man, Mike Sallows, Doctor Withers began nighttime journeys to campsites under bridges, in parks, and on the streets to establish identity, build trust, and provide basic medical care. Soon, others from Mercy Hospital in Pittsburgh joined to expand care to include social services, legal aid, and housing (Varma, 2018). It is particularly important for street medicine providers to be flexible and take a nonjudgmental, advocacy approach that encourages self-determination and applies the "Golden Rule." Street medicine includes conducting a needs assessment, iteratively reassessing, and listening to those served. A developmental approach builds on assessments and establishing relationships with community resources. Consider a records system, supportive organization, staffing, and funding (NHCHC, 2019). Start small and move forward with higher community presence, collaborative specialist services, follow-up systems, and transitional primary care. The eventual goal for street medicine/ health care is one of 24/7 coverage that provides continuity of care with a multidisciplinary team (NHCHC, 2019).

One VA initiative, the Anywhere to Anywhere program, aims to increase care to veterans no matter where they live by providing access to telehealth where they might have limited internet access. The Accessing Telehealth through Local Area Stations (ATLAS) program offers healthcare virtual appointments for problems that do not require hands-on exams for primary care, nutrition, mental health counseling, or social work services. The ATLAS sites began in select locations in Iowa, Michigan, North Carolina, and Wisconsin, with more sites scheduled to open nationally by 2023 (Office of Public and Intergovernmental Affairs, 2020). Other corporations have collaborated with the American Legion and Veterans of Foreign Wars to provide convenient locations and private areas for veterans to receive telehealth care through VA Video Connect, which is the VA's secure videoconferencing platform. Telehealth resources have been implemented nationally to improve veterans' access to care (Boyle et al., 2020). Using the VA Video Connect system allows for on-demand and distant services. Telepsychiatry, drug abuse counseling, e-consultations, and healthcare access for emergent health conditions such as COVID-19 for veterans without equipment and/or internet connectivity are possible through this service.

COVID-19 Employment and Housing Efforts

The COVID-19 pandemic forced temporary or permanent closing of thousands of businesses creating an unprecedented rise in unemployment. The Federal Reserve predicted that unemployment rates due to the pandemic would go as high as 32% putting about 67 million Americans employed in positions at high-risk for layoffs (VA.org, 2020). Veteran unemployment was up nearly 12% amid the coronavirus surge in April 2020. Younger post-9/11 veterans seeking jobs had unemployment rates of 13%, while Vietnam-era or earlier veterans reported 17% rate in unemployment, the highest of any other veteran's group (Shane, 2020).

Altogether, more than one million veterans filed for jobless benefits in the midst of the pandemic's first wave. Female veterans were more severally affected than males, with 14% filing for unemployment benefits compared to 11.4% of male veterans (Shane, 2020). Additionally, unemployment and poverty contribute to housing instability with foreclosures, evictions, and homelessness. Some programs to assist the veteran with employment and housing are the Homeless Veterans Community Employment Services (HVCES) that provides vocational assistance, job development and placement, and ongoing support to improve employment outcomes (VA Employment Programs for Homeless Veterans [EMPHV], 2020). The

Compensated Work Therapy (CWT) Program assists homeless veterans in returning to competitive employment through Sheltered Workshop, Transitional Work, and Supported Employment. The Vocational Rehabilitation and Employment (VR&E) Program helps veterans with service-connected disabilities through skills-building employment services and may include comprehensive rehabilitation evaluation to determine abilities and assistance finding and job retention (EMPHV, 2020). See Table 20-1 for veteran employment and unemployment benefits resources. The National Health Care Council for the Homeless Comparative Data (2020) reported on COVID-19 testing results, testing capacity, clinic closures, telehealth visits, and virus disparity for health centers that receive homeless funding only and included some 202,155 clients. Overall, services have progressively increased from the clinic closures in April–May 2020. Yet those sites that have not fully opened had few testing sites and implemented telehealth care (National Health Care Council for the Homeless Comparative Data, 2020). See Table 20-1 for the COVID-19 response for homelessness response system.

Congressional short-term steps have provided some financial relief to Americans. However, additional assistance for housing vouchers under the HUD-VA Supportive Housing program, rehabilitation, and employment programs is needed to boost program capacities to foster veterans' employment and to prevent loss of shelter during this widespread disaster.

Courtesy of U.S. Department of Veterans Affairs.

Box 20-3 **EBP: Video-Based Care Eliminates Barrier of VA Setting**

Article: Slightam, C., Gregory, A. J., Hu, J., Jacobs, J.,, Gurmessa, T., Kimerling, R., Blonigen, D., & Zulman, D. M. (2020). Patient perceptions of video visits using Veterans Affairs telehealth tablets: Survey study. *Journal of Medical Internet Research, 22*(4), e15682. doi:10.2196/15682

Summary: The VA distributed video-enabled tablets to provide video visits to veterans with health access barriers. Patient preferences were measured at baseline and at three to six months later. Qualitative themes were assessed, two-thirds of tablet recipients preferred (194/604, 32.1%) or thought they were "about the same" (216/604, 35.7%) as in-person care. Qualitative themes for preference for video-based care were perceived improvements in access to care, perceived differential quality of care, feasibility of obtaining necessary care, and technology-related challenges. Veterans who reported the barrier of feeling uncomfortable or uneasy in the VA setting were more likely to prefer video-based care (adjusted odds ratio 2.22, 95% CI 0.88–2.26; $P < .001$).

Box 20-4 **EBP sidebar: Companion Animals Are Key Factors in Sheltering Decision**

Article: Lee, S., & Willson, P. (2017). Soldiers on the streets: How homeless Vietnam veterans decide to seek healthcare. *The Internet Journal of Advanced Nursing Practice, 16*(1). https://ispub.com/doi/10.5580/IJANP.47907

Summary: To investigate homeless male and female veterans' ($N = 8$) relationships with their companion animals, a mixed method design was used that included face-to-face interviews and the Comfort from Companion Animals Scale (Zasloff, 1996). Primary themes were that homeless veterans (1) have a strong, unyielding bond with their companion animals that overrides personal needs, and (2) homeless veterans with companion animals have difficulty finding housing or employment and will refuse opportunities for placement if companion animals are not permitted, thereby impacting the decision-making process of whether or not to exit homelessness if terminating the human/animal relationship was required.

Housing

The differences between younger and older veterans who are experiencing homelessness impact housing options. Younger veterans tend to have higher rates of transitory homelessness because of having some income stability and the ability to find employment, warranting different housing interventions, whereas older veterans have higher rates of mental health issues. Generally, the younger the veteran, the less permanent the intervention needs to be. For example, younger veterans have better results using GPD/SSVF interventions as opposed to HUD-VASH since they are often able to work and, with early physical and mental health care, can prevent escalations of health-related issues. Offering permanent subsidy resources to young veterans risks creating dependence and limiting their lifelong potential. Older veterans, on the other hand, need the permanency of intervention as their health status and income are unlikely to substantially change. Homeless veterans are biologically older than their chronological age. In assisted-living-type settings, the resident's average age is 54 years, which means they are not eligible for Medicare. HUD-VASH is their only option and that is not service enriched to any degree to support veterans who need assistance with activities of daily living.

The VA has five different housing support programs that are augmented by municipal partnerships and initiatives. The programs include rapid re-housing, short-term benefits, transitional housing with specific care, and long-term and sustainable accommodations (Cusack et al. 2019). Each initiative is operationalized through local resources within each community and is presented using a supportive housing framework (Gabrielian et al., 2014) to evaluate initiatives in terms of housing (affordable, permanent, independent) and support (flexibility, voluntary, tenant-centered, coordinated services). Flexibility denotes types of housing available (single adult, families). Voluntary indicates that an individual may self-refer in and out of the program. Tenant-centered denotes the degree of self-determination by the housing members. Coordinated services refers to the community resources and services provided at the housing site. Under housing, affordable, permanent, and independent are the aspects of housing provided.

Permanent subsidized housing with multiple voluntary supportive services is a key ingredient for the four programs presented in distinct geographic areas. These programs illustrate successes in sheltering the homeless based on the Housing First approach where the first step is to connect people experiencing homelessness to safe, secure, and permanent housing without any preconditions or barriers, and the second step is to offer flexible supportive services that focus on housing stabilization and quality of life (San Diego Housing Commission, 2019). A brief description of each community housing initiative, including characteristic criteria that represents *housing* and *support*, follows.

Community First! Village

Community First! Village is a 51-acre community in metro Austin, Texas, that provides 500 affordable, permanent RV/park/micro-homes in a supportive community setting for people exiting chronic homelessness (see **Figure 20-3**). Community First! Village was developed by Mobile Loaves & Fishes to support unsheltered people living on the streets. This community also allows the surrounding community to work with the homeless. Community First! Village offers laundry, restroom, and shower facilities; outdoor kitchens; public transportation; movie theater; car services; organic farm and farmer's market; screen printing; memorial garden and prayer labyrinth; health center; walking trails; woodworking and art shops; entrepreneur resources; community park; gathering room; and welcome center. Since 2005, this residential program has become the largest community-based model in the United States providing people who are homeless both a home and a supportive community (Mobile Loaves & Fishes, 2020).

Figure 20-3 Community First! Village.

Courtesy of Mobile Loaves & Fishes.

Mobile Loaves & Fishes Community First! Village:

Weblink: https://mlf.org/contact-us/

Contact information: 9301 Hog Eye Road, Suite 950, Austin, TX 78724

Phone: 512-328-7299

Fax: 512-328-7223

Supportive Housing Checklist:
Housing

- Affordable—yes, much less than the cost of traditional housing
- Permanent—yes, providing residents pay their rent, abide by civil law, and follow community rules, 87% retention rate
- Independent—yes, with community support and engagement

Support

- Flexible—must be chronically homeless, must have been sleeping in a place not meant for human habitation (e.g., on the streets) and/or in an emergency homeless shelter for a cumulative period of twelve months over three years and lived in the Austin metro area for the last year. Registered sex offenders are excluded.
- Voluntary—yes
- Tenant-centered—yes, individual
- Coordinated services—supported services and amenities

Harbor Care, Nashua, NH

Harbor Care, a nonprofit organization serving veterans and other at-risk populations across the state of New Hampshire, achieved an effective end to veteran homelessness in Nashua in 2017 (see **Figure 20-4**). With more than 90 percent of veterans served connected to the

Figure 20-4 Harbor Care.

Reproduced from Bi-State Primary Care Association. (n.d.). *Harbor care.* bistatepca.org

local VA Medical Center, Harbor Care maintains this feat through partnerships with city officials, nonprofit agencies and community organizations, and the federal government. Believing that housing is health care, Harbor Care utilizes a Housing First approach to create sustainable systems of care that ensure all veterans have near-immediate access to transitional and permanent housing. If the veteran elects to receive health care outside the VA system, the agency offers its own Federally Qualified Health Center for the Homeless, located in walking distance from its VA-funded veteran transitional housing facility. Dedicated transportation is also provided at each facility—Buckingham Place and Dalianis House—for 60 veteran households to ensure healthcare appointments are maintained.

Beyond housing, Harbor Care provides wrap-around supports to veterans and their families though a Department of Labor–funded veteran employment program and a HUD-funded SSVF program. As the largest provider of homeless veteran–specific housing in New Hampshire, Harbor Care includes a newly built 26-unit permanent housing project in Plymouth, NH—the first of its kind in New Hampshire—and a third transitional housing project in Manchester, New Hampshire. This housing is combined with the aforementioned veteran-services programming serving 300 veteran households a year. The programs include homeless prevention, rapid re-housing, and case management. Harbor Care's regional success in ending veteran homelessness is being replicated statewide, with approximately 35 veterans across New Hampshire identified as homeless, all with a path to permanent housing clearly defined.

Of note, among all veterans experiencing homelessness, there are those who are not eligible for VA services, particularly health care and other supports that address social determinants of health, who experience the most difficulty ensuring long-term housing. This speaks to the critical impact reliable health care has on overall outcomes for this special population.

Harbor Care:

Weblink: https://www.harborcarenh.org/permanent-supportive-housing

Contact Information: 77 Northeastern Boulevard, Nashua, NH 03062

Phone: 603.882.3616

Email: hope@nhpartnership.org

Supportive Housing Checklist:
Housing

- Affordable—yes, Housing First model of care; veteran housing financial assistance
- Permanent—yes, 500 units of crisis, transitional, permanent supportive, and income-based rental housing and homeless prevention/rapid rehousing services
- Independent—yes, with federal and community stakeholders and partnerships

Support

- Flexible—yes, permanent housing and housing vouchers; Women's services
- Voluntary—yes,
- Tenant-centered—yes, sustainable systems of care that ensures near-immediate access to transitional and permanent housing
- Coordinated services—yes, shares a common board of directors, CEO, and related infrastructures that offer a wide range of services in a collaborative manner; maternal, substance abuse, mental health, and wellness programs

Bud Clark Commons with Home Forward and Health Share of Oregon

Bud Clark Commons (BCC) in Portland, Oregon, is an architectural award-winning eight-story dignified space that provides 130 apartments and supportive services for the most vulnerable homeless residents. Three primary programs within BCC are a transitional shelter for men, a 90-bed facility with 45 beds reserved for veterans (storage area, kitchen, and common space), and a day center with an array of resources and services (Office of Policy Development and Research, 2020). The Centers for Outcomes Research and Education (CORE) reviewed Medicaid claims data to determine the relationship of housing after homelessness and health. To provide an even deeper analysis, CORE used personal surveys with the residents to learn more about their health status, healthcare use, and levels of trauma they had experienced in their lives and whether that changed after having permanent housing. In the year before they moved into BCC, residents on Medicaid averaged total healthcare costs of $1,626 per month. In the year after moving in, average costs were $899 per month, a 45% decline. Total Medicaid cost reductions were greater than one-half of a million dollars in the first year following resident move-in (BCC, 2014). Services most frequently used were case manager, computer lab, counseling, social activities, and group meetings (CORE, 2014). Housing First supports recovery and provides a stable housing for the most vulnerable including families.

Bud Clark Commons:

Weblink: https://www.centralcityconcern.org/services/housing/

Contact information: 665 NW Hoyt St., Portland, OR 97209

650 NW Irving Street, Portland, OR 97209.

Phone: 503.280.4700

Fax: 503.280.4710.

Supportive Housing Checklist:
Housing

- Affordable—yes, location is north of downtown and convenient to other resources
- Permanent—yes, studio apartment with bathroom and kitchenette
- Independent—yes, permanent supportive housing with resident retention at more than 80%

Support

- Flexible—yes, open to individuals and families
- Voluntary—yes, they use a vulnerability assessment tool used to prioritize housing and healthcare needs
- Tenant-centered—yes, common rooms, group rooms with internet and one meal served daily, and the recipient of an architectural award
- Coordinated services—yes, coordinated and convenient health clinic, mental health, chemical addictions, and unemployment services

Swords to Plowshares

Since 1974, Swords to Plowshares, a not-for-profit organization, has addressed homeless, low-income, and at-risk veterans in the San Francisco and Oakland, California, area (see **Figure 20-5**). Services include employment and job training, supportive and permanent housing, counseling, case management, and legal services. The mission is to "heal the wounds of war, to restore dignity, hope, and self-sufficiency" to veterans to rebuild their lives. The three areas of support are: housing, health and wellness, and financial stability (e.g., employment and legal services). Housing services help veterans with emergency and temporary housing, transitional housing

Figure 20-5 Swords to Plowshares

Reproduced from Wikia.org. (n.d.). *Swords to Plowshares*. https://sfhomeless.wikia.org/wiki/Swords_to_Plowshares

at three locations in the Bay Area for veterans with TBI; PTSD; and substance use, depression, and mental health issues. Permanent supportive housing provides 400 units in San Francisco with on-site services, such as staff, activities, and meals. Rent and moving costs are offered, as well as assistance with unpaid rent and utilities, to ensure veterans remain sheltered. The service centers also provide a mailing address, food boxes, and hygiene kits.

Swords to Plowshares:

Weblink: https://www.swords-to-plowshares.org

San Francisco Service Center, 1060 Howard Street, San Francisco, CA 94103

Oakland Service Center, 2719 Telegraph Avenue, Oakland, CA 94612

Phone: (415) 727-VETS (8387) or (415) 252-4788

Supportive Housing Checklist:
Housing

- Affordable—yes, access for all veterans
- Permanent—yes, ranging from temporary, transitional to permanent housing with assistance for preventing eviction with utility and rent assistance
- Independent—yes, independent living for individuals and families

Support

- Flexible—assistance with enrolling in multiple programs based on needs and goals
- Voluntary—yes
- Tenant-centered—community environment with shared responsibilities and activities
- Coordinated services—case management, counseling, support groups, access to health care, referrals

Summary

Community-based, nonprofit, veteran peer-support groups offering transitional housing, a sense of community and camaraderie, and structured, substance-free environments with fellow veterans seem to be most effective for homeless and at-risk veterans. Government funding is limited, and services are often stretched to capacity. Community groups provide additional support, resources, and opportunities, such as housing, employment, and health care. Veterans have many opportunities to participate in services, which improve chances of overcoming homelessness (NCHV, 2020). A systematic meta-analysis of 31 studies looked at the risk factors for homelessness among U.S. veterans by Tsai and colleagues and found the strongest risk factors were substance abuse disorders and mental illness, followed by low income and other income-related factors (Tsai et al., 2015). Therefore, substance use disorders, mental illness, and low-income policies and programs should by targeted in efforts to end homelessness among veterans. Until the root causes are addressed, homelessness will continue to be a significant problem. To facilitate primary prevention, the incidence of homelessness has to be quantified and documented, yet the homeless are reticent to be counted.

References

American Addiction Centers (2020, August 31). *High rate of substance abuse among veterans and treatment options*. https://www.rehabs.com/veterans-drug-abuse/

Blais, R. K., & Geiser, C. (2019). Depression and PTSD-related anhedonia mediate the association of military sexual trauma and suicidal ideation in female service members/veterans. *Psychiatry Research*, 279, 148–154. doi:10.1016/j.psychres.2018.12.148

Blumer, H. (1969). *Symbolic interactionism: perspective and method*. Prentice-Hall.

Boyle, L., Filips, J., Schultz, S., Yadack, A., & Aslam, M. (2020). Using telehealth technology to improve access and quality of mental health care to older veterans. *The American Journal of Geriatric Psychiatry, 28*(4), S20. doi:10.1016/j.jagp.2020.01.040

Carroll, T. D., McCormick, W. H., Smith, P. N., Isaak, S. L., & Currier, J. M. (2020). PTSD, religious coping, and interpersonal antecedents of suicidal desire among military veterans: An initial examination of moderation models. *Psychology of Religion and Spirituality, 12*(3), 304–310. doi:10.1037/rel0000270

Cooper, S. A., Szymanski, B. R., Bohnert, K. M., Sripada, R. K., & McCarthy, J. F. (2020). Association between positive results on the Primary Care-Posttraumatic Stress Disorder Screen and suicide mortality among U.S. veterans. *JAMA Network Open*, 3(9), e2015707. doi:10.1001/jamanetworkopen.2020.15707

Council of Economic Advisers. (2019, September). *The state of homelessness in America*. https://www.whitehouse.gov/wp-content/uploads/2019/09/The-State-of-Homelessness-in-America.pdf

Department of Veterans Affairs & Department of Defense. (2017). *VA/DOD clinical practice guideline for the management of posttraumatic stress disorder and acute stress disorder, Version 3*. https://www.healthquality.va.gov/guidelines/MH/ptsd/VADoDPTSDCPGFinal.pdf.

Dunphy, L. M., Winland-Brown, J. E., Porter, B. O., & Thomas D. J. (2015), *Primary care: The art and science of advanced practice nursing* (4th ed.). F.A. Davis

Elnitsky, C. A., Fisher, M. P., & Blevins, C. L. (2017). Military service member and veteran reintegration: A conceptual analysis, unified definition, and key domains. *Frontiers in Psychology, 8*, 369. https://doi.org/10.3389/fpsyg.2017.00369

Evans, W. N., Kroeger, S., Palmer, C., & Pohl, E. (2019). Housing and Urban Development Veterans Affairs supportive housing vouchers and veterans' homelessness: 2007–2017. *American Journal of Public Health, 109*(10), 1440– 1445. doi:10.2105/ajph.2019.305231

Gabrielian, S., Yuan, A. H., Andersen, R. M., Rubenstein, L. V., & Gelberg, L. (2014). VA health service utilization for homeless and low-income Veterans: A spotlight on the VA Supportive Housing (VASH) program in greater Los Angeles. Medical Care, 52(5), 454–461. doi:10.1097/MLR.0000000000000112.

Garfield, R., Orgers, K., & Damico, A., (2021). *The coverage gap: Uninsured poor adults in states that do not expand Medicaid*. Kaiser Family Foundation. https://www.kff.org/medicaid/issue-brief/the-coverage-gap-uninsured-poor-adults-in-states-that-do-not-expand-medicaid/

Gates, G. J, & Herman, J. (2014). Transgender military service in the United States. *UCLA: The Williams Institute*. https://escholarship.org/uc/item/1t24j53h

Glenn, J. J., Dillon, K. H., Dennis, P. A., Patel, T. A., Mann, A. J., Calhoun, P. S., Kimbrel, N. A., Beckham, J. C., & Elbogen, E. B. (2020). Post-traumatic symptom severity mediates the association between combat exposure and suicidal ideation in veterans. *Suicide and Life-Threatening Behavior, 2020*(00), 1–6. https://doi.org/10.1111/sltb.12678

Grant, J. M., Mottet, L., Tanis, J. E., Harrison, J., Herman, J. L., & Keisling, M. (2011). *Injustice at every turn: A report of the National Transgender Discrimination Survey*. National Center for Transgender Equality and National Gay and Lesbian Task Force. 2011. https://www.thetaskforce.org/injustice-every-turn-report-national-transgender-discrimination-survey

Harrison-Quintana, J., & Herman, J. L., (2013). Still serving in silence: transgender service members and veterans in the National Transgender Discrimination Survey. *LGBTQ Policy Journal, 3*, 39–52. https://lgbtq.hkspublications.org/2013/10/21/still-serving-in-silence-transgender-service-members-and-veterans-in-the-national-transgender-discrimination-survey/

Kim, J. C., Matto, M., & Kristen, E., (2019). Safer housing for homeless women veterans. *Journal of the American Academy of Psychiatry and the Law Online*, JAAPL.003854-19. http://jaapl.org/content/early/2019/06/11/JAAPL.003854-19

Kranke, D., Floersch, J., & Dobalian, A. (2019). Identifying aspects of sameness to promote veteran reintegration with civilians: Evidence and implications for military social work. *Health & Social Work, 44*(1), 61–64 doi:10.1093/hsw/hly036

Lee, S., & Willson, P. (2017). Soldiers on the streets: How homeless Vietnam veterans decide to seek healthcare. *The Internet Journal of Advanced Nursing Practice, 16*(1). http://doi-org/10.5580/IJANP.47907

Livingston, W. S., Fargo, J. D., Gundlapalli, A. V., Brignone, E., & Blais, R. K. (2020). Comorbid PTSD and depression diagnoses mediate the Association of Military Sexual Trauma and Suicide and Intentional Self-Inflicted Injury in VHA-enrolled Iraq/Afghanistan Veterans, 2004-2014. *Journal of Affective Disorders*, 274, 1184–1190. https://doi-org/10.1016/j.jad.2020.05.024

Lofgreen, A. M., Tirone, V., Carroll, K. K., Rufa, A. K., Smith, D. L., Bagley, J., Zalta, A. K., Brennan, M. B., Van Horn, R., Pollack, M. H., & Held, P. (2020).

Improving outcomes for a 3-week intensive treatment program for posttraumatic stress disorder in survivors of military sexual trauma. *Journal of Affective Disorders, 269*, 134–140. doi:10.1016/j.jad.2020.03.036

McCarthy, J. F., Bossarte, R. M., Katz, I. R., Thompson, C., Kemp, J., Hannemann, C. M., Nielson, C., & Schoenbaum, M. (2015). Predictive modeling and concentration of the risk of suicide: Implications for preventive interventions in the U.S. Department of Veterans Affairs. *American Journal of Public Health, 105*(9), 1935–1942. https://doi-org./10.2105/AJPH.2015.302737

Metraux, S., Clegg, L. X., Daigh, J. D., Culhane, D. P., & Kane, V. (2013). Risk factors for becoming homeless among a cohort of veterans who served in the era of the Iraq and Afghanistan conflicts. *American Journal of Public Health, 103*(Suppl. 2), S255–S261. http://dx.doi.org/10.2105/AJPH.2013.301432

Mobile Loaves and Fishes. (2020). *Community First!* Village. https://mlf.org/community-first/

National Coalition for Homeless Veterans. (2020). *Background and statistics.* http://nchv.org/index.php/news/media/background_and_statistics/

National Coalition for Homeless Veterans. (2021). *House committee votes unanimously to expand HUD-VASH.* http://nchv.org/index.php?/news/headline_article/OTH-HUD-VASH

National Conference of State Legislators. (2020, May 22) *Veteran Homelessness: Overview of state and federal resources.* https://www.ncsl.org/research/military-and-veterans-affairs/veteran-homelessness-an-overview-of-state-and-federal-resources.aspx

National Health Care for the Homeless Council. (2019, May 22). *Overcoming challenges in street medicine.* Conference presentation, Grand Hyatt Washington. https://nhchc.org/wp-content/uploads/2019/08/overcoming-challenges-in-street-medicine-final.pdf

Nichter, B., Hill, M., Norman, S., Haller, M., & Pietrzak, R. H. (2020). Impact of specific combat experiences on suicidal ideation and suicide attempt in U.S. military veterans: Results from the National Health and Resilience in Veterans Study. *Journal of Psychiatric Research, 130*, 231–239. https://doi-org/10.1016/j.jpsychires.2020.07.041

O'Flaherty, B. (2019). Homelessness research: A guide for economists (and friends). *Journal of Housing Economics, 44*, 1–25. doi:10.1016/j.jhe.2019.01.003

Office of Public and Intergovernmental Affairs. (2020, November 2). *Walmart reopens five VA telehealth access points after COVID-19 shutdown.* https://www.va.gov/opa/pressrel/pressrelease.cfm?id=5556

Payne, R. K. (2019). *A framework for understanding poverty: A cognitive approach* (6th ed.). Aha!Process, Inc. https://www.amazon.com/Framework-Understanding-Poverty-Cognitive-Approach-dp-1948244187/dp/1948244187/ref=dp_ob_image_bk

Sayer, N. A., Orazem, R. J., Noorbaloochi, S., Gravely, A., Frazier, P., Carlson, K. F., Schnurr, P. P., & Oleson, H. (2014). Iraq and Afghanistan war veterans with reintegration problems: Differences by Veterans Affairs healthcare user status. *Administration and Policy in Mental Health Services Research, 42*, 493–503. doi:10.1007/s10488-014-0564-2

Slightam, C., Gregory, A. J., Hu, J., Jacobs, J., Gurmessa, T., Kimerling, R., Blonigen, D., & Zulman, D. M. (2020). Patient perceptions of video visits using Veterans Affairs telehealth tablets: Survey study. *Journal of Medical Internet Research, 22*(4), e15682, 1–17. https://doi-org./10.2196/15682

Tsai, J., Hoff, R. & Harpaz-Rotem, I. (2017). One-year incidence and predictors of homelessness among 300,000 U.S. Veterans seen in specialty mental health care. *Psychological Services, 14*(2), 203–207. doi:10.1037/ser0000083

U.S. Department of Housing and Urban Development. (2020). *The 2019 Annual Homeless Assessment Report (AHAR) to Congress: Part 1: Point-in-time estimates of homelessness.* https://www.huduser.gov/portal/sites/default/files/pdf/2019-AHAR-Part-1.pdf

U.S. Department of Housing and Urban Development. (2018). *The 2018 Annual Homeless Assessment Report (AHAR) to Congress: Part 1: Point-in-time estimates of homelessness.* https://files.hudexchange.info/resources/documents/2018-AHAR-Part-1.pdf.

U.S. Department of Veterans Affairs. (2020a). *2019 National veteran suicide prevention annual report.* Office of Mental Health and Suicide Prevention. https://www.mentalhealth.va.gov/docs/data-sheets/2019/2019_National_Veteran_Suicide_Prevention_Annual_Report_508.pdf

U.S. Department of Veterans Affairs. (2020b). *Veterans experiencing homelessness.* https://www.va.gov/HOMELESS/endingVetshomelessness.asp

U.S. Department of Veterans Affairs. (2020c). *Veterans Justice Outreach Program.* https://www.va.gov/HOMELESS/VJO.asp

U.S. Department of Veterans Affairs. (2021). *How to apply for a discharge upgrade.* https://www.va.gov/discharge-upgrade-instructions/

U.S. Interagency Council on Homelessness. (2015, June 26). *Breaking the cycle of veteran incarceration and homelessness: Emerging community practices.* https://www.usich.gov/tools-for-action/breaking-the-cycle-of-veteran-incarceration-and-homelessness/

VA National Center on Homelessness Among Veterans. (2017, June 22). *Homeless evidence and research synthesis (HERS) Roundtable Proceedings: Rural veterans and homelessness.* https://www.va.gov/HOMELESS/nchav/docs/Rural_HERS_proceedings.pdf

Varma, R. (2018, November 13). *What you need to know about street medicine movement and homeless healthcare.* https://medium.com/@DrRohitVarma/what-you-need-to-know-about-street-medicine-movement-and-homeless-healthcare-bf33eaf04efa

CHAPTER 21

Identifying Soul Injury: A Self-Awareness Inventory

Deborah L. Grassman, Abi Katz, Josephine F. Wilson, and LuAnn J. Conforti-Brown

Few people have been with 10,000 dying veterans; five VA hospice nurses have. The lessons they learned reveal a process for attaining personal peace, and ironically, these lessons have come from people who were trained for war. Those 10,000 veterans showed the nurses a wound that lurked in their souls—a wound that was different than the PTSD that many of them had. Although the wound could often be described as a "moral injury" (a violation of deepest-held beliefs that causes moral confusion), many of the wounds extended *beyond* the definition of moral injury. Some veterans called their wound is a "Soul Injury." The lessons were so profound that the nurses started a nonprofit organization, Opus Peace, to bring the Soul Injury message to the rest of the world.

At first glance, it may seem odd that the phenomenon of *Soul Injury* is emerging from the hospice field. However, dying people know things others do not; perspectives shift dramatically as death approaches. The day before a person is given a terminal diagnosis, they take their life for granted; the day *after* they are given the diagnosis, they wake up. Things that did not seem important yesterday, suddenly seem urgent to complete. And things they thought were important fade in priority. That is the gift that death is: it awakens people to how their life *matters*. Another shift in perspective that sometimes occurs is people become more honest—in fact, the *unvarnished* truth often surfaces. As one veteran described it: "Now, while I'm dying, is no time for me to be lying to myself." It is at this point that a Soul Injury might come to light and the person is ready to deal with it—possibly for the first time in their lives.

Healthcare providers who are sensitive to how military service influences aging veterans understand how military experience sometimes complicate peaceful dying. The previous chapter "Identifying the Unique Needs of Veterans That Influence End-of-Life Care" outlines those influences. Many of those influences surround Soul Injury, Moral Injury, and PTSD. This chapter will provide a brief overview of these three wounds of suffering and then familiarize the reader with an instrument to help identify Soul Injury and use the instrument as a tool to facilitate relevant conversations about serious illness and death.

Wounds of Suffering: PTSD, Moral Injury, Soul Injury

Although not labeled as "PTSD," symptoms of PTSD have been described since early recorded history. In the Bible, Job reports his response to the trauma of losing his children, wealth, and health. He describes the classic nightmares of PTSD: "My bed shall comfort me, my couch shall ease my complaint. Then, God, you affright me with dreams and visions terrify me, so that *I should prefer choking and death rather than my pains*" (*New American Bible,* 1970). In more recent decades, the aftermath of war was often described as "battle fatigue," "shell shock," or "soldier's heart." It was not until 1980 that the *Diagnostic and Statistical Manual* (DSM) codified PTSD as a diagnostic category with identified symptoms to meet the criteria (American Psychiatric Association, 2013, pp. 271–276).

Although morals and ethics have been recorded by philosophers for centuries, it was not until the 1900s that psychologists like Jean Piaget, and later Carol Gilligan and Lawrence Kohlberg started to study and report on moral development in professional publications (Piaget, 1932; Gilligan, 1977; Kohlberg, 1981). Andrew Jameton first conceptualized the term "moral distress" in 1984 (Jameton, 1984, p. 6). The term *moral injury* was subsequently coined by VA psychiatrist Jonathan Shay and colleagues in the 1990s based on numerous discussions they had with veterans (Shay, 1994). Shay recognized the moral damage experienced by veterans and believed that much of the distress they suffered represented an inner conflict between their moral beliefs and their actions during military service. Both the VA and the Department of Defense have adopted the term "moral injury" and define it as events that are considered morally injurious if they transgress deeply held moral beliefs and expectations (U.S. Department of Veterans Affairs, 2016).

Distinguishing Soul Injury, Moral Injury, and PTSD is important because they have different causative factors that require a different approach to maximize effectiveness. All three might have overlapping symptoms such as anxiety, depression, and/or uncontrolled anger that make differential diagnosis difficult. Two or all three diagnoses may exist simultaneously. **Table 21-1** contrasts these three wounds to help make the distinction.

An example might help to clarify. John Drinkard is a Marine Corps veteran who has studied and lived Soul Injury, Moral Injury, *and* PTSD. In speaking to an audience of hospice workers, he said: "I could tell you about the three helicopter crashes I was in and the PTSD I have suffered after Vietnam, but I won't because PTSD treatments have taught me how to manage my triggers and calm my mind. I could tell you about the moral injury I suffered because I felt betrayed by my country. I had joined the Marine Corps to go to Vietnam and fight for God and country. When I got there, I discovered there was no God and country in that war. It was all a bright, shining lie. But working with a group of other veterans who also had moral injury helped me release my bitterness. If I was dying and if you came to visit *me*, the issue that might surprise you is my "father wound"—a wound that occurred when I was 9 years old. I had just been discharged from the hospital with a diagnosis of an enlarged heart. On the way home, my dad stopped to socialize with a friend. I told him I didn't feel good and wanted to go home. My father berated me for expressing my needs, completely devaluing and degrading me. The John I knew *disappeared* that day. The loss of self and the shame I felt from my father's onslaught created an insidious Soul Injury that was much greater than the 'enlarged heart' I had just suffered. That incident does not meet the criteria for PTSD nor Moral Injury; it *does* meet the criteria for Soul Injury—a wound I had buried alive because it paled in comparison to all the traumas I experienced in the war. In my 70s, I learned about Soul Injury and how to grieve the losses of that 9-year-old boy, and to learn how to extend self-compassion" (Drinkard, 2018).

Table 21-1 Soul Injury, Moral Injury, and PTSD

Soul Injury	Moral Injury	PTSD
Definition An overlooked, unassessed emotional, spiritual, or psychosocial wound that traumatically or insidiously separates one from their own sense of self. Soul Injury is not listed in the *Diagnostic and Statistical Manual* (DSM) because it does not indicate a pathological diagnosis.	**Definition** Violation of deepest-held beliefs and expectations, causing moral confusion. Moral Injury is not listed in the *Diagnostic and Statistical Manual* (DSM) because it does not indicate a pathological diagnosis.	**Definition** A mental health issue that some people develop after experiencing or witnessing a life-threatening event such as combat, a natural disaster, a car accident, or sexual assault. PTSD is well defined and outlined in the DSM-V and has been well researched for decades.
Caused by Barriers that interfere with accessing a person's deepest self. Releasing the barriers restores wholeness. The primary barriers are: ■ Unmourned loss and hurt ■ Unforgiven guilt and shame ■ Diminished self-compassion	**Caused by** Situations or events: ■ Without clear right/wrong choices ■ Overt or covert coercion to act against one's moral beliefs ■ Trusting people who fail to do the right thing ■ Surviving in ways that violate personal conscience	**Caused by** Events that result in identified symptoms that meet DSM-V diagnostic criteria from: ■ Exposure to actual or threatened violence, death, serious injury, or sexual assault via direct experience ■ In-person witnessing, or learning about a loved one's traumatic event
Impacts Personhood, causing one to fear being real and/or experience their full potential so they can be who they are meant to be	**Impacts** Beliefs and values, separating one from a sense of trust in others and/or themselves	**Impacts** The brain (especially the amygdala and limbic system) separating one from a sense of safety in the world
Symptoms (Commonly develops *insidiously* before the wound becomes recognizable): ■ Lying, hiding, masking personal thoughts and feelings from others and/or self ■ Disconnecting from a perception of one's own inner goodness and beauty ■ Feeling empty or that a part of self is missing ■ Having a vague or profound sense of worthlessness, inadequacy, or loss of meaning ■ Yearning to be someone else, belong, approved of, "normal," "good enough," etc. ■ Using numbing agents to shut down the part of self holding loss, hurt, guilt, or shame	**Symptoms** (Can develop with one serious breach of trust or a series of smaller betrayals): ■ Feelings of grief, guilt, remorse, shame, outrage, despair ■ Loss of trust in others and/or themselves due to betrayal ■ Self-isolation ■ Fear of being judged ■ Bitterness due to "unfairness" in a world that should be "fair"	**Symptoms** (Often develop suddenly after trauma, but can occur gradually over time): ■ Intrusive memories, distressing dreams, dissociative reactions, physiological and psychological distress when triggered ■ Avoidance of memories and external reminders ■ Adverse changes in cognitions and mood (exaggerated negative beliefs about self and others, persistent negative emotional state and inability to experience positive emotions, feeling detached from people and activities) ■ Irritability, angry outbursts, recklessness, hypervigilance, sleep disturbances, etc.

(continues)

Table 21-1 Soul Injury, Moral Injury, and PTSD *(continued)*

Soul Injury	Moral Injury	PTSD
Treatment ■ *Soul Injury Self-Awareness Inventory* to identify unresolved losses and hurts ■ *Anchoring Heart Technique* to learn how to allow emotional pain and peace to sit side by side together ■ Identification of "favorite numbing agents" ■ Learn how to self-compassionately *feel* the helplessness of an uncontrollable situation ■ Integrative letter-writing to re-own, re-home, and re-vitalize scattered piece of self	**Treatment** ■ Discussion with a trusted other who will not judge the action ■ Dialogue with a benevolent moral authority ■ Methods for forgiveness and self-forgiveness ■ Guided imagery ■ Meditation ■ Collective rituals	**Treatment** ■ Individual psychotherapy ■ Group psychotherapy ■ Antidepressant and anti-anxiety medications ■ Exposure/Desensitization therapy ■ Somatic therapies (bio-feedback, eye movement desensitization reprocessing (EMDR), yoga, etc.) to retrain the stress response of the amygdala
Examples of Adverse Events That Can Cause Soul Injury ■ Name-calling ("fat-so," "dumbo," "lazy," "fag," "n____," etc.) as a child and the label was incorporated into personal identity ■ Birth issues: a girl with parents who wanted a boy and regularly reminded of that, not being the "favorite" sibling, born with a parent who abandoned them, born with the "wrong" sexual orientation, adopted, raised by a non-parental relative, etc. ■ Young adult who cannot get "launched," older adult with a midlife crisis, loss of dreams, etc. ■ Personal identity issue with a life transition (feeling "lost," "forgotten who I am") after divorce, death of a loved one, retirement, lay-off from a job, etc. ■ Perfectionism to prove one is "good enough" ■ Snobbish behaviors or bullying with feelings of superiority ■ Becoming a loner to avoid dealing with feelings of inferiority ■ Having PTSD, bipolar, depression, or other	**Examples of Adverse Events That Can Cause Moral Injury** ■ Military combatant accidently or intentionally kills a child, civilian, unarmed enemy ■ Military combatant betrayed by his/her country (called "murderer," "baby killer," spit upon, etc.) ■ Altering testimony, witness account to "save my own skin"; victim of being falsely accused. ■ Not protecting or standing up for someone ■ Woman aborts a pregnancy in spite of her religious beliefs (or man with certain religious beliefs unable to stop the abortion) ■ Victims of crime; perpetrators of crime with remorse ■ A supervisor who has to lay off good, loyal workers to meet fiscal responsibilities	**Examples of Trauma that can Cause PTSD** ■ The DSM-V lists the following examples of at-risk populations: ■ Military combat ■ Violent personal assault (sexual, physical, robbery, mugging) ■ Kidnapping or taken hostage ■ Terrorist attack ■ Torture ■ POW or concentration camp prisoners ■ Natural or man-made disasters ■ Severe auto accidents ■ Terminal diagnosis

Soul Injury: An Overview

Soul Injury is defined as:

- A wound to our sense of self—our real self *beyond* the façade, affecting our deepest personhood
- A wound that stifles full potential because it separates a person from who they are *meant* to be

Sometimes these wounds accompany trauma. More often, Soul Injuries occur insidiously, gradually corroding a sense of self.

The word "soul" as it is used with the term "Soul Injury," should not be misconstrued to have a religious connotation. Rather, the word "soul" is used to identify that piece of self beyond the body, beyond the brain, that is the *essence* of who a person is. People find meaning and purpose when they are able to stay connected to this deepest part of self. Life circumstances, however, cause people to become separated from who they really are—in other words, a Soul Injury emerges with accompanying symptoms that might include:

- Feelings of emptiness or that a part of self is missing or defective
- A loss of meaning and a sense one does not matter
- Longing to be enough: "good enough," "pretty enough," "smart enough," etc.
- Use of numbing agents to avoid feeling uncomfortable emotions

Soul Injuries occur when barriers are created that interfere with accessing a person's deepest self. Releasing the barriers restores wholeness. The primary barriers are:

- Unmourned loss and hurt
- Unforgiven guilt and shame
- Diminished self-compassion

Losses include any failure or disappointment. Failure to acknowledge a loss exiles that part of self into unconsciousness. Left unmourned, dashed hopes and expectations might solidify into a wall that separates a person from their full potential of who they are meant to be. Unresolved guilt adds layers to the wall. Without insight and self-compassion, shame cements the wall into a seemingly impenetrable fortress. The result is a Soul Injury.

We are not taught how to lose, how to mourn, how to forgive, or how to compassionately listen to our deepest self. Our educational systems value achievement and success—teaching us how to hold on to and how to control. Therefore, we do not learn how to mourn losses and hurts. We are not taught how to use self-compassion to transform shame. Instead, we are taught to numb out feelings of loss, hurt, guilt, and shame.

You only get to die once. Don't miss the opportunity to be present!

The Soul Injury concept provides a non-pathologized term to describe a phenomenon in everyday language with practical applications. After a hospice medical director attended a Soul Injury conference, he said: "We use a Red-Yellow-Green triage system for symptom management: Red means symptoms are out of control; green means we have symptoms under control. When I heard the talk on Soul Injury, I realized that after we get our patients into the green zone, that's not enough. There's something more . . . and I realized that day that the 'something more' is *Soul Injury!*" This physician now values Soul Injury and uses the term among their team members to address it.

Like this physician, hospice providers might forget that the goal of hospice care is *not* symptom management. Symptom management is an essential vehicle to achieve the goal of *healing*. Dying people are fertile ground for healing because they become awakened to what is important and what is not. Responding to the symptoms of *Soul Injury* is an essential vehicle to achieve the goal of healing, and it starts with a conversation. The Soul Injury Self-Awareness Inventory helps clinicians initiate a conversation that creates a safe emotional environment that allows people to let go of fear and denial so they can be *present* for the mystery that death is.

Soul Injury Self-Awareness Inventory (SISAI)

The Soul Injury Inventory (Opus Peace, n.d.-b) is a tool that was developed:

- To increase personal self-awareness for healthcare professionals and caregivers; healthcare providers need to be able to identify their own personal, insidious Soul Injuries in order to authentically bring wholeness to care for others with a Soul Injury
- As an educational tool to raise awareness about Soul Injuries in patients and families, providing relevant issues for team meetings that allow alternative discussions to emerge
- As a tool that opens the door to meaningful conversations, helping the hospice care provider quickly uncover "unfinished business" that left unfinished could have a negative impact on patient outcome
- To establish metrics that validate the relevance of Soul Injury so it will become incorporated into healthcare curricula

The Soul Injury Inventory should not be understood as providing any type of diagnosis or healthcare recommendations. Screening tools such as the *Soul Injury Self-Awareness Inventory* (see **Box 21-1**) are designed to enhance awareness of one's own experiences for the purpose of raising awareness of feelings and experiences related to possible *Soul Injuries*. Highlighting these experiences may offer an opportunity to reflect on them at greater length, consider their relevance in a broader life context, and provide a gateway to meaningful conversations with healthcare professionals.

Box 21-1 Soul Injury Self-Awareness Inventory

Courtesy of Opus Peace.org

Many people have acquired *Soul Injuries* at one time or another. The definition of *Soul Injury* is:

1. A wound that separates one from their sense of self—their real self *beyond* the façade
2. An aching wound perpetuated by unmourned loss/hurt, unforgiven guilt/shame, and diminished self-compassion that is often manifested as a sense of emptiness, a loss of meaning, or a sense that a part of self is missing
3. A long-lasting response to a person or a situation that causes one to feel defective, inadequate, or incomplete

Circle the answer that most closely reflects your experience most of the time:

1. I am not able to be my real self.
   1 Always true 2 Often true 3 Sometimes true 4 Never true
2. I engage in some activities to help me avoid uncomfortable feelings.
   1 Always true 2 Often true 3 Sometimes true 4 Never true
3. When I avoid uncomfortable feelings, it often causes problems with people in my life.
   1 Always true 2 Often true 3 Sometimes true 4 Never true
4. I have a hard time facing loss, change, disappointments, or transitions.
   1 Always true 2 Often true 3 Sometimes true 4 Never true
5. Guilt and/or shame haunt me.
   1 Always true 2 Often true 3 Sometimes true 4 Never true
6. I feel defective, inadequate, or unworthy.
   1 Always true 2 Often true 3 Sometimes true 4 Never true

7. Self-compassion is difficult for me.
   1 Always true 2 Often true 3 Sometimes true 4 Never true
8. I struggle to find meaning in my life.
   1 Always true 2 Often true 3 Sometimes true 4 Never true
9. Have you identified a possible *Soul Injury?* Yes ______ No ______ Not Sure ______
10. Do you think a past *Soul Injury* is affecting you now? Yes ______ No ______ Not Sure ______

Using the Tool to Facilitate Meaningful Conversations

The Self-Awareness Inventory tool uses a 1–4 Likert Scale to measure responses that range from "always true" to "never true." Two additional questions inquire about whether they think they have identified a possible *Soul Injury* and whether they think a past *Soul Injury* is still affecting them. Scoring implications for further possible actions include:

- 8–16: Consider consulting a professional who specializes in loss, grief, forgiveness, and self-compassion.
- 17–24: Explore www.OpusPeace.org or www.SoulInjury.org website for more information about the impact that Soul Injury might be having on your life.
- 25–32: You have probably worked hard to achieve and maintain a strong sense of self.

The lower the score, the more likely there are issues of loss, hurt, grief, guilt, and shame. These issues often reflect unfinished attachments that might complicate peaceful dying or could complicate bereavement recovery.

Usage of the Soul Injury Self-Awarness Inventory (**Box 21-2**) is not limited to people who are facing life-limiting illnesses, nor is it restricted to use with veterans. The inventory precipitates meaningful conversations no matter what the issue or stage of life might be.

The first statement, "I am not able to be my real self," asks about the ability to be authentic. It invites dialogue about facades, self-betrayal, expectations from others, "appearances," etc. Often, the question provides family members with an opportunity to offer insight about the person's "real self" in ways that allows self-exploration.

Statement 2: "I engage in some activities to help me avoid uncomfortable feelings" invites people to look at their *fear* of "uncomfortable" feelings. Although emotional hurts are often talked about, fear of feeling the emotional hurt is usually overlooked. It is the fear of *feeling* uncomfortable emotions that causes those feelings to become covered up, hidden, buried alive. It is the fear of experiencing the hurt that is at the root of utilizing numbing behaviors (internet surfing, work-a-holism or other addictions, stoicism, staying busy, shopping, video games, comfort foods, taking care of others, etc.).

Statement 3: "When I avoid uncomfortable feelings, it often causes problems with people in my life." Avoiding uncomfortable feelings can impact relationships. Engaging in a conversation about how *fear* of emotional distress impacts relationships is something many people have never thought about. In fact, people sometimes think that avoiding "negative" feelings is desired—the way to "be happy." This might contribute to shallow relationships that lack intimacy. As people are dying, regrets commonly surface. When the layers of regret are peeled back, regrets almost always reveal their misuse of numbing agents that disconnected them from people they loved and people who loved them, and also disconnected them from themselves—a Soul Injury.

Box 21-2 ***Soul Injury*** **Self-Awareness Inventory**

Purpose

Raise awareness about the phenomena of *Soul Injury* in your own life and the lives of others. This is important for several reasons:

- Identifying a *Soul Injury* brings it out of unconsciousness where it can insidiously lurk and sabotage lives without our even knowing it.
- Learning how to release UNMOURNED LOSS/HURT and UNFORGIVEN GUILT/ SHAME helps remove barriers that prevent us from connecting with our "real" self—the self we were meant to be.
- Grieving and forgiving are not routinely taught in families, communities, educational programs, or healthcare systems. This perpetuates barriers that keep us from connecting with our deepest self.
- Acknowledging and validating the presence of a *Soul Injury* cultivates self-compassion so that self-identity is strengthened and inner goodness/beauty affirmed.

How to Use the *Soul Injury* Self-Awareness Inventory Personally

- Complete the inventory for yourself.
- Contemplate your own story and the losses you have sustained.
- Reflect on the "numbing agents" you use to avoid feeling emotional pain (internet surfing, work-a-holism, stoicism, staying busy, shopping, video games, comfort foods, taking care of others, etc.).
- Consider how FEAR of feeling emotional pain might be controlling your life and causing you to be less "you."
- Discern relationship problems that might be caused by your fear of feeling emotional pain.
- Become curious about how you face change and transition.
- Pay attention to ways in which you feel guilty, ashamed, defective, inadequate, or unworthy.
- Search for the next deeper meaning for your life—a meaning that yields more "you."

How to Use the *Soul Injury* Self-Awareness Inventory with a Trusted Other Person(s)

- Initiate a conversation about the topic of *Soul Injury* with someone else.
- Discuss the words or images that come to mind with the term *"Soul Injury."*
- Query each other about possibilities for unmourned loss/hurt and unforgiven guilt/shame that the other person might not be able to see within themselves.
- Explore with each other how FEAR of emotional pain may be sabotaging your lives.
- Consider how your *Soul Injury* may be impacting your relationship with each other.

How to Use the *Soul Injury* Self-Awareness Inventory in a Professional Setting with Clients

- Have them complete the inventory.
- Have them identify ONE survey question on the inventory to discuss.

Reproduced from Opus Peace.org. (n.d.). *Soul injury self-awareness inventory*. https://opuspeace.org/BlankSite/media/Documents/Soul-Injury-Inventory-Instructions.pdf

Statement 4: "I have a hard time facing loss, change, disappointments, or transitions." Losses, changes, and transitions are fraught with uncertainty, loss of control, and unknowns. People have not been taught how to navigate change, how to let themselves experience disappointments and failures. These can be threatening and frightening. Certainly, death is the greatest transition that any of us will experience. If someone has already had a difficult time letting go of control or facing loss and change, then a hospice provider can anticipate that this person may be at higher risk for complicated dying.

Statement 5: "Guilt and/or shame haunt me." This statement offers opportunities to seek and extend forgiveness. After answering this question, one woman asked if she could obtain a blank inventory to give to her adult daughter. The inventory was provided and she gave it to her daughter, saying: "I'd like you to take this inventory and afterward let's talk about how my alcoholism caused a Soul Injury in you when you were a child." This woman reported that her relationship with her daughter dramatically changed because now there is no more fear; they are both open to talking about their hurtful past.

Statement 6: "I feel defective, inadequate, or unworthy." Feelings of not being "enough"—good enough, pretty enough, strong enough, giving enough, competent enough, etc. are at the core of many Soul Injuries, undermining a person's sense of self. These stories often originate in childhood and not unusually surface unbidden at the end of life, complicating peaceful dying. Paradoxically, helping a person self-compassionately *feel* their childhood helplessness often brings insight and relief.

Statement 7: "Self-compassion is difficult for me." Self-compassion starts with achieving a sense of self. In his book, *The Body Keeps the Score,* Dr. Bessel Van Der Kolk writes about the area of the brain that gives us a sense of self (2014). Dr. Van Der Kolk has devoted his career to responding to people who have been traumatized. He reports that there is a central corridor of the brain (anterior and posterior cingulate, medial and orbital prefrontal cortex, insula) that is responsible for giving a person a sense of "self." This part of the brain registers *sensations*. When these brain structures are not activated, the person has difficulty interpreting internal states and has difficulty assessing the significance of the internal sensation. After trauma, brain scans show markedly lower activity in this corridor of the brain, which in turn means there is an interruption in their ability to achieve a sense of self. Conversations that explore ways to self-validate help people better connect to their personhood.

Statement 8: "I struggle to find meaning in my life." As people are dying, they often embark on a life review process. It happens rather naturally as memories surface. Also, family members frequently visit and review memories of their time together. In the stories lie clues to the person's life meaning. Thus, life review helps people develop insight to better understand the meaning in their lives—especially if the family does it with the patient. Missed opportunities and lost dreams can be grieved; achievements validated.

Validation of the Soul Injury Self-Awareness Inventory

The Soul Injury Self-Awareness Inventory has been validated in two separate studies with healthcare professionals and caregivers. In the first study, 365 healthcare professionals and caregivers completed the Soul Injury Inventory during an Opus Peace training. The types of trainings differed by theme, including "Forgiveness and Loss" (attended by 8.2% of the 365 professionals who completed the Inventory), "The Hero Within" (attended by 12%), a 3-day comprehensive Soul Injury program (attended by 8.7%), "PTSD" (attended by 2.2%), "Soul Injury" (attended by 70.8%), and "Suicide Loss Support Group" (attended by 6.3%). Of the 365 participants who completed the Soul Injury Inventory, 75.1% were women. Ages of the participants were reported by range, 18–30 (11%), 31–50 (34%), 51–65 (35%), 66+ (14%), unreported (6%). Most of the 365 worked in the healthcare field (83.9%), 6.3% worked in allied fields such as the ministry or were caregivers, 5.7% were veterans, and 4.1% were volunteers in hospital or hospice settings.

The 365 participants were a largely homogeneous cohort. The mean Soul Injury Self-Awareness Inventory score (that is, the sum of the answers for questions 1–8) was 23.5 (SD = 4.0). No significant differences between men and women, among age groups, among type of profession, or among type of training were found. Of the entire group of 365, 18 (4.9%) scored between 8 and 16, indicating a high degree of Soul Injury; 190 (52.1%) scored between 17 and 24, indicating some impact of Soul Injury; and 157 (43.0%) scored between 25 and 32, indicating little impact of Soul Injury and a strong sense of self.

In this study, a factor analysis of the responses to the first eight questions on the Soul Injury Self-Awareness Inventory revealed that all eight questions contributed significantly (with communalities all greater than 0.53) to a single factor with an eigenvalue of 3.85 that accounted for 43.4% of the variance. This indicates a strong factor structure for the Inventory that appears to measure a single factor, Soul Injury.

Further validation included chi square analyses of the responses ("Yes," "No," "Not Sure") to questions 9 and 10 on the Inventory by participants who scored 8–16, 17–24 or 25–32 to questions. On Question 9, "Have you identified a possible Soul Injury?" a significant effect ($p < .001$) was found. Over 83% of participants who had an Inventory score of 8–16 answered "Yes, I have identified a possible *Soul Injury*," whereas 64% of those with a score of 17–24 gave that answer, and only 36% of those with a score of 25–32 answered "Yes." Similarly, with Question 10, "Do you think a past *Soul Injury* is affecting your life now?" the chi square analysis revealed a significant relationship ($p < .001$) between level of Soul Injury (as demonstrated by the Inventory score) and the participant's answer to Question 10. Whereas 89% of the participants who scored between 8 and 16 answered "Yes, a past *Soul Injury* is affecting my life now," 58% of the participants who scored 17–24 and less than 24% of the participants who scored 25–32 answered "Yes" to this question. These analyses indicate that the Soul Injury Self-Awareness Inventory is quite sensitive to perceptions of *Soul Injury*.

The second validation study involved comparing responses on the Soul Injury Self-Awareness Inventory responses by 29 individuals who attended an Opus Peace training, before and after the training. These 29 participants were 72.4% female and age of the participants were reported by range, 31–50 (21%), 51–65 (43%) and 66+ (36%). Of these 29 participants, 48.3% were healthcare professionals, 10.3% were clergy, 10.3% were veterans, and the rest (31.1%) were volunteers or caregivers. The mean Inventory scores (that is, the sum of answers for questions 1–8) did not significantly differ before and after the training, showing excellent test-retest reliability. Superb internal consistency and construct reliability was also demonstrated with these data (Cronbach's alpha = .791). A factor analysis of responses to questions 1–8 again revealed one factor with an eigenvalue of 3.36 that accounted for 42.0% of the variance. All eight questions had communalities greater than 0.62.

These two validation studies, taken together, demonstrate that the Soul Injury Self-Awareness Inventory is an excellent, invariant measure of *Soul Injury*. These analyses were conducted with Soul Injury Self-Awareness Inventory data from healthcare professionals and other caregivers, including clergy. In the near future, *Soul Injury* data from veterans will be secured. The validation studies conducted to date support the phenomena of *Soul Injury*.

Responding to Soul Injury

The Opus Peace founders summarize the process for addressing the inner work needed to address Soul Injuries:

> Cultivate in me the willingness to
> re-own, re-home, and re-vitalize

scattered pieces of myself so wholeness can be restored.

Grow in me the honesty, courage, and humility

to release my fear of who I am and who I am not.

Fuel me with your grace (Opus Peace, n.d.-a).

Self-Help Tools

- Learning how to mourn losses creates a safe space for "negative" feelings. Acknowledging and validating uncomfortable feelings provide permission to stop denying or numbing unwanted feelings. This helps people re-own their humanity and extend self-compassion to the part of self carrying the burden—a burden that has often been buried *alive*.
- Leaning how to use a somatic technique that allows emotional pain and peace to sit side by side together *without* fear helps diminish emotional distress so it does not have to be banished into unconsciousness. The *Anchoring Heart Technique* is such a technique. It is an age-old somatic practice that can be done whenever a person is upset or in need of grounding. When a person is calm, their energy usually resides low and deep within themselves. Anxious energy, however, usually rises; breathing becomes shallow; voice pitch gets higher. When told bad news, there is often a gasp and a clasping of the chest with an open palm, *unconsciously* anchoring oneself. The Anchoring Heart Technique simply utilizes this technique *consciously* while breathing deeply and taking a moment to feel unwanted feelings.
- Exercises to identify "favorite numbing agents" provide insight about behaviors used to avoid and deny uncomfortable feelings, as well as the loss of self that results when this occurs.
- Learning how to seek and extend forgiveness to self and others provides self-compassion as issues of regret, remorse, and resentment are identified.
- Integrative letter-writing can be used to re-own, re-home, and re-vitalize scattered pieces of self so a Soul Injury can be unburdened. Utilizing gestalt therapeutic concepts, aspects of self that have previously been silenced into unconsciousness can be brought into the open. For example, this is a letter that a Vietnam veteran wrote to the part of self that had been raped when he was a child. He says this letter was "transformative":

  Dear Bill:

  I know you remember that summer when my 12-year-old soul was fractured every week for three months. It started when the door closed behind my little brother and me while a 17-year-old boy pulled out a knife and told us he would kill us if we told what he was about to do. At that age, I didn't even know what rape was. The feelings I've held in my body? I have pushed them out and I am taking a huge risk in naming them today. That summer day that began with so much curiosity, fun, and innocence was changed into: cold terror, suffocating horror, unimaginable pain, feelings of dirt and shame, overwhelming helplessness, violated safety, and RAGE—rage so big that for years afterward I plotted how I would kill him if I saw him again. And fear, fear that I would do it. All of the feelings—too many and too much for an innocent 12 year-old kid to carry.

  Sincerely, Billy

- Ceremonies and rituals. Ceremonies are an effective way to both prevent *and* respond to *Soul Injuries*. A well-designed ceremony acknowledges the hardships that have been incurred, provides information about how to face the challenges, and integrates the experience symbolically. Well-designed ceremonies are effective because they access the *unconscious;* they access the deepest levels of our soul.

Summary

Raising awareness about the phenomena of *Soul Injury* in our own life and the lives of others is important for several reasons:

- Identifying a *Soul Injury* brings it out of unconsciousness where it can insidiously lurk and sabotage lives without our even knowing it.
- Learning how to release unmourned loss/hurt and unforgiven guilt/shame helps remove barriers that prevent people from connecting with their "real" self—the self they were meant to be.
- Grieving and forgiving are not routinely taught in families, communities, educational programs, or healthcare systems. This perpetuates barriers that keep people from connecting with their deepest self.
- Acknowledging and validating the presence of a *Soul Injury* cultivates self-compassion so that self-identity is strengthened and inner goodness and beauty affirmed.
- The Soul Injury Self-Awareness Inventory is a valid and useful tool to develop personal insight for professionals to develop insight into one's own experiences and for the purpose of assisting others in raising awareness of feelings and experiences related to possible *Soul Injuries*.

References

American Psychiatric Association. (2013). *Diagnostic and statistical manual of mental disorders* (5th ed.). Author.

Drinkard, J. (2018, July). *Presentation for NHPCO webinar.* https://www.wehonorveterans.org/soul-injury-and-opus-peace-tools-deborah-grassman

Gilligan, C. (1977). *In a different voice.* Harvard University Press.

Jameton, A. (1984). *Nursing practice: The ethical issues.* Prentice-Hall.

Jung, C. G. (1958). *Answer to Job.* Princeton University Press.

Kohlberg, L. (1981). *Essays on moral development: The philosophy of moral development* (Vol. 1). Harper and Row.

New American Bible. (1970). Job 7:13. Confraternity of Christian Doctrine.

Opus Peace. (n.d.-a). *Home.* https://opuspeace.org.aspx

Opus Peace. (n.d.-b). *Soul Injury Inventory.* https://opuspeace.org/Survey.aspx

Piaget, J. (1932). *The moral judgement of the child.* Routledge.

Shay, J. (1994). *Achilles in Vietnam.* Scribner.

U.S. Department of Veterans Affairs. (2016). *Moral injury in the context of war.* National Center for PTSD.

Van der Kolk, B. (2014). *The body keeps the score.* Viking Press.

CHAPTER 22

Moral Stress and Injury in the Military and Veterans

Deborah J. Kenny and Jessica Zumba

Introduction

The terms *moral distress* and *moral injury* are becoming well known and more widespread, especially in nursing and healthcare literature. This chapter begins with a discussion of the definitions of moral injury, moral distress, and moral outrage. Moral injury will be discussed from the perspective of war, the military, and humanitarian efforts. Moral distress is somewhat more challenging to define because it is used in many different contexts, but more so within a healthcare environment. Moral outrage, in and of itself, is also defined but will not be discussed in depth. The differentiation and overlap of moral injury and PTSD symptoms will be described, and finally, suggestions for treatment of moral injury and recommendations for care will be given. Secondary traumatization and compassion fatigue will not be introduced or addressed in this chapter because it is generally considered a different stress mechanism than moral distress.

Moral Injury

Moral injury has been a term that is usually associated with war and wartime scenarios. Although some would argue that moral injury is a signature wound of 21st-century wars, in fact, it has only recently begun to be recognized as a distinct concept (Shay 2014). Conceptually, psychological injury based on conscience and values has been documented as a part of war for millennia. Perhaps the first mention of moral injury (though not using that term) was in Homer's *Iliad*, where Homer describes an incident during the Trojan War. Achilles was an officer who cared, not just for himself, but for the army and its people. On the other hand, Agamemnon was a selfish commander, who refused to return the daughter of a priest of Apollo and then ultimately took a prize that rightfully belonged to Achilles. Achilles struggled much over this betrayal and left the Trojan War for several years. As a result of his moral injury, Achilles lost concern for his comrades, then eventually for all humanity (Butler & Cape, 1999/1925). This story serves as the backdrop for the moral injury of veterans of modern wars.

Because of the relatively recent recognition of injury to conscience during war, early definitions of the term vary. Moral injury was first used in reference to leadership. Shay (1994) first coined *moral injury* as a betrayal of moral character by someone in a position of authority, usually involving high-stakes circumstances. An example of this would be a commander ordering troops to kill non-combatants or civilians. He later expanded this to include the betrayal of moral character by oneself (Shay, 2014), such as killing civilians without an order. However, Shay did not differentiate between moral injury in such a situation and a reaction to a physical threat. Instead, he included this within the PTSD umbrella. Litz et al. (2009) offer a definition of moral injury that encompasses the entire range of offenses that profoundly violate moral values or expectations of moral actions. They went further to provide a framework for moral injury that includes the act and its consequences. These consequences include internal conflict and resultant feelings of shame, guilt, and anxiety. More recently, Farnsworth et al. (2017) expanded the definition of moral injury as a holistic response to an individual's attempts to manage the experience of a past morally injurious event. The evolution of this definition from an action that is contrary to one's beliefs and values to the spiritual, psychological, and somatic reactions to an event confuses the picture of what moral injury is. All those attempting to conceptualize moral injury propose that more research is needed to define it fully. All agree that something happens to a person who acts or witnesses events that conflict with their deeply rooted values, even if condoned by the military culture in which they are residing.

> "Daylight came [long pause], and we found out we killed a lot of fishermen and kids. . . . So you know in your heart it's wrong, but at the time, here's your superiors telling you that it was okay. . . . And they would have award ceremonies . . . I'd be standing like a [expletive] jerk and they'd be handing out [expletive] medals for killing civilians." (Shay, 1994, p. 4)

The literature on moral injury during war is vast, and it is still nebulous. However, one word that repeatedly appears in the literature is *betrayal* (Gilligan, 2014; Blinka & Harris, 2016; Jordan et al., 2017; Wortmann et al., 2017; Currier et al., 2019). This betrayal is based on threats upon which action might violate values. This is opposed to threats involving fear and imminent physical danger. The dissimilarities in value threat versus physical danger create a different effect on an individual's psyche (Litz et al., 2009).

Drescher et al. (2011) assert that military service in and of itself may require an individual to execute actions during war that would be illegal under other circumstances. Service members train for situations in which they must kill others. At times, this could lead to inappropriate aggressiveness in the face of real or perceived threats to themselves or other service members. This aggressiveness may be an instantaneous situational reaction that the service member learned in their training. It may be only after the event that the impact on the servicemember is either minimized or it becomes a foundation for the effects of moral injury.

In contrast to the traditional belief that moral acts' emotional processing takes all options into consideration, Mullaney and Regan (2019) suggest that ethical decision making during a war may be subconscious. They described the Recognition-Primed Decision Model, developed by Klein (1985) where an individual might find themselves in an unfamiliar and potentially dangerous situation, quickly scan cues for patterns to which they can act according to a trained script, and then respond within seconds, before they can cognitively process the scene (**Figure 22-1**). Because battlefield decisions are often made in the face of a rapid and flawed interpretation of the circumstances, and it occurs without deliberate and rational cognition, it could potentially set the stage for acts that could be later questioned as immoral (Doris & Murphy, 2007).

There is some disagreement as to moral injury's distinctiveness (Farnsworth et al., 2014; Bryan et al., 2016; Gray et al., 2017; Molendijk et al., 2018; Farnsworth, 2019). Some argue about whether it falls inside the scope of PTSD (Molendijk et al., 2018) or under its umbrella (Smith et al., 2013; Wachen et al., 2016). What is clear is that moral injury can only occur if an individual already has an integrated central value system (Litz et al., 2009; Gilligan 2014; Farnsworth et al., 2017) and an action involves a violation of those deeply held moral ideals and beliefs (Farnsworth et al., 2014; Drescher et al. 2011; Litz et al. 2009; Currier et al. 2019; Molendijk et al. 2018, Jordan et al., 2017). Gilligan (2014) discusses moral injury as "a shattering of trust that compromises our ability to love." (p. 90)

Moral Injury in Military Healthcare Providers

In health care, military providers often are also victims of moral injury during war. The general goal of care providers is to alleviate suffering and provide healing of injured service members. It has been suggested that providers do not see the same types of carnage that warfighters themselves see, and because of that, their suffering is not seen as such or at least perceived as serious. That premise could not be further from the truth. As severely injured patients are brought into hospitals, whether on the battlefield or farther down the transportation line, providers see a bigger picture of battle consequences. Only frontline medics may witness actual acts of killing and injury, but providers behind the lines will get many of those with raw injuries from many different skirmishes. In treating these injuries, they will perceive their seriousness and the potential long-term quality of life issues. Not only do they have to treat injuries, but they also have to cope with the very anxious comrades of the injured who are at the doorstep wanting the providers to save their buddy. Providers may be at the point of care where resources are scarce, and they have to determine who does or does not get the support. They are in positions to make decisions about who lives and who may not live. Said one nurse who had deployed:

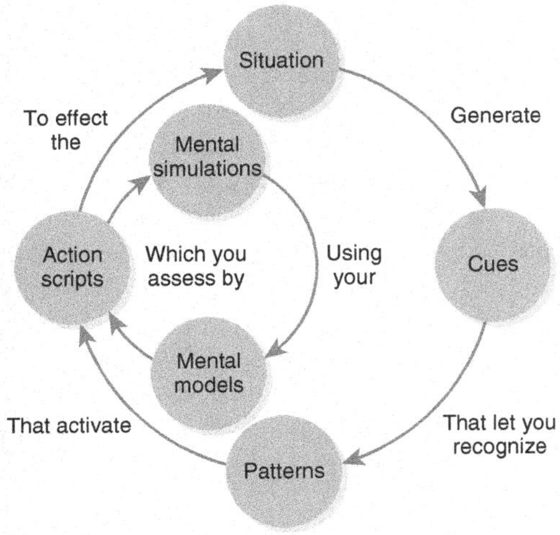

Figure 22-1 Recognition-Primed Decision (RPD) model.

Reproduced from Klein, G. (2002). *Intuition at work*. Doubleday.

> And I think—I just got the thing, too, that we saw some horribly wounded people. I know it's not for us to decide, but were we really doin' them any favors, with the massive injuries—maybe we should have let 'em—some of 'em go. I mean, I had one guy who had two drains in his head, an ICP monitor, and half his skull was out. I don't know how he did but I'm just like—the long-term prognosis—like I say, we don't know how they end up doin'. Or they're missin' both their legs and one arm, long-term. Are we really doin' them any favors. (Kenny & Kelly, 2019).

Deciding who may or may not get care can give rise to an interruption of professional values of providing the best care available for everyone. Providers are asked to care for enemies simultaneously, knowing they are using resources meant for service members. They care for unintended victims of war, such as bystander women and children. They may be caring for local civilians who understand the Americans have a better health system than they do and flood their system and resources. Some providers in the war zone have stated they never have the follow-up regarding whether the service member they treated lived, died, or recovered. After a patient is evacuated back to stateside care, providers may be caring for severely injured servicemembers and wonder about the futility of the care or the quality of life for that service member and their family. One WWII nurse, when interviewed, was quietly astounded when she asked for help with psychological wounds, yet told she had not really been to war, that she could not possibly be morally wounded. The psychiatrist remarked,

> Their involvement with hundreds of patients, along with the protected environment and discipline of a hospital—all gave them the skills and mechanisms they needed to cope with their troubles. In other words, their status as clinicians and the hard work and long service in the cause of human suffering had left them less vulnerable than the average soldier. Their profession has somehow rendered them insensate. (Norman, 1999, pp. 241–242).

Even in more recent wars, healthcare professionals seeking help with the sequelae of war may be told they did not experience the real war and should not have issues. Fry et al. (2002) developed a moral military distress model based on a study of military nurses. They described military distress as similar to that of civilian providers. However, contextual barriers, such as dangerous settings and different patient conditions (age, battle casualties, mass casualties) place the providers at an increased risk for moral suffering.

Moral distress is compounded when health professionals must also deal with wartime scenarios where they are faced with unique ethical issues such as scarce resources, care for enemies, or long-term care of local patients. Sometimes they may also come under enemy fire for which they must protect their patients and take part in the combat situations. As war evolves, standard ethical conventions must also evolve.

> The changing modes of warfare create difficulties for the established conventions of war. They also create new dilemmas for medical personnel, who may be called upon to lend their expertise to the prosecution of war rather than simply to relieve the suffering it causes. (Gross, 2004, p. 23.).

Gross (2004) states that certain humans' rights to medical care can differ according to the threat they posed. He gives an example of enemy combatants. Uninjured, they have no rights to medical care, but once injured, they have a right to the same medical care as one's own service members. However, once they recover and again pose a threat, then their rights go away. Even so, while caring for the enemy, medical personnel are put in danger when they are assaulted both verbally and physically, yet they are expected to care for them (Thompson & Mastel-Smith, 2012; Kenny & Kelley, 2019; Mark et al., 2009; Agazio & Goodman, 2017). Said one nurse who was stationed on a hospital ship in Iran:

> It was very difficult when some of those prisoners were resentful. They were angry and mistreating the staff on the ship. Some of that turmoil was, "Look, I'm here to provide you,

> probably, the best care in the world, and you're throwing things at me and spitting at me." There was an emotional struggle with that.

Distress seen in practitioners working in the Veterans Healthcare Administration (VHA) facilities seemed to center around veterans' needs in getting the care they needed. Many veterans they cared for had traumatic brain injuries (TBI) or post-traumatic stress (PTS) and would miss appointments either because they forgot or did not want to go. The nurses sometimes acted as liaisons between the patients and family members. Often, the family members had unrealistic expectations of their injured service member, and nurses found themselves trying to explain the true situation.

> The family—the thing that kept pushing me with his family was, the mom would come in and—with traumatic brain, a lot of times, they will respond to something, but it's not that they understand. So when she would come in, he would look over at the door, or if she said something, he was responding. So we finally had a family meeting with her, to explain to her that he was not responding to her, but he was just responding, and that he wasn't going to come out of this.

Other practitioners felt moral angst because veterans learned fairly quickly how to "game" the system in an effort to get a higher disability rating and, thus, more compensation. Still others reported seeing older veterans who were clearly affected by exposures or injuries that never got reported and so were not getting the care they deserved.

Moral Distress in Nursing. Beginning in the 1970s and 1980s, nurses recognized that bioethics played a significant role in their practice. Smith and Davis (1980) started to explore ethics in the context of nursing from a perspective of conflict with roles and decisions of which they had no or little input. The term *moral distress* had its roots in nursing, as described by Andrew Jameton (1984). He defined *moral distress* as ". . . when one knows the right thing to do, but institutional constraints make it nearly impossible to pursue the right course of action" (p.6). It has since further evolved and refined to include initial moral distress. A person feels frustration and anger because of workplace constraints, followed by reactive distress that occurs when a nurse fails to act because of the limitations. The concept has been recognized as extremely complex, and a single definition of the term seems elusive. Hamric et al. (2012) described moral distress as when providers are "repeatedly exposed to situations in which they feel unable to carry out what they believe to be ethically inappropriate action. . . ." (p. 1). Morley et al. (2019) suggested the term is too narrow in its scope and should be expanded to include any moral event from a range that includes organizational constraints, conflict, tension, dilemmas, and uncertainty.

Because of the multitude of definitions of moral distress, Hamric et al. (2012) further concluded some of the confusion might be caused by limited research on moral distress in the medical professions and the simultaneous use of the same concept in other professional fields. This muddiness creates difficulties in generalizing any particular definition to a specific institution or occupation. Even within nursing, there seems to be no consensus about moral distress and what constitutes it (Hamric et al., 2012). Corley (2002) asserted that by its nature, caring for patients is an ethical undertaking. When organizational constraints prevent nurses from acting ethically, they can suffer moral distress. Nevertheless, as described in the nursing and medical literature, moral distress and moral conflict seem to differ from the moral injury seen in war veterans. Even the moral injury suffered by healthcare professional veterans who were deployed differed from that in the civilian medical literature. Perhaps the differences may be due to the degree of moral conflict, but the symptoms can be the same.

However, as mentioned previously, moral distress in the civilian healthcare world is compounded when unique ethical challenges present themselves, such as the coronavirus pandemic of 2020. The situation of scarce physical resources, allocation of limited resources, loss of life, unsupportive leadership, unpreparedness for decisions that might have to be made, or witnessing those decisions are all risk factors for moral injury (Williamson et al. 2020). Healthcare providers and responders worldwide are currently facing these challenges, and their environment is being described as a war zone (Dishman, 2020; Zak & Hesse, 2020).

Moral Outrage. Moral outrage differs from moral injury and moral stress in that it is defined by Batson et al. (2009) as ". . . anger provoked by the perception that a moral standard or principle has been violated" (p. 155). The primary difference between this and moral injury is that outrage is externally directed as the perception of an event someone else committed. In contrast, moral injury is inwardly directed and perpetrated by actual behavior that violated moral principles. For example, the public reaction toward soldiers of the incident at Haditha, Iraq, where 24 innocent civilians were slain in 2005 after an IED had exploded and killed a U.S. Marine, was one of anger and disgust at the marines' action. On the other hand, after the fact, the marines themselves experienced shame and guilt at their actions. This and other reports of war incidents, such as My Lai in Vietnam, have been brought into our living rooms through the media and have fueled public moral outrage, some of it justified. By no means can these incidents be rationalized, but the reports fail to mention the incidents' other casualties. Those military servicemen's reactions differed; some experienced shame, some guilt, some isolated themselves, some lashed out, some dulled their pain with drugs and alcohol, and some committed suicide.

Differences Between Moral Injury and PTSD

Jinkerson (2016) describes moral injury as a "particular type of trauma that is characterized by guilt, existential crisis, and loss of trust that may develop following a perceived moral violation" (p. 122). Others characterize moral injury as akin to being "shattered" (Gilligan, 2014; Litz et al., 2009). Both PTSD and moral injury can have the same symptoms (see **Table 22-1**). These would include such symptoms as flashbacks, nightmares, depression, anger, difficulties coping, substance abuse, and suicidal ideation. However, moral injury also has differences. Some of the emotions that may be associated with moral injury include guilt due to the violation of personal standards and shame as a result of the abhorrence of one's behaviors (Farnsworth et al., 2014). Maguen and Burkman (2013) found that killing in war generally produced feelings of post-deployment anger, but it was much more pronounced in those who had killed (advertently or inadvertently) non-combatants. Yan (2016) suggested that the magnitude of moral injury can be observed as a positive correlation between veteran exposure to morally injurious events in war and a lifetime of physical and internal conflict, higher rates of depression, and a greater prevalence for post-traumatic stress disorder. Moral injury manifestations may present as aggressive or self-harming behaviors, suicidal ideations or attempts, substance use, avoidance, over-compensation (i.e., giving large amounts of money to charities and being unable to cover basic needs), and social disconnection (Brémault-Phillips et al., 2019).

Kinghorn (2012) described the advent of moral injury as very timely because it compels a new look at the interplay between psychological combat trauma and human moral

Table 22-1 Symptomatology Comparisons

Moral Injury	PTSD	Moral Distress	Moral Outrage
Shame	Flashbacks	Stress	Anger
Guilt	Nightmares and recurrent dreams	Guilt	Disgust
Loss of trust	Hypervigilance	Shame	Disdain
Suicidal Ideation	Emotional distress	Emotional numbness	
Anger	Irritability, anger		
Numbness	Trouble concentrating, memory problems		
Detached	Emotionally numb		
Avoidance	Suicidal ideation		
Substance abuse			
Suicidal ideation			
Anguish			
Loss of self-worth			
Non-redeemability			
Hyper- or hypo-spirituality			

agency. He goes on to state that the guilt and shame associated with moral injury can propel an individual on to the typical PTSD flashbacks, nightmares, avoidance, hypervigilance, negative mood changes, but this is a deeper psychological wound for which the current clinical psychology structure cannot provide. While it may be helpful to differentiate between moral injury and PTSD, the important difference lies in the cause. Both are psychological traumas, but moral injury is caused when an individual witnesses or actually violates intensely held internal beliefs. In contrast, PTSD is generally caused by fear of imminent physical harm or threat. Some of the literature described the symptomatology of moral injury as similar to PTSD; however, there is one important difference. In terms of violations of conscience, those who have suffered moral injury, or even distress, often see themselves as irredeemable and unworthy. Those who have been in wartime scenarios may have seen or done things that are not understood by a civilian culture that may not understand or recognize the moral challenges they have faced.

Stigmatizing mental health, calling it shameful, and placing negative labels on those who suffer from it has been a part of military culture in the United States for years. American culture generally does not disparage veterans who have visible physical wounds such as amputations or burns. In fact, they tend to be honored for their service. On the other hand, those who have psychological or moral wounds tend to be viewed as less than honorable or with some disdain (Kinghorn, 2012). Veterans and service members dealing with mental health instability are often afraid to speak with their providers at the VHA for fear of being labeled or stigmatized. There may be other potential professional and personal ramifications, thus leading them to seek care outside of the military or veteran healthcare system where they are often unable to relate to civilian providers due to military/civilian cultural differences (Ross et al., 2015). As U.S. military engagements and humanitarian missions continue overseas and at home, more is learned about veterans and service members' mental health. Over the past several decades, research and our understanding of Trauma and post-traumatic stress disorder (PTSD) have grown exponentially, and yet, we have barely scratched the surface. As we continue to learn about the effects of trauma, particularly the different types of traumas (i.e., person vs. person, person vs. environment, person vs. self) on the individual and their functioning, we are learning that service members engaged in actions that contradict deep-rooted beliefs and ideals often struggle with a different kind of stress reaction. Traditionally, traumatic events experienced by service members that cause impairment in function have been labeled as PTSD. However, psychiatrist Jonathan Shay instead suggests that engaging in actions that contradict our own morality can cause a moral injury, a distinct syndrome from PTSD, but often comorbid (Litz et al., 2009; Shay, 2011; Shay, 2014).

Highlighting the Research Gap:Female Veterans and Families

In the ongoing conflicts in Iraq and Afghanistan, plus other operations in the global war on terrorism, female veterans have been directly involved in combat despite combat jobs being closed to them before 2016. Many female service members serve alongside their male counterparts as medics, truck drivers, military police, fuelers, pilots, engineers, nurses, civil affairs, and other occupations under enemy engagement. With females now allowed to formally take on combat roles in the military, there is beginning research on female veterans' moral injury. For example, Nillni et al. (2020) examined PTSD and moral injury, finding that both may adversely affect perinatal outcomes. Thus, screening not just for depression but also for PTSD and moral injury is vitally important in women of childbearing age. We are gaining new information daily; however, most of the research addressing moral injury in war does not adequately explore female veterans. How does moral injury impact women? What factors put them most at risk for moral injury? What types of events are they encountering that contribute to moral injury? How do we assess and effectively treat moral injury in female veterans?

Even though all genders of veterans are at risk for experiencing moral injury events, distinctly different physiological and psychological mechanisms comprise males and females. The result is that female combat veterans are thereby generalized with the predominantly white male randomized-control veteran group who report betrayal as the most heinous of moral injury (Wisco et al., 2017). This gap in the research is of great significance. Even more is needed now that combat jobs such as infantry, artillery, and combat engineer have been opened to female service members. Moreover, when it comes to the impact of moral injury in war on families, the research is grossly underrepresented, presenting a unique challenge for providers.

Legal Issues

There may be some questions by providers over whether they are mandated reporters if one of their patients discusses a possible war crime or atrocity. An exhaustive search of the literature found different viewpoints. The proper procedures and statutes are confusing at best.

If the person being treated is currently in the military, and they are being treated on the Department of Defense (DoD) military installation by a military, civilian, or contract provider, and the person being treated discloses "a possible, suspected, or alleged violation of the law of war, for which there is credible information, or conduct during military operations other than war that would constitute a violation of the law of war if it occurred during an armed conflict" (DoD, 2006) should be reported through a chain of command. However, the more recent DoD Instruction 6490.08 (DoD, 2011) states that only minimal information should be given to meet the disclosure's demands. If an active military member receives care through a civilian provider, then subsequently receives care in the military installation and records of the civilian provider are obtained, they are subject to the reporting instruction. Suppose the person being treated is receiving care through the VHA. In that case, no similar directives could be found on mandated reporting except in the case of child abuse (Department of Veterans Affairs, 2017). No guidance could be found for civilian providers treating veterans. The international community is far less clear in its disclosure rules. The International Humanitarian Law states there is no statute of limitations on war crimes. Given the lack of clear guidelines, it is best practice for a provider to ask what must be done before a patient potentially discloses a war crime and to what extent they are protected by provider-client privilege.

Treatment for Moral Injury

Gilligan (2014) describes the ethics of caring as coming with a cost. She states, "It is grounded less in moral precepts than in psychological wisdom, underscoring the costs of not paying attention, not listening, being absent rather than present, not responding with integrity and respect" (p. 103). Hoge (2011) iterates that veterans often describe their care as less than satisfactory and that there is a split between their experiences and what is perceived by healthcare providers. He further states a need for military cultural competency and calls for enhancing treatment with complementary therapies such as yoga or acupuncture. However, he does not differentiate between trauma caused by combat violence and moral injury (Hoge 2011). On the other hand, Currier et al. (2017) described moral violation as included in the constellation of PTSD and that understanding veterans' needs in the community setting was vital. They did differentiate symptoms of moral injury as opposed to PTSD caused by a physical threat.

Due to the complex nature of moral injury and its effect on multiple domains of life, Levi-Belz and Zerach (2018) promote the necessity for ongoing suicide assessments as moral injury exposure puts veterans at higher risk for suicidal ideation (Bryan et al., 2013; Tripp & McDevitt-Murphy, 2017), even years after exposure. In addition to increased depression, PTSD, social and occupational functioning, and suicidal ideation, interestingly, spirituality was found to be both a risk factor and a protective factor for moral injury, with ongoing spiritual fitness and spiritual well-being assessments being recommended (Brémault-Phillips et al., 2019). Moral injury may contribute to the severity of PTSD, but it does not predict the severity. Veterans are typically screened for PTSD, but not for moral injury. It may be helpful to also screen all veterans for this as well. As each morally injurious event occurs, and as the veteran tries to reconcile it with their values, moral residue can be present. As the veteran experiences more events, the level of residue can rise to a point where the veteran cannot continue to cope or function normally. Farnsworth (2019) suggests that providers should explore the objective perspective of an injurious event and both their and the client's moral judgments of the event. As a service member attempts to define the meaning of an event for themselves, they consider its morality and how it ought to be. If the event and their thoughts about its morality conflict with their values, they then suffer a moral injury. This may be exacerbated if the provider judges the conflict and projects this to the veteran. It has been suggested that civilians should bear some of the moral responsibility for war. The military goes to war for the good of a civilian community. After war, they must return to that community. Suppose the community only supports war in a shallow way, but turns its back on service members who may have committed atrocities. In that case, we will have a new generation of "Vietnam veterans" who already felt moral angst when they returned and then were further disenfranchised by the very community that states it supports them. If any provider expresses negative feelings regarding a service member's moral injury, the veteran may feel judged, trust will be lost, and the service member may feel further condemned (Litz et al., 2009). What veterans want is merely for healthcare providers to listen to their stories without judgment or assumptions and to help them make sense of the confusion they are feeling (Gilligan, 2014; Shay, 1994).

Moral Resilience

Much of the literature on moral distress and resilience is written in the context of health care. It is especially present in recent nursing literature. However, though in the term, *"self-transcendence,"* moral resilience appears in many of Viktor Frankl's writings, but more specifically in terms of making meaning of life events or transcending the self (Frankl, 2000). Bonanno (2004) followed up by stating that resilience is more common than thought, as most are exposed to some type of violent or traumatic event throughout their lives. Lützen and Ewalds-Kvist (2013) took this one step farther and described moral resilience as " . . . choosing to attribute meaning to every situation . . ." (p. 320). Definitions for the term *moral resilience* seem to be as elusive as a definition of moral injury in the healthcare literature. However, in essence, as defined by Baratz (2015), moral resilience is the ability of an individual to remain true to their convictions and values when they have been tested. Rushton (2016) offers many suggestions for building moral resilience, including mindfulness practices, recognizing an individual's ability to be purposeful in maintaining moral convictions and potential objection to an action, making meaning when situations create moral distress, and being able to reconsider one's moral values and viewpoints. These suggestions may be used to build moral resilience that can be used at any time, either before or after an event that may cause moral distress. However, it is recognized that in the military, objection to an order by a superior officer that has the potential for moral injury may also have unforeseen consequences such as risking lives, putting one's career at risk, and creating further distress. This is a point that providers need to consider when treating veterans.

Screening

Screening Tools

There is a need for the development and scrutiny of reliable and evidence-based assessments. Two such assessment tools are the Moral Injury Questionnaire-Military Version and the Impact of Killing Treatment, which are currently being investigated to assess for validity and reliability for use with military populations (Currier et al., 2015; Burkman et al., 2019. The newest scale, the Moral Injury Symptom Scale–Military–Short Form (MISS-M-SF), is a 10-item tool that screens for symptoms most associated with moral injury. In a study of veterans, it showed good reliability and validity (Koenig et al., 2018). In this population, the tool accurately identified the symptoms related to the psychological and spiritual aspects of moral injury. Regarding treatment modalities and interventions for moral injury, presently, mindfulness, yoga, self-awareness, acts of service, compassion training, and social connection are evidence-based interventions that have been shown to improve outcomes for veterans suffering from moral injury (Brémault-Phillips et al., 2019).

Strategy

Treatment Strategies

Litz et al. (2009) suggest providers focus on (1) establishing a strong working alliance and trusting and caring relationship; (2) preparation and education about moral injury and its impact, as well as a collaborative plan for promoting change; (3) an emotion-focused disclosure of events surrounding the moral injury; (4) a subsequent careful, directive, and formative examination of the implication of the experience for the person in terms of key self and other schemas; (5) an imaginal dialogue with a benevolent moral authority (e.g., parent, grandparent, coach, clergy) about what happened and how it impacts the patient now and their plans for the future or a fellow service member who feels unredeemable about something they did (or failed to do) and how it impacts his or her current and future plans; (6) fostering reparation and self-forgiveness; (7) fostering reconnection with various communities (e.g., faith, family); and (8) an assessment of goals and values moving forward. Farnsworth et al. (2017) suggest that some treatments used to treat PTSD may not be fully effective on moral injury. Furthermore, they indicate that Acceptance and Commitment Therapy (ACT) might offer an approach to moral injury. ACT espouses a program of immediate positive actions and self-compassion.

As trauma is pervasive in our lives in many forms, there is beginning to be a body of literature about trauma-informed care for the treatment of PTSD. Much of the literature is written about care for children who have experienced trauma and violence or for adults who experienced childhood trauma. Some of the literature is not medically focused but examines other disciplines such as law and social work. The military/veteran literature also ran the gamut of care for children and families, military sexual trauma, mental health, and PTSD. Again, the literature is confusing as some discussed trauma-informed care as care for an individual who has experienced trauma. Some discussed trauma-informed care as an organizational approach to victims of trauma. However, trauma-informed care delivery is based on the five pillars of safety, trustworthiness, choice, collaboration, and empowerment (Currier et al., 2017). These pillars may differ, but what was lacking was addressing moral injury. Herzog et al. (2020) stated that a framework for trauma-informed care is necessary for treating victims of violence. Nowhere in their paper was moral injury mentioned as part of a cause for PTSD. However, there are several principles inherent in the care of persons who have experienced trauma. In the Substance Abuse and Mental Health Services Administration (SAMHSA) Treatment Improvement Protocol for Trauma-Informed Care (SAMHSA, 2014), trauma is defined as resulting

> ... from an event, series of events, or set of circumstances that is experienced by an individual as physically or emotionally harmful or life-threatening and that has lasting adverse effects on the individual's functioning and mental, physical, social, emotional, or spiritual well-being. (p. 7, SAMHSA, 2014)

It makes no mention of moral injury, though it could be inferred by using the term *emotionally harmful*, but this is not specified. Whether individual or organizational, the principles do not seem to apply to moral injury. It is only implied and does not include what the veterans iterated in Shay's (1994) book *Achilles in Vietnam* described they needed most, and that is a provider simply listen to them.

We would caution that if moral injury interventions fall outside of your scope of practice, establishing a listening and non-judgmental relationship with the veteran is the most important first step in gaining the veteran's trust even to accept help. Then an appropriate referral should follow. This does not mean that any provider should let the relationship go once a referral is made. The trust relationship should continue.

Conclusion

Moral injury is a very complex constellation of feelings and reactions. Shay's (1994) first conceptualizations of moral injury, may be too simplistic for the complex collection of causes and consequences. However, it contains certain criteria that must be present. Those criteria are a defined moral order, betrayal, and by someone in authority. Moral injury should not be considered a syndrome, but rather as a continuum ranging from mild moral distress to frank moral outrage. The practitioner should be aware of this continuum. It is also a continuum that runs from mild emotional distress to serious and permanent psychological injury. It needs to be addressed as theoretically and realistically as possible to recognize how emotions are involved and expressed as moral injury. Shay (1994) expressed the veterans' requests simply and eloquently. *"The advice that veterans consistently give to trauma therapists is 'Listen! Just listen'"* (p. 189). Rather than assuming the best treatment for a veteran with moral injury, we recommend that providers be aware that this is something that veterans may be struggling with but may not want to talk about. It is essential to gain their trust before they are willing to open up about moral injury.

Gaining an understanding of military culture and explicitly asking clients about moral injury in war, and being prepared to address the wide array of emotional responses are necessary steps towards improving the quality of life for veterans and service members. It is vital that healthcare providers working with military and veteran populations explore their own implicit biases, familiarize themselves with military culture, and learn therapeutic ways to address moral injury. Most veterans are now reporting moral injury as the most distressing and long-lasting warzone experience (Currier et al., 2015; Ross et al., 2015). Researchers and clinicians need to continue to gain knowledge of moral injury in war and its impact on the service member, veteran, and family. As a provider, there is a moral obligation to support and promote whole-person recovery, and to listen to their stories, experiences and feelings without judgment.

References

Agazio, J., & Goodman, P. (2017). Making the hard decisions: Ethical care decisions in wartime nursing practice. *Nursing Outlook, 65*(5S), S92–S99. doi:10.1016/j.outlook.2017.06.010

Baratz, L. (2015). Israeli teacher trainee's perceptions of the term moral resilience. *Journal for Multicultural Education, 9,* 193–206. doi:10-1108/JME-12-2014-0041

Blinka, D., & Harris, H. W. (2016). Moral injury in warriors and veterans: The challenge to social work. *Social Work & Christianity, 43*(3), 7–26.

Bonanno, G. A. (2004). Loss, trauma, and human resilience: Have we underestimated the human capacity to thrive after extremely aversive events? *American Psychologist, 59*(1), 20–28. doi:libproxy.uccs.edu/10.1037/0003-066X.59.1.20

Brémault-Phillips, S., Pike, A., Scarcella, F., & Cherwick, T. (2019). Spirituality and moral injury among military personnel: A mini-review. *Frontiers in Psychiatry*, 10, 276.

Bryan, C. J., Bryan, A. O., Anestis, M. D., Anestic, J. C., Green, B. A., Etienne, N., Morrow, C. E., & Ray-Sannerud, B. (2016). measuring moral injury:

psychometric properties of the moral injury events scale in two military samples. *Assessment, 23*, 557–570. doi:10.1177/1073191115590855

Burkman, K., Purcell, N., & Maguen, S. (2019). Provider perspectives on a novel moral injury treatment for veterans: Initial assessment of acceptability and feasibility of the Impact of Killing treatment materials. *Journal of Clinical Psychology*, *75*(1), 79–94.

Butler, S. & Cape, J. (1999). *Homer: The Iliad*. Dover Publications, Inc. (Original work published 1925)

Corley, M. C. (2002). Nurse moral distress: A proposed theory and research agenda. *Nursing Ethics, 9*, 636–650. doi:10.1191/0969733002ne557oa

Currier, J. M., Foster, J. D., & Isaak, S. L. (2019). Moral injury and spiritual struggles in military veterans: A latent profile analysis. *Journal of Traumatic Stress, 32*, 393–404 doi:10.1002/jts.22378

Currier, J., Holland, J., & Malott, J. (2015). Moral injury, meaning making, and mental health in returning veterans. *Journal of Clinical Psychology, 71*(3), 229–240.

Currier, J. M., Holland, J. M., Drescher, K., & Foy, D. (2015). Initial psychometric evaluation of the moral injury Questionnaire—Military version. *Clinical psychology & psychotherapy*, 22(1), 54–63.

Currier, J. M., Stefurek, T., Carroll, T. D., & Shatto, E. H. (2017). Applying trauma-informed care to community-based mental health services for military veterans. *Best Practices in Mental Health, 12*(1), 47–64.

Department of Defense (2006). *Department of Defense Directive 2311.01E: DoD Law of War Program*. https://www.esd.whs.mil/Portals/54/Documents/DD/issuances/dodd/231101e.pdf

Department of Defense (2011). *Department of Defense Instruction 6490.08: Command Notification Requirements to Dispel Stigma in Providing Mental Health Care to Service Members*. https://www.jag.navy.mil/distrib/instructions/DODI6490.08.Cmd_Notification_Mental_Health.pdf

Department of Veterans Affairs. (2017). *Reporting cases of abuse and neglect*. Veterans Health Administration

Dishman, L. (2020, April 20). Describing a coronavirus "war zone," nurses sue New York and two hospitals over safety issues. *Fast Company*. Retrieved from https://www.fastcompany.com/90496358/see-the-26-world-changing-ideas-awards-winners-that-are-building-a-better-world

Doris, J. M., & Murphy, D. (2007). From My Lai to Abu Ghraib: The moral psychology of atrocity. *Midwest Studies in Philosophy, 31*, 25–55.

Drescher, K. D., Foy, D. W., Kelly, C., Leshner, A., Schutz, K., Litz, B. (2011). An exploration of the viability and usefulness of the construct of moral injury in war veterans. *Traumatology, 17*(1), 8–13. doi:10.1177/1534765610395615

Farnsworth, J. K. (2019). Is and ought: Descriptive and prescriptive cognitions in military-related moral injury. *Journal of Traumatic Stress, 32*, 373–381. doi:10.1002/jts.22356

Farnsworth, J. K., Drescher, K. D., Evans, W., & Walser, R. D. (2017). A functional approach to understanding and treating military-related moral injury. *Journal of Contextual Behavioral Science, 6*, 391–397 http://dx.doi.org/10.1016/j.jcbs.2017.07.003

Farnsworth, J. K., Drescher, K. D., Nieuwsma, J. A., Walser, R. B., & Currier, J. M. (2014). The role of moral emotions in military trauma: Implications for the study and treatment of moral injury. *Review of General Psychology, 18*, 249–262 http://dx.doi.org/10.1037/gpr0000018

Frankl, V. E. (2000). *Man's search for ultimate meaning*. Perseus Books.

Fry, S. T., Harvey, R. M., Hurley, A. C., & Foley, B. J. (2002). Development of a model of moral distress in military nursing. *Nursing Ethics* 9, 373387. doi: 10.1191/0969733002ne522oa

Gilligan, C. (2014). Moral injury and the ethic of care: Reframing the conversation about differences. *Journal of Social Philosophy, 45*(1), 89–106.

Gray. M. J., Nash, W. P., & Litz, B. T. (2017). When self-blame is rational and appropriate: The limited utility of Socratic questioning in the context of moral injury: Commentary on Wachen et al. (2016), *Cognitive and Behavioral Practice, 24*, 383–387.

Gross, M. L. (2004). Bioethics and armed conflict: Mapping the moral dimensions of medicine and war. *Hastings Center Report, 36*(6), 22–30.

Hamric, A. B., Borchers, C. T., & Epstein, E., G. (2012). Development and testing of an instrument to measure moral distress in healthcare professionals, *AJOB Primary Research*, 3(2), 1–9, doi:10.1080/21507716.2011.652337

Hoge, C. W. (2011). Interventions for war-related posttraumatic stress disorder: Meeting veterans where they are [Editorial]. *Journal of the American Medical Association, 306* 549–551.

Jameton, A. (1984). *Nursing practice: The ethical issues*. Prentice-Hall.

Jinkerson, J. D. (2016). Defining and assessing moral injury: A syndrome perspective. *Traumatology, 22*(2), 122.

Jordan, A. H., Eisen, E., Bolton, E., Nash, W. P., & Litz, B. T. (2017). Distinguishing war-related PTSD resulting from perpetration- and betrayal-based morally injurious events. *Psychological Trauma: Theory, Research, Practice, and Policy, 9*, 627–634.

Kenny, D. J., & Kelley, P. A. (2019). Heavy burdens: Ethical issues faced by military nurses during a war. *Online Journal of Issues in Nursing, 24*(3). Manuscript 1.

Kinghorn, W. (2012). Combat trauma and moral fragmentation: A theological account of moral injury. *Journal of the Society of Christian Ethics, 32*(2), 57–74.

Koenig, H. G., Ames, D., Youssef, N. A., Oliver, J. P., Volk, F., Teng, E. J., Haynes, K., Erickson, Z. D., Arnold, I.,

O'Garo, K., & Pearce, M. (2018). Screening for moral injury: The Moral Injury Symptom Scale–Military Version short form. *Military Medicine, 183*, e659–e665. doi:10.1093/milmed/usy017

Levi-Belz, Y., & Zerach, G. (2018). Moral injury, suicide ideation, and behavior among combat veterans: The mediating roles of entrapment and depression. *Psychiatry Research, 269*, 508–516.

Litz, B. T., Stein, N., Delaney, E., Lebowitz, L., Nash, W. P., Silva, C., & Maguen S. (2009). Moral injury and moral repair in war veterans: A preliminary model and intervention strategy. *Clinical Psychology Review, 29*, 695–706.

Lützen, K., & Ewalds-Kvist, B. (2013). Moral distress and its interconnection with moral sensitivity and moral resilience: Viewed from the philosophy of Viktor E. Frankl. *Bioethical Inquiry, 10*, 317–324. doi:10.1007/s11673-013-9469-0

Maguen, S., & Burkman, K. (2013). Combat-related killing: Expanding evidence-based treatments for PSTD. *Cognitive and Behavioral Practice, 20*, 476–479

Mark, D. D., Connelly, L. M., Hardy, M. D., Robison, J., Jones, C. C., & Streett, T. A. (2009). Exploring deployment experiences of Army medical department personnel. *Military Medicine, 174*(6), 631–636.

Molendijk, T., Kramer, E., & Verweij, D. (2018). Moral aspects of "moral injury": Analyzing conceptualizations of the role of morality in military trauma. *Journal of Military Ethics, 17*(1), 36–53 doi:10.1080/15027570.2018.1483173

Morley, G., Bradbury-Jones, C., & Ives, J. (2019). What is "moral distress' in nursing? A feminist empirical bioethics study. *Nursing Ethics*, 1–18. https://doi.org/10.1177/0969733019874492

Mullaney, K., & Regan, M. (2019). One minute in Haditha: Ethics and non-conscious decision making. *Journal of Military Ethics, 18*, 75–95 doi:10.1080/15027570.2019.1643593

Nillni, Y. I., Shayani, D. R., Finley, E., Copeland, L. A., Perkins, D. F., Vogt, D, S. (2020). The impact of posttraumatic stress disorder and moral injury on women veterans' perinatal outcomes following separation from military service. *Journal of Traumatic Stress, 0*, 1–9.

Norman, E. M. (1999). *We band of angels.* Simon & Schuster.

Ross, P. T., Ravindranath, D., Clay, M., & Lypson, M. L. (2015). A greater mission: Understanding military culture as a tool for serving those who have served. *Journal of graduate medical education*, 7(4), 519–522.

Rushton, C. H. (2016). Moral resilience: A capacity for navigating moral distress in critical care. *AACN Advanced Critical Care, 27* 1110119. doi:http://dx.doi.org/10.4037/aacnacc2016275

Shay, J. (1994). *Achilles in Vietnam: Combat trauma and the undoing of character*. Scribner.

Shay, J. (2014). Moral injury. *Psychoanalytic Psychology, 31*(2), 182.

Smith, S. J., & Davis, A. J. (1980). Ethical dilemmas: Conflicts among rights, duties, and obligations. *The American Journal of Nursing, 80*, 1462–1466. https://www.jstor.org/stable/3462695

Smith, E. R., Duax, J. M., & Rauch, S. A. (2013). Perceived perpetration during traumatic events: Clinical suggestions from experts in prolonged exposure therapy. *Cognitive and Behavioral Practice, 20*, 461–470. https://doi.org/10.1016/j.cbpra.2012.12.002

SAMHSA (2014). *Trauma informed care in behavioral health services*. Treatment Improvement Protocol (TIP) Series 57. HHS Publication No. (SMA) 13–4801. Substance Abuse and Mental Health Services Administration.

Thompson, S., & Mastel-Smith, B. (2012). Caring as a standard of nursing when deployed military nurses provide services to enemy insurgents. *International Journal for Human Caring, 16*(4), 22–26.

Wachen, J. S., Dondanville, K. A., Pruiksma, K. E., Molino, A., Carson, C. S., Blankenship, A. E., . . . STRONG STAR Consortium. (2016). Implementing cognitive processing therapy for posttraumatic stress disorder with active-duty U.S. military personnel: Special considerations and case examples. *Cognitive and Behavioral Practice*, 23, 133–147. https://doi.org/10.1016/j.cbpra.2015.08.007

Williamson, V., Murphy, D., & Greenberg, N. (2020). COVID-19 and experiences of moral injury in frontline key workers [Editorial] [Epub ahead of print]. *Occupational Medicine, 70*, 1–3. doi:10.1093/occmed/kqaa052

Wisco, B. E., Marx, B. P., May, C. L., Martini, B., Krystal, J. H., Southwick, S. M., & Pietrzak, R. H. (2017). Moral injury in U.S. combat veterans: Results from the national health and resilience in veterans study. *Depression and Anxiety, 34*(4), 340–347.

Wortmann, J. H., Eisen, E., Hundert, C., Jordan, A. H., Smith, M. W., Nash, W. P., & Litz, B. T. (2017). Spiritual features of war-related moral injury: A primer for clinicians. *Spirituality in Clinical Practice, 4*, 249–261.

Yan, G. (2016). The invisible wound: Moral injury and its impact on the health of Operation Enduring Freedom/Operation Iraqi Freedom veterans. *Military Medicine, 181*(5), 451–458.

Zak, D., & Hesse, M. (2020, April 28). Nurses are trying to save us from the virus, and from ourselves. *Washington Post.* https://www.washingtonpost.com/lifestyle/style/nurses-are-trying-to-save-us-from-the-virus-and-from-ourselves/2020/04/27/7713f79e-84aa-11ea-878a-86477a724bdb_story.html

PART IV

The Military Family

CHAPTER 23	Impact of Parental Military Service on Military-Connected Children	403
CHAPTER 24	Military Spouses	421
CHAPTER 25	Second Service: Military and Veteran Caregivers Among Us	433
CHAPTER 26	Supporting the Sidelines: Encounters with Stress and Loss Related to Military Service	443

CHAPTER 23

Impact of Parental Military Service on Military-Connected Children

Konstance Mackie, Catherine Hernandez, Heather Johnson, and Alicia Gill Rossiter

While walking home from school, a first grader asked his mother, "Mommy, where am I going to go to school for second grade?" She replied, "Here at your same school." "Mommy, where am I going to do third grade?" "I don't know yet, son." The mother paused for a moment then told him, "But I have good news . . . Wherever we go, you can take three of your favorite people with you. His eyes opened widely, and his entire face lit up, as he began listing his best friends from school: "David, Kenneth . . ." The mother chuckled, "No, son. Unfortunately, you cannot take your favorite friends, but you can take your favorite family members—Mom, Dad, and sister."

Military-connected children (MCC) encounter a great deal of uncertainty throughout their lives. Their transient lifestyle can blur family roles and fragmented friendships because children of active duty members who complete a twenty-plus year career in the military will typically transition between six and nine different schools from kindergarten through high school. They also often endure multiple, and sometimes extended, periods of absence from their family members (Department of Defense Education Activity [DoDEA], 2018; Huebner, 2019). Historically, the military family has not been recognized for the role they play in supporting the service member. For those who have served, the phrase "If the military wanted you to have a family, they would have issued you one in your duffel bag" was a common rebuke when a service member voices any issues or concerns with a spouse or child. Yet for those who serve and do have families, military service does have an impact on the family members on the home front supporting the service member. While there is a fairly robust range of research on service members and veterans and the impact of military service on their physical and psychological health, there is a paucity of research regarding the impact of military service on the children of veterans.

The term *military brat* is often used to describe the child of someone serving in the military. While the word *brat* often comes with negative connotations, military children usually view this term as one of endearment, as military brats have a reputation for being resilient. The phrase is rife with rumors regarding its exact definition and origin. One story is that BRAT is an acronym for British Regiment Attached Traveler, the term given by the British to family members who were allowed to travel with their soldier. Another theory is that it's an abbreviation for barrack rat, or child who lives in the military barracks. Speculations are that it could also be an acronym for born, raised, and trained, or born rough and tough (Lange, 2017).

Crunching Numbers

Military children are those whose parents, guardians, or siblings are serving in the Air Force, Army, Coast Guard, Marines, or Navy on Active Duty or in the Reserve or National Guard (NG). In addition, it includes children whose parents, guardians, or siblings have served in the military and are now veterans or deceased. According to Military OneSource (n.d.-a), 37.3% (n = 486,485) of active duty military members have children, while 41.5% (n = 332,932) of members of the Reserves and NG have children. There are currently 677,755 children ages 0–18 years from active duty military families, and there are 440,393 children ages 0–18 years from Reserves and NG families. Children in the 0–5 years age group make up 44.8% (n = 303,849) of all children of active duty members and 36.2% (n = 159,603) of all children of Reserves and NG members. Children who are 6–11 years old comprise 33.8% (n = 229,079) of all children of active duty members and 35.8% (n =157,511) of all children of members of the Reserves and NG. Children ages 12–18 years comprise 21.7% (n =144,827) of all children of active duty military members and 28.0% (n =123,279) of all children of members of the Reserves and NG (Military OneSource, n.d.-a).

Why is this significant? The children of veterans and those who have separated from the military after a period of service all receive care in the civilian sector by providers who may not be aware of their connection to the military. In addition, based on services at each Military Treatment Facility (MTF), care for active duty dependents may be outsourced to providers in the community for both primary and/or specialty care (Bushatz, 2020). In 2020, the Defense Health Agency announced plans to outsource health care for pediatrics, retirees, and other family members to TRICARE civilian network providers in order to focus on the mission-readiness of active duty military members (Bushatz, 2020). Military children will no longer be seen in several military clinics scheduled for this outsourcing of care. As a result, more families will be accessing their health care through local civilian providers. Of the 343 military healthcare facilities that were assessed, 50 have been slated to begin outsourcing healthcare services, and an additional 26 facilities are under review (Bushatz, 2020).

Pros and Cons of Military Life

The military lifestyle brings with it challenges and benefits. Since the events of September 11, 2002, there is now a generation of children who have lived their entire lives while the United States has been at war. For the first time in history, we have parents and children who have served during the same conflict. Some of these children have endured repeated deployments of their loved ones or have even lost a loved one (Huebner, 2018; Panton, 2018; Rossiter et al., 2018; Vasterling, 2015). Relocations every two to four years cause military members and their families to move away from their core support systems. These support systems include extended family members, close friends, schools, healthcare facilities, and familiar cultures. Deployments cause family members to worry for their loved ones' safety. With each deployment comes risks for potential life-changing physical and/or psychological injuries or death in combat zones or related to accidents secondary to hazardous occupations. The stress of the military lifestyle has been shown to increase the risk of physical and mental health issues not only in the military member, but also in their family members. Moreover, military members contend with increased rates of divorce and suicide, which no doubt have a profound affect on their children (Huebner, 2018; Vasterling, 2015).

Academics

Educational considerations, such as errors in grade placement or gaps in curriculum, can cause problems with report card grades, progression, and the timeline to graduation. Attending new schools with different teaching styles requires military children to adapt in order to succeed. Ineligibility for favorite sports, activities, or clubs can occur when a student must wait for a new school year to begin. Credit bleed due to the new school not accepting the previous school's coursework and different graduation requirements in their gaining schools (the new schools) are additional examples of these challenges (Military Child Education Coalition [MCEC], n.d.).

Relocations

Relocations every few years present even more challenges for military children. Temporary lodging and finding permanent housing can wreak havoc in familiar routines. Changes in childcare providers (especially when babies/children have bonded with their caregivers) and separating from their families add to this stress. Packing and unpacking comfort items (toys, etc.), acclimating to a new environment, and culture shock are just some of the many adjustments that military children must work through (MCEC, n.d.). In addition, changing healthcare providers can lead to inconsistencies and decreased continuity of care during important times of development in pediatric patients.

Social Issues

Military children must find a new support system wherever they go, especially with relocations. Missing old friends, making new friends, and trying to fit in with new peers are inevitable for these children. Dealing with the "military" label and people's political opinions can further complicate social issues for military children, and they may experience possible developmental regression. All of these can cause difficulties in making and maintaining relationships with new peers (MCEC, n.d.). Conversely, the military-connected child has an opportunity to reinvent themselves with every move while limiting the influence of destructive peer groups (MCEC, n.d.). Overall, MCC are more likely to engage in risky sexual behaviors and substance use than their civilian counterparts, if the military family is not supported (Bello-Uto & DeSocio, 2015; Cramm et al., 2019).

Family Dynamics

Family dynamics deeply affect how a family will function. MCC live with a sense of pride, patriotism, and respect for the role their parent plays in providing for the safety and security of the nation. Most military families are geographically separated from their extended families. Because of this, military families make strong connections with other military families. The camaraderie enjoyed by military members and families is very strong, as military members and families lean on each other for support in their homes away from home. Neighbors often become each other's second families. Predeployment emotions, coping with separation, anxiety about their parents during deployment, and handling changes in family dynamics are some challenges that military children contend with. Older children are likely to take on more responsibilities, such as helping with caretaking responsibilities for younger siblings and household chores/maintenance, when a parent is deployed. Reintegration (the return of the military member from deployment) can be positively or negatively affected by existing family dynamics (MCEC, n.d.).

Benefits

Military families benefit from the many services afforded to them as a member of the military community. Job security, financial stability, health benefits, community services such as daycares, fitness centers, clubs, etc., and a community of service members and families who promote resiliency and provide support (MCEC, n.d.). The military lifestyle brings with it worldwide travel and exposure to different cultures. Many military families get to live where others vacation! These opportunities provide enriching lifetime experiences for military children and often result in these children becoming well-rounded individuals who are resilient and can adapt easily to changes (MCEC, n.d.).

Gold Star and Blue Star Families

It is worth mentioning Gold Star and Blue Star Families in consideration of military children. Gold Star families are the survivors left behind when a military member dies while on active duty. This concept originated in World War I, when families displayed a banner with a blue star for every immediate family member who went off to war. If that family member died during service, then the blue star was replaced with a gold star. Today, the gold star represents not only family members who die in combat zones, but also those who die during the line of duty in their day-to-day jobs, even during periods of leave, also known as vacation time off during their time of military service. With increased survival rates of the wounded in battle, Blue Star families are now more common (Blue Star Families, 2020; Hedayat, 2019; Military OneSource, 2019; PsychArmor, n.d.). An increasing number of military members are returning from the combat zone with visible and invisible wounds. Sadly, many of these current service members and veterans may have mental health issues, such as post-traumatic stress disorder (PTSD), survivor's guilt, or other complications, such as substance abuse disorders. They may also return with changed personalities as a result of physical injuries such as traumatic brain injuries (TBI). Many have sustained disfiguring injuries, such as burns and amputations. Blue Star families are the immediate family members who provide care for these military members and veterans, and this deeply affects the children in those families (Blue Star Families, 2020; Hedayat, 2019; Military OneSource, 2019; PsychArmor, n.d.).

Services for Military Children

Families of active duty members receive full medical and dental benefits and live close to or on military installations (bases). Therefore, resources are more readily available for families of active duty members. An active duty military member can retire after 20 years of service, affording their spouses and children (children until the age of 22 years, if enrolled in college full-time) continued medical and dental coverage through TRICARE and the TRICARE Dental Program (Volkin, 2020).

Family members of the Reserves and NG receive full medical and dental benefits only when the military member is called up for times of temporary active duty service. Reservists and NG members and their families may live in locations that are remote from military installations, so resources are not as readily available for their children. They will have to utilize civilian healthcare insurance to fill in the gaps in coverage while the military member is not on an active duty assignment (Volkin, 2020).

However, one does not have to travel far beyond their computer in the comfort of home to locate resources for military children. The MCEC has many resources for all children regarding education and coping with changes that come with the military lifestyle (MCEC, n.d.). Behavioral health resources are available, many free of charge, and families can self-refer for these services (a provider's referral is not necessary to access behavioral health services). Behavioral health services can be accessed through Military OneSource online, or military families can call 800-342-9647 for access. Resources are also readily available at the click of a mouse for many other needs, such as parenting resources, family relationships, and moving and housing, as well as information for members of the Reserves and NG (Military OneSource, n.d.-c).

Family Care Plans

Military obligations often require service members to be away from their families. This can be for short periods of time (weeks to months) for temporary training (temporary duty travel [TDY], temporary additional duty [TAD], or temporary duty under instruction [TDI]), or longer periods of a year or more for deployments or unaccompanied assignments. Single parent homes, those in which both parents are servicemembers (dual military), families with certain custody agreements, and those with dependent family members are required to create a Family Care Plan (FCP) at each assignment (Department of the Navy, 2016). These care plans outline care for the dependent(s) in the service member's absence, such as expectations for child/dependent care, medical care, finances, schooling, and require documents to be drafted for power of attorney and other legal aspects for temporary guardianship that must be considered well in advance of the service member parent's absence (Military OneSource, 2020b). Creating a care plan can be a lengthy process and requires frequent revision with changes in family dynamics and/or relocations. Additionally, it should be noted that FCPs are more of a checklist for the member and command, therefore, are not legally binding, and the accompanying legal documents must be completed (Department of the Navy, 2016).

The Impact of Military Service on Children

Studies exploring the impact of parental military service on children are beginning to emerge, and the overwhelming consensus determined that repeated, lengthy deployments can have a cumulative negative impact on the mental health of each family member. Until recently, research on the stress an individual is exposed to from the military lifestyle has focused on the service member, however data continues to emerge that associates parental military service to a list of unexpected comorbidities (Bello-Utu & DeSocio, 2015; Cramm et al., 2019; Creech et al., 2014).

Physical and Psychological Risk Factors

Physical and psychological risks to military-connected children (MCC) are numerous and may include delays in attainment of developmental milestones, such as verbal communication, and increases in incidence of psychosocial conditions such as anxiety, depression, and behavioral problems. Incidences of physical and non-physical victimization (bullying) increase during parental deployment as well as rates of substance use and risk-taking behaviors, which include physical violence, gang involvement, weapon carrying, and suicidal thoughts and attempts (Alfano et al., 2016; Bello-Utu & DeSocio, 2015; Gilreath et al., 2016). Additionally, MCC are at risk for declining academic achievement and disordered eating during stressful times (Estrada et al., 2017; Quattlebaum et al., 2019).

Imperative to each child's healthy growth and development is the mitigation of risk through the healthcare provider's thoughtful screening and consideration of individual and family risk factors. As with all well child visits, it is important to be cognizant of and to screen for the attainment of developmental milestones. The following section will serve as a review of age-related milestones and growth and the potential impact of military service on the MCC during these developmental stages.

Infants (Newborn–12 Months)

The at-home parent of a newborn grapples with the same stressors as a single parent when their loved one is deployed. Missed milestones may signal neglect or issues with maternal/child bonding. The risk of neglect or ineffective bonding is increased with depression or anxiety in parents (Panton, 2018). Signs of neglect or ineffective bonding could be evident in the baby not gaining weight appropriately. It is important to ascertain whether this is due to parental lack of knowledge, as with first-time parents and the possibility of improper mixing of formula, or ineffective coping secondary to a spouse's deployment or relocation to a new duty station.

Babies should gain 1 ounce/day from birth–3 months, then 0.5 ounce/day from 3-6 months of age. At 5 months, babies should be twice their birth weight, and at 12 months, they should be triple their birth weight. Assess cues for missed milestones such as not being able raise their head when lying on their stomach by age 3 months (head lag), not trying to pick up a toy by the age of 6 months, no reactions to noises/voices, not laughing by the age of 5 months, and not sitting up by the age of 6 months. Psychologically, infants are developing trust. Increased clinginess and emotional expressions are normal during this stage of development and it is not uncommon for the infant to develop a fear of strangers by the age of 6 months or separation anxiety by the age of 8 months (Barkley & Associates, 2018; CDC, 2019; Panton, 2018). An excellent tool that parents can use to track their babies' milestones is the CDC's Milestone Tracker App that can be downloaded onto smartphones (Centers for Disease Control and Prevention [CDC], 2019).

Toddlers and Preschoolers (Ages 1 Year–5 Years)

Toddlers should weigh four times their birth weight by the age of 24 months. During the ages of 3 years to 5 years, they should grow 2.5 inches per year. Verbal children may begin to complain more often of stomachaches and headaches. When stressed, this age group may manifest with anxiety, withdrawal, increased excitement, heightened emotional responses, aggression regression, and sleep disturbances (Panton, 2018).

Talk with parents about childcare arrangements, and encourage the parent left on the home front to maintain their routine. Children will require increased affection for reassurance.

If regression, such as toileting accidents in a previously toilet-trained child, or clinginess, irritability, sadness, and increased aggression persist or worsen, then parents should be encouraged to seek further evaluation (Panton, 2018).

Ask how the family is doing at each visit, and be prepared to address behavioral concerns, such as eating and sleeping problems, as these are common with children experiencing the absence of a parent. Remind parents that heightened emotions are to be expected, because toddlers cannot always put into words how they may be feeling. Affection and patience go a long way during these tough times. Remind parents to ask for help from a trusted friend, so that they can get a break from time to time. Playgroups can serve as an excellent way to get to know other parents with similarly aged children who they can swap babysitting with. Parents can find these resources by searching local social media groups or asking around at local schools and daycare centers (Barkley & Associates, 2018; Panton, 2018)

School Age Children (Ages 6 Years–12 Years)

School-age children should gain five to seven pounds and grow two to three inches per year. They may complain more frequently of vague, somatic issues, such as stomachaches or headaches. Psychological symptoms may include anxiety, confusion, anger, depression, resentment, increased moodiness, and emotional withdrawal (Barkley & Associates, 2018; Panton, 2018).

With school-age children, depression and anxiety caused by stress may erroneously be diagnosed as attention deficit hyperactivity disorder, causing them to possibly be prescribed unnecessary medications (Hamilton et al., 2018). Warning signs include frequent vague, somatic complaints, such as headaches and stomachaches, decline in academic performance, withdrawal from activities or friend groups, increased aggression, sadness, anxiety, and anger. Encourage the family to include children in discussions about family plans to include relocation and deployment. Encourage children to talk about what they are feeling. Consider having children help with putting together care packages and making a count-down calendar. Encourage peer support groups if available at school or within the military community. Be mindful of the MCC who live far from military installations as they may be the only child in his or her class who has a parent who is deployed. For these children, peer support services may be limited or nonexistent and the knowledge and expertise of school personnel and providers in the community may be lacking. School psychologists and social workers are another resource. Limit children's exposure to violent or disturbing events in the media (Barkley & Associates, 2018; Panton, 2018).

Adolescents (Ages 13 Years–18 Years)

Adolescents may report more frequent somatic complaints. They may exhibit signs of self-harm. Cyclical vomiting may be seen with substance abuse, especially marijuana. There may also be signs of eating disorders (Panton, 2018). Encourage parents to acknowledge their teens' feelings. Ask how the family is coping with the deployment. Screen for substance abuse, disordered eating, depression, anxiety, and suicidal ideation. Teens may be engaging in or feeling pressured to take part in risky behaviors. Discuss these concerns with teens in privacy, without their parents in the same room.

Teens are likely to take on more family responsibilities in the absence of a deployed parent. When the deployed parent returns home, there may be adjustment issues as the teen has likely been regarded as more mature by the at-home parent as they will most likely have taken a greater role in maintaining the household and helping with younger siblings. This could become problematic when the deployed parent still thinks of the teen as the younger child they left behind at the time of their deployment. Know that even the safe return of the deployed parent brings stress with these changed family dynamics. Warning signs in teenagers include changes in school performance, different friendships, changes in eating habits, sleep disturbances, personality changes, talk of self-harm or suicide, or withdrawal from friends and family (Barkley & Associates, 2018; Panton, 2018).

The Deployment Cycle

The deployment cycle has been described in various articles throughout the literature. Of note, it has been determined that the deployment time period resembles a cycle rather than a solitary event (National Child Traumatic Stress Network

[NCTSN], 2015). Pincus and colleagues (2001) had previously separated the deployment cycle into five phases, which included: (1) pre-deployment, (2) deployment, (3) sustainment, (4) redeployment, (5) post-deployment. However, more recently, researchers have streamlined the deployment cycle to include three phases: (1) pre-deployment, (2) deployment, and (3) reunification (see Appendix). Each phase includes a general timeline for expected duration and commonly associated emotions and/or behaviors that may be displayed (Pincus et al., 2001; Rossiter et al., 2018).

Pre-deployment

The pre-deployment phase begins when the member is notified of an approaching deployment (Pincus et al., 2001). The length of time from notification to the actual departure can vary widely, from weeks to a year or more, however typically the service member is given a few months' notice of an upcoming deployment (Pincus et al., 2001; Rossiter et al., 2018). During the pre-deployment phase, the service member may begin detaching from the family and may be away for extended periods of time for required pre-deployment training. Some families have cited feeling that the member is already "psychologically deployed" during this time (Pincus et al., 2001). The spouse and children can experience denial, anger, sadness, and frustration and may struggle with the many aspects of getting affairs in order before the service member physically departs (Pincus et al., 2001; Rossiter et al., 2018).

Deployment

The deployment phase begins with the physical departure of the service member to the conflict area and typically lasts from 4 to 12 months (Rossiter et al., 2018). During this phase, children may experience feelings of loneliness, fear, sleeplessness, anxiety, adjustment to the new family dynamics, and detachment. Unfortunately, during this time, children may be at higher risk for neglect due to increased demands placed on the at-home caregivers, time and attention (Trautmann et al., 2015).

Reunification

The reunification phase begins when the service member from deployment and typically lasts from 9 to 12 months (Rossiter et al., 2018). Children may experience anticipation, apprehension, excitement, and emotional adjustment. While many people have viewed videos and pictures on the news and the internet of the joyful return of service members to their family post-deployment, the reunification period can be a tumultuous time. The at-home parent and children are at an increased risk for abuse during this time (Pincus et al., 2001, Rossiter et al., 2018). The happy homecoming can be frustrating, as return dates or locations may change frequently and anticipation and expectations run high.

Additionally, there may be animosity if the family is unable to greet the service member immediately on their return. Justifications for this are varied and may include sick children, work requirements, inability to travel, or various other factors. Upon the military member's return, adjustment within the family unit are inevitable and include reallocation of roles within the family, realignment of chores and household responsibilities, and changes in the way discipline is managed and rules are enforced, all of which may lead to discord (Pincus et al., 2001).

Familiarity with the deployment cycle provides a strong guideline to help the military family successfully navigate the various stages and avoid potential pitfalls associated with deployment. Support should focus on being proactive versus reactive. Finally, during this time, it is important to consider the child's age, developmental stage, and family dynamics as highly significant predictors of resiliency

(Bello-Utu & DeSocio, 2015; Pincus et al., 2001; Rossiter et al., 2018).

Risks to Children

Children are at greatest risk for neglect when a parent deploys, and at greatest risk for abuse upon the parent's return (Rossiter et al., 2018). Service member parents who have returned from deployment with injuries, including invisible wounds of war such as PTSD and TBI may expose their family to secondary trauma from their experiences (Bello-Utu & DeSocio, 2015; NCTSN, 2015). In their study of 174 military families, Chesmore and colleagues (2018) found that fathers with symptoms of PTSD reported increased psychosocial symptoms in their children, when compared to the mother's reporting. Furthermore, Christie and colleagues (2019), completed a systematic review of 27 studies that discovered a clear association between parental PTSD and suboptimal parenting practices. The researchers found that parents with PTSD often practiced inconsistent and more severe discipline, reported lower satisfaction with parenting, and frequently suffered from detachment/impaired bonding with the child. One of the greatest predictors of child resilience is the mental health of the at-home parent/caregiver, therefore, it remains valuable to assess the mental health of both parents when possible (Bello-Utu & DeSocio, 2015).

The Exceptional Family Member Program

Military service members are most effective when they know that their families are supported especially during their absence at trainings or deployments. Distress at home takes the focus away from achieving the military mission and could put the military member and his or her team at risk if the individual is distracted by or distraught over issues at home. The Department of Defense (DOD) is dedicated to ensuring that family members with exceptional needs are supported so that service members can train and deploy with as few distractions as possible.

The Exceptional Family Member Program (EFMP) is designed to (1) facilitate military moves (also called Permanent Change of Station [PCS]); (2) ensure that a child's health and educational needs are considered during the assignment process; and (3) provide support and referrals for programs to support the individual and family with special needs (Aronson et al., 2016; DOD, 2017). Each service branch—Army, Navy, Air Force, and Marine—administers its own EFMP program. This section discusses the overarching program, and service members should refer to guidance from their individual service branch for tailored direction.

Although the EFMP is not exclusively a program for children, most of those enrolled are children. The primary purpose of the program is to ensure EFMP members have adequate medical and educational support at their new duty stations. Identifying exceptional family members and enrolling the family member in the EFMP program is mandatory for the service member. Qualifying medical, educational, and mental health conditions do not necessarily fall into what most would consider serious or severe (**Table 23-1**).

There is a common misconception that the EFMP program is a medical program, since most of the qualifying conditions are medical. However, it is a readiness program that falls under the purview of the Office of the Under Secretary of Defense for Personnel and Readiness. The EFMP program provides information and referrals to help families make informed decisions that may impact their quality of life, including educational, social, community, housing, legal, and financial services (DOD, 2017). Managing medical transitions of care falls outside of the scope of this program, even though the healthcare and educational requirements of the child are

Table 23-1 Qualifying Conditions for the Exceptional Family Member Program (EFMP)

Special Educational Needs
- Individualized Education Program
- 504 Plan
- Individualized Family Service Plan or other Early Intervention Services

Special Medical Needs
- Medical or physical conditions requiring follow-up from a primary care manager (including pediatricians) more than once a year
- Potentially life-threatening conditions
- Chronic medical or physical conditions lasting ≥ 6 months
- Any specialty care
- Asthma or other respiratory-related diagnosis with chronic recurring symptoms with any of the following:
  - Scheduled use of inhaled or oral anti-inflammatory agents or bronchodilators
  - Emergency room or clinic visits for acute asthma exacerbations or other respiratory-related diagnosis within the past year
  - One or more hospitalizations for asthma, or other respiratory-related diagnosis within the past 5 years

Mental Health Conditions
- Current and chronic mental health condition (last 6 months or longer) (such as bipolar, conduct, major affective, or thought or personality disorders)
- Inpatient or intensive outpatient mental health service within the last 5 years (> one visit per month for more than 6 months)
- Current intensive mental health services
- Includes mental health care from any provider, including primary care

Attention Deficit Disorder or Attention Deficit Hyperactivity Disorder (ADD/ADHD) with one or more of the following:
- Comorbid psychological diagnosis
- Requires multiple medications, psycho-pharmaceuticals (other than stimulants) or higher than usual doses of medication
- Requires management or treatment by a mental health provider
- Necessitates care by a specialty consultant more than twice a year
- Involves modifications of the educational curriculum or the use of behavioral management staff

Any chronic condition that necessitates:
- Adaptive equipment (such as an apnea home monitor, home nebulizer, wheelchair, custom-fit splints/braces/orthotics (not over the counter), hearing aids, home oxygen therapy, home ventilator, etc.)
- Assistive technology devices (such as communication devices) or services
- Environmental or architectural considerations (such as medically required limited numbers of steps, wheelchair accessibility, or housing modifications and air conditioning)

Modified from Department of Defense. (2017). *DOD instruction 1315.19 The exceptional family member program (EFMP)*. Executive Services Directorate. https://yokosuka.tricare.mil/Portals/133/131519p.pdf

taken into consideration during the assignment process. Civilian and military healthcare providers have a large role in identifying children who should be enrolled in EFMP. Healthcare providers help to ascertain the type and frequency of treatments and services and complete appropriate DOD documents to track these. The healthcare provider may also need to coordinate referrals for medical, psychological, dental, or educational evaluations for enrollment in EFMP or to update information for an upcoming transition (DOD, 2017). TRICARE, the health care program for active duty service members, some veterans, and retirees and their families, outlines the procedures for medical case management and transitions of medical care (Defense Health Agency, 2019a, 2019b).

Military OneSource is a primary reference for all military-related information. The EFMP & Me Online Tool is a resource for military families, healthcare providers, and leaders, which includes information and checklists for enrolling, planning, and transitioning an EFMP family member (Military OneSource, n.d.-b). The local Family Support Center or EFMP office are additional means of getting accurate information related to the program and enrollment (Military OneSource, 2020a).

Education and the Military Child

Military children are undeniably affected by their parents' military service in many ways, but one often overlooked aspect is the child's educational opportunities. Frequent relocation brings with it various other challenges of the military child, such as the transfer of school courses and credits, qualification for extracurricular activities, and meeting the varying educational requirements of different locations (DoDEA, 2020). The Military Interstate Compact Act was developed for this exact reason. In collaboration with the National Center for Interstate Compacts and the Council of State Governments, the Department of Defense aimed to address the educational transition issues of military families in which rigid restrictions were inadvertently penalizing military children (National Military Family Association [NMFA], 2020). The Act addresses enrollment by allowing use of unofficial school records to enroll a military child in school, placement by allowing the child to continue in the grade level they were in or take comparable courses to what they were taking before the move, attendance by allowing the child to miss school days for deployment-related reasons, and waiving some graduation requirements for students who transfer during their senior year of high school. The Interstate Compact Act has been adopted by all 50 states and the District of Columbia, and more information can be obtained from the student's area School Liaison Officer (SLO), or from the Military Interstate Children's Compact Commission at http://www.mic3.net/interactive-map.html (NMFA, 2020).

Factors Affecting Resilience

In their systematic review of military child coping, Bello-Utu and DeSocio (2015) concluded that the MCC resilience was based on three common themes: (1) age and/or development of the child, (2) at-home parent/caregiver mental health, and (3) previous cumulative risk and resiliency. Identified protective factors for MCC include a strong family relationship, school involvement, parental engagement/attentiveness, and community support (Kelly & Paul, 2018; Tunac De Pedro et al., 2018). Engagement with children of veterans, deceased military members, and Reservists and National Guardsmen is especially significant and challenging, as these families typically live in civilian communities, are remote from military installations, and are often isolated from military support services normally available to active duty family members (Huebner, 2019; Rossiter et al., 2018). MilitaryOneSource.mil (2020c) discusses five protective factors that increase military family resilience, including: (1) parental resilience, (2) knowledge of parenting and childhood development, (3) social connections, (4) parental support, and (5) promoting social and emotional competence in the children. Families should attempt to engage in resources early to build a proactive support network and maintain optimal communication within the family unit.

I Serve 2

Healthcare providers have successfully utilized clinical guidelines and pocketcards, and integration of a pocketcard during patient assessment has been reported to improve healthcare quality and are associated with improved patient outcomes (BootsMiller et al., 2004; Rossiter et al., 2018). In 2017, a group of Advanced Practice Nurses and Nurse Researchers, all of whom have served in the military, were MCC, and/or are parents of MCC themselves, created the *I Serve 2: A Pocketcard for Healthcare Providers Caring for Military Children* (see Appendix) to serve as a guideline and resource for providers caring for MCC. The pocketcard was modeled after the U.S. Department of Veterans Affairs *Military Health History Pocket Card for Health Professions Trainees and Clinicians* and the American Academy of Nursing *Have You Ever Served?* initiative in hopes that providers could use all three resources in tandem when caring for the military family unit. The *I Serve 2: A Pocketcard for Healthcare Providers Caring for Military Children* honors the tremendous sacrifices MCC make as well as acknowledges the stressors they endure in support of a parent(s) military service and why it important that those who work with or care for MCC to be aware of this.

The front of the pocketcard prompts the provider to ask every patient, or the parent of a young child, "Do you have a parent, sibling, or other family member that has ever served in the military?" Siblings were included in the ask as research shows an even greater impact on the mental health of children when a sibling was deployed as compared to the deployment of a parent or other family member (Tunac De Pedro et al., 2018). Additional questions are provided to help the provider ascertain whether the parent, sibling, or other family member is active duty, Reserve, National Guard, or a veteran; when and where they served; where the family is in the relocation or deployment cycle. This information will give the provider a better idea about possible risks and exposures as well as the need for potential resources and referrals. In addition, it includes a brief overview of the deployment cycle highlighting common emotions and behaviors that may be associated with each stage of the cycle. In addition, it may alert providers as to risks associated with deployment and should prompt the providers to assess for risk factors such as depression, anxiety, suicidality, and abuse/neglect. Finally, a list of resources for providers and family members rounds out side one of the pocketcard. For states or other organizations interested in utilizing the pocketcard when asked, the authors have amended this section to include state, community, and/or institutional specific resources to ensure these families have information for resources in their local area.

Once the MCC child has been identified, side two of the pocketcard includes the ICARE support strategy—Identify, Correlate, Ask, Ready Resources, and Encourage and Educate—that prompts the provider to ask age-appropriate questions (Rossiter et al., 2020). This allows the provider to identify and address any physical, psychological, and/or behavioral issues the MCC might be experiencing in order to mitigate the impact of parental military service, provide referrals for additional services and supports, and engage the parent and child with resources either on a military installation or in the community.

Resources for Caring for Military-Connected Children

- *I Serve 2: A Pocketcard for Healthcare Providers Caring for Military Children*
- Military OneSource: Around the clock resource for information and support. It is free for military families (Military OneSource, n.d.-d).
- Family Advocacy Program (FAP): Works with military families to build resilience and prevent abuse in the home (Military

OneSource, 2020d). FAP also works closely with Child Protective Services to investigate and follow reported cases of child abuse and/or neglect (Military One Source, 2020e).

- Yellow Ribbon Events: Initiative from the Department of Defense that aims to engage service members and families to resources throughout the deployment cycle, including during the reintegration phase. More information can be found at https://www.yellowribbon.mil/ (Yellow Ribbon Reintegration Program, n.d.)

References

Alfano, C. A., Lau, S., Balderas, J., Bunnell, B. E., & Beidel, D.C. (2016). The impact of military deployment on children: Placing developmental risk in context. *Clinical Psychology Review, 43*, 17–29. doi:10.1016/j.cpr.2015.11.003

Aronson, K. R., Kyler, S. J., Moeller, J. D., & Perkins, D. F. (2016). Understanding military families who have dependents with special health care and/or educational needs. *Disability and Health Journal, 9*(3), 423–430. doi:10.1016/j.dhjo.2016.03.002

Barkley & Associates. (2018). *Pediatric primary care nurse practitioner certification review/clinical update continuing education course 2018*. Barkley & Associates, Inc.

Bello-Utu, C. F., & DeSocio, J. E. (2015). Military deployment & reintegration: A systematic review of child coping. *Journal of Child and Adolescent Psychiatric Nursing, 28*, 23–24. doi:10.1111/jcap.12099

Blue Star Families. (2020). *Deployment resources*. BlueStarFam.org. https://bluestarfam.org/for-mil-families/deployments/deployment-resources/

BootsMiller, B. J., Yankey, J. W., Flach, S. D., Ward, M. M., Vaughn, T. E., Welke, K. F., & Doebbeling, B. N. (2004). Classifying the effectiveness of Veterans Affairs guideline implementation approaches. *American Journal of Medical Quality, 19*, 248–254.

Bushatz, A. (2020, February 19). *Here's the list of military clinics that will no longer serve retirees, families*. https://www.military.com/daily-news/2020/02/19/pentagon-releases-list-health-clinics-closing-retirees-military-families.html

Centers for Disease Control and Prevention. (2019, December 09). *CDC's milestone tracker app*. https://www.cdc.gov/ncbddd/actearly/milestones-app.html

Chesmore, A. A., He, Y., Zhang, N., & Gewirtz, A. H. (2018). Parent discrepancies in ratings of child behaviors following wartime deployment. *Journal of Traumatic Stress, 31*, 79–88. doi: 10.1002/jts.22257DOI: 10.1002/jts.22257

Christie, H., Hamilton-Giachritsis, C., Alves-Costa, F., Tomlinson, M., & Halligan, S. L. (2019). The impact of parental posttraumatic stress disorder on parenting: a systematic review. *European Journal of Psychotraumatology, 10*(1), 1550345. doi:10.1080/20008198.2018.1550345

Cramm, H., McColl, M. A., Aiken, A. B., & Williams, A. (2019). The mental health of military-connected children: A scoping review. *Journal of Child and Family Studies, 28*, 1725–1735. doi:10.1007/s10826–019-01402-y

Creech, S. K., Hadley, W., & Borsari, B. (2014). The impact of military deployment and reintegration on children and parenting: A systematic review. *Professional Psychology: Research and Practice, 45*(6), 452–464. http://dx.doi.org/10.1037/a0035055

Defense Health Agency. (2019a). *DHA-PI 6025.20 medical management (MM) program within the Military Health System (MHS)*. https://health.mil/Reference-Center/Policies/2019/08/27/DHA-PI-6025–20-Medical-Management-MM-Program

Defense Health Agency. (2019b). *Special needs*. https://www.tricare.mil/CoveredServices/SpecialNeeds/SNResources

Department of Defense. (2017). *DOD instruction 1315.19 The exceptional family member program (EFMP)*. Executive Services Directorate. http://www.dtic.mil/whs/directives

Department of Defense Education Activity. (2018). *All about DoDEA educational partnership*. https://www.dodea.edu/Partnership/about.cfm

Department of Defense Education Activity. (2020). The Military Interstate Compact Act. https://www.dodea.edu/Partnership/interstateCompact.cfm

Department of the Navy. (2016). *Preventive law series: Family care plan*. [PDF File]. https://www.jag.navy.mil/legal_services/documents/FAMILY_CARE_PLANS_Mar_2016.pdf

Estrada, J. N., Gilreath, T. D., Sanchez, C. Y., & Astor, R. A. (2017). Associations between school violence, military connection, & gang membership in California secondary schools. *American Journal of Orthopsychiatry, 87*, 443–451. doi:10.1037/ort0000181

Gilreath, T. D., Wrabel, S. L., Sullivan, K. S., Capp, G. P., Roziner, I., Benbenishty, R., & Astor, R. A. (2016).

Suicidality among military-connected adolescents in California schools. Suicidality among military-connected adolescents in California schools. *European Child & Adolescent Psychiatry, 25*, 61–66. doi:10.1007/s0087-015-0696-2

Hamilton, L., Ling, C., & Rossiter, A. G. (2018). Impact of parental military service on the health of military-connected children: A case study. *Journal of Pediatric Health Care, 32*(6). doi:10.1016/j.pedhc.2018.07.001

Hedayat, S. (2019, September 24). *What is a gold star family?* https://www.uso.org/stories/2471-what-is-a-gold-star-family

Huebner, C. R. (2019). Health and mental health needs of children in US military families. *Pediatrics, 143*(1), 1–13. doi:10.1542/peds.2018–3258

Kelly, D. & Paul, M. (2018). Veterans-by-proxy: A conceptual framework of ambiguous loss among children of combat veterans. *Journal of Family Social Work, 21*, 4–5, 255–270, doi:10.1080/10522158.2017.1321605

Lange, K. (2017, April 13). "Military Brat:" Do you know where the term comes from? *Stars and Stripes Guam*. https://guam.stripes.com/education/%E2%80%98military-brat%E2%80%99-do-you-know-where-term-comes

Military Child Education Coalition. (n.d.). *Resources*. https://www.militarychild.org/resources

Military OneSource. (n.d.-a). *2018 Military demographics profile* [PDF File]. https://www.militaryonesource.mil/data-research-and-statistics/military-community-demographics/2018-demographics-profile

Military OneSource. (n.d.-b). *EFMP & Me*. https://efmpandme.militaryonesource.mil/

Military OneSource. (n.d.-c). *Featured content*. https://www.militaryonesource.mil/

Military OneSource. (n.d.-d). *Get free 24/7 support for your MilLife*. https://www.militaryonesource.mil/all-the-ways?gclid=Cj0KCQjw6uT4BRD5ARIsADwJQ1-LWiyUK-94tvFyp7SdW_3c0ySHrCZZQTV1qSi_vk4PosLIdlx-h0BtUaAu9TEALw_wcB

Military OneSource. (2019, November 13). *Honoring gold star families*. https://www.militaryonesource.mil/family-relationships/survivor-casualty-assistance/support-after-loss/honoring-gold-star-families

Military OneSource. (2020a). *The exceptional family member program: A program for families with special needs*. https://www.militaryonesource.mil/family-relationships/special-needs/exceptional-family-member/the-exceptional-family-member-program-for-families-with-special-needs

Military OneSource. (2020b). *Preparing your family care plan*. https://www.militaryonesource.mil/family-relationships/relationships/parents-guardians/preparing-your-family-care-plan

Military OneSource. (2020c). *Five protective factors for mil-parents: Ways to secure more parenting wins*. https://www.militaryonesource.mil/family-relationships/parenting-and-children/parenting-infants-and-toddlers/ways-to-secure-more-parenting-wins

Military OneSource. (2020d). *The family advocacy program*. https://www.militaryonesource.mil/family-relationships/family-life/preventing-abuse-neglect/the-family-advocacy-program

Military OneSource. (2020e). *How to report child abuse or neglect in the military*. https://www.militaryonesource.mil/family-relationships/family-life/preventing-abuse-neglect/how-to-report-child-abuse-as-a-member-of-the-military

National Military Family Association. (2020). *Military child education*. https://www.militaryfamily.org/info-resources/education/

Panton, J. (2018). Caring for military children: Implications for nurse practitioners. *Journal of Pediatric Health Care, 32*(5), 435–444. https://doi.org.ezproxy.hsc.usf.edu/10.1016/j.pedhc.2018.02.007

Pincus, S. H., House, R., Christenson, J., & Adler, L. E. (2001). The emotional cycle of deployment: A military family perspective. *US Army Medical Department Journal*, 4(5)

PsychArmor Institute. (n.d.). *About us*. https://psycharmor.org/about-us/

Quattlebaum, M., Burke, N. L., Higgins Neyland, M. K., Leu, W., Schvey, N. A., Pine, A., . . . Tanofsky-Kraff, M. (2019). Sex differences in eating related behaviors and psychopathology among adolescent military dependents at risk for adult obesity and eating disorders. *Eating Behaviors,33*, 73–77. doi:10.1016/j.eatbeh.2019.04.001

Rossiter, A. G., Cogan, A. M., Cervelli, L., & Ling, C. G. (2020). Treating military-connected children in the civilian sector: Information and resources for clinicians. *Archives of Physical Medicine and Rehabilitation, 101*(4), 735–737. doi:10.1016/j.apmr.2019.12.003

Rossiter, A. G., Patrician, P. A., Dumas, M. A., Ling, C. G., Johnson, H. L., & Wilmoth, M. C. (2018). I Serve 2: Identifying and caring for military-connected children in civilian primary care settings. *Journal of the American Association of Nurse Practitioners, 30*(11), 614–620. doi:10.1097/JXX.0000000000000084

The National Child Traumatic Stress Network. (2015). *Child maltreatment in military families: A fact sheet for providers*. [PDF File]. https://www.nctsn.org/sites/default/files/resources//child_maltreatment_military_families_providers.pdf

Trautmann, J., Alhusen, J., & Gross, D. (2015). Impact of deployment on military families with young children: A systematic review. *Nursing Outlook, 63*(6), 656–679. doi:10.1016/j.outlook.2015.06.002

Tunac De Pedro, K., Astor, R. A., Gilreath, T. D., Benbenishty, R. & Berkowitz, R. (2018). School climate, deployment, and mental health among students in military-connected schools. *Youth & Society*, 50 (1), 93–115. doi:10.1177/004118x155922

Vasterling, J. J., Taft, C. T., Proctor, S. P., Macdonald, H. Z., Lawrence, A., Kalill, K., ... Fairbank, J. A. (2015). Establishing a methodology to examine the effects of war-zone PTSD on the family: The family foundations study. *International Journal of Methods in Psychiatric Research, 24*(2), 143–155. doi:10.1002/mpr.1464

Volkin, M. (2020). *5 things to consider when choosing active or reserve duty.* https://www.military.com/join-armed-forces/5-things-to-consider-when-choosing-active-or-reserve-duty.html

Yellow Ribbon Reintegration Program. (n.d.). *About the yellow ribbon reintegration program.* https://www.yellowribbon.mil/

Appendix

I Serve 2

I SERVE 2: A POCKETCARD FOR HEALTHCARE PROVIDERS CARING FOR MILITARY CHILDREN©

I CARE Support Strategy for Military Children

- **Identify:**
  - Military children in your practice/community
  - Risk factors, mitigating aspects and patterns of coping
  - If the parent is Active Duty, Reservist, or National Guard in order to gauge services available
- **Correlate:**
  - Developmental stage, healthcare concerns in context of the individual child
  - Family and teacher concerns about child
- **Ask**
  - How the child is coping
  - Assess risks for physical, psychological, behavioral, social, and academic concerns
  - Conduct a vulnerability and safety assessment
  - How will the family ensure a smooth deployment and reintegration
  - What you can do to reduce unnecessary visits during deployment (e.g. medication refills, referrals, etc.)
- **Ready Resources**
  - Engage partnerships within the school system
  - Ready a list of local and national resources for military families
  - Encourage families to engage resources well in advance of deployment
  - Determine accessibility to military installation services
- **Encourage and educate**
  - Prevention strategies
  - Strong families and healthy problem solving
  - Early engagement with resources
  - Healthy expectations during and after deployment

I CARE created by Dr. Heather Johnson and Dr. Catherine G. Ling and adapted by Dr. Alicia Gill Rossiter DOI: 10.1111/1745-7599.12003

For additional information on I Serve 2 refer to: I Serve 2: Identifying and caring for military connected children in civilian primary care settings—Dr. Alicia Gill Rossiter* (arossite@usf.edu), Dr. Patricia A. Patrician, Dr. Mary Anne Dumas, Dr. Catherine Gaines Ling, Dr. Heather L. Johnson, and Dr. Margaret C. Wilmoth. DOI# 10.1097/JXX.0000000000000084. DOI: 10.1016/j.outlook.2016.05.01. https://doi.org/10.1016/j.pedhc.2018.07.001

Questions that can be asked of parents and military children at well child/acute care visits:

Correlate/Ask

- Has anyone expressed any concerns about you (or your child?)
- Have you noticed any of the following?
  1. Increased stress
  2. Anxiety, sadness
  3. Emotional or physical outbursts
  4. Crying/ overly emotional
  5. Difficulty sleeping, nightmares
  6. Difficulty concentrating
  7. Change in academic performance or appetite
  8. Clingy or distant
  9. Increase in behavioral issues at home, school, with peers
  10. Increase in complaints of stomach aches, headaches, or other physical symptoms

Ready Resources

- Who do you turn to for support? Where is this person located?
- What resources are available to you in the:
  1. Military
  2. Community
  3. School/day care
  4. Religious affiliations
  5. Sports/ service organizations

Vulnerability/ risk assessments

- Where do you live? On or off a military instillation?
- Do you feel safe in your home?
- Are you concerned about your child?
- Tell me about the relationship with your parents.
- Tell me about a typical day at home/school
- How do you feel about your parent's job in the military?
- How have things been since your parent returned from deployment?

Point of Contact: Dr. Alicia Gill Rossiter arossite@usf.edu

I SERVE 2: A POCKETCARD FOR HEALTHCARE PROVIDERS CARING FOR MILITARY CHILDREN©

Military children make tremendous sacrifices in support of a parent(s) military service. Over 2 million children have a parent who is serving or has served in the Armed Forces. While "resilient" is the word used to describe most military children, it is important that we recognize the stresses/stressors of military life—that military children serve too—in order to support and care for them.

★ I SERVE 2 ★

Ask your patients & their parents:

"Do you have a parent, sibling, or other family member who has ever served in the military?"

If the patient answers 'yes' ask:

- Is the military member:
  - Active duty?
  - Reservist?
  - National Guard?
  - Veteran?
- Has your parent deployed? Where? When?
- Where are you in the deployment cycle?
- What is your time for relocation (PCS)?

PREDEPLOYMENT (3 MONTHS BEFORE DEPARTURE): DENIAL, ANGER, SADNESS, FRUSTRATION
DEPLOYMENT (4 MONTHS TO 12 MONTHS): LONELINESS, FEAR, SLEEPLESSNESS, ANXIETY, ADJUSTING TO BEING ALONE, DETACHMENT, HIGH RISK FOR NEGLECT
REUNIFICATION (9 TO 12 MONTHS): APPREHENSION, ANTICIPATION, EXCITEMENT, EMOTIONAL READJUSTMENT, HIGH RISK FOR ABUSE

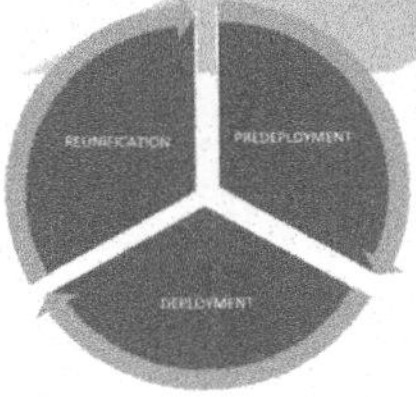

RESOURCES

MILITARY ONE SOURCE: WWW.MILITARYONESOURCE.MIL

BLUE STAR FAMILIES: WWW.BLUESTARFAM.ORG/RESOURCES/DEPLOYMENTS/DEPLOYMENT-RESOURCES/

CHILD MIND INSTITUTE: WWW.CHILDMIND.ORG/TOPICS/CONCERNS/MILITARY-FAMILIES/

MILITARY.COM: HTTP://WWW.MILITARY.COM/SPOUSE/MILITARY-LIFE/MILITARY-RESOURCES/FAMILY-SUPPORT-SERVICES.HTML

MILITARY CHILD EDUCATION COALITION: WWW.MILITARYCHILD.ORG

NATIONAL MILITARY FAMILY ASSOCIATION: WWW.MILITARYFAMILY.ORG

U.S DEPARTMENT OF EDUCATION: WWW.ED.GOV/VETERANS-AND-MILITARY-FAMILIES

MILITARY INTERSTATE CHILDREN COMPACT: WWW.MIC3.NET

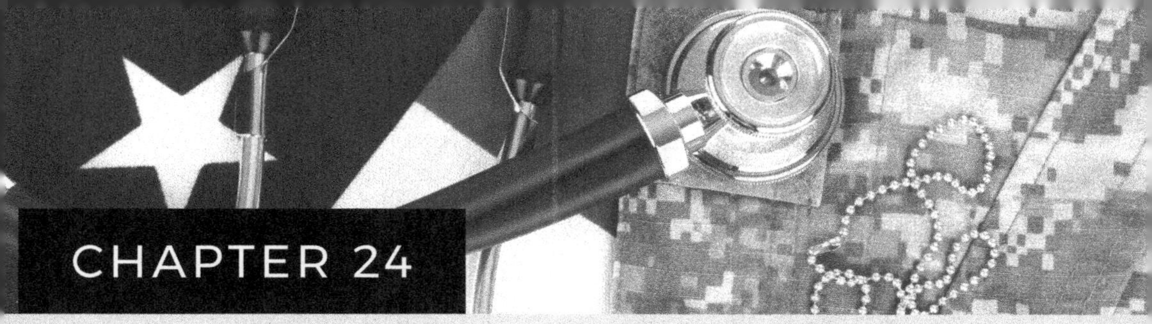

CHAPTER 24

Military Spouses

***Definition**: Spouse refers to male or female married or unmarried partners of service members. Historically, spouses have been majority female. Changes to include more male partners are due to the repeal of Don't ask Don't tell, an increase in women service members, and an increase in opportunities for women in war-fighting billets or positions.*

Catherine G Ling

Introduction

Military spouses have been vilified or canonized in popular media when the truth is more complex. It is critical to understand their roles and community context as they have the greatest impact on the longevity of service of active duty, Reserve, and National Guard members. Military spouses are an under-recognized vulnerable population. They experience multiple deployment and move cycles with care-taking responsibilities. These cycles and responsibilities have costs: physiologic and psychologic stress, chronic under- and unemployment, and social isolation. These costs contribute to a non-communicable disease burden and are not necessarily balanced by access to care. While all spouses have access to health insurance, that does not equate to access to care. Additionally, these partners are key to family resilience.

The Importance of the Military Spouses—Looking at the "So What"

Military spouses play a critical role in the health and longevity of military service members, military children, and the quality of life for veterans. Spousal contentment with military life is the leading cause for service members leaving active duty (Blue Star Families, 2019). Additionally, spousal well-being is a primary factor in children's ability to successfully navigate the military parent's deployment and service (Arnold et al., 2017; Chandra et al., 2011; Kritikos et al., 2020). These pivotal roles also point to military spouses being a factor in national security (Dunham, 2020; Koehlmoos et al., 2020).

Civilian providers will see more military spouses. Military Health Systems have limited facilities and services for families and veterans (Blue Star Families & Institute for Veterans and Military Families, 2019). A secondary consequence with every move is the need for spouses to reestablish primary care for themselves and their families. Therefore, it is critical that health providers know the distinctive healthcare needs of military spouses and how to provide culturally informed care (Borah & Fina, 2017). Implications for spousal care reinforce the need for integration of trauma-informed care and routine assessment of social determinants of health into routine clinical practice.

Historical Perspective

Military spouses have played a critical and understated role in supporting their military members since militaries were organized. The historical roles of spouses are primarily captured in diaries and letters in American colonial and early national periods (Alt & Stone, 1991; Huffman, 2020). These spouses fell into roughly three groups: officer wives, enlisted wives, and "camp followers" (unmarried or widowed women who followed the troops from camp to camp). The role of each was to provide comfort and support to service members. That support took the form of cooking, creating or mending uniforms, doing laundry, providing medical care, and nursing in addition to more personal comforts (Alt & Stone, 1991; Albano, 1994; Schultz, 1992). Martha Washington is the best-known Revolutionary War spouse. She spent every winter encamped with the Colonial Army providing counsel and support to General Washington while feeding, nursing, and caring for his officers (Pine, 2014; Alt & Stone, 1991). There is little written record of the work of slaves who accompanied many of the wives. It is not implausible to attribute the work of the wives to these unnamed women.

While spouses were not explicitly addressed by military regulation, they were seen as being critical to the health, good order, and discipline or conversely as a disruptive force. This perception can be found in diaries and letters from Revolutionary War through the westward expansion (Alt & Stone, 1991; Pine, 2014; Reilly, 2016; Schultz, 1992). Spouses were key to providing medical care during pre–World War I. The diaries and writings of these wives speak of deprivation but they also speak of finding joy in some aspect of where they were whether it was the company, environment, or time with their spouse (Handy-Marchello, 2006; Huffman, 2020). Martha Washington's quote "The greater part of our happiness or misery depends on our dispositions and not our circumstances" speaks to a thread that continues to this day—military spousal life is what you choose to make of it.

Contemporary Spouse

Contemporary military spouses live in a unique context. The military spouse is part of an all-volunteer force. This profession dictates where they live and how much time their spouse will spend with their family. The non-military spouse will have to face employment challenges while navigating a society where the vast majority of two-parent families have dual income. These spouses face a constant cycle of reinventing, reinvesting, and service. Ironically, they are labeled as a dependent in the military system—the same term that is used for a child. Popular media representations are stereotypical and do not reflect the full complexity. This section will speak to demographics, education, and employment to get a more clear picture of the contemporary spouse.

National Guard and Reserve

National Guard and Reserve spouses face some of the same issues faced by active duty spouses but have their own set of supports and challenges (**Table 24-1**). Keep in mind the following elements that impact these families as they move into and out of active duty status depending on the deployment or activation of their service member.

Table 24-1 National Guard/Reserve Spouses

National Guard and Reserve Spouses	
Supports	**Challenges**
Uninterrupted employment or education	Limited access to military family supports
Consistent community	Potential family economic disruption with activation/deployment
Established support systems	Lack of military cultural immersion
Uninterrupted services like health care and housing	Unrecognized in community

Data from Blue Star Families & Institute for Veterans and Military Families. (2019). *2019 military family lifestyle survey: Comprehensive report.* https://bluestarfam.org/wp-content/uploads/2020/03/BSF-2019-Survey-Comprehensive-Report-Digital-rev200305.pdf; Bommarito, R. K., Sherman, M. D., Rudi, J. H., Mikal, J. P., & Borden, L. M. (2017). Challenges facing military spouses during postdeployment reintegration: A review of the literature and current supports. Military *Behavioral Health, 5*(1), 51–63. https://doi.org/10.1080/21635781.2016.1243494; Faber, A. J., Willerton, E., Clymer, S. R., MacDermid, S. M., & Weiss, H. M. (2008). Ambiguous absence, ambiguous presence: A qualitative study of military reserve families in wartime. *Journal of Family Psychology, 22*(2), 222–230. doi:10.1037/0893-3200.22.2.222

Demographics

In general, military spouses are young and female caring for young children. The diversity of who is a military spouse evolved as women have moved into broader opportunities within the military; they are bringing their spouses and families with them. Additionally, with the end of the "Don't Ask, Don't Tell" policy barring gay service members in 2010 and the SCOTUS decision from 2015 upholding same sex marriage has further expanded the definition of who is a military spouse. See **Figures 24-1** and **24-2** for a full comparison. Unmarried partnerships are beginning to be recognized as well though for the purposes of this text married partners are the point of reference because they are reliably represented in the data and literature.

Education

There are notable differences in the education attainment of military spouses when compared with their civilian counterparts (see **Figure 24-3**). The comparative group is married civilian women as this group most closely matches the majority of military spouses. With those caveats, the following percentages are time matched and gender matched where possible (Bureau of Labor Statistics, 2014;

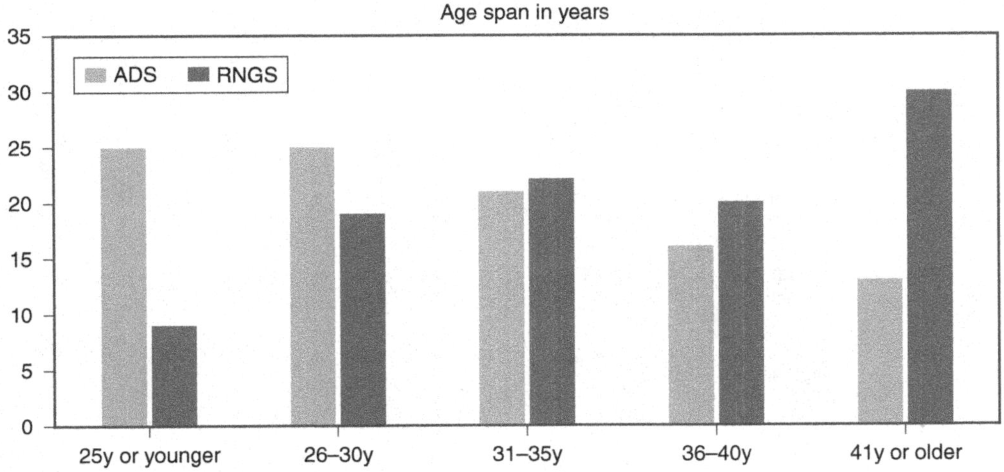

Figure 24-1 Age of Military Members in Years.

ADS = Active Duty Servicemember
RNGS = Reserve National Guard Servicemember

Department of Defense, 2014). Broadly, military spouses have higher education attainment early but that tapers off at higher levels. Approximately 44% of military spouses have some college or an associate degree versus 30% for married civilians with only 10% of military spouses having up to and completed a high school diploma versus 31% for civilian married women (Bureau of Labor Statistics, 2014; Department of Defense, 2018). This education accomplishment begins to reverse with advanced degrees; 38% of civilians attain a college degree compared with 30% of military spouses. Professional and graduate degrees demonstrate an even more enhanced disparity with 37% civilian attainment compared with 15% of military spouses (Bureau of Labor Statistics, 2014).

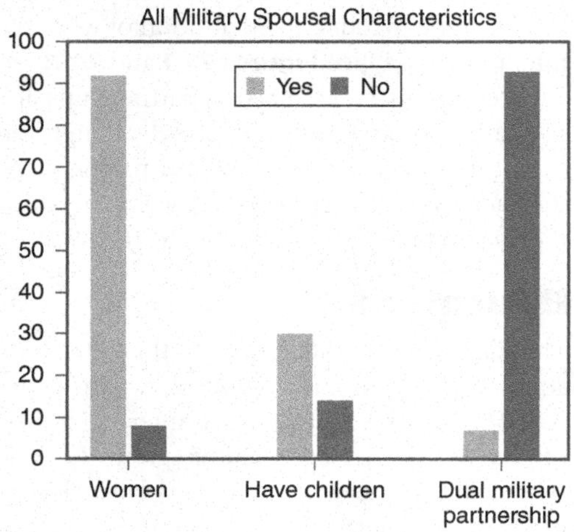

Figure 24-2 Men/Women - Dual/Single mil member - With children/Without

Reasons for these trends include availability of scholarships and financial aid, access to institutions offering advanced degrees, cost and availability of child care, timing and support for obtaining higher education, and post-graduation opportunities (Friedman et al., 2015; Ott & Morgan, 2018). Access to online institutions, increasing mentorship, and geographic separation for the spouse are some of the ways these challenges can be mitigated.

Occupations/Employment

Occupation and employment are critical elements of family well-being and security along with adult identity and self-worth (Green et al., 2013; Trewick & Muller, 2014). For military spouses, they balance their career with that of their active duty partner. Military spouses are

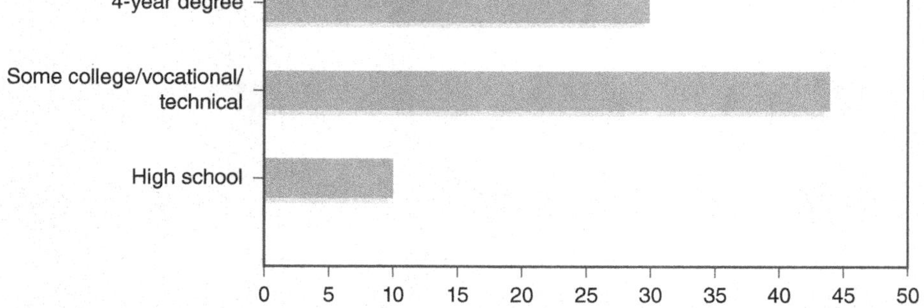

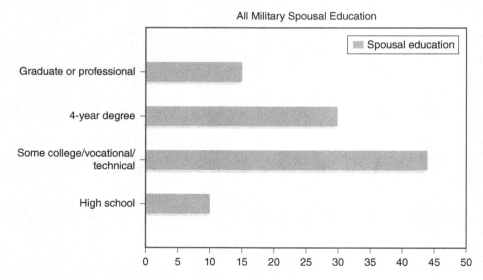

Figure 24-3 Education level.

employed in a variety of fields and disciplines from engineering to research to retail to health care. Military life presents a significant challenge to maintenance of spousal employment. Military spouses experience under- and unemployment at exponentially higher rates than civilians. Over the last 10 years, spouses experienced unemployment rates well above the national average (see **Figure 24-4**). This level has remained steady throughout economic recession, recovery, and economic boom.

US = US average unemployment rate

RNGS = Unemployment rate average for Reserve and National Guard Spouses

ADCS = Unemployment rate average for Active Duty Spouses

Reported as percentage

Reasons for unemployment include restricted opportunities, licensure/relicensure regulation, access to and affordability of child care, recent PCS, and limited professional network to name a few (Friedman et al., 2015). At the core of these reasons are frequent moves and availability of opportunities where bases are located. For example, the military family moves from San Antonio to Honolulu. The spouse is a teacher who must meet criteria to be licensed in Hawaii, find an opening, and navigate the interview. The probability that the spouse has a professional network that can identify openings is limited. If there are children in the family, their care needs must be addressed. If the military parent is on a deployable platform, the spouse will be responsible for all issues that arise with child and home care. Military spouses have been heard to joke that it is not a deployment until you have had three major appliances fail including having the car break. Being in Hawaii, the probability that extended family can be part of a care plan are limited.

Those same reasons also contribute to spousal underemployment. Underemployment is defined as working below educational preparation and experience or part-time when full-time work is sought (Friedman et al., 2015; Meadows et al., 2016). One study estimated that 40% of working military spouses were underemployed (Lim & Schulker, 2010). This contributes to a significant pay and hours gap found between military spouses and matched civilians (Meadows et al., 2016). Underemployment can be a double-edged sword in building a career. It can prevent any gaps in active experience, but the spouse also runs the risk of being "stuck" in working at that lower

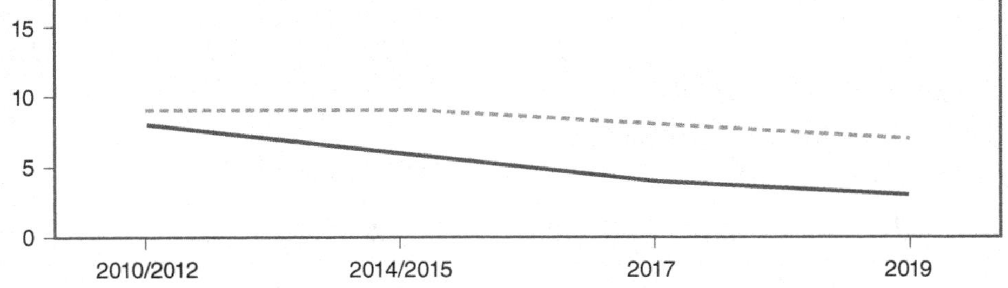

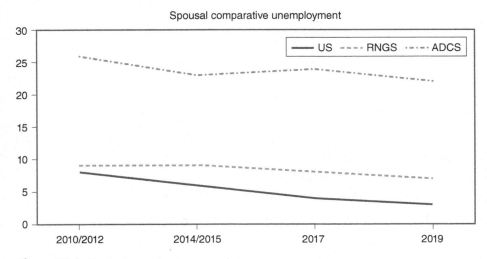

Figure 24-4 Unemployment rate comparison.

skill level that is not commiserate with education or experience, and this could potentially harm long-term employment.

One type of military family that does not face these challenges is the dual military family. In these families, both spouses are actively serving. While these families have employment stability and each have opportunity for growth and promotion, there are still challenges (Huffman, 2020). These challenges include child care, deployment backup plans, and arranging moves that keep both spouses in the same city or state (Woodall et al., 2020). The services are under no obligation to colocate married service members and colocation challenges increase if the spouses are in different branches; there is not always a navy base near an army post.

Given the challenges with paid work, some spouses choose volunteerism as an occupation. Volunteerism allows spouses to create a work record and professional identity while maintaining control over scheduling. Volunteering allows these spouses to contribute to their community with flexibility in setting hours. Some of the volunteer opportunities provide support at unit level and connection to the military society. Other opportunities include mentoring, care taking, fundraising, and continued practice without stricture of employment, though state and federal licensure and regulation will still apply. A few military-specific examples of volunteer organizations that benefit from spousal volunteerism are the Navy Marine Corp Relief Society, Scholarships for Military Children, Family Readiness Groups, and the Ombudsman program.

Programs to Promote Military Spousal Education and Employment

During OIF/OEF and in conjunction with the Obama Administration's Joining Forces initiatives, several programs have begun or evolved to support and promote spousal work and education opportunities. MyCAA, eMentor, post- 9/11 GI bill transference, and scholarships that provide in-state tuition for military spouses are just a few. Fees associated with establishing spousal professional licensure are now considered a reimbursable moving expense per the Defense Authorization Act of 2018 and the ceiling amount was raised in 2020. Spouses are also eligible for unemployment following a move. Additionally, efforts have and are being made to extend licensure recognition across state lines in regulated fields such as nursing, education, and real estate. However, when moving into a new state, the prospective licensee must look at the State Licensing Board's fine print regarding military spousal eligibility. There may still be associated fees for practice and professional recognition in that state beyond license recognition.

Health and Well-Being

The health and well-being of military spouses is not an exhaustively studied topic. The majority of published literature regarding these spouses has been in conjunction with caretaking, mental health, and home safety in relationship to the actions of their service member. Only 11% of research published in the last 20 years about military service members and their families focuses primarily on the spouses (December search in Pub Med). Yet, military life does impact spousal health and well-being (Corry et al., 2019; Mailey et al., 2018). Military life with deployment cycles and accessible resources are discussed here as they impact spouses. Full discussion of deployment and military culture/lifestyle are discussed elsewhere in this text (Chapter XX and Chapter YY).

Impact of Military Life Cycle

The military life cycle includes permanent changes of station (PCS), military life span, entry to retirement, impact on spousal health, and well-being. The PCS or moving cycle is the most obvious impact on spousal health and well-being. With each move, spouses must reestablish work, leisure, education, and community activities for themselves and any children. At a basic level, they must reestablish a home, routines, and services. In addition to finding and integrating into routines with new schools, jobs, day care, and neighborhoods; they must learn new geography and find their usual food staples in a new grocery store. They will need to establish routine maintenance and care with a new dentist, mechanic, and hairdresser. These new contacts are then multiplied by the number of household members who are non-active duty. The physical act of moving and the associated tasks listed previously are stress inducing. PCS also exacts a fiscal cost that is not reimbursed. By one estimate, the average military family pays over $5,000 out of pocket with each PCS to cover moving-related expenses (Jowers, 2020). So, the PCS presents both disruption and opportunity for change.

In addition to the ongoing PCS cycle, military life also occurs along a spectrum or time span. At enlistment or commissioning (entry points to becoming an enlisted service member or officer), there is a significant training period preparing for the next level of work. Spouses may or may not be able to accompany. This creates periods of uncertainty and waiting. Additionally, prior to each career point is an evaluation for advancement during which the spouse waits for test and selection results along with the service member. This is stressful in an abstraction in support of the partner but also each of these career milestones has implications for where they will live, increase or decrease in pay, deployments, or if the family will transition to civilian life.

The final and longest phase of military life is after they leave the military and become veterans. As a spouse of a veteran, many military-based supports that an active duty spouse may have had ready access, will no longer be available. For example, military families can often obtain primary care at the same military treatment facility as their service member. Spouses do not have standing to receive health care at a Veterans Affairs (VA) facility, though their service member may have direct access to care within the VA. In addition to establishing a civilian-based life, the spouse may be reentering or entering fully the workforce. One study found that money and spousal employment were some of the highest areas of concern for veterans and their families (Blue Star Families & Institute for Veterans and Military Families, 2019). While there are transition courses for service members that retire, this is not the case for spouses or if the military member separates from service in other ways.

Deployment Cycle

Like the military life cycle, the deployment cycle has an impact on military spouses' health and well-being. As referenced in Chapters XXX, the deployment cycle consists of preparation, separation. and reintegration phases. In each phase, spouses have different roles and tasks. Roles include primary decision maker, mediator, problem solver, primary or sole caregiver, and journalist (recording and reporting the news of the day). Much like with military life, spouses who are grounded in community or occupation and have health-enhancing behaviors in response to these cycles, decrease risks for military children and improve mission readiness of the service member (O'Neal, Lucier-Greer, et al., 2016; Paley et al., 2013). Conversely, spouses can experience exacerbations if they have unmet or evolving physical or behavioral health issues and their ill health negatively impacts both the military children and the service members (O'Neal, Mancini, et al., 2016; Verdeli et al., 2011).

Since September 11, 2001, over one million service members have deployed. Some of these deployments are routine and some are combat tours. Service members and their families are experiencing multiple deployments for months at a time with varying downtime. The number, length, and dangerous nature of these deployments is now being found to have a cumulative impact on health behaviors along with physical and mental health (Donoho et al., 2018; Fish et al., 2014; Mailey et al., 2018; Paley et al., 2013). Research has found an inverse relationship between health behaviors (physical activity, nutrition, and sleep) and NCD risk and the length and frequency of military partner deployments (Fish et al., 2014; Mailey et al., 2018; Paley et al., 2013). Mediating factors were found to be community support to include meaningful work and community integration (Kritikos et al., 2020; Padden et al., 2011).

Frequent deployments and military lifestyle have also been found to take a toll on mental health. That toll can be compounded by their partner's experiences. Service members accumulate macro- and micro-traumas during deployment that become part of them. Spouses incur secondary trauma through association and through negotiating the challenges of military life (Bjornestad et al., 2014; Steenkamp et al., 2018). Longer and more frequent partner deployments are associated with increases in spousal rates of depression and risk of self-harm (Eaton et al., 2008; Faulk et al., 2012). Spousal suicide data began being collected and released in 2017 and suicide attempts among military spouses was found to be 6.8 per 100,000; a rate that is lower than their civilian counterparts (Under Secretary of Defense for Personnel and Readiness, 2019). With this increased recognition of risk, it should be noted that behavioral health resources are readily accessible on base or post and are reserved primarily for active duty. This leaves spouses, children, and veterans to access care in the community.

Availability of Resources

The previous example speaks to the availability of resources for military spouses. All active duty military spouses are enrolled in one of the TRICARE health plans. While service members receive comprehensive care with military facilities, spouses may or may not have access to the same services or necessary specialty care. With frequent moves, spouses can experience interrupted or breaks in continuity of care. Spouses also experience geographic variation in type of care available.

While TRICARE provides insurance benefits, those benefits do not necessarily cover all of the costs or have the appropriate level specialty. This is particularly salient when specialty care is needed. Not every location has ready access to developmental pediatrics or adolescent behavioral health. Even when care is established in an area, it will need to be reestablished with the next move. This will involve a potential lag in care with wait lists and reevaluation. All of this assumes a degree of health literacy, availability of disposable income to bridge gaps in care, and the ability to navigate multiple healthcare systems. Additionally, spouses may leave their healthcare networks during a deployment in order to access social and family support. While out of network, they will access care through urgent and emergent services (**Table 24-2**).

Given the costs and challenges associated with navigating military life and obstacles associated with continuity of employment and education, some military families choose to create a stable home base and have the service member "geo-batch' or be a geographic bachelor. This means the service member will live at the assigned base and the spouse will maintain a home base in a separate location. This solution has additional financial costs and relationship strains, but when weighed against the benefits of stability, this may be a reasonable solution.

Specific Population Considerations

Some military spouses face additional challenges. Caregivers, male spouses, and Gold Star Spouses all have unique aspects to their lives as spouses.

Table 24-2 Health Access

Issue	Mitigating factors
Community/ Organization translation	TRICARE coverage Command/Unit supports Networks (formal/ informal)
Navigation	Multisystem interaction with different resources
Insurance does not equal access	Limited coverage Extensive out of pocket Limited availability to on-base/post resources

Caregivers

The 5.5. million military spouses are caregivers because they provide daily, in-person care for their severely ill or injured service member or veteran (Ramchand et al., 2014). They are either thrust into that role or they piece by piece assume the role as the service member's need evolves. Caregiving includes helping with activities of daily living like bathing and feeding, coordinating and transporting to providers and therapists while providing home-based therapies and treatments as prescribed (Ramchand et al., 2014). These spouses also face challenges with making their homes adaptive to their service member's needs, creating flexible work that allows them to care and parent.

For veterans with a 70% disability who need daily care, spouses can apply for the VA's Program of Comprehensive Assistance of Family Caregivers (https://www.caregiver.va.gov/support/support_benefits.asp). This program provides support for significantly injured or ill service members and their caregivers. These supports include a stipend, training, respite care resources, and access to health insurance for the spouse if there is no other source. Caregiving has a toll. These spouses have limited support networks and are four times more likely than civilian counterparts to experience depression (Ramchand et al., 2014). Tailoring supports while providing education options, employment opportunities, and extending benefits while understanding that caregiving needs are going to evolve as the wounded warrior ages.

Male Spouses

There are increasing numbers of women entering military service and they are bringing their spouses with them as are same-sex couples. Male spouses experience many of the same issues faced by female spouses; under- and unemployment lack of community resources, and difficulty in accessing specialty health care (Weinstock, 2016). However, there are some differences. Male spouses are frequently mistaken for the service member so they are treated differently and, in some cases, more respectfully. Males also tend to be more isolated than female spouses. Some of the isolation is by choice; they choose not to integrate into spouses' clubs or unit family activities. Other isolation is caused by a structure that has been set up for and by women. One group of male spouses at an overseas installation set up a support network called "Dependabros" (Manfre, 2020). As the number of women and men on active duty begins to equalize, integrating and welcoming all spouses will be critical.

Gold Star Spouses

The final special group is Gold Star Spouses. These are the widows and widowers of service members killed while on active duty. The Gold Star family designation began during World War I when families would fly a flag with a blue star if they had a family member serving in the military. That blue star was replaced with a gold one if the service member was killed. President Woodrow Wilson was thought to be the first to use the term *Gold Star Mother* in honoring those who lost sons in that conflict (Budreau, 2008). Currently, there are over 400,000 surviving Gold Star spouses.

These widows and widowers are of all ages with a sharp increase in those under 40 years old from OIF/OEF. They can be found in communities across the country. They are eligible for a variety of benefits that need to be adapted to meet the needs of these younger partners who have borne the ultimate cost of almost 20 years of war with an all-volunteer force. The benefits include education assistance for the widow or widower, access to health care, and stipends (Military OneSource, 2020). There are, however, significant constraints that are undergoing legislative review. One example is that if the surviving spouse remarries before the age of 57, they forfeit their benefits (Gold Star Wives of America, Inc, 2020). Given the younger ages of OIF/OEF survivors, this provision causes undue hardship. Organizations like Gold Star Wives of America are working on behalf of these spouses with Congress.

Summary

Military spouses make a unique contribution to the support of our national security. They face unique challenges in education, occupation, health maintenance, familial relationships, and responsibilities while navigating military life and culture. Providers caring for these spouses need to assess not only what phase of military life they are experiencing but also what resources they can access and what requirements associated with their spouse's service need to be met. Understanding that context is critical.

It is appropriate that as this chapter that started with the definition of a military spouse and calls for providers to listen to these partners should end with a letter from a spouse. The following is an excerpt from a letter written by a World War II spouse who had just dropped her soldier off to go to war. This description of separation rings as true today as it did then.

My Darling,
You have only been gone a few hours and already the house is waiting for you . . . I began mentally putting away our life together to make room for the new one alone . . . it wasn't till I picked up the shirt you'd worn last night that the feel of you was unbearable . . . I'm going to bed—I'll pretend we're together . . . And if I dream about you, tomorrow will be a lovely day.

(**Litoff & Smith**, 1995, p.12)

References

Alt, B. S., & Stone, B. D. (1991). *Campfollowing: A history of the military wife*. Praeger.

Arnold, A. L., Lucier-Greer, M., Mancini, J. A., Ford, J. L., & Wickrama, K. A. S. (n.d.). How family structures and processes interrelate: The case of adolescent mental health and academic success in military families. *Journal of Family Issues*, *38*(6), 858–879.

Bjornestad, A. G., Schweinle, A., & Elhai, J. D. (2014). Measuring secondary traumatic stress symptoms in military spouses with the Posttraumatic Stress Disorder Checklist Military Version: *The Journal of Nervous and Mental Disease*, *202*(12), 864–869. doi:10.1097/NMD.0000000000000213

Blue Star Families & Institute for Veterans and Military Families. (2019). *2019 military family lifestyle survey: Comprehensive report*. https://bluestarfam.org/wp-content/uploads/2020/03/BSF-2019-Survey-Comprehensive-Report-Digital-rev200305.pdf

Bommarito, R. K., Sherman, M. D., Rudi, J. H., Mikal, J. P., & Borden, L. M. (2017). Challenges facing military spouses during postdeployment reintegration: A review of the literature and current supports. *Military Behavioral Health*, *5*(1), 51–63. doi:/10.1080/21635781.2016.1243494

Borah, E., & Fina, B. (2017). Military spouses speak up: A qualitative study of military and Veteran spouses' perspectives. *Journal of Family Social Work*, *20*(2), 144–161. doi:10.1080/10522158.2017.1284702

Budreau, L. M. (2008). The politics of remembrance: The Gold Star mothers' pilgrimage and America's fading memory of the Great War. *Journal of Military History*, *72*(2), 371–411.

Bureau of Labor Statistics. (2014). *Educational attainment and earnings of women*. https://www.bls.gov/opub/ted/2014/ted_20140603.htm

Chandra, A., Lara-Cinisomo, S., Jaycox, L., Tanielian, T., Han, B., Burns, R., & Ruder, T. (2011). *Views from the homefront: How military youth and spouses are coping with deployment*. RAND. doi:10.7249/RB9568

Corry, N. H., Radakrishnan, S., Williams, C. S., Sparks, A. C., Woodall, K. A., Fairbank, J. A., & Stander, V. A. (2019). Association of military life experiences and health indicators among military spouses. *BMC Public Health*, *19*(1), 1517. doi:10.1186/s12889-019-7804-z

Department of Defense. (2018). *2018 demographics: Profile of the military community*.

Donoho, C. J., LeardMann, C., O'Malley, C. A., Walter, K. H., Riviere, L. A., Curry, J. F., & Adler, A. B. (2018). Depression among military spouses: Demographic, military, and service member psychological health risk factors. *Depression and Anxiety*, *35*(12), 1137–1144. doi:10.1002/da.22820

Dunham, C. (2020). It takes a family: How military spousal laws and policies impact national security. *Journal of National Security Law & Policy*, *11*(1), 1–31.

Eaton, K. M., Hoge, C. W., Messer, S. C., Whitt, A. A., Cabrera, O. A., McGurk, D., Cox, A., & Castro, C. A. (2008). Prevalence of mental health problems, treatment need, and barriers to care among primary care-seeking spouses of military service members involved in Iraq and Afghanistan deployments. *Military Medicine*, *173*(11), 1051–1056. doi:10.7205/milmed.173.11.1051

Faber, A. J., Willerton, E., Clymer, S. R., MacDermid, S. M., & Weiss, H. M. (2008). Ambiguous absence, ambiguous presence: A qualitative study of military reserve families in wartime. *Journal of Family Psychology*, 22(2), 222–230. doi:10.1037/0893-3200.22.2.222

Faulk, K. E., Gloria, C. T., Cance, J. D., & Steinhardt, M. A. (2012). Depressive symptoms among US military spouses during deployment: The Protective effect of positive emotions. *Armed Forces & Society*, *38*(3), 373–390. doi:10.1177/0095327X11428785

Fish, T. L., Harrington, D., Bellin, M. H., & Shaw, T. V. (2014). The effect of deployment, distress, and perceived social support on Army spouses' weight status. *U.S. Army Medical Department Journal*, 87–95.

Friedman, E., Miller, L., & Evans, S. (2015). *Advancing the careers of military spouses: An assessment of education and employment goals and barriers facing military spouses eligible for MyCAA*. RAND. doi:10.7249/RR784

Gold Star Wives of America, Inc. (2020). *Home: United we stand . . .* https://www.goldstarwives.org/

Green, S., Nurius, P. S., & Lester, P. (2013). Spouse psychological well-being: A keystone to military family health. *Journal of Human Behavior in the Social Environment*, *23*(6), 753–768. doi:10.1080/10911359.2013.795068

Handy-Marchello, B. (2006). *Army officers' wives on the Great Plains, 1865–1900*. http://plainshumanities.unl.edu/army_officers_wives/

Huffman, A. (2020). *Influential military wives from the Revolutionary War to today*. https://www.wearethemighty.com/MIGHTY-MILSPOUSE/influential-milspouses-revolution-to-now/

Jowers, K. (2020). Military families lose about $5,000 out of pocket for each PCS move, survey finds. *Army Times*. https://www.militarytimes.com/pay-benefits/2020/06/23/military-families-lose-about-5000-out-of-pocket-for-each-pcs-move-survey-finds/

Koehlmoos, T. P., Banaag, A., Madsen, C. K., & Adirim, T. (2020). Child health as a national security issue: Obesity and behavioral health conditions among military children: Study examines obesity and behavioral health among military children. *Health Affairs*, *39*(10), 1719–1727. doi:10.1377/hlthaff.2020.00712

Kritikos, T. K., DeVoe, E. R., Spencer, R., Langer, D. A., Nicholson, J. V., Mufti, F., & Tompson, M. C. (2020). Finding meaning in times of family stress: A mixed methods study of benefits and challenges amongst home-front parents in military families. *Military Psychology*, *32*(4), 287–299. doi:10.1080/08995605.2020.1754122

Lim, N., & Schulker, D. (2010). *Measuring underemployment among military spouses*. RAND.

Litoff, J. B., & Smith, D. C. (Eds.). (1995). *Since you went away: World War II letters from American women on the home front*. University Press of Kansas.

Mailey, E. L., Mershon, C., Joyce, J., & Irwin, B. C. (2018). "Everything else comes first": A mixed-methods analysis of barriers to health behaviors among military spouses. *BMC Public Health*, *18*(1), 1013. doi:10.1186/s12889-018-5938-z

Manfre, M. (2020). *Dependabros do it their way*. https://militaryfamilies.com/military-spouses/dependabros-do-it-their-way/

Meadows, S. O., Griffin, B. A., Karney, B. R., & Pollak, J. (2016). Employment gaps between military spouses and matched civilians. *Armed Forces & Society*, 42(3), 542–561. doi:10.1177/0095327X15607810

Military OneSource. (2020). *Gold star & surviving family members: Support after loss*. https://www.militaryonesource.mil/family-relationships/gold-star-surviving-family/support-after-loss/

O'Neal, C. W., Lucier-Greer, M., Mancini, J. A., Ferraro, A. J., & Ross, D. B. (2016). Family relational health, psychological resources, and health behaviors: A dyadic study of military couples. *Military Medicine*, *181*(2), 152–160. doi:10.7205/MILMED-D-14-00740

O'Neal, C. W., Mancini, J. A., & DeGraff, A. (2016). Contextualizing the psychosocial well-being of military members and their partners: The importance of community and relationship provisions. *American Journal of Community Psychology*, *58*(3–4), 477–487. doi:10.1002/ajcp.12097

Ott, L. E. & Morgan, K. (2018). Impact of military lifestyle on military spouses' educational and career goals. *Journal of Research in Education*, *28*(1), 30–61.

Padden, D. L., Connors, R. A., & Agazio, J. G. (2011). Stress, coping, and well-being in military spouses during deployment separation. *Western Journal of Nursing Research*, *33*(2), 247–267. doi:10.1177/0193945910371319

Paley, B., Lester, P., & Mogil, C. (2013). Family systems and ecological perspectives on the impact of deployment on military families. *Clinical Child and Family Psychology Review*, *16*(3), 245–265. doi:10.1007/s10567-013-0138-y

Pine, J. T. (Ed.). (2014). *Wit and wisdom of America's first ladies: A book of quotations*. Dover Publications.

Ramchand, R., Tanielian, T., Fisher, M., Vaughan, C., Trail, T., Batka, C., Voorhies, P., Robbins, M., Robinson, E., & Ghosh Dastidar, M. (2014). *Hidden heroes: America's military caregivers*. RAND. doi:10.7249/RR499

Ramchand, R., Tanielian, T., Fisher, M., Vaughan, C., Trail, T., Batka, C., Voorhies, P., Robbins, M., Robinson, E., & Ghosh-Dastidar, B. (2014). *Military caregivers: Who are they? And who is supporting them?* RAND. doi:10.7249/RB9764

Reilly, R. F. (2016). Medical and surgical care during the American Civil War, 1861–1865. *Baylor University Medical Center Proceedings*, *29*(2), 138–142. doi:10.1080/08998280.2016.11929390

Schultz, J. E. (1992). The inhospitable hospital: Gender and professionalism in Civil War Medicine. *Signs*, *17*(2), 363–392.

Steenkamp, M. M., Corry, N. H., Qian, M., Li, M., McMaster, H. S., Fairbank, J. A., Stander, V. A., Hollahan, L., & Marmar, C. R. (2018). Prevalence of psychiatric morbidity in United States military spouses: The Millennium Cohort Family Study. *Depression and Anxiety*, *35*(9), 815–829. doi:10.1002/da.22768

Trewick, N., & Muller, J. (2014). Unemployment in military spouses: An examination of the latent and manifest benefits, quality of life, and psychological well-being. *Australian Journal of Career Development*, *23*(2), 47–56. doi:10.1177/1038416213520306

Under Secretary of Defense for Personnel and Readiness. (2019). *Annual suicide report: Calendar year 2018* (D-30C1C14; pp. 1–47). Department of Defense. https://www.google.com/url?sa=t&rct=j&q=&esrc=s&source=web&cd=&ved=2ahUKEwiQ6vGRlu3tAhUGwlkKHRU3CIAQFjAIegQIDRAC&url=https%3A%2F%2Fwww.dspo.mil%2FPortals%2F113%2F2018%2520DoD%2520Annual%2520Suicide%2520Report_FINAL_25%2520SEP%252019_508c.pdf%3F_ga%3D2.86818399.619987331.1571340363-160498055.1571340363&usg=AOvVaw2bOBJY29Pbd1CTeYVro5se

Verdeli, H., Baily, C., Vousoura, E., Belser, A., Singla, D., & Manos, G. (2011). The case for treating depression in military spouses. *Journal of Family Psychology*, *25*(4), 488–496. doi:10.1037/a0024525

Weinstock, M. (2016). *Staff perspective: male military spouses—"invisible" family members?* https://deploymentpsych.org/blog/staff-perspective-male-military-spouses-%E2%80%9Cinvisible%E2%80%9D-family-members

Woodall, K. A., Richardson, S. M., Pflieger, J. C., Hawkins, S. A., & Stander, V. A. (2020). Influence of work and life stressors on marital quality among dual and non-dual military couples. *Journal of Family Issues*, *41*(11), 2045–2064. doi:10.1177/0192513X20903377

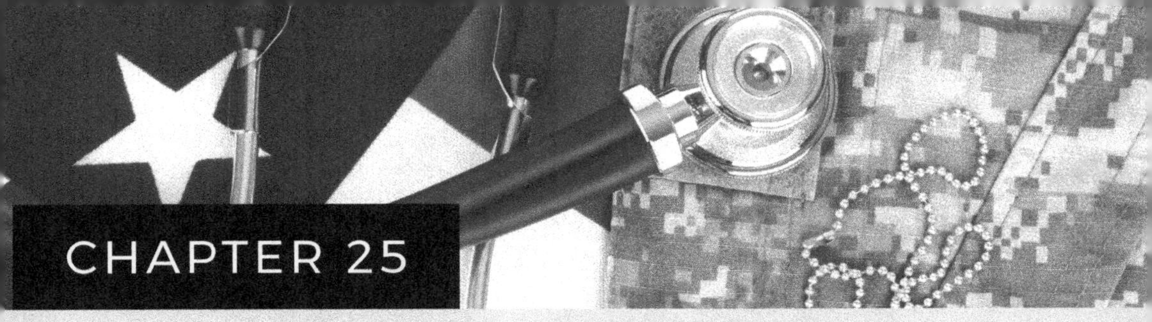

CHAPTER 25

Second Service: Military and Veteran Caregivers Among Us

Roxana E. Delgado, Kimberly Peacock, Christi Luby, and Mary Jo Pugh

Who Are Military and Veteran Caregivers

Military life is a life of sacrifice for both the service member and their family. While military spouses do not serve actively in the military, that does not mean they don't *serve* the military. Military spouses make countless sacrifices to support their service member and are often referred to as someone who serves out of uniform. Military service includes selflessness, support, and leadership. Service means the individual gives up their sense of self for the betterment of those who serve alongside them, and the mission at hand (Citroen, L.). This chapter will illustrate how the military family also lives a life of service, dedication, and sacrifice, sometimes in the ultimate way: becoming a military caregiver. A military and veteran caregiver (MVC) is defined as an individual (spouses, parents, or friends) that provides assistance to a service member or veteran with activities of daily living (ADLs) or instrumental activities of daily living (IADLS) (AIDLs) (Ramchand, 2014). This chapter will also provide great value and insight into the world of the MVC.

Since the beginning of this country's history, military families have received the notification when their loved one has been injured. In an instant, lives are changed. Typically, these family members drop everything, leave the life they know, and rush to be by the side of their injured service member, often in a faraway military hospital.

During the adjustment period, family members take on new roles, adapt to new schedules, and learn new ways of handling many of life's obstacles. They are forced into a new world: caregiving. Caregiving becomes their *second service*. Caregiving is, by nature, an emotional and often difficult topic to write about. This chapter will describe the MVC, examine caregiver needs, and discuss the impact of caregiving on the physical and psychological health associated with caring for a wounded, ill, and injured service member. Additionally, current initiatives and programs addressing caregiver needs as well as resources for healthcare providers who may care for the MVC will be discussed.

This chapter highlights the words of Senator Elizabeth Dole, "America cannot fulfill her sacred vow to serve those who have borne the battle if steadfast support is not given to their hidden heroes—military and veteran caregivers."

Characteristics of Military and Veteran Caregivers

As discussed earlier, MVC are a diverse group of spouses, parents, siblings, or friends with one characteristic in common: caring for a service member or veteran that served in the U.S. Armed Forces. A marked distinction of the MVC population is the era of war, denoted mostly by the veteran's service period: before or after the wars in Iraq and Afghanistan, also known as pre- and post-9/11 veterans. Caregivers assisting veterans may have unique characteristics, given their pre- or post-9/11 status. According to a large-scale nationwide needs assessment among military caregivers, Ramchand and colleagues (2014) were able to identify the top challenges and needs among military caregivers. The research team stratified the caregivers by era of war (pre- and post-9/11) and compared these caregivers to civilian caregivers. The comprehensive report, also known as the "RAND Report," showed that military caregivers, particularly the post-9/11 population, had the worst health-related outcomes. The RAND Report shed light on the challenges military caregivers face, especially given their young age and the sudden transition to the new role and associated responsibilities. The key findings of the RAND Report (Ramchand, 2014) are: (1) post-9/11 military caregivers differ from other caregivers; (2) caregivers perform a variety of caregiving tasks and face heavy burdens; (3) society needs to start planning now for caregivers' futures; and (4) most relevant programs and policies serve caregivers only incidentally.

Military caregivers represent an estimated 5.5 million people who are an essential part of recovery for our nation's wounded, ill, and injured service members and veterans. These "hidden heroes," may spend up to 80 hours per week assisting loved ones with health-related events and facilitating daily activities. This can impact the individual caregiver and the subsequent well-being of the family unit, as caregivers may put off caring for their own health to prioritize the needs of others. As such, the MVC population may experience periods of isolation, guilt, sleep-deprivation, and financial stress. Many also face diminished educational and professional opportunities. This scenario generates a greater incidence of depression and suicidal ideation among military caregivers (Malik et al., 2019; Sander et al., 2019).

Often, caregivers do not realize what is happening to them physically, mentally, or emotionally while taking care of their loved ones. The MVC population experiences worse physical and mental health issues than civilian caregivers and non-caregivers. The MVC population's unique characteristics may not be represented by the existing body of literature, which has focused on family caregivers of patients in hospice or patients with a diagnosis of cancer, dementia, Parkinson's, Alzheimer's, and other specific diseases/disabilities (Epstein-Lubow, 2014; McLaughlin et al., 2016; Gan et al., 2010; Razani et al., 2007). The young age and long lifespan of service members and veterans with traumatic brain injury (TBI) and other injuries make this population unique in light of the extant literature. The limited evidence regarding military caregiving suggests that these caregivers may experience a health decline for a longer period of time than any other group.

Needs of Military and Veteran Caregivers

Have you ever put together a puzzle? Try to recall the steps necessary to build the puzzle. Do you gather the straight edges, find the corner pieces, and sort the pieces into like colors? Often, you develop a method and procedure that when followed and used persistently, leads to the completion of the puzzle. For MVC, finding their way as caregivers is much like assembling a jigsaw puzzle. They develop their own methods and procedures, and each piece of their puzzle tells a portion of their caregiver journey. Just like a puzzle, no two pieces—no two journeys—are exactly the same. Each journey may present unique challenges and opportunities. One of the opportunities that healthcare providers may be able to identify is the incorporation of the MVC in the treatment plan. The *Caregiver Perceptions About Communication with Clinical Team Members* (CAPACITY) is an instrument that may be used to assess this opportunity and that can inform the healthcare provider and the MVC (VanHoutven et al., 2017), a benefit for the MVC and healthcare provider relationship.

Implications of Caregiving

For almost four decades, military spouses have been studied using qualitative research. These spouses have reported and exhibited an array of symptoms of chronic stress (anxiety, hypervigilance, somatic complaints, sleep disorders, and agoraphobia) that have been associated with their partner's post-traumatic stress disorder (PTSD) and/or combat injuries (Carmassi et al., 2019; Chwalisz & Stark-Wroblewski, 1996; George, 1986; Klippel & Sullivan, 2018; Schulz & S.R., 1999; Tooth et al., 2005). These past reports have used terms like *indirect traumatization*, *secondary PTSD*, and *vicarious traumatization* to discuss these issues (Luby, 2015a). Most of this research has occurred outside of the United States.

Due to the post-9/11 conflicts, researchers within the United States have increased their focus on the interpersonal difficulties and trauma reported in U.S. military and veteran households, such as marital discord, domestic violence, divorce, substance abuse issues, and suicide rates in both service members, and more recently, their family members. When a family member becomes the caregiver, another set of issues emerge. The toll of these biopsychosocial issues is increasing as the years of military engagement and multiple deployments have increased. Therefore, it is difficult to describe caregiving in military and veteran populations if we don't depict the variability within the MVC community. Each individual situation and experience are unique based on roles and relationships, type of injury, and the chronicity of their injury.

The next section of this chapter describes and explains various scenarios in military caregiving. Each case is hypothetical, but based on real-life caregiving scenarios. Each case represents a unique set of variables to offer a breadth of learning experiences and to capture the reality of caregiving. Each case presents opportunities for you, the healthcare provider, to examine your clinical practice and the experiences of caregivers accompanying the veterans you serve. We hope these case scenarios represent your patients and serve as a bridge between this book and the clinical setting. We encourage you to reflect on your patients and the caregivers that support them and begin to explore opportunities to better serve them.

Case Scenarios

Case Scenario 1

Mary is a 28-year-old married to John, a service member who was deployed to Iraq. After four months into his deployment, John is catastrophically wounded by an explosive formed projectile (EFP), a type of improvised explosive device (IED). Mary was notified within hours of the explosion while John was being medically evacuated. In the meantime, Mary is waiting for further word while also caring for their children, a 3-year-old boy and a 5-year-old girl. Seventy-two hours later, Mary was notified that John will be arriving at one of the Military Treatment Facilities (MTF) that specialized in trauma. Unfortunately, the MTF is 800 miles from their duty station and home. Mary joins John and had to leave their two children with family for the time being. John received catastrophic wounds and he is assigned to the MTF for at least 6 months until he is stable and recovers from his injuries.

Case Scenario 2

Elizabeth is a 28-year-old married to David, a service member who was deployed to Iraq. After 12 months of deployment, John returns home. Mary and their two children, a 3-year-old boy and a 5-year-old girl, are excited and filled with emotion. Finally, John was able to come home and be with his family. A week after John's return from deployment, Mary notices a change in John's behavior. He is irritable and not the same person as when he left. Mary asked John repeatedly if everything was okay, and he insists that all is fine. A year later, Mary and John's family life is adversely affected by John's symptoms that may very well be associated with a number of medical conditions that have not been identified and that Mary and John do not know about (i.e., PTSD, depression, TBI). Mary wants to know more about what is causing her husband's change after his deployment. She asked medical providers, and at first, she wasn't able to get a definite answer. However, Mary was persistent and became John's best advocate, so during a medical visit she engaged the medical provider. Fortunately, John was sent for a full evaluation and diagnosis.

Case Scenario 3

The parents of Charlie received a phone call on June 29, 2009, that changed their lives forever. Their son, a 22-year-old service member was catastrophically wounded by an IED and he was being medically evacuated, but with a slim prognosis of survival. The parents traveled to be at their son's bedside and after 6 weeks, they realized that the long-lasting effects of Charlie's injury will require long-term care and specialized medical equipment and assistance.

Case Scenario 4

Stella has been married to Paul for 45 years. Together, they have three adult children. Paul is a Vietnam veteran and served for 10 years. After military service, Paul worked as an entrepreneur and spent the rest of his adult life in a fruitful career. Paul, now in his early 60s, develops a terminal illness that may be associated with exposures (i.e., environmental, chemical, biological) incurred during his military service. Stella, a professional with a full-time job and not at retirement age, becomes Paul's caregiver. For the next year, Stella and Paul will face a set of challenges that will result in an abrupt change, not only in Paul's health, but also in the couple's financial situation.

Case Scenario 5

David is a young adult and the child of Paul, a Vietnam veteran. David started noticing changes in his father and decided to accompany his father to his various medical appointments. Paul was diagnosed with a neurological degenerative disease that will affect Paul's memory and independence. David knows that his father served in Vietnam but they have never discussed his experience or anything from his time in war. David doesn't know much about the type of benefits his father may be entitled to or even if he was ever evaluated for conditions that are now affecting his health and well-being. David is now faced with more questions than answers and all he knows is that he needs to act quickly given his father's illness.

Reflecting on the previous case scenarios, you may find yourself a bit confused by the difference between all the cases. In some scenarios, the injury required the veteran to be medically evacuated to receive specialized care, while in other scenarios, there was no apparent injury and the veteran exhibited the symptoms post-deployment. Notice that in the examples, the caregivers are a spouse, parents, and an adult child. However, it is possible that you may encounter caregivers that are friends (i.e., neighbors, church members), siblings, and young children. The role of the caregiver will be impacted by the caregiver's access to the MTFs and/or the the VA to accompany the veteran and will also play a role in the caregiver's rights to advocate for the care recipient.

As you contemplate the role of the family caregiver in your clinical practice, we would like to emphasize that the caregiver should be viewed as a vital healthcare resource. Often, it is the caregiver who knows everything that is going on with your patient. Caregivers typically keep track of prescriptions and appointments; which tests are completed or need to be performed; and facilitate communication among doctors on the Veteran's medical team. Additionally, caregivers are usually the ones preventing miscommunication and tracking the majority of paperwork associated with the veteran's care.

These scenarios demonstrate that caregiving isn't one-size-fits-all. Recent studies suggest that military caregivers are assisting veterans with multiple conditions, injuries, and/or illnesses, which adds to the complexity of care for a prolonged period of time that could last decades (Ramchand, 2014; Tanielian et al., 2017). How are we addressing the unique characteristics and needs of the MVC population when compared to other types of caregiving?

Caregivers Assisting Veterans with Polytrauma

Polytrauma occurs when there are injuries to more than one body part or organ system. Polytrauma is frequently associated with blast injuries, but not all individuals with polytrauma have been exposed to a blast. One very common condition in polytrauma is TBI, which frequently occurs together with other disabling injuries, including amputation, spinal cord injury, burns, and neurosensory conditions (e.g., vision and hearing deficits or loss). This complex constellation of injuries results in diverse healthcare needs for the patient and a high level of coordination and integration of clinical care and other support services.

Significant advances in protective gear, medical technology, and development of clinical practice guidelines for combat casualty and en route care ("Joint Trauma System: DoD Center of Excellence for Trauma,") has led to improved survival of U.S. service members who sustained polytrauma in recent combat operations. Recognizing the importance of providing early coordinated and comprehensive rehabilitation services to support recovery from polytrauma, the VA developed a specialized Polytrauma System of Care. The Veteran Affairs Polytrauma program describes its healthcare model as "the hallmark of care for polytrauma is a patient-centered, interdisciplinary approach that works with the injured individual, caretaker, and family to comprehensively address the injury and sequela that affect the injured service member's life" (VeteranAffairs).

When a service member returns home with the signature wounds of war, their spouses and partners provide long-term medical assistance or become companions (Tanielian et al., 2013). As such, family caregivers are affected directly and indirectly. This indirect exposure to trauma has been studied extensively in professional caregivers and clinicians. Past studies have noted how military spouses seem to experience similar symptoms to professional caregivers. When military spouses and caregivers experience cumulative, prolonged exposure to stressors and/or triggers, like the clinician, they also may begin to feel biopsychosocial exhaustion, distress, inefficacy, cynicism, or apathy. Unfortunately, research examining the long-term impacts of caregiving in the military caregiver population that is generally younger and has decades of caregiving in their futures. Prior to Luby (2015), there was a lack of research focused on ways to measure these constructs in the non-healthcare support network of service members. However, Luby identified ways to measure the military caregiver's indirect exposure to combat trauma and operational stress, and direct exposure to deployments, reintegration, and living with veterans with PTSD, TBI, etc. By studying these multiple factors, this research filled a gap in the traumatology literature and led to a better understanding of how these issues affect the overall well-being of this unique population in their roles as military spouse and veteran caregiver.

Health and Well-being Based on a Psychosocial Construct

A multiphase, mixed-methods study focused on spouses in their role as a partner within the service member–spouse dyad and their role as a veteran caregiver. It also looked at a factor not considered in previous studies—the effect of these spouses acting as the social support system to other military spouses and veteran caregivers (Luby, 2015b). The study also compared the symptoms experienced by professional caregivers to nonprofessional/familial caregivers.

The Secondary Traumatic Stress Theory and Compassion Fatigue Model both begin with an indirect exposure to trauma coupled with a therapeutic expression of empathy by the professional caregiver (Figley, 1995, 2002). The degree of empathy experienced increases the risk of the professional caregiver experiencing secondary traumatic stress and compassion fatigue (Bride, 2004; Figley, 1995, 2002). Empathy predisposes a professional who is listening to a client's stories of fear, pain, and suffering to the possibility of feeling similar fear, pain, and suffering (Figley, 1995).

When this logic was superimposed onto the military spouse participants (Luby, 2015b), there was a convergence with constructs found in the compassion fatigue model (Figley, 1995) and secondary traumatic stress theory (Bride, 2004), such as emotional distress, arousal, and social avoidance. However, using both qualitative and quantitative research, a more comprehensive understanding of the spouses' symptoms associated with their roles emerged. There was a divergence that suggested other culturally relevant constructs existed specific to the military spouse participants. Through qualitative feedback, spouses and caregivers expressed distinct differences in their phenomenon to the professional healthcare providers.

Using a three-phase mixed-method process, this study bridged the gaps found in previous mono-method studies. Analysis of the lived experiences helped establish themes and operationalize constructs. The themes helped identify the specific differences between professional and nonprofessional caregivers. For the literature, Luby (2015) originally identified 10 *a priori* biopsychosocial content domains as empathy, secondary traumatic stress, compassion fatigue, psychological distress, burnout, caregiver burden, role strain, social support, social isolation, and quality of life. Items representing these 10 content domains were organized into four distinct components of well-being (psychological, social, spiritual, physical). The lived experiences provided triangulation and authentication of findings in the literature. New items were developed to assess the spouses' and caregivers' specific issues surrounding self-efficacy, exhaustion, emotional separation, and disengagement. Then quantitative tests established reliability and validity to create a new instrument specific to the issues affecting this specific population. Four constructs emerged (role overload, intrusive arousal, social avoidance, emotional distress) using items specific to the nonprofessional caregiver.

As with Figley and Bride's professional caregiver model and theory, the caregiver's expression of empathy to the primary sufferer is influenced by possible risk factors that affect overall health and well-being. However, unlike the trained professional, the untrained nonprofessional caregiver expresses sympathy almost immediately when they step in to help others. Luby (2015) theorizes that unlike the clinician, the spouse is an informal caregiver and lacks the training to disengage and lacks the ability to emotionally distance, or to physically separate, from their family member or friend. While trained empathy may be a protective factor for the unemotional union between professional and client or patient, the untrained caregiver or spouse is predisposed to quickly move from empathy to feelings of sympathy or suffering with another. This risk factor of sympathy and lack of training, coupled with the inability to permanently remove themselves physically and emotionally from the situation, sets the stage for distinguishing, and often more emotionally intense, differences found in spouses from the very beginning of the military spouse helper's interaction with the sufferer (Luby, 2015b).

Current Initiatives and Programs

The following are a sample of current initiatives and programs focusing on family caregivers as critical partners in the plan of care for veteran patients. We hope you will find these resources helpful in your clinical practice as you incorporate the MVC into your team.

Caregiver Experience Journey Map

The Caregiver Experience Journey Map (**Figure 25-1**) is a collaborative work between the Elizabeth Dole Foundation, Philips, and the Department of Veterans Affairs ("Military & Veteran Caregiver Experience Map"). The Caregiver Experience Journey Map provides a comprehensive description of the stages of a military caregiver journey and depicts the significant phases and "landmarks" that may be pivotal in the trajectory of the caregiver.

Understanding the nature of the veteran's medical conditions may benefit not only the patient but also the family members and, in many instances, the caregiver. Evidently, caregivers have been struggling with maintaining a balance between their new role and responsibilities with their own life cycle. The Caregiver Experience Journey Map also describes the impact of the military caregiver journey on the caregiver's psychosocial well-being. The Journey Map provides a snapshot of a caregiver trajectory and important events that may alter the pathway. Healthcare providers can use this tool to identify the caregiver's phase during their trajectory. Additional information about the Caregiver Experience Journey Map can be found at https://caregiverjourney.elizabethdolefoundation.org.

Health Assessment for Loved Ones

The Health Assessment for Loved Ones (HALO; Luby 2015 began from a need's assessment involving community-based participatory research gathered from the perspective of the military spouse. Participants' feedback helped adapt and form culturally relevant items to create a culturally sensitive instrument that truly resonates with those directly exposed to

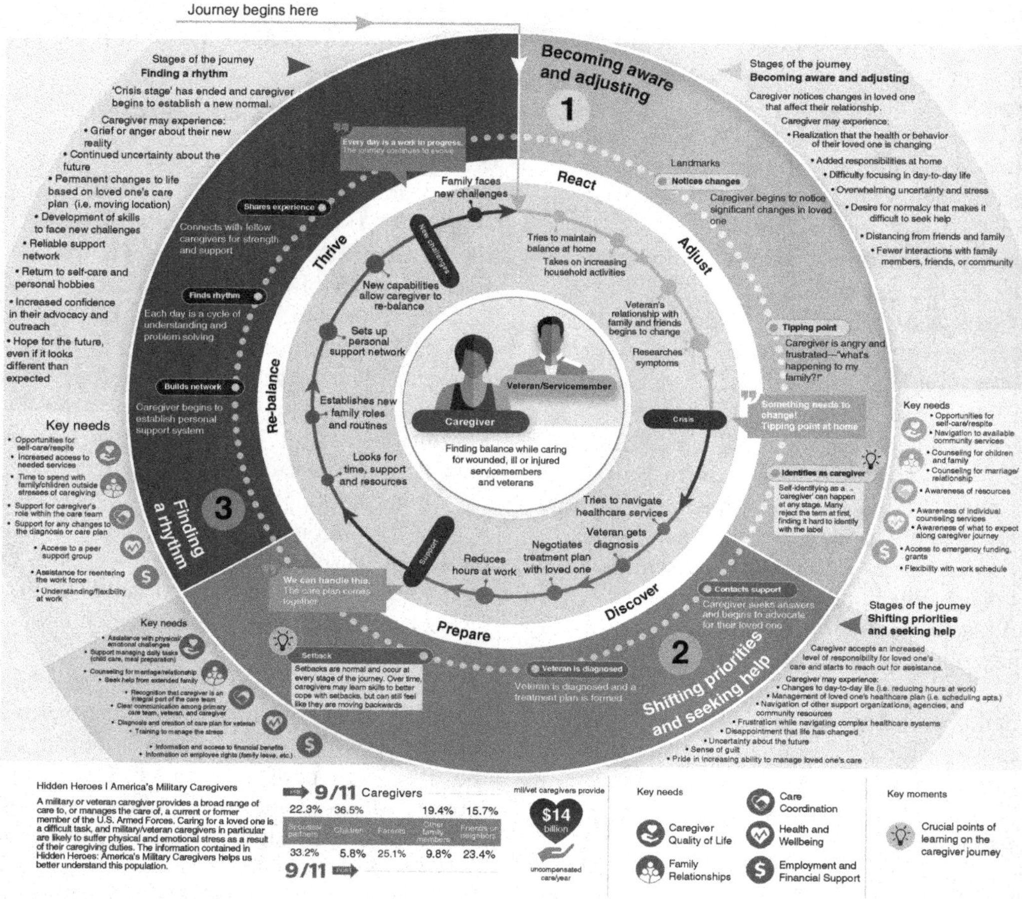

Figure 25-1 Military & Veteran Caregiver Experience Map. A detailed view of the Caregiver Experience Map is available at https://caregiverjourney.elizabethdolefoundation.org/.

deployment and reintegration stress, and indirectly exposed to combat trauma and operational stress. Because this instrument was created by spouses for spouses, the community acceptance has been very promising.

The HALO is a valid and reliable instrument that is easy to take and score. It is not a diagnostic tool but may be used as a self-help tool by spouses and caregivers to build awareness. It may also be used by practitioners to provide trauma-informed care as a complement to current treatment or to evaluate interventions for the nonprofessional and familial populations. The HALO may also be used as a part of a comprehensive care model that involves the spouse being included in the service member's care team and treatment.

The new biopsychosocial framework created from this study uses a wellness approach to health and is grounded in behavioral and public health theories. This adapted theory helps explain familial helpers and caregiver's unique phenomenon and may be used to increase culturally competent preventions and interventions. This new grounded theory provides trauma-informed care to bring awareness of trauma's effect on nonprofessional caregivers and helps to address symptoms, identify possible triggers, and to hopefully prevent the long-term effects of secondary traumatic stress.

Luby's (2015) findings suggest military spouses and veteran caregivers do exhibit similar symptoms to those seen in professional caregivers and first responders, as well as some other specific issues and risk factors. It agrees with Charles Figley's (1995, 2002) and Brian Bride's (2004) early studies with professional caregivers, noting that when empathy and "co-suffering" or sympathy are experienced too often and/or for too long, it leads to apathy, burnout, and compassion fatigue. Therefore, Luby places emphasis on educating nonprofessional caregivers and helpers on the differences between empathy (*imagining the feelings of another*) versus sympathy (*sharing in the feelings with another*), and training spouses to practice empathy.

Luby's (2015) framework uses a strengths-based approach and suggests prevention and interventions should focus on increasing the biopsychosocial assets and protective factors in an effort to decrease the risk factors of helping. Some examples she suggests include developing programs to: (1) teach skills to increase self-efficacy in the caregiving role; (2) provide actual self-care therapy and techniques, not just advisement to *practice* self-care; (3) train caregivers about empathy and how to practice empathy; (4) involve the caregiver from the beginning in a comprehensive care model; and (5) bring continual awareness of the careful balancing of needs—between the helper and those being helped. Through these types of programs, spouses feel supported and understood, which in turn, increases their acceptance and participation in the care of the veteran.

Military spouses and veteran caregivers are the frontline helpers, advocates, and defenders of our nation's defenders. They deserve culturally competent care, and specific resources and support created with them in mind. Spouses and caregivers usually know their service member has been adversely affected long before those serving them and serving alongside them know. They are often an untapped and underutilized asset within the military and veteran communities. By protecting their health, and increasing their well-being, providers automatically better serve those who serve our nation.

Conclusion

Military and veteran caregivers are a valuable asset in the healthcare system. The service MVC provide by assisting wounded, ill, and injured service members and veterans may affect their health and well-being, requiring additional support and resources. Almost three decades of research have demonstrated that caregiving can be stressful and in turn adversely harms both the caregiver and the care recipient. One of the most essential aspects of caregiving is navigating the healthcare system. Healthcare providers can be a source of support to improve the awareness and education among MVC so they can successfully care for the service member and veteran. The resources listed in this chapter are an attempt to focus on the family caregiver as part of the patient's therapeutic plan of care in the clinical setting. The most important clinical practice implication of this chapter is that healthcare providers can change the course of caregiving for both the caregiver and the care recipient by respecting the role that each has in managing ongoing care beyond the classic boundaries of professional patient care.

References

Bride, B. E., Robinson, M. M., Yegidis, B., & Figley, C. (2004). Development and validation of the secondary traumatic stress scale. *Research on Social Work Practice, 14*, 27–35.

Carmassi, C., Corsi, M., Bertelloni, C. A., Pedrinelli, V., Massimetti, G., Peroni, D. G., . . . Dell'Osso, L. (2019). Post-traumatic stress and major depressive disorders in parent caregivers of children with a chronic disorder. *Psychiatry Research, 279*, 195–200. doi:10.1016/j.psychres.2019.02.062

Chwalisz, K., & Stark-Wroblewski, K. (1996). The subjective experiences of spouse caregivers of persons with brain injuries: A qualitative analysis. *Applied Neuropsychology, 3*(1), 28.

Epstein-Lubow, G. (2014). A family disease: Witnessing firsthand the toll that dementia takes on caregivers. *Health Affairs, 33*(4), 708–711. doi:10.1377/HLTHAFF.2012.1351

Figley, C. (1995). *Compassion fatigue: Coping with secondary traumatic stress disorder in those who treat the traumatized*. Brunner/Mazel.

Figley, C. (2002). *Treating compassion fatigue*. Brunner-Routledge.

Gan, C., Gargaro, J., Brandys, C., Gerber, G., & Boschen, K. (2010). Family caregivers' support needs after brain injury: A synthesis of perspectives from caregivers, programs, and researchers. *NeuroRehabilitation*, 27(1), 5–18. doi:10.3233/nre-2010-0577

George, L. K., & Gwyther, L.P. . (1986). Caregiver well-being: A multidimensional examination of family caregivers of demented adults. *The Gerontologist, 26*, 253–259.

Joint Trauma System: DoD Center of Excellence for Trauma. https://jts.amedd.army.mil

Klippel, C., & Sullivan, G. (2018). Older adults as caregivers for veterans with PTSD. *Generations, 42*(3), 41–46.

Luby, C. (2015a). Health assessment for loved ones: Development and validation of a new instrument to measure well-being in military spouses. In E. C. f. U. o. Texas (Ed.).

Luby, C. (2015b). *Health assessment for loved ones: The development and validation of a new instrument to measure well-being in military spouses*. Open Access Theses & Dissertations. 1093.

Malik, A. A., Mohsin, S., Azam, N., Pervaiz, F., Sharif, A., Younis, F., & Mahmood, H. (2019). Frequency of depression and general mental health among primary caregivers of disabled persons with blast injuries: a cross sectional study. *Pakistan Armed Forces Medical Journal, 69*, S187-S193.

McLaughlin, C., McGowan, I., Kernohan, G., & O'Neill, S. (2016). The unmet support needs of family members caring for a suicidal person. *Journal of Mental Health, 25*(3), 212–216. doi:10.3109/09638237.2015.1101421

Military & Veteran Caregiver Experience Map. https://caregiverjourney.elizabethdolefoundation.org

Ramchand, R., Tanielian, T., Fisher, M. P., Vaughan, C. A., Trail, T. E., Epley, C., Voorhies, P., Robbins, M.W., Robinson, E. & Ghosh-Dastidar, B. (2014). *Hidden heroes: America's military caregivers*. http://www.rand.org/pubs/research_reports/RR499.html:

Razani, J., Kakos, B., Orieta-Barbalace, C., Wong, J. T., Casas, R., Lu, P., . . . Josephson, K. (2007). Predicting caregiver burden from daily functional abilities of patients with mild dementia. *Journal of the American Geriatrics Society, 55*(9), 1415–1420. doi:10.1111/j.1532-5415.2007.01307.x

Sander, A. M., Boileau, N. R., Carlozzi, N. E., Hanks, R. A., & Tulsky, D. S. (2019). Emotional suppression and hypervigilance in military caregivers: Relationship to negative and positive affect. *Journal of Head Trauma Rehabilitation*. doi:10.1097/HTR.0000000000000507

Schulz, R., & S.R., B. (1999). Caregiving as a risk factor for mortality: The Caregiver Health Effects Study. *Journal of the American Medical Association, 282*(23), 2215–2219.

Tanielian, T., Bouskill, K. E., Ramchand, R., Friedman, E. M., Trail, T. E., & Clague, A. (2017). *Improving support for america's hidden heroes: A research blueprint*. https://www.rand.org/pubs/research_reports/RR1873.html

Tanielian, T., Ramchand, R., Fisher, M. P., Sims, C. S., & Harris, R. (2013). *Military caregivers: Cornerstones of support for our nation's wounded, ill, and injured veterans*. http://www.rand.org/pubs/research_reports/RR244.html: Rand Corporation.

Tooth, L., McKenna, K., Barnett, A., Prescott, C., & Murphy, S. (2005). Caregiver burden, time spent caring and health status in the first 12 months following stroke. *Brain Injury, 19*(12), 963–974. doi:10.1080/02699050500110785

VanHoutven, C. H., Miller, K. E. M., O'Brien, E. C., Wolff, J. L., Lindquist, J., Kabat, M., . . . Voils, C. I. (2017). Development and Initial Validation of the Caregiver Perceptions About Communication With Clinical Team Members (CAPACITY) Measure. *Medical Care Research and Review*, 1–23.

VeteranAffairs. (n.d.). *Polytrauma/TBI system of care: What is polytrauma*? Retrieved from https://www.polytrauma.va.gov/understanding-tbi/definition-and-background.asp

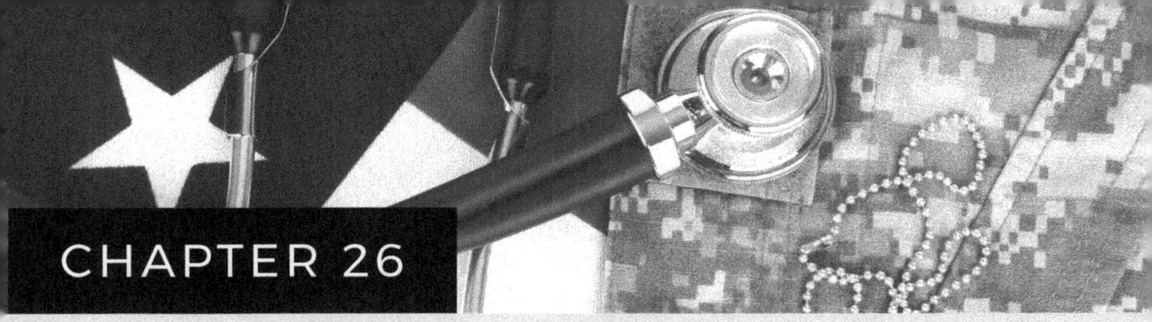

CHAPTER 26

Supporting the Sidelines: Encounters with Stress and Loss Related to Military Service

Jeanne Grace

Encounters with Stress: Stressors for Military Members and Families

The military experience has impacts far beyond those on the individuals who serve. Immediate family members, other relatives, and the community of service colleagues are also affected. The exemplar military stressor is the risk of death or injury in combat; however, the actual stressors and risks are broader, more frequent, and much more complex. Exposure to those stressors and to the resources intended to mitigate them varies according to the circumstances of each person in the service member's support network.

Between 2006 and July 1, 2020, 17,645 U.S. service members died while on active duty. Of that number, 4,577 died as a result of hostile action in combat zones. Ninety-three percent of the remaining deaths occurred in the United States. Over 31% of all deaths resulted from accidents and 24% resulted from self-inflicted injuries (Mann & Fischer, 2020). Since 2015, deaths during training exercises have exceeded combat deaths each year. (Annenberg, 2018; Ritchie, 2018) An analysis of military deaths from 1980 to 2010 concluded that only logging and commercial fishing were more hazardous occupations than military service (Planes, 2018). Data from the Bureau of Labor Statistics (2019) and Department of Defense (2020a) suggest this remains true.

Most of the data on potentially permanently disabling injuries comes from combat theater operations. Between October 7, 2001, and July 28, 2015, over 52,000 service members were wounded in action. Based on the experience in Operation Iraqi Freedom, about 15,000 of those injuries were likely severe enough to require medical evacuation to Europe or the United States for treatment.

A similar number of medical evacuations were required for non-hostile injuries in the same theaters over the same time period (Goldberg, 2010). More than 1,600 service members experienced amputation of an arm or leg because of a battle injury. Across both combat and non-combat settings, more than 8,000 service members received severe or penetrating traumatic brain injuries (TBI). More than 39,000 service members not previously deployed and more than 138,000 service members deployed to combat theaters had at least two clinic visits or a hospitalization with post-traumatic stress disorder (PTSD) as the diagnosis (Fischer, 2015).

Thus, no military assignment can be considered totally safe. Family members need to find a way to balance their respect and support for their loved one's choice to serve against their concerns about the risks that service engenders. Often, family members will rationalize that their loved one is safer than others because of their skill level, prior experience, or particular assignment. This rationale is disrupted by combat zone deployments or when a service colleague in the same unit is injured or killed, regardless of location. In the words of one spouse, "that was real tough, because then it was real" (Lapp, et al., 2010).

Deployment to a combat zone poses additional stressors, particularly on the service member and their immediate family. In 2018, 51.5% of active duty service members were married (Department of Defense, 2019a). Family relationships are altered when one member of the family unit is no longer in residence. During the pre-deployment period, all family members share uncertainty about the specific leave date and are engaged in tasks of preparation. When the deployment occurs, a new normal emerges on the home front as the remaining spouse takes on previously shared responsibilities. Meanwhile the deployed member establishes a new "family" of colleagues in a dangerous place and focuses on the mission, while trying to maintain engagement with family at home (Wood et al., 1995). The deployed member may suffer moral injury as a result of combat experiences or enacting policies perceived to be unjust. The possibility that they may return with PTSD is a legitimate concern for both the deployed member and their family. The transforming experiences of the deployed family member, as well as the experiences of their family members during the absence, make it likely that no family member is quite the same person at the end of deployment as when it started. When the deployed service member returns, family roles must be renegotiated and the mutual transformations acknowledged (Yablonsky et al., 2016) Many families report that the first three months after reunion are the most stressful part of the deployment cycle (Lester & Flake, 2013). These stressful experiences, moreover, recur through multiple deployments.

Almost 38% of service members are parents, and 62% of them have children between birth and five years old (Department of Defense, 2019a). When the family includes young children, the non-deployed spouse has increased parenting duties. These include helping children stay connected with the absent service member, recognizing the ways in which children express their stress, establishing caring routines, taking care of oneself, nurturing, and managing reunification (DeVoe & Ross, 2012; Zero to Three, 2008). The impact of parental absence on children depends on their developmental stage. Infants and toddlers are apt to express their feelings of disruption and distress through regression and other altered behaviors (Zero to Three, 2008). Forty-seven percent of military parents have school-aged children (Department of Defense, 2019a). During parental absence this age group is more apt to exhibit initial anxiety, depression, and school difficulties; however, most then adjust and display more independence and responsibility (Lester & Flake, 2013). In a study of Army families with a member deployed to a war zone, younger age of the at-home parent predicted increased parental and school-aged child stress

(Flake et al., 2009). All children will pick up on the stress of the remaining parent (O'Grady et al., 2018)—hence the importance of parental self-care and extra-family supports.

Deployment has an additional impact for children with a single parent or two active duty parents who are both deployed. Often, these children are sent to live with grandparents or other relatives, disrupting usual routines, school, friendships, and health care. The additional burdens on these temporary caregivers are added stressors. Extended family may also be called on to provide additional support when a non-deployed spouse chooses to relocate from a military base to live with family during the deployment. Family supports are more available, but the support services provided through the military base are less so.

For families of Reserve and National Guard members, deployment is less predictable in timing and duration. Multiple deployments of Guard or Reserve units to combat zones is a 21st-century phenomenon. Members come from scattered, often rural, communities and "soldier" is not their primary identity. They experience the additional stress of disrupted civilian employment or education (Blow et al., 2017). Non-deployed spouses have described the pre-deployment period as having lives "on hold" and reported loneliness during the deployment because they lacked community peers living the same experience (Lapp et al., 2010).

Service members also experience noncombat temporary assignments (TDY) away from their home base for training and other purposes. These may result in family separations that last up to a year. Although families have less concern about the service member's safety during this sort of temporary duty, the family dynamics are otherwise similar to those of combat deployments. The at-home partner "pulls double duty" and children react to a missing parent.

Whether or not active duty military families experience combat zone deployments or TDYs, they will experience duty reassignments or permanent changes of station (PCS). These are typically on a three-year cycle and involve relocation from one military base to another. These moves can be across the United States or to or from an overseas assignment. These frequent relocations may impede the civilian spouse from developing their own career or even finding consistent employment. Families heading to or returning from overseas postings face significant waits before their household goods and vehicles are available. Some returnees report culture shock as they re-encounter American civilian life.

Military families with children move three times more often than civilian families (AASA, the School Superintendents Association, 2019). Military children are faced with developing new friendships and meeting the expectations of different school systems on a regular basis. When children attend an on-base school, their peers have had similar experiences and are accustomed to accepting newcomers. Almost 80% of military children, however, attend U.S. public schools, where the response may be less informed or welcoming (AASA, the School Superintendents Association, 2019).

When military service ends, anticipating and reentering civilian life brings its own stressors. Although service members have developed valuable attitudes and skills, they must figure out how to apply their experience to civilian opportunities for employment or further education. Housing, finances, and health care must be arranged, and relocation is often involved. When the veteran has a service-related health condition, Veterans Administration care and civilian care need to be coordinated.

Military Impact on Coping Strategies

In classic stress-coping theory, coping is defined as an individual's constantly changing cognitive and behavioral efforts to manage specific demands appraised as potentially exceeding one's resources. Coping is preceded by, and is a response to, cognitive appraisal of a situation relevant to well-being. Primary appraisal assesses the risk (i.e., what is at stake in the situation). Secondary appraisal assesses what can be done about the risk. Subsequent research has classified the many cognitive and behavioral strategies people may use to respond to those appraisals and to attempt to reduce their stress into systems of general categories. These systems focus on the target of the coping strategy (problem, emotion, appraisal) or whether the strategy is active or avoidant (Folkman & Moskowitz, 2004). Individuals tend to use different strategies depending on the nature of the primary and secondary appraisal and the severity of the stress. Different types of strategies may be used simultaneously or sequentially (Folkman et al., 1986).

Military service presents unique challenges to coping strategies. For service members and their families, the public is personal. Governmental policy decisions determine the need for and nature of deployments and thus the everyday activities of service members. Federal budget decisions about maintenance, training, and equipment impact service member safety, and the quality of life for immediate family members. Key aspects of some stressful military situations are out of the control of the persons affected, resulting in secondary appraisal that the situation cannot be altered. This, in turn, limits the coping strategies available to manage the resulting stress.

Military families are a minority cultural group in the United States. In June 2020, there were slightly more than 1,360,000 active duty military service members and 800,000 members of the Reserves and National Guard (Department of Defense, 2020a; Department of Defense, 2020c). Together with their

Box 26-1 Examples of Coping Strategies

Problem-focused—addressing the problem causing stress

- Making a plan of action
- Concentrating on next step
- Seeking instrumental support
- Gathering additional information about the problem, seeking advice
- Confronting others to change situation
- Avoidant—behavioral disengagement

Emotion-focused—easing the negative emotions associated with the stressor (can be active or avoidant)

- Seeking emotional support
- Humor
- Self-control—keeping feelings to oneself
- Avoidant—emotional disengagement, denial, use of drugs or alcohol or food to feel better, distraction to avoid thinking about stressor

Meaning-focused—cognitive strategies used to manage the meaning or threat potential (primary and secondary appraisal) of the situation

- Determining causes
- Seeing opportunities for growth in adversity
- Positive reinterpretation
- Drawing on values, beliefs, and goals in face of chronic stressor

Data from Folkman, S., & Moskowitz, J. T. (2004). Coping: Pitfalls and promise. *Annual Review of Psychology, 55*, 745–774. https://doi.org/10.1146/annurev.psych.55.090902.141456

immediate families, they comprise only 1% of the U.S. population. In June 2020, roughly half of the active duty military personnel stationed in the United States were concentrated in four states: California, Virginia, Texas, and North Carolina (Department of Defense, 2020b). Military personnel and families living on base or in nearby communities have easy formal and informal access to peers who understand their situation and can provide instrumental and emotional support. Extended family members living elsewhere—for example parents and siblings of the service member—may be the only ones in their social circles with a current military connection. Seeking out peers for emotional support requires more effort and intentionality.

Kuo (2011) summarized the ways cultural group membership can be expected to impact coping. Cultural beliefs influence primary and secondary appraisal, the appropriateness of various coping mechanisms, and what institutional mechanisms are seen to be helpful. For close-knit groups such as military units, the desired goals of coping are survival of the group as well as reduction in individual stress. Military families take care of each other. In that context, however, hesitancy to socialize above one's rank may limit social support for service members and their families. Cultural ideals of service members and families as strong and resilient may cast stigma on persons seeking help, especially from institutional sources.

Studies of coping during deployment generally identify the ability to maintain communication with the deployed family member and keeping busy at home as helpful strategies (Lapp et al., 2010; Wood et al., 1995; Zero to Three, 2008). Individuals vary in the other coping strategies they find most helpful. Avoidant coping strategies are often associated with poorer mental health and family relationship outcomes (e.g., (Blow et al., 2017). In a study of Israeli Defense Force members and spouses (Desivilya & Gal, 1996), however, researchers identified a subset of couples who were task-oriented and not particularly introspective. Both spouses addressed military vs. family conflicts with avoidant coping and were judged to be well-adjusted as families Lapp et al. (2010) identified spouses of deployed National Guard members who benefited from family group websites and those who preferred to restrict their incoming information.

Opportunities to Assess Health Needs

Active duty military and their dependents who are seeking civilian health care can be identified by their TRICARE health insurance. National Guard and Reserve members and their dependents, as well as retired service members and their dependents may also be covered by various TRICARE products or by the U.S. Family Health Plan. Extended family members do not have identifying insurance but may seek care for anxiety or stress-related somatic symptoms related to their concerns about their military family member. New problematic behaviors in military children and teens should raise the question, "What has changed in this child's life?" Rossiter and associates have developed the *I Serve 2: A Pocketcard for Healthcare Providers Caring for Military Children* (see Chapter 23) to assist pediatric healthcare providers in identifying and assessing the unique needs of children in military families (Rossiter et al., 2018).

Resources

The Armed Services provide many supportive resources to members and their families, including on-base confidential counseling, family life activities, and electronic newsletters for extended family members and friends. There is content specific to each of the uniquely military stressors discussed in this chapter. The services are described and accessible via https://www.militaryonesource.mil.

During World Wars I and II, families displayed service flags with a blue star for each member serving in one of the branches of the military. That image carries forward in the identification of families that include a service member as Blue Star Families. Blue Star Mothers of America is a nonsectarian, nonprofit organization that offers social support for mothers of sons or daughters on active duty in, or honorably discharged from, the U.S. military. There are multiple local chapters with regular meetings in most states (see https://www.bluestarmothers.org). Fathers and family associates are also welcome.

Zero to Three is a mental health advocacy group for infants and children. Their resources for military and veteran families include downloadable apps and videos. https://www.zerotothree.org/parenting/military-and-veteran-families-support

Military REACH is a group of human development and family studies scholars who appraise research of interest to professionals working with military families. The output includes TRIP (translating research into practice) critical appraisals of military family research studies, research briefs, and "best practices" comprehensive reviews of selected narrowly focused topics (see https://militaryreach.auburn.edu/#/).

Encounters with Loss: Bereavement and Grief

The death of any individual has far-reaching and long-lasting impact on all the close relationships in that person's life: spouse/partner, children, parents, siblings, and potentially close colleagues as well. Bereavement may be understood as the state of having lost a significant other. Grief denotes the emotional and physical responses to bereavement. These responses include initial emotional numbness, shock or disbelief, followed by distress about separation from the lost loved one, yearning to be reunited, intrusive thoughts about death, and preoccupation with memories of the deceased. Anger, sadness, despair, and sometimes guilt and loss of interest in life may also occur. Physically, grief may manifest with inability to sleep, loss of appetite, intense fatigue, and disorganization of daily routines (PDQ Supportive and Palliative Care Editorial Board, 2017). These responses may also occur when the loss is severe disability, rather than death.

For most persons, the symptoms of grief are initially intense and cause some impairment of social, work-related, or other aspects of the bereaved person's life. Over time, grief symptoms typically become less intense, occur less frequently, and result in less disruption of everyday living. This period of reorganization, or creating a "new normal," typically takes between six months and two years (PDQ Supportive and Palliative Care Editorial Board, 2017). Members of the deceased's immediate family are called on to make both emotional and instrumental adjustments to the absence of their loved one. Extended family members may experience less instrumental impact on their activities of daily living, but their emotional loss is still profound.

While terms like *closure* and *getting over it* are often used, bereavement is better understood as a chronic condition. One need only listen to aging World War II veterans talk about their comrades who never came home to understand that the loss remains. Just like the newly diagnosed type 1 diabetic, the newly bereaved person puts much emotion and effort into managing symptoms and the altered circumstance of their life. With successful use of coping strategies, over time, bereavement becomes a part of the background pattern of everyday life, rather than the focus of all attention. There is some evidence that successful coping strategies cycle between those oriented to managing the loss and those aimed at restoration (mastery of the "new normal"; Folkman & Moskowitz, 2004). There will be foreseeable and unexpected exacerbations, when grief symptoms return and require more attention, but there will also be new occasions for relationship and joy.

Box 26-2 Lessons Learned from Loss—One Mother's Experience

1. You must find a way to forgive your loved one for dying.
2. You must find a way to forgive the world for going on without your loved one.
3. You must find a way to forgive yourself for going on without your loved one.
4. Nos. 1, 2 and 3 are processes, not one-time accomplishments. Some processes take more work than others, depending on the circumstances and survivor.
5. Beyond the physical loss of my loved one, I most fear he will be forgotten. When you talk to me about him and we share memories, I know part of him lives on in your heart. Written memories, especially ones that I did not share, are particularly precious.
6. When my loved one died, the loss was the major context of my life for several months, even after I returned to work and social activities. Any encounter with people who might or might not know was exhausting because of its ambiguity. It was very helpful when such encounters were resolved right away with "I heard. I'm so sorry. I've been thinking about you."
7. It may seem to you that my loss is the perfect illustration of God's will, the need for federal budget reallocations, the effects of environmental pollution or the need for gun control. I may eventually find a similar meaning. But my loss is fundamentally the loss of the person who is my loved one. Please keep your agenda off it.
8. Ann Finkbeiner (1996) says that "nothing is normal about the loss of a child." Parents do what they do—and what they do varies widely—because it seems like the only thing to do at the time. She's right.
9. Don't be afraid of talking about my loved one for fear of reminding me of my loss. Trust me, I haven't forgotten. See No. 5 above. There is a special place in my heart for those who continue to acknowledge his birthday and death date.
10. Cooperating with the press in coverage of the loss is like taking a ride on the back of a tiger. Your agenda and the press's agenda are not the same. Sometimes, both agendas can be met and you come back from the ride still on the back of the tiger. But there's always the risk that only the press agenda will be met, and you'll come back inside the tiger.
11. Bereavement is not a competition event and degree of personal tragedy cannot be ranked like the difficulty of ice-skating jumps. Every loss is personal and very individual. How can you possibly know "exactly how I feel" when I'm not even sure all the time how I feel?
12. From a bereaved colleague: "Don't ask me how I'm doing unless you're prepared to hear the truth."
13. Managing the grief symptoms of bereavement is physically exhausting! When I could anticipate having to deal with some aspect of my loss (e.g., reviewing paperwork, dispositioning personal effects), I learned to keep my schedule light for the rest of the day.
14. Anniversaries do not represent closure. At some level, I believed that if I grieved "well" through the first year, I'd get bereavement "time off" for good behavior. As a friend said, "I thought I'd stop crying after the anniversary." The day after the first anniversary of my loss, my child was still dead. Getting through the "firsts" just assures you that you will probably survive the "seconds" and "thirds," too. Bereavement usually gets more manageable over time: experience and practice do help.
15. There is no "perfect" way to observe holidays and milestone dates, so feel free to maintain traditions or go in new directions. Just don't agonize about the choice. See No. 8 above.
16. When I first read parent accounts of the loss of a child, I was surprised to note how little one parent wrote about the grief experience of the other parent. I understand that now. The most difficult grief to be present to is borne by the people I love most. I cannot tell you how my husband and surviving children are coping, only that they seem to have found a way. Hopefully, we can grieve in whatever way works for each of us without increasing each other's pain.

Dr. Grace's oldest son, Capt. William "Bill" Grace, USAF, died in an aviation training accident.

Unique Aspects of Bereavement for Military Families

The death of an active duty service member, either by hostile action or accident, is likely to be either violent or unexpected—circumstances that qualify as a triggering event for PTSD whether directly witnessed or happening to a significant other (American Psychiatric Association, 2014). Bereavement involving a traumatic death does not necessarily cause the survivors to experience PTSD, but it does challenge any belief that the world is a safe and predictable place (Finkbeiner, 1996).

For survivors of a military casualty, the personal becomes public. Mourning—the public expression of grief—will be a matter of community-wide interest. Families attempt to plan disposition of the body and remembrance rituals consistent with their culture and religious background and appropriate to honor the spirit of their lost loved one. They will also face community expectations for what constitutes appropriate military recognition and may be involved in military rites inconsistent with their own beliefs. Multiple agendas are in play. The bereaved family wants their loved one to be remembered. The media want to present a narrative that engages their audience. The military command wants to re-inspire military colleagues and families to maintain their endeavor. The civilian community wants to express general gratitude for those who have chosen military service. Sadly, hate groups may also see a military funeral as a publicity opportunity for their viewpoints.

For the purposes of providing military honors and family benefits, the Armed Forces distinguish at least three categories of military death not caused by a preexisting medical condition. Highest consideration goes to service members killed serving in combat, during an international terrorist attack, or as part of a peacekeeping force. The next level of consideration is for other deaths occurring to persons while on active duty ("line-of-duty") or during National Guard/Reserve training. The final level is deaths related to the service member's misconduct, for example drunk driving. Survivor benefits are adversely affected by this determination. Self-inflicted deaths may be judged either "line-of-duty" (service-related aggravation of a preexisting condition) or the result of the deceased's own misconduct (Secretary of the Air Force, 2015).

Residence on base or in a nearby community allows surviving dependents of active duty casualties access to institutional supports, including bereavement counseling, and also to associates who knew the deceased and share their loss. Current Armed Forces policy allows families situated on a domestic base to remain in federal housing or continue their housing allowance for up to a year. Children of deceased service members can remain in base schools until graduation or family relocation (Department of Defense, 2015).

Extended family of active duty casualties and families of deceased National Guard or reserve members are more likely to live in communities unfamiliar with the military knowledge or terminology that was so central to their loved one's life and death. Media reporting errors that result can increase the bereaved family's sense of isolation from their civilian neighbors.

Assessing for Further Mental Health Needs

Uncomplicated grief is a human condition, not a mental disorder. When significant impairment in daily living continues for an extended period following the death of a significant other, assessment for complicated/prolonged grief, major depression, or PTSD is indicated. Assessment and differential diagnosis may be appropriate after as little as one month post-loss, since traumatic bereavement can trigger an episode of major depression or PTSD, concurrent with uncomplicated grief.

A consensus group of psychiatrists proposed that prolonged or complicated grief be included as a recognized disorder in the most recent update of the *Diagnostic and Statistical Manual of Mental Disorders* (DSM-V). The hallmarks of this disorder are yearning for and preoccupation with the deceased loved one, severe or increasing emotional pain, difficulty accepting the death of the loved one and inability to experience positive mood. "Prolonged" has been proposed as the persistence of these symptoms as disabling disrupters of usual social and work activities for either six months or one year, with the further understanding that the persistence of symptoms is beyond what is culturally appropriate for the bereaved person. The prevalence of this disorder is estimated at one in ten mourners (Lundorff et al., 2017)

Complicated/Prolonged grief disorder was only included in DSM-V as a potential diagnosis requiring further study. However, the note cautioning against diagnosing major depressive disorder within two months of bereavement was removed (Bryant, 2014). Depression and grief can coexist. They can be distinguished from each other by pattern, ability to experience positive feelings and benefit from social support, content of thoughts, and impact on self-esteem. In a major depressive episode, negative emotions are constant, not triggered by any specific thoughts. The depressed person cannot anticipate happiness and withdraws from sources of social support. There is a general feeling of worthlessness and hopelessness, driving suicidal thoughts. In contrast, the sadness and pain of grief tends to come in waves, triggered by thoughts of the deceased. Grieving persons can experience pleasant emotions and socialize to receive support. Their self-esteem is generally intact. Any intrusive thoughts are specifically about the lost person, and any thoughts of death are specific to being reunited with that person (Kavan & Barone, 2014). The differentiation of major depression from grief is important for treatment. Pharmacological treatment with antidepressants is more effective in reducing depression symptoms than it is in reducing grief symptoms. Effective complicated/prolonged grief therapies include several manualized cognitive approaches (PDQ Supportive and Palliative Care Editorial Board, 2017).

Effective therapies for complicated/prolonged grief have much in common with effective therapies for PTSD. The two disorders can be distinguished from each other on the basis of core symptoms, emotional valance, and duration since the traumatic event. Primary complicated/prolonged grief disorder symptoms are bittersweet thoughts of, and yearning for, the lost significant other. Primary PTSD symptoms are intrusive, consistently negative thoughts about the traumatic triggering event. These thoughts lead to a state of hyperarousal and threat, and avoidance of stimuli associated with the traumatic event. The diagnosis of PTSD can be made within a month of the triggering event's occurrence. By contrast, the response to the bittersweet thoughts of complicated/prolonged grief disorder is predominantly sadness at loss, and the minimum duration for diagnosis is six months of continued almost daily disability (Maercker & Znoj, 2010).

Supports for Grieving

The service flags that contributed to naming Blue Star Families had gold stars for family members who died in military service. The Armed Forces officially recognize only families of those killed in combat, by terrorism, or during peacekeeping missions as Gold Star Families. The voluntary organizations for bereaved family members are more inclusive. American Gold Star Mothers welcome all mothers (birth or adoptive) whose sons or daughters died while on, or as a result of, active duty or who are missing in action. Fathers and other relatives are welcomed as associate members. There are local chapters and an annual weekend gathering in Washington, DC (see https://www.goldstarmoms.com).

Gold Star Wives is an organization with similar objectives for widows and widowers of persons who died while serving in the Armed Forces or as a result of injuries incurred during that service. In addition to peer and child supportive services, members advocate legislatively for military survivor benefits (see https://www.goldstarwives.org).

There are multiple Gold Star Family groups. Some adhere to the military definition, welcoming only survivors of service members who died from hostile action. Others accept survivors of service members who died during a period of declared conflict, regardless of cause of death. Still others share the open approach of the Gold Star Mothers and Gold Star Wives groups.

Each branch of the Armed Services provides immediate support to survivors following the death of a service member by means of an assigned casualty assistance officer. Long-term case management services are provided as needed via service-specific survivor outreach programs. The Department of Defense provides contact information for military and non-military sources of support via Military OneSource. Three resource guides are

- *A Survivor's Guide to Benefits: Taking Care of Our Families*, https://www.militaryonesource.mil/products#!/detail/149
- *The Days Ahead, Essential Papers*, https://www.militaryonesource.mil/products#!/detail/33/the-days-ahead–essential-papers–english-version (Also available in Spanish: https://www.militaryonesource.mil/products#!/detail/35/the-days-ahead--essential-papers-spanish-version)
- *National Resource Directory*, https://www.nrd.gov/ (Comprehensive guide for services for service members, families, and veterans, as well as survivors.)

References

AASA, the School Superintendents Association. (2019). *Fact sheet on the military child.* https://www.aasa.org/content.aspx?id=8998

American Psychiatric Association. (2014). *diagnostic and statistical manual of mental disorders* (5th ed.). American Psychiatric Association.

Annenberg, M. F. (2018, June 24). U.S. military training nearly four times deadlier than combat. https://www.ozy.com/acumen/us-military-training-nearly-four-times-deadlier-than-combat/87491

Blow, A. J., Bowles, R. P., Farero, A., Subramaniam, S., Lappan, S., Nichols, E., . . . Guty, D. (2017). Couples coping through deployment: Findings from a sample of National Guard families. *Journal of Clinical Psychology, 73*(12), 1753–1767. doi:10.1002/jclp.22487

Bryant, R. A. (2014). Prolonged grief: Where to after Diagnostic and Statistical Manual, Edition 5? *Current Opinion in Psychiatry, 27*, 21–26. doi:10.1097/YCO.0000000000000031

Bureau of Labor Statistics. (2019, December 17). *Hours-based fatal injury rates by industry, occupation, and selected demographic characteristics, 2018.* https://bls.gov/iif/oshcfoil.htm#rates

Department of Defense. (2015). *A survivor's guide to benefits. Taking care of our families.* https://www.militaryonesource.mil/products#!/detail/149

Department of Defense. (2019a). *Profile of the military community—2018 demographics.* Department of Defense. https://www.militaryonesource.mil/data-research-and-statistics/military-community-demographics/2018-demographics-profile

Department of Defense. (2019b). *The days ahead: Essential papers for families of fallen service members.* https://www.militaryonesource.mil/products#!/detail/33/the-days-ahead--essential-papers--english-version

Department of Defense. (2020a, June 30). *Active duty military strength by service.* https://www.dmdc.osd.mil/appj/dwp/dwp_reports.jsp

Department of Defense. (2020b, June 30). *Number of military and DoD Appropriated Fund (APF) civilian personnel permanently assigned by duty location and service/component.* https://www.dmdc.osd.mil/appj/dwp/dwp_reports.jsp

Department of Defense. (2020c, June 30). *Selected Reserve personnel by Reserve component and rank/grade.* https://www.dmdc.osd.mil/appj/dwp/dwp_reports.jsp

Desivilya, H. S., & Gal, R. (1996). Coping with stress in families of servicemen: Searching for "win-win" solutions to a conflict between the family and the military. *Family Process, 35*, 211–25.

DeVoe, E. R., & Ross, A. (2012). The parenting cycle of deployment. *Military Medicine, 177*(2), 184–190.

Finkbeiner, A. K. (1996). *After the death of a child: Living with loss through the years*. Simon and Schuster.

Fischer, H. (2015). *A guide to U.S. military casualty statistics: Operation Freedom's Sentinel, Operation Inherent Resolve, Operation New Dawn, Operation Iraqi Freedom, Operation Enduring Freedom*. Congressional Research Service. https://sttc.brictly.com/file/4768af8865780f20.pdf

Flake, E. M., Davis, B. E., Johnson, P. L., & Middleton, L. S. (2009). The psychosocial effects of deployment on military children. *Journal of Developmental and Behavioral Pediatrics, 30*, 271–278.

Folkman, S., & Moskowitz, J. T. (2004). Coping: Pitfalls and promise. *Annual Review of Psychology, 55*, 745–774. doi:10.1146/annurev.psych.55.090902.141456

Folkman, S., Lazarus, R. S., Dunkel-Schetter, C., DeLongis, A., & Gruen, R. J. (1986). Dynamics of a stressful encounter: Cognitive appraisal, coping, and encounter outcomes. *Journal of Social and Personality Psychology, 50*(5), 992–1003.

Goldberg, M. S. (2010, April). Death and injury rates of u.s. military personnel in Iraq. *Military Medicine, 175*(4), 220–226.

Kavan, M. G., & Barone, E. J. (2014, November 15). Grief and major depression—controversy over DSM-5 changes in diagnostic criteria. *American Family Physician, 90*(10), 693–694. http://www.aafp.org/afp

Kuo, B. C. (2011). Culture's consequences on coping: Theories, evidences, and dimensionalities. *Journal of Cross-Cultural Psychology, 42*(6), 1084–1100. doi:10.1177/0022022110381126

Lapp, C. A., Taft, L. B., Tollefson, T., Hoepner, A., Moore, K., & Divyak, K. (2010). Stress and coping on the home front: Guard and Reserve spouses searching for a new normal. *Journal of Family Nursing, 16*(1), 45–67. doi:10.1177/1074840709357347

Lester, P., & Flake, E. (2013, Fall). How wartime military service affects children and families. *The Future of Children, 23*(2), 121–141.

Lundorff, M., Holmgren, H., Zachariae, R., & Farver-Vestergaard, I. (2017). Prevalence of prolonged grief disorder in adult bereavement: A systematic review and meta-analysis. *Journal of Affective Disorders, 212*, 138–149.

Maercker, A., & Znoj, H. (2010). The younger sibling of PTSD: Similarities and differences between complicated grief and posttraumatic stress disorder. *European Journal of Psychotraumatology, 1*(1), 5558. doi:10.3402/ejpt.v1i0.5558

Mann, C. T., & Fischer, H. (2020, July 1). *Trends in active-duty military deaths since 2006*. https://fas.org/sgp/crs/natsec/IF10899.pdf

O'Grady, A. E., Whiteman, S. D., Cardin, J.-F., & Wadsworth, S. M. (2018, April). Changes in parenting and youth adjustment across the military deployment cycle. *Journal of Marriage and Family, 80*, 569–581. doi:10.1111/jomf.12457

PDQ Supportive and Palliative Care Editorial Board. (2017, April 20). *Grief, bereavement, and coping with loss. Health professional version*. https://www.cancer.gov/about-cancer/advanced-cancer/caregivers/planning/bereavement-hp-pdq

Planes, A. (2018, October 3). *Dying for a paycheck: These jobs are more dangerous than military service*. https://www.mysanantonio.com/business/fool/article/Dying-for-a-Paycheck-These-Jobs-Are-More-5320369.php

Ritchie, E. I. (2018, May 14). Training kills more troops than war. Here's what's being done about it. *Orange County Register*. https://www.military.com/daily-news/2018/05/14/training-kills-more-troops-war-heres-whats-being-done-about-it.html

Rossiter, A. G., Patrician, P. A., Dumas, M. A., Ling, C. G., Johnson, H. L., & Wilmoth, M. C. (2018). I serve 2: Identifying and caring for military-connected children in civilian primary care settings. *Journal of the American Association of Nurse Practitioners, 30*(11), 614–618. doi:10.1097/jxx0000000000000084

Secretary of the Air Force. (2015, October 8). *Air Force instruction 36-2910 line of duty (LOD) determination, medical continuation (MEDCON), and incapacitation (INCAP) pay*. http://static.e-publishing.af.mil/production/1/af_a1/publication/afi36-2910/afi36-2910.pdf

Wood, S., Scarville, J., & Gravino, K. S. (1995, Winter). Waiting wives: Separation and reunion among Army wives. *Armed Forces and Society, 21*(2), 217–236.

Yablonsky, A. M., Barbero, E. D., & Richardson, J. W. (2016). Hard is normal: military families' transitions within the process of deployment. *Research in Nursing and Health, 39*, 42–56. doi:10.1002/nur.21701

Zero to Three. (2008). Young children on the home front. https://www.zerotothree.org/parenting/military-and-veteran-families-support

PART V

Preparing Professionals to Care for Service Members, Veterans, and Their Families

CHAPTER 27 To Know Them Is to Care for Them Better: Educating Healthcare Providers on Caring for Veterans 457

CHAPTER 28 It Starts with One Question—Have You Ever Served? 471

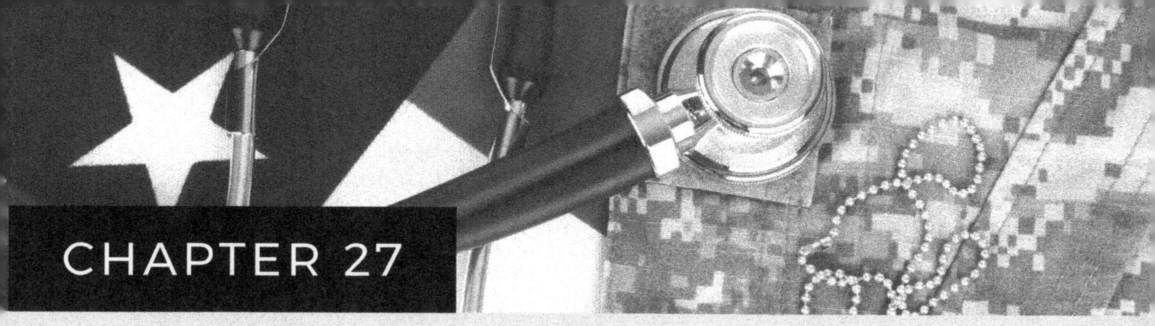

CHAPTER 27

To Know Them Is to Care for Them Better: Educating Healthcare Providers on Caring for Veterans

Kent D. Blad and Tracy Dustin

The question is asked: How many have a veteran in their family, among friends, or in their neighborhood? A safe guess would be that there are very few out there who do not know or who have not been impacted by a veteran. Because of this fact, most healthcare providers will, at some point in their careers, care for these wonderful heroes in our veteran patients.

There probably is not a veteran in existence where their service did not impact their life forever, in one way or another. There is a large difference between treating active military personnel and veterans with service associated injuries and wounds, as compared to treating civilians in our populations.

Having cared over many years for World War I, World War II, Korea, Vietnam, and Gulf War (Operation Desert Shield/Storm) veterans, as well as many veterans from the current conflicts, the authors will share many lessons and pearls of wisdom that have been gleaned through their practice in this chapter. Each conflict, each war, brings with it a distinct set of healthcare challenges for those who have served. Healthcare providers must be aware of how to care for these varying needs and challenges, both seen and unseen. Because of the small percentage of impact of the current conflicts on our nation's population, a generation of care providers exists where very few have ever been exposed to the horrors of war. If current healthcare providers are not made aware of how best to care for our veterans, the nation will have a population of patients that will not receive optimum care. This chapter will discuss details on establishing an undergraduate level education program targeted toward caring for veterans. Specifically, this chapter will discuss the process of initiating a program within health care based on caring for the veteran patient, including appropriate resources needed to do so. In addition, material on integrating student learning activities into a healthcare program that will achieve the appropriate student learning outcomes related to caring for this population of veterans will be presented.

Introduction to the Program

The authors of this chapter initiated an educational program specifically designed to teach nursing students about caring for the veteran patient. The material in this chapter can easily be translated to any healthcare discipline caring for the veteran patient. This program was designed as a semester-long course that involves senior-level nursing students. This program involves both classroom and clinical components that aid in teaching students how to best care for the veteran patient. The premise of this course is to present the diversity and culture of our veteran patients. Funding for this program is provided by tuition monies, through student fees, mentoring grants, and often by very generous donors. The clinical settings in which we present are in local and rural areas. Also, the program includes a nine-day field experience in Washington, D.C., with students and faculty. It culminates and concludes with a three-day Honor Flight to Washington, D.C., where students serve as guardians or escorts to an individual veteran. The credit hours for this course are a total of 6 credit hours. The didactic portion is 2.5 and the clinical portion is 3.5 credit hours.

The foundation of the program is based solely on the veterans themselves, with the culture of the military and veterans being a major component. A motto was created for this course, which states: "To know them is to care for them better." We also institute the motto that the VA Healthcare Administration uses, which is from Abraham Lincoln (Gettysburg Address): "To care for him who shall have born the battle and for his widow, and his orphan." In this course students must learn the long-term impact of military service on a veteran's life and health.

The focus is on presenting the veteran's experience and health issues, which must become humanized and become real to these students. Most nursing students have never had exposure to veterans to this point in their young careers. Therefore, the goal of this program is to have participants learn to understand the veteran and their culture to provide more competent nursing care in any facility or healthcare setting. Emphasis is placed on the point that veterans are a different population and have different issues that affect their lives and needs for appropriate health care.

Veterans penetrate all healthcare systems. Of the approximate 18 million veterans in the United States (United States Census Bureau, 2018), only half actually receive care through the VA healthcare system. There are approximately nine million veterans who get their care at other facilities across the nation (U.S. Department of Veterans Affairs, 2019). No matter where a healthcare provider serves in their career, caring for veterans is a distinct reality.

The student learning outcomes or objectives of this program are twofold. First is to prepare participants to better care for the veteran patient by understanding the unique healthcare needs of that population through providing direct clinical-related experiences with the veteran patients. The second goal is to culturally prepare students to better care for the veteran patients through exposure to health, cultural, and sociopolitical elements of the veteran population.

Student Learning Activities

Many student learning activities, assignments, and requirements are present in this program. Besides attendance in class, veterans themselves are used to educate, rather than textbooks. The goal is to provide individual and group meetings and interviews with many veterans of various wars and conflicts, presenting unique healthcare challenges faced from each conflict. Among current warriors and veterans, the most common healthcare issues are post-traumatic stress disorder (PTSD) and other mental health conditions, which include suicide, traumatic brain injury (TBI), and amputations and polytrauma..

The following is a partial list of a variety of learning activities used over the years to educate students on veterans:

1. As part of this program, students are introduced to the culture of the military, using a training module called the Military Cultural Awareness Training (MCAT), produced by the U.S. Department of Veterans Affairs (2012). The MCAT is a series of modules on military cultural training. These modules of cultural training include an introduction to the branches of the military, to the service members and veterans, to different military conflicts and disaster support, as well as introducing students to ranks and titles and military customs. Included are a pre-test and a post-test that are available in written format as well as online.
2. Included in course learning activities, students get many opportunities to teach each other. Individual students research and report on many military-related items, including various military conflicts of the United States and various Veteran Service Organizations (VSOs). Each student is required to put their research in brochure format and present their research and the brochure at an appropriate time. See example that follows.
3. Students do a cultural appreciation media activity such as viewing a film on the military or history, viewing a play, reading a book, or whatever media they choose related to veteran culture and then report to each other on a summary of the activity and lessons learned through the experience.
4. Students research and report on a veteran's memorial in Washington, DC, in preparation for visiting those memorials later in the semester. See example that follows.
5. Students are required to do a reflective writing assignment at the end of the program. The student shares in their reflective writings the impact of this program and what has been gained in learning how to best care for the veteran patient. See template that follows.
6. In order to assess cultural competence, a clinical and cultural skills evaluation tool is used to ensure that students understand the importance of this culture. See template that follows.
7. Students also are required to meet and interview a veteran of their choice and, while in Washington DC, present the story of that particular veteran and lessons learned from meeting with their veteran.
8. As a culminating learning activity experience, students, in small groups (2–3 students per group), prepare and design scholarly products, such as podium presentations, poster presentations, and journal articles that are of professional quality. Many of those are submitted, accepted, and presented at professional meetings.

Clinical Experiences

Students complete 147 clinical hours during the course of this program. Included in the clinical hours are any time spent with a veteran in a cultural or clinical setting. Clinical experiences are widely varied and include any setting where veterans receive health care. Students spend time in a variety of clinical settings that are unique to the veteran's healthcare needs. The following are settings that have been used for this educational experience:

1. VA PTSD and mental health clinics, which are very unique to our veteran healthcare system.

2. Amputation clinics and physical therapy units for those individuals who have experienced amputation.
3. Motorized wheelchair clinics.
4. Homeless veteran clinics.
5. State veteran homes.
6. Wounded warrior transition units.
7. Rural community hospitals. Over 25 percent of Utah's veterans live in rural counties (Utah Department of Health, 2018). Students have gone to rural community hospitals to help care for these veterans.
8. The VA system contracts with hospice agencies to do home visits. Students learn valuable lessons about the importance of caring for veterans at the end of life.
9. As a culminating experience in our clinical settings, Students participate in an Honor Flight event. Honor Flight is a national organization that was started in 2005 and is dedicated to providing a veteran with honor and closure. The goal of the Honor Flight is to take veterans to Washington, DC, especially World War II, Korea, and Vietnam veterans, to experience their memorials and to be honored for their service. There is an Honor Flight hub in most states. For Utah, the Honor Flight, because of the distance to Washington, DC, is a three-day excursion where a one-on-one guardian attends to each veteran. Students serve as guardians for an individual veteran. Often that veteran is a family member of the student, which increases the impact of that experience and lessons learned by the student.

Program Field Experiences

During the course of this program, our students participate in many field experiences, where exposure to individual and groups of veterans is made a focus. Within the state of Utah, students are accompanied to rural, suburban, and urban settings to meet, interview, and have discussions with individual veterans as well as panels of veterans. Wherever a veteran can be found, meetings and experiences are set up for the sharing of the veteran stories and pearls of wisdom. As an example, the following advice was presented to students by a World War II veteran who met with this course of students during a field experience:

> My name is Lester Dean Lee. In the Army, I was a Staff Sergeant. Students enrolled in the nursing program need to realize that it is a different ball game when caring for the needs of most veterans. The unseen wounds with which many veterans are afflicted require nursing care of a special nature involving the deeper understanding of the psychic nature of a veteran who has come face to face with the unthinkable horrors of war. So, in addition to compassion, to empathy, nurses need to strive to find ways and means to treat unseen wounds. A nurse will need to know: 1. the extent of the burden which a veteran carries like a yoke around the neck as a result of his or her military experience; 2. the ease or difficulty experienced in adjusting from military to civilian life; and 3. how happy or unhappy he or she is with life at the present time (L.D. Lee, personal communication, 2012).

Continuing with field experiences, students travel to and participate for 8–9 days in Washington, DC, in a variety of experiences. While there, students are exposed to and immersed as much as possible in the military and veteran culture there. The following includes activities that have been experienced, based on availability, that help in educating students in caring for veterans:

1. A visit to Walter Reed National Military Medical Center, where our current Wounded Warriors (ill or injured) reside,

exposes our students to the sacrifices made by our servicemen and-women.

2. A visit to the Washington, DC, VA Medical Center and the War-Related Injury and Illness Study Center, where research is being done with the heroes of our nation, teaches students about current research and the needs of our warriors.
3. A visit to Arlington National Cemetery allows students the opportunity to lay a wreath at the Tomb of the Unknown Soldier.
4. A visit to the many memorials at Arlington National Cemetery allows students to present their research about each memorial to other students in the class. That becomes a very powerful and impactful experience as these students see the sacrifice that has been made by many veterans throughout the years.
5. A visit and tour of the Pentagon allows students to learn about the headquarters of our U.S. military.
6. A meeting with a Utah senator or house representative on Capitol Hill gives students the opportunity to discuss what is currently being proposed and presented as far as legislation to help care for our veterans.
7. A visit to the VA Central Office, a cabinet position for the secretary of the VA, allows students to meet with the chief nursing officer of the VA System and her assistants who present what healthcare options and programs are available for veteran patients.
8. Many of the veteran memorials and museums that honor our nation's heroes are visited to further educate students on U.S. veteran history.
9. A very unique opportunity exists each year where students meet with a Holocaust survivor and hear a presentation of that survivor's experience. Students are allowed to ask questions of the Holocaust survivor, to experience during that meeting how the American military played a part in bringing freedom and liberty to those people.
10. A tour of the capitol of the United States is given, where various symbols and military history are discussed.
11. Students also are given the opportunity to take advantage of various war sites around the area. Civil War sites in Gettysburg, Pennsylvania, and a visit to Fort McHenry, Baltimore, Maryland (the birthplace of "The Star Spangled Banner"), help to bring a visual reality to students learning about our nation's military history in defending freedom.

Available Resources

What resources are available to initiate this type of a program? Where can one find information on caring for our nation's veterans? Many valuable resources exist at each of our Veterans Administration (VA) hospitals, outpatient clinics, and facilities. VA facilities are located in every state in the nation and in most major populated cities. The VA provides very unique clinical experiences for students, including PTSD and mental health clinics, which are very few in our civilian clinics and hospitals. Other unique clinical opportunities include polytrauma clinics, prosthetic clinics, amputation clinics, motorized wheelchair clinics, and others that teach many unique healthcare needs about our Wounded Warriors that have experienced healthcare issues in the combat setting. Another valuable resource is the Office of Academic Affiliations, which provides a military health history guide for clinicians that can be found at https://www.va.gov/oaa/pocketcard/overview.asp. This guide is used to help train and educate providers on appropriate questions to ask when addressing various healthcare issues from the varying wars and conflicts over the years.

How does one contact the VA? Appropriate contact would go through the Human Resources department of any VA facility, asking for the individual in charge of non-paid WOC (without compensation) students. The individual will provide guidance on where and how to go about having students placed in that facility. Paperwork and training are required before students are placed.

Volunteer Opportunities

Many volunteer opportunities exist for students to work with and serve our veterans. In searching for volunteer veteran service opportunities, the www.va.gov (search "volunteer") website provides multiple resources that are available in communities. The following are examples, among many, of available resources for service and volunteering:

1. Stand Down for the Homeless: Stand Downs are typically one- to three-day events providing supplies and services to homeless veterans, such as food, shelter, clothing, health screenings and VA Social Security benefits counseling. These take place at over 200 locations across the United States.
2. Fisher Houses: places that house veteran families, while the veteran (or active military) is in the hospital.
3. Federal and state veteran cemeteries: many service projects can be done at veteran cemeteries to help beautify the grounds, especially at times such as Memorial Day and Veterans Day. Veteran families deserve a beautiful place of peace and solace as they have paid the ultimate sacrifice.
4. *Still Serving* (ssv.org): a website with veteran service opportunities available. The site also contains a video program that looks at vets who are still serving vets. Many ideas are presented for opportunities to give back.
5. Veteran Service Organizations (VSOs): Currently there are over 100 VSOs that are recognized by the VA. The list of these organizations is lengthy and can be found at https://www.va.gov/vso. These provide many opportunities for service. Examples of common veteran service organizations include the American Legion, Veterans of Foreign Wars, Disabled American Vets, Iraq and Afghanistan Veterans of the US, Purple Heart, Medal of Honor, Wounded Warriors, and many others.

Finding Veteran Opportunities

Where can one find veterans to meet with, talk to, share stories, and help educate students? Many resources and places exist that can help in accessing veterans to meet with and visit with participants. Veterans can be found through family members, friends, people in our neighborhoods, and coworkers. In addition, the following can provide opportunities for meeting veterans to present to students:

1. VA facilities: provide access to veterans from a wide variety of wars and cultures.
2. VSOs: these organizations are all dedicated to veterans and their causes. Many of them are run by and populated by veterans. These provide a valuable resource for finding speakers to present and share with individuals or groups in the classroom or smaller settings.

Additional Veteran Educational Resources

Many additional educational resources exist that can help in initiating or maintaining a curriculum on veteran culture and care. Within nursing organizations, there are many veteran care resources, such as written materials, webinars, video clips, etc. Those organizations include the American Association of Colleges of Nursing, the American Association of Nurse Practitioners, the American Organization of Nurse Executives, the

American Nurses Association, the National League for Nursing, the office of Nursing Services with the VA system, and the VA Nursing Academy.

Lessons Learned

As faculty teaching veteran material to a variety of students over many years, the authors have learned many lessons in creating and maintaining a successful veteran course. What has been done that works best in meeting the educational outcomes of a veteran-related program? What learning activities impact the student the most about caring for veterans in a healthcare setting? The most important lesson learned, which has had the biggest impact on students, has been that of continuous contact with the student and veterans. Students enter this program knowing very little about veterans and exit knowing much more. This contact creates a strong knowledge base for the student, but more importantly, a strong passion to help care for veterans. Students gain an understanding and appreciation for another's culture outside of their own, which has a very positive impact on providing care of those in that culture. In addition, students learn that not only do the cultural concepts apply to veterans, but also those same concepts and learned lessons can transfer to patients of any culture. Having witnessed on many occasions, students are never the same for the better, after being exposed to our nation's heroes and learning the make-up and characteristics of these individuals. Other valuable lessons learned include the following:

1. The goal of a veteran program is never to make students experts on veterans, but advocates. Students are to be veteran advocates, not experts.
2. The key to this program's success is immersion. Immerse students in the veteran culture at all times and in all places, as much as possible.
3. Expose students as much as possible to veterans as individuals and in groups. Use individuals and groups of veterans as the textbook for the program. With every veteran that dies, a library closes, use them while available.
4. Rather than having faculty do all of the lecturing and teaching, have students do much of the teaching and leading discussions with each other as much as possible. Allow students the opportunity to do the research on the various wars/conflicts, veteran healthcare issues, veteran memorials, or anything related to veterans.
5. Have student assignments within the program include many presentations to the class by students in the class.
6. Have presentation assignments include handouts that have been produced by the students which can be shared with fellow students, as well as future classes. Students have also been known to share those handouts at family events and other events in group settings.
7. Listen to students each time about ways to make improvements in the program for the future.
8. With so many factors that go into a program like this, be flexible with learning activities and schedule, knowing that perfection is not always achievable.
9. Use resources that are already available, don't reinvent, and don't think that you need to reinvent. Use resources presented in this chapter. As a veteran program is initiated and put in place, resources will become more readily known and made available.
10. Listen to students about activities that make the greatest impact and maintain that in the curriculum from course to course. Survey students often, verbally and written, on what is working or not. Maintain those things that they say work and eliminate the items that don't have an impact. In summary, make changes

as needed to a veteran program as it is taught.

11. Always remember, as much as students can be exposed to veterans and immersed in the culture, the more successful the program will be.

To put it into perspective from a student's point of view who completed this program, the following story is shared from Shannon Reynolds (2014). Her story is an example of the impact that the outcomes of this program can have on those that complete it. The main lessons learned from this course are shared in the story.

> I started doing home health medications for a gentleman named Bob. And the lady that offered me the job, the lady that helped me get the job, and the nurse that took me to Bob's house the first time all warned me that Bob hated new people, he wouldn't even look at me, he wouldn't smile, he'd hold his g-tube just so I wouldn't give him medications. He just hated everybody new. That's what I was told. So I was really worried going into it, just unsure of how he would approach this situation, and how I should approach this situation. But I went to his house with another nurse who showed me around and surely enough he glanced at me when I walked in and looked away. I was like, "okay, I expected that." And then as we were preparing the medications, I noticed a photo above his television of a veteran and I asked the nurse if he was a veteran. She quickly said, "No." I explained that I was wondering because of the picture on the top of the TV. She said, "That's not Bob," and then she looked at the picture a little more closely and then said, "Actually, I don't know, I've never asked him." So this nurse has been working with Bob for a year, he had had a stroke that left him with an inability to speak. He can nod his head yes or shake his head no and that was about it. When we were giving Bob his medications, I said, "Bob, are you a veteran?" and he looked at me and smiled and nodded his head. So this is the first time I've met him and he's smiling at me and looking at me and so I went on to ask him about which branch he served in, asking yes or no questions. Did you serve in the Marines? In the Navy? It turns out he served in the Army. I just asked him more about it and tears came to his eyes and I asked him if he had served overseas. I told him that we would talk about it later. I told him I would be back the next day to give him his medications. When I was leaving, he grabbed my hand and looked at me and smiled again. The nurse and the aide that were there were just shocked, saying, "He never smiles at anybody or grabs anyone's hand ever!" And so they were just amazed and from that time forward, Bob and I were really dear friends. Each time I went he would smile, he would grab my hand. And I just loved spending time with him and I loved when I got to give him his medications. And it was all because of that one question that I had asked, it was because I had shown interest in him and because I knew more about our veterans that I was able to care for him better and that I was able to come closer to him as a patient and as a person. It made a complete difference in the care that I gave to him both from what I did for him and also what he did for me. It changed my life and I'm hoping that I made some kind of impact on his. A couple of months later, he got super sick. He was switched to hospice care

and I was with him the night before he passed away and I was able to sit with him for a few hours and hold his hand and be there for him while he suffered and struggled. It was a really tender experience to do that and to just be with him when he needed it the most; and really, it all goes back to that one question. It goes back to that; by understanding our veterans we can care for them better. We can make that connection with them and they can change our lives and we can help change theirs.

Transitioning from Combat to Classroom

In concluding this chapter, the question is asked: What happens if one has a veteran as a student in the classroom? How does one approach them? Do they get treated any differently than the normal everyday student or do they get treated the same?

In transitioning from combat to the classroom, unique challenges in the veteran student exist. Many that have served in a combat or military environment have an extreme challenge to assimilate back to civilian life. In addition, many faculty or staff do not understand the issues that veterans face after serving in such an environment. Faculty need to have an increased knowledge about the needs of these veterans. The need is to remember that the wounds of war, visible or invisible, that some veterans experience make adjustment back to civilian life much more difficult. The other important concept to address is that no veteran that has ever served is not impacted by that service, for the better or the worse, for the rest of his or her life. Their service and experience cannot be erased, so they do need to be cared for differently.

What faculty competencies are needed in order to help these veterans as they transition into the classroom? Training programs exist to help healthcare faculty to actualize veterans to the classroom. Those programs are highly recommended to any teachers in this situation. One program is named the Green Zone Training (GZT), with the reference listed here (Nichols-Casebolt, 2012). Any are welcome to access that reference in order to implement that training into a program. Another training, with the outcomes being equal, is the Got Your Six program (D'Aoust et al., 2016. These are excellent programs that have been implemented and tested to train healthcare faculty in having veteran students in the classroom. From the research, faculty need to 1. be competent in having an appreciation for the contributions of our veterans to our society, 2. care about and have empathy for veterans, and 3. faculty need to be team players and include veterans in the teaching team as these curriculums are taught. Faculty need to be trust builders, with a level of trust between these veterans and those that come in contact with them. In summary, faculty are asked and expected to become as culturally competent as possible about veterans and the military culture.

Continuing with the concept of combat to classroom, what are unique characteristics about veteran students? Veteran students do not need a lecture on maturing into an academic setting as do the younger students that are coming out of high school or soon thereafter. If the veteran student is currently on active duty or reserves, then flexibility is needed with assignments and deadlines due to their military requirements. Faculty are encouraged to listen to the student's ideas on how they, the veteran student, can be successful while considering their military work experience, especially if it is in the medical field. Many of our healthcare veteran students have been medics or in other healthcare fields in the military. That experience, real-world experience, can be very valuable as they learn in our programs.

A presentation exists, *15 Things Veterans Want You to Know for Healthcare Providers*, on a website (https://www.youtube.com/watch?v=5rPFsX-saBM) that is very valuable for any that are learning about military culture or teaching veteran students in a classroom environment. The concepts presented were gleaned from surveying many veterans about their service. This presentation emphasizes 15 things that veterans want you, as healthcare providers or teachers, to know about military culture. The concepts introduced apply to students and faculty about any that have served in the military. In any setting, a conversation can be initiated with the following in mind. The following is a summary of those 15 things that veterans want you to know:

1. We are not all soldiers. So, ask the veteran, what branch did you serve in? Soldiers refer to a member of the Army. The Navy are sailors. Marines like to be called marines. A member of the Air Force is an airman. And a member of the Coast Guard is a guardian.
2. The Reserves are a part of the military. The Reserves and the National Guard have been used frequently, most recently in our conflicts in Afghanistan, Iraq, the Middle East, and other places. They are a very valuable part of the military.
3. Not everyone in the military is infantry. Not everyone carries a weapon. Not everybody shoots the weapon. Therefore, an appropriate question would be: What did you do in the service? What was your assignment? For every infantryman carrying a weapon, man or woman, there are at least five individuals in support roles of that one infantry.
4. Leadership is very important to the veterans. There are leaders at every level in the chain of command. They are very used to a chain of command and being able to use their supervisors and that chain to achieve results.
5. We as veterans are always on duty. There are times when we cannot get our service or our experience out of our minds and we have that sense of duty and are always on the lookout for the need to protect.
6. We take pride in our appearance and conduct. The military has a very strict code of conduct and dress code and so on. Be appreciative of that.
7. We do not all kill someone, and those who have don't necessarily want to talk about it. So that is not something that you would want to ask or bring up with our veterans in our military unless they choose to bring it up.
8. We do not all have PTSD. Yes, PTSD is a major concern among our military and our veterans. Currently the PTSD rate is about 11–20%, but outside of that, not every military member suffers from PTSD.
9. Those of us who do have an invisible wound are not dangerous and we are not violent.
10. Often it is really hard for us to ask for help. In the military, often asking for help is considered a sign of weakness and the mission of the military is that of others and mission before self.
11. Our military service changes us for life and that's okay. As I mentioned earlier, there is no one that has served in the military that forgets about that service and it will affect them for the rest of their lives for the better, or for the worse.
12. We differ in how much we identify with the military after we leave active duty. So maybe you ask the veteran: How has your military service shaped you? With veteran students, take the time to care or simply ask some of these questions. By doing so, you will develop that trust that is so important in a relationship with that student.
13. Our families served with us. Our families are the unsung heroes, and families have to learn the power of flexibility, bravery, strength, and resilience that help define us and our military families.
14. We would die for each other and we would die for our country. We would and

we do. So be appreciative of the sacrifice that is made by these individuals who have been willing to put their lives on the line for our freedoms.

15. We've all made this sacrifice for one reason: to serve something more important than ourselves.

If these concepts are understood and realized, the teacher will be in tune with the students that have served in the military or might be currently serving.

In summary of this chapter, a couple points need to be re-emphasized. Veterans penetrate all healthcare facilities across the United States. Only one third of veterans seek their health care in VA facilities; two thirds get their health care in all other private or public facilities. Military culture and healthcare are very unique and need to be understood in order to better care for veterans. If any are to better care for veterans, a better understanding of these individuals and their culture is crucial. Immerse and expose students to veterans. Veterans have unique needs when transitioning from a military to an academic setting.

References

Blad, K. & Ulberg, R. (2017). N404/N390R *Syllabus: Advanced public and global health: Nursing care of the veteran patient clinical sections*. BYU College of Nursing, Provo, UT. (found in AACN Joining Forces Toolkit).

Carlson, J. (2016). Baccalaureate nursing faculty competencies and teaching strategies to enhance the care of the veteran population: Perspectives of the Veteran Affairs Nursing Academy (VANA) Faculty. *Journal of Professional Nursing*, 32(4), 314–323.

D'Aoust, R. F., Rossiter, A. G., Itle, E., & Clochesy, J. M. (2016). Got your six: Supporting veterans' move into professional nursing. *Nursing Education Perspectives*, 37(6), 340–342. doi:10.1097/01.NEP.0000000000000081.

Moss, J. A., Moore, R. L., & Selleck, C. S. (2015). Veteran competencies for undergraduate nursing education. *Advances in Nursing Science*, 38(4), 306–316. doi:10.1097/ANS. 0000000000000092.

Nichols-Casebolt, A. (2012). The green zone: A program to support military students on campus. *About Campus*, 17(1), 26–29. doi:10.1002/abc.21070.

Sikes, D., Francis-Johnson, P., Jones, M. M., Opton, L., Casida, D., Allen, P. E. (2018). Actualizing veterans' education in nursing. *Journal of Professional Nursing*, 34, 189–194.

United States Census Bureau (2018). *Veteran status.* https://data.census.gov/cedsci/table?q=veteran&g=&table=S2101&tid=ACSST1Y2018.S2101&lastDisplayedRow=30&mode=

U.S. Department of Veterans Affairs (2012). Military Cultural Awareness Training (MCAT). VA Learning University, Washington D.C.

U.S. Department of Veterans Affairs (2019). *Veterans Health Administration*. https://www.va.gov/health/aboutvha.asp

Utah Department of Health (2018). *Rural Veterans Health Access Program*. https://ruralhealth.health.utah.gov/rural-veterans-health-access-program-rvhap/

Voelpel, P., Escollier, L., Fullerton, J. & Rodriquez, I. (2018). Transitioning veterans to nursing careers: A model program. *Journal of Professional Nursing*, 34, 272–279.

Appendix

Culture Practicum Skills Assessment

Type: Student completed
Due: Mid-experience **and** End of experience
Points:

The purpose of the practicum cultural skills evaluation is to guide students in understanding the principles and skills they should be learning during this term to become a culturally competent nurse. This is a self-reflective process. At the end of their cultural practicum experience, students should have made progress and have met minimal levels of the following skills. **It is suggested students should have at least two bullet points listed in "Improvement Plan."**

Culture Skill	Mid-term Progress: Strength	Mid-term Progress: Weaknesses	Improvement Plan (2 bullet points)	Progress
Identifies and articulates cultural needs and beliefs				
Asks appropriate questions to understand culture and beliefs				
Adapts and provides care that is culturally appropriate when working with people				
Provides cultural-specific information (teaching-using translation services, as appropriate)				
Respects and distinguishes differences of opinion, values, and/or practices. (does not stereotype, recognizes ethnocentrism)				
Strives to provide culturally competent care as Christ would.				

(Based on Purnell's Model for Cultural Competency and King's and Baxter Magolda's Intercultural Maturity Model)

Final Reflective Writing

TYPE: Individual
DUE: **Monday, June 17, 11:59 pm**
POINTS: 100

Expected Learning Outcome

The purpose of this assignment is to allow students to reflect on their experiences and identify how they have impacted learning and life, helping to internalize what they have learned. Reflective self-assessment and writing is an excellent lifelong skill to develop and use for self-improvement and analysis. Students will analyze and synthesize their experiences during this course and how the lessons they learn from those experiences apply to current and future nursing practice.

The assignment will be accomplished through a series of steps.

1. Review the reflective writing questions (below) prior to practicum and cultural experiences in GHHD.
2. Seriously consider the reflective writing questions during practicum and cultural experiences. Carrying around a notepad may be helpful to record your thoughts and impressions.
3. Identify the impact that these experiences have on your personal values and future nursing practice.
4. Paste the question at the beginning of each response.
5. Respond in writing to each of the five reflective writing questions by describing experiences and impressions, assessing your understanding and growth, and applying lessons learned.
6. Polish writing to present it professionally.

Reflective Writing Questions

1. Analyze the most meaningful **cultural** experience you had in this course and the impact it will have on your future nursing experience in providing culturally competent care to populations different than your own (including populations who have lower socio-economic status, less educated, diverse race/ethnicity, religion, and other social determinants).
2. Articulate and analyze the most meaningful **nursing** experience you had in this course related to public and global health (within individuals, family, and communities), and how it will impact your current and future nursing practice and lifelong learning goals.
3. Evaluate how your **attitudes** (personal, professional, spiritual, etc.) toward your population of interest have changed as a result of your experiences in this course and how these changes will impact your current and future nursing practice and personal life.
   a. How will it impact your outlook on advocacy, creating social change and how you will provide service and care to those in need?
4. As you reflect on your public and global health experience and your previous reflective answers, evaluate and synthesize your understanding of the healer's art as it relates to global health and human diversity and empowering others.

Commonly Asked Questions Regarding the Reflective Writing

To whom am I writing?

Your audience is you and your faculty member. Your writing should be clear, concise, and professional. Your reflections may be shared in other forums, such as N400 orientations, College of Nursing publications, etc.

Do I need to use APA format?

You may want to incorporate ideas or information from your reading assignments. If so, please use APA formatted citations and references, but you do not need to use APA headings, title page, abstract, etc.

What length should my paper be?

The length of the entire reflective writing assignment should be five to six pages, double-spaced. Responses to each question should be one to two pages, double-spaced.

Reflective Writing Grading Rubric

Content	*Incomplete Response (0–79%)*	*Satisfactory Response (80–89%)*	*Comprehensive Response (90–100%)*	*Points Earned*
Description of Experience(s) Related to Reflective Writing Questions 1, 2, 3, 4	Incomplete description of experience(s) **0–12 points**	Satisfactory description of experience(s) **12–16 points**	Comprehensive description of experience(s) **17–20 points**	____/20
Analysis to questions 1, 2, 3, 4	Incomplete evidence of critical examination of experience(s) **0–21 points**	Satisfactory evidence of critical examination of experience(s) **22–26 points**	Comprehensive evidence of critical examination of experience(s) **27–35 points**	____/35
Reflection on questions 1, 2, 3, 4	Incomplete evidence of purposeful contemplation and learning **0–21 points**	Satisfactory evidence of purposeful contemplation and learning **22–26 points**	Comprehensive evidence of purposeful contemplation and learning **27–35 points**	____/35
Mechanics and Format	Many errors and much rework needed **0–6 points**	Minimal errors and writing could be more concise or clear **7–8 points**	Free of errors and writing is concise and clear **9–10 points**	____/10

TOTAL POINTS: ________/100

COMMENTS:

CHAPTER 28

It Starts with One Question—Have You Ever Served?

Rita D'Aoust, Linda Schwartz, and Alicia Rossiter

Over the past decade, the U.S. Congress enacted two key legislations—the Veterans Access, Choice, and Accountability Act (2014) and the MISSION Act (2018) to improve access of care for veterans within the Veterans Administration (VA). In response, the VA expanded the use of community-based provider networks to ensure veterans receive timely and accessible health care. In 2017 alone, the VA reimbursed community providers for 19 million veteran claims for care (GAO, 2019). Recent estimates imply that more than 30 percent of veterans receiving care through the VA used community-care (Mattocks et al., 2021). This is a significant shift as prior to these legislations, nearly all care was provided at a VA setting. Recent reports indicate that one in three veterans receive some type of care in community-based provider networks (Mattocks et al., 2021).

The Congress and the VA realized the success of expanding care to the civilian sector and the urgent need to expand this community care option. In an attempt to reduce veteran wait and travel times, Congress authorized $10 billion in funding to expand and streamline this access to community providers and healthcare services (GAO, 2019). By fiscal year 2021, the VA estimates that at least 1.8 million veterans would elect to use community care (GAO, 2019). As this trend has steadily increased, it clearly illustrates that community care is and will continue to be a vital resource in the continuum of care for America's veterans.

While the expansion of access to care is an improvement, there are concerns that this transition and the complex cultural and occupational needs of America's military and veterans' populations would be overlooked. Military service has many unknown challenges, dangers, and exposures to hazardous agents and environments (Collins et al., 2013). As troops return from deployments and seek care in the community, concerns continue to emerge about the special occupational and culturally specific healthcare needs of this population. Initially, approved community-based providers experienced delays with the VA managing claim adjudication and reimbursements. The VA has diligently addressed the backlog and delays in order to meet veteran access needs.

Community Health Care Providers (CHCP) may be unfamiliar with the complexities and the risks encountered by military personnel and the consequences these may pose for both short- and long-term health and quality of life. Historically, asking about military service has rarely been recognized or utilized as a factor of health assessments or care. The effort to increase awareness about the importance of asking the question "Have you served in the military?" is essential to identify occupational risks associated with service and for unique risks due to deployment. It is important to ensure the unique and often complex healthcare needs of the veteran and families are met. All civilian healthcare providers and staff should be competent to screen and refer for determination of service-associated disabilities, provide care as a CHCP, or access resources and services that do not require service-associated disability. It is evident that you, the reader, have made a commitment to serve veterans, and their families, in your care.

Have You Ever Served? Initiative

Studies indicate most primary care providers do not report an overall high level of knowledge and comfort with any of the usual veterans' health issues (Maiocco et al., 2020; Fredericks & Nakazawa, 2015). The veteran population is frequently overlooked by civilian providers as it is assumed that veterans are treated at the VA, although less than 50 percent of veterans receive VA-based care (Vest et al., 2018). Healthcare providers seldom inquire about military service or any details about exposures and/or duty assignments due to lack of knowledge and comfort level about military service and its health associated risks. Vest and colleagues (2018) recommend education for all providers, specifically around the impact of military service and health-related sequelae, and barriers to providers screening and eliciting this information. These studies indicate a hesitancy and perception that this information was too intrusive. However, compared to the standard questions about alcohol consumption, tobacco use, and sexual activities, recognizing military service as an occupational hazard seemed both timely and appropriate. Experts noted this was a public health issue rather than a "nice to know" matter. Simply asking the question "Have you ever served in the military?" on intakes, patient assessments, or health histories is key to effective diagnosis, treatment, and care (Collins et al., 2013). The importance surrounding asking this question is rooted in the premise that it is important to make both the provider and the veteran aware of aspects and exposures encountered in military service and the potential increased risk for certain mental and physical conditions that require treatment and/or interventions (Viet Nam Veterans of America, 2020).

In 2013, as part of the First Lady Michelle Obama and Dr. Jill Biden Joining Forces initiative, the American Academy of Nursing launched the program, "Have You Ever Served?" which included a pocket card for providers to utilize when caring for veteran patients (https://www.haveyoueverserved.com/about.html). This tool served to further increase provider awareness during intakes, patient assessments, and/or health histories and is key to the effective diagnosis, treatment, and care of the veteran. The Substance Abuse and Mental Health Service Administration (SAMSHA) adopted the "Have You Ever Served?" initiative as a best practice for the 2019 and 2020 Governor's and Mayor's Challenge to Prevent Suicide among Service Members, Veterans and Their Families." Teams comprised of interagency military, first responders, and civilian teams from 27 states and 19 cities used this tool to develop and implement a comprehensive plan to prevent suicide among service members and veterans in their locale. For all practical purposes, this program is a crucial public service that has been instrumental in improving the understanding and care of America's military members, veterans, and their families.

While originally created in 2014, as new information is identified and made available, the contents of the original pocket card have been revised and updated. In the 2020 edition of the "Have you ever served?" Pocket Card (see **Figure 28-1**), the primary question posed on the front panel of the pocket card was expanded to include family and significant others: "Have you or someone close to you ever served in the military?" Questions about military service are more inclusive: When did you serve? Which branch? and What did you do while in the military? Deployments can be to any part of the world and encompass a vast array of assignments. Military and veterans are an occupational group with a vast array of specialized and diverse norms which do play an important role in their mindset and personality. This initial discussion can be an "ice breaker" which has the potential to begin to build the trust and confidence in the interview and future encounters.

Military Health History Pocket Card for Clinicians

HAVE YOU EVER SERVED?

WWW.HAVEYOUEVERSERVED.COM

Have you or has someone close to you ever served in the military?

- When did you serve?
- Which branch?
- What did you do while you were in the military?
- Were you assigned to a hostile or combative area?
- Did you experience enemy fire, see combat, or witness casualties?
- Were you wounded, injured, or hospitalized?
- Did you participate in any experimental projects or tests?
- Were you exposed to noise, chemicals, gases, demolition of munitions, pesticides, or other hazardous substances?

Have you ever used the VA for health care?

- When was your last visit to the VA?
- Do you have a service-connected disability or condition? Do you have a claim pending? If so, what is the nature of the claim?
- Do you have a VA primary care provider?

Do you have a safe place to go when you leave today?

- Do you need assistance in caring for yourself or members of your household?

American Academy of Nursing

Figure 28-1 Have You Ever Served? Pocketcard Front Panel

Courtesy of American Academy of Nursing.

The questions "Do you have a safe place to go when you leave today?" and "Do you need assistance in caring for yourself or members of your household?" were recently added to the schedule of questions. These items were included to address concerns about veteran homelessness, health insurance, domestic violence, food insecurity, and financial well-being, all of which are prevalent in both the military and veteran communities. State and federal VAs have many established relief and support programs to address these issues and can be easily accessed by contacting respective State Departments of Veteran Affairs or local VA facilities.

Often healthcare providers have asked "Now that I know my patient is a veteran, what do I do next?" Vital information on additional resources with contact information and Internet links to assist clinicians using this tool are on the back panel (see **Figure 28-2**). National veteran organizations to include the VA are listed as resources for providers as well as veterans and their family members to utilize as appropriate. Additional space is available for state and local governments who may be using the card to list their state specific agencies or resources.

In the first inner panel, questions and information about areas of concern for all military and veterans are identified. Questions to elicit this information about the Post-Traumatic Stress, Military Sexual Trauma, Blast Concussions, and Traumatic Brain Injuries are

AMERICAN ACADEMY OF NURSING

transforming health policy and practice through nursing knowledge

Have You Ever Served in the Military?

Managed and designed by the American Academy of Nursing, *Have You Ever Served in the Military?* is an awareness initiative to improve veterans' health.

Nurses are uniquely positioned to facilitate this change and ensure that vital information is obtained and recorded to improve the health care provided to our veterans and their families. To learn how you can be more involved, visit **HaveYouEverServed.com.**

RESOURCES FOR PROVIDERS:

National Association of State Directors of Veterans Affairs (NASDVA): Each state or territory has a local "boots on the ground" agency tasked with assisting veterans. Learn more: http://www.nasdva.us/Links.aspx

Veterans Experience Office (VEO) Hotline: 1-855-948-2311; Calls are answered 24/7, 365 days a year by an agent who has extensive training on VA programs and services.

Women Veterans Call Center: 1-855-829-6636 (1-855-VA-Women); Mon-Fri 8 a.m. - 10 p.m. ET; Sat 8 a.m. - 6:30 p.m. ET. Information regarding services the VA provides for women Veterans, including in crisis situations such as suicidal behavior, homelessness, sexual trauma, and domestic violence.

Military Environmental Exposures: Information on the most current environmental hazards; https://www.va.gov/health-care/health-needs-conditions/chemical-hazardous-materials-exposure/.

Veterans Crisis Line

1-800-273-8255 PRESS 1

V.05-2020

Figure 28-2 Have You Ever Served? Pocketcard First Inner Panel (Resources)

Courtesy of American Academy of Nursing.

General Areas of Concern for All Veterans

Post-Traumatic Stress

Have you ever experienced:

- A traumatic or stressful event which caused you to believe your life or the lives of those around you were in danger?
- Trauma-related thoughts or feelings?
- Nightmares, vivid memories, or flashbacks of the event?
- Feeling anxious, jittery, watchful, or easily startled?
- A sense of panic that something bad is about to happen?
- Feeling numb or detached from others?
- Difficulty sleeping or concentrating?

Military Sexual Trauma

- During military service did you receive uninvited or unwanted sexual attention, such as touching, pressure for sexual favors or sexual remarks?
- Did anyone ever use force or threat of force to have sexual contact with you against your will?
- Did you report the incidents to your command and/or military or civilian authorities? Is this an on-going problem?
- Would you like some help with this?

Blast Concussions/Traumatic Brain Injury

- During your service, did you experience:
  heavy artillery fire, vehicular or aircraft accidents, explosions (improvised explosive devices, rocket-propelled grenades, land mines, grenades), or fragment or bullet wounds above the shoulders?
- Did you have any of these symptoms immediately afterwards:
  loss of consciousness or being knocked out, being dazed or seeing stars, not remembering the event, or diagnosis of concussion or head injury?

Suicide Risk

Certain observable cues (affective and behavioral) should prompt the clinician to remain alert to the possible presence of suicidal ideation:

- shame
- humiliation
- irrational thinking
- paranoia
- agitation
- anxiety
- insomnia
- irritability
- despair
- profound social withdrawal
- neglecting personal welfare
- deteriorating physical appearance
- feeling trapped
- feeling that there's no way out
- feeling that life is not worth living
- feeling that there is no purpose in life
- feelings of failure or decreased performance
- sense of hopelessness or desperation

Figure 28-3 Have You Ever Served? Second Inner Panel (General Areas of Concerns)

Courtesy of American Academy of Nursing.

presented first (Collins et al., 2013). Questions about "Suicide Risk" were included at the request of the Military Order of the Purple Heart because the rates of suicide in the Veteran/Military Community were especially troubling and estimated to be 21-22/day or more. This selection of questions was not placed first on the card as a clinician would not typically ask these questions at the beginning of an assessment. These questions are provided to prompt clinicians to be alert for observable cues and behaviors which might suggest emotional distress such as depression or suicidal ideation or risk of suicide which may need to be explored further before the patient leaves the interview (see **Figure 28-3**).

In the panel titled "Common Military Health Risks," there is a listing of eight important exposures, Estimated Time/Period of Military Operations, and Geographic Locations, where toxic containments and hazardous substances were determined to have existed (see **Figure 28-4**). Adjacent are listings of health conditions known or thought to be associated with those with specific exposures. Many exposures are unknown and specific health conditions have not been associated with a contaminate. The VA does recognize those substances and the diseases listed. The science for some of these exposures is not precise and continues to cry out for more research to determine health effects. Unfortunately, many of these issues are not on any research agenda because there is a mistaken notion that veterans receive "free care" for all their needs.

Common Military Health Risks

Radiation Exposure/Nuclear Weapons (WWII: Amchitka, Alaska, Hiroshima, Nagasaki, POW in Japan; Korea; sub-mariners exposed to nasopharyngeal radium treatment; Gulf Wars; Bosnia; Afghanistan): High risk for cancer.

Agent Orange Exposure (Korea & Vietnam): High risk for cancers (including respiratory and prostate cancer), chloracne, type 2 diabetes, ischemic heart disease, soft tissue sarcoma, peripheral neuropathy, spina bifida in veterans' biological children.

Camp Lejeune Water Contamination (January 1, 1957–December 31, 1987): Veterans and families stationed at Camp Lejeune exposed to chemical contaminants in the groundwater and wells are at risk for the following cancers (bladder, blood dyscrasia, breast, esophageal, kidney, leukemia, lung, multiple myeloma, myelodysplastic syndromes, non-Hodgkin's lymphoma) and conditions (female infertility, hepatic steatosis, miscarriage, renal toxicity, scleroderma).

Hepatitis C (Vietnam): Transfusions prior to 1992, battlefield exposures to blood and human fluids, group use of needles, razors, toothbrushes, and other personal items and injecting drugs such as heroin or cocaine increase risk. It is recommended to have regular screening for Hepatitis C or HIV.

Exposure to Open Air Burn Pits (Vietnam; Iraq; Afghanistan): High risk for respiratory illnesses and wide variety of cancers, including leukemia.Veterans of Iraq and Afghanistan were exposed to high levels of particulate matter associated with Burn Pits. Early respiratory symptoms are often misdiagnosed as allergies, flu or common colds. On biopsy, titanium and plastics have been found in patients' lungs which compromise respiratory function and becomes constrictive bronchiolitis.

Gulf War Syndrome (Gulf Wars): Characterized by fibromyalgia, chronic fatigue syndrome, headaches, gastrointestinal problems, cognitive impairment and pain, high rates of brain and testicular cancers, and neurodegenerative diseases (ALS, MS).

Depleted Uranium (Gulf Wars; Bosnia; Afghanistan): Inhaled or ingested microfine particles (heavy metal toxicity). Risk for respiratory and kidney diseases.

Infectious Diseases (Iraq & Afghanistan): Malaria, typhoid fever, viral hepatitis, leishmaniasis, TB, rabies

Figure 28-4 Have You Ever Served? Pocketcard Outside Panel (Common Military Health Risks)

> I used to think I was lucky to have this "free care" until somebody reminded me that I had paid a mighty high price for it! I thought about it and he was right. I gave my hopes and dreams; my future and my every day. When I struggle to walk, I am reminded of how different my life is because of that firefight in Vietnam. I did not die but, in many respects, I did give my life for my Country and that care.
>
> Vietnam Veteran who served in Long Binh '68

The Unasked Question No More

It is the hope of the editors and authors of this book that we have provided readers with the confidence to ask all patients who enter their facility "Have you ever served in the military?" and the knowledge needed to adequately and appropriately assess their health status and needs. Each chapter in this book provides you with the tools needed for your veteran patient toolkit as well as for their family members. It can be a daunting challenge to provide culturally competent care to every patient in your facility; however, the payoff for our veteran population and their family members is a matter of national security. In addition, it is the debt of gratitude owed for the service and sacrifice of those who have served in harm's way. Finally, this book provides information on sequelae associated with military service, resources, and how to access resources and obtain service-associated disability determination.

Very few veterans who visit their healthcare provider have the stereotyped appearance of the young amputee or the older gentleman wearing a gold embroidered "I Am a Veteran" cap. They represent one of every six average-looking adult male (and an increasing number of female) patients. And because they served their country, many are at risk for potentially serious problems that are not being addressed by our medical community. This is not because of indifference, but because of an oversight in training. Until the question "Have you ever served in the military?" becomes part of routine medical history, patients who have been wearing their "I Am a Veteran" caps when visiting their healthcare provider will have good reason to continue doing so (Brown, 2012).

References

Brown, J. L. (2012). The unasked question. *JAMA, 308*(18), 1869-1870.

Collins, E., Wilmoth, M., & Schwartz, L. (2013). "Have you ever served in the military?" Campaign in partnership with the Joining Forces initiative. *Nursing Outlook, 61*(5), 375-376.

Fredricks, T. R. & Nakazawa, M. (2015). Perceptions of physicians in civilian medical practice on veterans' issues related to health care. *The Journal of the American Osteopathic Association, 115*, 360–368.

Government Accountability Office. (2019). VA HEALTH CARE: Estimating Resources Needed to Provide Community Care. Retrieved from https://www.gao.gov/products/gao-19-478#summaryAO-19-478.

Maiocco, G., Vance, B., & Dichiacchio, T. (2020). Readiness of non-veteran health administration advanced practice registered nurses to care for those who have served: a multimethod descriptive study. *Policy, Politics, & Nursing Practice, 21*(2), 82-94.

Mattocks, K. M., & Yehia, B. (2021). Evaluating the Veterans choice program: lessons for developing a high performing integrated network. *Med Care*, 55, 1-3.

Vest, B. M., Kulak, J., Hall, V. M., & Homish, G. G. (2018). Addressing patients' veteran status: primary care providers' knowledge, comfort, and educational needs. *Family medicine, 50*(6), 455.

Viet Nam Veterans of America. (2020). Leave No Veteran Behind . . . The Mission Continues America's Aging Veteran Population and the Covid-19 Pandemic. Vietnam Veterans of America. https://vva.org/wp-content/uploads/2020/08/Press-Release-20-06.pdf.

Index

Note: Page numbers followed by *b*, *f*, *t* indicate boxes, figures and tables respectively.

A

Absent Without Leave (AWOL), 127
abuse disorders, and chronic pain, 246–247
AC. *See* active component
ACA. *See* Affordable Care Act
ACAA. *See* Airline Carrier Access Act
academics, 405
Acceptance and Commitment Therapy (ACT), 397
ACEs. *See* childhood adverse experiences
Achilles in Vietnam, 397–398
ACS. *See* American College of Surgeons
ACT. *See* Acceptance and Commitment Therapy
active component (AC), 31–32
active duty (AD). *See* active component (AC)
active service, 123–124
activities of daily living (ADLs), 433
acupuncture, 245
ADA. *See* Americans with Disabilities Act
additional veteran educational resources, 462–463
ADLs. *See* activities of daily living
adolescents, 409
Advanced Trauma Life Support (ATLS), 157
AE. *See* Aeromedical Evacuation
Aeromedical Evacuation (AE), 168
aeromedical evacuation crew, 169
Affordable Care Act (ACA), 115
AFSC. *See* Air Force specialty code
Agent Orange, 123, 188–189
Air Force specialty code (AFSC), 8
Airline Carrier Access Act (ACAA), 144
Alcohol Use Disorder Identification Test-Consumption (AUDIT-C), 322
alpha stim therapy, 245
American College of Surgeons (ACS), 157
American Gold Star Mothers, 451
American Academy of Nursing, 472
The American Psychiatric Association (APA), 269
Americans with Disabilities Act (ADA), 140, 144
America's military, 471, 472
America's veterans, 471
amputation, 160
ANAM. *See* Automated Neuropsychological Assessment Metrics
animal welfare, 147–150
APA. *See* The American Psychiatric Association
appeal options for disability claims, 131–132
Armed Forces, 31
Armed Forces Vocational Aptitude Battery (ASVAB), 8
arousal and reactivity, marked alterations in, 271
assess health needs, opportunities to, 447
ASVAB. *See* Armed Forces Vocational Aptitude Battery
ATLS. *See* Advanced Trauma Life Support
Automated Neuropsychological Assessment Metrics (ANAM), 206
autonomic reactivity, 277
available resources, 461
avoidance and numbing, 270
AWOL. *See* Absent Without Leave

B

baby killers, 258
bad conduct discharge (BCD), 126–127
bad paper, 127
battlefield acupuncture, 245
battlefield medicine, 19–20
BCC. *See* Bud Clark Commons
BCD. *See* bad conduct discharge
behavioral therapies, chronic, 245
BEP. *See* Brief Eclectic Psychotherapy
bereavement for military families, unique aspects of, 450
Biden, Jill Dr., 472
bilateral stimulation (BLS), 281
biofeedback, 245
biopsychosocial-spiritual assessment, 79–81, 81*t*
  biological domain, 81–83, 82*t*
  psychological domain, 83–84, 83*t*
  social domain, 84, 84*t*
  spiritual domain, 84, 85*t*
biopsychosocial stressors, 301
bladder pain syndrome (BPS), 60
Blast Concussions, 473
blast injuries, 158–159, 159*t*, 207–209
  mechanisms of, 208*t*
BLS. *See* bilateral stimulation
Board of Veteran Appeals (BVA), 108, 131
borderline personality disorder (BPD), 300, 308
BPD. *See* borderline personality disorder
BPS. *See* bladder pain syndrome
Bride, Brian, 441
Brief Eclectic Psychotherapy (BEP), 282
Bud Clark Commons (BCC), 371
burns, 160–161
BVA. *See* Board of Veteran Appeals

C

camp followers, 422
cancer pain, 237–238
cannabinoids, for chronic pain, 241
CAPACITY. See Caregiver Perceptions About Communication with Clinical Team Members
Caregiver Experience Journey Map, 439, 440*f*
Caregiver Perceptions About Communication with Clinical Team Members (CAPACITY), 435
caregivers, 429
caregiving, implications of, 435
CASEVAC. *See* casualty evacuation
casualty evacuation (CASEVAC), 166
CAVC. *See* U.S. Court of Appeals for Veterans Claims
CBOC. *See* Community-Based Outpatient Clinics
CBT. *See* Cognitive Behavioral Therapy
CCATT. *See* Critical Care Air Transport Team
The Centers for Outcomes Research and Education (CORE), 371
CHAMPUS. *See* Civilian Health and Medical Program of the Uniformed Services
CHCP. *See* Community Health Care Providers
childhood adverse experiences (ACEs), 275
children, impact of military service on, 407
children, risks to, 411
CIR. *See* Community-Integrated Rehabilitation
Civil War (1861–1865), 47
Civilian Health and Medical Program of the Uniformed Services (CHAMPUS), 35
civilian healthcare system, 13–14
civilian life, transition to, 356
civilian providers, MST resources for, 350
classroom, transitioning from combat to, 465–467
clinical experiences, 459–460
Clinical Institute for Withdrawal Assessment for Alcohol revised scale (CIWA-Ar), 324
clinical practice guidelines (CPGs), 156
clinical setting, behaviors encountered in, 277
CoC. *See* Continuum of Care
Cognitive Behavioral Therapy (CBT), 307, 308
Cognitive Behavioral Therapy for Suicide Prevention (CBT-SP), 307
Cognitive Processing Therapy (CPT), 281
Colonial Army, 422
Columbia-Suicide Severity Rating Scale Screener (C-SSRS), 297–298
Combat and Operational Stress Reaction (COSR), 362–363
combat injuries, 435
Commissioned Officers O-1 up to O-10, 8
Common Military Health Risks, 475
Community-Based Outpatient Clinics (CBOC), 14
Community First! Village, 369, 369*f*
Community Health Care Providers (CHCP), 472
Community-Integrated Rehabilitation (CIR), 211*t*, 212
Community Living Centers, 14
community reintegration (CR), definition of, 204
comorbidities, 337
companion animals, case study, 145–147, 146*f*
Compassion Fatigue Model, 438
The Compensated Work Therapy (CWT) Program, 366–367
comprehensive assessment, for females, 72
Comprehensive Medical Readiness Program, 156
contemporary spouse, 422
Continuum of Care (CoC), 357
CONUS (continental United States—lower 48), 4
coping strategies, military impact on, 445–447, 446*b*
CORE. *See* The Centers for Outcomes Research and Education
COSR. *See* Combat and Operational Stress Reaction
COVID-19 employment and housing efforts, 366–367
CPGs. *See* clinical practice guidelines
CPT. *See* Cognitive Processing Therapy
CR. *See* community reintegration, definition of
Critical Care Air Transport Team (CCATT), 169
crunching numbers, 404
culture practicum skills assessment, 468–470
current initiatives and programs, 439
CWT Program. *See* The Compensated Work Therapy Program

D

DADT. *See* "Don't Ask, Don't Tell, Don't Pursue"
DBT. *See* Dialectical Behavior Therapy
DD. *See* dishonorable discharge
DD Form 214 (Certificate of Release/Discharge from Active Service), 124
de-escalation techniques, 278–279
Dean Lee, Lester, 460
decision-making process, 359
DEERS. *See* Defense Enrollment Eligibility Reporting System
Defense Authorization Act of 2018, 426
Defense Enrollment Eligibility Reporting System (DEERS), 35
Defense Health Agency (DHA), 19, 404
demographic characteristics, 299
demographics, 423, 423–424*f*
Department of Defense (DOD), 336, 354, 359, 395, 411, 412
Department of Veteran Affairs, 68
  healthcare issues women, 70–71
  institutional barriers faced by female veterans, 69–70
Dependabros, 429
Dependents Medical Care Act (1956), 35
deployment, 410

and combat-related experiences, 301
and dwell time, frequency of, 273–274
conditions of, 273
cycle, 36–37, 41, 409–410, 427
depression, 54–56
developing PTSD, risk and protective factors for, 275
DHA. *See* Defense Health Agency
Diagnostic and Statistical Manual (DSM), 376
Diagnostic and Statistical Manual of Mental Disorders (DSM-V), 451
Dialectical Behavior Therapy (DBT), 308
disability-priority treatment groups, VA criteria for, 133
barriers to benefitted entitlements, 134–135
military sexual trauma, 135–136
Other Than Honorable discharges, 133–134
resources, 135
Discharge Under Honorable Conditions, 124
dishonorable discharge (DD), 127
documentation, 341
DOD. *See* Department of Defense
domestic violence. *See* intimate partner violence
"Don't Ask, Don't Tell, Don't Pursue" (DADT), 10–11
"Don't Ask, Don't Tell" policy, 423
Drinkard, John, 377
drinking behaviors, 321, 321*t*
DSM. See Diagnostic and Statistical Manual
dysuria, acute, 59

E

EACE. *See* Extremity Trauma and Amputation Center of Excellence
Early intervention, 322
EBT. *See* evidenced-based treatment
ECHO program. *See* Extended Care Health Option program
education, 423–424, 423*f*
military child, 413
EFMP. *See* Exceptional Family Member Program
EFP. *See* explosive formed projectile
Elizabeth Dole Foundation, 439
EMDR. *See* Eye Movement Desensitization and Reprocessing
emerging and adjunctive therapies, 282–283, 284–286*t*
emotional support animals (ESAs)
case study, 144–145
salve for hidden wounds, 144
emotionally harmful, 397
Employer Support for Guard and Reserve (ESGR), 42
En Route Patient Staging System (ERPSS), 169
Enlisted E-1 up to E-4, 8
Enlisted Noncommissioned Officers (NCOs) E-5 up to E-9, 8
Enrollment Act (1863), 106
Enrollment Priority Groups, 128
Priority Group 1, 128
Priority Group 2, 128
Priority Group 3, 128
Priority Group 4, 128
Priority Group 5, 128–129
Priority Group 6, 129
Priority Group 7, 129
Priority Group 8, 129
entitlements, 35–36
vs. veteran benefits, 129–130
EOD. *See* explosion ordinance disposal
era of service, 11–12
ERPSS. *See* En Route Patient Staging System
ESAs. *See* emotional support animals
ESGR. *See* Employer Support for Guard and Reserve
Estimated Time/Period of Military Operations and Geographic Locations, 475
evidence-based psychotherapies, 281–282
evidenced-based treatment (EBT), 280
Exceptional Family Member Program (EFMP), 411–413, 412*t*
Executive Order 9981, 66
explosion ordinance disposal (EOD), 273
explosive formed projectile (EFP), 435–436
Extended Care Health Option (ECHO) program, 36
Extremity Trauma and Amputation Center of Excellence (EACE), 179, 180
Eye Movement Desensitization and Reprocessing (EMDR), 281–282

F

facilitate meaningful conversations, tool to, 381–383
factors affecting resilience, 413
Fair Housing Act (FHA), 144
Family Advocacy Program (FAP), 414–415
Family Care Plan (FCP), 407
family-centered medical homes (FCMHs), 23
family considerations, 283
family dynamics, 405–406
family involvement, 325
Family Readiness Groups, 426
FAP. *See* Family Advocacy Program
FCMHs. *See* family-centered medical homes
FCP. *See* Family Care Plan
female veterans, caring for, 65–89
biopsychosocial-spiritual assessment, 79–81, 81*t*
biological domain, 81–83, 82*t*
psychological domain, 83–84, 83*t*
social domain, 84, 84*t*
spiritual domain, 84, 85*t*
Department of Veteran Affairs, 68
healthcare issues, 70–71
institutional barriers faced by, 69–70
emerging issues, 84
homelessness, 86–87
intimate partner violence, 87–88, 88*t*
military sexual trauma, 85–86
integrative health care, 71–72
and military service, 10
physical health, 72
physical exam, 73–79, 75*t*, 76–78*t*
well-woman exam, 73, 74*t*
rethinking veterans, 67–68
U.S. military, changing profile of, 66, 66–67*f*
FHA. *See* Fair Housing Act

Figley, Charles, 441
finding veteran opportunities, 462
focused assessment of females, 72
Frankl, Viktor, 396
further mental health needs, assessing for, 450–451

G

general discharge, 126
Gilligan, Carol, 376
Global War on Terrorism (GWOT), 4
Gold Star and Blue Star Families, 406
Gold Star Mother, 429
Gold Star Spouses, 429–430
Gold Star Wives, 451–452
Green Zone Training (GZT), 465
grieving, supports for, 451–452
guilt and shame, 254–255
guilt, shame/soul injury practice considerations, 255–256
Gulf War, 113, 457
Gulf War I (1991), 51
Gulf War Illness, 189–190
GWOT. *See* Global War on Terrorism
GZT. *See* Green Zone Training

H

HALO. *See* health assessment for loved ones
Harbor Care, Nashua, NH, 369–370, 370*f*
"Have you ever served in the military?,"465–466
"Have You Ever Served?," 462–465, 473–475*f*
HCSDB. *See* Health Care Survey of DoD Beneficiaries
health and well-being, 426
health assessment for loved ones (HALO), 439–441
Health Care Survey of DoD Beneficiaries (HCSDB), 27
Health Related Behaviors Survey (HRBS), 320
healthcare costs, 176–177, 177–178*t*
healthcare needs, 360–362
helping veterans seek assistance, 287–288
herbicidal exposure, 188–189
HOME Program. *See* Home-Based Mental Health Evaluation Program
Home-Based Mental Health Evaluation (HOME) Program, 309
Homeless Veterans Community Employment Services (HVCES), 366
Homeless Vietnam Veteran (HVV) Healthcare Utilization Theory, 360, 361*f*
homelessness, female veterans, 86–87
honorable discharge, 124, 126
housing, 368–369
HRBS. *See* Health Related Behaviors Survey
human-animal bond, benefits of, 140–141
HVCES. *See* Homeless Veterans Community Employment Services
HVV Healthcare Utilization Theory. *See* Homeless Vietnam Veteran Healthcare Utilization Theory
hypnosis, 245

I

"I Am a Veteran" caps, 476
I Serve 2, 414, 418–419
  initiative, 53
IADLS. *See* instrumental activities of daily living
identifying Soul Injury
  facilitate meaningful conversations, tool to, 380–382*b*, 381–383
  responding to, 384–385
  self-help tools, 385–386
  suffering, wounds of, 376, 377–378*t*
  validation of the Soul Injury self-awareness inventory, 383–384
IED. *See* improvised explosive device
IM. *See* integrative medicine
Impact of Killing Treatment, 396
improvised explosive device (IED), 436
inattention and distraction, 277–278
incarceration, 354, 356–357*t*
infants, 408
injuries, types of, 158
  amputation, 160
  blasts, 158–159, 159*t*
  burns, 160–161
  internal trauma, 159–160
  orthopedic trauma, 160
  penetration injuries, 159
  soft tissue injury, 159–160
  spinal cord injuries, 161
injury severity score (ISS), 157
instrumental activities of daily living (IADLS), 433
integrative health care, 71–72
integrative medicine (IM), 245–246
The International Humanitarian Law, 395
interpersonal therapy (IT), 282
The Interstate Compact Act, 413
intimate partner violence (IPV), 87–88, 88*t*
intrusive symptoms, 269–270
IPV. *See* intimate partner violence
Iraq and Afghanistan Wars (2001–2014+), 51–53
Irritability and Anger, 278
ISS. *See* injury severity score
IT. *See* interpersonal therapy

J

jigsaw puzzle, 435
jobs in military, 8–9
JOES. *See* Joint Outpatient Experience Survey
Joint Outpatient Experience Survey (JOES), 27

K

know the law, follow the law, 341, 342*t*
Kohlberg, Lawrence, 376
Korea War, 457
Korean Conflict (1950–1953), 49

L

legal issues, 394–395
lessons learned, 463–465
lethal means, access to, 301–302
Lincoln, Abraham, 123, 458
loss, encounters with, 448, 449*b*

M

MACE tool. *See* Military Acute Concussion Evaluation tool
Maintaining Internal Systems and Strengthening Integrated Outside Networks (MISSION) Act (2018), 112
male spouses, 429
managing and helping children, 288
Mann, Ron, 255
marijuana, VA and, 241, 243*b*
massage therapy, 246
MDORP. *See* Mobile Device Outcomes-Based Rehabilitation Program
means safety counseling, 309–310, 311*f*
MEDEVAC. *See* medical evacuation
medical evacuation (MEDEVAC), 166–168, 167*t*
  acronym, 4
medications, 15
meditation, for chronic pain management, 246
Memorial Affairs. *See* National Cemetery Administration
MHS. *See* Military Healthcare System
MI. *See* Motivational Interviewing
mild traumatic brain injury (mTBI), 95, 205, 205*t*
Military Acute Concussion Evaluation (MACE) tool, 162, 206
military and civilian sexual assault definitions, laws/guidelines, differences between, 345–346
military and veteran caregiver (MVC), 433–435, 437, 439
military and veterans, moral stress and injury in
  differences between moral injury and PTSD, 392–394, 393*t*
  legal issues, 394–395
  military healthcare providers, 389–392, 389*f*
  moral resilience, 396
  research gap, highlighting, 394
  screening, 396–397
  strategy, 397–398
  treatment for, 395–396
military brat, 403–404
military caregiver *vs.* civilian caregivers, 222
  financial, 222–223
  health-related quality of life, 223–224
  mental health, 223
  sleep, 224
military children, services for, 406–407
military-connected children, parental military service on
  academics, 405
  adolescents, 409
  benefits, 406
  children, impact of military service on, 407
  crunching numbers, 404
  deployment, 410
  deployment cycle, 409–410
  education/military child, 413
  Exceptional Family Member Program, 411–413, 412*t*
  factors affecting resilience, 413
  Family Care Plans, 407
  family dynamics, 405–406
  Gold Star and Blue Star Families, 406
  I Serve 2, 414
  infants, 408
  military children, services for, 406–407
  military-connected children, resources for caring for, 414–415
  military life, pros and cons of, 404–405
  physical and psychological risk factors, 407–408
  pre-deployment, 410
  relocations, 405
  reunification, 410–411
  risks to children, 411
  school age children, 409
  social issues, 405
  toddlers and preschoolers, 408–409
military culture, 3–16
  branches of service, 6
  era of service, 11–12
  female veterans, and military service, 10
  gender identity, 10–11
  jobs, 8–9
  joining military, 9–10
  language, 3–4
  medications, 15
  military families, 12–13
  military healthcare system, 13–14
  Military/Warrior Ethos, 4–6, 5*t*
  mindset, 4–6
  National Guard, 6–7
  nonprescription substances, 15–16
  ranking, 8
  Reserves, 6–7
  sexual orientation, 10–11
  Special Operations Command, 7–8
  Veterans Health Administration, 14
military discharge, 124
Military Ethos, 4–6, 5*t*
military families, 12–13
military families benefit, 406
Military Healthcare System (MHS), 7, 13–14, 19, 20*f*, 421–422
  access to care for military members and families, 25–26, 25*t*
  education and training, 26
  mission of, 23–24
    healthcare missions between services, 24
  in OCONUS and CONUS medical home within, 21–23, 22–23*t*
    role 1–4, 20–21
  patient satisfaction and loyalty, 26–28
  scope and allocations of care, 24–25
  Tricare insurance, 26
The Military Interstate Compact Act, 413
military language, 3–4
military life cycle, 426–427
military life, pros and cons of, 404–405
military members and families, stressors for, 443–445
Military Occupation Specialty (MOS), 8, 273
military occupational exposures, 187–200
  Agent Orange, 188–189
  burn pits, 191
  depleted uranium, 190–191
  ears
    military background, 194
    military hearing conservation programs, 194–195
    veteran auditory health assessment, 195, 195*b*

military occupational exposures (*Continued*)
  eyes
    military background, 192–193
    military ocular health and injury prevention programs, 193
    veteran ocular health assessment, 193–194, 193*b*
  Gulf War Illness, 189–190
  herbicidal exposure, 188–189
  musculoskeletal
    military background, 197–198
    veteran musculoskeletal health assessment, 197*b*, 198
  neurological
    military background, 198–199
    veteran neurological health assessment, 199, 199*b*
  pulmonary
    military background, 195–196
    veteran pulmonary health assessment, 196–197, 196*b*
  toxic exposures during military deployments, 187–188
  in United States, 191–192
military rank, 8
Military REACH, 448
military sexual trauma (MST), 10, 57–58, 85–86, 135–136, 259, 271–272, 364–365, 473
  comorbidities, 337
  sexual assault and sexual harassment, 336
  how to prepare for sexual assault patients, 338–339
military spousal education and employment, programs to promote, 426
military spouses
  caregivers, 429
  contemporary spouse, 422
  demographics, 423, 423–424*f*
  deployment cycle, 427–428
  education, 423–424, 424*f*
  Gold Star Spouses, 429–430
  health and well-being, 426
  historical perspective, 422
  impact of military life cycle, 426–427
  importance of, 421–422
  male spouses, 429
  National Guard and Reserve, 422, 423*f*
  occupations/employment, 424–426, 425*f*
  programs to promote military spousal education and employment, 426
  resources, availability of, 428, 429*t*
  specific population considerations, 428
military to civilian life, transition from, 93–102
  community/society/system issues
    health care related, 98–99
    logistics of transition, 99–100
  individual considerations
    belonging, 96–97
    demographics, 94
    information/skills, 95–96
    psychological factors, 95
    purpose/meaning, 96
  interpersonal considerations, 97–98
  relationship with veterans administration, 100–101
  resilience and growth, 101–102
Military Treatment Facility (MTF), 404, 436
military veterans, PTSD in
  arousal and reactivity, marked alterations in, 271
  autonomic reactivity, 277
  avoidance and numbing, 270
  clinical setting, behaviors encountered in, 277
  deployment and dwell time, frequency of, 273–274
  deployments, conditions of, 273
  developing PTSD, risk and protective factors for, 275
  emerging and adjunctive therapies, 282–283, 284–286*t*
  evidence-based psychotherapies, 281–282
  family considerations, 283–287
  helping veterans seek assistance, 287–288
  inattention and distraction, 277–278
  intrusive symptoms, 269–270
  irritability and anger, 278–279
  managing and helping children, 288
  military occupational specialty, 273
  military sexual trauma, 271–272
  moral injury, 272
  negative cognitive and mood symptoms, 270
  polytrauma, 274–275
  screening, 275–277, 276*t*
  suicidal thoughts, 279
  supporting family members, 288
  training and culture, 273
  traumatic brain injury, 274
  traumatic experience, 269
  treatment, 279–281
  veterans, resources for family members of, 288–289
  veterans, unique about PTSD in, 273
military/veteran caregivers among us
  Caregiver Experience Journey Map, 439, 440*f*
  caregiving, implications of, 435
  case scenarios, 435–437
  current initiatives and programs, 439
  health assessment for loved ones, 439–441
  military and veteran caregivers
    characteristics of, 434
    needs of, 435
  polytrauma, caregivers assisting veterans with, 437–438
  psychosocial construct, health and well-being based on, 438–439
mindfulness, for chronic pain management, 246
mindset, defined, 4–5
MISSION Act (2018). *See* Maintaining Internal Systems and Strengthening Integrated Outside Networks Act (2018)
Mobile Device Outcomes-Based Rehabilitation Program (MDORP), 179
moral distress, 376, 390, 391–392
moral injuries, 255
moral injury, 272, 376, 377–378*t*, 387–394, 393*t*
  treatment for, 395–396
Moral Injury Questionnaire-Military Version, 396
moral outrage, 392
moral resilience, 396
MOS. *See* Military Occupation Specialty
Motivational Interviewing (MI), 283

MST. *See* military sexual trauma
mTBI. *See* mild traumatic brain injury
MTF. *See* Military Treatment Facility
multimorbidity, 177–179
murderers, 258
MVC. *See* military and veteran caregiver

N

NAEMT. *See* National Association of Emergency Medical Technicians
Narrative Exposure Therapy (NET), 282
National Association of Emergency Medical Technicians (NAEMT), 156
National Cemetery Administration (NCA), 108
The National Coalition for Homeless Veterans (NCHV), 358
National Defense Authorization Act (2008), 131
National Guard, 6–7, 31, 33, 35
  Reserve training, 450
National Guard and Reserve, 422, 423*f*
National Hospice and Palliative Care Organization (NHPCO), 251, 260
National Resource Directory, 182
National Vietnam Veterans Art Museum in Chicago, 255
Navy enlisted classification (NEC), 8
Navy Marine Corp Relief Society, 426
NCA. *See* National Cemetery Administration
NCHV. *See* The National Coalition for Homeless Veterans
NCOs E-5 up to E-9. *See* Enlisted Noncommissioned Officers E-5 up to E-9
NEC. *See* Navy enlisted classification
negative cognitive and mood symptoms, 270
NET. *See* Narrative Exposure Therapy
Neurobehavioral Symptom Inventory (NSI), 206
NHPCO. *See* National Hospice and Palliative Care Organization
Nightingale, Florence, 140
Non-suicidal self-injury (NSSI), 299–300
nonprescription substances, 15–16
NSI. *See* Neurobehavioral Symptom Inventory
NSSI. *See* Non-suicidal self-injury

O

Obama, Barack, 426
Obama, Michelle, 472
Occupation and employment, 424–426, 425*f*
OCONUS (outside the continental United States), 4
OEF. *See* Operation Enduring Freedom
often forgotten, 259
OIF. *See* Operation Iraqi Freedom
OIF/OEF/OND military women, 51–52
OIF/OEF/OND women veterans, 52–53
Ombudsman program, 426
OND. *See* Operation New Dawn
Operation Enduring Freedom (OEF), 4, 114–115, 325, 354
Operation Iraqi Freedom (OIF), 4, 325, 354
Operation Iraqi Freedom, 114–115, 443
Operation New Dawn (OND), 4
opioid therapy
  for chronic pain, 243–244
  for pain management, 241
opioid use disorder (OUD), 302
orthopedic trauma, 160
OTH discharge. *See* Other Than Honorable discharge
Other Than Honorable (OTH) discharge, 126, 133–134, 358–359
  bad conduct discharge, 126–127
OUD. *See* opioid use disorder
outside the continental United States. *See* OCONUS (outside the continental United States)
overactive bladder, 59

P

pain
  acute, 236–237, 237*t*, 238
  cancer, 237–238
  chronic, 237, 238, 238*b*
    abuse disorders related to, 246–247
    impact on veterans and their families, 246
  definitions of, 236
  descriptors, 236
  management, in VHA, 239–240, 240*b*
    complementary therapies, 245–246
    integrative medicine, 245–246
    interventions, 244–245
    pharmacological, 240–244, 242*t*
  physiology, 236
  veterans and, 238–239
patient-centered care, 296
patient-centered medical home (PCMH), 21–23, 22–23*t*
Patient Movement (PM) system
  inter-theater, 165–166, 166*f*, 168–169
    Aeromedical Evacuation, 168
    aeromedical evacuation crew, 169
    Critical Care Air Transport Team, 169
    En Route Patient Staging System, 169
    regulation center, 168–169
  intra-theater, 165–168, 166*f*
    Aeromedical Evacuation, 168
    medical evacuation, 166–168, 167*t*
  introduction to, 164–165
  physiological stressors of flight, 169, 172–173
  summary, 173
patient movement regulation center (PMRC), 168–169
PCMH. *See* patient-centered medical home
PCS. *See* permanent changes of station
PCS. *See* post-concussive symptoms
PCT. *See* polytrauma clinical triad
PCT. *See* present-centered therapy
PE. *See* Prolonged Exposure Therapy
Pearl Harbor Day, 48
pelvic organ prolapsed (POP), 59
penetration injuries, 159
permanent changes of station (PCS), 426–427

pharmacologic treatments, 308
Phoenix, 116–117
PHTLS. *See* Prehospital Trauma Life Support
physical and psychological risk factors, 407–408
physical exam, female veterans, 73–79, 75*t*, 76–78*t*
physical health conditions, 300–301
physiological stressors of flight, 169, 172–173
Piaget, Jean, 376
PM system. *See* Patient Movement system
PMRC. *See* patient movement regulation center
polytrauma, 157–158, 274–275
polytrauma care across continuum, 155–183
  admission, 174–176, 174*t*, 175*b*
  clinical treatment considerations, 161–162
  considerations for war-injured service members
    healthcare costs, 176–177, 177–178*t*
    multimorbidity, 177–179
    support system considerations, 180–181
    technological advancements, 179–180
  discharge, 176
  emergency response
    damage control resuscitation, 163–164
    pain management, 164
    triage, 163
  hospital care, 173
  injuries, types of, 158
    amputation, 160
    blasts, 158–159, 159*t*
    burns, 160–161
    internal trauma, 159–160
    orthopedic trauma, 160
    penetration injuries, 159
    soft tissue injury, 159–160
    spinal cord injuries, 161
  Patient Movement system, 170–171*f*
    inter-theater, 165–166, 166*f*, 168–169
    intra-theater, 165–168, 166*f*
    introduction to, 164–165
    physiological stressors of flight, 169, 172–173
    summary, 173
  rehabilitation, 173–174
  resources
    for caregiver and family members, 183
    for healthcare providers, 181–182, 182*b*
    for veteran/service member, 182–183
  risks to service members
    environmental exposure risks, 162
    infection risks and considerations, 162–163
  training
    civilian sector training opportunities, 157
    clinical practice guidelines, 156
    Comprehensive Medical Readiness Program, 156
    planning and response, 157
    Trauma Combat Casualty Care course, 156
polytrauma, caregivers assisting veterans with, 437–438
polytrauma clinical triad (PCT), 210, 210*f*
Polytrauma Rehabilitation Centers (PRCs), 173–174
Polytrauma System of Care (PSC), 173–174
POP. *See* pelvic organ prolapsed
post-acute care, 308–309
Post-Assault Clinical Flow Sheet, 340, 347–349
post-concussive symptoms (PCS), 274
post-traumatic stress (PTS), 268, 391, 473
post-traumatic stress disorder (PTSD), 50, 56–57, 268–269, 325, 337, 354, 360–363, 376, 377–378*t*, 388, 389, 392–394, 393*t*, 395, 397, 411, 435, 438, 444, 450, 451, 459
  healthcare practice tips for veterans, 252–254
  screening, 275–277, 276*t*
  treatment, 279–281
PRCs. *See* Polytrauma Rehabilitation Centers
pre-deployment, 410
Prehospital Trauma Life Support (PHTLS), 156
present-centered therapy (PCT), 282
Primary Care PTSD screen (PC-PTSD), 275
Problem-Solving Therapy (PST), 307–308
program field experiences, 460–461
Prolonged Exposure Therapy (PE), 281
protective factors, 302–303
PSC. *See* Polytrauma System of Care
PST. *See* Problem-Solving Therapy
psychiatric conditions and symptoms, 300
psychologically deployed, 410
psychosocial construct, health and well-being based on, 438–439
PTS. *See* post-traumatic stress
PTSD. *See* post-traumatic stress disorder
PTSD at-risk environments, 252, 253*b*
"pulls double duty," 437

Q

Qigong, for chronic pain management, 246

R

RAND Report, 434
RBANS. *See* Repeatable Battery for the Assessment of Neuropsychological Status
RCs. *See* reserve components
RCT. *See* 2005 randomized control trial
Recognition-Primed Decision (RPD) Model, 388, 389*f*
Red-Yellow-Green triage system, 379
reduce veteran homelessness, federal policies to, 357–358
Rehabilitative Lower Limb Orthopedic Analysis Device (ReLOAD), 179
ReLOAD. *See* Rehabilitative Lower Limb Orthopedic Analysis Device
relocations, 405
Repeatable Battery for the Assessment of Neuropsychological Status (RBANS), 206

reserve components (RCs), 32–35, 33–34*t*
access flowchart, 42*f*
impact of 9/11 on, 41–43
Reserves, 6–7
National Guard personnel, 50–51
resources, 447–448
availability of, 428, 429*t*
for veteran community, 135
reunification, 410–411
Revolutionary War, 422
risk stratification, 303, 304–306*f*
RPD Model. *See* Recognition-Primed Decision Model

S

SA. *See* sexual assault
SAC. *See* Standardized Assessment of Concussion
Safety Planning in the Emergency Department (SPED), 307
safety planning interventions, 306
Sallows, Mike, 366
SAMHSA. *See* Substance Abuse and Mental Health Services Administration
SAPR Program. *See* Sexual Assault Prevention and Response Program
SASQ. *See* Single Item Alcohol Screening Questionnaire
SBIRT. *See* Screening, Brief Intervention, and Referral to Treatment
Scholarships for Military Children, 426
school age children, 409
SCMHs. *See* soldier-centered medical homes
screening, 322–324, 323*t*, 396–397
Screening, Brief Intervention, and Referral to Treatment (SBIRT), 319, 322
SDM. *See* Shared Decision Making
SDV. *See* self-directed violence
Secondary Traumatic Stress Theory, 438
secondary traumatization, 283
self-directed violence (SDV), 299, 303, 307
self-help tools, 385–386
self-transcendence, 396
The Sequential Intercept Model, 355
service animals, case study, 141–143
Service-Connected Disability, 100–101, 132, 132*f*
service members (SMs), 280
service members and veterans (SMVs), 221
clinical recommendations, 224–225
assistance with managing cognitive and emotional difficulties, 225
assistance with obtaining needed services and with everyday needs, 226–227
assistance with self-management of emotions and stress, 225
military caregiver *vs.* civilian caregivers, 222
financial, 222–223
health-related quality of life, 223–224
mental health, 223
sleep, 224
unique characteristics of military caregivers of individuals with TBI, 221
family strain and deployment-related changes, 221–222
increased medical complexity, 221
navigation of complex healthcare systems, 222
sexual assault (SA), 335–336
barriers to reporting, 337–338
diagnosing MST, 339–340, 340*t*
documentation, 341
follow-up and referrals, 341
know the law, follow the law, 341, 342*t*
traumatic effects of, 336–337
treating MST, 340–341
sexual assault patients, how to prepare for, 338–339
Sexual Assault Prevention and Response (SAPR) Program, 336
sexual harassment, 336
Shared Decision Making (SDM), 280, 283
Shay, Jonathan, 376
SI. *See* suicidal thoughts/intention
SI. *See* Symbolic Interactionism
sidelines, supporting
assess health needs, opportunities to, 447
bereavement for military families, unique aspects of, 450
coping strategies, military impact on, 445–447, 446*b*
encounters with loss, 448
encounters with stress, 443–445
further mental health needs, assessing for, 450–451
grieving, supports for, 451–452
resources, 447–448
Single Item Alcohol Screening Questionnaire (SASQ), 322
SISAI. *See* Soul Injury Self-Awareness Inventory
SIT. *See* stress inoculation training
sleep disorders, 209
SMs. *See* service members
SMVs. *See* service members and veterans
social issues, 405
SOF. *See* Special Operations Forces
soft tissue injury, 159–160
soldier-centered medical homes (SCMHs), 23
soldierization, 4–5
Soul Injury, 376, 377–378*t*, 379–380, 384–385
Soul Injury Self-Awareness Inventory (SISAI), 380, 380–382*b*
validation of, 383–384
Spanish-American War (1898–1902), 47
Special Operations Forces (SOF), 7
specialized consideration, 257
Specific Population Considerations, 428
SPED. *See* Safety Planning in the Emergency Department
spinal cord injuries, 161
STAI. *See* State-Trait Anxiety Inventory
Standardized Assessment of Concussion (SAC), 206
State-Trait Anxiety Inventory (STAI), 206
STB. *See* suicide thoughts and behavior
stoic veteran, healthcare practice tips for, 251
stoicism, 251
strategy, 397
street medicine/health care, 365–366

stress-coping theory, 445
stress inoculation training (SIT), 282
stubbornly independent, 252
student learning activities, 458–459
Substance Abuse and Mental Health Services Administration (SAMHSA), 338, 397, 472
substance use disorders (SUDs), 300, 303, 320*t*, 354, 357
  drinking behaviors, 321, 321*t*
  early intervention, 322
  family involvement, 325
  prevalence and risk factors, 319–321
  screening, 322–324, 323*t*
  suicide, 326, 332
  trauma and substance abuse, 325–326, 327–331*t*
  withdrawal and delirium tremens, signs and symptoms of, 324, 324*t*
  withdrawal interventions and safety, 324–325
SUDs. *See* substance use disorders
suicidal thoughts/intention (SI), 279
suicide, 325
suicide ideation and suicide attempt, 363–364
suicide risk, evaluation of, 299
suicide risk identification, evaluation, stratification/management, 296–297
suicide risk management, 303, 306
suicide risk screening, 297–299, 298*f*
suicide thoughts and behavior (STB), 58
supporting family members, 288
Supportive Services for Veteran Families Program, 358
Swords to Plowshares, 371–372, 372*f*
Symbolic Interactionism (SI), 359–360

T

Tactical Combat Casualty Care course (TCCC), 156
Tactical Emergency Casualty Care (TECC), 156
tai chi, for chronic pain management, 246
TBI. *See* traumatic brain injury
TCCC. *See* Tactical Combat Casualty Care course
TCDD. *See* 2,3,7,8-tetrachlorodibenzo-p-dioxin
TECC. *See* Tactical Emergency Casualty Care
technology-based modalities, 309
"Thank You" Is Not Enough, 256–257
Theater Validating Flight Surgeon (TVFS), 169
thermotherapy, for chronic pain management, 246
TNCC. *See* Trauma Nursing Core Course
toddlers and preschoolers, 408–409
total force concept, 50
TOUGH project. *See* Trauma Outcomes and Urogenital Health project
toxic exposures during military deployments, 187–188
training and culture, 273
transgender veterans, 365
transition of care for wounded warriors, 19–20
translating research into practice (TRIP), 448, 450
trauma and substance abuse, 325–326, 327–331*t*
Trauma Nursing Core Course (TNCC), 157
Trauma Outcomes and Urogenital Health (TOUGH) project, 60–61
  clinical care environment, 61
  healthcare system, 60–61, 61*b*
  interventions, 60
  therapeutic relationships, 60
traumatic brain injury (TBI), 274, 300–301, 391, 434, 438, 444, 473
  as chronic condition, 209
  clinical recommendations, 224–225
    assistance with managing cognitive and emotional difficulties, 225
    assistance with obtaining needed services and with everyday needs, 226–227
    assistance with self-management of emotions and stress, 225
  common post-concussion symptoms, 209
    behavioral/mental health diagnoses, 210
    chronic pain, 210
    cognitive symptoms, 209–210
    polytrauma clinical triad, 210, 210*f*
    sleep disorders, 209
    visual symptoms, 210
  definition and severity levels, 204, 205*t*
  environments of care, 206
  impact on caregivers, 220
  incidence of, 219–220
  mild, 205, 205*t*
  military caregiver *vs.* civilian caregivers, 222
    financial, 222–223
    health-related quality of life, 223–224
    mental health, 223
    sleep, 224
  military/civilian divide, 203–204
  moderate and severe, 206
  polytrauma system of care, 207, 207*f*
    blast injuries, 207–209
  screening, 206
  treatment considerations and resources, 210–212, 211*t*
  unique characteristics of military caregivers of individuals with, 221
    family strain and deployment-related changes, 221–222
    increased medical complexity, 221
    navigation of complex healthcare systems, 222
traumatic experience, 269
treating MST patients, 338
Tricare, 35–36, 37*t*
  related health benefits, 36, 38–40*t*
TRICARE Dental Program, 406
TRICARE health plans, 428
Tricare Inpatient Satisfaction Survey (TRISS), 27
Tricare insurance, 26
TRIP. *See* translating research into practice
TRISS. *See* Tricare Inpatient Satisfaction Survey
Trojan War, 387

2,3,7,8-tetrachlorodibenzo-p-dioxin (TCDD), 188
2005 randomized control trial (RCT), 307
2019 National Veteran Suicide Prevention Annual Report, 295
TVFS. *See* Theater Validating Flight Surgeon

U

uncomplicated grief, 450
undesirable discharge, 126–127
Uniformed Services, 31, 32*t*
Uniformed Services University of the Health Sciences (USUHS), 26
urinary tract infections (UTIs), 59
urological deployment hazards, 58–59
  acute dysuria, 59
  bladder pain syndrome, 60
  overactive bladder, 59
  pelvic organ prolapsed, 59
  urinary tract infections, 59
U.S. Air Force, 6
U.S. Army, 6
US Congress, 471
U.S. Court of Appeals for Veterans Claims (CAVC), 108, 131
U.S. Department of Veterans Affairs (VA), 107–109, 108*f*
U.S. Marine Corps, 6
U.S. Navy, 6
U.S. Special Operations Command (USSOCOM/SOCOM), 7–8
USUHS. *See* Uniformed Services University of the Health Sciences
UTIs. *See* urinary tract infections

V

VA. *See* Veterans Administration
VA. *See* Veterans Affairs
VA claims, 130–131
VA healthcare system, 109–112
  eligibility and enrollment for care, 109
  mission of, 109
VA Justice Programs (VJP), 355
VACAA. *See* Veterans Access, Choice, and Accountability Act
VBA. *See* Veterans Benefits Administration
VCCP. *See* Veterans Community Care Program
Vet Centers, 14
veteran benefits, 123
  active service, 123–124
  character of discharge, 124–126
    bad paper, 127
    dishonorable, 127
    general, 126
    honorable, 126
    undesirable, 126–127
  DD Form 214, 124, 125*f*
  discharge, 124
  length of service, 124
  vs. entitlements, 129–130
veteran community, taking care of, 127
  appeal options for disability claims, 131–132
  claims, 130–131
  disability rating and priority systems of care, 132–133
  eligibility for care, 127–128, 128*b*
  Enrollment Priority Groups, 128
    Priority Group 1, 128
    Priority Group 2, 128
    Priority Group 3, 128
    Priority Group 4, 128
    Priority Group 5, 128–129
    Priority Group 6, 129
    Priority Group 7, 129
    Priority Group 8, 129
  Service-Connected Disability, 132, 132*f*
veteran healthcare providers, resources and support for, 259–260, 260–261*b*
Veteran Homelessness Demonstration Program, 358
Veteran/Military Community, 474
veteran population, 472
Veteran Service Organizations, 135
veteran suicide prevention, challenges in, 310–312
veterans and pain, 238–239
Veterans Access, Choice, and Accountability Act (VACAA), 116–117
Veterans Administration (VA), 336, 354, 355, 358–359, 376, 461–462, 471, 472, 473, 475
Veterans Affairs (VA), 427
Veterans Benefits Administration (VBA), 108, 133
Veterans Community Care Program (VCCP), 112
veterans, definition of, 122–123
veterans, educating healthcare providers on caring for
  additional veteran educational resources, 462–463
  available resources, 461–462
  classroom, transitioning from combat to, 465–467
  clinical experiences, 459–460
  finding veteran opportunities, 462
  lessons learned, 463–465
  program field experiences, 460–461
  program, introduction to, 458
  student learning activities, 458–459
  volunteer opportunities, 462
veterans experiencing homelessness, assessing and addressing health care for
  accessing health care, decision-making process used by homeless veterans in, 359
  Bud Clark Commons, 371
  civilian life, transition to, 356–357
  Community First! Village, 369, 369*f*
  COVID-19 employment and housing efforts, 366–367
  demographic characteristics of, 353*f*
  Harbor Care, Nashua, NH, 369–370, 370*f*
  healthcare needs, 360–362
  Homeless Vietnam Veteran (HVV) Healthcare Utilization Theory, 360, 361*f*
  housing, 368–369
  incarceration, 355–356, 356–357*t*
  military sexual trauma, 364–365
  psychiatric needs, 362–364
    Combat and Operational Stress Reaction, 362
    post-traumatic stress disorder, 362
    suicide ideation and suicide attempt, 363–364

veterans experiencing homelessness, assessing and addressing health care for (*Continued*)
  psychosocial risks, 354
    post-traumatic stress disorder, 354
    substance use disorders, 354
  reduce veteran homelessness, federal policies to, 357–358
  risk factors leading to, 354
  street medicine/health care, 365–366
  Swords to Plowshares, 371–372, 372*f*
  Symbolic Interactionism, 359–360
  transgender veterans, 365
  Veterans Administration, 358
Veterans Healthcare Administration (VHA), 14, 107–118, 123, 360–365, 391, 394, 395
  caring for veterans in 21st century, 112–113
  eligibility for healthcare services and programs, 107
  "for those who have borne the battle," 104–105
  Operation Enduring Freedom, 114–115
  Operation Iraqi Freedom, 114–115
  pain management in, 239–240, 240*b*
    complementary therapies, 245–246
    integrative medicine, 245–246
    interventions, 244–245
    pharmacological, 240–244, 242*t*
  Phoenix, 116–117
  U.S. Department of Veterans Affairs, 107–109, 108*f*
  VA healthcare system, 109–112
    eligibility and enrollment for care, 109
    mission of, 109
Veterans' Health Care Eligibility Reform Act (1996), 123
Veterans Integrated Service Networks (VISNs), 109–110, 110*f*
  organizational structure, 111*f*
veterans receiving community-based care, suicide risk evaluation and management
  access to lethal means, 301–302
  biopsychosocial stressors, 301
  demographic characteristics, 299
  deployment and combat-related experiences, 301
  evaluation of suicide risk, 299
  means safety counseling, 309–310, 311*f*
  non-pharmacologic treatments, 306–308
    Cognitive Behavioral Therapy for Suicide Prevention (CBT-SP), 307
    problem-solving therapy, 307–308
    safety planning interventions, 306–307
  pharmacologic treatments, 308
  physical health conditions, 300–301
  post-acute care, 308–309
  protective factors, 302–303
  psychiatric conditions and symptoms, 300
  risk stratification, 303, 304–306*f*
  SDV thoughts and behaviors, history of, 299–300
  specific psychiatric conditions, treatment options for suicidal behavior in individuals with, 308
  suicide risk identification, evaluation, stratification, and management, 296–297
  suicide risk management, 303, 306
  suicide risk screening, 297–299, 298*f*
  technology-based modalities, 309
  veteran suicide prevention, challenges in, 310–312
  warning signs, 302
veterans, unique about PTSD in, 273
VHA. *See* Veterans Healthcare Administration
Vietnam War (1964–1973), 49–50, 457
Virtual Lifetime Electronic Record (VLER), 26
virtual reality exposure therapy (VRET), 282
VISNs. *See* Veterans Integrated Service Networks
VJP. *See* VA Justice Programs
VLER. *See* Virtual Lifetime Electronic Record
volunteer opportunities, 462
VRET. *See* virtual reality exposure therapy

W

Walker, Mary Dr., 47
warning signs, 302
Warrant Officers WO-1 up to CWO-5, 8
Warrior Ethos. *See* Military Ethos
Washington, George, 105
We Honor Veterans (WHV) Partners, 260
"welcoming home" vietnam veterans, 258–259
well-woman exam, 73, 74*t*
WHO BIC. *See* World Health Organization Brief Intervention and Contact
WHV Partners. *See* We Honor Veterans Partners
Wilson, Woodrow, 429
withdrawal and delirium tremens, signs and symptoms of, 324, 324*t*
withdrawal interventions and safety, 324–325
WMSM. *See* Women military service members
women, in military
  first, identification, 53
  health issues
    depression, 54–56
    military sexual trauma, 57–58
    posttraumatic stress disorder, 56–57
    suicide thoughts and behavior, 58
  "healthy solider effect," 51–52
  historical review of, 46
    1950–1961, 49
    Civil War (1861–1865), 47
    Gulf War I (1991), 51
    Iraq and Afghanistan Wars (2001–2014+), 51–53
    Reserves/National Guard personnel, 50–51
    Spanish-American War (1898–1902), 47
    total force concept, 50
    Vietnam War (1964–1973), 49–50
    World War I (1917–1918), 48
    World War II (1941–1945), 48

military children
identification, 53
possible deployment consequences, 54, 55*t*
Trauma Outcomes and Urogenital Health project, 60–61
clinical care environment, 61
healthcare system, 60–61, 61*b*
interventions, 60
therapeutic relationships, 60
urological deployment hazards, 58–59
acute dysuria, 59
bladder pain syndrome, 60
overactive bladder, 59
pelvic organ prolapsed, 59
urinary tract infections, 59
Women military service members (WMSM), 45
Women Veterans Health Program, 69
World Health Organization Brief Intervention and Contact (WHO BIC), 309
World War I, 48, 107, 406, 422, 429, 448, 457
World War II, 48, 254, 258, 259, 448, 457, 460

Y

Yellow Ribbon Events, 415
yoga, for chronic pain management, 246
yoga practice, 282